THE ULTIMATE
DIVAN of HAFEZ

For a complete list and descriptions of our over 600 titles
go to
amazon.com/author/smithpa

THE ULTIMATE
DIVAN of HAFEZ

Newly Revised, Centered
Translation, Introduction, Appendix

Paul Smith

NEW HUMANITY BOOKS
Book Heaven
Booksellers & Publishers

First Edition, Limited to 1000 copies in 2 vols. 1986

First Revised e-book Edition 2005.

First Revised paperback edition 2012.

NEW HUMANITY BOOKS
BOOK HEAVEN
(Booksellers & Publishers for over 40 years)
47 Main Road Campbells Creek Victoria 3451
Australia

Introduction & Poems first published in

Divan of Hafez. (2 vols.)
Translation & Introduction by Paul Smith .
New Humanity Books.
Melbourne. Australia 1986.

ISBN 9781794120488

Poetry/Mysticism/Sufism/Middle Eastern Studies/
Sufi/ Poetry/Persian Literature/Oracles

INTRODUCTION:

THE ULTIMATE
DIVAN OF HAFEZ

APPENDIX:

HAFEZ~of~SHIRAZ

The Life, Poetry & Times of the Immortal Persian Poet

(In Three Volumes)

BOOK ONE: THE EARLY YEARS

(The Opening 180 Pages)

Hafez & Abu Ishaq

(Brit. Mus. Add. 7468, f 34b)

INTRODUCTION

1. THE LIFE OF HAFEZ

Hafez was born in Shiraz in south-western Persia (modern Iran) in 1320 A.D., twenty two years before the birth of Chaucer and a year before the death of Dante. He was named Shams-ud-din, which means 'Sun of Faith,' Mohammed. Later when he began to write poetry he selected Hafez for his pen-name or '*takhallus.*' 'Hafez' is the title given to one who has learnt the whole of the *Koran* by heart and Hafez claimed to have done this in fourteen different ways.

Physically Hafez was small and ugly but even as a young boy he began to show the great gifts that would finally take him to the height of artistic and spiritual achievements. He was loving and helpful to his parents, brothers and friends, and he had a wonderfully ironic sense of humour that caused him to continually see the humorous side of everyday life. Even at this early age he was fascinated by the poetry and prose of Persia's great poets and writers and stories about the spiritually advanced souls and Perfect Masters. He loved the *Koran,* which his father read to him and he began to memorize it. He discovered he was blessed with a remarkable memory, and before he was nine he had memorized the *Koran.*

As a boy his favourite poets were Nizami and Sadi, Shiraz's most loved poet of the time, who had died about thirty years previously. All of Shiraz was singing his beautiful songs, his *ghazals,* and telling his magical stories, and Hafez was no exception. He dreamed of becoming a great poet like Sadi or like Nizami, Farid ud-Din Attar, or Rumi, all of whom he admired.

Then a change occurred in his life. His father died and left his family in difficult circumstances. Baha-ud-din's business of being a coal merchant had failed because he had suffered from a long illness, and Hafez's mother could only raise enough money to pay back all the debts. His two older brothers left home to work in Isfahan and young Hafez and his grief-stricken mother went to live with his uncle, Sadi, who fancied himself a poet like his famous namesake.

Because of the poverty that they now experienced, Hafez had to leave day-school and he began work in a drapery shop and later managed to find work at night in a bakery. Half of his salary he gave to his mother and the other half he used to go to school at night where he learned calligraphy and a wide variety of subjects.

Hafez was twenty years old in 1340, and was still working in the bakery and studying at day and until this time had not gained much success as a poet. He had become skilled in jurisprudence and had learnt all the sciences, including mathematics and astronomy. One of his teachers Obeyd Zakani, the controversial poet and jester and social commentator would become a life-long friend. For the past ten years Hafez had been constantly studying all of the great poets and the lives and works of the great Spiritual Masters. He was fluent in Arabic and had also learnt Turkish.

Then, one day at the bakery, one of the workers who delivered bread was sick, and Hafez had to deliver to a certain quarter of Shiraz where the prosperous citizens of Turkish origin lived. While taking the bread to a particular mansion, Hafez's eyes fell upon the form of a young woman who was standing on one of the mansion's balconies. Her name was Shakh-e-Nabat which means 'Branch of Sugarcane'. Her unveiled beauty (as she was of the Turkish upper-class) immediately intoxicated Hafez and he fell hopelessly in love with her. Her beauty had such a profound effect on him that he almost lost consciousness. At night he could not sleep and he no longer felt like eating. He learnt her name and he began to praise her in his poems.

Hafez heard that she had been promised in marriage to one of the princes of Shiraz (who would later become the king… Abu Ishak) and realized how hopeless was his quest for her love. Still, the vision of her beauty filled his heart, and his thoughts were constantly with her. Then one day he remembered the 'promise of Baba Kuhi'. Baba Kuhi was a Perfect Master-Poet who had died in Shiraz in 1050 and had been buried about four miles from Shiraz at a place called 'Pir-i-sabz,' meaning 'the green old man,' on a hill eventually named after him. This *ruba'i* poem of his could easily have been composed by him about Hafez and how he felt for Nabat at that time…

The work isn't finished without love's fire, my dear:
heart isn't perfect unless consumed entire, my dear.
Burn every day and night like the moth and candle...
day is Beloved's face; night, hair to admire my dear.

The promise that Baba Kuhi had given before he passed into Eternal Existence forever was that if anyone could stay awake for forty consecutive nights at his tomb he would be granted the gifts of poetry, immortality, and his heart's desire. Hafez, interested in the third of these, vowed to keep this vigil.

Every night Hafez would go to work at the bakery, then he would eat, and then in the morning walk past the house of Nabat, who had heard some of the poems that he had composed in praise of her. She had noticed him passing her window, each day more weary, but with a fire in his eyes that had lit the lamp of her heart for him. By this time Hafez was in a kind of trance. Everything that he did was automatic, and the only thing that kept him going was the fire in his heart and his determination to keep the lonely vigil.

Early on the morning of the fortieth day the Angel Gabriel (some say Khizer) appeared to him. Gabriel gave Hafez a cup to drink which contained the Water of Immortality, and declared that Hafez had also received the gift of poetry. Then Gabriel asked Hafez to express his heart's desire. All the time that this was happening, Hafez could not take his eyes off Gabriel. So great was the beauty of the Angel that Hafez had forgotten the beauty of Nabat. After Gabriel had asked the question, Hafez thought: "If Gabriel the Angel of God is so beautiful, then how much more beautiful God must be." Hafez answered: "I want to be united with the Beauty of God!" On hearing this, Gabriel directed Hafez to a certain street in Shiraz where there was a shop where perfumes were made and sold and a little fruit that was owned by a man named Mahmud Attar. Gabriel said that Attar was the Perfect Master, the *Qutub*... a God-realized soul, who had sent Gabriel to Hafez for Hafez's sake, and that if Hafez would serve Attar faithfully, Attar promised that one day Hafez would attain his heart's desire.

So Hafez joined the small select circle of Attar's disciples, but it wasn't until forty years later Hafez that received the mantle of God-realization from Attar. Unlike Mahmud Attar who always remained veiled as to his true identity, Hafez's fame spread far and wide, and as will be seen further on, it was only Hafez's quick tongue and sense of humour that constantly saved him from death or imprisonment.

The story of Hafez's vigil had made him known throughout Shiraz and the poetry that he now wrote, in praise of his beloved and out of longing to gain his heart's desire became known and sung throughout Shiraz. Nabat had lost her heart to him but the difference in their status caused many problems. Hafez saw and thought of her beauty as a reflection of God's Beauty... the Beauty of her Creator. As his love for her increased, it increased his desire for his Beloved (God) Whom he now saw as her higher Self, and it was to this higher Self manifesting through her grace and beauty that he composed his *ghazals*.

He also saw the wisdom and mercy of God manifesting through his Master Mahmud Attar, and he composed many poems praising his Master and begging Attar to fulfil the promise of Union with God. When Hafez went to visit Attar, Attar would ask Hafez to recite his latest poem, then Attar would spiritually analyze it for the sake of Hafez and the other disciples, (this practice continued for forty years). Then, the disciples would put tunes to the *ghazals* and the songs would soon be sung throughout Shiraz by the minstrels (such as Hajji Ahmed) and the masses and the fame of Hafez continued to grow.

Soon Hafez's poems were being sung at Court and the new king, Abu Ishak, who had much love for good poetry and art, wine and philosophy, sent an invitation to Hafez to come and recite some of his *ghazals*. Hafez accepted and a strong friendship grew between the them. Abu Ishak was intoxicated by the verse and knowledge and humour of this young man and introduced him to many of the notable people who frequented his court. Hafez was introduced to painters and other poets including Persia's greatest satirist, the infamous Obeyd Zakani, the author of 'Cat and Mouse' and many other works critical of the upper levels of society and hypocritical clergy and false Sufis and ribald stories and poems as well as many beautiful *ghazals* that would have influenced Hafez. When he was later forced by the vicious dictator Mubariz to leave Shiraz and his friends he would compose the following *ghazal*...

I am leaving the land of Shiraz, as my life will be taken...
ah, because of this unavoidable despair my heart's broken.
I go beating my head with my hands, feet sinking in shit:
what will happen to me... on this road, what will happen?
Now, I cry out like the nightingale that is lost in love...
now, like the heartsick bud, my collar has been torn open.
If I leave this city I'm leaving what I have for an unknown:
when I go through those city gate... my life is gone then.
As I leave my Self... heart and friends, Shiraz behind me...
I go on, hopelessly looking back and remembering... when.
There is no strength in my hands left to hold the reins...
can legs go on... when strength from them has been taken?
I'm so sick today and heart's aching from the pain of love:
no help, wise friends... parents' advice I should have taken.
O Obeyd, this is not a journey that I wanted to make...
sky pushes me and then the chain of Fate pulls me... again.

Jahan Malek Khatun, the daughter of the previous monarch, Abu Ishak's oldest brother, Masud Shah... who is perhaps the greatest female poet Persia/Iran has produced... and who was a close friend and pupil of Hafez and constantly sought his help with her poetry, would poignantly state in the preface to her large Divan... "Everyone wishes for recognition in this world and to leave the world something worthwhile to be remembered by. When someone dies that one will be forgotten but if that one leaves a memory in people's minds they never forget such a one. Poems and literature are the best way to be remembered in the world. I am... Princess Jahan, the daughter of Masud Shah and I preferred... I sometimes had to choose a lonely path. Don't choose to be alone but also don't choose to open your heart. I composed poems all day long. Sometimes untalented and lazy people teased or found fault with me. Only some people are able to compose poetry. If composing poems is so bad we wouldn't have so many poets. At first I thought it wasn't a good occupation because it was disapproved of and not liked in the society that I lived in. After sometime I realized that our Prophet Mohammed's daughter composed poems and other women too, including his wife Ayesha. I began to compose poems everyday... it became my pleasure.

If mine you will be, it is my pleasure:
and if you kill me, it is my pleasure.
You may never be mine I know but if
you remember me, it is my pleasure!

"Composing poems isn't easy... you have to learn a great many things about it. I've done my best but if there are problems with my poems, forgive me. If I didn't do as well as I could and my poems are not as good as they should be then please forgive me."

And finally, among many other poets were the much older Khaju Kirmani, Abu Ishak's official Court poet and author of many *masnavis* and *ghazals* of the first order and Emad of Kirman the Sufi and Court poet of Shah Shuji a later ruler whom Hafez came into conflict with. He would also have met ministers, judges, scholars and the highest members of the orthodox clergy, who having heard of Hafez and his poetry, eyed him with jealousy and suspicion, for Hafez had been free in his criticisms of their deceit and hypocrisy.

Abu Ishak was a humble but powerful ruler, who was also a great patron of the arts which flourished during his reign that lasted for ten years.

For Hafez, during this period, his life must have seemed to have been split in two, and this is reflected in many of his *ghazals*. On one hand there is the pursuit of knowledge and truth through the intellect and on the other hand is his growing desire for Union with God. More and more, he recognized the fruitlessness of trying to *know* God, and more and more his heart told him to let go of the mind and give full rein to feelings.

Although Hafez had reached, while still in his thirties, the height of Shiraz society, and he had the ear of famous and powerful men including the Shah and his advisors, there was a rebellious streak in him. He had a wanderlust, a vagrant soul that prompted him constantly to give it all away and become like one of the God-intoxicated outcasts that he had seen on the back-roads and on the outskirts of Shiraz. These were the kalandars, the dervishes dressed in rags, indifferent to the world, singing the praises of God and living on the few scraps of food that may be thrown their way. He knew, however, that this was not the answer for him. He had his master Attar, whom he had to obey, and he had responsibilities to his wife (not Nabat) and child and to the people of Shiraz who were singing his songs, and who more and more, looked to him for some direction in their relationships to God and to each other. As time passed, he realized that he must somehow steer a middle course and that responsibilities were there to be fulfilled; that desires for anything other than God must be abandoned and that one must become mad for God inside, while on the outside showing no pain or sign at all.

This period of Hafez's life was not without problems for the young teacher. It seems that through a set of circumstances that are unclear, he fell into debt and had to leave Shiraz for two years and stay in Isfahan.

Although Hafez now had notoriety, friends in high places and enough money to live on, he also had a secret life that consisted of his love for Shakh-e-Nabat who still inspired him, and his love and obedience and relationship to Attar, who with his small group of disciples was unknown to the majority of the population. Hafez was torn between the mind and the heart, and with Attar's guidance he tried to balance and integrate the two, but this process was a long drawn-out painful one, which was to last for the next thirty years.

During the late 1340's Abu Ishak became worried by the growing power of the tyrannical ruler of Yazd and Kirman, Mubariz al-Din Muhammad ibn Muzaffar. Twice Abu Ishak invaded Kirman and he failed both times. In 1350 he tried to take Yazd but again he failed; and after failing one more attempt at taking Kirman, he was defeated two years later. Mubariz now invaded his enemy's camp and after a nine-month battle resisted by the brave Shirazis he captured Shiraz in 1353 and Abu Ishak fled to Isfahan.

In 1353 when Mubariz entered Shiraz he plundered, murdered and raped and immediately, with the help of the false Sufi Shaikh Ali Kolah and his thousands of blue-robed followers, closed the taverns and wineshops, which was a sign of his puritanism against the liberated citizens of Shiraz.

Mubariz Muzaffar was a stern, cruel and ruthless ruler who was famous for executing many of the city's citizens with his sword in one hand and the *Koran* in the other.

Unable to earn a living at the college, Hafez who was an excellent calligrapher, began to copy manuscripts of other poets to receive enough money for his family to survive.

But the tyrant's death was soon to follow. In 1358 while he was conquering Tabriz, his son Shuja who could no longer bear his father's madness and cruelty took him prisoner and to repay him for his atrocities and to prevent him from escaping, blinded this dictator.

Hafez was re-instated and resumed his duties as a teacher at the college. While the poems of Hafez written during this oppressive reign of Mubariz Muzaffar were poems of protest at the atrocities that he committed. With the coming to power of Shah Shuja, Attar had begun to internalize Hafez's consciousness and Hafez's poems became more subtle, 'spiritually impressionistic,' for Hafez had begun to experience the inner realms of consciousness.

While the poems that he wrote during the time of Abu Ishak could be called 'spiritual romanticism' and those under Muzaffar the dictator: protest poems, the poems of the following period had begun to break new ground, and he was creating an impressionistic way of writing that was completely new, fresh, vibrant and subtle.

But the period of Shah Shuja's reign was also not without problems for Hafez. Shah Shuja, who also knew the *Koran* by heart and considered himself something of a poet, grew jealous of Hafez although it was because of their common interests that a friendship had developed between them in the beginning.

Hafez's enemies, the orthodox clergy, the false Sufi Ali Kolah and his many followers and some other poets who were jealous of him, had made Shiraz an unsafe place by constantly slandering him and complaining about him to Shah Shuja, who was now completely under their sway for the previous prime minister Haji Kivam was no longer at court to protect him having died when Mubariz invaded the city.

Hafez was about to go into hiding but this proved to be unnecessary because early in 1363 Shah Shuja's brother Shah Mahmud who was the ruler of Abarguh and Isfahan took Shiraz.

Shah Shuja retaliated by invading Isfahan and this produced a treaty between the two brothers. But this was not to last, for in the next year Shah Mahmud with the help of Uvays the ruler of Baghdad since 1355, attacked Shiraz and after eleven months of fierce fighting by the weary Shirazis he entered the city.

The enemies of Hafez, wary of the new ruler, refrained from their persecution of him. His popularity with the citizens of Shiraz, who called him 'The Tongue of the Hidden' and 'The Interpreter of Mysteries' had grown, and by now had spread over all of Persia.

By 1369 the danger in the situation became critical and Hafez and his wife packed some provisions and late one night fled the city, taking the road to Yazd. They were to spend the next two years there, and many of the poems written during this bitter time were full of homesickness for Shiraz, where Hafez's Master was, and where his friends, including Shakh-e-Nabat, waited for his return.

Back in Shiraz, Shah Shuja had become embroiled in the bitter controversy over whether Hafez should be allowed to end his exile and return to Shiraz. The people were calling for the return of their favourite poet and champion, and on the other side Hafez's enemies continued to slander him. Shuja had become wary and weary of the influence of the clergy upon him and decided to deal them a blow by allowing Hafez to return, and by doing this, not only would he put them in their place, but again gain the love and respect of the common people. He sent a message, asking Hafez to come back to Shiraz.

On returning he was once again re-instated to his position at the college and he resumed his old life and his relationship with his Master, Mahmud Attar. It was late in 1375 and Hafez had been obeying his Master for 35 years and still he had not gained his heart's desire. When he once again complained to Attar about this, Attar replied: "Patience is the key to Joy."

One day in 1381 Hafez went to visit Attar. Hafez's patience had come to an end. When he was alone with Attar he began to weep and when his Master asked him why he was weeping, Hafez through desperation cried out: "What have I gained by being your obedient disciple for nearly forty years?" Mahmud Attar replied: "Be patient and one day you will know." Hafez cried: "I knew I would get that answer from you," and left the room.

It was exactly forty days before the end of their forty year relationship. Hafez went home and entered a circle that he drew on the ground. Through love and desperation he had decided to enter self-imposed 'Chehel-a-Neshmi,' in which the lover of God sits within a circle for forty days and if the lover of God can succeed in this difficult practice, God will grant whatever he desires. The love and strength and bravery of Hafez was so great that he succeeded in never leaving the circle, no matter what God had in store for him.

On the fortieth night Attar again sent to him the form of the Angel Gabriel as he had done forty years earlier, who asked him what was his heart's desire. Hafez replied: "My only desire is to wait on the pleasure of my Master's wish."

Before dawn appeared on the last day Hafez left the circle and rushed towards the house of his Master, Mahmud Attar. Attar met him at the door and embraced him, gave him a drink of two year old wine and made him God-realized. Hafez had finally attained his heart's desire after forty long years.

During the remaining eight years of his life, Hafez wrote half of the poems that bear his name. He no longer wrote of his desire for the Beloved, for now he was the Beloved. He wrote of the Unity of God, of the temporality of the world and its works and of the stages of the Path to God-realization and he gave advice to others how to best avoid the traps of the Path. The poems written after Realization are written from the Authority of Divine Knowledge and have a Perfect detachment and Merciful involvement that sets them apart from the other poems that were written from various stages on the road to the Truth.

Quickly Hafez gathered his disciples around him and began to teach them, using his poems to illustrate the various Spiritual points that he wanted them to understand. Because his fame had become so widespread and people were travelling from all parts of Persia and other countries to be in his presence, he had to seclude himself to a degree to be able to continue to teach his chosen disciples, and to write his ghazals that were eagerly awaited by his many devotees, and his enemies who continued to plot against him.

It is 1387 and Hafez, head bent, is kneeling (and coughing) before the golden throne of Timur the Lame who has plundered and murdered his way across Persia (killing all the inhabitants of Isfahan, all 70,000 and piling their heads outside the city in a huge gruesome pyramid). Hafez's clothes are badly torn, his turban's disheveled... he coughs a heavy cough as he squints and looks up to see standing before that throne the forty-two year-old Timur, the dictator, thick-necked... a stocky, strong-looking bull of a man, bristling with anger and worldly power. Advisors and clerics stand behind him as his Court recorder (his son) writes down all that happens and all that is said in a book to be entitled *'I am Timur, the World Conqueror'*. The following account from my novel/biography *Hafez of Shiraz: Book 3 The Final Years* is taken from that account.

He looks down at the old, famous and *infamous* poet, brought before him and shouts, his great voice, booming out...

"I know of *you* Hafez... any other poet here today... I would not know from even Adam. Tell me, old man, did *you* compose this:

Last night I saw that on Winehouse door angels knocked,
they took the clay of Adam and it into a cup they shaped.
Inhabiting eternal harems, veiled and pure Angelic ones...
upon me lying in dust, a sweet intoxicating wine poured.
Thank God, between us there is peace and contentment:
to this... many a cup of gratitude dancing huris drained.
No wonder a hundred harvests of fantasy led me astray,
when from Path, aware Adam by a grain was betrayed.
The heavens could not bear that Trust's heavy burden...
they threw dice, and on mad lover, helpless me, decided.
That is no true fire that makes the candle's flame dance,
it is where the moth's harvest by that Fire is annihilated.
Pardon the seventy-two arguing sects, because unable to
see the Truth, on the door of illusion they have pounded.
No one has like Hafez torn the veil from Thought's face,
since the tips of long hair, Speech's Brides first combed.

"Amir Timur, my eyes are very weak and I can hardly see you, but, your voice is clear and you recite my poem... beautifully."

"Hafez, in this poem you are being blasphemous because in the second couplet you have said:

Inhabiting eternal harems, veiled and pure Angelic ones...
upon me lying in dust, a sweet intoxicating wine poured.

"Here, you have said that God has a *harem*. On top of this sacrilege you've brought disgrace on the Almighty for you've stated that His women have left His *harem* to be with *you* in the dust by the side of the road drinking wine and enjoying yourselves with *you!*"

Timur juts out his formidable chin and waits... as Hafez, coughing up phlegm onto the polished floor finally clears his throat and answers in a voice that captures all who hear it, reverberating for the rest of their lives.

"Amir Timur, I've uttered no blasphemy or disgraced the Almighty in that couplet. In the first line of that couplet I've said... *Inhabiting eternal harems, veiled and pure Angelic ones.* The two words *inhabiting eternal* mean that the *harem* that I am talking about is not an ordinary *harem* but what I'm meaning is a mysterious... a secret *harem*. I talk here of a *harem* which has a secret mystery that isn't known... a *harem* in which chastity... purity is the rule. Also, I haven't said that there are *women* in God's *harem*... as a matter of fact I haven't mentioned women at all. I've talked about the 'inhabitants of the *harem*' and not the 'women of the *harem*'. I haven't talked about a worldly *harem* but about a *harem* that's so sacred no stranger can enter. It was at midnight in spring that this poem came to me. It was beautiful weather and one could smell the flowers in the atmosphere. Ecstasy filled my heart and the nightingales were singing. While I composed this *ghazal* I was so full of ecstasy and joy that I could feel that I was involved in the essence of Creation. It seemed as though angels of paradise were alive inside me and I'd become an angel. While I was in that ecstatic state that *ghazal* came to me."

Timur frowns.

"In the second line of that couplet you state that angels of paradise have drunk *wine* with you, don't you? Drinking wine is forbidden... as you well know!"

Hafez looks down at his feet and then stretches his old, bent back and smiles in the direction of his accuser and clears his throat again (spitting black-blood on the floor) and replies.

"O Amir... this... er... drinking of wine, is an expression of the Sufis and doesn't mean the drinking of wine in any worldly sense. It refers to gaining knowledge from those who've achieved... perfection. As with the drinking of ordinary wine (which is prohibited, which is the cause of intoxication)... the gaining of true knowledge from the Perfect Master also causes a similar intoxication for that one who is seeking God. The Winehouse for the Sufi is that place where this divine type of wine is taken. The Winehouse is that place where true knowledge is gained. At midnight during that Springtime I became so full of ecstasy that (as I've already said)... the presence of angels *came*... and they spoke to me. They seemed to be telling me the secrets of Creation. And so... when I say in that *ghazal* that they were drinking wine with me... I'm telling of my *feelings* at that time."

Timur is fascinated now and leans forward and asks the old, rheumy poet.

"Tell me... *what* were those secrets... that they told to you... eh?"

Once again Hafez clears his terribly infected throat and looks up from his old, battered boots in the direction of the 'world conqueror' and sweetly smiles and replies.

"Amir Timur, it was at midnight that the angels of Paradise revealed the secrets of the Universe into my *creative imagination*. But, you *must* understand... that it was merely a feeling that was created by my imagination and as it was impossible for me to tell of those images in my mind, I told them... finally, in this poem. When a mystic on the Spiritual Path is deep in thought, he experiences some feelings that he cannot talk about... feelings impossible to explain. One can't tell in words these feelings, for one can only tell of coldness or softness or of something rough. When you talk of these sensations others can understand what you're saying. Inner feelings and those of a Spiritual nature cannot be described in the same way. If one tries to describe these, even the fact that we're trying to describe them will be questioned by the one who hears such an attempt. It's my opinion that even one who's on the Spiritual path when he hears late at night the song of a nightingale and the sound of the call to prayer when the atmosphere is full of the scent of flowers... that one has feelings that he can't describe with words. So... this is why at that time I couldn't tell what those angels of my creative imagination told me... and so... that is the reason why I can't tell to you now what those secrets were that they were talking with me about. If this wasn't so, I'd have also put all of that into the poem."

"Hmmm..." Timur begins, "an answer to which I suppose there's no argument, my clever poet. Now, there's another matter that I wish to take up with you. I've saved this city with the agreement that each of its citizens pay a tax... and you, O you *famous poet* are the only one not to pay that tax. For a some time I've been waiting to catch up to you!"

Hafez looks up and smiles. His eyes ablaze with Divine light and love. Timur is taken aback, steps a little backwards and sits down and thinks for a second or two, then he points at Hafez and shouts with not nearly so much force as before...

"Are you not the poet who wrote those lines that are sung all over my kingdom, even by my own soldiers, who pay with their lives if I hear them singing them?"

Hafez smiles mischievously.

"I've composed so much, it's all a matter of taste! Amir, please, *what* is the poem?"

Timur scowls, leans forward, elbows on knees, then recites in his booming voice.

If that Turkish beloved of Shiraz would take this heart in hand...
for that one's Hinduish mole I'd barter Bokhara and Samarkand.
Hafez looks thoughtful.

"Ah, yes! You recite so well and for a change, so very accurately. As before, it was composed *some time ago*... please, and what do you find... ehem... offensive in that... old *ghazal* of... yours truly?"

Timur, furious, jumps to his enormous, hairy feet again and limps over... advisors and officials and members of the Court jump or lean back in fear of the consequences. Timur pulls his great scimitar from its scabbard and holds it aloft and thrusts forward his great, gold-encrusted chest and bellows.

"With the blows of this scimitar I... have conquered most of the known world. I have laid waste thousands of towns to enrich my twin capital cities of Bokhara and Samarkand and you, you... who can't even pay your tax... you, you who would give them both away for the black mole on some loved one's cheek!"

The onlookers gasp as one then silence reigns as the almost scarlet faced Timur bends over the pathetic-looking form of the sick, small, ugly, old poet. Hafez blinks, then smiles his ironical smile as he opens his bloodstained chained hands and looks with a twinkle in his eye into those bloodshot eyes of the so-called master. The Perfect Master, Hafez, quietly replies...

"It's because of such *extravagant generosity*... you can see me... in this state of poverty... that I... am in today!"

Timur's mouth drops open in astonishment as do all the other mouths of those in attendance... then Timur splutters, now his great chest begins to heave and finally it reaches his throat and he begins to roar with laughter! Those surprised *others* (Timur rarely laughs) finally, cautiously follow suit. Hafez grins and eventually drops his old head. Now Timur has recovered and shouts to the Court...

"Ah, I respect so much a fearless and witty man! Even if I'm not so appreciative of his poetry."

He laughs again, they all laugh. He staggers back and sits on the throne, holding his stomach and shouts.

"Treasurer, fill up his purse... we can't have such an 'infamous' poet wandering the city totally poverty-stricken! Dismissed!"

Hafez nods... as he is unchained and a large purse is thrust into his hands and as he slowly limps, coughing, (and still spitting) towards the door. The Perfect Master, Hafez, had outwitted the so-called master, Timur, the dictator. Two months after their meeting Timur headed north once again to his twin-capitals of Bokhara and Samarkand, that were being besieged by the Tuqatmish, an engagement that was to occupy his attention for the following four years. Hafez had (through that encounter) subtly changed the situation and he and Shiraz had been left in peace once again.

It was early 1388 and in two short years Hafez's time to leave his physical form would come. He continued to write, but now at a faster pace for he could see that his old body was preparing to blend with the dust of Shiraz. The poems that he wrote during this period are beautiful for their insight into the Nature of God, their compassion and understanding and their poignant love for the people of Shiraz and the whole world, and because of his knowledge of his impending death.

By 1390, his body was racked with a sickness that he had been suffering for many years. The small ugly form had served him well for 70 years and this old cloak that his soul wore, had been the vessel that had helped to steer him to the Realization of the Existence that has no beginning or end.

The news rapidly spread through the city that their most loved (and hated) citizen had passed away. Thousands walked towards his home where he lay, surrounded by his closest disciples. However, his lifelong enemies, the hypocritical orthodox clergy had also heard the news of the death of their rival and castigator.

Later, Hafez's body was carried towards the Muslim burial ground in the rose-bower of Musalla, on the banks of the Ruknabad, which he loved and praised in his poems, and to where he often had walked and sat down to write many of his *ghazals*.

The Ulama of Shiraz, with his fellow clergy, refused to allow for Hafez's body to be buried as a Muslim and claimed that his poetry was impious. The long knives that they had been trying to drive into his back were now fully on show, for he was no longer there to defend himself against them with his sharp wit and sense of irony.

The followers of Hafez and the many citizens of Shiraz began to argue with those who followed the orthodox point of view, and in the heat of the argument, someone suggested that they should ask the poet himself for the solution. The clergy, by now afraid of the size and fervour of Hafez's supporters, reluctantly agreed to the suggestion of tearing up many of his poems into couplets and placing them into a large urn, and to call on a small boy in the crowd to select one couplet from it. The couplet that was selected was…

Don't you walk away from this graveside of Hafez, because,
although he is buried in mistakes he is travelling to Paradise.

Even after death, Hafez had, with tongue in cheek, outwitted his bitter rivals, and this practice of consulting his *Divan* as an oracle has continued from this incident, shortly after his death, down into this present age.

The tomb of Hafez was surrounded by a garden of roses and his body was laid at the foot of a cypress tree which he had planted.

Soon after his death Hafez's popularity had reached such proportions that even the orthodox Muslims claimed him as one of their own.

It is thought that Hafez never collected all of his poems together during his lifetime (although some scholars say that he did, and the collection was lost) even though many of his friends constantly asked him to do so. After his death two collections of his *ghazals* and other poems were assembled. One was an edition by a friend and student, Muhammad Gulandam, who also wrote a preface to this edition which although quite long deserves to be quoted here. After giving due praise to the Prophet and the wisdom and power of eloquent speech he goes on...

"And now to move on without any extravagant ceremony to the pen-name of those words and the subject of these introductions, the one owner of the attributes... the lord, the greatest master, the fortunate, the late, the martyr, the glory of the learned, master of the expert writers, the mine of spiritual subtleties, the treasury of divine knowledge, the sun (shams) of the community and of the faith (ud-din)... Mohammed, the Hafez of Shiraz, may God preserve his tomb and promote his rank in heaven for his lustrous, delectable poetry is the envy of the fountain of life and those daughters of his thoughts are the object of envy for the beautiful *huris* and *paris* of paradise. His heart-ravishing couplets obliterate Sahban's words and his exquisite creations cause neglect of Hassan's beneficence...

Like string of pearls and the gardens of Paradise
and security of heart and favour of sleep's sighs.
(Qayravani)

With beautifully real words he sweetened the palates of ordinary people and with profound meanings he salted mouths of the upper class. By him were opened doors of understanding to the leaders of the exoteric and also from him enlightened matters were increased for those masters of the esoteric. At each event he said words that befit the occasion and for every delicate meaning he created such rare expressions. He said many real things in few words and he comprehended many kinds of innovations in his compositions.

Sometimes he led the intoxicated of love's alleyway on the road of mutual love and flirting and smashed the glass of their patience on the rock of impermanence...

If you go to our school wash all pages white,
because in the book, never love's learning is.

Sometimes he encouraged dreg-drainers to be devotedly attending upon the Perfect Master in companionship in the holy place of the Winehouse...

As long as wine and Winehouse name and trace shall be,
the dust of path of the Perfect Master... our face shall be.

The overflowing of the clear stream of his fine nature which is like 'the sweet easily-swallowed, pleasant to drink' *[xxxv, 12]*, has extended and is spreading to those low and high and the benefit of his excellent and bountiful words which are 'like a niche within it is a lamp' *[xxiv, 35]*, has illuminated all far and near. The legitimate magic of his nature tied a knot in the tongue of eloquence and poetic necklace of his thought is surpassing the merchandise of sea and the mine. Drops of the flowing fountains of his brilliant genius and worth water the gardens of meetings of friends with that pure flowing water and 'everything's from water... it makes everything alive' *[xxi, 30]*. The breeze from the rosegarden of his intelligence in the gardens of souls spreads the meaning of the verse... 'Contemplate the works of God's mercy, how He gives life to the earth after its death' *[xxx, 50]*. His eloquent words like the breathing of Christ have given life to dead hearts and the drops from his Khizer-endowed pen has made a miracle appear on the throne of language. See how the spring wind has acquired such fineness from the breeze of his virtues and cheeks of the hyacinth and the wild rose have taken beauty and fresh tenderness from his lustrous poetry... and the form of the box-tree and the straightness of the free cypress have received elegance, symmetry and motion from the firmness of his mind's judgement...

You feeble versifiers, why are you envious of Hafez?
God's gift, sweet words pleasing heart and mind, is.

Without pretence he strung on the thread of poetry every pearl and gem existing in the jewelry shop of nature for the sake of the elegant beauty of the virgins of his heart's *harem*... so, when he saw himself in the clothing and robes of expression and ornament of metaphor, he opened his tongue and claimed…

Majnun's time has passed, now it's our turn…
every one gets five days term: five days, yours.

He contended with proponents and opponents with style and grace and he participated in gathering and parties of the common folk and the upper-class and in the private meetings of religious and political figures, king and beggars and the learned and the uneducated and in each place and opportunity he caused tumult and stirred up excitement and enthusiasm.

Last night Hafez, secluded, Winehouse's guest became:
he broke his promise and the winecup his quest became.

And he was safe and secure from the flaw of skepticism and the disturbance of sensuality… and the hand of misappropriation never touched his reputation's skirt and no one could lift the finger of betrayal and fraud and the cheek of ecstasies was protected from corruption of reproach and blame, guarding piety and preserving sincerity, as he said…

If my garment is soiled… what is the difference?
whole world is witness to innocent ways: Yours.

Then in a short time the loaded camels of his world-conquering *ghazals* reached the borders of Turkistan and India and caravans of his heart-pleasing words quickly traveled the districts and frontiers of both Iraks and Azerbaijan. The strong wind blows and the much-traveled man goes gently with the ease of the Messiah… the journey of stories goes forward and imagination travels by night. The Sufis without his stirring *ghazals* wouldn't become excited and the parties of wine-lovers without the sweetmeats of his taste-arousing, delightful speech wouldn't come alive…

Ghazal-singing of Hafez went so far… by Heaven
the melody of the music of Venus… was forgotten.
The gift of speech in the ghazal in such a way he gave
as no other poet gave… in that form of versification.
When your heart his sweet-flowing poetry has, say…
"To Hafez's soul, God's countless mercies be given."

However, because of diligent study of the *Koran* and attention to piety and doing good works and his investigation of the *Kashaf* and

Miftah, and reading the *Matali'* and *Misbah* and his acquisition and scrutiny of the canons of literature and the appreciation of the works of the *divans* of the Arab poets... he did not finish collecting his scattered *ghazals* and he was never busy in assembling and fixing their couplets.

He, who has written these pages... (may God forgive me whatever has passed)... during college and at lectures with the refuge-of-religion, our master and lord, the teacher of mankind, adornment of the community and religion, slave of God... Haji Kivam (may God exalt his rank to the summit of the highest heaven)... many times when we were talking together, he would often mention in the course of our conversation that Hafez should tie these precious gems of spiritual profit into one necklace and that he should join on one thread these rare gems and pearls so that it would become an elegant and magnificent necklace of the people of the time and a belt and scent-box of the brides of all times. That excellent one... (Hafez) had entrusted the raising of this building to the inappropriateness of circumstances and fortune and offered as an excuse the hostility and treachery of the people of that time until in the year 792/1390 he gave his life to the guardians of the eternal fate and to be carried from the cloak of existence out of the narrow passage of death.

His pure soul joined those dwellers of the higher world and he became a companion of the beautiful black-eyed *huris* of Paradise...

In 'abjad' of year of B and S and Z (=792/1390),
from day of auspicious flight of most laudable,
he was going towards that highest Paradise...
Shams-ud-din Mohammed, the incomparable
of the epoch. When I passed his pure dust, the
purity and light of his tomb, to me was visible.

And after some time the old, just claims of companionship and the necessities of the promises of friendship with him and the encouragement of sincere loved ones and the instigation of loyal friends, (from brilliance of whose faces the page of ecstasy is given beauty and by the beauty of whose education the goods of all accomplishments receive perfection)... inspired and made this poor one, me, to arrange this book, the *Divan,* and assemble it and organize it eventually, like this. My hope is that by the benevolence of the Giver of Existence and the Source of the Good and Generosity... this author and copier and collector and hearer... in showing kindness for these difficult times and in the course of this study, would be blessed with a new life and limitless joy and that He would let the mistakes pass by the excellence of the content and sweet grace of the perfection... and so he gives a proper submission to the Omnipotent."

Another collection was made by the poet Kasim e-Anvar who died in 1431. His collection consisted of 569 *ghazals* and was called the '*Divan e-Khwaja-e Hafez.*'

The change of consciousness in the world brought about by Hafez during his lifetime had been great, but his influence on the world and on art and poetry had just begun and we are still being greatly affected by it.

2. THE SPIRITUALITY OF HAFEZ

"There is no equal of Hafez in Poetry. He was a Perfect Master."
Meher Baba.

In the opening chapter of this introduction, I wrote a out how at the age of sixty-one Hafez experienced God-realization at the hands of his Master, the Perfect Master Mahmud Attar, after serving Attar faithfully for forty years.

Before proceeding further in this discussion on Hafez's spirituality and its influence on his life and work, and on the stages of the Path to God, in relation to Hafez, and on what it means to be the *Qutub*... Perfect Master (Man-God) and Avatar (God-man, Christ, Rasool, Buddha etc.), I will first define God-realization and the clearest and best definition that I know is that by Meher Baba in 'Discourses Vol. ii.' "To arrive at true self-knowledge is to arrive at God-realisation. God-realisation is a unique state of consciousness. It is different from all the other states of consciousness because all the other states of consciousness are experienced through the medium of the individual mind; whereas the state of God-consciousness is in no way dependent upon the individual mind or any other medium. A medium is necessary for knowing something other than one's own self. For knowing one's own self no medium is necessary. In fact, the association of consciousness with the mind is definitely a hindrance rather than a help for the attainment of real-isation. The individual mind is the seat of the ego or the consciousness of being isolated. It creates the limited individuality, which at once feeds on and is fed by the illusion of duality, time and change. So, in order to know the Self as it is, consciousness has to be completely freed from the limitation of the individual mind. In other words, the individual mind has to disappear but consciousness has to be retained . . . The consciousness which was hitherto associated with the individual mind is now freed and untrammeled and brought into direct contact and unity with the Ultimate Reality. Since there is now no veil between consciousness and the Ultimate Reality, consciousness is fused with the Absolute and eternally abides in It as an inseparable aspect promoting an unending state of infinite knowledge and unlimited bliss...

"God-realisation is a personal state of consciousness belonging to the soul which has transcended the domain of the mind. Other souls continue to remain in bondage and though they also are bound to receive God-realisation one day they can only attain it by freeing their consciousness from the burden of the ego and the limitations of the individual mind. Hence the attainment of God-realisation has a direct significance only for the soul which has emerged out of the time-process . . . It is possible for an aspirant to rise up to the mental sphere of existence through his own unaided efforts, but dropping the mental body amounts to the surrenderance of individual existence: This last and all-important step cannot be taken except through the help of a Perfect Master who is himself God-realised."

When Hafez was twenty one and he became a disciple of the Perfect Master Attar, Hafez's consciousness was that of a 'normal' person. He was conscious of the 'gross' world, of its sights and smells and sounds. I shouldn't really call Hafez a 'normal' person because he was in fact spiritually inclined from an early age and was fascinated by stories about the great Perfect Masters and saints of the past and he read all the Perfect Master-Poets and also learnt all of the Koran by heart. Already at an early age his thoughts dwelt constantly on God and he experienced great longing to be united with Him. Then at the age of twenty-one an incident occurred that was to become the 'point' of departure for him towards the spiritual Path to God-realization. He saw the beautiful woman Shakh-e-Nabat, 'Branch of Sugarcane,' and fell in love with the beauty of her. In her he saw the mirror of the beauty of his own true Self, the beauty of God. As Ibn al 'Arabi says in *Futuhat* II, 326': "And if you love a being for his beauty, you love none other than God, for He is the beautiful being. Thus in all its aspects the object of love is God alone. Moreover, since God knows Himself and he came to know the world, He produced it ad extra of His image. Thus the world is for Him a mirror in which He sees His own image, and that is why God loves only Himself, so that if He declares: 'God will love you,' it is in reality Himself that He loves."'

Hafez loved Nabat all his life, but it was not a lustful or possessing love that 'wants' an object for oneself, but a creative love for the Beauty of God, which eventually led him to his Master Attar; and it was this Beauty which he praised in his poetry, and in the 'Beloved' he recognized God's Beauty as symbolised in the being whom he loved, his 'Branch of Sugarcane.' This love of Hafez was so great that it became Divine. For forty years he obeyed and loved Attar, and over this period his ego and his desires were completely worn away.

Much has been written about Hafez's 'philosophy' of life which has been called 'rind' or unreason. It is true that Hafez approached the Truth or God through this subjective approach in which he advocated being an outcast, an outsider, outside formal religious rituals (although he probably participated in them under fear of death), to get intoxicated on God's love, to turn the back on reason and trying to 'know God,' and not to care what the world may say or think, for the relationship with God the Beloved is a personal one, a relationship between the lover and the Beloved; and the only way to gain the Beloved's special glance is to dare and dare again by surrendering everything at the Beloved's feet - everything, including the mind. This surrenderance that Hafez advocates in his life and poetry is of course a surrenderance of all inner thoughts and desires and eventually surrenderance of the whole of the ego. Hafez, as seen in the first chapter, was a responsible man, who was a husband and father and worked all of his life in a variety of occupations. He did not throw away his responsibilities and become a mad seeker searching for God. For Hafez, true love for God was an inner thing and the outer must be looked after also, so that it would in no way interfere with this surrenderance which is the most difficult surrenderance of all. Hafez continually in his poems, criticizes those who make a show of their love for God, the false Sufis in their blue robes or patched garments, and the priests on the pulpits preaching one thing to the masses but in private acting in a completely different way. For Hafez, the path was an inner path, walked down in the midst of everyday life, but fulfilling one's obligations in this world to family, friends and the state, and inwardly fulfilling one's obligations to God, by dedicating all of one's thoughts, desires and actions to the Beloved and not holding back even one.

This was not the only approach that Hafez advocated. The other way he followed all his life was an objective approach which showed that he never underestimated intelligence, when it is used to gain the Objective of everlasting value. The other approach that Hafez believed in was that of Pure Reason and as only the Perfect Master, the Complete Man, has knowledge of the Truth and has experienced the Secret of Life and has attained true detachment, peace and happiness, then one should recognize this fact and use all of one's intelligence to follow and gain the Secret of such a Master of Knowledge. The two paths are one, because the heart and the mind have to be balanced to achieve the balance that allows the soul to manifest itself.

In the poems of Hafez and the other great Master Poets who proceeded him, there is much imagery of a sensual nature if viewed only in a physical sense. This imagery concerns the power and allurements of wine and praises and describes the various features of the Beloved: the lip, hair, eyes, neck etc. All these symbols are used by Hafez to describe the aspects of God and the different stages the lover must pass through to gain Union with the Beloved (God). As has been explained by many of the commentators of this kind of Love poetry, there are many types of 'love.' There are the kinds of human love from the most lustful, to the highest kind that becomes selfless and eventually leads to Divine Love, which can only be gained by the Grace of God.

Those who have entered the Spiritual Path have been fortunate enough to have received from God this gift, and they have made God the Objective of all their love and striving and praise and poetry (if they write poetry as Hafez did).

The subject of the *ghazals* and other poems is this love (wine) which the Beloved feels for the lover and which the lover longs for, and experiences flowing from the Beloved's cup (heart) to him, filling his heart (cup) to overflowing. If the lover cannot feel this flow of love from God, this causes him great pain and despair.

The sensual imagery that Hafez and others use is the cloak which they use to dress this inner experience. By using such sensuous imagery Hafez spiritualizes the physical form and uses a language which is understandable to all, even the most gross conscious (even if he doesn't 'get' the essence of the poem, it still infiltrates his unconscious) and raises human love into the possibility of the Divine. Through such imagery Hafez expresses the agony and the ecstasy of his direct experience of God and makes these experiences available for all to share, whatever the stage of the reader's consciousness may be at the time of 'experiencing'- the poem.

This imagery of the whole of creation that Hafez raised to the Sublime, became recognized symbols used in later poetry and gave rise to later arguments (mainly by Western scholars, whose intellects were like steel walls between themselves and the true 'heart' of Hafez poetry) as to whether Hafez's poetry was to be regarded in a physical or a spiritual sense. Hafez himself many times throughout his *Divan* states that the symbols he uses are for spiritual states, that the Beloved, the Winebringer, Friend, Minstrel, Rose, are all God and that wine is Divine Love, the Truth. The scholars that have argued against Hafez's own statements have obviously been blinded by their own egos and have read Hafez's poetry as they wanted to, and not as he wanted them to. (I recommend that the reader of this English version familiarize him or herself with the meaning behind Hafez's symbolism by consulting the Glossary at the end of this introduction, before reading Hafez's poetry.)

When one reads the poems of Hafez in this context, as he wrote them and wanted them read, then every line, couplet and poem of Hafez becomes clear and tells the tale of Love in a universal and beautiful way, in such a human fashion (for love needs the form to express itself through), that Hafez talks to everyone, for everyone at some time has felt some kind of love. Hafez tells us of all the stages of love from the human to the Hu (=God) man, but always from the understanding that the goal of all life is to eventually be able to Love in the Divine way, and to experience the Love of God, and to become united with one's own true Self.

Ever since Hafez dropped his physical body in 1391 there has been a continuing discussion and argument among the various religionists and scholars of Persian Literature as to what was the 'religion' of Hafez. This is a hollow argument for a number of reasons: 1. God (or the Perfect Master) does not belong to a religion, all the religions belong to God. 2. Hafez was always concerned with the essence of Truth and continually denounced those who believed in the 'shell':

Pay regard to the jewel and leave the shell alone;
By that way... a bad reputation is left to its own.
from his 'The Wild Deer' masnavi.

3. Hafez was the lover or disciple of the Perfect Master Attar, and so Attar (until Hafez was God-realized) was Hafez's 'religion.'

Hafez is claimed by many Sufis to have been a Sufi. In the true sense of Sufism (love of God, respect for the essence of all paths to God, the need for a Perfect Master to help one to attain unity with the Beloved) Hafez was a Sufi, a true Sufi. But Hafez recognized that any approach to God can become abused and many 'Sufis' at the time when Hafez lived were doing this, and he continually criticizes their hypocrisy and deceit. It is claimed that Hafez was a Shi'ite Muslim because he wrote poems in praise of Mohammed and of Ali, their first Imam. What true Christian would not praise the bravery of Peter, and in this manner Hafez praised Ali - and so he definitely understood it in its essence. One could also call Hafez a Christian for in many of his poems he praises Jesus, but he also praises Abraham and Moses, so was Hafez a Jew? Zoroaster was also praised by Hafez, and Noah, and in fact all the Perfect Masters and the Godman Who were known in Persia at that time - for the religion of Hafez was the existence of God in human form, and this is the foundation of all true religions and Hafez was brave enough in an often strict Muslim country to recognize this and to declare it for all to hear.

The 'religion' of Hafez was the love of God in human form and beyond all form, and this 'religion' Hafez proclaims in all his poetry, and this 'religion' Hafez lived throughout his life. To try to put Hafez into a box labeled this or that 'religion' is an impossible task because God is impossible to classify; God can only be lived and 'religion' is the creation of man, and God is the Creator of all of mankind. As Hafez says...

O God, You are the remedy of those without remedy.
You know the remedy for me... and for those like me.
from his 'The Wild Deer' masnavi.

3. THE POETRY OF HAFEZ

"Not all poets were men of God-realization, however talented they were. Not all God-realized ones were poets, however high they were held in esteem and love. It was given to some of them to be God-realized and yet to have Nature's gift to express their thoughts and experiences in poetry. Hafez was one of them. Throughout the running thoughts of many of his compositions there is an underlying meaning which reveals his experiences belonging to specific states and stages of spirituality, the path of involution of consciousness from that of man to God. This he has done in the choicest of words, similes and metaphors in the everyday language of the time. He is looked on as the best poet of Iran to have balanced the most abstract with the most dense. Although Hafez had his mind always soaring the heights of divinity, he was careful to have his feet well set on the surface of the world and its affairs." Adi K. Irani.

While considering Hafez the poet, one should never forget at all times Hafez the man, and Hafez the Perfect Master. One should remember Hafez as a man: his weaknesses, his desires, his strengths, and his life as a husband and a father and his love for 'Branch of Sugarcane;' his various occupations as an assistant in a bakery, calligrapher and lecturer in Koranic studies and his work as a teacher; his friendship with the people of his time, be they beggars or kings, wise or foolish; his fame and his fortune and misfortune - all have an influence on his poetry that should not be forgotten.

The same can be said to an even greater degree about his spirituality. One should always remember his love for, and dedication to his Master, Attar; and that from about the time Hafez first began to write he was on the Path to God, which for the next forty years he traversed.

For the last ten years of his life he was a God-realized being, who was conscious of both God and mankind, of the Reality and the illusion, and for the last years of his life he was experiencing the Bliss, Knowledge and Power of God within himself; and at the same time the sufferings and happiness of others. All of this formed the basis of his poetry, and its influence cannot be over-estimated.

'The range of subjects covered by Hafez in his *ghazals* and other poems includes human and Divine love, Fate and fortune, the beauty of the Creation and its existence as an illusion. Also included are the subjects of youth and old age, hypocrisy and sincerity, war and peace, hope and hopelessness, greed and generosity, fear and bravery, God-intoxication and ordinary drunkenness, envy and jealousy, friendship and faith, the law of man and God's law, the worthlessness of material power and wealth, the power of God and the Perfect Masters and the Godman, the desperation caused by separation from the Beloved and the bliss of Union. He writes of the beauty and fragility of all life, the grief of losing loved ones; the need to make the most of every opportunity; the worthlessness of the intellect for discovering Truth and the worth of the heart; the wisdom of being able to laugh at oneself and to be honest with oneself and all others; the need to be serious about loving God; praise of God in all His aspects, as the Perfect Master and also His invisible aspect; the value of silence, prayer, wakefulness and constantly remembering the Beloved the traps of the externalities of formal religions, the unity of the essence of all religions; and many more subjects too numerous to mention.

Through the poetry of Hafez marches many of history's famous and infamous personalities. Some are dictators at whom Hafez laughs for being so stupid as to believe in material power. And there are the Perfect Masters and the Godman and the saints who are praised by Hafez for their wisdom, love and miraculous abilities. There are also the fools and the dreamers and the kings and the poets and the painters, soldiers, craftsmen, singers, thieves and magicians, the mad and the God-mad, the hypocrites and the sincere lovers of God.

Often, with his friend and fellow-poet Obeyd Zakani, he criticized the false Sufis such as Shaikh Ali Kolah who wore blue robes and plotted to get rid of anyone not agreeing to their fundamentalist dogmas and false ascetics like Abdullah bin Jiri who decked himself in rags and with others paraded their holiness in the market-place. He also criticized and threw in their faces, the ravings of the hypocritical clergy in their pulpits, and the power-hungry fanaticism of the false masters, the judges, police, cruel kings and their devious off-siders.

He also recognized the worth of honest men in positions of power and wrote poems to them (and has been criticized by some people because of this).

Very few poets of Persia (or the whole world)... except for Obeyd Zakani, have equaled Hafez in his revolt against the deceit and hypocrisy of people on all levels of society, wherever he saw it.

The sincerity of Hafez, whether he is writing about love and wine, or hypocrisy and deceit, exists in every line that he ever wrote, and is one of the many reasons why his poetry was loved by so many people during the time that he lived, and has been loved ever since. It is obvious that each poem comes straight from the heart and each poem subtly divulges the deepest feelings and thoughts that he experienced.

In the poetry of Hafez a new language was created, rich and colourful, simple and exact, beautiful and sparkling, fiery and profound. It seems as though all the great poetry of Persia and the rest of the world that preceded him, had culminated in his poetry; and he added to it an individuality that was sweet, sure, fluid and graceful, making it timeless enough to be still modern. If God had taken form as a Poet, it seems He would have been happy to have written as Hafez wrote.

Not only did Hafez have the great gift of being able to weave words together in a completely original way and express his ideas profoundly, but he also invented words and techniques which became a part of the common language and poetry of Persia. And in all this great tapestry of words and rhymes, of symbols and technical dexterity, the meaning or content which Hafez wanted to convey always came through loud and clear, for he never allowed any form or word or technique to hinder the expression of the content; in fact, he used his great skills in all these areas to give clarity, beauty and power to the meaning which he wanted the reader to experience.

"The work of Hafez, from beginning to end, is one series of beautiful pictures, ever revealing and most inspiring. Once a person has studied Hafez he has reached the top of the mountain, from whence he beholds the sublimity of the immanence of God." Inayat Khan.

GHAZAL

The form of poetry which Hafez nearly always used and which he loved more than any other was the *ghazal* (pronounced 'guz'el'). Hafez perfected this form and revolutionized it to such an extent that it is said that most *ghazals* written in Persia afterwards were either poor copies or became so involved in the form that they lost meaning and originality.

There is really no equivalent to the *ghazal* in English poetry, although as Masud Farzaad, the great Iranian authority on Hafez says, the sonnet is probably the closest. As a matter of fact, the *ghazal* is a unique form and its origin has been argued about for many centuries.

Some say that the *ghazal* originated in songs that were composed in Persia to be sung at court before Persia was converted to Islam, but not one song has survived to prove this. It is also possible that originally the *ghazals* were songs of love that were sung by minstrels in the early days of Persian history and that this form passed into poetry down the ages. I find this explanation plausible for the following reasons: firstly, the word *ghazal* means 'a conversation between lovers.' Secondly, the *ghazals* of Hafez, Sadi and others were often put to music and became songs, which have been popular in Persia from ancient times until now.

Whatever the origin, by the fourteenth century the *ghazal* had become a mature form of poetry. Among the great *ghazal* writers of the past were Nizami, Farid ud-Din Attar, Rumi, and Sadi; but with the *ghazals* of Hafez this form reached its summit.

The form of the *ghazal* at first glance seems simple, but on a deeper inspection it will be found that there is more to it than one at first sees.

It is usually between five and fifteen couplets ('beyts' or 'houses'), but sometimes more. A 'beyt' is 'a line of verse split into two equal parts scanning exactly alike.' Each couplet has a fixed rhyme which appears at the end of the second line. In the first couplet which is called the 'matla' meaning 'orient' or 'rising,' the rhyme appears at the end of BOTH lines. This first couplet has the function of 'setting the stage' or stating the subject matter and feeling of the poem. It reminds me of the 'Image' in the 'I Ching.' The other couplets or *beyts* have other names depending on their positions and often remind me of the 'changing lines' in the hexagrams of the 'I Ching.' One could say that the opening couplet is the subject, the following couplets the actions: changing, viewed from different angles, progressing from one point to another, larger and deeper, until the objective of the poem is reached in the last couplet. The final couplet is known as the 'maqta' or 'point of section.' One could compare this to the 'Judgement' in the 'I Ching.' This couplet almost always contains the 'takhallus' or pen-name of the poet, signifying that it was written by him and also allowing him the chance to detach himself from himself and comment on what effect the actions of the subject matter in the preceding couplets had on him. Often the poet uses a play on words when he uses his own pen-name: ('Hafez' or example means: a preserver, a guardian, rememberer, watchman, one who knows the *Koran* by heart).

In the *ghazal,* Hafez found the ideal instrument to express the great tension between the opposites that exist in this world. Having the strict rhyming structure of the same rhyme at the end of the second line of each couplet (after the first couplet) the mind must continually come back to the world and the poem and the rhyme. But by being allowed to use any word at the end of the first line of each couplet, one can be as spontaneous as possible and give the heart its full rein. This of course happens also in the first line of the first couplet, for whatever word (or rhyme sound) that comes out in the first line sets the rhyme for the rest of the *ghazal.* So the 'feeling' created by the rhyme is one that comes spontaneously from the heart, and this spontaneity is allowed to be expanded from then on in the non-rhyming lines, and to contract in those lines that rhyme, when the mind must function as an 'orderer' of the poem. This expansion and contraction, feeling and thinking, heart and mind, combine to produce great tension and power that spirals inward and outward and creates an atmosphere that I would define as 'deep nostalgia.' This deep nostalgia is a primal moving force that flows through all life, art and song, and produces within whoever comes into contact with it when it is consciously expressed, an irresistible yearning to unite the opposites that it contains. So, the subject matter of Hafez's *ghazals* is the movement of the opposites towards unity: grief and bliss, lover and Beloved, fear and bravery, desire and patience, separation and union, madness and sanity, youth and old age, drunkenness and sobriety, life and death, slave and king, the outcast true lover of God and the hypocritical laws of the church, friendship and loneliness, rose and nightingale, the church and the winehouse, the world that is passing and God Who never dies, the Perfect Master of Knowledge and the ignorant disciple, and so on in every *ghazal*.

Hafez, however, not only points out and explains these opposites, but also shows the invisible connection between the two; and this connection is there in all of his poetry, in every line and couplet; and this connection is connected to a point of Unity which flows through all the opposites and makes one yearn even more to be united with that Unity.

This optimism in Hafez's poetry can only be the result of one who has loved, and it is this love which is the unifying thread running through all his poems (even the ones criticizing the hypocrites, who Hafez feels for because they are the furthest from this Unity). This takes us along with him, for we ourselves recognize in his feelings, feelings that we have also experienced; and the same 'deep nostalgia' which he expresses is an expression of an area existing in everyone's soul, for it is the soul itself which is longing to be united with Itself, and the humour of this predicament has an irony which is not missed by Hafez, and which is there in his poems all the time. Like a screwdriver, Hafez screws his *ghazals* into the mind and the heart, and not content with that he goes further, he aims for the soul: the essence of everyone and everything. It is no wonder that people say: "Read Hafez and go mad," for Hafez creates in the reader such a longing to be drunk with the wine of Unity, that one becomes mad for God; and like Hafez, will not be content until this Union takes place.

MASNAVI

The *masnavi* is the form used in Persian poetry to write epic ballads or romances. Each couplet has a different rhyme with both lines rhyming with the same rhyme at the end of each line. This is to allow the poet greater freedom to go into a longer description of the subject he has chosen to present. All of the great long narrative poems of Persia were composed in this form which is a Persian invention and is not known in classical Arabic poetry. The most famous poems written in this form are the 'Shahnama' (Epic of the Kings) of Firdausi, the 'Five Treasures' of Nizami, the 'Seven Thrones' of Jami and the great 'Masnavi' of Rumi.

In the 'Book of the Winebringer' masnavi, Hafez also uses what appears to be a device that he invented in relation to the *masnavi* form. He invents an internal rhyme structure in most of the couplets by beginning many of them with "Winebringer, come" or "Give," and produces a kind of chant that is not dissimilar to the repetition of a word or words that he places at the end of many (if not most) of his *ghazals*. Many scholars have hailed Hafez's *masnavi* 'The wild Deer' as his masterpiece, but while agreeing with them that it is indeed a masterpiece, one could also say the same about the 'Book of the Winebringer' and many of the *ghazals* and other poems of Hafez.

QASIDA

This kind of poem resembles a *ghazal* in many ways except that it is longer than the *ghazal* and is often as long as a hundred couplets. In the first couplet, both the lines rhyme, and the same rhyme runs through the whole poem, the rhyme-word being at the end of the second line of each couplet (after the first couplet) as in the *ghazal*. The *qasida* is usually written in praise of someone and is often read in his or her presence, so it is stated that it shouldn't be too long or it might weary the listener. It has a number of sections: i. *matla* - the beginning, ii. *taghazzul* -introduction, iii. *guriz* - the couplets in praise of whoever it is written to, iv. *maqta*- the end. In the *qasida,* the *takhallus* or pen-name of the poet usually does not appear , and if it does it is not necessarily near the end or at the end as in the *ghazal.* Any metre may be used except that used for the *ruba'i* 'The Falcon with the Golden Wing,' I have placed amongst the poems in the *qasida* section because of its length, (and because it is in the *qasida* section in some editions) but it could equally go in the section for *ghazals* as in fact it is a long *ghazal,* or more accurately, a cross between a *ghazal* and a *qasida.*

MUKHAMMAS

The *mukhammas* consists of verses of five lines. In the first verse, all of the lines rhyme. In the verses that follow, the first four lines rhyme with each other and the last line rhymes with the rhymes of the first verse. A close inspection of this form shows that it is also as with the *ghazal,* a spiral, and probably originated from the *ghazal.* There are other forms in Persian poetry similar to it, with six and seven lines in each verse. In some ways a *mukhammas* is like an extended form of the *ghazal,* but unlike the *ghazal* it is a totally rhymed poem and doesn't have the freedom of the *ghazal,* where one can be spontaneous because of the lack of rhyme in the first line of each couplet after the first. As far as I know Hafez only wrote one *mukhammas.*

BINO RHYME

The bino rhyme is the same as the *masnavi* except it is a short poem. Each couplet contains a different rhyme and both lines rhyme at the end. Sometimes the poets pen-name appears in the last couplet which resemble the *ghazal* in content but not in rhyme-structure.

RUBA'I

The *ruba'i* is a form already known in the West because of the 'Rubaiyat of Omar Khayyam' which incidentally contains many *ruba'is* of Hafez and Attar and other Persian poets, including Omar Khayyam, for it was an anthology of *ruba'i* poems collected down the ages and named after Omar Khayyam. Persians consider the rubaiyat of Omar to be greatly inferior to , those of Hafez and other Persian poets.

The *ruba'i* is a poem of four lines in which usually the first, second and fourth lines rhyme and sometimes with the 'radif' or refrain after the rhyme words. It is composed in metres called 'ruba'i metres.' Each *ruba'i* is a separate poem in itself and should not be regarded as a part of a long poem as was created by FitzGerald when he translated those he attributed to Omar Khayyam.

It is possible that the *ruba'i* originated from the first two couplets of the *ghazal*, but this is unlikely because of the different metre. Sometimes the *ruba'i* consists of rhymes at the end of each line but this is unusual. The length of the line, as in the other forms written by Hafez, should always be the same. This of course adds to the beauty of the poem on the page and also allows the calligrapher laying out the poems to experiment with different symmetrical designs on the page.

QIT'A

The *qit'a* or fragment must consist of at least two verses and is similar to a *ghazal* or a *qasida* but in the first verse, the double-rhyme does not appear. It can be composed in any metre except for that of the *ruba'i*. It can be a fragment from a *qasida* or a *ghazal*, or it may be complete in itself. Hafez often used this form to write obituaries on people whom he knew.

TARJI-BAND & TARIKH-BAND

These two kinds of strophe (band) poems consist of a series of stanzas each containing a variable but equal, or nearly equal, number of couplets all in one rhyme, these stanzas being separated from each other by a series of isolated couplets that mark the end of each strophe. If the same couplet (or refrain) is repeated at the end of each *band*, or strophe, the poem is a *tarji-band*, or 'return-tie': if on the other hand the couplets concluding each band is different, each rhyming internally in a rhyme different from the preceding and succeeding bands, the poem is called a *tarikh-band*, or 'composite-tie'.

As I stated in the first chapter of this introduction, the practice of using the *Divan of Hafez* as an oracle and spiritual guide began even before Hafez's body was buried and has continued over the centuries to the present day. This first known instance of when his poems were used in this way was so successful that probably no day has passed since that day, when someone, somewhere in the world, has not asked Hafez's advice on a particular problem. Housewives ask Hafez to help them, and also businessmen, kings and queens, politicians, poets, artists, soldiers, and of course seekers of spiritual Truth and knowledge. All over the world, people are still asking Hafez for advice on a great variety of problems and are receiving instant help from the Divinely inspired poet and Perfect Master. Hafez's immortality is a fact of life, evident every moment of the day in the effect that he has on all who read his work, whether they are ignorant or spiritually advanced, rich or poor, educated or not.

Why do people continue to consult the poems of Hafez to gain advice? Masud Farzaad in his book 'Hafez and his Poems' gives some of the reasons: "What strikes me as the most essential characteristic of the man Hafez is that his emotional and intellectual reactions in the face of life's situations were above all, rational. And being lord both of language and literary design, he succeeded in transforming the dictates of this crystalline common sense into poems of unsurpassable beauty in a language that is second to none in the beauty of her poetry. We have now lost the clues to most of the particular situations which made him feel, think and write as he did; but reading any poem of his, we do recognize in it the universalization of some experience which we ourselves or our acquaintances have had, are having, or are quite likely to have in the future.

"This is, I believe, the basic reason for the rise and the continuation of the time-honoured practice called *[tafa'ol]* or seeking a fore-knowledge of one's fortune by random reference to his book of collected lyrics. Ordinary men and women are sure, after centuries of trial, that the particular type of dilemma in which they may find themselves at any time, confronted Hafez too; and that he not only had something sensible to say about it, but also said it so clearly and beautifully that they can hardly help enjoying it and remembering it long afterwards.

"Like all men of good sense and deep sensibility, Hafez finds himself on more than one occasion a stranger among his fellows; at war with some his social superiors; hating and hated by hypocrites; struck dumb by loud, unscrupulous, mendacious mediocrities; wondering why such people and things should be. He finds that (to borrow an immortal phrase from Shakespeare) "cold reason" has, in his own case at least, failed to solve the problem of life's complexities, where all the most essential facts seem perpetually and deliberately to be hidden behind a psychological curtain more solid and more effective than any iron curtain. Furthermore, no means other than this same poor, inadequate reason has been vouchsafed to man for the solution of this painful riddle.

"Finding himself and his fellow-humans incapable of answering these burning question he tries two diametrically opposite solutions. One, as symbolized by *Wine* (and sometimes *Love*) is the path of unreason, of the unconscious. The other as symbolized by the *Elder of the Wise Men* *(pir e morghan)* is objective; for this is the path of Pure Reason, and he is the Complete Man who knows the truth, and the secret of life; and is incidentally (or perhaps, consequently) cheerful, tranquil, and tolerant: a man in short, whom every seeker should strive to resemble as nearly, or at least as closely as possible." So, Hafez has experienced all the ups and downs of ordinary people: the sorrows, joys, anguishes, betrayals, and longings, and after much questioning arrived at the twin-solutions of unreason, or drunkenness, or love, and Pure Reason; that is obedience to the Perfect Master and the following of his example and guidance.

Hafez is 'everyman,' for he has walked every step of the path to the Truth; and when he finally discovered the Truth after forty years of searching, loving, suffering, patience, and obedience to his Master, Mahmud Attar, he then also became a Perfect Master. Then, in the poems that he wrote after this Realization, he retraced many of the steps he had taken and gave perfect advice on how to avoid the traps along the Way. Hafez wrote of all the stages and situations while experiencing them, and afterwards wrote about them from the Authority of Godhood. In this sense he was truly 'Every-man.'

But all of this still does not explain why, when one opens Hafez's *Divan* with a nagging problem in the mind or heart, the couplet or the whole poem that appears is a subtle and sometimes powerful explanation or piece of advice that is exactly what was needed. My explanation for this is twofold: It is contained in the nature of what it means to be God-realized, to have true Immortality, and secondly it is a gift that Hafez, out of his Divine Generosity and Wisdom, has given to all mankind for all time.

All souls who have not realized their own True Self (God) have individualized minds that are subject to time and space. All Perfect Masters and the Godman have experience of Universal Mind that is not subject to time and space but exists forever in the Present. The poems of Hafez exist in that aspect of Universal Mind that is Hafez's own Divine Individuality. The *Divan* or the physical book of Hafez contains the symbol of that Divine Individuality in the physical world. When we ask Hafez to help us in all honesty and respect, the book of Hafez is one medium through which the God-realized of the time extend their help and knowledge. Through our sub-conscious mind they direct us without us understanding the process, to open the book at a certain page and couplet that will help and guide us. This is one of the reasons why Hafez's poems are always 'modern.' They never date because they are connected with Existence in the Eternal Now, God's Existence.

Every Perfect Master and the Godman in each appearance, through compassion and love leaves a 'gift' for all mankind to help us through this 'long dark night.' It might only be one line of Truth that has rung through the centuries and helped dispel fear and hopelessness as when Mansur Hallaj stated: "I am the Truth"; or John the Baptist's example of bravery; or Rumi's great collection of poems and stories; or Francis of Assisi's respect for all forms of life; or Zoroaster's... "Good thoughts, good words, good deeds;" or in the case of Baba Kuhi, a promise that Hafez remembered. With Hafez it is his *Divan*, and contained in this great gift is the possibility of help in our darkest hours, our longest nights, our struggle to see the Light. Hafez has given us a book in which to find a Friend, and a Friend in a book; and even before his physical form was buried he had made clear to us all by an obvious example, that he wishes this gift to be accepted and used whenever it is needed.

There have been many famous instances in history where Hafez's *Divan* has been consulted with remarkable and sometimes humourous results. Many are contained in a small book titled *Latify-i-Ghaybiyya* that was written by Muhammad b. Muhammad of Darab and finally published in Tehran in 1886.

The first instance records the experience of Shah Isma'il the Great who founded the Safawi dynasty and made the Shi'a creed Persia's official faith. He was so energetic in doing this that he ordered the tombs of anyone suspected of leaning towards the Sunni faith to be wrecked. One day he visited Hafez's tomb and with him was a fanatical and ignorant priest who was called Mulla Magas ('Magas' means 'fly' in Persian). The Mulla told the Shah that Hafez was orthodox in belief (Sunnite) and also a drunkard. The Shah was not too sure of the wisdom of this advice so he consulted Hafez's *Divan* and opened it at the following...

At morning Gemini placed before me the Koran's preserving:
which means... "The slave of the King I am," I was swearing.

The Shah was pleased with this answer, considering that the famous poet was loyal to him. Happily, he opened the book once again and received... a couplet that was intended for his companion...

Fly, in presence of the Simurgh is not the place for you to be;
you will not keep your position and cause us a plight to keep.

'Fly' in Persian is 'magas,' and upon hearing this answer it is most likely that the priest disappeared in a hurry.

Another example refers to a king of the same dynasty named Shah Tahmasp who dropped a ring that he greatly valued when he was playing with it one day. All his servants were ordered to search for it everywhere but it couldn't be found. Eventually he asked Hafez and received the following...

Heart finding the Hidden Secret, cup of Jamshid's might has;
and for seal-ring that was lost, concern that is only slight has.

On hearing this couplet the king clapped his hands from such a happy surprise at the appropriateness of it, and the ring which had become caught in his sleeve fell into his lap.

The third story is about another king of the Safawi dynasty, Shah Abbas the Second (A.D.1642-1667), who received the following couplet when he was contemplating a campaign against Adharbayjan where Tabriz is the capital...

Hafez, with your sweet verse you have captured Irak and Fars:
come, for now the turn of Baghdad... also Tabriz's moment is.

The king was so happy with the reply that he decided to take Hafez's advice and was successful in his campaign.

There is another story about the same king. He had a servant who was named Siyawash who bore the brunt of the jealousy of his fellow-servants. They went to the king, slandering him... and tried to have him put to death. The king asked Hafez and the answer was...

The King of the Turkans, listened to suggestions of enemies...
his, great shame for way Siyawash he did cruelly mistreat... be.

Another instance is given by the author of this little book, about his own experience. In 1642 he reached Ahmadabad which was at that time the capital of Gujerat in India. While he was there he became friendly with a well-known person of the district, a certain Kan'an (Canaan) Beg who had a brother by the name of Yusuf (Joseph) Beg. Yusuf, who was in the army, had only recently been posted as missing in battle. His brother was extremely upset until Hafez was consulted and a couplet was received which proved to be true, for later his brother returned. The couplet received was...

That lost Joseph will return again to Canaan: do not grieve;
sorrow's cell becomes a blooming rosegarden... do not grieve.

Imam-quli Khan had a son called Fath-Ali Sultan who was extremely handsome and known to the author, Muhammad of Darab. He visited Hafez's tomb on a day towards the end of the month of Rajab which is set aside for people to visit Hafez's tomb and ask the poet for help. The handsome youth was dressed in a green coat lavishly embroidered with gold and was a bit tipsy from drinking some wine. He opened the *Divan* of Hafez and received this couplet from Hafez...

When you pass by intoxicated in your garment scattering gold...
give a present of a kiss to Hafez, who wears the wool of poverty.

The youth cried out: "What's one kiss? I make a promise to give you two!" A week passed and again he visited the tomb and the couplet that he received was...

You said: "I'll become drunk and will give you two kisses:"
your promise never ends, but for me, will one or two start?

On reading this he called out: "What's two kisses? I promise to give you three!" He left again without fulfilling his promise. When another week had passed he returned and received...

Three kisses you promised as my portion from your two lips,
if you do not give to me, to me then indebted you should be.

On reading this the youth fell upon Hafez's tombstone kissing it again and again and again.

There are many other instances in history recording Hafez's *Divan* being used as an oracle. Those recorded by the Moghul Emperor Jahanger are famous and it is said that Queen Victoria never made an important decision without consulting Hafez first.

For my own case, out of the many thousand times that I have been helped by Hafez I will record two here that seem appropriate. many years after I began reading Hafez I read that his *Divan* was used as an oracle and I could not make up my mind if Hafez wanted his *Divan* used in this manner, and so I asked him. The couplet I received which was the first time I consulted the *Divan* as an oracle was...

I'll only relate about the Friend in the Friend's presence;
and words of friend... the friend will trustfully preserve.

I take this couplet to mean that Hafez will not divulge God's Secrets to those unworthy, but will still be a friend to them and help them in other matters; and if one sees the Friend (God) in Hafez and in the words of Hafez, then it is God in the person Who sees this.

Sometime later I consulted Hafez again and asked whether he wanted me to try to make an English version of his book of poems. The answer was...

After serving pleasure and loving those fair moon-faced,
work with your heart on the verse of Hafez... then recite.

As my adopted daughter's name is Chanthan which means 'moon-flowered face' this again seemed very appropriate at the time and I immediately set to work on this long and difficult and immensely rewarding task of bringing the poetry and life of Hafez to the world that is still going on now after thirty-four years and completing his *Divan*, a radio play... a stage play and a musical and a number of film-scripts and a children's novel on his fascinating and inspiring life as well as a three volume novel-biography! Once you begin with Hafez he never lets you go, like love... he is irresistible!

METHODS OF CONSULTATION.

There are a number of methods of consulting the *Divan* of Hafez for advice. The simplest and most popular is to think of the question or the wish, close the eyes and open the book. Whatever poem the eyes first set upon is the one that is read. For an answer that is more exact, the person who is consulting the *Divan* should use the same method but also place a finger on the page and whatever couplet it falls upon is Hafez's reply. The other couplets in the poem can then be read for a more detailed explanation if the situation calls for it. There are very detailed methods for using the Persian text to gain an answer, but these complicated methods do not apply to a translation because the length of the lines and number of letters in a line are different.

If you are using an e-book version of this book simply using the cursor move the box on the right of the screen past this Introduction etc. then close your eyes and press it down and when the 'feeling' comes to stop, stop... and whatever poem is in the majority on the screen is IT. For a more detailed answer... when you stop, place your finger on the screen and the couplet it falls on (or nearest to) is your answer and the poem it is a part of is the one to read. (Note: I'm sure e-book readers will find many other ingenious methods of consulting Hafez, The Oracle.)

5. HAFEZ'S INFLUENCE ON THE EAST AND WEST

The influence of Hafez's life and poetry upon the art, literature and the consciousness of the East and the West is a subject that is vast and almost unexplored and would take years of research and hundreds of pages to fully uncover. We will attempt only to point out the way by showing the golden thread of Hafez's influence over the past six hundred years. It has woven together the art and consciousness of the East and West, and has helped to precipitate some of the advances in these areas in a way that is sometimes subtle, yet sometimes so obvious that it is a great wonder that it has rarely been given its due recognition.

One of the reasons why Hafez has not been fully appreciated is that many of the scholars studying his work and its effect have had no understanding of his role as a Perfect Master or even that he *was* a Perfect Master, and how a Perfect Master influences mankind's consciousness. Dr. Abdul Ghani Munsiff: 'It is only when it comes to appraising the esoteric side of his poetical mind, that all his biographers without any exception, have failed miserably in giving Hafez his due in the domain of mysticism and spirituality. All of them have paid learned tributes to his poetic genius and have written many an interesting treatise comparing and contrasting his favourite Muse with that of other luminaries from the literary firmament of Iran. Even such an eminent Orientalist as Moulana Shibli Nomani (India) consciously or unconsciously forgets to think of Hafez as something more than a poet or higher than a free thinker. He like many others, easily disposes of the question of the poet's mystical experiences and spiritual flights on the ground of rare gifts of poetical imagination and fancy, therefore, very inconsiderately puts him in the category of Epicurean philosophers like Omar Khayyam."

There have been exceptions to this, but rarely have these exceptions come from the ranks of scholars and literary historians. Among the exceptions was Doulat Shah who in 1476 said: 'Void of difficulty and plain is his speech, but in truths and divine knowledge its meanings are endless. Far below his degree, is the rank of poet. In knowledge, outward and inward, unequalled.' Later in the early 19th century Goethe was the first Westerner to recognize his true spiritual and poetic status. In the late 19th century Herman Bicknell and H. Wilberforce Clarke began the first of the English translations that gave some recognition to his spirituality, and in the twentieth century, the leader of the Sufi movement Inayat Khan paid him the respect he deserved. Meher Baba, continually throughout his life pointed out that Hafez was a Perfect Master and had not gained the true recognition that he deserved. However, these exceptions are few and far between and for the most part the biographers, translators and scholars generally have not understood Hafez and have failed to see the great influence that he has had down the ages. The 'coin of history' that I spoke about at the beginning of this introduction, not only has two sides, but also an edge that links both sides; and without that edge of God in human form, the evolution and involution of the consciousness of mankind (true history) would never roll on to its eventual Divine Destination.

The influence of poetry upon painting and painting upon poetry has never been properly documented. While paintings have been inspired by poems and poems by paintings and both have influenced each other when movements in art-consciousness such as 'romanticism' and 'impressionism' have happened, most of the time the study of both of these ways of artistic expression is limited to a specialized analysis of the history of one particular form without an understanding of the influence of the other form upon it. This narrow approach has caused a state of appreciation of the arts where people often receive a history of a particular art-form that is one-sided and untrue. The cross-pollination between the various art forms is something that is known to all true artists and is one of the reasons why art progresses, is revitalized, and expands the consciousness of the individual and all mankind.

HAFEZ'S INFLUENCE ON EASTERN AND WESTERN ART

Persian painting is the world's greatest example of book illustration, or the art of illuminated miniature painting. Its greatest period began in 1330-6 (ten to sixteen years after the birth of Hafez) with the monumental and widely recognized masterpieces that have been called the 'Demotte Shahnama.' These paintings are the culmination of the 'realistic' Chinese-influenced painting of the previous hundred years and justly deserve their status as some of the world's finest miniatures.

In the 'Demotte Shahnama' (and a later series of miniatures for the book 'Kalila wa Dimna,' a book of animal fables imported from India and painted 1360 -74), some of the paintings transcend the limitations of 'realism,' and these two series of miniatures closed a period of painting that in many instances had become tired, two-dimensional and gross.

Until this time Persian illuminated miniature painting usually took as its subject-matter works that had very little spiritual content. Above all, the 'Shahnama,' an epic poem on the kings and heroes of Ancient Persia, was illustrated. Other works illustrated were natural histories, animal fables, scientific anthologies, bestiaries, general histories and encyclopaedias.

During the second half of the fourteenth century there occurred a change in Persian painting, not only in content but also in style. B.W. Robinson writes about this change in 'Persian Drawings' published by Little, Brown and Company, Boston 1965: 'Strangely enough it is under the Muzzaffarid dynasty (1353-93) at Shiraz - a minor dynasty in a provincial city - that we find the first dated examples of Persian book illustrations which, though comparatively simple, and unsophisticated, are yet close kin to the magnificent works of the fifteenth - and sixteenth - century artists...' Robinson goes on to cite the difference between the style of the paintings painted under the ruler-ship of Abu Ishak and the later paintings painted under Shah Shuja etc. Robinson finally asks the question: 'How did this fundamental and revolutionary change come about?'

Many authorities on Persian painting have recognized that this shift in consciousness from the 'realist/Chinese influenced' paintings of the 13th century that culminated in the two masterpieces previously mentioned in the mid 14th century, changed during the last half of the 14th century and that this change happened in Shiraz. They sometimes mention that Hafez lived there during this time but they never make the connection' between this change and the influence of Hafez, and his poetry. Hafez must have known many of the painters and he, of course, was the most famous poet of the time.

In his *ghazals,* Hafez had expressed new ways of seeing the Creation and the inner realms of consciousness as symbols of God's Beauty he described this in *ghazals* that were at first spiritually 'romantic', spiritually 'impressionistic ' then spiritually 'surrealistic.' The change that occurred in Persian painting from the mid-fourteenth century the mid-sixteenth century followed exactly the same pattern. The content also became internalized, for the painters of these great periods in Persian painting saw that theirs was an art that had the responsibility and visionary possibility of seeing the Creation with 'the eye of God.'

The 'romantic' period of Persian miniature painting dates from Junayd's illustrations to Khwaju Kirmani's *'Divan,'* painted in 1396. Junayd has been called the first great spiritual 'romantic' painter, along with an unknown landscape painter who painted miniatures for an 'Anthology' (1398 lived at Bihbahan near Shiraz. In these paintings the Chinese and Mongol influences had been integrated and also a truly original style had emerged that we now call 'Persian painting.'

Like the 'romantic' poems of Hafez, these works have a great respect nature as a representation of the beauty of the Creator and a love of colour, a subtlety, simplicity and clarity of vision, a naturalness and sympathy, had not appeared before. The 'realistic' works of the past were often thickened with dull colours and often awkward and heavy. Their themes we this world, mostly a depiction of history, of objects merely for their sake and rarely in praise of, or in search of the underlying hand of Divine.

With the change in consciousness brought about by Hafez, these painters of the 'romantic' style had begun to see the world through 'the eye of the Creator,' and by doing so had paved the way for the next stage. Subject-matter had also changed. Most of the illustrated masterpieces of the next two hundred years were the works of the great Master Poets: Sadi, Hafez, Nizami and others. The content and form had become spiritualized.

These 'romantic' paintings generally represented one scene at a time began to distort the horizon line and perspective in such a way that the previous paintings that were definitely seen on the level of the eye man, these paintings are usually viewed from a position above the scene pictured, but close enough to see everything that was going on. Because of this and other qualities, Persian painting from this period on is said to be viewed with 'the eye of God.'

The next important advance in Persian painting dates from the work of Persia's most famous Master Painter, Bihzad, whose paintings first appeared about 1478.

Dr Mulk Raj Anand in his book 'Persian Painting,' Faber and Faber, London 1930, mentions that the artistic achievement that Bihzad attained was the result of the spiritual romanticism of the work that preceded him. His art became the transformation of the great spiritual works of Sadi, Hafez, Nizami, Jami and others. Dr Anand also says that Bihzad tried to achieve the spiritual ideal of these Masters through the art of painting: as a way to realize absolute beauty. For Bihzad, according to Dr Anand: '... the full perception of beauty is regarded as the realization of the Supreme beauty in the spiritual world.'

Bihzad illustrated the books of the great Master Poets and achieved an intensity of colour, mood and structure that until then had not been attempted. Here we have the second stage in Persian painting containing dynamic patterns and a fantastic reality, a world that is simple and direct and available for all to enter. The colours are sometimes intense and sometimes subtle, pure and full. All figures are of the time, easily recognizable. All buildings and spaces are carefully balanced. Perspective as we know it has completely vanished. Through these paintings we can view the scenes depicted on many levels, inside rooms and outside. What is on the horizon and in the foreground is equally perceptible. The painter and the viewer are looking with the 'eye of God' and the vision that one sees in an impression of the subtlety, intensity and beauty of the Divine Creator's Creation. This spiritual 'impressionism' that Bihzad achieved can be easily likened to the spiritually 'impressionistic' poems of Hafez that were written by him before and after God-realization.

The third stage in the development of the great periods of Persian painting flowed from this Master/Painter and combined the elements that were in his paintings with a new quality.

The painters that were the pupils of the Master Bihzad followed his example in style and technique. Shaikh Zadeh developed Bihzad's formal elements until they became more important than the human element. He still produced masterpieces of design, colour and subtlety (which remind me of the paintings of Cezanne) and occasionally... controlled passion (as in his wonderful painting for a *Divan* of Hafez).

Sultan Muhammad also illustrated Hafez's *Divan*, but with a sense of drunken abandonment, with an intensity of passion and colour that could only come from a God-intoxicated soul. Not only are his paintings sublimely spiritual, many of them are also spiritually 'surreal.' In the paintings of Sultan Muhammad we see the emergence of the third stage in Persian painting. The colour is even more intense than in Bihzad's work, and the objects are clearer. In a state of 'vision' he paints the rocks with faces, with their souls showing them crying out for further evolution. The faces of many of the humans in his paintings are strange, surreal, haunting. Angels manifest in the paintings and demons, earth spirits, fantastic birds and fabulous creatures. The sky swirls in symbolic spirals and the scenes seem to be happening in other worlds, worlds of visions in which the Spirit underlying all of Creation, all levels, becomes apparent.

By the 1580's the great periods of Persian painting had ended and the paintings that were to follow gradually lost the impetus of change and there began a process of refinement until eventually the influence of European painting turned them into lifeless shadows of their European models.

Early in the 20th century two large exhibitions of Persian miniature painting were held in Europe. The first in Paris in 1903 and then in Munich in 1910. These exhibitions were to have an influence on European painting and in particular on the 'Fauves'; Matisse coming under their spell more than any other painter. Matisse said in 'The Path of Colour' (from 'Matisse on Art' by Jack D. Flann, Phaidon 1973): 'Persian miniatures, for example, showed me all the possibilities of my sensations. I could find again in nature what they should be. By its properties this art suggests a larger and truly plastic space... Thus my revelation came from the Orient.'

From the beginning of the 16th century some of the best of the Persian painters left for India and started a revolution in painting there that we now know as 'Moghul painting.'

In 'Moghul painting' we see that the advanced stages of Persian painting combined with the best elements of Indian miniature painting. This produced a new intensity of mood, colour, and form, as well as a greater variety of subject-matter. All the great works of Persia's Master-Poets are again painted. Hafez, Sadi, Nizami, Jami and others are there in all, their glory, as well as miniatures depicting the love of Radha and Krishna and Rama and Sita, and the great esoteric love poems of India's 'Bhakti' poets. This union between the mystical side of Hinduism (Vedanta) and Islam (Sufism) not only occurred in miniature painting, but had happened before, and during the early part of the 15th century had become evident in the poetry of many of India's great Master-poets. Hafez again was a major influence in this integration and this change in consciousness.

HAFEZ'S INFLUENCE ON EASTERN POETRY, LITERATURE AND CONSCIOUSNESS

Hafez was the last Master-Poet of Persia, excluding one. That one was Jami, born in 1414, died in 1492. Jan Rypka in 'History of Iranian Literature:' p.287 says: 'He took Hafez and Nizami (sometimes Amir Khusrau) as his models ...'

The influence of Hafez can be seen throughout Jami's poetry and also throughout the most important Persian poets of the centuries that followed.

Baba Fighani (b.late 15th C.) and Lisani (d.1534) who was called 'the little Hafez' were both emulators of Hafez, as was Niziri of Nishapur (d.1604) who went to India and had a considerable influence there. Another Persian poet who went to India (in 1626) and was considered a great master of the 'Indian style,' and whose fame rested on his *ghazals*, was Sa'ib (b.1601), who was also an admirer of Hafez.

Visal (b.1779 d. 1846) was one of the most influential Persian poets of the 19th century. A large proportion of his 'Divan' are direct parallels to the ghazals of Hafez and Sadi.

With the exception of the last great Master-poet, Jami, and the minor (but significant) poets mentioned above, it is as though throughout the 15th and 16th centuries Persia's spiritual/artistic centre moved into the art of painting, and the spiritual/poetic heart moved into India. There, a succession of Master-Poets appeared over the following three to four centuries. These poets, though not all being God-realized, brought about a spiritual/artistic shift in consciousness which can be likened to, and can also be seen to be a continuation of, the tremendous spiritual/artistic upsurge that took place from the 11th century to the 14th century in Arabia, and in particular in Persia.

The enormous changes in consciousness that this succession of Master-Poets produced reached India and much of Asia and parts of Europe in great waves, and with each wave of love, changes occurred.

The spiritual symbols used by Hafez and others quickly became the language of the poets of India, with the local equivalents also explored. The fusion of Vedanta and Sufism meant that in one poem the poets would sometimes praise Krishna, Rama, Mohammed and even Jesus as incarnations of the one God.

During the early years of the 15th century one of India's greatest and most popular poets, Kabir, was born at Benaras. Kabir became a disciple of the Perfect Master Ramananda and eventually Kabir gained God-realization. Evelyn Underhill in her introduction to Tagore's translation of 'One Hundred Poems of Kabir' (Macmillan 1915) says of Ramananda: 'Ramananda ... appears to have been a man of wide religious culture, and full of missionary enthusiasm. Living at the moment in which the impassioned poetry and deep philosophy of the great Persian mystics, Attar, Sadi, Jalalu'ddin Rumi and Hafez, were exercising a powerful influence on the religious thought of India, he dreamed of reconciling this intense and personal Mohammedan mysticism with the traditional theology of Brahamanism.'

During his lifetime Hafez's poems/songs were widely known in India and exerted a strong religious and poetic influence. After his death this influence did not wane and was quickly carried as far west as Spain.

There are many similarities between Kabir and Hafez, even though as Perfect Masters they each possess Divine Individuality. Both praised the one God and scorned religious ritual and fanaticism and were the most controversial figures of their times who bore the brunt of persecution from the orthodoxy. Another similarity was their philosophy of 'the outsider.' This was the path of the vagrant, the God-intoxicated vagabond, the lover of God who denounced reason as the path to the Truth, and embraced love and renunciation of worldly desires as the only true way.

Kabir praised Ram and Rahim in one breath and in doing so fought the religious separatism and hatred that was throughout the Hindu and Muslim communities at the time. This brave stance brought about a new wave understanding between the communities and a fundamental mystical revival.

Hafez praised Jesus, Mohammed, Abraham and Zoroaster, and by doing this he reasserted the right of each individual to follow the one God in whichever appearance he accepted.

Babur, who reigned in India from 1525-1530 was an accomplished poet in the Persian language. He obtained most of his ideas for his *ghazals* from Hafez and Jami.

The influence of Hafez and other Master poets can be seen in the poetry of the great poet and martyr of India, Sarmad, who died in 1657. He says in one of his poems: 'I care not what people think of me and say; I have adopted in my odes the style of Hafez ...' Translated by Bankey Behari, from his 'Sufis, Mystics and Yogis of India' Bhavan, India 1962.

Bullah Shah was born in the Punjab in 1680 and died in 1752 and was a disciple of Shah Inayat. Bullah Shah saw God as Mohammed, Jesus, Krishna and Rama and the influence of Hafez, Rumi and others is obvious throughout his beautiful poems, as stated by Bankey Behari: 'Bullah Shah was much influenced by the works of the Iranian Sufis - Jami, Rumi, Sadi, Hafez and of some Arabian saints.'

Shah Latif (1689-1752) was the greatest of the known Sufi-saints of Sind. He always carried a copy of the *Koran* and Rumi's *Masnavi* with him. Latif, like Bullah Shah and Nazir (to follow) '... drew a wealth of knowledge and experience from the writings of the Sufis of Iran like Hafez, Rumi, Sanai, Sadi and others, and from the Arabian Saints, like Rabia, Ibn Arabi and others.' Bankey Behari.

The influence of Hafez and the other Master/Poets of Persia crossed through all language barriers in India. Not only were there poets writing in Hindi, Sindhi and Punjabi who came under this influence, but in Urdu (which in the 17th century came to be written in the Persian script) a whole line of *ghazal* writers also became influenced by Hafez's verse.

The Urdu *ghazals* employed the same imagery as Hafez and the others, and also added to this Vedantic philosophy and Indian imagery. With Vali (b. 1668) the *ghazal* found a firm foothold in Urdu. Vali's poetry reached Delhi in 1720 and immediately had a tremendous impact.

Mir was born in 1723 at Agra, he was the son of a dervish. Throughout all of Mir's poems rings the bell of truth, the pain of the heart in search of love. Mir was the first great Urdu poet. He was soon followed by a poet who has been called the Chaucer and Shakespeare of India, Nazir.

Nazir was born in Delhi in 1735 and died in 1846. In his poems he praises Krishna and Ali and Mohammed. Bankey Behari states: '... again we have the echo of Hafez in Nazir's lines...' and 'Nazir got enough material from Khusru, Sadi, Hafez and Rumi to make his choice and cleverly he made'.

The next great Urdu poet in relation to Hafez and his influence on Urdu poetry is Ghalib. Ghalib was born in 1797 at Agra and began writing poems in Urdu at the age of ten. Man of his works were written in Persian. He is considered by many scholars to be with Mir and Nazir among the greatest of the Urdu poets. The influence of Hafez is evident in much of his poetry. Aijaz Ahmed in his introduction to *Ghazals of Ghalib* Columbia University Press 1971 states: '... the tradition of poetry that reaches its first greatness with Hafez and Rumi in Persia... ends its Classical phase with Ghalib in Delhi'.

Probably the last great poet who wrote in Persian and Urdu was Sir Muhammad Iqbal (1877-1938). Iqbal was a noted lawyer and philosopher as well as a poet, and he has been called 'the father of Pakistan' because he encouraged his fellow Muslims in India to such an extent that this eventually led to Pakistan becoming an independent nation. This imminent poet/philosopher gained notoriety in 1915 when his long poem in Persian *Asrar-e Khudi* (Secrets of the Self) was published. In this poem Iqbal attacked Hafez for Iqbal's belief that Hafez preached ascetic inaction. Iqbal later explained that the verses he wrote on Hafez were really only illustrating and criticizing a literary principle, shortly afterwards Iqbal praised Hafez as one of the world's greatest poets and excluded from the poems the lines criticizing Hafez. Many of Iqbal's poems resemble those of Hafez as well as Shelley and Pindar and it is through the rhymes and metres that he inherited from Hafez, Ghalib and others that he expounded his philosophy of Action and realization of the Self.

In the 19th century the Hindu philosopher and religious reformer Debendranath Tagore was called 'Hafez-e-Hafez' because he knew the whole of Hafez's *Divan* by heart. His son, Rabindranath, India's most famous poet of the 20th century was influenced by Hafez and other Persian Master Poets.

If we follow the golden thread of Hafez's influence into Turkey we will see that yet again Hafez was to be a major influence in another country's poetic and spiritual development. From the early 15th century onwards there were very few Turkish poets who did not come under the influence of Hafez's poetry.

One of the first influences on the Second Period of Ottoman Turkish poets (1450-1600) were Jami and his friend, the statesman Mir 'Ali Shir Nawa'i. Nawa'i (b. 1439 - d.1501) wrote prose and verse in the Turkish language. E.J.W. Gibb in vol. 2 of his *History of Ottoman Poetry* pub. Luzac and Co. 1902, states: 'Like all other Persian and Turkish lyric poets of the time, Newa'i also was of the school of Hafez.'

The first Turkish poets to 'give form to Turkish poetry' and one of the three masters of the early classical age, and considered by most critics to be 'the true founder of Ottoman Poetry,' was Ahmed Pasha (d.1497). In his work on Turkish poetry Gibb says of him: 'His favourite model for the *ghazal* at any rate, was evidently Hafez, echoes from whose *Divan* may be heard on well-nigh every page he wrote.'

The next great Turkish poet is the great Baqi (1526-1600) who has been called 'the sultan of poets' and 'the greatest poet of the people.' Gibb says of Baqi: 'Frequent echoes from the lyrics of Hafez tell clearly enough where the Ottoman singer went for his inspiration, and whom he chose as model...'

The poet Vehbi (d. 1809), a Romanticist and the first Turkish poet to write occasional verses was also among the many Turkish poets influenced by Hafez: 'Of the Iranian Masters his favourite seems to have been Hafez, whom he frequently quotes and sometimes imitates.' Gibb.

The 'New Ottoman' poet, the first to state the need to return to the thinking and language of the ordinary people was the remarkable reformist poet of the 19th century, Ziya Pasha (1829-1880). Gibb translated one his autobiographical poems into literal English: 'I was assisted in my studies by certain poets, one of whom induced me to read a considerable part of Hafez. My whole nature was enthralled in what I read; it was as though my closed eyes were opened.'

Of the modern poets, Yahya Kamal Beijatli (1884—1958) has written a beautiful poem on 'The Death of Hafez.'

HAFEZ'S INFLUENCE ON WESTERN POETRY, LITERATURE AND CONSCIOUSNESS

We will now follow another thread of Hafez's influence as it travels even further west in a direct line that carried it to Spain shortly after Hafez's death in Shiraz.

Towards the end of the 14th century and early into the 15th century Timur's conquests caused immense destruction and loss of life in Persia and India. The poorest people in both of these countries were the Gypsies. Although poor in material wealth, they were rich in the arts of song and dance. Hafez's *ghazals* were being sung by rich and poor alike all over Persia and India. When Timur crushed his bloody fist down upon the masses, many of these wanderers (Gypsies) headed west and some finally ended up in the early 15th century in sunny Spain, and in particular in Andalusia. In his essay on Andalusian Gypsy music ('deep song') Federico Garcia Lorca in *Deep Song and other Prose* trans. by Christopher Maurer (New Directions 1980, agrees with the Spanish composer and music historian Manuel de Falla that: '... in the year 1400 the Gypsies, pursued by the hundred thousand horsemen of the great Tamerlane, fled from India. Twenty years later these tribes appeared in different European cities and entered Spain with the Saracen armies then periodically arriving (from Egypt and Arabia) on our coast. On arriving in Andalusia the Gypsies combined ancient, indigenous elements with what they themselves bought and gave what we now call deep song its definitive form.'

Lorca then says how much the poems of Hafez and other Asiatic poems moved him when he read them as translated by Don Gaspar Maria De Nava into Spanish and published in 1838, and how they reminded him of the 'deepest' poems of his countrymen. Lorca gives five examples from Hafez's *ghazals* to illustrate the closeness (almost identical) between them and Gypsy poems ('siguiriya'), saying: 'But where the resemblance is most striking of all is in the sublime amorous *ghazals* of Hafez.' Lorca shows through these examples the close similarities in symbology and sentiment between the two.

Many of Spain's greatest poets and composers were influenced by this Andalusian Gypsy music. It was influential on Debussy and later Lorca fell under its spell. Lorca wrote a number of *ghazals* ('gacela').

The Gypsies fled not only to Spain early in the 15th century but to all over Europe and the song and poetry that they brought with them was probably influential throughout Europe from the grassroots level of 'popular music' such as drinking songs.

The more literate members of European and American society would have to wait another 200-300 years for Hafez to be translated into Latin, then English, German, Russian, French, Spanish and other European languages. With these translations Hafez would influence many of the great figures in the Arts in England, Europe and America.

The first translation of a Hafez *ghazal* into Latin was published in 1680. Almost a hundred years later the first translation into English appeared. This first translation by the famous Orientalist and 'father' of Persian studies in the East, Sir William Jones, had an immense immediate and long-term influence, corn parable only to the later translations of Khayyam by FitzGerald, which it definitely helped to bring about. Soon the translation of Persian poetry into English became so fashionable and voluminous (particularly in the case of Hafez) that within a short time Hafez, like Horace, became a household name. Within one hundred years poets of both hemispheres began using 'Hafez' as a pen-name to gain a wider audience and eventually Hafez became so well-known that even Sherlock Holmes quoted him with Horace to give a solution to a problem.

Jones called his version *A Persian Song* and it was so well received that it was soon included in *The Oxford Book of 18th Century Verse*. G.H. Cannon Jnr. states in his book *Sir William Jones, Orientalist: An Annotated Bibliography of His Works* (Honolulu: University of Hawaii 1952... 'It was immensely popular at once and continued to be popular for decades... and definitely stimulated... Byron, Swinburne (and) Moore and Gatty.' Byron was influenced by this poem and imitated its rhyme-structure and later Swinburne perfected the stanza. By the turn of the century six other translations of Hafez (including others by Jones) had appeared since the first successful attempt by Jones, and by 1905 another twenty-two translations were published including two complete versions of the *Divan*.

Not only did the English Romantic poets of the early 19th century fall under Hafez's spell, but in the mid-nineteenth century E.B. Cowell introduced Hafez to Edward FitzGerald who called Hafez 'the best Musician of Words' and later went on to translate Omar Khayyam (possibly because so many versions of Hafez's poems already existed). Among Cowell and FitzGerald's friends were Carlyle and Tennyson who were extremely interested in Hafez. This interest in Hafez became even greater as the century progressed into the Victorian Age with Hafez influencing Swinburne and Burne-Jones, to whom John Payne dedicated his complete version, published in 1901, with the words: '... which owed its completion to his urgent instance.' By the turn of the century Hafez had become a 'fad' in England, consulted as an oracle by Queen Victoria.

From 1905 until now approximately another eighty translations into English have appeared; proof that the interest in Hafez has not waned in English-speaking countries.

Let us go back to early in the 19th century and follow the thread of Hafez into another country and culture: Germany. In 1812-13 a translation into German by Von Hammer-Purgstall appeared. During the first half of 1814 one of the greatest influences on the Romantic movement in Europe, Goethe, read it and immediately recognized Hafez as his Spiritual Master and as a poetic genius. Although the translation was romantic in the 'gross' sense, the genius and intuition of Goethe understood the immense Spiritual content of the poems and Goethe set about praising and clarifying the spiritual status and the verse of Hafez. To do this and to write a *Divan* of his own (inspired by Hafez's example), Goethe began his *West-Eastern Divan* which was to become a vessel in which he could pour his experiences as they happened and his belief in the deeper aspects of life and love. This book became an impressionistic poetical diary of the years 1814-18, and through the *Divan* of Hafez (using page numbers of Von Hammer's trans. as ciphers) he corresponded with the woman he loved, Marianne, who also wrote poems that were recorded in his own *Divan*.

In his 'West-Eastern *Divan* Goethe says of Hafez in the section called *The Book of Hafez*: 'In his poetry Hafis has inscribed undeniable truth indelibly...' Trans. by J. Whaley, and later: 'This is madness, I know well, Hafez has no peer!' In another poem he states: 'In you true source of joy and poetry shows, From you unnumbered wave on wave outflows.' And: 'In the word we see the bride, Bridegroom is the spirit. For this wedding sanctified Hafez takes the merit.'

Goethe's *West-Eastern Divan* appeared in 1819 to a mixed reception, its admirers included Alexander Von Humbolt, Hegel and Heine. Goethe's interest in Hafez led to many excellent German translations in the years that followed and caused many writers and philosophers in Germany and other countries in Europe to view Hafez in a more spiritual light.

A German philosopher who was deeply interested in Goethe and Hafez was Fredrich Nietzsche (1844-1900) who saw Hafez and Goethe as ideals and spent many years studying them both. In his book *The Joyful Wisdom,* Nietzsche praised Hafez for 'mocking divinely'. He would also say following about Hafez in *The Will to Power...* 'Only the most enlightened of beings can benefit from the deepest human joys because within such beings resides a unique force of freedom and rapture. Their awareness rests in the house of spirit and their soul mates with their awareness, meaning that which shines in the soul is known with awareness. This unity of spirit and mind is the legacy of Hafez.'

Frederick Junger (b.1898), the German poet, essayist and short story writer who was an outspoken critic of Nazi Germany was another German writer who was influenced by the poems of Hafez.

The influence of Hafez has also threaded its way through the literature of Russia. Russia's greatest poet Aleksander Pushkin (1799—1837) was the founder of Russia's modern literature. The Age of Pushkin is considered the 'Golden Age' of Russian literature. According to the letters of Pushkin the Eastern style of Saadi and Hafez was a model that he believed had to be Europeanized. 'To Pushkin, Hafez and Sadi were not merely '... names familiar' the latter he regarded a sage worthy of quoting, while the former - a poet worthy of imitation, though Pushkin's verses *From Hafez* are actually unconnected with the great Persian bard.' From *Six Centuries of Glory* by Michael J. Zand, Moscow 1967. In Pushkin and Hafez's poetry, both the spiritual and physical planes art fused. Both used simple words and images with no artificiality, nothing being forced which results in an impression of spontaneity. Pushkin used parallel themes within a single poem that are so balanced that the content and the form are indivisible, a style that is similar to that of Hafez. While Pushkin was influenced by Hafez and the 'Eastern Style' - that later Russian poet, Fet (1820 -1892) was, according to Zand, '... infatuated with Hafez which resulted in many subtly conceived renderings and imitations of Hafez's poems...' Fet's passionate lyric poetry was a great influence on the later Russian

Symbolist poets, Blok in particular. Fet was a close friend of Turgenev and Tolstoy. In 1859 Turgenev gave Fet a German translation of Hafez and Fet immediately began work on translating some of these versions into Russian. Twenty-seven different translations by Fet were published separately in 1860 in the periodical *Russkoe Slovo*.

Early in the 20th century, this 'infatuation' with Hafez by Russian poets once again showed. *Ghazals* inspired by Hafez were created by V. Ivanov (1866-1949) a leading Symbolist poet and V. Bryusov (1873-1924) the controversial poet, critic and novelist who played a major role in the Symbolist Movement in Russia.

Sergei Yesenin (1895-1925) ranks with Pushkin and Mayakovsky as one of Russia's three most popular poets. According to Zand: 'This early century Russian 'Hafeziana' actually links up with Yesenin's 'Persian motifs,' though while mentioning the names of Sadi, Firdawsi, Khayyam, he never directly alludes to Hafez.' Russian interest in Hafez has continued over the past eighty years with many translations and scholarly and critical works appearing in Russia and elsewhere. Some of the most important discoveries in 'Hafez studies' have recently appeared in the former U.S.S.R.

A year after Pushkin's death in 1837 and about twenty years after Goethe's *West-Eastern Divan* appeared, another of the great figures in 19th century literature came under the spell of Hafez.

The thread of Hafez's influence reached America in 1838 when Ralph Waldo Emerson read in German Goethe's *West-Eastern Divan*. Emerson immediately became interested in Hafez and sought out Von Hammer Purgstall's German translation of Hafez's *Divan*. On obtaining a copy Emerson immersed himself in a study of Hafez and other Persian poets. For him, Hafez and Sadi became the ideal poets. For fourteen consecutive years Emerson read the *Divan of Hafez* through completely and quoted Hafez in many of his essays, including those on 'Fate,' 'Power' and 'Illusion.' Hafez became Emerson's ideal and he says of him in *Journals*: 'He fears nothing. He sees too far; he sees throughout; such is the only man I wish to see and be.' Many of Emerson's poems, including 'Bacchus' were influenced by Hafez, and Emerson translated some of Hafez's *ghazals* into free-form English verse from the German translation.

Of the many compliments that Emerson paid Hafez a number stand out, for they could also be applied to Emerson himself: 'Hafez defies you to show him or put him in a condition inopportune or ignoble. Take all you will, and leave him but a corner of Nature, a lane, a den, a cowshed ... he promises to win to that scorned spot the light of the moon and stars, the love of man, the smile of beauty, and the homage of art.' 'Sunshine from cucumbers. Here was a man who has occupied himself in a nobler chemistry of extracting honour from scamps, temperance from sots, energy from beggars, justice from thieves, benevolence from misers. He knew there was sunshine under those moping churlish brows, and he persevered until he drew it out.'

It was Hafez's joyful humanity and love of Nature, his freedom of thought and spirit and sincerity and self-reliance that attracted Emerson to Hafez. Hafez's perception of beauty in man and Nature was also an attraction, and from Hafez Emerson learnt of the inspirational quality of women. Emerson was also inspired by Hafez's thoughts on love and friendship and often quoted Hafez on friendship Emerson also learnt much from Hafez about the Law of Compensation (Karma) and quotes Hafez on this. For Emerson, Hafez was like Shakespeare, above the preachers and the philosophers as he states in the following poem from *Works*:

'A new commandment,' said my smiling Muse,
'I give my darling son, Thou shalt not preach,'
Luther, Fox, Behman, Swedenborg grew pale,
and, on the instant, rosier clouds up bore
Hafez and Shakespeare with their shining choirs.

In his *Essay on Persian Poetry* 1858 Emerson states: 'That hardihood and self-equality of every sound nature, which result from the feeling that he spirit in him is entire and as good as the word, which entitle the poet to peak with authority, and make him an object of interest and his every phrase and syllable significant, are in Hafez, and abundantly fortify and enoble his tone.' Further on he states: '...Hafez is a poet for poets whether he writes, as sometimes with a parrot's, or as at other times, with an eagle's quill.'

Another poet who was interested in Hafez early in the 19th century was he great Victor Hugo of France. Hugo, along with Goethe, Pushkin, Byron and Emerson can be considered one of the greatest influences on the Romantic Movement in Europe. He was also influential on the later Impressionist and symbolist poets of France. Hugo was born in 1802 and died during 1885. M. Darwish in his Introduction to *Poems from the Divan of Hafez* (Javidan Pub. Iran 1963) states that Victor Hugo translated some of Hafez's *ghazals*. In 1826 at the age of twenty-four Hugo published a collection of poems titled *Les Orientales* which were inspired by a number of Eastern poets, among them were Hafez and Sadi. Some of Hugo's poems seem to be direct parallels in style and content to those of Hafez. It is as though he read some of Hafez's *ghazals* and transposed them into the French context.

Another French poet and artist who was influenced by Hafez was Tristan Klingsor (b.1874). Klingsor was a member of the original Symbolist group and published *Scheherazade* in 1903, a collection of poems inspired by Hafez and other Persian poets.

During the 20th century a few Australian poets were influenced by Hafez. Early in this century A.B. 'Banjo' Paterson wrote a poem *Wisdom of Hafez* in which he used various couplets from a number of Hafez's *ghazals* to write a satire on horse racing. In 1974 Francis Brabazon, the first great mystical poet to appear in Australia, published a book of modern *ghazals* titled *In Dust I Sing* (Beguine Library, Berkeley, U.S.A.) Although not *ghazals* in the strict sense, 'the form is based on the Persian *ghazal*, perfected by Hafez 600 years ago and carried down in the Urdu language to the present day,' Brabazon. Many of Brabazon's earlier poems have also been influenced by Hafez.

Hafez was not only a poet for the masses, rich and poor alike, but he was also as Emerson stated 'a poet for poets.' As can be seen from this, many of the most influential poets, artists, writers and philosophers of the past 600 years have come under his irresistible spell. It seems that Hafez was instrumental in helping many of these great figures in literature to align themselves with the true Spirit within themselves and all of mankind.

In THE POETRY OF HAFEZ I told about the three different stages that Hafez's poetry went through during his journey to Divine Consciousness, and how he used these later, after gaining God-realization, to enlighten others. I, along with others, have called these stages 'romanticism,' 'impressionism' and 'surrealism,' and I have prefixed the terms for each of these stages with the word 'spiritual' so that the reader will not confuse them with the Movements in art and literature which occurred in Europe from the late 18th century up until the present time. But, I believe that there is a connection between them, as can be seen by the influence of Hafez upon many of the great figures in literature as mentioned above, and in the nature of the work of the Perfect Master in raising the consciousness of mankind through his possession and use of Universal Mind.

It should be understood that in Hafez's 'spiritually romantic' early poems that he wrote from about the age of twenty-one, he viewed and symbolized the Creation and all that it contains, its beauties and its horrors, as symbols to disclose the Truth that manifests it all. Hafez's principal aim was to praise the beauty of God's Creation and to discover its inner meaning.

Hafez's conscious 'spiritually romantic' poems written after God-realization, towards the end of his life, used the symbols of Creation to praise the Creator and to show His Glory and shower His Grace and to disclose Truth by using the everyday symbols in the world around us as shadows of the higher Reality that he was experiencing.

The Romantic Movement in Europe during the late part of the 18th century and during the beginning of the 19th century rejected the neoclassicism, rationality and realism of the 'Age of Reason' and sped in the opposite direction, that of feeling, passion and sentiment. I have termed this early Romanticism 'gross,' and examples of it can be clearly seen in many of the early translations of Hafez's *ghazals* where the spiritual quality is unseen and his poems are interpreted usually only in a physical sense.

In the works of Goethe, Hugo, Pushkin and Emerson we see somewhat of a spiritualization of the Romantic Movement take place. All these great writers came under the influence of Hafez and other Eastern Master/Poets.

Goethe's *West-Eastern Divan* is really a collection of impressionistic poems that were greatly influenced by Hafez and were imbued with Goethe's theory of light and colour which he expressed in his book *Theory of Colours*. Once again we see Romanticism moving into the next stage... Impressionism.

Impressionism and Symbolism became the next major stage in art consciousness as Romanticism, as Goethe predicted, turned in on itself and became an end as well as a means.

Throughout the Symbolist Movement in Russia we again see Hafez's influence. The French Symbolists also drew on the Orient, and from their predecessors, including Hugo. Many of Rimbaud's poems are on the surface reminiscent of Hafez and one wonders whether he read him in French translation. Rimbaud's famous statement: 'One must be completely modern' seems to be a distant echo of Hafez's often quoted couplet:

In this dusty world of ours, to hand comes not one true man...

it's necessary to make a new world and a new man is necessary.

The imagery, symbols, light, colour and magical qualities of the Impressionists and Symbolists are reminiscent of Hafez's 'impressionist' and 'surrealist' periods. The Symbolists were later to inspire the Surrealists, and among them Lorca was directly influenced by Hafez.

In Hafez's 'romanticism' his consciousness was not directed at the object, but at what the object represented in the spiritual sense. The aesthetic aspect only mattered in that a beautiful vessel makes one more aware of what it might contain. Romanticism in Europe usually directed its attention at the aesthetic and horrific aspects of the Creation and at the effect that these had upon the onlooker... i.e. the artist. For the Romantics the poet was the seer, the visionary who contained within himself the possibility of perfecting his own consciousness. For Hafez the poet was fortunate to be a dog on the leash of his Master (God in human form), another individual outside of his own ego, but as close to his true Self as his jugular vein. It was his Master who could perfect his consciousness, not himself. The Romantic's master was his own perception. Hafez's Master was his Master's command.

In Hafez's 'impressionistic' poems he expresses his experience of the 'subtle world,' a world of subtle light and colour and subtle smells and music: a Paradise. This is not to be confused with the world as we understand it, but a state in which the consciousness of the individual involutes. This 'gross' or physical world we experience is really a shadow of this subtle inner realm.

The Impressionists and Symbolists directed their attention at expressing their experience of the energy, light, colour, smells, symbols of the physical world, outside themselves.

Hafez expressed his experience of an inner world and how its images, sounds, smells were shadows of an even greater Reality.

The light that the Impressionist saw was not a subtle light, but a more intense experience of physical light. The symbols the symbolist expressed were not from a higher state of consciousness, but from a forced freeing of the imagination. The bubble of 'gross-consciousness became distorted and they experienced 'visionary states' which clothed the physical world in light, colour and mystery which was always there in the 'spiritually romantic' sense. By doing this they believed that they had created a new way of seeing. What they had actually done was to create another way of seeing and expressing the physical world.

Hafez actually existed in a different state of consciousness and expressed his experience of it, and its limitations in relation to the greater Reality. It was Hafez's quality of actually experiencing this other 'subtle world' that drew many of the symbolists to his poetry.

The Surrealists of the 20th century through the sub-conscious mind, by means of dreams, trances, imagination and chance, sought to express by juxtaposing opposite symbols, an *idea* of truth, beauty, unity. The subject-matter of the Surrealists was the mind, and in particular the sub-conscious, the hidden, strange, mysterious side of the psyche. Hafez's 'surrealistic' poems are written from a deeper state of consciousness than the 'subtle' realm, the 'subtle' being a shadow of the Mind-state which he now inhabited. This is a state of pure vision - 'face to face with God.' The images that Hafez juxtaposes are images of the Divine Emanation - Universal Mind. There is no conscious or sub-conscious, only a consciousness that all is God and emanates from the Creator. The opposites are shadows, an illusion created, imagined to be flowing from His Unity, through Mind. The Surrealists explore the 'gross' mind in an effort to know the opposites that exist there, the conscious and sub-conscious. Hafez expresses pure Divine Archetypes, while the Surrealist manufactures or discovers psychological archetypes as they appear in the sub-conscious. Hafez knows, the surrealist dreams, imagines, explores through chance. Hafez is face to face with his Master - God. The Surrealist is in the dark with his master, the sub-conscious.

The 'stream of consciousness' method used by many modern writers has also been pre-empted by Hafez. This method of trying to create the flow of the consciousness of the characters in some modern novels (and in free-form poetry and 'action painting') should really be called 'stream of incoherent consciousness' for the consciousness they depict is not an awareness of a greater Reality, but merely a record of thought and feeling processes. They are usually lacking in any purpose other than to record.

According to Michael J. Zand in *Six Centuries of Glory*, Moscow 1967: 'Hafez's *ghazals* mostly present a wisp of themes, as it were held together by very relative, at times elusive associations that impart a certain unity to the whole *ghazal* - a unity of emotion and tonality rather than logic or reason. Compressing the long logical sequences leading from one *beyt* (couplet)-theme to the next, until they are reduced to an associative allusion of interrelationship, the poet involves the reader in the process of immediate perceptive reconstruction of this interrelationship, in the process of active co-experience, co-creation, i.e. the stream-of-consciousness. We may state, without incurring the danger of modernization, that in these *ghazals* Hafez applied quite consciously and consistently a method of revealing his hero's inner condition at which European literature first arrived only in the 20th century.'

Masud Farzaad states in *Haafez and his Poems...* 'by the simple process of association of ideas (which 'Modern' psychology 'discovered' and labeled several centuries after Hafez knew about it and used it) he has linked every verse with the next one in every single one of his poems.'

The Abstract Expressionist tried to intellectually experience and express the idea of an abstract state of non-existence, beyond the mind - a false 'fana' (annihilation of the mind). Abstract Expressionism was an intellectual interpretation of 'fana' or 'nirvana' - but without the existence of God, merely an idea, not an experience. Such a true experience can only be given or passed on by a God-realised Master, for as Jesus said, 'No one gets to the Father but through Me.' Hafez states...

Don't place your foot down in the street of Love without a Guide;
by myself, for myself, a hundred moves I willed; and it wasn't to
be.

The soul must explore the false approach before it finds and explores the true path. The Age of Reason gave away to the Age of Intellect which finally put men on the moon and painted black paintings and found that nothing had changed, consciousness remained the same.

All these Movements in art/consciousness were pale intellectual shadows of Spiritual states of higher consciousness that were expressed by Spiritual Masters, be they artists or not.

Many of the poets and artists mentioned above who were influenced by Hafez and many others, have also been influenced by an aspect of Hafez that has been called 'rind' or 'unreason.' It is understandable that at the end of the Age of Reason Hafez's 'philosophy of unreason' would effect many of them.

According to Steingass' *Persian-English Dictionary* 'rind' means: 'sagacious, shrewd; a knave, rogue; a *Sufi;* dissolute; a drunkard, debauchee; one whose exterior is liable to censure, but who at heart is sound; a wanderer, traveller; and insolent, reckless, fear-nought fellow.' Zand states: 'The image of the *rind* is deeply rooted in the early mediaeval social and cultural history of Central Asia and Iran... Hafez raised this image to the level of great poetic generalization, transforming it into an expression of the proud, free human personality opposing a society cramped with hypocritical morality and hideous personal and social relationships... Hafez hurled and individualistic challenge at the very foundations and establishments of evil. In the power of his individualistic revolt of a man delighting in life, against a crippling life, Hafez has no equal not only in the mediaeval literature of the Near and Middle East, but probably in the mediaeval literature of the world.'

There are two aspects of the *rind* as portrayed by Hafez that I now wish to comment upon. Firstly, Hafez used this image of himself as a form of protest as stated by Zand above. Secondly, he used this image as a symbol of an inner, spiritual stance. The spiritual hero in this sense, rejects the formal religious path of aestheticism and religious rituals, and is placed outside formal religion.

The path of Hafez's outsider is one of denunciation of selfish desires, scorn for Reason as a method of knowing God and a belief in unreason (or love) as being the best approach. For Hafez the true hero is the one who has lost consciousness of any desire other than to please his own Master. In this sense he is outside formal religion and outside his own path and has abandoned himself and the world and has embraced the Will of God as his Master, ceaselessly moving with this Will and always longing to fulfil it.

It was this duel image of the rind that appealed to Goethe who became a wanderer, awaiting on the pleasure of God and his own inspiration when he wrote his *West-Eastern Divan*. This image also appealed to Emerson as can be seen by the quotes by him earlier in this chapter. It also appealed to Nietzche and influenced many of the great writers of Russia where this 'outsider' features as one of the heroes of Russian literature. Rimbaud's vagrant stems from this image, as does Hesse's hero in the 20th century. A distant echo can be seen in the 'beat' poets and in the heroes of Kerouac's *On the Road*.

Hafez's outsider's stance was a spiritual one that saw through falseness in the world and exposed it for what it was. The outsider in Western literature was usually a victim of the outside world and his reaction to its beauty and its tyranny was to walk the path of aloneness and from this to gain an outside perception of himself and the world.

The difference between them is obvious. Hafez's 'madness' or 'intoxication' is because of his love for God and is channeled towards God on earth in physical form, while many of the outsiders in Western literature's 'madness' is because of a feeling of being alone in the world and searching for the meaning of this.

Hafez is intoxicated by God's Love and does not try to understand 'how' or 'why'. The other 'outsider' is over-awed by God's Creation and can't escape it. One has a Master and is overwhelmed by the Master's Godhood; the other is alone, still searching, overwhelmed by the loneliness and magnitude of the search and the cruelty of the world - a brave lonely victim. Hafez is a victim of the love of God in human form and is frightened of only one thing - losing his Master's blessing.

Hafez's only desire is God, and all else is false. The other 'outsider' desires that which is yet to be found: some distant Nirvana, escape, or some shadowy imagined 'master'.

Through Mohammed, the Age of Pure Reason commenced which finally became distorted through the ego into a pale shadow, the Age of Reason; which Hafez tore away with the Age of Unreason, which then became distorted through the ego into the Age of Intellectual Expressionism

And now we stand in the morning of the Age of Intuition, already dawned by the 'New Coming Messiah,' and so begins the involution of consciousness. All past experiences will be concentrated into the experience of knowing through the logic of the heart. All thoughts of diversity will eventually become feelings of unity. How? Through, as always, the releasing of Divine Love, Knowledge and Power on Earth by the Manifestation of God on Earth in human form.

The 'rind' will become the norm and the outsider will eventually be come whoever is outside the inner approach to God, outside the desire to fulfil the command of the Divine Master, outside the Truth. Perhaps this will, for quite some time, become an impossibility.

With the dawning of the Age of Intuition, where heart and mind are becoming more balanced and inner meanings appreciated, it is likely that he will from now on have a much greater influence than he has had in the past. For his Vision is not in the past, but in the never-ending Present, and that Present is with us now, as always, but perhaps it is clearer to all of us now, if only we ask God to help us to be open to it. 'The picture that Hafez drew represents a wider landscape though the immediate foreground may not be so distinct. It is as if his mental eye endowed with wonderful acuteness of vision, had penetrated into those provinces of thought which we of a later age were destined to inhabit.' Gertrude Bell.

ACKNOWLEDGEMENTS:

'Discourses Vol. 11' by Meher Baba. Sufism Reoriented 1967. U.S.A.
'Creative Imagination in the Sufism of Ibn 'Arabi' by Henry Corbin, Trans. by Ralph Manheim. Princeton University Press. 1969. U.S.A.
'Hafez and his Poems' by Masud Farzaad. London.
'Divan of Hafez' Translation & Introduction by Paul Smith. 2 vols. New Humanity Books. 1986. Melbourne. Australia.

GLOSSARY

NOTE: Please read this Glossary carefully before reading Hafez's Divan so that the spiritual meaning of his poetry may be understood. As there are many shades and levels of meaning in Hafez's poems it is necessary to understand the symbols in the context of each poem. Sometimes Hafez uses the symbol in a spiritual sense, sometimes in a physical sense and sometimes both. For Hafez, everything in Creation is a symbol of a higher Reality. In this Glossary I have explained only those symbols which appear most frequently. I have not arranged this Glossary alphabetically as is usual, but in a manner which I hope the reader will find less boring and more enjoyable and enlightening. Other explanations are given in the Notes to the Divan.

THE SKY: Sometimes Hafez describes the sky as an 'inverted bowl' and 'the blue dome.' The sky symbolizes fate: unpredictable, untrustworthy, always changing.

THE SUN: The Beloved, God. The bright face of the Beloved. The Power of God's Light revealing the Truth.

THE MOON: The Beauty of the true Beloved also (in context) the false beauty of the Creation, physical beauty. The Moon cannot be seen unless the light of the Sun is upon it (i.e. the Light of God). The sickle-shaped Moon represents the bent shape of the poor suffering lover and when waning, old age and death. The half (split) Moon symbolizes the opposites existing in the psyche, and throughout Creation. The full Moon usually means the Beloved, showing fully the Beauty of God. Sometimes Hafez uses the Moon as the hand of Fate as in the *ghazal* on the death of his wife.

SATURN: A great distance - also, misfortune.

JUPITER: The mind, reason, intellect.

MARS: Tyranny.

VENUS: Music, dance and song. The sky's minstrel. Good fortune.

PLEIADES: Sometimes used as a symbol for the tears of the lover and sometimes as a necklace of jewels to place around the Beloved's neck. Other meanings in context.

SIRIUS: A false master. Ignorance. Obscurity.

THE WIND: The bringer of bad news, misfortune. Sometimes it symbolizes one who brings news of death.

THE BREEZE: The bringer of messages from and to the Beloved. Often the messenger who brings good news. Divine inspiration.

THE SEA: The ocean of love to be crossed by the lover. The immensity of Divine Love, of which human love is but a mere drop. The turbulent sea represents the difficulties the lover must endure on the voyage to God.

THE BOAT: The form, energy and mind of the lover of God of whom the Perfect Master is the Captain. Sometimes the boat represents the Perfect Master who sails us to the Divine Shore.

THE PEARL DIVER: The lover of God, the seeker of the Truth.

THE PEARL: God, Divine Knowledge, the Truth, the lover's true Self.

THE SHELL: The outer form, the physical illusion, the false, the ego.

THE DESERT: The long period that the lover of God must pass through when the lover's thirst for God's Grace remains unquenched.

THE HILLS AND VALLEYS: The ups and downs experienced by the lover on the Path of Love.

THE FIELD: The world, whereupon the Game of Love is played.

POLO: Hafez sometimes uses the game of Polo as a symbol for the Game of Love. The horseman represents the Beloved and the ball symbolizes the lover's mind and sometimes the lover's heart. The Beloved's long curling hair symbolizes the polo-mallet that strikes the ball (the lover's heart).

THE GARDEN: The special place in the world (and in the inner realms) where the lovers see, meet and converse with the Beloved. The Presence of the Beloved.

THE ROSE: The true Beloved, i.e. God. The Perfect Master whose heart has expanded like the rose. Sometimes the rose signifies a beautiful woman. The rosebud sometimes signifies the lover, whose heart has yet to become expanded by Divine Love, i.e. love that is still young.

ROSEWATER: The Grace of God. Divine Mercy. Kindness shown by the Perfect Master.

THE TULIP: The humble, faithful, tragic lover of God. The tulip, blood-streaked, cup-shaped, often symbolizes the heart of the grief-stricken lover.

THE VIOLET: The patient obedient servant or disciple of the Perfect Master (the rose). In Persian gardens violets are often planted in rows leading up to the rosebushes, i.e. like attendants, or lovers waiting to serve the Beloved.

THE HYACINTH: The Beloved's hair is often compared to the hyacinth because of its beautiful perfume.

THE LILY: The lily often symbolizes a gossip, its long yellow stamen representing a tongue.

THE ARGHAVAN: The arghavan or Judas tree has crimson flowers. This represents the mature, long-suffering lover.

THE NARCISSUS: A proud beautiful one, jealous of the Beloved's (the rose's) beauty. Sometimes Hafez refers to the Beloved as the narcissus, telling the Beloved not to be so proud and to call on the lover. Often the eyes of the Beloved are symbolized by the narcissus.

THE CYPRESS: The cypress symbolizes the form of the Beloved because of the tall, upright stature of the cypress and because like God Who never changes, the cypress remains green all throughout the year.

THE CYPRESS CONE: The lover's heart.

THE NIGHTINGALE: The lover of the Beloved (the rose). It also symbolizes the poet who sings of the beauty of the Beloved.

THE PARROT: The poet who talks to the Beloved in the hope that the Beloved will reward him with sugar (Love, Grace).

THE FALCON: God. The Perfect Master or the Beloved, who preys upon the lover who is a mere fly by comparison.

THE KITE AND THE CROW: Ignorance, false poets, false masters.

THE PARTRIDGE: False pride, pomposity. Often the partridge symbolizes an earthly king, or person in power, who prides himself on his position.

THE HOOPOE OR LAPWING: The messenger of the Perfect Master. A faithful servant.

THE MOTH: The lover, who wishes to extinguish himself in the flame (Love) of the candle (God).

THE PATH, STREET, HIGHWAY: The Path of the love of God in human form i.e. the Perfect Master. The Spiritual way. The path that leads to the Winehouse, wherein is found the Perfect Master. The journey through the inner realms of consciousness to the true Self (God).

THE WINEHOUSE: The place where the lover goes to be with the Beloved, the Perfect Master. The dwelling of the Perfect Master. Sometimes the Winehouse symbolizes the inner Self of the lover.

THE WINE: Truth, Love, Grace, Knowledge. As ordinary wine changes a person's personality, so Divine Wine changes the inner consciousness and brings the lover closer to God and intoxicates the lover with God's Love and Truth. The more the lover drinks of this wine, the more he becomes addicted to it and the more he loses his reasoning. Wine (in the ordinary sense) was forbidden to Muslims and by using wine as a symbol for personal love for God and from God (as Jesus did), Hafez points out the difference between formal and personal religion. The love for the Perfect Master that Hafez advocated could result in persecution by the orthodox clergy of the time: hence, the symbol was an apt one.

THE CUP: The heart of the lover of God and sometimes the Beloved, from whom flows the wine of Divine Love.

THE FLAGON AND WINECASK: The Perfect Master, God.

THE WINEBRINGER: The Beloved, the Perfect Master, the Godman, or anyone who brings to the lover (the drunkard) God's Love, Truth and Beauty. Sometimes Hafez means Destiny, which brings the cup from which we must drink.

THE FRIEND: God, the Perfect Master.

THE BELOVED: God, the Perfect Master. God perceived in beautiful human form as in the female (Nabat in Hafez's case... his 'Muse'.).

THE BELOVED'S HAIR: The attraction of God's Grace. The Mystery that conceals the Divine Essence. The hair sometimes symbolizes the world with its problems (tangles) and mysteries, in which sometimes we get trapped.

THE BELOVED'S CURLS: The beauties of God's Manifestation. The charms of the Beloved. The twists of Fate.

THE BELOVED'S EYE: The Power of God. One glance and we can become annihilated in His Love.

THE BELOVED'S EYEBROW: The eyebrow of the Beloved is often compared with the arch towards which one prays (in the direction of Mecca) in a Mosque. Sometimes Hafez describes it as a bow which the Beloved uses to shoot arrows (glances) from the eye into the lover's heart (target).

THE BELOVED'S DOWN (ON CHEEK OR LIP): This symbolizes the attractions of Divine Love. It also symbolizes the sprouting forth of Life.

THE BELOVED'S LIP: The lip of the Beloved will heal the lover because from it the lover can taste the Water of Everlasting Life and the Wine of Divine Love.

THE BELOVED'S MOLE: An attraction of the Beloved, full of Mystery. The Perfect imperfection?

THE WINEMAKER: God in human form; the Messiah, Rasool, Avatar e.g. Adam, Jesus, Mohammed, Noah.

THE WINESELLER: The Perfect Master. God in human form.

THE KING, SOVEREIGN, MONARCH: God in human form, same as above. Hafez often used these titles when speaking of the Messiah (the first Perfect Master,) and many of the poems in which he used these titles were mistaken by commentators to be about kings who lived when Hafez lived. By using such symbology Hafez could openly praise his Master and the king of the time would not be jealous, but pleased, for he would think that they were about him.

MONARCH'S CROWN: God's Glory.

THE SLAVE: The lover of God (the King), who is bound by God's Beauty, which is sometimes represented by the long flowing (chainlike) hair of the Beloved.

THE PAINTER, THE ARCHITECT: God the Creator.

THE RUIN: This world, wherein one can find the Treasure (the Perfect Master, the Truth). It also symbolizes the lover's body which though ruined through searching and longing for God, still contains the jewel of the Soul.

THE INN, HOTEL: The world, where we must stay awhile before passing on.

THE SUFI: The Muslim mystic. Hafez often talks of true and false Sufis. (See Chapter 2 of the Introduction and various Notes to the poems).

THE SUFI'S GARMENT: Hafez advises us to soak our coat of religion in the wine of Divine Love.

THE DERVISH: The true lover of God, the real mystic.

THE KALANDAR: Like the dervish, a true lover of God.

NOTES

1. LOVE AT FIRST

COUPLET 1. The opening couplet of this *ghazal* is supposed to have brought much criticism to Hafez, because the first line was said to have been taken from words composed by Yezid ibn Moawiyah, the second Khalif of the Ommiad line, who is hated by the Shi'ites because he caused the death of Ali's son Husain whom they regard as the third Imam and rightful successor. Hafez's reply to this accusation was: "Who would not take away a pearl from the mouth of a filthy dog?" COUPLET 3: A description of 'the dark night of the soul.' The whole of this *ghazal* is a description of the soul through the inner stages of consciousness to Godhood. See chapter two of the introduction. COUPLET 4. THE BELL CLANGS: The bell of death?

NOTE: Because of the way of laying out a *Divan* by the last letter of the rhyme word and so on... this *ghazal* is always appearing first in every *Divan of Hafez*. Obviously Hafez made sure it was so. It is said that this *ghazal* contains in microcosm the whole of the *Divan* as is said of the first *sura* of the *Koran*.

2. DAILY BREAD.

COUPLET 9: Jam (Jamshid) was a king of ancient Persia who possessed a magic cup in which he could see the state of the whole world. This is a similar symbol to Alexander's Mirror in which the world was reflected. Both are symbols for Universal Mind - or a Guide or Master who guided their actions. This Master in relation to Alexander was called Khizer - meaning a Perfect Master who has gained immortality and the ability to appear anywhere at any time or to direct someone to do his bidding in relation to one who has no Master. Both Jamshid and Alexander ended their lives not gaining the Water of Life (God-realization) because their attachment to power and pride stopped them from taking the advice of their Guide. See *ghazal* No. 6 couplet 5 and *ghazal* 165, c. 3. See: 'The Epic of The Kings' translated by R. Levy, Routledge Keegan and Paul 1967, and the other translations; also: 'Iskandarnama. A Persian Alexander Romance' translated by M.S. Southgate. Columbia University Press 1978. 'The Book of Alexander the Great' by Nizami. Trans. H. Wilberforce Clarke 1881.

3. IT COULD BE.

COUPLET 9. Khwaja Haji Kivam was an advanced soul and an advisor to Abu Ishak and was a patron and friend of Hafez. It is said that one day when Hafez visited him he saw in a winecup the image he expresses in this couplet. Haji Kivam died in 1353 A.D at the siege of Shiraz by the tyrant Mubariz Muzaffar. See introduction and index.

4. THE MOMENT'S JOY.

COUPLET 1. SUFI: See GLOSSARY of Terms and symbols.
COUPLET 2. PURE BIRD: God in the Beyond State i.e. God the Father in Christian terminology. The word that Hafez uses is 'Anka.' Hafez means that one cannot reach to the Pure Existence of God without God in human form as an intermediary, a Perfect Master or the Godman. "No one reaches the Father but through Me." Jesus Christ. COUPLET 3. ADAM: The first Perfect Master, or God-realized soul i.e. the first Hero or Beloved of lovers, who consciously united as the first Divine lover, with the first perfected woman Eve, to begin the history of the Godman on this earth. Their 'sin' or mistake was only seen as such by others who could not comprehend their Consciousness. Their 'mistake' was that when they were accused by others of committing only a gross or lustful act, they refused to answer, to deny it: thus paving the way for the concept of 'original sin.' Hafez uses the symbol of a grain of wheat or barley, instead of an apple. The grain is likened to the mole on the cheek. COUPLET 9. JAMSHID: See explanation to no. 2 couplet 9.

6. DESTINY'S DESIGN.

COUPLET 5. ALEXANDER'S MIRROR: See explanation given to no. 2, couplet 9. DARA (DARIUS): Darius III d. 330 B.C. Darius was defeated by Alexander who had invaded Persia in 331 B.C. See 'The Epic of The Kings' (Shahnama). KARUN: The Korah of the Bible and the uncle of Moses. It is said that he was the richest man in Israel, having so much wealth that the keys to his treasure houses were heavy burdens for several men. Karun tried to have Moses stoned for a false charge of adultery. Moses commanded the earth to swallow him up. Karun and his palaces and wealth fell into a great pit and are said to be still sinking (see *ghazal* 36 couplet 11). God then said to Moses: "You had no mercy on Karun, although he asked for pardon three times. If he had asked Me only once, I would have spared him." See The Bible, Numbers xvi; the *Koran,* xxviii, 76.

7. NEWS OF THE ROSE

COUPLET 6: Hafez refers to the humility of the Godman or Perfect Master, using Noah as the example as he does elsewhere.

8. FAIR EXCHANGE

COUPLET 1. TURKISH: Hafez compares the Beloved to a Turk because of their beauty and fair complexion. BOKHARA AND SAMARKAND: Once a part of Persia, then a part of the U.S.S.R. now independent. It is said that some time after writing this, Hafez was brought before Timur. See the end of my *Hafez of Shiraz... A Novel/Biography* Book 3 (Shiraz Books 2008) for a full account of this famous encounter (recorded by one of Timur's sons) and see chapter one of this Introduction or visit my website... Hafezofshiraz.com.

COUPLET 2. RUKNABAD: A stream or canal four feet wide, a mile to the north of Shiraz. Its water is said to be very pleasant. A branch of this stream passes by the tomb of Hafez. JOSEPH: Joseph of Egypt was a Perfect Master who was also extremely handsome. He was the symbol of God's perfect beauty. ZULAIKHA: Zulaikha was the wife of Potiphar. She fell in love with Joseph and could not contain her great love for him. The story of their love was told by many Persian, poets. Jami's version is the best and most famous.

10. GUIDING LIGHT

COUPLET 1: OUR MASTER: Some translators say that this refers to the Prophet Mohammed, but it could also be Attar, Hafez's Master.

11. MURDERER

COUPLET 1. MONACH: Beloved, Perfect Master or Godman. Hafez often refers to the Master as King, Monarch, Sovereign.

14. FRESH

NOTE: This *ghazal* appears only in some editions but Sudi who is considered the greatest commentator on Hafez's *Divan* included it in his edition. As well as being popular in Iran it is very popular in India, especially in Kashmir (see the chapter of my novel *The First Mystery* set in Kashmir). It is still sung by the boatmen on the Ganges.

15. THIRSTY

COUPLET 2. KERBALA: The saying 'the thirsty ones of Kerbala' refers to the seventy followers of Husain, the son of Ali, the first Imam of Shi'ite Islam, who was to Mohammed what Peter was to Jesus. Husain and his followers were killed at Kerbala by the Caliph's troops, who feared Husain would gain popularity as the Imam. They were called 'thirsty' because during the fight they were cut off from the Euphrates river, and because they were thirsting so much for God that they were prepared to give up their lives. Husain was the third Imam and his brother Hasan was the second. Imam means: Leader of Islam.

17. THE MORNING CUP.

COUPLET 10: see explanation to *ghazal* 2 couplet 9.

20. DON'T GIVE UP HOPE

COUPLET 1. CHIEF: Hafez uses the word 'Khwaja' which has a number of meanings. 1. It is a term of respect as in English 'Kind Sir.' 2. It means a particular kind of Master. A Khwaja personality Perfect Master is one who rarely leaves his home - 'a stick in the mud.' It is his or her personality not to travel but to remain in the one place and allow the world to come to him. Hafez was of this type, and is usually given the title of 'Khwaja.' A 'Kalandar' type of Perfect Master has the opposite type of personality. He is always on the move and inwardly gives exact attention to every detail. A 'Khizer' Perfect Master has the ability to appear to anyone at anytime in any form he pleases or to send someone to do his work, be his agent, whether consciously or without knowing. COUPLET 8. ASAF: Solomon's chief minister who Hafez criticizes here for losing Solomon's seal-ring that originally belonged to Jam. Hafez sometimes uses Asaf to signify a Chief or Master or a prime-minister like Givam ud-Din.

22. YOUR TREASURY

COUPLET 6. MAJNUN: Majnun (about 721 A.D.) which means 'madman' whose real name was Qays, was the famous lover of Layla who came from another tribe in Arabia. Majnun fell in love with Layla when they were children at school together. Unable to contain his love, one day he expressed it and Layla's father, enraged by the scandal of this 'madman' in love with his daughter, refused to allow them to see etch other. Majnun's father, who was the leader of his tribe, tried to reconcile them but to no avail. Layla also loved Majnun. Majnun wandered the hills living with wild animals and composing songs in praise of Layla. Finally their human love became so great that it was transformed into Divine Love by a Perfect Master. Majnun became so undernourished that he finally starved to death. Layla threw herself on his grave and died there. Their souls mingled with their dust. Many stories and poems have been written about them, the most popular being that by Nizami. Possibly their story which came through Spain into Europe inspired Massuccio Salernitano whose story inspired Luigi Da Porto, whose story inspired Shakespeare to write his play Romeo and Juliet. See my translation of *Layla & Majnun*. Shiraz Books. 2006

24. THAT ONE

COUPLET 2. THE SEAL: The Seal of Prophecy.
COUPLET 6. JESUS' BREATH: Hafez states it was Jesus' breath that could raise the dead... a popular belief in Sufi and Eastern Poetry.
NOTE: In this *ghazal* Hafez states that Mohammed was the Rasool or Messiah come again, with the same Divinity as that of Adam (the first Perfect Master) and Solomon and Jesus etc.

26. TONIGHT

COUPLET 1. THE NIGHT OF POWER: The night on which the *Koran* was manifested and on which God looks favourably towards those who pray and all wishes are granted. The most sacred night of the Muslim year, the exact date is not known. See *Koran* xiiv, 1-6; liii, 6.
COUPLET 7. ANT: Solomon's Master (Asaf?) appeared to him in the form of an ant. Solomon was about to crush the ant when it spoke to him and made him understand that God was in everything, even an ant, and that the Power of God was much greater than Solomon's power. This was the last lesson Solomon had to learn and so he received God-realization and it is because of this that the ant was called 'Solomon's steed.'

32. THE HOUSE OF HOPE.

COUPLET 3. ANGEL OF BEYOND: Gabriel
COUPLET 6. PATHWAY'S MASTERMIND: The Perfect Master.

34. LAWFUL WINE

COUPLET 8. FAME: Hafez was famous in his lifetime in many countries (see introduction) but it made him uncomfortable for he became so popular with the people that his life was often in danger from the clergy and the various rulers.
COUPLET 10. CENSOR: The Persian word means a kind of policeman who policed the anti-wine laws at that time.

35. 'GOD IS THE GREATEST.'

COUPLET 5. THEY: They, with a capital 'T', for whenever Hafez uses this word this way, he means Fate or Destiny as directed by the Perfect Masters who jointly control all the affairs of the Creation and direct all of its workings from the inner Spiritual levels of Consciousness.
COUPLET 10. LAND OF DARKNESS: The Water of Life is in the 'Land of Darkness' or the form, or the world, because God (Light) needs the dark to manifest Himself through: the reason for Him manifesting the Creation. This is also symbolical of the 'Dark Night' of the wayfarer on

the Spiritual Path, which must be passed through before the Light of Divinity or Eternal Life shines within and is recognized.

KHIZER: See previous explanations and also introduction.

36. PERFECT MASTERS (DERVISHES)

COUPLET 1. DERVISHES: To Hafez, dervish was the word he used to signify a spiritually sincere seeker or one who had attained Realization. He preferred to be called a 'dervish,' rather than a 'Sufi,' which often meant a ritualistic connection with a sect which had little to do with the essence of Sufism: the love of God, respect for all approaches to God and the belief in the need to have a Perfect Master to attain God-realization. In this poem Hafez uses the word 'Dervishes' with a capital 'D' because be means all those true lovers of God who have reached the goal and have become Perfect Masters.

COUPLET 3. RIZVAN: The angel who keeps the door to the Palace of Paradise.

COUPLET 11. KARUN: See note to *ghazal* 6 couplet 10.

COUPLET 12. ASAF: Hafez uses the name of Asaf (who was Solomon's Chief advisor and Perfect Master) to signify the Chief of the Masters of the period in which Hafez lived.

40. YOUR EYE'S PRESCRIPTION

COUPLET 6. GARDENER: God.

41. LOVE'S OCCUPATION.

COUPLET 9. KHUSRAU PARVIZ AND SHIRIN: Shirin was said to be the beautiful daughter of the Byzantine Emperor, Maurice. She married Parviz (A.D.591) and became the queen of Persia. It was Parviz who invaded Jerusalem and carried away the true cross. A sculptor by the name of Farhad fell in love with her and she with him. Farhad made an agreement with Parviz that if he could cut a pass through a mountain for a water-channel, he would be given Shirin. After many years he achieved this remarkable feat (it still exists today) but on hearing that he had succeeded Parviz sent a messenger to tell him that Shim had committed suicide. On hearing this lie, Farhad threw himself off the mountain and died. King Parviz was violently put to death by his son who then proposed to Shirin. Shirin promised to marry him if she could once again see her husband's body. When she was taken to the corpse she pulled out a dagger and killed herself, falling across the body of Parviz. This tragic love story is very popular in Persian legend and poetry.

42. NO CHOICE

COUPLET 1. ANCIENT ONE: God in human form i.e. Jesus, Adam, Mohammed, Krishna, Meher Baba, Zoroaster, Buddha etc.

43. THIS TALE

COUPLET 5. DAY PRIMAL: This couplet refers to the Covenant that God made on the First Day i.e. before the Creation, in God's Imagination. God created (in His Infinite Imagination) all the souls that were possible to create, and He asked them: "Am I NOT your God?" This of course was something of a trick question, and not without a sense of humour. Some, out of love, not wishing to be rude by not answering answered: "Yes!" (In other words: You are NOT our God). These were the lovers of God. Others did not answer. God then manifested all of the souls into creation, some of them being lovers (Hafez claims to have remembered saying "yes" and so was one of these), and others, those who had to learn from the lovers to try to love and to say "yes" to God, even though to try is the best that one can do. The word in Persian for 'yes' has a number of meanings: it also means 'mistake' or 'calamity' or 'curse.' Hafez claims to have loved God from before the Creation was formed, and claims that this burden (love) must be taken up if one is to reach the goal and give the correct answer, whatever that may be.

49. ILLEGAL WINE AND FORGED COIN

COUPLET 2. 'EXPLAINING OF EXPLAINER'S': Hafez was known to have annotated this book which was said to be the greatest commentary written on the *Koran*, the 'Kashf-i-Kashshaf' by Jaru-I-lah as Zamakhshari (b.1074 d. 1144). Hafez's edition has been lost to us, or perhaps it is hiding away somewhere in a library in Iran or Tashkent. Hafez must have been teaching *Koranic* studies when he annotated it, as is obvious from this couplet.
COUPLET 3. PURE BIRD: The Anka. See previous explanation to *ghazal* 4 c. 2.
POLE TO POLE: From mountaintop to mountaintop in the Spiritual sense. From Master to Master.
COUPLET 7. CITY'S FORGER: Maybe Hafez means the false poets who stole his poems and claimed them as their own.

50. BETWEEN HEAVEN AND HELL

COUPLET 4: See previous note to *ghazal* 49, couplet 2.

51. THE LOVER'S NEED

COUPLET 5: This couplet examines the meaning of the 'cup' as previously discussed in relation to Alexander's 'mirror' and Jamshid's 'cup'. See note to *ghazal* 2 couplet 9.
COUPLET 6. THE SAILOR: The Perfect Master.
THE PEARL: Divine Knowledge, or Grace.

53. FASCINATION

NOTE: This *ghazal* is said to have been written when Hafez was still a youth. Maybe it was written shortly after he first saw the woman he fell in love with: Shakh-e-Nabat, or 'Branch of Sugarcane.' See introduction.

54. REASON

COUPLET 4: Hasan, Bilal and Suhaib were all among the first disciples of Mohammed. Bilal, the black slave from Abyssinia, was the first to call the people to prayer and died in 641 A.D. Hasan was famous for his devotion. He died in 728 A.D. Suhaib was supposed to have taught the Scriptures to Mohammed. Abu Jahal (d. 624) was one of Mohammed's enemies. He was born in Mecca.
COUPLET 5. ABU LAHAB: He was Mohammed's uncle and his greatest enemy. See the *Koran* for details.
COUPLET 7. DAUGHTER OF THE GRAPE: Love.

55. THE CHOICE

COUPLET 4. THE GARDEN OF IRAM: This was said to have been created by King Shudad, the son of Ad who was the grandson of Iram, who was the son of Shem, Noah's son. The tribe of Ad settled in the desert near Aden and Ad started to build a fabulous city which was finished by his son Shudad. Shudad created a wonderful garden around his palace which he thought would rival the Garden of Paradise. When it was finished he set out to admire it and when he came near to it all were destroyed by a great sound that came from God. It is said that the ruins still exist near Aden. Hafez means: what is the use of a beautiful setting if you can't enjoy it. A lesson which Shudad must have learnt.
COUPLET 8. PARADISE'S KAUTHER: Kauther is said to be the main river in Paradise, from which all other rivers and streams flow. Its water is said to be pure and sweet and around it are countless cups for one to use to drink from it, and on drinking, one thirsts no more. Some of its waters lead to a great lake that take a month to go around. In this couplet Hafez states that he prefers the pleasure of today, rather than that of tomorrow.

57. CONCEAL THE WINECUP

COUPLET 5. KISRA: Cyrus, also the title of the Sassanian Kings. PARVIZ: KHUSRAU, PARVIZ AND SHIRIN: Shirin was said to be the beautiful daughter of the Byzantine Emperor, Maurice. She married Parviz (A.D.591) and became the queen of Persia. It was Parviz who invaded Jerusalem and carried away the true cross. A sculptor by the name of Farhad fell in love with her and she with him. Farhad made an agreement with Parviz that if he could cut a pass through a mountain for a water-channel, he would be given Shirin. After many years he achieved this remarkable feat (still exists today) but on hearing that he had succeeded Parviz sent a messenger to tell him that Shirin had committed suicide. On hearing this lie, Farhad threw himself off the mountain and died. King Parviz was violently put to death by his son who then proposed to Shirin. Shirin promised to marry him if she could once again see her husband's body. When she was taken to the corpse she pulled out a dagger and killed herself, falling across the body of Parviz. This tragic love story is very popular in Persian legend and poetry. Nizami's great poem (not trans. into English) is the greatest portrayal of this story.

COUPLET 6. INVERTED BOWL: The sky, fate.

COUPLET 7. When Nadir Shah (d.1747) went to war with Afghanistan he made a pilgrimage to Hafez's tomb and consulted the *Divan*. This was the couplet he received. He attacked Baghdad and Tabriz and took them back from the Turks. For the use of the *Divan of Hafez* as an oracle see the introduction.

58. A GLIMPSE OF UNION

COUPLET 8. KALANDARS: Kalandars are lovers of God who have given up attachment to desires and live only for God. The name comes from a Master named Kalandar Yusuf. The word means 'pure gold.' Kalandars are continually on the move and care nothing for their own condition, as they are only concerned with praising God. Hafez says that the real meaning of Kalandarship is scrupulous attention to detail and never giving in. In other words, the outer appearance doesn't matter, and a true Kalandar is inwardly meticulous in giving up all his desires to God. For further explanation of 'Kalandar,' in relation to the Kalandar type of Perfect Master, see note to *ghazal* 20 couplet 1. John the Baptist was probably a Kalandar-type Perfect Master. See *ghazal* 107: 'The True Kalandar.'

60. PARADISE

COUPLET 7: This was the couplet that was received when there was an argument over whether Hafez should be buried in a Muslim burial ground. This couplet then began the use of Hafez's *Divan* as an oracle... which has continued ever since. See Introduction.

61. PURE WINE

COUPLET 5. HURIS: Huris are the angels of Paradise in beautiful female form. Paris are the angels of Paradise in handsome male form.

62. AUTUMN WIND

COUPLET 2: Wadi Aiman is the name of the valley near Mt. Tur, Sinai. where Moses saw God appear in the form of a burning bush.

64. OPEN KNOWLEDGE

COUPLET 5. JAMSHID'S CUP: See note to 'DAILY BREAD' Couplet 2. COUPLET 9. KING: God.

66. THE HIDDEN SECRET

COUPLET 4. BREATH FROM YEMEN: This is symbolical of God's Mercy and refers to Uvais Karani, from Yemen, who was a Perfect Master at the time of Mohammed, who didn't need to see Mohammed to accept him as the Divine Prophet. A breeze from Yemen is said to be cool, joyful and merciful, refreshing. In honour of Mohammed who had lost his teeth in the battle of Ohod, Uvais Karani pulled out his own teeth. Mohammed said of Uvais: "Truly, from the quarters of Yemen, I perceive the perfume of God (Uvais Karani)."

68. BEYOND THE VEIL

COUPLET 5. JESUS-BREATH: See note to 'THAT ONE' (above)...couplet 6.

69. THE NIGHTINGALE'S LAMENT

COUPLET 4. MASTER SANAAN: Sanaan (d. 1159 A.D.) was a Shaikh who had over four hundred followers. He fell in love with a Christian girl and supposedly left the path of Islam. Some of his followers went to a Perfect Master and asked for advice, for Sanaan had given all his money to her and had pawned his religious garment to buy her the wine that she wanted. Finally for her sake, he started looking after pigs. The Perfect Master rebuked Sanaan's disciples for not having enough faith in their leader and sent them back with advice on how to bring him back to God through prayer. This happened, and the girl became Sanaan's disciple, for he was now a Master, having experienced that which it was necessary for him to experience to gain God. See Farid ud-Din Attar's 'Conference of the Birds' English translation by C.S. Nott p.p. 34-44 pub. Shambhala.

COUPLET 5: This couplet also refers to Sanaan, who was known to have still said his prayers even though he had embraced the Christian faith for the sake of the woman he loved. KALANDAR: Kalandars are lovers of God who have given up attachment to desires and live only for God. The name comes from a Master named Kalandar Yusuf. The word means 'pure gold.' Kalandars are continually on the move and care nothing for their own condition, as they are only concerned with praising God. Hafez says that the real meaning of Kalandarship is scrupulous attention to detail and never giving in. In other words, the outer appearance doesn't matter, and a true Kalandar is inwardly meticulous in giving up all his desires to God. John the Baptist was probably a Kalandar-type Perfect Master.

72. BE KIND TO MY HEART

COUPLET 4. SHIRIN AND FARHAD: See note to 'CONCEAL THE WINECUP' couplet 5 (above). LAYLA AND MAJNUN: Majnun (about 721 A.D.) which means 'madman' whose real name was Qays, was the famous lover of Layla who came from another tribe in Arabia. Majnun fell in love with Layla when they were children at school together. Unable to contain his love, one day he expressed it and Layla's father, enraged by the scandal of this 'madman' in love with his daughter, refused to allow them to see each other. Majnun's father, who was the leader of his tribe, tried to reconcile them but to no avail. Layla also loved Majnun. Majnun wandered the hills living with wild animals and composing songs in praise of Layla. Finally their human love became so great that it was transformed into Divine Love by a Perfect Master. Majnun became so undernourished that he finally starved to death. Layla threw herself on his grave and died there. Their souls mingled with their dust. Many stories and poems have been written about them, the most popular being that by Nizami. Possibly their story which came through Spain into Europe inspired Massuccio Salernitano whose story inspired Luigi Da Porto, whose story inspired Shakespeare to write his play Romeo and Juliet. See my Layla and Majnun (Shiraz Books 2006 & e-book).
COUPLET 9: KARUN: The Korah of the Bible and the uncle of Moses. It is said that he was the richest man in Israel, having so much wealth that the keys to his treasure houses were heavy burdens for several men. Karun tried to have Moses stoned for a false charge of adultery. Moses commanded the earth to swallow him up. Karun and his palaces and wealth fell into a great pit and are said to be still sinking. God then said to Moses: "You had no mercy on Karun, although he asked for pardon three times. If he had asked Me only once, I would have spared him." See The Bible, Numbers xvi; Koran, xxviii, 76.

73. THE HEART'S PURPOSE

COUPLET 7. BIRD OF PARADISE TREE: The Angel Gabriel.

75. FESTIVAL DAY

COUPLET 2. DAUGHTER OF THE VINE: The wine of Love.
COUPLET 7. ARK OF NOAH: The Perfect Master.

76. GRIEF OF SEPARATION

COUPLET 1. OLD MAN OF CANAAN: The Perfect Master, or perhaps Joseph's father Jacob.

77. THE ANSWER OF THE ROSE

COUPLET 5. IRAM'S GARDEN: This was said to have been created by King Shudad, the son of Ad who was the grandson of Iram, who was the son of Shem, Noah's son. The tribe of Ad settled in the desert near Aden and Ad started to build a fabulous city which was finished by his son Shudad. Shudad created a wonderful garden around his palace which he thought would rival the Garden of Paradise. When it was finished he set Out to admire it and when he came near to it all were destroyed by a great sound that came from God. It is said that the ruins still exist near Aden. Hafez in this couplet means: what is the use of a beautiful setting if you can't enjoy it. A lesson which Shudad must have learnt.
COUPLET 6. JAMSHID'S CUP: See note on 'DAILY BREAD', couplet 2 (above).

81. MY DESIRE

COUPLET 3. NIGHT OF POWER: See expl. to 'TONIGHT' couplet 1 (above).

82. THE INVISIBLE MESSENGER

COUPLET 1. SABA: A land in Arabia also called Sheba... symbolically the home of the Beloved.

83. BROUGHT TO COMPLETION

COUPLET 4. HARUT: One of the angels (the other being Marut) who were sent by God to Babylon in the time of David; for God wished to prove to them that it was passion and lust that caused humans to sin. They fell in love with Zuhra, a singer, who they taught the great Name of God. They worshipped her and killed her husband. By the Power of the Name which she now knew, she descended to the heavens and became

Venus. The two angels by the wrath of God were placed in a pit outside Babylon, head downwards, from where they taught people magic and sorcery.

84. TO THE RESURRECTION'S DAYS

COUPLET 7. IMAM: A religious leader in Shi'ite Islam. Not one of the original Imam's, as was Ali, Hasan etc. A similar instance would be Peter, appointed by Jesus, and a Pope, a thousand years later, appointed by the Church elders. Hafez often criticized such 'leaders' and received their wrath because of it, and almost lost his life on a number of occasions.

87. COMMOTION IN THE WINEHOUSE

COUPLET 2. WINE: Hafez once again states that wine is a symbol for the Truth, Love, or Grace of God.
COUPLET 6. MAJNUN AND LAYLA: See expl. to 'BE KIND TO MY HEART' couplet 4 (above). MAHMUD AND AYAZ: Mahmud (b.967 d.1030 A.D.) of Ghezni was the famous Sultan who conquered India. Ayaz his favourite slave was also famous for his faithfulness and honesty and courage. Mahmud loved Ayaz so much that it could be said that this love transformed the relationship into one where Ayaz was the Master and Mahmud the slave. Such is the nature and power of love. There are many stories about Mahmud and Ayaz in Persian literature pointing this out. See 'The Mathnavi' by Rumi, translated by R.A. Nicholson, published by Luzac, 3 Vols. There does not seem to be any similar love story in the world's literature.

91. BEYOND CURE

COUPLET 7. SAFA FROM MERVEH: These are the names of the two mountains near Mecca that Hagar, the handmaiden of Abraham ran back and forth to, after being sent into the desert with their son Ishmael. This occurred after Abraham had prayed to God for direction, as Sarah his wife became jealous because Hagar had been able to bear Abraham a child. Dying of thirst, Hagar ran from mountain to mountain imploring God to help her and her son. She did this seven times. At last she heard her son cry out and found a stream manifested where he was lying. Gabriel appeared and informed her that the stream would continue to flow, and that Abraham would return and build a house there (which became the Kaaba) and that it would become a place of pilgrimage. Gabriel also said that her son would become a prophet. Pilgrims still run seven times between the two to commemorate this.

97. IN ALL PATHS

COUPLET 3. MANY JOSEPH OF EGYPT: This means that many a beautiful one, even perfect in beauty, has fallen into the trap of the Beauty of God.

99. DIVINE WISDOM

COUPLET 6. PHYSICIAN: Hafez sometimes calls the Perfect Master the 'Physician' and when he does it is spelt with a capital 'P'.

100. IT'S A PITY

COUPLET 3. *KORAN'S FIRST CHAPTER*: The *Fatiha*. 'SINCERITY': Chapter cxii of the *Koran*. CHARM OF YEMEN: A prayer that Mohammed taught while travelling to Yemen.

102. PLUNDER

COUPLET 12. OBSCURE SIRIUS: Suhra or Sirius is an obscure star in Ursa Minor. Hafez likens it to a false Master.

104. BY THE GRACE OF GOD

COUPLET 3. HEAVENLY HOUSE: The Kaaba. VINE'S DAUGHTER: Love, wine.
COUPLET 6. ABU LAHAB: Mohammed's uncle and greatest enemy. MUSTAFA: A title of Mohammed, meaning: 'The Chosen One.'

105. TRAP OF FAITH

COUPLET 6. TWO NOBLE RECORDERS: The two angels who write in the Record-book, man's good and bad actions.

107. THE TRUE KALANDAR

COUPLET 6. KALANDARSHIP: See expl. to 'THE NIGHTINGALE'S LAMENT', couplet 5 (above).

109. WISE WORDS

COUPLET 1: One of the well-known couplets of Hafez often quoted by Meher Baba.
COUPLET 9. Hafez often calls the Master the Minstrel.

111. YOUR SUPREME MAJESTY

COUPLET 5. KHIZER: See introduction and expl. to 'DON'T GIVE UP HOPE' couplet 1 (above) and 'A GLANCE FOR A VICTIM' couplet 3 (below).

112. A DRUNKARD'S PRAYER

COUPLET 2. 'Bringer of darkness' and 'Splitter of morning' are both attributes of God.

113. THE HOPE OF UNION

COUPLET 1 and 3. 'GOD'S MONTH': Ramazan, the ninth month of the Muslim year, during which there is a rigorous fast. On the 27th, the *Koran* manifested and this is called 'The Night of Power' - but the exact day that this falls on is not known. The 'Day of Surrender' is the first of the month.
COUPLET 5. 'SPLITTER OF MORNINGS': God.
COUPLET 7. KING SHUJA: Shah Shuja (d.1384) was the Sultan of the Muzaffar dynasty whose capital was Shiraz. He opened the doors of the winehouses and is praised by Hafez for doing this. See introduction.
COUPLET 8. THE OPENER: God.

114. FARRUKH

NOTE: 'Farrukh' which means 'auspicious, blessed, beautiful' is possibly a nickname for Mahmud Attar or Prophet Mohammed or even for Shakh e-Nabat.
COUPLET 5. ARGHAVAN: The Syrtes or 'Judas' tree, that has crimson flowers signifying the pain and depth of mature love.

117. A LOST SON

NOTE: It is said that this was written by on the death of his son.
COUPLET 4. CAMELDRIVER: The Master, God.

120. A RESOLUTION

COUPLET 6. ANCIENT PROMISE: The Covenant with God on the First Day in Eternity. See expl. 'THIS TALE' couplet 5 (above).

121. RETURN OF THE ROSE

COUPLET 1. NOTHING TO GODHEAD: From God in the Beyond State without Form, to God in the state of form: as the Perfect Master or the Godman i.e. Jesus, Adam, Attar, Mohammed.

COUPLET 5. ZOROASTER: A daring statement by Hafez, (to create a new faith out of the faith of Zoroaster i.e. to drink wine, liquid fire, love) as at that time he was living in a strictly Muslim country. In this statement Hafez recognizes the Mastership of Zoroaster who lived about 6000 B.C., not 500 B.C. as is often stated by historians confusing him with the last of the Zoroastrian priests. NIMROD: Nimrod built a great fire and threw Abraham into it. God turned it into a bed of roses. Nimrod built the tower of Babel.

COUPLET 7. SOLOMON: The Perfect Master who had the ability to travel on the wind and also to understand the language of the birds. DAVID: Another Perfect Master, famous for the songs he composed and sang. The Perfect Singer.

COUPLET 8. IMAD UD-DIN MAHMUD: Shah Abu Ishak's advisor and a friend of Hafez who seems to have been a Master. He is likened in this couplet to Solomon's chief advisor Asaf (the Asaph of the Psalms) who was famous for his wisdom, even though at one time he lost Solomon's seal-ring and caused Solomon much trouble. See expl. to *ghazal* 20 couplet 8.

122. BUBBLE OF DECEPTION

COUPLET 1. SUFI: Hafez here of course is talking about a false Sufi. See Introduction.

COUPLET 4. IRAK AND HIJAZ: These are musical notes which are played at breakfast time. Irak is a cheerful note and Hijaz is a sad note. Hafez may also be referring to the actual places.

COUPLET 8: In this couplet Hafez alludes to the popular tale of the Sufi poet and Court poet of Shah Shuja, Emad Kermani, (see Introduction) who trained his cat... that by pretending to be devout and practice meditation lured a partridge (Shah Shuja) into its trap and ate it. Hafez is warning inexperienced people of the cunning and tricks of those claiming to be holy (false Sufis and others).

123. THE MAD HEART

COUPLET 1. JAMSHID'S CUP: See expl. to *ghazal* 2 couplet 9.

COUPLET 6. THAT FRIEND: Hafez's Master Attar, who Hafez is quoting, means the Perfect Master and martyr Mansur Hallaj (d.919 A.D.), who was sentenced to death for saying: "I am the Truth (Anal Haq)." (See *ghazal* 217 couplet 6 where Hafez makes the same statement, which must have made it difficult for him from then on, i.e. if he made this poem public). Much has been written about Hallaj and his famous (and infamous) statement. If the reader wishes to follow up his life and writings, a list is given below. To me, the meaning of this couplet in its context is that it was Hallaj's Karma or Fate to make that true statement and suffer the consequences; but it does not mean that others who experience the same, God-realization, have to proclaim it to the whole world, unless they have a particular role to play in this creation by doing so. On Mansur Hallaj's life and sayings see: 'Muslim Saints and Mystics' by Farid ud-Din Attar trans. by A.J. Arberry R.K.P. pp. 264-272; 'The Kashf al-Mahjub: The Oldest Persian Treatise on Sufism' by Hujwiri. trans. by R.A. Nicholson, Luzac, U.K. 'Diwan of al Hallaj' trans. into French by Louis Massignon, Paris 1955 (Documents Spiritual S.10); 'The Passion of Hallaj' by Louis Massignon, Princeton University Press.

COUPLET 8. WHITE-HANDED SEER: Moses. When Moses threw down his staff it became a snake, and when he placed his withered hand into his armpit and pulled it out it was luminous. See Exodus vi 1-6; vii, 10-12 and the *Koran* vii, 104-105. The magician who was ineffective was Samiri (see Index) and Reason that has no power over Love.

124. DAUGHTER OF THE VINE.

COUPLET 1: The daughter of the vine is the wine of love.

125. LISTEN CLOSELY

COUPLET 1. JAMSHID'S CUP: Universal Mind, or the heart, or the true Guide. See previous notes.

129. ONLY A MEMORY

COUPLET 4. FARHAD: See note to *ghazal* 41, couplet 9.
COUPLET 8: See note to *ghazal* 122, couplet 4.

133. BEHIND THIS SCREEN.

COUPLET 10. 'THE HAFEZ': 'Hafez' means 'One who knows the Koran by heart' and also 'preserver' and 'guardian.'

135. THE SIGH AT MIDNIGHT

COUPLET 4. THEY: They, with a capital 'T', See note to *ghazal* 35, couplet 5.

136. A CONVERSATION

COUPLET 8: The conjunction of Jupiter and the moon is said to be auspicious.

LOVE'S PAIN AND REMEDY

COUPLET 1. PARI-FACED: See note to *ghazal* 61, couplet 5.
COUPLET 7. MANSUR: See note to *ghazal* 123, couplet 6.

139. DETERMINED IN LOVE

COUPLET 8. BLUE GOWNS: False Sufis, making a show of their belief like Shaikh Ali Kolah. See Introduction.

140. PERFECT MASTER'S DISCIPLE

COUPLET 3: Solomon, who knew the language of the birds, made the hoopoe the king of the birds and sent a message to Sheba (Saba) to Bilquis the queen. When the mandate reached her she said to her advisors: "Truly I have received a merciful letter from Solomon. It says: 'In the Name of God the Merciful and Compassionate, don't be proud, come while you are submissive.' "The hoopoe had already been to Sheba earlier and on returning had told Solomon that Bilquis wasn't a worshipper of the true God, being at that time a worshipper of the sun. When the hoopoe delivered Solomon's mandate she knew that Solomon must have been a Master for he could direct the birds and the power of his letter was greater than that of the sun, so she submitted to Solomon. The hoopoe after this became known as 'Solomon's messenger.'

144. WHAT EXCUSE?

COUPLET 10. Jamshid: See note to *ghazal* 2, couplet 9.
KAY KHUSRAU: Kay (great king) Khusrau was the third king of the ancient Kayanian dynasty. See 'The Epic of the Kings' by Ferdowsi, trans. by Reuben Levy, Pub. by R.K.P., and other translations of Ferdowsi's epic tale of the heroes and kings of Persia (see Bibliography).

146. PRESERVE

NOTE: 'Hafez' means 'one who knows the *Koran* by heart' and also 'guardian' and 'preserver.
COUPLET 3. CORD: The Promise.

147. THE WISE BIRD

COUPLET 2. PARI AND HURI: Male and female angels... or more correctly, angels in beautiful male and female forms.

148. HIDDEN LONGINGS

COUPLET 6. MOON: 'Moon' with a capital 'M' because Hafez means the Friend, the Beloved, the Perfect Master.

151. FALLEN FOR A CUP

COUPLET 5: Wine destined to be Hafez's since the First Day, before Time began, because he was even then a lover of God.

152. IF IT IS NOT

COUPLET 3. ABU LAHAB: Mohammed's uncle and bitterest opponent.

154. THE RETURN

COUPLET 1. LAPWING: Another name for the hoopoe (bird)

158. THREE CUPS

COUPLET 1. CYPRESS, ROSE, TULIP: Hafez's financial situation when exiled in Isfahan was desperate until he received a letter passed on by friends in Shiraz from the king of Bengal in India, Ghiyasud-din Purbi. The king had become very sick from a disease and thought he was going to die. In his *harem* there were three beautiful women named, Cypress, Rose and Tulip whom he loved more than the others. He asked them to wash his body and they happily did so, and he quickly recovered. Because of this, the king's love for them increased. His other dependants were jealous and derisively called them 'body-washers.' This was revealed to the king and he composed the first line to the first couplet but could not complete the second line. He called in all of India's best poets, but none could complete the poem. Hafez's fame had already reached India, and the king was informed that he would have to send the line to the famous poet. The king sent Hafez the line and his problem, and it finally found him after a year of travelling. Hafez completed the poem in one night and sent it back to the king and received a sizable gift for his effort which was to be of help in the time that he spent in Isfahan.

COUPLET 8. SAMIRI: Samiri came from Samra where he recognized some traces of Gabriel. Picking up the dust of Gabriel's path he placed it in an idol, a calf of gold and silver, which came alive. Because of this, many left Moses and followed him. See Exodus vi, 1-6; vii, 10-12; *Koran* ii, 50; xx, 96. See also note to *ghazal* 123, c.8.

159. PATIENCE AND VICTORY

COUPLET 4. KHWAJA: See note to *ghazal* 20, couplet 1.

160. YOUR BEAUTY

COUPLET 2. FORTUNATE BIRD: The Persian word is 'Huma' which is a lucky, happy Bird, signifying the Beyond State of God: God in the formless aspect. Even if its shadow should fall on you, you will become extremely fortunate. A symbol for God's Grace.
COUPLET 5. IDOL: Hafez often calls the Beloved 'Idol.'

161. YOUR RUBY LIP

COUPLET 4. 'A' OF YOUR FORM: Hafez uses the 'Alif' which in the Arabian/Persian lettering is a straight vertical line.

163. INSIDE THE CUP

COUPLET 1. JAMSHID: He was the king of the Pishadi dynasty whom the Persians believe founded Persepolis which is called 'The Throne of Jamshid.'

165. GLANCE FOR A VICTIM

COUPLET 3. KHIZER: Khizer is often called: "The Green One" for he was said to have drunk from the Fountain of Immortality and gained Eternal life. He has been identified with Elias, St. George, Phineas, the Angel Gabriel, the companion of Mohammed on a journey which is told in the *Koran,* viii, 59-8 1, and throughout the literature of Mysticism has appeared to many great seekers who eventually became Perfect Masters. Many commentators have been confused by his periodic appearances throughout history. They do not understand that one of the Perfect Masters or the Rasool or Avatar of the age (whatever age it is) has the function and ability (can unlock the 'office' of Khizer) to appear to anyone in need at any time or place in the form that he wishes to take. When an aspirant is without a Master or his or her Master has died (as in the case of Francis of Assisi), one of the Perfect Masters appears to the aspirant to guide him or her to a Perfect Master (as Attar did to Hafez) or to help with a problem, or to give God-realization (as in the case of Francis). Many times throughout his poems Hafez calls to Khizer to come and help him as he did earlier in his life or talks of Khizer having appeared to him.

166. THE FOUNDATION OF GENEROSITY

COUPLET 1: Solomon was a Perfect Master, his advisor was Asaf.

167. SOME GOOD NEWS

COUPLET 3. RIZVAN: The angel who keeps the door to the Palace of Paradise. The Huri of Paradise in this context.

172. HIDDEN DEFECTS

COUPLET 2. MASTER OF THE WINESELLERS: The first Perfect Master - the Godman.
COUPLET 8. 'ROSECOLOUR': Probably a nickname for Hafez's Master, Mahmud Attar who was said to have a ruddy complexion.

174. I REMEMBER THAT TIME

COUPLET 7. ABU ISHAK: Abu Ishak was the king of Shiraz and a friend of Hafez who loved poetry and the arts. He reigned from 1343-53. He was a generous man and a profligate and in the end this was his downfall, as Hafez remarks in this couplet. There is a turquoise-mine in Nishapur that bears his name.

175. DUST OF THE PATH

COUPLET 2: This couplet is written on the slab in Hafez's tomb at Shiraz.
COUPLET 3. FIRST MASTER: The first Perfect Master, the Godman.

178. THE REAL PROVIDER

COUPLET 2. CIRCLE: The inner circles of the Man-God (Perfect Master) and of the God-Man (Rasool, Messiah, Avatar) consisting of twelve male disciples and two female disciples.
COUPLET 7. NIGHT OF POWER: See note to 'TONIGHT' couplet 1 (above).

185. A LOVERS DESTINY

COUPLET 7. MAJNUN, LAYLA: See note to 'BE KIND TO MY HEART' couplet 4 (above).

186. THE BOOK OF LOVE

COUPLET 4. THE PRETENDER: Satan, or the false ego.

187. REMEMBER

COUPLET 2. JESUS: Jesus' breath is said by Hafez to give life to the dead.

188. HEARTSIGHS

COUPLET 2. SOLOMON'S SEAL-RING: See note to *ghazal* 20, couplet 8. See also the *Koran xxxvii, 33*.
COUPLET 6. PHOENIX: The Huma Bird. See note to *ghazal* 160 couplet 2.

190. THE TALE OF ABSTINENCE

COUPLET 5. This couplet has become well-known for being one of the last couplets quoted by Meher Baba.

191. UNION WITH BELOVED

NOTE: Notice the similarity of this *ghazal* and nos. 217 and 218. It was probably written at the same time, shortly after Hafez had gained God-realization. See introduction.

199. COME WHAT MAY

COUPLET 4. JAMSHID: Fourth king of Pishadi dynasty, lived 800 B.C.? See note to *ghazal* 163 couplet 1 and *ghazal* 2 couplet 9. BAHMAN: Bahman was another member of the Kayanian house and is well-known to the Persians as Ardisher Dirazdast, the Artaxerxes Longimanus of the Greeks and Romans. Some say he is the same person as Ahusuerus of the Book of Esther. He rose to the throne in 464 B.C. and was the grandson of Darius. The historians of Persia state that he reigned for over a hundred years. KOBAD: Kay Kobad was the founder of the second dynasty the Kayanian. The hero Rustom, son of Zal, placed him on the throne.
COUPLET 5. KAUS: Kay Kaus was the son of Kay Kobad mentioned above. KAY: This probably refers to Kay Khursau, third king of the Kayanian dynasty. See: 'The Epic of the Kings' by Firdowsi translated by R. Levy. R.K.P. for the above, and other trans. (see bibliography).
COUPLET 6. SHIRIN AND FARHAD: See note to *ghazal* 41, couplet 9.
COUPLET 9. MUSALLA AND RUKNABAD: See note to *ghazal* 8 couplet 1.

201. THE LOVER'S CONDITION

COUPLET 5. KHIZER: See 'A GLANCE FOR A VICTIM', couplet 3 (above) for explanation.

202. KEY TO THE TREASURE

COUPLET 3. SUHAIB: Suhaib, native of Mosul, who was educated at Constantinople, came to Mecca, gained his freedom and embraced Islam. He fled with Mohammed to Mecca, in 622 A.D.
COUPLET 6. WADI AYMAN: See note to 'THE FLY AND THE FALCON' couplet 3 (below). JETHRO: Jethro was the father-in-law of Moses and gave Moses knowledge of the book of Adam, and other spiritual knowledge.

203. ONE DAY

COUPLET 4. THE PHEASANT: Beloved, God, Perfect Master.

204. THE HAPPIEST SPRING

COUPLET 7. KAUTHER: The main river in Paradise.
COUPLET 10. AZAR: Azar was the father of Abraham and an idolater who sold idols.
COUPLET 11. SULTAN UVAYS: Sultan Uvays of Baghdad (d.1374 A.D.). See ghazal no 497 and introduction, chapter one.

206. THE FLY AND THE FALCON

COUPLET 3. WADI AYMAN: Where Moses saw the burning bush i.e. God in the form of fire. WADI AYMAN is also spelt Wadi-i-Aiman.

209. THE BEST ADVICE

COUPLET 1. THEY: 'They' with a capital 'T', meaning the Perfect Masters and the appearance of God in human form as the Rasool, Christ, Buddha, Avatar, who control the Fate and Destiny of all in Creation.

217. THE NIGHT OF UNION

NOTE: This ghazal was written during the night that Hafez received God-realization from his Master Attar. For more information see the introduction to this book.
COUPLET 6. ANAL HAQ: Mansur Hallaj (d.919 A.D.), was sentenced to death for saying: "I am the Truth (Anal Haq)." (Hafez makes the same statement, which must have made it difficult for him from then

on, i.e. if he made this poem public). Much has been written about Hallaj and his famous (and infamous) statement. If the reader wishes to follow up his life and writings, a list is given below. To me, the meaning of this couplet in its context is that it was Hallaj's Karma or Fate to make that true statement and suffer the consequences; but it does not mean that others who experience the same, God-realization, have to proclaim it to the whole world, unless they have a particular role to play in this creation by doing so. On Mansur Hallaj's life and sayings see: 'Muslim Saints and Mystics' by Farid ud-Din Attar trans. by A.J. Arberry R.K.P. pp. 264-272; 'The Kashf al-Mahjub: The Oldest Persian Treatise on Sufism' by Hujwiri. trans. by R.A. Nicholson, Luzac, U.K. 'Diwan of al Hallaj' trans. into French by Louis Massignon, Paris 1955 (Documents Spiritual 5.10); 'The Passion of Hallaj' by Louis Massignon, translated into English... pub. by Princeton University Press.

218. REALIZATION

NOTE: For information on this all-important *ghazal* and the previous one, see the introduction to this book, chapters one and two.
COUPLET 3. NIGHT OF POWER: See note to *ghazal* 26, couplet 1. Hafez also means it was the 'Night of Power' for him because he received the Power of a God-realized soul.
COUPLET 4. LAT AND MANAT: The Arabs worshipped as companions of God three goddesses which they call God's daughters. Lat was the idol of the tribe of Ihakif and Manat was the idol of the tribes of Hudhail and Khuzaah.

221. PLAYING AT LOVE

COUPLET 11. Hafez of course knew the *Koran* by heart and also wrote an annotation of as-Zamakashari's famous commentary.

222. THE CLAY OF ADAM

COUPLET 4: Adam was the first Perfect Master or Qutub. COUPLET 5. THAT TRUST'S BURDEN: Love.

227. A FLEETING TREASURE

NOTE: This is said by many to be composed on the death of his wife.

230. LOVE'S MYSTERY COMES

COUPLET 6. JOSEPH, ZULAIKHA: Joseph of Egypt was a Perfect Master who was also extremely handsome. He was the symbol of God's perfect beauty. Zulaikha was the wife of Potiphar. She fell in love with

Joseph and could not contain her great love for him. The story of their love was told by many Persian poets. Jami's version is the most famous.

233. DOES IT MATTER?

COUPLET 3. JAMSHID: A King of Ancient Persia who had a cup in which he could see the whole world (Universal Mind) but... even that will not get you Unity if you do not experience Love

234. THE BURNING HEART

COUPLET 2. PARI-FACED: Face of an angel in the male form.

235. THE WINESELLER CAME

COUPLET 1. ANCIENT WINESELLER: Mohammed or the New Coming Messiah. The Godman (Avatar).

237. THE RING OF SERVICE

COUPLET 5. KING OF THE TURKANS: Afrasiyab, the king of Turan. The Perfect Master or Beloved is likened to him... for he killed his son-in-law Siyawash, whom Hafez represents as himself.

238. THE ONLY REMEDY

COUPLET 3: Hafez taught *Koranic* studies in a college for some of his life.
COUPLET 4. SAMIRI: Samiri came from Samra where he recognized some traces of Gabriel. Picking up the dust of Gabriel's path he placed it in an idol, which came alive. Because of this, many left Moses and followed him. See Exodus vi, 1-6; vii, 10-12; *Koran* ii, 50; xx, 96.

241. THE STAR

COUPLET 1. THE STAR: Mohammed.

242. WHERE IS ONE?

COUPLET 8. FAKHR-UD-DIN ABDU-S-SAMAD: According to the commentators a friend of Hafez not known to them.

246. HAPPINESS AND GOOD FORTUNE

COUPLET 3. SOLOMON: The Perfect Master the ability to travel on the wind and understand the language of the birds. JAMSHID: See note to 'DOES IT MATTER', couplet 3 (above). KAY KHUSRAU: An ancient Persian King i.e. worldly power that doesn't last.

247. COMPLAINT

COUPLET 1. SWEETHEART: The Beloved.

248. SMILE A SWEET SMILE

COUPLET 8. KHWARAZM OR KHUJAND: Both well-known for their beautiful ones.

249. DESTINY'S ORIGINAL ORDER

COUPLET 2. FARHAD AND SHIRIN: See note to *ghazal* 41 couplet 9.

252. AGAIN TO THE GARDEN

COUPLET 1. KHUTAN: A village in Turkey noted for its beautiful ones.

254. MINSTREL OF LOVE

COUPLET 9: The *Fatiha* is the *Koran's* first chapter.

255. THE ROBBER OF THE ROAD

COUPLET 5. SIRIUS: See note to *ghazal* 102 couplet 12.
COUPLET 6: The Director is of course God, the Perfect Master.
COUPLET 8. SAMIRI: See note to *ghazal* 158 couplet 8 and 123 couplet 8.

264. THE OLD WINESELLER

COUPLET 6. JAM AND KAY: Both Jamshid and Kay Khusrau had worldly power because they were kings, but today they are only dust. Hafez again points out the power of love (wine) over power and wealth.

265. THE DRUNKARDS GIFT

COUPLET 1. THEY: The Perfect Masters who control Fate.

268. LOVE LET LOOSE

COUPLET 2. DAUGHTER OF THE VINE: The wine of love.

270. MY EXISTENCE

COUPLET 5: The Zinda river is the river of Isfahan.

277. HAIL!

COUPLET 5. 'DARLING OF EGYPT': Joseph.

278. HIGHEST OF THE HIGH

COUPLET 6: Round cakes of silver and gold: the moon and the sun.

282. THE PARROT

COUPLET 10: CHINESE IDOL. To the Persians the physical beauty of the Chinese was the epitome of the beauty of the human form, as can be attested in Persian miniature painting. Perhaps Hafez is meaning that the beauty of the physical form is difficult not to desire in the Path to God. Perhaps Hafez is referring to the woman he loved 'Branch of Sugarcane'. See Introduction.

284. DO NOT GRIEVE

COUPLET 1: Joseph was of course a Perfect Master.
COUPLET 7: Noah was a God-conscious soul.
NOTE: Down the centuries this has been and still remains one of the most loved and quoted of the *ghazals* of Hafez. People often send it to friends who are depressed.

290. DON'T DENY

COUPLET 4. PARROT: Poet, Hafez.

292. FROM SEPARATION COMES UNION

COUPLET 5. HURIS: The Huris are the angels of Paradise that are in female form and are extremely beautiful.

293. THE NIGHT OF POWER

COUPLET 1. NIGHT OF POWER: See note to *ghazals* 26 couplet 1 and 218 c 3.

294. THE ADVICE TO LOVERS

COUPLET 13. MAJNUN: See note to *ghazal* 22 couplet 6.
COUPLET 15. ZAHIR: Zahir was a poet who lived in the time of Tughral III and died at Tabriz in 1201. A.D. SALMAN: Salman was a contemporary of Hafez who lived in Baghdad and died in 1377 A.D. He was a famous Court poet of the time. KHWAJU: Khwaju Kirmani was a poet who lived until 1345 A.D. and was popular at that time. It is likely that Hafez knew him well. For more information on these three poets see: 'A Literary History of Persia' by Edward G. Browne. Cambridge University Press and my novel/biography 'Hafez of Shiraz' 3 vols. Shiraz Books 2006-8.

NOTE: Possibly Hafez was thirty four years old when he wrote this *ghazal* - for he mentions in couplet 7 that he had been loving his Master Attar, the Beloved, for fourteen years. Hafez was born in 1320 and followed and loved Attar for 40 years, and then Attar gave him God-realization and Hafez became a Perfect Master. He lived for about nine more years and wrote half of his poetry in this time, while God-realized. See first chapter of the introduction for further information.

295. SHAME AT LAST

COUPLET 5: When Hafez was alive the Chinese were considered to be the greatest painters and had a great influence on Persian painting.

301. A NIGHT LIKE THIS

COUPLET 3: Hafez means since gaining his true home, the Presence of the Beloved, and uses the symbol of the *Kaaba* to express this, as he often does.

306. THE CONDITION OF BLEEDING HEARTS

COUPLET 3. PLATO: In this couplet Hafez praises Plato as a master and calls him 'one who is with wine'.

309. THROW ME IN

COUPLET 6: It's necessary to take the veil off love and to experience it (love).

310. ENOUGH TO LIVE BY

COUPLET 1. ARAXES: A river near the Euphrates and the Tigris.
COUPLET 2: SALMA: The name of a lovely Arabian woman and a name for the Beloved.
COUPLET 8: Hafez means that the other lovers or poets are successful and he, the fly, is not.

311. DON'T ASK

COUPLET 6. ALEXANDER AND DARIUS: Jam (Jamshid) was a king of ancient Persia who possessed a magic cup in which he could see the state of the whole world. This is a similar symbol to Alexander's Mirror in which the world was reflected. Both are symbols for Universal Mind - or a Guide or Master who guided their actions. This Master in relation to Alexander was called Khizer: meaning a Perfect Master who has gained immortality and the ability to appear anywhere at any time. Both Jamshid and Alexander ended their lives not gaining the Water of Life (God-realization) because their attachment to power and pride stopped them from taking the advice of their Guide. See: 'The Epic of The Kings' translated by R. Levy, Routledge Keegan and Paul 1967, and the other translations; also: 'Iskandarnama. A Persian Alexander Romance' translated by M.S. Southgate. Columbia University Press 1978. DARA (DARIUS): Darius III d. 330 B.C. Darius was defeated by Alexander who had invaded Persia in 331 B.C. See 'The Epic of The Kings' (Shahnama).

316. TRUE TO PROMISE

COUPLET 3: See note to 'DON'T ASK' couplet 6 (above).
COUPLET 8. RARE ONES: Perfect Masters.

318. BLESSED WITH UNITY

COUPLET 2. KHWAJA: See note to 'DON'T GIVE UP HOPE' couplet 1 (above).

319. TULIP SEASON

COUPLET 3. WISEMAN: The Perfect Master.

322. SHIRAZ

COUPLET 2: See note to *ghazal* 8 couplet 2 for Ruknabad.

COUPLET 3. JAFARABAD: A district to the east of Musalla that has ceased to exist. For Musalla see note to *ghazal* 8 couplet 2.

COUPLET 5. SWEET ONES: The God-intoxicated and the God-realized.

NOTE: It is obvious from this *ghazal* and whenever Hafez mentions Shiraz in others, how much he loved his home and how beautiful it must have been in his time.

323. TAKEN

COUPLET 1: By 'Idol' Hafez means the Beloved.

COUPLET 2: A Pari is an angel in the male form.

324. THE DERVISH

COUPLET 1: Hafez preferred to be called a 'dervish' rather than a 'Sufi', for many of the Sufis (such as Shaikh Ali Kolah) were pretenders and he often called them tricksters and hypocrites. Some, of course were true lovers of God and these he praised.

COUPLET 7. KHIZER: Here Hafez attests to the fact that the Khizer Perfect Master's form does not live forever. It is the role or function that is passed on from one Perfect Master to another who becomes Khizer. Hence the misunderstanding over the years by many writers.

326. A VOICE FROM THE INVISIBLE

COUPLET 1: The king Hafez means in this couplet is probably Shah Shuja (d.1384 A.D.) who was addicted to wine and no one was punished for drinking it during his reign. See introduction. The King mentioned in couplet 8 of this *ghazal* is God: The King of kings.

327. OPENLY DRINKING

COUPLET 1. SHAH SHUJA: See previous note and also the introduction to this book.

328. BITTER WINE

COUPLET 4. BAHRAM: Bahram Gur 420 A.D. was one of Persia's greatest kings and was known for his physical strength and courage. While hunting a wild ass (gur) with his lasso he leaped with his horse into a pool and was never seen again. See: 'The Epic of The Kings' by Ferdowsi. In this couplet Hafez means: let go of the form and take up the cup that gives knowledge to the mind, i.e. don't be an ass (gur). COUPLET 5. SOLOMON AND THE ANT: Hafez means here to be humble, for no matter how great one is, we can always learn, even from the smallest of creatures.

331. COMBINATION OF BEAUTY AND GRACE

NOTE: It is possible that this *ghazal* was written about Hafez's son who was fourteen years old at the time as mentioned in couplet 4. See *ghazal* 117 which is on his son's death. In this poem he seems to have a premonition of this, or it could be that his son was sick at the time. Or it might have been written about the woman Hafez fell in love with when he was 21 years old, 'Branch of Sugarcane,' Shakh-e-Nabat. It is possible that she was fourteen years old when he first saw her and he could have written this *ghazal* shortly afterwards.

334. TRAVELLING COMPANION

COUPLET 4: Salma is an Arabic name for the Beloved.

335. FRESH LIFE

COUPLET 6. KAABA: In this couplet Hafez means the beauty of the Beloved, or True Home: Divine Place. He often uses the *Kaaba* as a symbol for the Beloved and sometimes for the heart.
COUPLET 8. JOSEPH: The Beloved, symbolized by the beauty of the Perfect Master, Joseph of Egypt.
COUPLET 9. CHIEF: The Perfect Master.

337. ROBE OF HONOUR

COUPLET 9. SULTAN OF LOVE: When They made Hafez a Perfect Master like Themselves.

338. THE PRECIOUS PEARL

COUPLET 3. RUSTOM: Rustom was the legendary hero of Ferdowsi's epic 'The Epic of The Kings' (Shahmana) and was renowned for his courage and acts of great strength: the Persian Hercules. WIKAS: Saad ibn Abi Wikas was the champion archer and one of the companions of Mohammed, who much admired his great skill.

339. CENSORSHIP, WINE AND THE BOOK

COUPLET 6: Chapter 1 of the *Koran* is called 'Praise' or 'The Opening' the Arabic words being *Al Hamd* and *Fatiha*. Chapter 112 of the *Koran* is called 'Constancy' or 'The Unity'... the Arabic words being *Ikhlas* and *Tauhid*.

343. *GHAZAL* TO HAFEZ

NOTE: This *ghazal* appears to have been written by Hafez's Master, Attar. Or, Hafez has written it, putting the words into the mouth of the Beloved. Another explanation is that Hafez as God wrote it to Hafez the man. The first explanation seems the most likely, and that Hafez was given it by Attar, who wanted to remain anonymous, so Hafez included it among his own poems, probably being very attached to it.
COUPLET 1: GUARD: Hafez also means guardian.

344. I SWEAR

COUPLET 1.SHAH SHUJA: See note to *ghazal* 326 couplet 1 and introduction to this book.

345. SING THE LOVE SONG

COUPLET 1. SHAH SHUJA: See note to *ghazal* 326 couplet 1 and introduction.

349. THE WATCHMAN

COUPLET 9. ALI: Ali, the son-in-law of Mohammed and the first Imam could be likened in role as Peter was to Jesus. Ali became God-realized and dropped his body in 661 A.D. His body is buried in Najaf Ashraf in Kufa.

358. THE GLORY OF GOD

COUPLET 3. ABRAHAM: See note to *ghazal* 121 couplet 5.
COUPLET 12. ELEPHANT: From loving the beautiful form Hafez became a lover of God.

359. EITHER: OR

COUPLET 4. ABRAHAM: See note to *ghazal* 121 couplet 5.
COUPLET 9: See note to *ghazal* 358 couplet 12.

360. SWEET IS THE CRY

COUPLET 3. SALMA: An Arabic name for the Beloved.
ZU SALAM: A sacred place between Mecca and Medina.

363. THE DOOR OF THE KING

COUPLET 1: Shah Yahya was the sixth of the Muzaffar dynasty (1353-1430).

365. A MAGIC CHARM

COUPLET 4. HALLAJ: See note to *ghazal* 123 couplet 6.

366. CHIEF OF THE AGE

COUPLET 10: JALALU-D-DIN: Hafez may be referring to Rumi the famous Author of the Masnavi and a Perfect Master. Hafez calls him the 'Truth Speaker'.

367. WINEHOUSE'S HIGHWAY

COUPLET 2. FIRST DAY: See note to 'THIS TALE' (above).

368. FAMILY FRIENDS

COUPLET 7. SONS OF OUR UNCLE: Lovers of God.

370. NEW WAY'S DESIGN

COUPLET 7: Kauther is the main river in Paradise.

375. PEACEFUL PLACE

COUPLET 1: Zu-Salaam is a thornless tree in an area between Mecca and Medina.
COUPLET 8: KAY KOBAD. See note to *ghazal* 199 couplet 4. JAMSHID: See note to *ghazal* 2 couplet 9.

376. WHAT CAN I DO?

COUPLET 5. RUSTOM: The hero or 'Hercules' of Persian history.
COUPLET 6. WADI-I-AIMAN: The place where Moses saw the burning bush. Also spelt Wadi Ayman.

380. THE SLAVE OF THE KING

COUPLET 1. THE PRESERVING: Maybe Hafez means by the preserving of the *Koran* by knowing it by heart.
COUPLET 12. SIMURGH: The Simurgh is the Bird that is God in the Beyond State. Everyone is, the Simurgh and the Simurgh is everyone. See

Attar's 'Conference of the Birds,' which is a story about how all the birds set out to find the Simurgh (God) and find that they are the Simurgh.

381. BELOVED'S STREET

NOTE: It is said that Hafez composed this *ghazal* while he was in Yazd, away from Shiraz.

384. THE ROSE SEASON

COUPLET 4: JAM, KAUS, KAY KOBAD: These three were all kings of ancient Persia. See previous notes.

385. EXISTENCE

COUPLET 2. RIZVAN: The gardener, the keeper of the gate of the Palace of Paradise.

388. GET UP!

COUPLET 10: Wadi-i-Aiman was the place where Moses saw the burning bush when he asked God to show Himself in the form of fire.

391. THAT DAY WILL BE HAPPY

COUPLET 4. ALEXANDER: See note to *ghazal* 2 couplet 9. Hafez means in this couplet that he is sick of being in the mind, and wishes to have Union with God through the heart, which he represents as the hand of Solomon, a Perfect Master.

395. DON'T FORGET TO REMEMBER

COUPLET 6. KARUN: See note to *ghazal* 6 couplet 10.

396. THE SOURCE OF A HAPPY HEART

COUPLET 2. ADAM AND EVE: See note to *ghazal* 4 couplet 3.

400. SUCH A CHIEF

COUPLET 9. ASAF: See note to *ghazal* 20 couplet 8.

403. IF

COUPLET 8. FALCON: God, the Perfect Master.

404. BEGGING

COUPLET 3. FARHAD, SHIRIN: See note to *ghazal* 41 couplet 9.
COUPLET 8. ASAF: The Perfect Master in the context of this couplet. Asaf was the son of Barkhuja and chief Minister of Solomon. He knew the great Name of God, understood the language of the birds and could travel on the wind. *See Koran*, xxvii, 386. It is most likely that he was Solomon's Master as he is reported to have taught Solomon these things. He is also famous for having lost Solomon's seal-ring.

406. IT'S NOT RIGHT

COUPLET 8: Ayaz was the slave and Beloved of King Mahmud. In this couplet Hafez calls his Beloved Ayaz.

407. WITH THE KORAN'S BLESSING

COUPLET 2. BIRD OF SOLOMON: The hoopoe or lapwing. See note to *ghazal* 140 couplet 3.
COUPLET 9. DIVAN: Divan has a number of meanings.: a collection of poems arranged alphabetically in a book, a council of wise people or an oracle, a couch on which lovers sit. In this couplet Hafez uses the first two meanings.

410. SOMETIMES

COUPLET 5. Aurang, Gulchihra, Mihr and Wefa were all famous lovers in Persian Literature and history.

412. A BANQUET

COUPLET 8. HAJI KIVAM: Haji Kivam was an advanced soul and possibly a Perfect Master (*Qutub*) and an advisor to Abu Ishak and was a patron and friend of Hafez. It is said that one day when Hafez visited him he saw in a winecup the image he expresses in this couplet. Haji Kivam died in 1353 A.D. See introduction.

416. THE SLAVE OF LOVE

COUPLET 4: The Tuba tree is a tree of Paradise. It is the lotus tree.

420. MY HOPE IS THIS

COUPLET 8. ADAM: The first Perfect Master, or God-realized soul i.e. the first Hero or Beloved of lovers, who consciously united as the first Divine lover, with the first perfected woman Eve, to begin the history of

the Godman on this earth. Their 'sin' or mistake was only seen as such by others who could not comprehend their Consciousness. Their 'mistake' was that when they were accused by others of committing only a gross or lustful act, they refused to answer, to deny it: thus paving the way for the concept of 'original sin.' Hafez uses the symbol of a grain of wheat or barley, instead of an apple. The grain is likened to the mole on the cheek.
COUPLET 9. The Minstrel is of course the Perfect Master.

427. MESSENGER OF GRACE

COUPLET 5. The Sidrah tree is a tree of Paradise.

429. A CONTRACT

COUPLET 7. The Ancient Winemaker is God in human form; as were Adam, Zoroaster, Rama, Krishna, Jesus etc.

435. AFTER LONG ABSTINENCE

COUPLET 2. CHIGIL: Chigil is a place in Turkey famous for its beautiful women.
COUPLET 9: Solomon had a seal-ring on which was engraved the Great Name of God. The ring was stolen by a devil or a demon.
COUPLET 10: Amin-ud-Din Hasan was the secretary and keeper of the seals to Sultan Uvays of Baghdad.

439. RESURRECTION

NOTE: This *ghazal* is inscribed on the slab of Hafez's tomb at Shiraz.

442. THIS LUNATIC SPHERE

NOTE: It is said that Hafez composed this *ghazal* when Timur invaded Persia in 1387. It is also possible that Hafez was looking into the future to this present time when he wrote it.

443. A CONSULTATION

COUPLET 3: See note to *ghazal* 435 couplet 9.
COUPLET 5. AFRASIYAB: The king of Turan, enemy of Persia and the slayer of Siyawash his son-in-law. See: 'The Epic of The Kings' by Ferdowsi.
COUPLET 10. ATABAK: A name for the Beloved.

444. THE OLD MAN'S ADVICE

NOTE: It is possible that this *ghazal* was written by Hafez as advice to his son.

445. ON TOP OF THE FIRE

COUPLET 9. MAHMUD AND AYAZ: See note to *ghazal* 87 couplet 6.

454. THE RAISING OF THE ROSE

COUPLET 12. KALANDAR: Farid ud-Din Attar says that one day an Arab was passing by a monastery of dervishes in Persia and they asked him in. On learning their doctrines he gave up the world and became a dervish. His family asked him why he had changed. He said: "Darvishu Kala:- 'Anda a' (the dervish said: 'Come in'. I did and I don't know what has happened to my possessions." Because of this, afterwards the Arabs called the Persian Sufis - 'Kalandar' - a play on the above words. See note to *ghazal* 58 c.8.

463. EXPECTATION

COUPLET 2. RAKHSH: Rakhsh is the famous horse of Persian Hero Rustom, known for its strength and bravery.

464. THE DESTROYER

COUPLET 1. SAMIRI: Samiri came from Samra where he recognized some traces of Gabriel. Picking up the dust of Gabriel's path he placed it in an idol, a calf of gold and silver, which came alive. Because of this, many left Moses and followed him. See Exodus vi, 1-6; vII, 10-12; *Koran* ii, 50; xx, 96.
COUPLET 7. DARI: The ancient Persian language spoken at court (420 A.D.). The word comes from 'dar' door. Hafez means... keep open the doorway of the old language, or the secret spiritual meanings.

467. A CITY SUCH AS THIS

COUPLET 1. BADAKHSHAN: The ruby of Badakhshan is lilac in colour and is known as the Balais ruby. RUKNI: The stream called Ruknabad in Shiraz. See note to *ghazal* 8 couplet 2. STRAIT: The mountain pass with the Persian name of 'Teng' from which the Ruknabad flows.

COUPLET 6. Siyamak was the son of Kayumars and father of Hoshang, the second king of the Peshdadian dynasty. Zhu was a descendant of the ancient kings of Persia whom Zal, the father of Rustom, raised to the throne. Zhu's son, Karshasp, was the last of the first dynasty, the Peshdadian, who ruled Persia for 2,400 years. See: 'The Epic of The Kings' (Shah-nama) by Ferdowsi.

496. DON'T COMPLAIN

COUPLET 1. KARUN: The Korah of the Bible and the uncle of Moses. It is said that he was the richest man in Israel, having so much wealth that the keys to his treasure houses were heavy burdens for several men. Karun tried to have Moses stoned for a false charge of adultery. Moses commanded the earth to swallow him up. Karun and his palaces and wealth fell into a great pit and are said to be still sinking. God then said to Moses: "You had no mercy on Karun, although he asked for pardon three times. If he had asked Me once, I'd have spared him." See the *Koran*, xxviii, 76.
COUPLET 3. MAJNUN: See note to 'BE KIND TO MY HEART' couplet 4 (above).
COUPLET 7. FIRIDUN: Like Jamshid, a king of Ancient Persia.

497. THE GREAT SULTAN

COUPLET 1. Ahmad Ilkhani was the grandson of Hasan Buzurg who was the ruler of Baghdad and died in 1356. Ahmad Ilkhani died in 1410 A.D. Hafez seemed to have a special affection for him.
COUPLET 4. Ahmad is another name for Mohammed.

499. THE RANSOM

COUPLET 1: Su-Add is a name for the Beloved taken from the opening line of a poem by Kab ibn Zuheir.
COUPLET 5: Arak is the name of the dwelling of the Beloved in pre-Islamic Arabic poetry.
COUPLET 6: Hima is a white salt barren place that occur in valleys in Arabia.
COUPLET 11. Nizami is the famous Persian Poet of the 12th Century. Author of 'The Book of Alexander' and 'Layla and Majnun' among other masterpieces. (See bibliography).

500. COME OUT

COUPLET 8. JOSEPH: The Beloved, the Perfect Master.

502. YOUR OWN FAULT

COUPLET 5. SIMURGH: The Simurgh is the Bird that is God in the Beyond State. Everyone is, the Simurgh... and the Simurgh is... everyone. See Attar's 'Conference of the Birds,' which is a story about how all the birds set out to find the Simurgh (God) and find that they together are the Simurgh (God)... so simple!

505. CROWN OF THE SUN

COUPLET 3. AFRASIYAB: See note to *ghazal* 443, couplet 5.
COUPLETS 3 and 10. KAY KHUSRAU: See note to *ghazal* 144, couplet 10.
COUPLET 11. SHAH YAHYA: See notes to *ghazal* 363 couplet 1 and 484 couplet 1 and introduction.
COUPLET 12. DARIUS: See note to *ghazal* 6 couplet 5.
COUPLET 13. JAMSHID: See note to *ghazal* 2 couplet 9.

514. GENEROSITY

COUPLET 9. HATIM TAI: Hatim Tai was an Arabian who was the chief of the tribe of Tai and was famous for his great generosity, his wisdom and his bravery. His tomb is in Arabia at Anwarz.

517. DRUNK WITH HAPPINESS

COUPLET 1: Pahlavi is one of the seven ancient languages of Persia.

522. DROWNING

COUPLET 13. CHIGIL: Chigil is a place in Turkey famous for its beautiful women. JALALU-D-DIN: The famous Perfect Master and author of 'The Mathnavi.' He was born in 1207 and dropped the form in 1273 A.D.

525. PERISH THE THOUGHT

COUPLET 10: It is said that Shah Shuja who was on good terms with Hafez but jealous of his poetry because the Shah was also a poet, accused Hafez of denying the Resurrection, an accusation which he based on this couplet. Hafez heard of this and put the words in the mouth of a Christian, (see couplet 9) and in this way saved himself.

533. SECLUDED

COUPLET 5. SECLUDED ONE: God.

534. GHAZALS OF IRAK

COUPLET 1. SULAIMA: Sulaima means 'little Salma.' Salma is an Arabic name for the Beloved.

535. THE MARKET'S PROFIT

COUPLET 3. BECOME A MAJNUN: Become a madman from love for the Beloved.

537. PRAYER OF THE EXILE

COUPLET 2. ARAK: See note to *ghazal* 499 couplet 5.

540. DELUGE

COUPLET 5. RUSTOM: See note to *ghazal* 338 couplet 3.

541. TWO-GALLON CUP

COUPLET 13: Rum is the past of Turkey that was included in the old Roman Empire. Rai is a ruined city near Teheran.

544. FOR SAKE OF LOVE'S EXISTENCE

COUPLET 10. DARI: One of the languages of Ancient Persia. In Persian the word 'Dari' comes from 'dar' meaning 'door'. ASAF: The Perfect Master.
COUPLET 16. LAYLA: See note to *ghazal* 22 couplet 6. Hafez uses the name of Layla to represent the Beloved, for she was the Beloved of Majnun who became God-intoxicated from his love for her. Hafez represents himself as the lover Majnun, as he often does.

549. DETACHMENT

COUPLET 6. SANAI: Hakim Sanai (b.1069, d.1131) was the famous Persian poet and Master who wrote: 'The Enclosed Garden of The Truth'. A translation by Major T. Stephenson. Weiser, N.Y.

522. CAPTURED

COUPLET 2. CIRCLE: Every circle of lovers.

555. THE DRUNKARD'S CRY

COUPLET 5: Hafez means purity and honesty is better than worldly generosity.

556. IT'S CERTAIN

COUPLET 5: A Brahmin is of course one of those who belong to the highest cast in India.

558. SPREAD YOUR WINGS

COUPLET 2: Tur was the mountain where Moses went searching for God in the form of fire.

559. THE STORY OF MY LONGING

COUPLET 2: Salma is an Arabic name for the Beloved.
COUPLET 3. THE KILLER: The Beloved.

561. HEART, FAITH AND YOUTH

COUPLET 1. Joseph of Egypt was a Perfect Master and extremely handsome. The ideal of Perfect Beauty.
COUPLET 2. SHIRIN: Shirin was said to be the beautiful daughter of the Byzantine Emperor, Maurice. She married Parviz (A.D.591) and became the queen of Persia. It was Parviz who invaded Jerusalem and carried away the true cross. A sculptor by the name of Farhad fell in love with her and she with him. Farhad made an agreement with Parviz that if he could cut a pass through a mountain for a water-channel, he would be given Shirin. After many years he achieved this remarkable feat (it still exists today) but on hearing that he had succeeded Parviz sent a messenger to tell him that Shirin had committed suicide. On hearing this lie, Farhad threw himself off the mountain and died. King Parviz was violently put to death by his son who then proposed to Shirin. Shirin promised to marry him if she could once again see her husband's body. When she was taken to the corpse she pulled out a dagger and killed herself, falling across the body of Parviz. This tragic love story is very popular in Persian legend and poetry.

562. THE SECRET

COUPLET 5. JAMSHID: Jam (Jamshid, sometimes seen as Noah) was a king of ancient Persia who possessed a magic cup in which he could see the state of the whole world. This is a similar symbol to Alexander's Mirror in which the world was reflected. Both are symbols for Universal Mind... or a Guide or Master who guided their actions. This Master in relation to Alexander was called Khizer... meaning a Perfect Master who has gained immortality and the ability to appear anywhere at any time. Both Jamshid and Alexander ended their lives not gaining the Water of

Life (God-realization) because their attachment to power and pride stopped them from taking the advice of their Guide

570. YOU SHOULD BE

COUPLET 10: One of the meanings of 'Hafez' is guardian.

571. JUICE OF THE GRAPE

COUPLET 6. NAJD: Najd is the area of Arabia where Layla lived: the home of the Beloved.
COUPLET 9. ZAT-I-RAML: A name in ancient Arabic poetry for where the Beloved lives.

572. THE ONLY GUIDE

COUPLET 1: Salma is an Arabic name poets use for the Beloved.

573. . DETACHMENT'S MIRROR

COUPLET 2: See the *Koran,* xix. 72.

574. SULTAN OF THE FAITH

NOTE: This *ghazal* is inscribed on Hafez's tomb at Shiraz.
COUPLET 4. ALI: The first Imam. See note to *ghazal* 349 couplet 9.
COUPLET 6: RIZA: Ali Musi Riza (b.765 A.D. - d.817 A.D.) was the eighth Imam. He was poisoned. He was buried in Mashad in Iran. For information on the different Imams see: 'Shi'ite Islam' by al-Tabataba'i, pub. by George Allen and Unwin 1975.

575. SELECT FRIENDS ONLY

NOTE: 'Our' and 'We' are spelt with capital 'O' and 'W' because Hafez is talking about God, Fate, the Perfect Masters, God in Human Form, who controls all happenings.
COUPLET 3. NOAH: See note to *ghazal* 7 couplet 6.
MOSES: Hafez here refers to the rod which was given to Moses which gave him the power to perform miracles (dividing of the sea etc.) but with also caused him to be caught up in the power he possessed.
COUPLET 4. SOLOMON: See note to *ghazal* 20 couplet 8. JACOB: The father of Joseph.
COUPLET 5. ABRAHAM: See note to *ghazal* 121 couplet 5
COUPLET 6. ZAKARIA: Zachariah of the Bible. JOHN: John the Baptist.

COUPLET 7: Mohammed lost his teeth in battle. JOB: Job of the Bible famous for his patience.
COUPLET 8. HASAN: Son of Ali, brother of Husain and the second Imam. He was poisoned. HUSAIN: See note to *ghazal* 15 couplet 2.
COUPLET 11. SHUDAD: See note to *ghazal* 55 couplet 4.

576. THE WILD DEER

COUPLET 6. KHIZER: See note to *ghazal* 165 couplet 3.
COUPLET 10. SIMURGH: See note to *ghazal* 380 couplet 12.
NOTE: Some scholars say that this poem was written on the death of Hafez's wife or a close friend.

577. BOOK OF THE WINEBRINGER

COUPLET 3. NOAH: The first appearance of the Godman after Adam who settled near Shiraz after coming down from Ararat.
COUPLET 5. ZOROASTER: God in human form after Noah.
COUPLET 7. JAMSHID: See note to *ghazal* 2 couplet 9.
COUPLET 11: Salsabil is a river of Paradise.
COUPLET 12. KAY: A king of Ancient Persia.
COUPLET 17. HURIS: Angels of Paradise in beautiful female form.
COUPLET 18. KAUS: Another king of Ancient Persia.
COUPLET 19. KAY KHUSRAU AND JAMSHID: Both kings of Ancient Persia.
COUPLET 32. KAY KOBAD: See previous notes. A king of Ancient Persia.
COUPLET 35. KAY AND KISRA: Both kings of Ancient Persia.
COUPLET 55. Rakhsh was the famous brave horse that belonged to Rustom. See: 'The Epic of The Kings' (Shahnama) by Ferdowsi.
COUPLET 56. RUSTOM: See note to *ghazal* 338 couplet 3.
COUPLET 72. MANUCHIHR: Manuchihr was a king of the Pishdadian dynasty. He succeeded Firidun and the prosperity of his reign was due to his chief minister Sam who was the son of Nariman, whose descendents Zal and Rustom were heroes in Iranian literature and history.
BUZURJMIHR: Buzurjmihr (d.580-590 A.D.), was the chief minister to Naushiravan the just, who imported chess and the fables of Bilpai from India.
COUPLET 73. NAUSHIRAVAN: Naushiravan the just was the son of Kubad and ascended to the throne in 531 A.D. and died in 579 A.D. Mohammed was born in 571 A.D. and said that he was born in the reign of a king who was just.

578. THE BOOK OF THE MINSTREL

COUPLET 1. MINSTREL: The Beloved.

COUPLET 23. The Iraki note is a melancholy note.

COUPLET 35. PARVIZ: A king of the Sassanian dynasty, ascended to the throne of Persia in 591 A.D. and died in 628 A.D. See note to *ghazal* 41 couplet 9. BARBUD: He was a minstrel to Parviz and this famous musician invented 'the barbud' a stringed instrument.

COUPLET 41. AFRASIYAB: Afrasiyab was the king of Turan and the enemy of Iran.

COUPLET 42: Salm and Tur were the sons of Firidun of the Pishdadian dynasty.

COUPLET 43. SHAIDA: Shaida was the fourth son of Afrasiyab (see previous note). PIRAN: Piran was a great general of Ancient Iran.

579. SOVEREIGN

COUPLET 1. IRAM: See note to *ghazal* 55.

COUPLET 6. DARA: See note to *ghazal* 6 couplet 5. SHUJA: This *ghazal* is said to be in praise of Shah Shuja. SHAH SHUJA: See note to *ghazal* 113 couplet 7.

COUPLET 11. ARDVAN: Ardvan was also called Artabanus (d.465-464 B.C.) was the minister of the Archamenian king Xerxes I of Persia and murdered him in 465 B.C. to become king for seven months. He was killed by Artaxeres.

COUPLET 22. SHAIGAN'S TREASURE: This was the name of a legendary treasure that is said to have belonged to Khusrau Parviz and was found in a place called Shaigan.

COUPLET 27: The Kayan kings were the monarchs of the second or Kayanian dynasty of Persia.

COUPLET 30. YELLOW PALACE: A palace built by Shah Shuja in his gardens at Shiraz. KAISER: The Emperor of Constantinople. KHAN: The Khan (king) of Tartary.

580. CHIEF OVER ALL THE WORLD

COUPLET 9. Haji Kivam a friend of Hafez and advisor of Abu Ishak was probably one of the Perfect Masters of the time.

581. THE FALCON WITH THE GOLDEN WING

NOTE: This *ghazal* is in praise of Abu Ishak. See note to *ghazal* 174 couplet 7.

COUPLET 19. POLESTARS: Two stars of Ursa Minor near the pole.

COUPLET 20. MAHMUD: See note to *ghazal* 87 couplet 6.

COUPLET 40. ALI: Ali, the first Imam (see note to *ghazal* 349 couplet 9) was famous for his great feats in battle with his double-pronged sword.

585. ONLY A BRIDGE

COUPLET 8. BAHRAM GUR: See note to *ghazal* 328 couplet 4.
COUPLET 11. 'FATIHA': The opening chapter of the *Koran* which is said to contain the whole of the *Koran* in concentrated form.

587. FROM ALI

ALI: See note to *ghazal* 349 couplet 9. Ali was the son-in-law of Mohammed and the first Imam. KHEIBER: Kheiber was a stronghold of the Jews near Medina. In 630 A.D. Mohammed took Kheiber and Ali pulled out the gates. KEMBER: Kember was Ali's slave who was freed. KAUTHER: Kauther is a river and spring in Paradise.

643. HAJJI AHMED

NOTE: Hajji Ahmed is said to have been a famous minstrel at the time who was a friend of Hafez.

748. MUZAFFAR THE DICTATOR

NOTE: This poem is about Mubariz al Din Mohammad ibn Muzaffar (d.1364 A.D.) who was the founder of the Muzaffar dynasty of Fars. He took Shiraz from Abu Ishak in 1353 and in 1359 his son Shah Shuja (d.1384 A.D.) dethroned and blinded him as Hafez states in couplet 10. SHUJA: See note to *ghazal* 113 couplet 7.
ABU ISHAK: See note to *ghazal* 174 couplet 7.

750. NEWS

COUPLET 3. ZAM-ZAM: The holy well at Mecca. KAUTHER: The main river and a spring in Paradise.

751. RELY ON GOD

COUPLET 3. YAZD: See note to *ghazal* 2 couplet 10. HURMUZ: A channel linking the Persian Gulf with the Gulf of Oman and the Arabian Sea. It contains an island called Hurmuz. Possibly a whole area was called Hurmuz during Hafez's time.

752. UPON THE THRONE

COUPLET 3. MANSUR MUZAFFAR: Shah Mansur (d.1393 A.D.) was the ruler of Irak and Persia. See introduction.

753. FIVE WONDERFUL PEOPLE

COUPLET 1. ABU ISHAK: See note to *ghazal* 174 couplet 7 and introduction.

COUPLET 3. SHAIKH MAJD UD-DIN: Shaikh Majd ud-Din Ismail was the judge of Shiraz at the time of Abu Ishak. Hafez wrote an obituary for him. See 778 and introduction.

COUPLET 4. SHAIKH AMINU-DIN: He was one of 'The Substitutes', who are seventy men who exist in all ages and who have reached Perfection but remain unknown at the time. He died in 1344. See introduction.

COUPLET 5. 'AZD: Azd ud-Din who died in 1355 was a judge and a professor. He wrote a book on religious law called 'Stations in the Science of Speech'. It became a famous work. Hafez probably attended his classes. He also wrote other books on philosophy and theology. See introduction.

COUPLET 6. HAJI KIVAM: See note to *ghazal* 3 couplet 9 and introduction. A great soul, friend and helper of Hafez who wrote a poem on his death (see no. 779). See introduction, chapter one.

759. LET US FLY TO GOD

COUPLET 5. HAJI KIVAM: See note to *ghazal* 3 couplet 9 and introduction.

760. A MESSENGER HAS COME

COUPLET 1. Rizvan is the gardener of Paradise and keeper of the gate to the Palace of Paradise. Salsabil is a river of Paradise.

766. A DREAM

COUPLET 5: Hafez believed that a thief had taken his mule and placed it as a gift in Masud Shah's stable. Possibly there is also a symbolical meaning to this humourous verse. Perhaps the Shah (the father of Jahan Malek Khatun) had plagiarized one of his poems.

769. HIDING OUT

NOTE: It is said that Hafez wrote this poem as a letter to a friend after he had been away from Shiraz for two years to escape his creditors. When he returned he stayed with Haji Kivam whose high position protected him. Some commentators say he went to Yazd, which he mentions in other poems.

COUPLET 8. SINCE B AND E WERE UNITED: When B and E are united you get BE! In Persian it is 'Kun'! This is the original creative Word spoken by God to manifest the creation. Since the beginning of Time is what Hafez means.

772. FRIDAY THE SIXTH

COUPLET 1. RABIU: The third month of the Muslim year.
NOTE: Commentators say that this obituary was written on the death of Hafez's son.

770. A SWEET BUY

COUPLET 1. 'Fawnheel' was a sweetmeat that was popular in Shiraz in Hafez's time.

773. FRUIT OF PARADISE

COUPLET 2. 'FRUIT OF PARADISE': In Persian the Arabic letters that make up this title have a numerical value of 778 which is the year after the 'Flight' of the Prophet in the Muslim Calendar and in our calendar 1376 - 7 A.D. It is said that it was written on the death of his wife. In all other poems on the death of friends and himself, Hafez uses this system or chronogram. I have given the dates in the Christian calendar. The Hijra dates from the 15th July 622 A.D.

775. MERCIFUL DIES NOT

NOTE: This poem was written on the death of Shah Shuja.

776. INCLINATION FOR PARADISE

COUPLET 1. TURANSHAH: Shah Shuja's prime-minister and patron of Hafez.
COUPLET 2. RAJAB: The seventh month of the Muslim year.

778. DEATH OF ISMAIL

COUPLET 1. ISMAIL: See note to 753 couplet 3 and introduction.
COUPLET 2. RAJAB: Seventh month of Muslim year.

779. DEATH OF GIVAM-UD-DIN

COUPLET 1. GIVAM-UD-DIN: Shah Shuja's prime minister and friend of Hafez. See notes to *ghazal* 3 couplet and 753 couplet 6.
COUPLET 2. ZU-L-KA'DAT: The eleventh month of the Muslim year.

780. ON YOUR DUST I WEEP

NOTE: It is said that this was written by about his son who had died.

781. A HYPOCRITE

NOTE: Possibly this poem refers to the following tale: An old man offered a camel at a low price, but no one was allowed to buy it without buying a cat with it. The price of the cat was greater than the camel.
COUPLET 3: Dara and Firidun were both kings of ancient Persia.

782. THE GREEN GRAIN

COUPLET 1. THE GREEN GRAIN: This may signify hashish, which Hafez condemns in this poem. SIMURGH: See note to *ghazal* 380 couplet 12.

784. SIXTH OF THE MONTH

COUPLET 1. HAJI KIVAM UD-DIN: See note to *ghazal* 3 couplet 9 and 753 couplet 6 and 777 couplet 1.
COUPLET 2. 'THE BEST OF MEN': Mohammed.
COUPLET 3. RABI'A: The fourth month of the Muslim Year.

786. SALMAN

COUPLET 5. SALMAN: See note to *ghazal* 294 couplet 13.

787. IT'S NECESSARY

COUPLET 4. FARKADS: Farkad major and minor are two stars in Ursa Minor.

790. DUST OF MUSALLA

NOTE: In this poem Hafez predicted his own death in 1389 A.D. It is inscribed on the slab of Hafez's tomb at Shiraz. Some commentators say that it was written by another poet and he died in 1390 or 1392.

791. THE LUTE AND THE CUP

COUPLET 3. The Puranas are the Hindu scriptures in the form of a dialogue in verse that were written after the Vedas. Their primary subject matter dealt with Vishnu and his incarnations. The Vedas are one of the collections of Indian sacred writings from the second millennium B.C., that form the scriptures of the Hindu faith. The Zend Avesta originally contained all the teachings of the Zoroaster who lived before 5000 B.C. but through a continuing mistake by many scholars is placed at 500 B.C. Aristotle for one, places Zoroaster 6000 years before Plato and Hermippus, 5000 before the Trojan war. From the original Avestan language evolved Sanskrit and also Pahlavi. It was the originator of all the Aryan languages. The Avesta (Zend Avesta) contains not only the cosmology, law and liturgy of Zoroastrianism but also the Gathas, a collection of songs or hymns which are the words of Zoroaster. The original Avesta was destroyed when Alexander conquered Persia and the Avesta as we know it today was recovered under the Sasasian kings (3rd-7th Century A.D.). It is this 'interpretation' of the ancient Avesta that has come down to us.

793. THAT ONE AGAIN

*Hatim Tai was an Arabian who was the chief of the tribe of Tai and was famous for his great generosity, his wisdom and his bravery.

TITLES

Alphabetical Index as a *Divan* by Title

SELECTED BIBLIOGRAPHY

Books consulted while working on this revised edition.
(See First Edition *Divan of Hafiz* 2 vols. Translation & Introduction by
Paul Smith. Published by New Humanity Books 1986 for a complete list of
the many versions of Hafiz etc. over the past 200 years in English.)

DIVAN OF HAFIZ. Translation & Introduction by Paul Smith. 2 vols.
New Humanity Books. 1986.

THE DIVAN - I - HAFIZ. Translated by H. Wilberforce Clarke. 2 vols.
1891. Reprinted by S. Weiser 1970.

THE POEMS OF SHEMSEDDIN MOHAMMED HAFIZ OF
SHIRAZ. Translated by John Payne. 3 vols. Villon Society.

DIWAN-I-HAFIZ. Translation and Commentary by M.G. Gupta
M.G.P. Publishers. Agra. 1997.

THE DIVAN OF HAFIZ. A Bilingual Text: Persian and English.
Translated from the Persian by Reza Saberi. University Press of America
2002.

THE COLLECTED LYRICS OF HAFIZ OF SHIRAZ Translated
by Peter Avery, Archetype Pub. U.K. 2007

HAFIZ OF SHIRAZ. by Paul Smith. Three Volumes. A 2000 page
Novel/Biography on the Life and Times of Hafiz. New Humanity Books
2000-12.

HAFIZ: THE ORACLE. (For Lovers, Seekers, Pilgrims and The God-
intoxicated) Translation & Introduction and Interpretations by Paul
Smith. New Humanity Books2006, 2011.

HAFIZ: THE BOY WHO BECAME THE WORLD'S GREATEST
POET. Paul Smith. New Humanity Books 2010.

MAST-HAFIZ (GOD-DRUNK HAFIZ). Rokneddin Homayoun
Farrokh. 8 vols. Saatar Publications 1975. (A huge mine of information on
Hafiz and his times.)

HAFIZ: AN INTRODUCTION. Robert McConkie Rehder.
Princeton University Degree Dissertation. 1970.

SHIRAZ IN THE AGE OF HAFEZ. The Glory of a Medieval City.
John Limbert. University of Washington Press. 2004.

SHIRAZ. Persian City of Saints and Poets. Arthur J. Arberry. University
of Oaklahoma Press. 1960.

OBEYD ZAKANI: THE DERVISH FOOL. A Selection of His
Poetry, Prose, Satire, Jokes & Ribaldry. Translation & Introduction &
Introduction by Paul Smith. New Humanity Books 2004, 2010.

HAFIZ'S FRIEND, JAHAN KHATUN: PERSIA'S PRINCESS
DERVISH POET. A Selection of Poems from Her *Divan*. Translated by
Paul Smith and Rezvaneh Pashai. New Humanity Books, 2005, 2010.

ONE HUNDRED GHAZALS AND ONE SAKI-NAMA OF KHAJU KERMANI. Khaju Kermani. Edited by Dr. Mahmud Tavosi. Navid Shiraz Publications. 1990.

EMAD KERMANI'S DIVAN. Khaju Emad ad-din Ali Faqhi Kermani. Editor Rokneddin Homayoun Farrokh. Ebne Sina. 1969.

A LITERARY HISTORY OF PERSIA. By Edward G. Browne. 4 vols. Cambridge University Press. 1920.

HISTORY OF IRANIAN LITERATURE. Jan Rypka and others. D. Reidel Publishing Company. 1968.

THE SHAHNAMA OF FIRDAUSI. 8 vols. Translated by Arthur George Warner and Edmond Warner. Kegan Paul, Trench, Trubner & Co. Ltd. 1923. (Available in Adobe Acrobat format from saladin20@yahoo.com)

THE TRAVELS OF IBN BATTUTA. (RIHLA) 3 vols. Translated by H.A.R. Gibb. Cambridge University Press. 1958.

A PERSIAN-ENGLISH DICTONARY (Comprehensive) by F. Steinglass. Oriental Books Reprint Corporation. 1973.

THE COMPLETE BOOK OF MUSLIM & PARSI NAMES. Maneka Gandhi & Ozair Husain. Indus. 1994.

THE CONFERENCE OF THE BIRDS. Farid ud-din Attar. Translated with Introduction by Afkham Daranbi, Dick Davis. Penguin Books. 1984.

THE ILAHI-NAMA or Book of God of Farid al-Din 'Attar. Translated from the Persian by John Andrew Boyle. Manchester University Press. 1976.

GOD SPEAKS. The Theme of Creation and Its Purpose, by Meher Baba. Dodd, Mead & Company. 1955.

THE QURAN. 2 vols. Translated by E.H. Palmer. Sacred Books of the East Series. Clarendon Press. 1880.

A DICTIONARY OF ISLAM by Thomas Patrick Hughes. W.H. Allen & Co. 1885.

THE KASHF AL-MAHJUB. The Oldest Persian Treatise on Sufism, by Al-Hujwiri. Translated by R. A. Nicholson. Luzac. 1911.

PERSIAN DRAWINGS From the 14th Through the 19th Century. Text by B.W. Robinson. Little Brown and Company. 1965.

EPIC IMAGES AND CONTEMPORY HISTORY. The Illustrations of the Great Mongol *Shahnama* by Oleg Grabar and Sheila Blair. The University of Chicago Press. 1980.

LAYLA & MAJNUN by Nizami. Translation & Introduction and Introduction by Paul Smith. New Humanity Books 2010.

THE TREASURY OF THE MYSTERIES by Nizami. Translation & Introduction and Introduction by Paul Smith. New Humanity Books 2005, 2010.

DIVAN OF SADI. His Mystical Love Poetry. Translated by Paul Smith New Humanity Books 2009.

DIVAN OF HAFEZ

1. LOVE AT FIRST

Hey, here Winebringer, circulate, offer the cup this way...
for love at first seemed easy, now problems come to stay.
Finally breeze sent musk-pod's scent from that forehead:
its twist of musky hair makes blood clot our hearts today.
Can wayfarers stay happy and secure in Beloved's house,
when suddenly the bell clangs to: "Lift your load! Away!"
With wine dye your prayer-mat if the Master commands;
this experienced traveller has understanding of the way.
The dark night and terrifying wave and fierce whirlpool...
do those light of burden on the shore know where we stay?
By acting upon my own desires I've ruined my reputation:
can the secret stay that way, when crowds tell it all day?
Hafez, if you desire the Divine Presence, do not be absent:
when you visit your Beloved... "Farewell" to the world say.

2. DAILY BREAD

Beauty of moon's glow comes from the bright face
of Yours;
its shining glory is coming from that dimple-place
of Yours!
From my longing to see You my soul is on the brink of my lip...
tell me, should it go out or stay back... which way's
of Yours?
The turning of Your glance did not give enjoyment to anyone...
it's best to be selling virtue's veil to that drunken race
of Yours.
Our chances are that our luck that is asleep will soon wake up,
for water falls on sleepy eye from the glistening face
of Yours.
Send by way of a breeze, a handful of roses from Your cheek...
so I may smell sweet dust of that garden's fragrance
of Yours.

Winebringers of the feast of Jam, Your long life is our desire;
although our cup has not been filled… by that grace
of Yours.
Tell to the Heartowner that my heart is completely shattered:
honestly my friends, this case of mine… is also a case
of yours.
These longings, constant companions, show out when my heart
is contained, and everywhere is that wild hair like lace
of Yours.
When passing, keep garment clear from our dust and blood;
victims are many, sacrificed, in that Pathway's Place
of Yours.
Soft breeze, say from us to those who live in the town of Yazd:
"May heads of all those blind to truth, be polo mace
of yours.
Although we may be far away in body, our thoughts are not;
servant of your king we are and we offer the praise
of yours."
King of kings and highest star, for God's sake give this gift…
so like the sky I may kiss the ground of that palace
of Yours.
Hafez makes a prayer, listen to it and then say this: "Amen!"
"May my daily bread be that sweet-lipped embrace,
of Yours."

3. IT COULD BE

Winebringer, make our cup brighter with the wine's light!
Minstrel, sing this: "For us the world now turns out right!"
In the cup we have seen reflected the face of the Beloved,
O ignorant one, you don't know our wine-drinking delight!
That one whose heart is alive with love, he will never die:
in the history of the world our immortality is right to write.
Glances and graceful sways of those straight shapes appeals,
until gracefully moving like pine, our cypress comes in sight.
O breeze, if you should pass by the rosebed of the Beloved,

be careful to give to the Beloved our message which I cite:
"Why did You purposely take our name from Your memory?
The time will soon come when our name is lost from sight."
In eyes of our Beloved that binds hearts, intoxication's best;
because They've handed our reins to intoxication's delight.
I doubt if on Day of Resurrection, the priest's lawful bread
will profit him any more than our unlawful liquid's red light.
Like the tulip in winter's air my heart closes from the cold:
Bird of Fortune, when in this cage of ours will You alight?
Hafez, keep on dropping the grain of tears from your eyes,
it could be the Bird of Union will take our bait one night.
The azure sea of the sky and the crescent moon like a boat,
are all drowned in our Haji Kivam's most favourable sight.

4. THE MOMENT'S JOY

O Sufi, come and see, for the cup's mirror is bright:
the ruby wine is bright, so come and use your sight.
Drunkard's intoxicated and Secret's behind the veil:
this situation is not in the snobbish puritan's sight.
The Pure Bird is prey no one wins; pick up your net,
nothing is caught in the cage here but wind's flight.
At Life's feast enjoy one or two cups and then leave;
seriously, don't look here for the perpetual delight.
Heart, youth's gone; although you plucked no rose,
use your old head skillfully... then do what is right.
Live in the moment's joy; when the water dried up
didn't Adam from the Garden of Safety take flight?
We on Your threshold are all owed much for service;
Sir, from pity look on Your slave from a great height.
Disciple of the cup of Jamshid is Hafez; O breeze go,
and take to the Master of Jam this servant's delight.

5. GIVE WINE

Get up Winebringer, and give a cup from the bowl;
throw dust upon the head of this sad earthly role.
Set the cup of wine in the palm, so that from off
this chest I may pull that patched-up blue stole.
Although the wise may believe us to be infamous,
a good name and fame have never been our goal.
Give wine, for so much dust has the wind of pride
thrown on desire's head, it is worthless as a hole.
The smoke from the sighs of my heart burning up,
consumed all those with ignorance as their goal.
The secret that is contained inside my mad heart
is not known by the high and low… not one soul.
With a Beloved so charming my heart is content,
who once from my heart the sweet quietude stole.
No one who has seen that silver-limbed cypress,
would look at the cypress of the field and knoll.
Hafez, all day and night be patient in difficulties:
you may in the end one day get your heart's goal.

6. DESTINY'S DESIGN

My heart reaches out, for God's sake help, friends of the Divine!
O what pain if all should soon know this hidden secret of mine.
The boat we inhabit is stranded, may fair-weather breeze rise up,
so that once again we may see the face of the Beloved so fine.
Favour for ten days is the fate of the stars: it's magic and trickery!
Friend, hold dear your friends, every moment is more lost time.
This, sang the nightingale nightly, surrounded by wine and roses:
"Bring wine of the Dawn and let's drink, drunken friends of mine."
True path of the two worlds is plain, as two true sayings show:
"To friends give generously, to enemies give endurance sublime."
If into the street of laurels and society I've not been admitted,
try and change it if you can, but do you know Destiny's design?
This bitter wine that the Sufi calls: "Mother of all grief and pain,"

when weighed against even a virgin's kisses is a far sweeter wine.
In times of hardship enjoy life's pleasures and Winehouse's wine;
this transforming Elixir can turn a beggar into Karun's goldmine.
Don't be proud, for like a candle you will be completely consumed
by this heart-stealing Guide, melted like wax by a touch sublime.
Alexander's famous companion a secret 'mirror' is Jamshid's 'cup';
that pure Guide was seeing all that was of Dara's realm's design.
Givers of life are the fair ones, who converse in sweet Persian...
Wineseller, to all the old Masters of Persia this glad news consign.
Please excuse Hafez, O you priestly shaikhs, so spotlessly attired;
because his poor old wine-stained coat is no arrangement of mine.

7. NEWS OF THE ROSE

The shine of Youth's time again upon the garden glows;
sweet-singing nightingale hears the glad news of the rose.
O breeze, if you reach again to the youths of the field,
see that greeting to cypress, rose and sweet basil goes.
If the Wineseller Master's apprentice shows shining grace,
my eyelashes sweep where dust of Winehouse door blows.
You, sweeping ambergris mallet of hair across the moon,
don't strike me madly off course... mind spinning woes.
That lot sniggering at those drinking wine-dregs, I fear
in the end with religion lost, to the very same place goes.
Be the friend of the Men of God, for in the Ark of Noah
was humble dust; not a drop touched as The Flood rose.
Leave the Sphere's house and stop seeking only bread,
such a black cup kills its guest when it's time to close.
To him, whose last bed is only a handful of earth, say:
"Towers you raise towards the sky, what use are those?"
O my moon of Canaan, now throne of Egypt is yours,
time for you has come to say goodbye to prison woes.
Hafez, go and drink wine and get drunk and be happy;
don't make the Koran a trap a deceit, as do all those.

8. FAIR EXCHANGE

If that Turkish One of Shiraz would take this heart in hand,
for that One's Hinduish mole I'd barter Bokhara, Samarkand.
Winebringer, the special leftover wine; for in Paradise won't be
found the bank of Ruknabad... nor Musalla's rosescented land.
No, these bold delectable gypsies who torment our whole city,
steal heart's patience like Turks who take pay from the hand.
The Beloved's beauty is not in need of all our imperfect love;
makeup, beautyspot and eyeliner, does a lovely face demand?
I know that beauty of Joseph, which growing daily brought out
Zulaikha from her veil of modesty which she had not planned.
You called me names, I'm happy; God bless, You did the best,
for a bitter answer is sweet from a ruby lip that's sugar bland.
O youth, listen... receive this good advice; for young learners
prize advice from old Masters... more than soul's command.
Let's talk of wine and minstrel, not look for Destiny's Design;
for this is a mystery that Reason hasn't power to understand.
You've rhymed a *ghazal* Hafez, stringing pearls; sing it sweetly,
so that upon your song Heaven flings Pleiades clustered band.

9. THE WIND OF HARD LUCK

Soft breeze, to the graceful gazelle go gently and say:
"You sent us to mountains and deserts, sent us away."
Sweet seller of such sugar, whose life be always long,
why not ask about the parrot who needs sugar all day?
Rose, perhaps pride in your beauty stops your heart
inquiring of the distressed nightingale, wailing away.
Kindness and real beauty catch men who see the truth,
not for deceit and cages will wise birds come to stay.
I don't know why it is that such unfaithfulness exists
in cypress-straight, dark-eyed, moon-faced; I can't say.
When you sit with the beloved tasting the aged wine,
think of us lovers biting the wind of hard luck's way.

This much can be revealed, your beauty is faultless,
but it's a pity loyalty and devotion you don't display.
It's no wonder that the poems of Hafez should cause
the dancing of the Messiah, for Venus is singing today!

10. GUIDING LIGHT

From the Mosque to Winehouse our Master came last night;
friends of Path, now that this has happened, what's in sight?
In the Ancient Master's Winehouse we shall also be staying;
this, Promise of Eternity beyond Time, as our Fate did write.
We disciples, how can we now turn our faces to the *Kaaba,*
when to the Wineseller's Winehouse our Master set his sight?
I wonder if our all night-long sighs, that burn away our heart
and rain down fire, will affect Your heart of stone one night?
If Wisdom knew how blessed is a heart chained by Your locks,
the wise would all madly pursue our long chains of delight.
On Your hair the wind blew, for me the world became black;
except for Your black wild hair as profit, our profit's slight.
Peace, the prey, fell into the trap of the Falcon of the heart;
You shook loose Your hair, again from hand prey took flight.
Your beautiful face's grace explains to us verses of the *Koran;*
so in our explanation… nothing but grace and beauty unite.
"Arrows of Our sighs pass beyond the Sphere, Hafez: silence!
have compassion for your soul, avoid arrow of Our Might."

11. MURDERER

To the attendants of the Monarch, who will be taking this prayer?
"In thanks for Sovereignty, don't send away from sight a beggar."
From the enemy with the nature of a demon, I take refuge in God;
maybe for God's sake, that blazing Light may be for me the helper.
If Your dark eyelash should be setting out straight for our blood;
O Fair One, consider its deceit and do not then be led into error.
When You enflame Your face, You consume the heart of the world:

if You are not kind, then from this can You ever be the gainer?
All night long I still have the hope that the breeze of the morning,
will with the greetings of the loved ones, be helpful to the lover.
Beloved, what commotion is this that in hearts of lovers You wake,
by Your face like bright moon, form like cypress, a heartstealer?
Sorrowful heart of Hafez bleeds because of separation from You;
how would it be if for a moment with Beloved it was the uniter?

12. WHERE?

Where's work's reward, where am I without recognition:
where?
See how long this path is, where is its final destination:
where?
What connection's the between drunkenness and pious virtue?
Where is lute's melody and the preacher's exhortation:
where?
My heart is sick of the cloister and the hypocritical patchcoat:
where's Wineseller's corridor, pure wine's intoxication:
where?
You have now gone; may the time of union be a sweet memory!
Where's that glance gone, where's that condemnation:
where?
What do the dark hearts of enemies gain from the Friend's face?
Where is extinguished lamp, candle of sun's radiation:
where?
Don't look at the dimple of that chin for that way is but a pit.
Heart, where are you hurrying; where's the destination:
where?
The dust of Your threshold is the supplier of balm for my eyes:
where can I go from here, where's there another location:
where?
O friend, do not look for an easy time or patience from Hafez:
what's an easy time, what's patience, sleep's relaxation:
where?

13. YOU WENT

You went, and You knew that we went with heart full of suffering;
where will such bad fortune take our Source, that us is nourishing?
We will decorate, like Your hair, with pearls our eyelashes scatter,
the messenger who will bring to us from You, the blessed greeting.
I have come in prayer: so You also please lift Your hand in prayer!
Mine: faith stays with You; Yours is: God our patience be helping.
I swear by Your head that if the world strikes swords on my head,
 desire for You out of this mind they could not possibly be taking.
 The heavens made me a wanderer, wandering in every direction;
 you know sky is jealous of Companionship our soul is cherishing.
 If all the people of the world should be tyrannical towards You,
 our Lord will demand justice from all for the tyranny they're doing.
 The day again will come when in safety my Beloved will come…
 that day will be happy when safely to our house Beloved is coming.
 Ever since we have sung praises of the beauty of Your lovely cheek,
 our book's leaves caused the rose's leaves with shame to be wilting.
 To who said these words: "Hafez has not gone on a long journey,"
 Say: "End of the journey, out of our head… will never be coming."

14. FRESH

Minstrel, the sweet song be singing,
 forever fresh, ever new:
give me wine that's heart-expanding,
 forever fresh, ever new.
With the Beloved covered in finery, secretly sit for awhile:
 from the lip sip the kiss of longing,
 forever fresh, ever new.
Call my silver-legged Winebringer for me and bring me wine!
 Quickly the flagon for me be filling,
 forever fresh, ever new.
When will you enjoy the fruit of life if you don't drink wine?
 To the Beloved wine be drinking…
 forever fresh, ever new.

For my sake, that charming heart-stealer's openly displaying
beauty, perfume and full colouring,
forever fresh, ever new.
O morning breeze, when you pass over the Beloved's street,
the story of Hafez's love be telling,
forever fresh, ever new.

15. THIRSTY

Since Your beauty has invited Your lover to be united with You,
heart and soul have fallen into ruin from Your hair and mole too.
That which from being separated from You souls of lovers endure,
no one has experienced, except for Kerbala's ones, a thirsty few.
O my soul, if my Bold One is practising loving and intoxication,
it is right to give up piety and with all soberness to be through.
The pleasurable time and the season of joy and the time of wine:
acknowledge it as plunder… as five days of leisure given to you.
Hafez, if you are helped by being allowed to kiss the King's foot,
you will in both worlds have the glory of grace and sublimity too.

16. STRANGER

I said: "O monarch of lovely ones, seeking mercy
is this stranger,"
reply… "Losing way because of heart's gluttony,
is this stranger."
I said: "Stay awhile with me;" the answer was: "Please excuse me.
Hoping one always home cares for one in misery,
is this stranger?"
Will the gently nurtured one who is asleep on the royal ermine be
grieved, if making thornbed with pillow of rockery
is this stranger?
O you, in the chain of whose hair are the souls of so many lovers…
that the musky mole falls on your cheeks glory,
is this stranger?

In that face like the moon's colour there appeared wine's reflection;
like the leaf of red arghavan on wild rose's purity;
is this stranger?
Strange is that down that's like a line of ants around your fair face:
yet in China's gallery, shading line not obviously,
is this stranger?
I said: "You, your hair as black as night is this stranger's evening;
be careful if at morning time… crying from injury
is this stranger."
The answer came: "Hafez, friends are in the state of astonishment:
it is no wonder if with grief and misery, weary…
is this stranger."

17. THE MORNING CUP

The morning comes up veiled by a thin cloud;
friends: morning cup, morning cup, out loud!
Dew trickles and streaks the face of the tulip;
friends, to drink wine, the wine, have vowed!
From orchard blows the breeze of Paradise;
drink forever pure wine, for it's now allowed.
On orchard, rose has placed its emerald throne;
go, get me wine that is like fiery ruby, proud!
Once more they have shut the Winehouse door;
"O open, door-opener," this, we cry out, loud.
At such a time as this, it's a wonder that they
now close Winehouse from this season's crowd.
Your ruby lip demands that the rights of salt
upon the wound of roasting hearts, is allowed.
O you fanatic, drink wine like the drunkard;
O you wise one, pray to God, don't be proud.
If you search for a trace of the Water of Life,
look in sweet wine, hear harp sounding loud.
If like Alexander you are searching for Life,
the Beloved's ruby lip is Life's raining cloud.

To the face of Winebringer of Paradise-form,
drinking pure wine in rose season, is vowed.
Hafez, do not worry or grieve; Bride Fortune
lifts the veil, finally, to view face is allowed.

18. THE MORNING OF FORTUNE

The morning of Fortune dawns; where's the cup like the Sun?
When is a more appropriate moment? Give winecup, be done!
A quiet house, the Winebringer friend and sweet subtle singer:
time of joy, cup's circulation and season of youth has begun.
For expanding soul's nature and for beautifying joy's jewel,
golden goblet is with melting ruby, a happy mixture's done.
Sweetheart and singer clap waving hands, drunkards dance;
Winebringer glances sleep from eyes of each wine-loving one.
A quiet seclusion, a pleasing place and mingling with friends;
who wins such a communion, a hundred doors open has won.
Nature's expert adorner, thinking of giving grace to the wine,
has happily in heart of the leaf of the rose the rosewater spun.
Since that Moon has with soul purchased the pearls of Hafez,
to ear of Venus reaches the sound of ribbed lute's melodic run.

19. HELL AND PARADISE

From garden of Union with You comes garden of Paradise;
from torment of separation from You is heat of Hell's fires.
In the beauty of Your cheek and fair form, have sheltered
Paradise and its Tree because: "Their safe refuge there lies."
Since all night long my eye is seeing the stream of Paradise,
in sleep is seen sight of Your intoxicating eye by my eyes.
All seasons chapters has Spring's description of Your beauty:
each and every book has Your grace mentioned by Paradise.
My heart's consumed, my soul hasn't achieved heart's desire;
if it attained its desire, blood wouldn't spill from my eyes.
Many are the salt-rights that are from Your lip and mouth

upon the wounded livers and hearts burning... full of sighs.
Don't think that in Your circle only lovers are intoxicated;
haven't you heard of the fanatic's mad griefstricken sighs?
From seeing Your face's lip, I knew that the ruby's shine
was produced by the sun, illuminating world and the skies.
Draw back the veil; how long will You practise seclusion?
except for the seclusion, what advantage in this veil lies?
Rose viewed Your face and then became burning with fire:
from Your fragrance, shamed became rosewater by desires.
In love with Your face Hafez drowns in the sea of calamity;
look, see he is drowning, come help, just once, for he dies.
"Hafez, do not allow that life should pass by in stupid waste;
try hard and understand the true value that to life applies."

20. DON'T GIVE UP HOPE

By soul of the Chief and ancient right and true covenant I swear:
my companion at breath of dawn is my prayer for Your welfare.
My tears that in volume are much greater than the flood of Noah,
have not washed from my heart Your love that is pictured there.
Come, do business, make a deal and purchase this broken heart;
although it may be broken, it's worth many that don't have a care.
Don't blame me for madness, because the Master appointed love
for me, when on First Day of Creation, Winehouse was my share.
Strive for the truth, so that out from your soul the sun may rise:
because the first dawn, being the false one, a black face did wear.
O heart, don't give up hope of the endless kindness of the Friend:
when you boast of loving, quickly stake your head then and there.
Because of Your direction, I became mad for mountain and plain:
but from compassion You don't loosen chain that on waist I bear.
Tongue of the ant was long when criticizing Asaf and rightly so:
he lost Jam's seal belonging to Solomon, and he looked nowhere.
Hafez, don't grieve and don't seek consistency from heart-stealers:
what fault is it of the garden, when this herb's not growing there?

21. THE HOME OF YOURS

This house of my eye is the home
of Yours;
courteously enter this house, home
of Yours.
Your mole and cheek steal hearts of Seekers,
this grain and snare hide rare charm
of Yours.
Nightingale, heart be happy, united with roses
for in the field is loving song, alone,
of Yours.
Remedy our sick heart with Your healing lip,
exciting is ruby dose in treasure tome
of Yours.
My body is so unworthy to do service for You;
my soul's essence, dust of doorstone
of Yours.
What a fine horseman You are, so magical that
the wild colt obeys, as whip is shown
of Yours.
What's my position, when even the juggling sky
is staggered by tricks stored in game
of Yours?
Now music of Your party makes the sky dance;
sweet verse of Hafez is melodic tone
of Yours.

22. YOUR TREASURY

Your Love is in my heart's holy place:
Yours.
My eye is mirror holder of form's face:
Yours.

I who do not bow to either of the two worlds,
my neck is beneath that load of grace:
Yours.
Paradise tree and you, form of Beloved and me;
Your way of thinking is your own case:
yours.
Me, I am in that holy place, where the breeze
holds the screen of the dignified space:
Yours.
If my garment is soiled, what's the difference?
Whole world's witness to innocent ways:
Yours.
Majnun's time has passed, now it is our turn:
every one gets five days term; five days:
yours.
Love's realm for the lover and a corner of joy,
given to me because of fortunate grace:
Yours.
If my heart and I become ransomed, no matter;
Your welfare's the objective of my case:
Yours.
Vision of the eye never be without Your image;
for its corner is a special secret place:
Yours.
Each new rose that came to adorn the meadow,
is in perfume and colour and all trace:
Yours.
So take no notice if he seems poor; for Hafez's
heart is the treasury of Love's embrace:
Yours.

23. THE WILL OF THE FRIEND

The head of our desire is on the threshold of the Almighty Friend:
all passing over our head, on the Will of the Friend will depend.
I haven't seen the equal to my Friend, although the moon and sun

I have placed as mirrors opposite Friend's face: they can't contend!
What news does the breeze give of our heart straining from grief,
which has wrapped it like petals of the rosebud, from end to end.
I am not a lone drinker in this cloistered world that burns lovers:
many a head is in this workshop for the winejar's clay to expend.
Perhaps You have been combing Your hair that scatters ambergris,
because the breeze is like civet and dust ambergris scent does send.
Every roseleaf in the garden is the sprinkling from off Your face,
every cypress on river's bank on Your graceful form does depend.
Tongue of speech becomes dumb when it's describing Your beauty:
what use is a reed's split tongue's babbling that can't comprehend?
Your face has come into my heart, now I know I'll have my desire:
for a happy omen's arrival, realization that is happy does portend.
Not only at this time has Hafez's heart been in the fire of seeking:
like tulip it was branded in Eternity… beyond beginning and end.

24. THAT ONE

That darkish coloured One, world's sweetness
is with that One;
laughing lip and eye bright, heart of happiness
is with that One.
Although all those sweet of mouth are the Sovereigns, that One
is Solomon of the Age, for Seal's powerfulness
is with that One.
The musky mole that is on that One's face of wheaten complexion:
mystery of that grain causing Adam's distress,
is with that One.
My Heartstealer's departed on a journey: friends, for God's sake
what to do with my heart, for healing compress
is with that One.
That One fair of face and with a pure garment, is perfect in skill:
truthfully, all that the Pure Ones spirits possess,
is with that One.
Who can one tell this enigma to? That stone-hearted One slew us:
yet Mary's son Jesus' breath, curing deathliness,

is with that One.
Hafez is one of the true believers, so regard him with due respect;
for many blessed spirits sympathetic forgiveness,
is with that one.

25. A REMEDY FOR MADNESS

From the threshold of the Friend, hopeful of a great favour am I;
I've done a great sin, but my hope in Friend's forgiveness does lie.
I know that the Friend will overlook and pass by this sin of mine;
for although Friend's nature is powerful, it is of the angels on high.
I have wept to such an extent that everyone who is passing by me,
on seeing streaming pearls of tears says: "What river does he cry?"
Like a ball we have played with our head at the end of Your street,
but none knew or said: "What ball and street's this?" So, no reply.
Your hair that does not utter any words, still draws my heart to it:
who would against Your hair that captures hearts a few words try?
It is a long lifetime since I have inhaled the perfume of Your hair;
yet in my heart's place of perfume, that perfume's scent does lie.
That mouth of which I don't see even a trace, it's as if it's nothing!
That waist that is only a thin hair, does my knowledge of it defy!
I wonder about the image of Your form, and how, though my tears
work continuously at washing and scouring, it never leaves my eye.
Hafez, the state that you are in is of one who is sick with madness;
remembering Friend's hair is remedy that to madness does apply.

26. TONIGHT

That which secluded ones call 'The Night of Power' tonight
is:
O my Lord, from what auspicious planet, this fortunate sight
is?
So that Your hair may not be touched by those who are unfit...
every heart in the circle's cry of... "O Lord, Lord," forthright
is.

I am a victim of the dimple of Your chin, because from all sides,
under the dimple of Your chin, neck of many a soul held tight
is.
Moon holds mirror for the face of the One Who is my Horseman:
dust of that One's horse's hoof, crown of sun's great height
is.
See sweat reflecting on Beloved's cheek: the longing sun's face,
for as long as it's day, daily longing with this sweat to unite,
is.
I will never give up the ruby lip of the Beloved, or the winecup;
pious ones excuse me, for the right religion, this, in my sight
is.
In that procession, when they fasten saddle on the wind's back,
how may I ride with Solomon whose mount an ant so slight
is?
The Water of Life is trickling out from my pen's eloquent beak!
Praise God: my pen a deep drinker, like black crow at night,
is!
That One shoots an arrow from under the eye at this my heart:
in that smile from under that lip, Hafez's food of Life to bite
is.

27. VISION'S GARDEN

From drunken me, the wish for piety and observance are far away,
for I was well known for drinking wine on Eternity's Original Day.
Every moment that I performed ablution in the fountain of Love,
four times upon all things that exist, "God is greatest" I did say.
Give wine, so I may give to you the knowledge of Fate's Mystery,
from Whose face I'm a lover and by Whose scent I'm drunk today.
The waist of the mountain is smaller than the waist of an ant here:
worshipper of wine, don't be hopeless of God's merciful doorway.
May that drunken narcissus stay and may the evil eye be far away;
underneath this dome of turquoise no one in happiness does stay.
May my soul be the ransom for Your mouth; for in vision's garden,
no rosebud sweeter than this rosebud did World's Maker display.

Hafez became a Solomon through the fortune of his love for You,
which means: of Union with You in hand he has only wind's spray.

28. BIGOTRY AND LOVE

In the bigot who shows piety, knowledge of our state
is not;
whatever he may say about us, a reason for us to hate
is not.
In the Path, whatever happens to the wayfarer is for his good:
the heart that's lost, in that Highway that is straight…
is not.
So that we may see how the game changes I will move a pawn:
on chessboard of drunken lovers, power of checkmate…
is not.
What is this high smooth roof that contains so many pictures?
in this world, knowing this mystery, one wise or great
is not.
Lord, who or what is this independence, this powerful force:
that there are hidden wounds but the strength to relate
is not.
You may say Lord of Secretaries doesn't know the account,
"For the sake of God" His Royal Signature, on the date
is not.
Say: "Come," to who wants to; "Speak," to who wishes to:
in this Court there's no arrogance, a stern porter at gate
is not.
The only unfitness here is because our formless-form isn't fit:
or, Your garment of glory's site, possible to overstate
is not.
It's the way of those of pure hearts to go to Winehouse door;
entry to Winesellers street, for whoever themselves rate,
is not.
I'm slave of Perfect Master, Whose generosity constantly flows;
unlike the priest and the bigot who rarely is, and of late
is not.

If Hafez doesn't sit in the highest seat it's due to his high spirit:
true Lover, drinking dregs, trapped by wealth and estate
is not.

29. LIFE'S AMULET

That messenger who has arrived from the land
of the Friend,
brought my life's amulet, written by the hand
of the Friend.
It gives a pleasant trace of the Friend's grace and greatness:
it makes happy mention of the glory so grand,
of the Friend.
I gave my heart for the good news, but I was very ashamed
of this meagre coin, which I gave to the land
of the Friend.
It is thanks to God, that with the help of Fortune's consent,
all my work's desire accords with the demand
of the Friend.
What power have sphere's movements and moon's revolutions?
Both turn obediently to the powerful command
of the Friend.
If the wind of calamity should smash the two worlds together,
we and the light of the eye, expand to the land
of the Friend.
O breeze of the morning… prepare eye-balm made of pearls
from dust of happy earth, blessed road's sand
of the Friend.
We'll always be at Friend's threshold, head down in prayer:
let's see who sleeps sweetly on chest and hand
of the Friend.
If the enemy speaks out against Hafez, what is there to fear?
Thanks to God, unashamed I'll take the stand
of the Friend.

30. FOREVER LAMENTING

Welcome, messenger of happiness; please, news be telling
of the Friend,
so with joy I may sacrifice my soul for the mentioning
of the Friend.
I'm forever lamenting and crying like nightingale in the cage does;
my nature's a parrot's, for sugar and almond I'm longing,
of the Friend.
That Friend's hair is the snare and that mole is the bait of that snare;
hoping for that grain, into the snare I am now falling...
of the Friend.
Until Judgement Morning one's hand from drunkenness shall not
raise, who in Eternity, like me a drop from the cup is drinking,
of the Friend.
Even a little explanation of my own longing I did not offer because
it's not best of manners to make the head begin aching,
of the Friend.
My inclination was towards Union and Friend's was to separation;
I gave up my desire so to fruition would come longing
of the Friend.
If this should happen, I woud put as salve into my eyes precious dust
of this path that is now honoured by the foot-stepping
of the Friend.
Hafez, patiently burn away for the Friend, and do not seek a remedy;
because there is no remedy for the pain, never resting,
of the Friend.

31. THE FRIEND

O breeze, if you reach to the land over there
of the Friend,
bring a scent of musky air from fragrant hair
of the Friend.
By that Soul I swear that I'd thankfully lay down my life,
if a message you would bring and deliver...
of the Friend.

If it happens that you cannot gain access to that Presence,
bring dust for my eyes from door and stair
of the Friend.
I am a lost beggar; where am I now, I who long for union?
Perhaps in sleep the form I will glimpse, there,
of the Friend.
Although the Friend wouldn't offer even a pittance for us,
for the whole world we wouldn't sell a hair
of the Friend.
What is it worth if his heart is free from the chains of grief,
for Hafez would still be slave, servant forever
of the Friend.

32. THE HOUSE OF HOPE

Come, for the House of Hope built on shaky sand
is;
bring the wine, for life's foundation like the wind
is.
I'm slave of that One's Will, Who under azure dome,
is free from all the colour that attachment's bind
is.
Can I tell you what good news last night given to me
drunk on Winehouse floor, by an Angel of Beyond
is?
"You far-sighted royal falcon resting in Paradise tree,
you shouldn't nest in the corner that this sad land
is.
From highest Heavens' fortress walls they call to you:
I do not know why, fallen in this trap, your kind
is."
Listen to this advice I give, think well and act on it;
this I know from One Who Pathway's Mastermind
is:
"Don't expect this deceitful world to keep a promise;
this hag, bride leaving thousand grooms behind,
is."

Don't let world's grief eat you, remember my advice;
for from a travelling Wayfarer this advice so kind
is.
Be content with what fate gives you, and don't frown;
door of free choice for you and me, tightly bound
is.
In the smile of the rose is no sign of faith or promise;
weep, loving nightingale; for this, lamentation's land
is.
You feeble versifiers, why are you envious of Hafez?
God's gift, sweet words pleasing heart and mind,
is.

33. LOST IN GRIEF

Since into the power of the breeze the tip of Your hair
has fallen,
my broken heart into two pieces, because of despair,
has fallen.
In the middle of the dark morning there is Your eye of sorcery,
this makes evident how hopeless my prescription's care
has fallen.
Have You knowledge of what that mole above curl of Your hair is?
It's really a dot of ink that on the curve of a 'j', there,
has fallen.
What is Your musky hair in the rosebed of Your cheek's garden?
It's really a peacock that into garden of Paradise's air
has fallen.
O Friend of the soul, my heart in its longing for Your fragrance,
as a grain of dust of the road, behind the wind however,
has fallen.
O no, this dusty body of mine cannot be rising up like the dust
from the end of Your street, because it there, forever,
has fallen.
O You of the breath of Jesus, the shade of Your cypress upon me
is shadow of the Soul that on bones, rotten and bare,
has fallen.

I have seen this: that one who believed his only place is the *Kaaba,*
thinking of Your lip, to dwell at Winehouse door, there
has fallen.
O dear sacred Soul, to Hafez whose heart is lost in grief for You,
a great friends hip from that Original Promise's share,
has fallen.

34. LAWFUL WINE

Rose inside, wine in hand, and Beloved to my wish
is;
king of the world is my slave on such a day as this
is.
Tonight please don't bring a candle into our gathering:
for tonight, on moon of Friend's face full emphasis
is.
In our belief the winecup is lawful; but, O my cypress,
rose of form, to be without Your face, this, amiss
is.
In our gathering do not mix rose perfume: our soul
each moment inhales scent Your hair's ambergris
is.
My ear's full of voice of reed and melody of the harp,
my eye upon Your ruby lip and circling cup's bliss,
is.
Don't talk about the sweetness of sugar or of candy,
for my desire, that sweetness of Your lip to kiss,
is.
Since treasure of grief for you filled my ruined heart,
corner of Winehouse, always now my house this
is.
You tell me about shame? Shame gave me my name!
You ask about fame? Fame to me shame's edifice
is!
I am a wine drinker, head spinning, looking for love;
in this city, is there a one who also not like this
is?

Don't inform the censor of my error, because he too
like me, always desiring a drink of the wine's bliss
is.
Hafez, never sit a moment without wine and Beloved;
season of rose, jasmine and of a celebration, this
is.

35. 'GOD IS THE GREATEST'

In my garden, there a need for the cypress and also the pine
is?
Less than whom, that beautiful shade-grown boxtree of mine
is?
O fair young beauty, what faith do you take for your religion,
where our blood more legal than mothers milk in your design
is?
Since you picture grief looming upon the horizon, drink wine!
we have made the right diagnosis and a certain cure the wine
is.
Why lift my head from threshold of Master of all Winesellers?
Because His head is Fortune and His door tranquillity benign
is.
In our Path, They purchase only the one whose heart is broken;
bazaar for believers in themselves over there at another line
is.
Yesterday, wine in your head, you promised to me intoxication;
today, what will you say when inside your head no more wine
is.
The story of love's pain is only one story; yet it is marvelous
that every time I hear about it… it never of the same design
is.
Come, for in separation, like the ears of those who are fasting
intent upon 'God is the Greatest', this expectant eye of mine
is.
Don't condemn Shiraz, water of Ruknabad, the pleasant breezes:
of the world's seven territories, their lustre the greatest shine
is.

It's a long way from Khizer's water of Life in land of darkness,
up to our water whose fountain 'God is the Greatest' as its sign
is.
We won't take away the honour of not having, and being content;
tell the king that what is provided, destined by Divine Design
is.
How strange it is Hafez, that the rod of sugar is your pen's reed;
pleasing to the heart more than honey... its every fruitful line
is.

36. PERFECT MASTERS (DERVISHES)

Paradise's Garden of Eternity is the sanctuary
of Dervishes;
the Ultimate Power's source is in the slavery
of Dervishes.
The Treasury of Seclusion containing a wonderful Talisman:
It's unlocking is in the glance, giving bravery,
of Dervishes.
The pleasure Rizvan has as doorkeeper of Paradise's palace,
is only a view of Garden's pleasing symmetry
of Dervishes.
That, by reflection of which dark base metal becomes gold,
is by the alchemy that is in the camaraderie
of Dervishes.
That grandeur to which high sun bows his glorious crown,
is the humble home of the dignified mastery
of Dervishes.
That great wealth, of which there is no fear of destruction,
hear the Truth told plainly: it is the treasury
of Dervishes.
When kings are altars to which worldly people pray for help,
it's because they serve the majestic ancestry
of Dervishes.
Pole to pole oppression's army stretches across the earth;
but, beginningless to endless Eternity is victory
of Dervishes.

Kings are offering prayers for fulfillment of their objectives;
desired object is mirrored from face's imagery
of Dervishes.
O wealthy man, do not proudly boast about all your riches;
life and gold come from benevolent treasury
of Dervishes.
Karun and his great treasure are still sinking into the earth;
you'll have heard, this results from effrontery
of Dervishes.
I'm the slave of the glance of the Asaf, the Chief of the age,
who is outwardly regal, wears inwardly, finery
of Dervishes.
Now you be full of respect here in such Blessed Company:
kings and angels stand respectfully in the gallery
of Dervishes.
Hafez, if you're seeking to gain the Water of Everlasting Life;
its fountain's source is in dust of the sanctuary
of Dervishes.

37. COME BACK

To Winehouse, cup in hand came that Friend of mine;
eye intoxicating all the drinkers and drunk on wine.
The hoof of Your horse showed the new moon's form,
Your high form lowered the height of the cypress pine.
Can I say: "I exist," when I don't know my true Self?
Can I say: "I'm not," when I'm expecting The Divine?
When you got up, the hearts of the companions sank;
when You sat, their cheers arose… to there combine.
If civet is musky, it's because it was near Your hair;
if indigo draws bow, it was near Your eyebrow fine.
My life like a candle, night to morning, burnt away:
burnt like a moth, not resting, until dawn did shine.
Come back, so that Hafez's spent life can come back;
though arrow doesn't return, sped from aim's twine.

38. THE REASON

Sleep of that seducing eye
of Yours, isn't for nothing:
that curl blowing to untie
of Yours: isn't for nothing.
Running from Your lip was mother's milk when I said:
"Sugar at that salt supply
of Yours, isn't for nothing."
Fountain of the Water of Life is Your mouth; but lip,
brink of pit of chin's lie
of Yours: isn't for nothing.
Your life be long, for I know so well Your eyelash's
arrow in bow of brow, eye
of Yours: isn't for nothing.
With pain and sorrow of separation you are upset:
O heart; wail, cry and sigh
of yours, isn't for nothing.
Last night, wind of Your street passed by rosegarden:
rose, torn collar and cry
of yours… isn't for nothing.
Though heart keeps love's pain secret from the crowd:
O Hafez, this weeping eye
of yours, isn't for nothing.

39. FREE TO BE CAPTURED

O preacher, go about your own work: what is all this commotion?
My heart fell from the hand: what has fallen to your occupation?
The connection with Beloved which God created from Nothing,
is a subtlety for which no created being has found an explanation.
The beggar of Your street is free of the eight abodes of Paradise:
Your captive that is bound is free of both the worlds' habitation.
Although the intoxication of love has made me drunk and ruined;

the foundation of my existence has grown by that intoxication.
Heart, don't complain of the injustice of your Beloved's violence,
for Beloved has openly warned you and this is true justification.
As long as Your lip does not caress my wish like the flute's reed;
like the wind in my ear is the whole of the world's admonition.
Hafez, go; explain no more stories and whisper no magical verse;
for I remember their charming conceits, in magical versification.

40. YOUR EYE'S PRESCRIPTION

Dew-fresh, bloodthirsty-ruby, lip of the Beloved fair of mine,
is;
yet to see You and surrender soul, sole aim forever of mine
is.
Those dark eyes and long eyelashes shame whoever sees them,
as with Your heart-stealing, which blame for despair of mine
is.
Cameldriver, don't take my load far from the gate; street's end
is a royal highway, where dwelling of the Beloved fair of mine
is.
I am possessed by my own ill fortune in this unfaithful period,
the love for that wildly intoxicated form, the affair of mine
is.
The essence-holder of the rose, its casket that sheds ambergris,
is small favour of pleasant fragrance that the Perfumer of mine
is.

Gardener, don't drive me away like the wind from Your garden,
that watered by tears, pomegranate-like, red and rare of mine,
is.
Your eye prescribes doses of rosewater and sugar from Your lip,
Physician of this sick heart, that sick with the care of mine
is.
Whoever taught Hafez subtlety, so he could beautify the *ghazal,*
is a sweet voiced subtle speaker, that the Friend fair of mine
is.

41. LOVE'S OCCUPATION

It's a long time since the love of beauties was an occupation
of mine:
the pain of such an occupation, is the sad heart's consolation
of mine.
To see Your ruby it's necessary to have an eye that can see the soul:
where is the place for the eye seeing the world's habitation
of mine?
Be my Friend, for the day's beautification and the evolution of time
come from Your moon-face, tears like Pleiades formation,
of mine.
Since Your love gave to me the lesson in the art of speaking in verse,
tongues of the people repeat these praises, this glorification
of mine.
O Lord, for me keep safely the condition of being in poverty because,
this blessing is the cause of the power and the high position
of mine.
O preacher, worshipper of rulers, don't go displaying your own pride,
for the Great King's dwelling is the heart full of desperation,
of mine.
O Lord Whose place of entertainment is the real *Kaaba* of my desire,
the rose and the wild rose were thornbush in the destination
of mine?
Who has taught Your imagination to freely sail over the ocean?
Perhaps its guide was the tears, like Pleiades constellation,
of mine.
Hafez, do not speak again of the tale of the power of Khusrau Parviz,
whose lip was drainer of dregs of the sweet Shirin concoction
of mine.

42. NO CHOICE

I'm the type, Wineshop is monk's cell for praying
for me;
praying at dawn to Winemaker is true praising,
for me.
If not for me the sweet harp of morning cup, why worry?
At dawn my crying song, is the excuse I am using
for me.
Thanks to God I have finished with the king and beggar:
beggar of dust of Friend's door is a king begging,
for me.
Through Mosque and Wineshop I desire union with You;
this idea is my only aim and God is witnessing
for me.
Being Your beggar is for me far better than being a king;
the true honour and glory is to You submitting,
for me.
Since the time that I laid my face on Your high doorstep,
above throne of the sun there's a pillow waiting
for me.
With death's sword I could cut away this tent of mine;
but, to stay by this fortunate door is remaining
for me.
Hafez, be good mannered and say this: "It's all my fault,"
even though in this there is really no choosing
for me.

43. THIS TALE

The red rose blooms and happily drunk is nightingale;
the invitation is to be merry, Sufis, wine lovers, hail!
The foundation of abstinence seemed as firm as a rock;
now see this marvel, it is broken by crystal cup so frail!
Bring wine, because in the Court of the Liberated One,
Oneness for slave, king, drunkard, censor, will prevail.

Since we have to depart from this hotel of two doors,
both high and low under life's archway go, so why wail?
To live in Bliss one must first have suffered from grief:
'Yes' to 'Am I *not* your God?' was 'curse' on Day Primal.
Don't worry what 'Is' and 'Is not', let mind be happy;
the end to all that is perfected is 'Is not', without fail.
Glory of being Asaf: wind as steed, language of birds,
wind swept away; the kind sir found them to no avail.
On the wing flies the feather, so don't leave the Path;
the arrow that flies high soon ends in the dusty trail.
Hafez, what thanks can the tongue of your pen speak?
For it speaks what from hand to hand goes: this tale!

44. THE VISIT

With a flagon in hand, singing a song and laughing, wine inside;
sweating all over, hair everywhere, garment torn down the side,
That eye looking for battle and mocking lips mouthing "O no;"
last night at midnight You came to my pillow, sat by my side.
To my ear You bent Your head and said in a sad soft whisper:
"My poor mad lover are you awake, or do you sleep?" You sighed.
If a wise man is given late at night such a drink, this is his Fate;
unfaithful to Love he would be if he praised wine, then denied.
Go away preacher, stop ranting about us drinking leftover dregs;
only this was given us, morning before Creation's clay was fired.
Whatever You have poured into our cup, we've swallowed it all;
either the wine of drunkards or the elixir of Paradise, we tried.
The laughter of wine in the cup and long curling hair of Beloved:
how many vows of repentance, like Hafez's have they untied?

45. WINE OF MANY COLOURS

A thousand hearts are captured by a single thread of hair;
path of thousands is blocked, a way out is no longer there.
So all can give up soul in hope of sweet smelling breeze,

You open musk pod then shut door when they come near.
I became frenzied by the Beloved's forehead like the moon;
it revealed eyebrow and turned, then veiled a face so fair.
The Winebringer poured into cup a wine of many colours;
in this container see how many images were created, so rare.
Lord, what magic the wine container does that blood sticks
to the neck, although it makes a sweet-glugging fill the air.
What sound was that the singer made in the centre of song,
that he keeps shouting truth to all who might like to hear?
The Magician who knew that this world is a trick of Illusion,
folded up equipment, and kept silent about the whole affair.
Anyone who has never tried to love yet wants union, Hafez,
would, without cleaning heart, the clothes of a pilgrim wear.

46. THE SOLUTION

When The Creator, form of Your fascinating eyebrow portrayed,
then He by Your glances, the solution of my poor condition made.
He took all peace from this heart and the bird of the garden's heart,
when both hearts to lament for You at morning, He did persuade.
Time planted me and cypress of the garden in the dust of the Path,
when it, garment of thin nargasin cloth for You had by hand made.
From our state and rosebud's heart, hundred knots were made loose
by rose's breeze, when it gave thread's end to Your Will, to braid.
Please do not tie a knot on my poor heart like that of the muskpod;
for my heart with Your hair loosening knots, a promise has made.
From Your perfume heart of one is filled if even for only one day
his heart, like rosebud from its longing for You, is totally remade.
Breeze of Union, You were the life that was given to another heart:
see mistake I made; my heart hoped that Your faith wouldn't fade.
I said: "On account of Your cruelty I'll soon depart from this city;"
Beloved laughed and said: "Go Hafez: your foot... who delayed?"

At this time, the only friend that of faults really free
is,
the flagon of the pure wine and the book of melody
is.
Go alone, for the pathway of salvation is very narrow:
take up the cup, for precious life without guarantee
is.
I am not the only one worrying about not working:
knowledge without practise the wise one's misery
is.
In this roadway full of commotion, to the eye of reason,
the world and all of its works without any stability
is.
The face of the old camel destined by Fate to be black
isn't white from washing, cleaning: this an old story
is.
Everything you see created is capable of deteriorating,
except for Love, which free from all inconsistency
is.
My heart had great hope that it would unite with You;
but in the pathway of Life, death involved in robbery
is.
Hold the moon-faced One's hair and don't tell about it;
the effect of Venus and Saturn, good luck and agony
is.
At no time whatsoever will they ever find Hafez sober;
because he, drunk with cup of beginningless Eternity,
is.

48. THE ESSENCE OF TORMENT

Since we have You in our imagination, for wine what need
is?

To winejar say: "Go away, the winehouse's ruin decreed
is."

Even if it's wine of Paradise, spill it: for without the Friend,
each mouthful that you give, the essence of torment indeed
is.

O no, Heartstealer has departed, and upon my weeping eye,
idea of a letter from that One, an image on water to read
is.

Eye, be awake; for one can't be safe from unceasing torrents:
where there's sleep, there also the torrents' greatest speed
is.

Openly the Beloved passes but keeps seeing only strangers,
and it is because of this that the Beloved, of a veil in need
is.

Since rose saw Your flushed cheek graced with much sweat,
dissolving in water from the heart's grief it hot with greed
is.

Don't go and search for any advice in the corner of my brain,
for this cell only filled with the hum of the harp and reed
is.

The Path: it's such a long Path, that compared to its vastness,
sky's surrounding ocean is only a mirage: a bubbling bead
is.

The valley and the plain are green; so come, let us not let go
hand from the Waterpool, for the world a mirage indeed
is.

At heart's banquet, a hundred candles are lit by Your face:
it's strange, a hundred veils on Your face always guaranteed
is.

Candle that illuminates the heart, without Your face that is
heart's remedy, my heart like roast meat, on fire to bleed
is.

If Hafez is a lover or a drunkard or a glancer, does it matter?
In time of youth for many strange occupations, the need
is.

49. ILLEGAL WINE AND FORGED COIN

Now that the palm of the rose the cup of the pure wine raises,
the nightingale with a hundred thousand songs sings its praises.
Ask for the book of songs and take the way out into the desert;
is this a time for college and 'Explaining of Explainer's' phrases?
Cut off attachments to the people and learn from the Pure Bird;
from Pole to Pole news of those sitting in quiet solitude blazes.
Intoxicated Head of College made this announcement yesterday:
"Wine's illegal: far worse, living off what's given to charities, is."
It's not your choice whether it is dregs or pure: drink, be happy,
for whatever flows from our Winebringer, the essence of grace is.
The story of the rival and the fantasies of all of the pretenders,
remind me of mat-weavers believing each stitch a gold trace is.
Hafez, keep silence and keep these subtleties like pure red gold;
because the city's forger of false coin, also banker of today is.

50. BETWEEN HEAVEN AND HELL

If You should gracefully call us, then given to us Your grace
is;
if You sternly dismiss us, in our heart of complaint no trace
is.
To describe You in a book is beyond the limits of possibility:
for description of You, beyond description of time and place
is.
One can see the face of our Beloved only with the eye of love:
because from Pole to Pole the radiance of the Beloved's face
is.
Read a verse of love from the page of the face of the Heartowner:
for that, the explanation of 'Explaining of Explainer's' base,
is.

O stony hearted Beloved, You are as unbending as the cypress:
what fountains flow to every direction from where our face
is!
O You: with no equal, to Whom Paradise's wealth is worthless;
because of this, between both heaven and hell my soul's place
is.
The enemy, who desires to be as eloquent in versifying as Hafez,
a tale of a swallow's low flight and the Bird of Infinite Space,
is.

51. THE LOVER'S NEED

To he who has chosen solitude, of the world's terrain
what need is?
One who has the Beloved's street, of desert and plain
what need is?
O Soul, by need of The Almighty of Whom You have knowledge,
I ask You for a moment to question: "For our pain,
what need is?"
Our need is the master of us and it has not a tongue to question:
in presence of the Merciful One, to ask and complain
what need is?
If You do intend to take our life there is no need for You to pretend:
to plunder when Yours is the whole of life's domain,
what need is?
The luminous mind of the Friend is the cup that shows the world:
then for me to reveal my need, I'll say once again...
what need is?
That time passed when I did bear the burden of the Sailor's favour:
but now that the Pearl has appeared, of ocean's strain
what need is?
When the lip of the Beloved that gives life has knowledge of you;
O lover, a beggar; to plead and beg like one insane,
what need is?
Monarch of beauty, I am burning; for the sake of God Almighty,
at least we beg of You to ask: "For the beggar's pain,
what need is?"

O pretender, go away: I have nothing that is in common with you!
When friends are present, of enemies who are inane
what need is?
Hafez, make an end to this poem, for what has worth shows itself
to argue and disagree with the pretender's dull brain,
what need is?

52. THE PATH OF A CONTENTED HEART

The garden's courtyard gives joy and friends' company
is pleasant;
rose's time is pleasant, so drinkers of wine's festivity
is pleasant.
By morning breeze our soul is pleasantly perfumed each moment;
yes, perfume of the spirit having true desire, truthfully
is pleasant.
See, the rose with the veil not lifted, gets ready for the departure:
nightingale, moan, for heartsick lovers' sorrowful plea
is pleasant.
To the bird that sings at night comes good news that to the Friend,
to be in Love's path, awake nightly, crying constantly
is pleasant.
From the tongue of the free lily to my ear came these special words:
"In closed world of ours, a work of those burden-free,
is pleasant."
There is no contentment for the heart in the market of the world;
if there is, the way of drunkenness and of vagrancy
is pleasant.
Hafez, path of a contented heart is in renouncement of the world,
if you don't keep thinking a world-possessor's security
is pleasant.

53. FASCINATION

Lord, that bright candle lights the night of whose dwelling?
Our soul burns while asking this: "That is whose darling?"
That one overturns my heart and my faith and my religion:
that's whose bedmate, I want to know, with whom is living?
May that lip of ruby wine be not far away from my lip!
It's wine of whose soul, giver of whose cup for drinking?
Every one devises a spell for that one; but it is not known
which way the tender heart goes; to whose magic-making?
That undrunk ruby wine, has made me so drunk and mad;
it's whose companion and cup: with whom is it associating?
O Lord, one so regal, face like the moon, forehead of Venus,
is whose peerless pearl and whose jewel beyond comparing?
Ask the destiny of companionship of that candle of delight;
before God ask: "That candle for which moth is burning?"
I said this: "The insane heart of Hafez burns without you!"
Hiding a smile: "For whom is he mad?" was the replying.

54. REASON

Because to show ability proudly before the Beloved disrespectful
is,
tongue should be silent, even if mouth, of Arabia's eloquence full
is.
Face of the Angel was hidden, and the demon gave exciting glances;
Reason, consumed by amazement, said: "This, more wonderful
is."
Don't ask the reason why the sphere became helper of the worthless;
because it gives without giving a reason and unreasonably helpful
is.
Faithful Hasan from Basra, Bilal Abyssinia, Suhaib from Syria,
unfaithful Abu Jahal from Mecca's dust: this strange and fateful
is.
In this world's field no one plucked rose without feeling the thorn;
even lamp of Mohammed, with Abu Lahab's flame that's lustful,
is.

I wouldn't buy the arch of the monastery or hotel for half a barley:
Winehouse is my palace; my pavilion, foot of Winejar that is full,
is.
The light of our eye that is the beauty of the daughter of the grape;
perhaps in the veil of glass and screen of grape, having an eyeful
is.
Look for remedy for your suffering in that ruby giver of gladness,
which in the crystal flagon and glass of Aleppo, a good mouthful
is.
Sir, I had a thousand reasonable explanations and as many manners:
now I'm drunk and ruined, only my lack of manners disrespectful
is.
Bring wine; for Hafez, always weeping and wailing in the morning,
begging at midnight, and continually asking God to be merciful,
is.

55. THE CHOICE

More pleasant than enjoying the garden and the Spring,
is what?
Where is Winebringer to ask this: "The cause of waiting,
is what?"
Every moment of happiness that comes your way, take as a gift:
no one is ever delayed, the end of all things be knowing
is what.
The bond of life is tied by only a single hair, so be intelligent:
take care of your own grief, for care of time's grieving
is what?
The meaning of the 'Water of Life' and of the 'Garden of Iram',
except for bank of the stream and wine pleasant tasting,
is what?
The sober one and the intoxicated one are both from one family:
to whose glance shall we give our heart, our choosing
is what?
What does the silent sky know of the secret within the screen?
Philosopher, to argue about who the screen is holding,
is what?

If God didn't make allowance for the slave's ignorance and error,
meaning of the Almighty's Grace and of this pardoning
is what?
Sober one desires wine of Paradise's Kauther and Hafez the cup:
now between these, that which the Almighty's preferring,
is what?

56. MOUNTAIN OF GRIEF

My moon left the city this week and to my eye it a year
is:
do you know separation, how difficult it is and what fear
is?
My eye saw its reflection in that cheek because of its grace;
it imagined that it, a musky mole on that cheek so clear,
is.
From that lip that's full of sugar, fresh milk keeps dripping;
although when it is giving glances, every eyelash a killer
is.
Although You are pointed out in the city as being generous,
it is a wonder how great Your negligence to the stranger
is.
Now I don't doubt the existence of the incomparable jewel;
for that which is on the point of Your mouth, the prover
is.
They gave me the happy message that You will pass by us:
don't change mind; it, an omen that couldn't be happier,
is.
How does separation's mountain of grief call for support of
Hafez's broken body, that from weeping, thin like a spear
is.

57. CONCEAL THE WINECUP

Though wine gives delight and breeze full of rose's scent

is,

do not drink wine to tune of harp for the censor apparent

is.

If a flagon and a companion be handed to you, drink carefully:

because it is a particular time, that full of dangerous intent

is.

Conceal the winecup in the sleeve of the old ragged garment;

for like flagon's eye shedding blood, this time a malcontent

is.

The cloak of religion we wash clean of winestains with our tears:

for the period of abstinence and to be with austerity content;

is.

The high blue vault of the sky, the sieve that splatters blood,

shedder of Kisra's head, sender of where Parviz's crown went

is?

Don't look for delight from the turning of that inverted bowl;

mixed with dregs of that vat, all purity that the flagon spent

is.

Hafez, with your sweet verse you have captured Irak and Fars:

come, for now the turn of Baghdad and also Tabriz's moment

is.

59. WHETHER SOBER OR DRUNK

O pious fanatic, so pure inside, do not criticize the lover of wine:

the sins of others They will not against you in the Records sign.

Whether I'm good or bad, you go away and take care of yourself:

in the end, what one reaps with what one sows, always combine.

Don't make me hopeless of promise of Mercy from Eternal Grace:

how do you know behind the screen who is saint or who is swine?

Whether they may be sober or drunk, all are seeking the Beloved:

whether it be a mosque or a church... every place is love's shrine.

I'm not the only one who has fallen out from the place of purity:

my father Adam also let his hand fall from the Eden of the Divine.
My head is laid in submission to the brick at the Winehouse's door:
critic, if this you do not understand, your head and brick combine.
The garden of Paradise is pleasant: but be extremely careful of this,
that you count as great gain, willow's shade and field's borderline.
Don't rely on your creations; on the day of beginningless Eternity,
do you know what the pen of the Creator to your name did assign?
If all this is in your disposition then excellent is your disposition!
If all this is in your nature then you have a nature that's truly fine!
O Hafez, if on the day of death in your hand you are holding a cup,
you, They will then from Winehouse's street to Paradise consign.

60. PARADISE

Now the rose breathes the breeze of the garden of Paradise,
together am I and wine of Joy, Beloved with Heavenly eyes.
Today, why shouldn't the beggar be boasting of a kingdom:
the feasting table is breadth of creation, roof is milky skies.
Maker of Life explains with Spring the only truthful story:
He who ignores today's beautiful glory, is tomorrow unwise.
With the Wine of Love fill the heart beyond overflowing:
for this rotten world is nothing but dust... everything dies.
This enemy is unfaithful: so don't try to get even a spark
from the hermit's candle, lit by lamp of a church that dies.
Don't criticize me for mistakes I've made due to ignorance:
do you know the pathways carved on my skull by the tides?
Don't you walk away from this graveside of Hafez, because,
although buried in mistakes... he is travelling to Paradise.

61. PURE WINE

O fanatic, never invite me to Paradise, and go far away;
God made me not of Paradise's people on that First Day.
Yours is the rosary and prayermat, austerity and chastity,
convent bell, prayercell; the Master's pure wine's my way.

Sinless Sufi, do not forbid me a drink; for the All Wise,
in Eternity, with pure wine mixed and kneaded our clay.
A true Sufi is not fit for Paradise if he has not like me,
given his coat of religion in Winehouse for wine, to pay.
Lips of Huris and pleasures of Paradise, don't please one
who let from his hand the garment of Beloved slip away.
One cannot reap one grain from the harvest of existence,
unless on illusion's path, seed is sown in God's highway.
Hafez, so that God's grace and generosity are given you,
give up Hell's troubles and Paradise; give them all away.

62. AUTUMN WIND

O fragrant breeze of morning, Beloved's place for resting
is where?
That Moon that takes lovers' lives, that Sorcerer's dwelling
is where?
The night is dark and in front is Wadi Aiman, the Valley of Safety:
where is fire of Sinai, and the promised place for seeing...
is where?
Whoever comes into this world is bearing the mark of a ruinous end:
you should go and ask in Winehouse: "One, not drinking,
is where?"
The bringer of happy news knows the sign: there are many subtleties,
but such a One Who understands the Mystery's meaning,
is where?
Every tip of each hair of mine has been tied to You for a reason;
but where are we, and the critic who is beyond reasoning...
is where?
The lover burned from pain of grief of being separated from You...
but You don't ask Yourself: "Lover who grief is suffering,
is where?"
Reason has given way to madness: where is that musky long hair?
Heart left us for the corner: Your eyebrow, heart-owning:
is where?

They are all ready: the cup and the Minstrel and rose, all are ready.
Bliss without Beloved is impossible: Beloved Who's willing,
is where?
My heart is sick and tired of the cell and the mosque of the shaikh...
where's the young Christian; house of Master, wine-making,
is where?
Hafez, don't grieve about Autumn wind blowing through the world:
if you think about it, the rose without thorn's wounding,
is where?

63. FORTUNE'S BEGINNING

That curve that Your bold eyebrow into Your bow
did throw,
towards my poor old powerless blood, a clever blow
did throw.
When You went into the meadow, sweating and drunk on wine,
Your face's sweat a great fire into the arghavan's glow
did throw.
For that one boastful glance that was thrown by the narcissus;
Your eye, a hundred calamities into the world let go:
did throw.
Because of that shameful one who compared Your face to a lily,
the lily by wind's hand, dust into her mouth, it is so,
did throw.
Last night I strolled by the meadow's feasting-place, intoxicated:
when rosebud into mind, idea of Your mouth's glow,
did throw.
The violet fastened up her curls that were knotted and twisted:
breeze, for all ears, story of Your hair's graceful flow,
did throw.
Out of austerity, I should never have looked at wine or minstrel;
now me to both, desire for all who to Winehouse go,
did throw.
Now I wash my cloak of religion with water of the ruby wine:
from off one's self, Eternity's lot, one never, I know,
did throw.

The two worlds were not existing when Love was in operation:
foundation of Love, Time down not some time ago,
did throw.
Line of Your face makes me the disaster I am: Glory be to God!
What pen was it that out, such a heart-stealing show,
did throw?
The world now turns to my desire; because the turnings of time,
let me into the Lord and Master's service finally go,
did throw!
Maybe the beginning of Hafez's fortune is in this disastrous state:
he into Winesellers wine, what Eternal Fate did throw,
did throw.

64. OPEN KNOWLEDGE

Every true wayfarer of the Winehouse's street, the way
knew;
and the knocking on another door, as a ruinous delay
knew.
Whoever has found a path to the threshold of the Winehouse,
the corridor's mysteries from winecup's generous spray
knew.
Time gave the crown of drunkenness to no one except that one,
who the great cup that contains the world to survey...
knew.
Don't look for anything from us except the love of a madman,
for being sane was sin that the Chief of our faith's way
knew.
Whoever reads Secret of both worlds from Winebringer's line,
secrets of Jam's cup and what road's dust does portray,
knew.
My heart didn't desire a safe life from Winebringer's dark eye:
way of the heart of that bold dark One, my heart I'd say
knew.
From oppression of my star of birth, my eye at each morning
is weeping so much the moon saw, and Venus far away
knew.

King of Glorious Majesty's the One, Who the sky's nine vaults,
as architecture of the archway of His Court's display,
knew.
The tale of the case of Hafez and cup he is secretly drinking,
not only police and censor, but the King Who all obey,
knew.

65. FIRE OF LOVE

From fire in my heart my chest from grief for Beloved fair,
burnt up;
such fire is in this room that the whole house everywhere
burnt up.
Because of separation from Heartstealer my body melted away;
in fire of Love my soul for Beloved's cheek, in its flare,
burnt up.
Whoever has seen chain of the curls' tip of one of Paradise-face...
his distraught heart, like distraught me full of despair,
burnt up.
See my heart, it's burning from the fire of my tears: candle's heart
last night in Love's desire like me, like the moth there,
burnt up.
Indeed, it isn't so strange that hearts of friends are on fire for me;
since I've been beside myself strangers hearts everywhere
burnt up.
Flood of the Winehouse took my religious cloak of pious austerity;
my house of reason also, the Winehouse cellar's red flare
burnt up.
The cup of my heart is broken because of the repentance I've made;
my liver, a flagon without wine and Winehouse, in fever
burnt up.
Enough of the past's talk, come back and witness; for my own eye
pulled off my head religion's cloak and it with a prayer,
burnt up.
Hafez, give up small talk, drink wine for awhile... for small talk
robs us of sleep and life passes us by, as the candle in air
burnt up.

66. THE HIDDEN SECRET

From the wine's sparkle the hidden secret the wise may
know;
the essence of each one's soul by means of this ruby, they
know.
Only the bird of the morning knows the value of the rosebud;
not all who read a page, the meaning it does convey,
know.
To my overworked heart, I offered this and that other world;
except for love for You, it did the rest as passing away,
know.
Stone and clay are made into ruby and precious stone by those
who value of merciful breeze's breath from Yemen's way
know.
That time has passed when I thought of what the people said;
ever since, my secret pleasure, men of Reason they say
know.
You who would learn Love's poetry from the book of Reason!
I am afraid that rare subtlety, you'll not by mind's way
know.
Heartstealer did not believe our ease was the business of time,
that one did surely, by our waiting heart, sick by delay,
know.
This pearl-strung poem, that from his soul Hafez has created,
comes for he does the guiding care of Master of the Day
know.

67. THE DISASTER OF LOVE

By alliance with grace, the world was by Your beauty
taken;
yes, by uniting in agreement, this world can still be
taken.
The candle wanted to divulge mystery of those in seclusion;
thank God that its tongue has by heart's fire, mystery
taken.

The rose wanted to claim colour and fragrance of the Friend;
its breath in its mouth has the breeze full of jealousy
taken.
From out of this hidden fire that is lying within my chest,
the sun in the sky is only a spark that's momentarily
taken.
I rested on the edge, apart, like on the circle of a compass;
Time's spiral into the central point, has me, finally,
taken.
Desire for the cup of wine burnt my harvest that day when
from image of Winebringer's cheek, fire had quickly
taken.
I wish to go to the street of the Masters, shaking my sleeve
of all the disasters that to Time's skirt will be finally
taken.
Drink wine; for whoever has seen how the world's work ends,
comes through grief lightly: full winecup justifiably
taken.
They have written with blood of tulip on petal of the rose:
"Such a one has red wine like the arghavan, maturely
taken."
Give wine in cup of gold, for dawn cup of morning drinkers
has like king with a golden sword, the world forcibly
taken.
Use every opportunity; for when disaster fell on the world
Hafez took to the cup: from grief to corner's security,
taken.
Hafez, since like water, grace is trickling from your poetry,
flow can exception to it by envious ones, be possibly
taken.

68. BEYOND THE VEIL

Winebringer come, for away the Beloved the veil
took;
the lamp to light, of those in seclusion so pale,
took.

The candle lifted its head again and enflamed its face;
this Master old in years, youth from mind's tale
took.
Beloved glanced in such a way that piety left the path;
Friend was so kind that cautious enemy to trail
took.
Safe shelter from such a sweet heart-stealing Speaker!
You may say: "Your mouth, speech sugar's tale
took."
To the great burden of grief that had broken our heart,
God sent a One of Jesus-breath, and our travail
took.
Each cypress-form boasting beauty over sun and moon,
when You came, pursuit of work of another detail
took.
The seven vaults of heaven are all shouting this story;
ashamed be short-sighted one, who short this tale
took.
Hafez, where did you learn this magic; that Beloved,
to turn it into amulet of gold, your verse's wail
took?

69. THE NIGHTINGALE'S LAMENT

A nightingale in beak, roseleaf of a colour that was pleasant
held,
and over that leaf that was sweet, forth a bittersweet lament
held.
I said: "At this time of union's joy why do you make complaint?"
Reply was this: "Me, the Beloved's beauty in this torment
held."
If the Beloved doesn't sit with us beggars, no reason to complain;
such wealthy Monarch rightly at length the poor mendicant
held.
If it is the path of Love that you follow, forget about reputation;
Master Sanaan pawned coat in Winehouse for what intoxicant
held.

Happy became that gentle Kalandar, who though in wanderings
was girdled by infidelity, still his prayers to the Omnipotent
held.
All our prayers and pleadings have no effect on Friend so beautiful;
happy is that one who from that Beloved, fortune's consent
held.
So now stand up, and scatter our soul on the brush of The Painter,
Who painted this wonderful picture the revolving firmament
held.
Beneath the palace's roof of that One with the nature of the Huri,
Hafez's flowing eye, Paradise's underground stream's current
held.

70. BROKEN PROMISE

You saw, except for cruelty, that one so fair
didn't have:
that one broke promise, pity for our despair
didn't have.
Lord, don't take that one; although the dove of my heart
was killed by one who respect for its Snare
didn't have.
Fate did me this heavy injustice; otherwise, the Beloved
showed the ways of kindness: another share
didn't have.
Everyone who has not endured contempt from such a one,
wherever he went, respect for him, all there
didn't have.
Winebringer, bring some wine; say to the 'man of morals':
"Don't stop us, such a cup Jamshid, I swear,
didn't have."
Wayfarers who didn't trek to Your Holy Doorway's Home,
sadly crossed desert; entrance to That Mecca
didn't have.
Happy time is given to drunkard who gives both worlds
from the hand; and any sorrow whatsoever,
didn't have.

Hafez, you take prize for poetry's craft: who claimed it
had no worth, knowledge about this affair
didn't have.

71. NO LAUGHING MATTER

Without the sun of Your cheek, my day bright
doesn't stay;
and any part of my life except the black night,
doesn't stay.
At the time of farewell to You, because Your face is distant,
my eye is weeping so much that in it any light
doesn't stay.
From my eye Your image went, and departing said to me this:
"It is a pity this corner's inhabitant of delight,
doesn't stay."
The moment is fast approaching when the spy, be he far away,
shall say: "That one left alone and not alright
doesn't stay."
What's the value after this if the Beloved troubled to see me:
for in my spent body, spark of life that's slight,
doesn't stay.
In being separated from You, if no water remains in my eye,
say: "Spill heart's blood, anything else is trite:
doesn't stay."
Medicine for my separation from You is to take being patient:
but can one take patience when strength to fight
doesn't stay?
Because of weeping and grieving, Hafez is no longer laughing;
for the feast, those who are sorrowful's appetite
doesn't stay.

72. BE KIND TO MY HEART

From weeping, pupil of my eye in blood is drowning;
see how all seekers sigh for You: it is so alarming!

Remembering Your ruby lip and wine-red drunken eye,
from grief's cup, ruby wine heart's blood is drinking.
If from the eastern district Your sunny aspect rises,
the aspect of my lucky star, fortune is welcoming.
The story of Shirin's sweet lip is the talk of Farhad,
twist of Layla's curls is Majnun's heart's homecoming.
Be kind to my heart that seeks Your cypress form,
speak to me: Your words are delightful, like singing.
Winebringer, with the circulating cup ease my soul:
from gravity of sky's revolutions the heart is grieving.
Ever since that enchanting One became out of reach,
from tears my garment is like river Jihun: soaking.
How can my sorrowful heart become happy again,
when its will is not allowed by the Power existing?
Hafez distraught, beside himself, seeks the Beloved;
as one poverty-stricken who Karun's gold is seeking.

73. THE HEART'S PURPOSE

Pupil of our eye is interested only in looking at Your face again;
that purpose of our overturning heart is to remember You, is plain.
My tearful eye wears pilgrim's clothes to circle Your inner temple;
but unlike my wounded heart's pure blood, it is impure, a stain.
Don't blame the bankrupt lover, if he doesn't own the latest coin,
if what he throws at Your feet is a heart of lead, don't complain.
His hand and his hand alone reaches that high cypress in the end,
whose spirit is so fine and whose search to the end does remain.
I will not converse with You about the life-giving breath of Jesus;
for I'm not the expert, He is, and Your Soulful lip is, for certain.
I am one, who though passionately on fire for You, does not sigh;
can anyone say I've an impatient heart that by Time has a stain?
May Bird of Paradise Tree be locked tight in a large cage like
the wild flying geese, if he from searching for You does abstain.
I said on that First Day, when I first saw Your mysterious curls:
"There is no end to their entwining that all the hearts enchain."
Longing to be united with You alone, Hafez's heart is not alone;
where's a heart still alive, whose desire is not the same for certain.

74. LOVE EVERY MOMENT

The Ocean of Love is a sea where a shore
is not;
without soul's surrender, remedy in store
is not.
Bring wine; don't frighten us with Reason's laws;
in this place, that Judge's punishable law
is not.
Every moment you give to Love becomes happy;
in good deeds, need of help from counselor
is not.
You ask Your own eye who has murdered us…
O Soul, blame on stars or on Fate's door
is not.
Your face like crescent moon only pure eyes see:
for all eyes, the new moon's splendour,
is not.
So take up the goods of the drunkard's highway;
this treasure, mapped out for all to score
is not.
In no way whatsoever do Hafez's tears move You;
I am amazed Your heart a hard stone core
is not.

75. FESTIVAL DAY

Winebringer, fortunate Festival day be
for You;
may promise You made, stay in memory
for You.
Let the daughter of vine be there, say: "Come out;"
our resolute breath set heart's chains free
for You.
I'm amazed that for so many days of separation,
You kept heart from friends, amazingly
for You!

Thank God Autumn wind didn't harm the garden
of jasmine and cypress, rose and box tree
for You.
May the evil eye be far from You; the separation
has returned natal fortune's star; lucky
for You!
Your glad footstep's arrival is joy of the gathering,
grief be in hearts that don't beat joyfully
for You.
Hafez, don't let this Ark of Noah slip your hand,
or your foundation, deluge ends quickly
for you.

76. GRIEF OF SEPARATION

I heard a saying that by the old man of Canaan they say
is said:
"Grief of separation from the Friend is such, it in no way
is said."
The tales of terror that the preachers tell about Judgment Day,
are only a hint of all the suffering when good-bye's day
is said.
Who can I ask where the Friend has gone, because all of the news
delivered by messenger the east breeze, in a confused way
is said.
"With wine that is very old, stopping heart's grief that is very old,
is seed of Joy's harvest," by the Winemaker old and grey
is said.
"Don't trust in knots the wind blows, even if it comes your way;"
this wise old saying, to Solomon by way of wind's way
is said.
For the ridiculous excuses the sky offers do not leave the Path:
who said this hag stopped telling tales; it by whom, say,
is said?
Come and drink the wine, because from the wise old Winemaker,
a story of Forgiveness by Merciful God to who disobey,
is said.

Don't ask 'how and why'; the happy slave accepts with the soul
each word said by this Monarch and never 'yea' or 'nay'
is said.
If anyone said that from thinking about You Hafez has returned,
don't believe it; for whoever said it, I didn't: a lie I say,
is said.

77. THE ANSWER OF THE ROSE

Bird of the garden said to opening rose at dawn of day:
"Less pride, in the garden many like you bloomed away."
The rose laughed this answer: "We are not hurt by truth,
but, harsh words to loved one, a lover would never say."
Should you desire the ruby wine from that jeweled cup,
many pearls pierced by point of your eyelash is the way.
For an eternity Love's perfume is never known to a one
whose head hasn't swept the Winehouse threshold's clay.
Last night in Iram's garden, in such soft and tender air,
as breeze stirred hyacinth's long locks at break of day,
I asked: "Throne of Jamshid, where's the revealing cup?"
The reply: "Sorry, that waking fortune has slept away."
Love's words are not those which come to the tongue;
Winebringer, give wine, send question and answer away.

78. YOU HAVE RISEN

My heart and faith are gone and the Heartstealer angrily
rises,
saying: "Don't sit with Me, for away from you all safety
rises."
Have you heard of one who sat happily for awhile at this feast,
and at feast's end not without regretting the company,
rises?
If the tongue of the candle boasts about that laughing face,
in payment, in Your lover's presence, it nightly, brightly,
rises.

Breeze of Spring from garden where rose and cypress embrace,
from admiration for Your cheek and form, passionately
rises.
You passed by intoxicated; from where angels are secluded,
commotion of the Resurrection from seeing You, loudly
rises.
The proud high cypress couldn't lift foot from being ashamed
before Your swaying height and form that so gracefully
rises.
Hafez, throw off religion's garment and maybe you'll gain life:
from religion's cloak of hypocritical sorcery, fire certainly
rises.

79. A STRANGE STORY

No one's seen Your face, but crowd of thousand watchers there
is:
though You're still in the bud, a nightingale for You everywhere,
is.
It is not really very surprising if to Your street I have come, at last;
because in this country, like me, many, O very many a stranger
is.
Though I'm far away from You, may no one be far away from You:
the hope that I always have here, of Union with You, forever,
is.
In Love there's no difference between the monastery and tavern:
wherever they may be situated, light of Beloved's face, there
is.
Wherever they are doing the work of the place where they worship,
the bell of the Christian monk with Name of the Cross, I swear i
s.
Where's one becoming a lover whose condition Beloved didn't see?
Sir, there is no pain and if there is, then Physician there to care
is.
When all's said and done, this crying of Hafez was not for nothing:
his story is a very strange one and his tale a tale of great wonder
is.

80. THE CAGE OF DESIRE

In the cage of Your curls my heart has caught
itself:
come and kill with one glance; this, it brought
itself.
If Your hand should bestow upon our heart its desire,
be ready at hand; for this kindness has taught
itself.
Sweet Idol, I swear by Your soul that in dark nights,
my desire is like that of the candle: to naught
itself.
Nightingale, when first you thought about love, I said:
"Don't, because that rose has only ever sought
itself."
Scent of the rose doesn't need China or India's musk,
for its pods of musk inside its own coat, caught
itself.
Don't go to the house of ungenerous ones of this time:
your own home's corner of contentment bought
itself.
Hafez burned away in the law of love and of surrender:
yet to the peak of loyalty, his soul has brought
itself.

81. MY DESIRE

To tell to You the condition of my heart
is my desire:
to know news that Your heart may impart
is my desire.
Notice the desire so fundamental: the tale well known;
to conceal from the watchers spying art,
is my desire.

A 'Night of Power' such as this that is precious and holy,
being with You until day sees night depart
is my desire.
O no, that pearl that is unique, that is tender and lovely,
in the dark night to pierce, know every part,
is my desire.
O breeze of the East give some help to me in this night,
for to blossom when morning does start,
is my desire.
For the sake of praising, to sweep the dust of the Path
with point from where my eyelashes dart,
is my desire.
Like Hafez, without regard for those who are censors,
verse beyond reason, loving, to impart,
is my desire.

82. THE INVISIBLE MESSENGER

O lapwing of the east wind, to Saba is where
I send you;
see how far it is and from here to over there
I send you.
It's a pity that a bird like you is in this dustpit of grief:
so to the nest where faithfulness fills the air,
I send you.
Say: "In Love's Path there's no such thing as near or far:
it's clear that I can clearly see You, my prayer
I send You:
Each morning and each evening caravans of good wishes,
in company of north wind, in east wind's care
I send You.
O my heart's conspirator, You are hidden from sight…
I whisper prayers to You, praises everywhere
I send You.
So that armies of grief don't devastate heart's domain,
my life and soul for ransom, in Your care,
I send You.

So that You'll hear from minstrels the tale of my desire,
words and *ghazals* set to melody with a flair,
I send You."
Winebringer, come; the Invisible Messenger brings joy:
"Bear pain patiently: remedy beyond compare
I send you.
Enjoy the creation of God reflected in your own face…
because that which displays God, as mirror,
I send you.
Hafez, in Our assembly the song We sing praises you:
hurry… for a horse to ride and coat to wear
I send you."

83. BROUGHT TO COMPLETION

O You, Who have left my sight, to God I am entrusting
You;
You burnt my soul… yet in my heart I am still holding
You.
As long as the hem of my shroud doesn't trail under the dust,
don't think I'll withdraw my hand from what's covering
You.
Show the altar of Your eyebrows so that in the morning I'll
raise hand in prayer and place it on the neck befitting
You.
And if it's necessary for me to go to visit Harut of Babylon,
I will learn acts of sorcery, which I'll use to be winning
You.
Through Your grace let me come to You; with heart on fire
I may then rain pearls from my eyes at the feet holding
You.
Over my chest I made a hundred streams flow from my eyes,
hoping I may sow love's seed in the heart of a resisting
You.
You spilled my blood and freed me from separation's grief
for Your glance that's like a dagger, thanks I'm offering
You.

Faithless Physician, my desire is that I should die before You:
ask about this sick one, for I'm still waiting, expecting
You.
And if my eye and my heart should show desire for another,
I'll set fire to that heart and pluck out eye for forsaking
You.
Hafez, wine, women, and drunken loving are not in Your line:
since you've brought this to completion, I'm pardoning
you.

84. TO THE RESURRECTION'S DAYS

Lord, cause my Beloved to return safely to this my place,
allow me to leave the clutches of this old trap's disgrace.
Bring the dust of the path that Beloved has travelled upon,
I'll make my eye that sees the world, its dwelling place.
O no, They have barricaded my path on all the six sides
by that mole and down and hair, cheek, form and face.
Today, while I am in Your hand, show me a little mercy:
tomorrow when I'm clay, will tears of repentance replace?
You who use your breath in words to talk and explain love,
I've no words for you but: "Peace to you, fortune's grace."
Dervish, don't be grieved under the sword of such friends,
for this type pay price of blood for those who they efface.
Set fire to religion's cloak: curve of Winebringer's eyebrow
shatters niche of prayer where the clergy loudly displays.
God forbid that I should complain about all Your violence;
the injustice of the fair is all kindness, all mercy and grace.
Hafez cannot cut short the praising of Your long hair's tip:
this chain of praise stretches out to the Resurrection's days.

85. IN THIS DARK NIGHT

Because of heart-soothing Friend I'm thankful, complaining as well;
if you understand love's subtleties, listen well to the tale that I tell.
Without reward and without any thanks was the service that I gave;
O Lord, don't allow lack of gratitude, in Whom we serve, to dwell.

To drunkards, mouths so thirsty, no one gives even a drop of water;
it's like: "Those recognizing the true lovers, told this place farewell."
O heart, beware, don't twist in the chains of that long flowing hair;
there you can see heads severed for no crime, of lovers uncountable.
The glance of your eye drinks our blood, and You also approve of it;
O Soul, it's not legal to condone one, through whom much blood fell.
In this dark night, the way and purpose of my destiny became lost;
come out O guiding Star, shine from the corner of that secret cell!
In every direction wherever I went there was nothing but more fear;
O beware of this great desert, for it is only an endless path as well.
of this path that is without an end, no end could ever be imagined,
for even in its very beginning a hundred thousand stages do dwell.
O Sun of all the lovely ones my heart is boiling and burning away;
for a moment's breath let me in the shade of Your protection dwell.
Although you have stolen my honour, Your door I'll never forsake;
Friend's violence, much more than enemies' favours, is acceptable.
Love will hear your heart cry out and will come to you, if like Hafez
your heart knows the *Koran* completely, in fourteen versions as well.

86. STILL INTOXICATED

I'm still intoxicated by the wisp of air of the fragrant hair
of Yours;
each moment I'm ruined by sorcery of deceitful eye's stare
of Yours.
O Lord, after such patience, I wonder if we will see a night in which
we will light our eye's candle in the eyebrows arch of prayer
of Yours.
The blackboard of the vision of the eye I hold to be sacred to the soul,
for it contains a likeness of what that dark mole does wear,
of Yours.
If You have the wish to perpetually beautify the world completely...
tell the breeze to momentarily lift the veil off face, so fair,
of Yours.
If You wish to efface from the world its way of coming and going:
shake Your head so thousands of souls fall from every hair
of Yours.

I have the kindness of the breeze to thank for the perfume of Beloved;
if not, here in the morning would I receive the slightest care
of Yours?
I always thought that the eye's black centre sought my heart's blood:
now it is sacred for it reminds me of the dark mole's snare
of Yours.
Praise be to Hafez's excellent spirit: for of this world and of the next,
nothing comes in his eye but dust of end of thoroughfare...
of Yours.

87. COMMOTION IN THE WINEHOUSE

Thanks be to God that the Winehouse door now open wide
is,
so that forever upon that door the face of my need applied
is.
The winejars are in a commotion, shouting from intoxication;
the term for the wine is 'The Truth' and it not misapplied
is.
Coming from Beloved is intoxication, commotion and pride;
coming from us, all helplessness, begging and lack of pride
is.
The secret that I haven't told the masses and will never tell,
I will tell to the Friend, Who of the secret never mystified
is.
Twist of hair, curl within curl, has an explanation which can
never be shortened; for this a tale that long from any side
is.
The burden of poor Majnun's heart is the curl of Layla's hair;
the cheek of Mahmud to the sole of the foot of Ayaz tied
is.
I've stitched up my eye like the falcon's eye from the world;
because upon Your adorable cheek, my eye now occupied
is.
Whoever happens to enter Your street also enters its House
through Your eyebrows arch, and with prayer preoccupied
is.

O companions, ask about the fire that's in poor Hafez's heart
from the candle, that by much burning, completely liquefied
is.

88. NOTHING

Value of the output of world's workshop is worthless:
is nothing;
bring wine, because this whole world and its business
is nothing.
Both heart and soul are desiring the Beloved's blessed presence;
that, is everything, and without that, life and happiness
is nothing.
Good fortune comes to the heart, without heart's blood and pain:
worth of Paradise's garden gained by blood and stress,
s nothing.
Do not look for shade beneath the tree of life or beneath the lotus,
for when you understand high and low, it O cypress…
is nothing.
Only five short favourable days you've been given in life's caravan;
rest peacefully awhile, for time and all it does express,
is nothing.
O Winebringer, we are waiting on the shore of the ocean of death;
use opportunity, wine from lip to mouth, more or less,
is nothing.
Don't worry about being hurt by what they say, be the happy rose,
for it is obvious that a passing world's powerfulness
is nothing.
O fanatic, be very careful, and do not be so enthusiastically right,
for the distance from cell to the Master's abode, I stress
is nothing.
I have been worn away to nothing from great grief and suffering;
there's no need to tell, for the need for one to confess:
is nothing.
Hafez is a name that has seal of approval, for it has been accepted;
but in drunkard's opinion, to have more or to have less:
is nothing.

89. A LETTER

What kindness it was when suddenly the ink-drops from Your quill,
  have recalled dues of our service according to Your gracious will.
You have written some greetings to me with the nib of Your pen;
  may the workshop of Time never be without Your writing to fill.
I don't say that it's a mistake that You remembered heartsick me:
  wisdom understands that there is no mistake in Your quill's skill.
Do not allow me to be despised, for I am so thankful that Fortune
  that is constant and favourable, is holding You as honourable still.
Come, because with the tip of Your hair I will make this promise:
  that if my head is leaving, never be lifting it from Your feet I will.
Your heart will only become aware of our condition at that time
  when the tulip blooms from dust of whom grief for You did kill.
The breeze of the morning is still telling the story to all the roses:
  how did spy allow an informer entry to Your sacred windowsill?
My heart is the dweller at Your door and I ask You to keep it safe;
  because of the reason that God kept You safe from grief's ill will.
This world's the place of ambush and You travel fast, so be careful:
  don't do this, or upon the king's highway the dust of You will spill.
Breeze of the breath of Jesus the Messiah, may Your days be happy:
  as Hafez's heartbroken soul is alive by what Your breath did instill.

90. THIS LONG DESERT

O Perfect Beloved, who unfastens the knot and then unveils
                    You?
O Bird of Paradise, who gives water and seed and never fails
                    You?
Sleep leaves my eyes and my heart burns when I think about this:
  whose breast is where You sleep, whose home is it that hails
                    You?
You suddenly left my embrace and also left me broken-hearted:
  I wonder, whose place became where sleep and rest entails
                    You?

The bitter cries of complaint that I've made You haven't heard:
O fair One, it is obvious an exalted habitation now avails
You.
You don't ask about the poor dervish and I'm so frightened that
there is not forgiveness or justice for whom You think fails
You.
O Palace that kindles the heart, that is the dwelling of my Love,
O Lord don't let happen that Time's ruinous calamity assails
You.
In this long desert the pool of water is far away in the distance:
beware, so desert ghoul's mirage, never deceitfully curtails
you.
That arrow of Your glance that You let fly at my heart, missed:
I wonder what device we will now see from what prevails
You.
O heart, how will you find your way in the pathway of old age?
In your youth you quickly wasted in mistakes what entails
you.
That eye, that wineseller, stopped the lover's heart in its path:
obviously that is intoxicating poison a certain One retails:
You!
Hafez is not the kind of slave who would run from his master;
show kindness and come back for I'm flailed by what ails
You.

91. BEYOND CURE

That Turk of an Angel's face, Who from me last night away
went,
what fault was it that One saw, and then towards Cathay
went?
Since that eye that sees all the world did depart from my sight,
tears from my eye, that to none, one can possibly convey,
went.
Last night, no candle sent any smoke out from its heart's fire,
like that which to this head from liver's burning decay
went.

Because I was far from that face, every moment a flood of tears
went from eye's foundation and a great deluge of dismay
went.
We fell from off our feet when the sorrow of separation arrived:
in grief we did stay, when out from the hand remedy's way
went.
The heart said: "One can reunite with that One through prayer.
for a long lifetime, my life as such a one who does pray,
went."
Why should I put on the pilgrim's robe, because Mecca isn't here?
Why make an effort to start running, for Safa from Merveh
went?
When the physician saw me yesterday, out of deep pity he said:
"I'm sorry, but beyond being cured your sickness today
went."
Friend, put down Your foot with intention of asking of Hafez,
before they say this: "He from this frail house of decay
went."

92. NOWHERE

Except for Your threshold, in the world my shelter
is nowhere;
my place of safety, except for this one door, there
is nowhere.
When the enemy draws out the sword we throw away the shield:
except weeping, lamenting and sighing, our rapier
is nowhere.
Why should I turn my face away from the Winehouse's street,
for in the world a better way for my feet, I swear
is nowhere.
If Time should send some fire into the harvest of my life, I say:
"Burn; for not worth a blade of grass, it I declare,
is nowhere."
I'm the slave of the fascinating narcissus eye of that fair form,
whose wine of pride's glance at anyone, anywhere,
is nowhere.

Because I see the many traps of the Path in every direction,
my shelter, except for the safety of Your long hair,
is nowhere.
You do what is desired, but don't go looking to do any injury:
in our Law, except for this, existence of a sinner
is nowhere.
The eagle of violence has drawn out his wing over every city:
body bent-bow of recluse, arrow-sigh of repenter,
is nowhere.
Don't give treasure of the heart of Hafez to each hair and mole;
such a trust to be under each black mole's power,
is nowhere.

93. HOUSE OF SALVATION

Winebringer, bring wine; month of fasting and prayer
has passed,
give the goblet, for the time of worship and honour
has passed.
Precious time has been wasted; let's pay back prayers not given,
before life of separation from goblet and Winebringer
has passed.
For how long upon the fire of repentance can one keep burning?
Give wine, for our over-long life lived in mad despair
has passed.
Come, for You make me so drunk with wine that I forget myself:
who is on plain of imagination, who when and where
has passed?
In the hope that a full winecup from You will be reaching to us,
my prayer at morning and evening for Your welfare
has passed.
To the heart that was dead a new life has reached into the soul,
since scent to place of scent from Your fragrant air
has passed.
The bigot's own conceit could never find the road to salvation;
but the drunkard, to House of Salvation from prayer
has passed.

Bigot, understand that you and seclusion alone need each other;
for to the lover the order to enjoy perpetual pleasure
has passed.
The coin that my heart had mined was all spent upon the wine,
it was a counterfeit coin that to the unlawful there,
has passed.
Don't advise Hafez again; the path of austerity's never been found
by a lost one, in whose throat a wine that is sweeter
has passed.

94. SINCE IN MY HEART

Since in my heart, grief for You a long residence
has taken;
like Your dark hair my heart into dark turbulence
has taken.
Your lip that is like a great fire is the Water of Life because,
that Water of Life us into a fire that's so immense
has taken.
It's a long time since the purest highest expanse of my soul,
to desire for Your shape and height of excellence
has taken.
I have become lover of Your form that is high and gracious,
since to height of splendor this lover's reverence
has taken.
Since we're here in the long shadow of Your great generosity,
why is it that Your shadow from us its influence
has taken?
Today the morning breeze is perfumed with ambergris scent,
perhaps my Beloved the path to desert's providence
has taken.
The ocean of my eyes drop tears that make a chain of jewels;
the world, into centre of pearls unique, immense,
has taken.
O my jasmine-breasted cypress, the poetry of Hafez is similar
to Your form's description the highest immanence
has taken.

95. AT YOUR FEET I DIE

My Monarch, You walk so well, head at Your feet:
I die;
my Turk, You sway sweetly, before You, complete:
I die.
You said: "When will you die before Me?" Why hurry?
You entreat O so sweetly, but before You repeat:
I die.
I'm a lover, drunk, exiled; where is Winebringer's form?
Sway Your fine fair form this way; when I see it…
I die.
Should You, causing lifetime's illness through separation,
enhance me one glance from eye's dark grey seat…
I die.
You said: "My ruby lip dispenses pain and sweet remedy."
Before pain came, and before Your remedy sweet…
I die.
You sweetly sway: may the evil eyes never see Your face.
I find one thought in my mind: that at Your feet,
I die.
Although Hafez's place isn't Your Secret Place of Union,
all Your places please; before Your places replete…
I die.

96. FROM FIRST TO FINAL DAY

For a long time that fire of desire for You is in this soul
of ours,
because of longing that is deep in the heart's desolate hole
of ours.
Pupils of my eyes are drowned in the bleeding water of the liver:
love's fountain for Your face, is in chest's lamenting bowl
of ours.
The Water of Life is but a trickle from that ruby that is like sugar;
that shining Moon's face reflects out the great sun's bowl
of ours.

Since I had heard that: "I blew My soul into him:" in this matter
I'm certain, that we're wholly Yours and You're the whole
of ours.
Love's mysteries are not manifested for every heart to understand:
knower of this spiritual mystery is the Owner of the soul
of ours.
Praiser of God, how long will you make explanation of the Faith?
Be silent; in both worlds, Beloved's company is faith's goal
of ours.
Hafez, until the Final Day give thanks forever for the favour that,
from First Day, Beloved was comforting Guest of the soul
of ours.

97. IN ALL PATHS

In all paths, the image of Your face is Way's Mate:
ours.
I am aware the perfume of Your hair is soul's state:
ours.
To sorrow of foolish intellectuals who argue against love,
fairness of Your face is ready reply to end debate:
ours.
Now listen well to what is said by the apple of Your chin:
"Many Joseph of Egypt fell into pit, bit that bait:
Ours."
Say to the watcher, guarding the door of the Secret Place;
"Those in the corner, one is dust of Court's gate:
Ours.
If like a beggar Hafez knocks at that door then open it;
longing for Moon-face, for years he had to wait.
Ours!"

98. THE FORBIDDEN GRIEF

If a mistake out from Your musky hair has passed,
it's past;
if cruelty from Your mole to our share has passed,
it's past.
If Love's lightning, harvest of wool-wearer burns,
it's burnt;
if King's violence to a beggar's despair has passed,
it's past.
If from Heartowner's glance, heart a burden bore, it's borne;
between the soul and Beloved whatever has passed,
it's past.
Because of slanderers, gossip bearers, reproaches still arise;
if with conspirators, something unfair has passed;
it's past.
In Love's Path, grief of the heart is forbidden: bring wine;
every trouble you see, into happy air has passed:
it's past.
O heart, in the game of Love it's difficult to keep feet firm;
if despair was, it was; and if cruel fear has passed:
it's past.
Don't blame Hafez for leaving cloister, for a free one's foot
can't be bound; and if he to elsewhere has passed:
it's past.

99. DIVINE WISDOM

Every one with insight, who for the heart content
went,
to a corner of Winehouse from the house of intent
went.
To the wayfarer with a half-filled cup, revealed mysteries
of beyond, that became in world of vision evident,
went.

Come, hear Divine Wisdom from my lips; for in my words,
some profitable subtleties that the Holy Spirit sent,
went.
From the star of my birth seek only a lover's drunkenness;
because with the star of my birth, this same intent,
went.
You rose up this morning because of the hand of another;
perhaps last night's wine, that your memory spent,
went.
Maybe the Physician, Jesus-breather, a miracle will work;
as long time, since a visit to me in my predicament,
went.
A thousand thanks that last night from Winehouse corner,
Hafez, to the corner of faith and prayer, obedient,
went.

100. IT'S A PITY

From Your lip of ruby not once have we tasted,
and You have gone:
our sight with Your moonlike face wasn't filled
and You have gone.
One could say that You've become greatly wearied by our company,
for You tied Your load before we had arrived,
and You have gone.
Often the *Koran's* first chapter and 'Charm of Yemen' we quoted;
then the chapter called 'Sincerity' we recited;
and You have gone.
You said: "Don't lift your head from what I've written or I'll leave."
Our head from what You wrote we haven't lifted:
and You have gone.
You gave a glance, saying: "I'll never leave the street of your desire."
In the end you can see how the glance we gained;
and You have gone.
You said: "Who wants Union with Me will renounce his own self;"
wanting Union with You ourself we renounced
and You have gone.

You went, moving proudly, into the meadow of beauty and of grace;
into Your rosegarden of Union we never moved;
and You have gone.
Grace of Your form is the effect of the Creation of God Almighty...
on Your face our glance we never fully effected;
and You have gone.
All night long we were weeping and we were wailing as Hafez does:
it's a pity, to wish you "farewell" wasn't granted;
and You have gone.

101. DEPARTED

O no, Beloved left me in grief, sorrow and pain
and departed;
like smoke upon fire the Beloved made us remain
and departed.
Not a cup of love's wine that gives joy was given to the drunkard,
who every separation You made to taste and drain:
and departed.
When I became Your prey You left me broken and wounded in
grief's sea... and then gave to Your steed its rein
and departed.
I said this: "Perhaps I'll bring You into the trap by practising."
You fled, frightening my steed of fortune again,
and departed.
When the blood of my heart found the straight place in my heart,
it ran rose-red by eye's road to desert's terrain,
and departed.
When the slave was not given the happiness of being of service,
he kissed threshold, caused service to maintain,
and departed.
The rose was secluded in the veil when the bird of the morning
came to the garden of Hafez, did then complain,
and departed.

There is no one who has not fallen victim to Your long dark hair;
who is there whose pathway is without the snare of some disaster?
It is as though Your bright face is the clear mirror of Divine Light:
O God, this is so; and in my mentioning this, no hypocrisy is there.
Fanatic tells me to turn away from Your face: O an excellent face!
He hasn't any shame before God, or before Your face that's so fair.
Candle of the morning, weep for your condition and also for mine:
For it is not hidden that your nightly burning I also openly share.
God's the witness and it's sufficient for me that God is the witness:
for my weeping isn't less than martyrs shedding blood: compare!
Narcissus tries to copy the movement of Your eye: O excellent eye!
But light of its eye hasn't news of its mystery and can only despair.
For God's sake do not make Your hair more beautiful; for no night
is there when we with morning wind, do not battle for Your hair.
Last night You went and I said: "O Fair One, keep Your promise:"
You said: "O kind sir, faith wasn't in this promise, you're in error!"
Since Your eye stole my heart from those sitting in corners secluded:
if I should follow behind You, then I can never be called… a sinner.
O candle that lights the heart, come back; for without Your face,
the effect of the Pure Light at the companions' banquet isn't there.
What difference does it make if the Perfect Master is my teacher?
There isn't a head in which God's Mystery is not contained there.
If in the presence of the Sun, one says: "I'm the fountain of light;"
Great Ones know that this of obscure Sirius is unworthy to declare.
It's known that one who helps the travelling stranger is respected;
O Soul, it seems that in Your city, no such custom do You share.
If the lover does not suffer the arrows of criticism, then who is he?
A shield against arrows of Destiny is not possessed by any warrior.
In the cloister of the pious fanatic and in the chamber of the Sufi,
except for the corner of Your eyebrow, there is no archway of prayer.
You Who have dipped Your hand into the blood of Hafez's heart,
it seems You have not thought of God's *Koran* that You plunder.

A glance that is not from radiance of Your face's light, bright
　　　　　is not;
on an eye is no favour, that from Your threshold dust's sight
　　　　　is not.
Those who possess true Vision are seeing Your face when they look:
　　O yes, any longing, in anyone that Your hair does not excite,
　　　　　is not.
Is it a wonder that because of my grief for You my tears are crimson?
　　There is not a storyteller who about his own actions, forthright
　　　　　is not.
The water of my eye receives the blessing of the dust of Your door...
　　there is not a door's dust that blessed by You day and night
　　　　　is not.
So that even a little grain of dust may not settle upon Your garment,
　　there is not a road that with my tears torrent, washed white
　　　　　is not.
Journey of Love is forbidden to those who are weak and immature;
　　for there is no danger, that in path's each step, left and right,
　　　　　is not.
So it doesn't boast everywhere of the evening scent of Your hair's
tip, there isn't a morning that with the breeze my wrangling fight
　　　　　is not.
It is not the right thing that the mystery should fall from the veil;
　　though in circle of drunken lovers, news not known outright,
　　　　　is not.
I complain about this unfortunate fortune because if I don't do this,
　　there is not another who sharing from Your street's delight
　　　　　is not.
O fountain of sweetness, from being ashamed of Your lip so sweet,
　　there is not a piece of sugar that downright melting in flight
　　　　　is not!
I'm not all alone with broken heart and bleeding liver due to You;
　　there is not a liver full of blood, that longing for Your sight
　　　　　is not.
In the desert of loving You, the brave lion turns into the crafty fox:

there is not a danger, that on this pathway of terrible fright,
is not.
Trace of my existence exists in that I am known and have a name,
no trace exists but this: from weakness, existence even slight
is not.
Except for this subtle point, that Hafez is still not pleased with You,
there is no subtle skill that completely in Your ability's might,
is not.

104. BY THE GRACE OF GOD

Life is a joy, because before eyes, Perfect Master there,
is;
in the Winehouse's garden, wonderful the climate's air
is.
It's best that all generous ones lay their heads at His feet;
to explain this further shows lack of respect and unfair
is.
The tale of Paradise with the fame of that heavenly House,
symbol explaining the vault of the vine's daughter rare
is.
The Spirit of our heart searches for the cup of ruby wine;
while the miser searching for gold and for silver forever
is.
In Eternity before Time, on everyone's head was written:
idol house and *Kaaba* there; here, Hell and Paradise fair
is.
No treasure can be attained without the snake; don't tell:
Abu Lahab's destructive flame, Mustafa's fortunate fare
is.
Jewel of Pure Essence is honorable, but work to do good,
for by birth or high lineage, no descent of honour There
is.
By this same Path, by the Grace of God, the heart of Hafez,
working hard, searching, striving day and night, forever is.

105. TRAP OF FAITH

Your hair's curve is trap of faith and unfaithfulness,
this is only a little that Your workshop does possess.
Your sweet loveliness is the miracle of all beauty; but,
the tale of Your glance is clearly pure magic I confess.
Your lip gives us long life like the miracles of Jesus...
but the tale of Your long hair is a rope of great stress.
May a hundred blessings be on that dark eye of Yours,
which in murdering lovers has a sorcery of expertness.
The science of love's form is truly a wonderful science,
for the seventh heaven is the seventh land's lowliness.
Don't think the speaker of evil died and saved his life;
with the 'Two Recorders' is account of his evilness.
Can one safely take one's life away from Your eye,
lying in ambush with bow of Your eyebrow's caress?
Hafez, you shouldn't sit feeling safe from that hair;
it takes heart and now intends to take faithfulness.
O heart, with soul draw that One's grace like Hafez:
for full of grace is that graceful One's gracefulness.
Hafez is drinking wine from out of the cup of love;
from this comes his mad loving and his drunkenness.

106. THE WINE FLOWS

The Fast is over and the Feast begun, hearts with joy are awake:
in the Winehouse the wine flows over, ask so the wine we can take.
Hour of the boasting sober ones is over, life's heaviness has gone:
the time has come now when joyful drinkers can happily partake.
Why should condemnation be upon he who like us drinks wine?
Because for the drunken lover, this is never a crime or a mistake.
That drinker of wine who has not a deceitful hypocritical face,
is better than a pious boaster, who hypocrisy's face can't forsake.
We are not hypocritical drunkards and not companions of deceit:
He Who knows hearts is witness to this, to our case He is awake.
We carry out the Commandments of God and don't hurt anyone;
whatever we may be told is 'unlawful', we never 'lawful' make.
Of what importance is it if you and I drink a few cups of wine?
Wine's blood of the grape; to make it, your blood they don't take.

This is not such a weakness that this weakness will cause injury;
if it were a sin, so what? Is there a man who never made a mistake?
Hafez, give away this 'How and Why' and drink wine for awhile:
can the power of talk of 'How and Why', His Divine Order break?

107. THE TRUE KALANDAR

My heart's tired of the world and all that is there in,
my heart contains only the Friend, Who dwells within.
If a fragrance from rosebed of union with You comes,
with joy, my heart like the rosebud, won't stay in skin.
The advice of me who became mad in Love's Path is
obviously the tale of a lunatic, a stone and a flagon.
Go and tell the preacher sitting alone: "Do not blame
us if our prayer-arch is that eyebrow's curve so thin."
Between *Kaaba* and form's temple there's no difference;
the Friend is everywhere, if you never lose sight of Him.
Kalandarship is not in shaving eyebrow, head and chin:
it's really a hair by hair responsibility, never giving in.
The true Kalandar, like Hafez, gives up all self-desire;
so easy it is, to give up the hair on the head and chin.

108. THE STATURE OF THE FRIEND

To talk about the cypress in view of Friend's form, is an ill will;
although cypress has a head that is held high, it borrows it still.
I don't imagine Your stature as being like that of the cypress;
for although the cypress is high, it grows wildly, beyond its will.
Image of that stature as like cypress, is still dwelling in my mind.
the reason is that the home of straight cypress is on river's frill.
East wind told tales to musk about Your hair and down and mole:
it's because of this, that like this, musk a sweet scent does distill.
There is a line on Your radiant face, but to fully comprehend if
it is crescent moon or eyebrow's bend is beyond a person's skill.
A thousand precious lives as ransom, would be given for the one
whose head into curve of the mallet of Your long hair does spill.
If you're looking for your heart's desire, seek it from that mouth;

like Hafez, don't seek it from eye that seeks to conquer and kill.

109. WISE WORDS

When hearing the Master's words, don't say: "That, faulty
is;"
my dear you're mistaken, faulty your knowledge obviously
is.
I do not bow down to this crazy world or to any other world;
praise be to God, for because of Him, our mind God-crazy
is.
I do not know who is inside this poor wounded broken heart,
for I am always silent; and it, upset and calling out loudly
is.
My heart broke the veil of patience: "Where is the Minstrel?
Come quick and sing songs and lighten the load that on me
is."
To this old world's weary work I never paid much attention;
for in my eyes Your face enlightened the illusion it really
is.
Because I imagined that I matured, I could not sleep at night;
a hundred winesick nights later, Wine house where to see
is?
By this means my bleeding heart has stained the lonely room:
to wash heart with wine from Your hand, allowed for me
is?
In the corridor of the Masters I am thought of as worthwhile,
for my heart is so much on fire that it burning constantly
is.
What was the tune that last night the Minstrel played to me?
Life has passed me by but still full of that song my memory
is.
Last night inside my heart, my love for You was so clear to me:
a voice spoke filling my heart, and it now longing deeply
is.
Ever since that time when the Beloved's words reached Hafez;
ringing the mountain of his heart, its great echo constantly

is.

110. THE REMEDY

For our pain there is no remedy.
Give Justice! Help!
our separation's end we can't see.
Give Justice! Help!
They've stolen faith and heart, now threaten the soul:
against such cruel deadly beauty,
give Justice! Help!
Help, they demand the soul as a payment for a kiss;
these heartstealers have no pity.
Give Justice! Help!
Look, these stony-hearted infidels drink our blood;
O Faithful to God, the remedy,
give. Justice! Help!
Day of Union, give help to the wretched: save them
from nights so long and deadly.
Give Justice! Help!
Each moment another new pain comes along the way
for this one's heart and soul: see!
Give Justice! Help!
Day and night, unselfish, weeping and burning away;
like this is Hafez, and also me!
Give Justice! Help!

111. YOUR SUPREME MAJESTY

It is fitting that all sweethearts to You praise pay:
as Crown over all the beloveds' heads You hold sway.
Your blissful eyes intoxicate the whole of Turkey;
tribute's paid to Your long curls by India and Cathay.
Your long dark hair's deeper than the depth of night;
whiteness of Your face outshines the brightest day.
Honestly, from this sickness of mine where is relief
if pain in my heart won't pay for remedy You outlay?

Water of Khizer's immortality flows from Your mouth,
Your lip is sweeter than Egypt's sugar by a long way.
O my soul; why do You with a heart of stone smash
my heart, that is as fragile as crystal, wasting away?
Your form is cypress, waist is hair-thin, chest is ivory;
Your cheek's down is Khizer; mouth, Life's Waterway.
Into Hafez's mind fell love for Your supreme majesty:
he wishes his obedient head, at Your dusty door lay.

112. A DRUNKARD'S PRAYER

If in Your law the flow of lovers' blood is considered right:
then, right to us is that which is also right in Your sight.
The blackness of Your hair explains: "Bringer of darkness,"
"The Splitter of morning" is because Your face is bright.
From my eyes down to lap flowed a deep river of tears;
so deep it was that no sailor could swim its great height.
Your lip that's like the Water of Life is food for the soul;
from such taste of the pure wine is this dust's appetite.
No one has ever escaped from that noose of Your curls;
from bow of Your eyebrow is shafted Your eye of light.
Don't look to me for repentance, piety, or good works;
who asks drunken lovers and madmen for what's right?
Despite a hundred ploys, Your ruby lip still gave no kiss;
nothing for my heart, many thousand pleadings despite.
Your welfare, is prayer of morning from Hafez's tongue;
and may it be continuous each day and also every night.

113. THE HOPE OF UNION

See the new moon of 'God's Month', demand the cup of wine:
it's month of assured safety, beginning year of peace sublime.
Against the fate of this gross world the beggar doesn't work;
O light of my eye, plant the ball of fortune to King's design.
Cherish the time of Union, for that moment compares with
'The Day of Surrender' and 'The Night of Authority Divine.'
Bring the wine, for his day in happiness and grace will pass,

whose 'Cup of Morning' the 'Light of Morning' will incline.
What appropriate devotion can come from me, so intoxicated,
that I don't know night cry from 'Splitter of Mornings' sign?
Heart, about your own work you do not care: when you lose
the key, I'm afraid that no one will open the door this time.
It is the age of Shah Shuja, season of wisdom and equality;
take it easy heart and soul, at morning and evening's time.
Like Hafez, stretch out night into day in the hope of Union;
rose of fortune blossoms from where 'The Opener' will shine.

114. FARRUKH

My heart, in desiring the face that's so fair
of Farrukh,
is amazingly tangled up like that long hair
of Farrukh.
There's no one except for the black Hindu of that hair,
who has enjoyed blessings from cheek, rare,
of Farrukh.
That Hindu has a good fortune, for that one is placed
by the side, but also the knee does share...
of Farrukh.
Cypress of the garden begins to tremble like a willow,
if it sees the heart and the stature and air
of Farrukh.
O Winebringer, give the wine of the arghavan's colour,
to toast narcissus eye of the sorcery there,
of Farrukh.
My poor form is now bent like bent bow of the archer
from continuing grief; as is eyebrow's stare of
Farrukh.
The perfumes of the musk of Tartary are put to shame
by breezes from the ambergris-scented hair of
Farrukh.
If the heart of anyone inclines towards another place,
my heart still inclines to the gracious air

of Farrukh.
I am the slave of the one who has made resolution to
be like Hafez, a servant of Hindu-black hair
of Farrukh.

115. FIRE OF GRIEF

You've seen heart, so again see what Love's grief repeatedly
has done;
what heart-breaking Beloved's departure to the lover truly
has done.
What an exciting game was played by magic-weaving narcissus;
intoxicating vision, drunkenness to the sober and ordinary
has done.
Twilight afterflow of bloodstreaked tears comes from such beauty;
see how this Love destroyed my luck; yes, this it obviously
has done.
With dawn, from direction of Layla's dwelling… a lightning flash!
No! See what to heartbroken Majnun's harvest, it totally
has done!
Wineseller, pure wine; for no one knows what Writer of the Invisible
does to movement of the compass of all Time… or already
has done.
No one knows what that One Who created this screen of azure sky
veils behind screen of Secrets; it's secret what the Divinity
has done.
Thoughts of Love struck and lit fire of grief in the heart of Hafez;
witness what that old Friend to friend like him, repeatedly
has done.

116. THE NIGHTINGALE'S TALE

Then nightingale told the tale to the east wind in the morning:
about what love for rose's face caused him, he was lamenting.
Love has caused my heart to bleed for that blooming face:
me, to be cut by that thorn from that rosebed it was causing.
I am the servant of whatever that graceful One may command,
Who gave freedom without any hypocrisy or any dissembling.
May the soft breeze of the morning be pleasant to that One,
Who made remedy for grief for those who at night are sitting.
I will never again complain about strangers, because whatever
they have done, it has really always been the Friend's doing.
If I had been hopeful of the King, then it was all my mistake;
if I sought faith from Heartstealer, tyranny was Your making.
In all directions, nightingales because of love were crying out;
while in the middle, I was given joy by the breeze of morning.
It drew back the veil of the rose and the curls of the hyacinth;
it, the tight knot of the coat of the rosebud was unfastening.
Respected ones of city becoming faithful to I who had gained
perfection of faith and fortune, was Father of Faith's doing.
Please take the happy news into the street of the Winesellers:
that Hafez, of all austerity and hypocrisy has been repenting.

117. A LOST SON

A nightingale drank the heart's blood and gained a rose;
the jealous wind's thorns struck the heart sharp blows.
The parrot was joyous from hoping for the sweet sugar;
but the torrent of decay tore away all hope that arose.
Forever your memory; my eyes freshness, heart's fruit!
You went so easily and now so hard for me it all goes.
O Cameldriver, my burden has fallen, a little more help;
relying on You, this journey was made with such woes.
Don't disregard my wet eyes or this my old dusty face;
this clay and straw hall of joy from azure sphere grows.
What a crying shame it is that the moon's envious eye
put my moonbrowed in the grave that the moon bestows.
Hafez, you forgot 'king to castle' and missed your move.
What to do, Time tricks again, I am careless I suppose.

118. THE PRICE OF WINE

Come, because the Turk of the sky, raid on the tray of fasting
has made:
The new crescent moon a hint that the cup will be circulating
has made.
That one took reward of fasting and gained the worth of pilgrimage,
who a pilgrimage to the dust of the Winehouse of true loving
has made.
The true dwelling that is ours lies over in corner of the Winehouse:
may God bless and do good to him who this precious dwelling
has made.
Happy be a prayer and supplication of him who from pain in the
head, with the water of the eye and the blood of the liver, scouring
has made.
Look at face of the Beloved and be grateful because of your eyesight:
for the eye looking only for true Vision, all this long gazing
has made.
What is price of wine that is like the ruby? It is the jewel of reason.
Come, for that one has made a profit, who such a bargaining
has made.
What a shame it is today the proud eye of the old priest of the city,
a glance full of contempt at all those who were dreg-drinking,
has made.
A prayer in those arches of prayer, curve of those eyebrows of Yours,
is made by one who his heart pure, in water that is bleeding,
has made.
If throughout assembly the head priest should make a search today,
give him the message that with wine the Sufi much cleansing
has made.
Hear story of love from Hafez and not from that one who criticizes;
even though that one, an art out of the example of explaining
has made.

119. LOVE'S PROMISE

A lover with bright wine the heart's clarification
made,
when early morning to Winehouse his destination
made.
When golden goblet of the sun became hidden from view,
new moon like eyebrow, sign of cup's celebration
made.
For curl of Your hair my heart paid soul, received terror;
I don't know what profit was by this speculation
made.
The respected Imam, a kind Sir who desired long prayers,
his coat in blood of vine's daughter, purification
made.
So, come to the Winehouse and see how high is my state,
though the critic's view of us his own degradation
made.
Look for the sign of love's promise in the soul of Hafez;
heart's house is for You, though You its violation
made.

120. A RESOLUTION

Like the breeze, my way to the end of Beloved's street
I'll make;
my breath to rain musk, by Beloved's perfume so sweet
I'll make.
All water from that face that I've gained by knowledge and faith,
scattered on the dust of the path at the Beloved's feet
I'll make.
Without wine and Beloved my life passed in such stupid waste:
from now on, through great effort, idleness to retreat
I'll make.
Where's breeze: for my life deeply steeped in blood like the rose,
as a sacrifice for perfume of Beloved 's hair so sweet,
I'll make.
Like the morning candle's love for Beloved, it is obvious to me,
that the gift of my life in that same manner; I repeat:

I'll make.
I will make myself ruined so that I will only remember Your eye:
strong and stable the Ancient Promise's foundation seat
I'll make.
Hafez, hypocrisy and disagreement don't give one purity of heart:
my path, that of drunkenness; my street, love's street:
I'll make.

121. RETURN OF THE ROSE

Now that to the field rose returns, from Nothing to Godhead,
and in worship the obedient violet lays down its humble head,
Drink the cup of morning-wine to tune of harp and tambourine;
kiss Winebringer's chin to music the flute and mandolin shed.
In rose's season don't sit without wine, loved one and harp;
for after only a week, like permanency of time… it has fled.
Earth is shining like the sky from zodiac's mansions of herbs,
for auspicious ascendant and a happy conjunction is spread.
In the garden create new faith out of the faith of Zoroaster,
now that the tulip is aflame like Nimrod's fire, blazing, red.
In the season of lily and rose the world is like Eden's garden;
but what's the worth when it's not an everlasting flowerbed?
When rose, like Solomon, mounts upon the wind and rides,
and bird's song at morning like a melody of David is sped,
demand cup brimming over, to memory of Chief of this Age;
to Solomon's Chief Imad ud-Din Mahmud, Hierarchy's Head.
Hafez, while his time is flourishing seek eternal joy and bliss,
shadow of his grace will to Eternity without end be spread.
Bring wine; for Hafez will forever beg for such a great Mercy,
as he is now, always will, from The Forgiver: The Godhead.

122. BUBBLE OF DECEPTION

Sufi set a trap and open the cover of his box of trickery
made;
he, a bubble of deception with sky that's full of sorcery,
made.
The sky, playing sport of cup and ball, broke the egg in his cap:
because he, a trick of slight of hand with One of mystery
made.
Winebringer come and bring wine, for the fair one of the Sufis
came with beauty and grace, and the display of flattery
made.
Where is this Minstrel who has constructed the melody of Irak;
who, resolution of turning from path of Hijaz's melody,
made?
Heart, come quickly and let us now flee to the shelter of God,
from what one of short sleeves and long-handed trickery
made.
Do not be deceptive for whoever did not play love truthfully,
love opened on the face of his heart, the door of reality
made.
When the porch of the Truth becomes opened wide tomorrow,
wayfarer will be ashamed, who his work that of jugglery
made.
Where do you go, O you partridge who struts about so proudly?
Do not be proud; hypocrite's cat, prayer that's illusory
made.
Hafez, do not blame intoxicated lovers; for God in Eternity,
me, to be beyond the habits of hypocrisy and austerity,
made.

123. THE MAD HEART

For Jamshid's cup request of me my heart for many a year
made,
begging for what it owned itself it pleas to a stranger near
made.
From the lost wanderers on the sea's sandy shoreline it searched,
for pearl too precious to be bound by shell time and sphere
made.
One who suffered to distraction, God being at all times with him
but he saw Him not, cried as from far off: "God, be clear
made!"
Last night I took my perplexing problem to the wise old Master,
who, with the benefit of insight, solutions to puzzles appear
made.
I saw him laughing and happy; while holding a cup, he was looking
in that mirror, and his perception a hundred secrets clear
made.
He said: "The crime of that Friend who glorified the gallows wood
was this: he who was given Secrets, available for all to hear
made.
But one whose heart like rosebud still hides the Secret of Truth,
has written on his mind this example: has it indelibly clear
made.
All of these shows of trickery which Reason has played out here,
were like tricks magicians before rod of white-handed Seer
made.
But if the Grace of the Holy Ghost decides once again to give aid,
others then will be able to make, whatever the Christ, here,
made."
I said: "When did God give you this cup that reveals all the world?"
He said: "Upon that day when He, this azure-blue sphere
made."
I asked him: "What use is the hair like chains of beautiful ones?"
He said: "Hafez unrestrained complaint, his mad heart's fear
made."

124. DAUGHTER OF THE VINE

Friends, repentance of being veiled, the daughter of the vine
made;
she went to Reason 'The Censor', and lawful her work's design
made.
She came out from veil to the banquet: become pure from her sweat,
so you may say to companions: "Why is it she a farewell sign
made?"
That they take her in the bond of Union is the right thing to be done,
the daughter who is intoxicated and who this veil to confine
made.
O heart, give this happy news that once again the Minstrel of Love
has sung song of drunkenness and drunkard's remedy, wine,
made.
Blossom has bloomed from my nature's clay and Beloved's breeze;
from fragrant red rose's leaf night's bird a song joyful and fine
made.
Even seven waters and a hundred fires will never remove the colour
that upon the old patchcoat of the Sufi, the blood of the vine
made.
Hafez, never give away being humble; because one that is envious,
offerings of reputation, wealth, heart, faith, at pride's shrine
made.

125. LISTEN CLOSELY

A glance at mysteries of Jamshid's cup at that moment
you can make,
when the dust of the Winehouse as your eyes pigment you can make.
Do not sit beneath the arch of the sky without music and the wine;
grief, leave the heart by winds ferment and instrument,
you can make.
The rose of your desire will open the veil and bloom at that moment,
when like morning breeze, for it serviceable achievement
you can make.
Go forward, advance some steps in the journey of the stage of love;
the gain is great that you can make, if this movement

you can make.
Come, for yourself in possession of delight, joy and an ordered life,
From blessings of the One with Vision's discernment,
you can make.
The beauty of the Beloved does not have either a veil or a screen: but
if path's dust you remove with tears, eyes fulfillment
you can make.
If you do not step out from the house that is the nature of the form,
how then is it that way to Street of the Omnipotent
you can make?
To beg at the door of the Winehouse is an alchemy that is wonderful:
if you practise this, dust into gold is accomplishment
you can make.
O heart, if you attain only once the knowledge of the light of purity,
like candle that laughs, of life and head abandonment
you can make.
But as long as you desire to have the beauty's lip and the cup of
wine, don't think that it's possible that another employment
you can make.
Hafez, if you listen closely to this advice that is of the highest,
your way along highway of Love full of enrichment,
you can make.

126. EXCEPT FOR YOUR HAIR

Now my hand will hold garment of that cypress tall and straight,
who tore me up both root and stem with swaying form, delicate.
There's no need for wine and minstrel; lift veil from off Your face
so fire of Your cheek will make me dance like rue-seed on hot-plate
Except for that face which they rub upon the hoof of Your horse
no face has the right to become mirror of the face of a happy fate.
Whatever has happened, I've expressed openly my grief's secret;
I have no more patience remaining: what to do, how long to wait?
O hunter, do not kill that musky deer; have a little consideration
for that dark eye; hold back the noose, please be compassionate!
I am a grain of dust who cannot raise the head from this doorway:
how then can I plant one kiss upon that high palace's front gate?

Hafez will not send songs to Khujand unless they reach perfection;
only fresh *ghazals* that fascinate heart are worthy for him to relate.
The heart of Hafez has no inclination except for Your long hair:
this heart bound by a hundred chains has no advice to propagate.
Hafez, do not take your heart away again from that musky hair,
because for the mad one it's better to be in an imprisoned state.

127. THE MYSTERY OF LOVE

To place the hand into the curve of that hair's curling,
can't be done:
trusting in Your promise and soft breeze of morning,
can't be done.
Whatever efforts I try to make, I make to try to see no one but You;
it is set up and laid down, that Fate to be changing,
can't be done.
With the heart's hundredth bleeding, Beloved's blessed garment fell
into my hands; fools oppose, but it away to be handing
can't be done.
Beloved's bright cheek cannot be compared to the moon in the sky;
incomparable to headless, and footless to be comparing,
can't be done.
The moment my swaying cypress starts dancing begins the Dance;
what's the use, because soul's coat in two to be tearing
can't be done.
What is there to say when Your nature is so subtle and is so tender?
so much in fact, that to carefully be humbly praying,
can't be done.
Beloved's face can only be seen by One Who has the Pure Vision;
unless the mirror's completely clean, in it to be seeing
can't be done.
I'm dying of jealousy because You are Beloved of the whole world:
but with God's creatures day and night to be fighting,
can't be done.
The Mystery of Love is beyond the bounds of human understanding;
to untangle such a Mystery with the mind's thinking,

can't be done.
Other than Your eyebrow there is no archway to pray to for Hafez:
it's our religion that unless it is You one is praising:
can't be done.

128. CONSUMED

You took my heart away, and hidden from me Your face
made;
O God, with whom has been sport like this in any place
made?
When the loneliness at dawn threatened to take away my soul;
me to think of You, Your endless kind deeds full of grace,
made.
Why don't I have a bleeding heart like that of the streaked tulip,
because Your narcissus eye, me, into a head-aching case
made?
Wind, if you have the remedy now is the time for you to give it:
the purpose of the pain of love's desire, my life to efface
, made.
Like candle burns up completely, You have also consumed me,
so that on me cup is weeping, stringed lute loud disgrace
made.
How can I speak of this suffering that consumes my poor soul?
"The Physician, design upon my powerless soul so base,
made?"
Can one ever speak about this matter to kind friends, by saying:
"Like this my Beloved spoke, like that a time and place
made?"
Not an enemy against the soul of Hafez, would have made that,
which the arrow of eye of the eyebrow-bow of that face,
made.

129. ONLY A MEMORY

Remember One, Who when parting, of us remembrance
didn't make;
who with farewell, our hearts with joy in preponderance
didn't make.
One of youthful fortune Who wrote decree of freedom for slaves,
I do not know why to this old slave, freedom's ordinance
didn't make.
We wash this papery garment i tears of blood, because the sky
to the foot of the true standard of justice, our guidance
didn't make.
In the hope that it could be a great echo happens to reach You,
in this mountain heart made cries even Farhad's grievance
didn't make.
It's possible if messenger of east wind learns his work from You:
for a movement that's faster than this, wind's performance
didn't make.
Since You took Your shadow from meadow, bird of the meadow
didn't nest in curl of the box tree's hair, and an appearance
didn't make.
Pen of Fate doesn't draw beautiful picture of that one's desire,
who a confession, that such beauty is by God's appliance,
didn't make.
Minstrel, change note and strike the path of the measure of Irak,
for in this path the Beloved went and of us remembrance
didn't make.
As *ghazals* of Irak are the melodies of Hafez; who has ever heard
such songs that set fire to the heart, and cries of grievance
didn't make?

130. DISTRAUGHT

The Heartstealer left and hint of hearts caught,
didn't make;
for city companion, journey's friend, a thought
didn't make.

It was either that my sorry fortune had left the Path of Love,
or You a trip along highway of True Support
didn't make.
I stood there like the candle and I offered my life for You…
but You, passage the morning breeze brought,
didn't make.
I said: "Perhaps weeping will soften and melt Your heart?"
My tears that on hard stone impression sought,
didn't make.
Although grief has broken the wing and feathers of my heart,
it, disappearance of passion of lover distraught,
didn't make.
Everyone who gazed upon Your face and then kissed my eye;
choice out of ignorance my eye's forethought
didn't make.
The split tongue of reed of Hafez's pen, while head's still on,
a mention of Your secret to crowds untaught,
didn't make.

131. LONGING TO DIE

I laid my face on Your path but me You did not pass by;
I hoped for kindness, but no glance came from Your eye.
O Lord, protect that young heartless beauty from arrows
of that One's lonely lovers: arrows caused by many a sigh.
Torrent of tears didn't wash hardness from Your heart:
no impression on that stone was made by rain from sky.
I was longing to die at Your feet, wasting like the candle:
but like morning breeze You didn't pass where I did lie.
O soul, what person is so stone-hearted and weak that he
didn't make himself the shield against arrows You let fly?
Last night my lamenting didn't allow fish or fowl sleep:
but see how that scornful One didn't open even an eye.
Hafez, your sweet song fascinates heart to such a degree,
that all who happen to hear… want it in their hearts to lie.

132. CHURCH AND WINEHOUSE

Preachers who at the altar and the pulpit a great display
make,
when into privacy they go, business of a different way
make.
My soul is full of amazement at such brazen-faced preachers,
who practise so little of what on pulpit a display they
make.
I've a difficulty to be put to the wise ones of the congregation;
"Why don't they do penance, who it the order of the day
make?"
You may say that they don't believe in the Day of Judgement,
since in the business of the Judge, fraud and deceit they
make.
Lord, place such upstart owners of new wealth on their asses,
because of having Turkish slave and ass, they boasts today
make.
I'm the slave of the Master of the Winehouse, Whose disciples,
independently fling dust on all riches that the world may
make.
You beggar of the monastery, leap up: in the Masters' dwelling
they give the pure liquid, that all hearts strong and gay
make.
Make your house empty of idols so it can be Beloved's home:
for the lustful, heart and soul a place for others to stay
make.
O no, these clever ones full of deceit who don't see the jewel,
equation that shell is worth the same as the pearl they
make.
At dawn from God's Throne came commotion as Wisdom spoke;
it could be said: "Angels, a song from Hafez's verse today
make."

133. BEHIND THIS SCREEN

Listen to song's words that with harp's strumming
They make:
"Secretly drink wine, then never any complaining
they make.
The honour of Love and the glory of lovers, they take away:
they forbid the young, and to the old, backbiting
they make."
They say: "Don't talk about the mystery of Love, don't listen."
It is a hard story that to all, constantly warning,
they make.
Outside the Door, we are handed deceptions by the hundred;
let us look behind screen and see the deceiving
they make.
They take all of the Master's time, these devoted followers;
only much trouble to the life the Wiseman's living
they make.
A hundred types of conquests can be bought by half a glance;
feel sorry for fair ones, small progress by flirting
they make.
With a great effort some tried for union with the Beloved;
and some others to the help of Fate, their trusting
they make.
I will tell to you clearly, don't trust in the Fortune of Time:
Time and the world are workshops where changing
They make.
There is nothing here but raw iron; but the fools think that
alchemist's stones from this old earth of grieving
they make.
Drink wine; for the Priest, the Hafez, Teacher and Moralist,
if you look at it all closely, a fine job of covering
they make.

134. THE VEIL THE SCREEN AND THE CURTAIN

Perfect Masters, Who, alchemy of dust with glance of an eye
make,
do They from corner of eye, a glance towards one such as I
make?
It's best for me to hide pain from those claiming to be physicians:
maybe They will to me from hidden treasury, remedy's supply
make.
Since wholeness doesn't come through being indulgent or denying,
it's best that we our actions, responsibility of Highest of High
make.
Since the Beloved is never lifting the veil from off the fair face,
why does imagination of each one a different tale to falsify
make?
Today, behind the curtain, there are many seditions taking place:
when the screen falls down, let's see the excuses they'll try
make.
Do not think it is a wonder if the stone cries out from this tale:
for the tale of the happy heart, those of heart a happy cry
make.
Drink wine, for a hundred hidden crimes committed by strangers,
are better than devotion, that they through a hypocritical lie
make.
The coat from which emanates the fragrance of Joseph the Beloved,
I'm afraid the jealous proud brothers will tear it, and an alibi
make.
Go to the street of the Winehouse so that those who are there now,
when they feel it's time, a prayer for your welfare to satisfy,
make.
Call me to You without enviers knowing: for Those Who are kind,
while doing God's work, a secret of Their generosity's supply
make.
Hafez, attainment of Union is forever beyond becoming attainable:
O God forbid, if Kings, no account of where the beggars lie,
make.

135. THE SIGH AT MIDNIGHT

If the lovely ones go on stealing all hearts in this way,
they will tear apart the faith of fanatics without delay.
Wherever that branch of that narcissus may blossom,
those rosy cheeks find their eyes hold narcissus all day.
When our Beloved begins to sing and starts the dance,
angels of the ninth heaven clap hands, shout and sway.
The sun of your fortune will show itself openly to you,
if the mirror that shines like the morning They display.
Lovers do not have any command over their own lives:
they carry out an order… that You happen to convey.
Pupil of my eye became completely drowned in blood:
such tyranny against man, where else do they do today?
O youth with the form of the cypress, strike the ball;
before they will make your form like the mallet play.
In these wet eyes of mine, much less than a mere drop
are the tales they tell of the Deluge, now and yesterday.
Look once from Your eyes… so that they may quickly
allow death to come to those whose hearts in grief lay.
Where is the festivity of Your cheek, so in faith to You,
lovers may give as sacrifice, life and soul without delay?
Heart, careless of mysteries, come out of grief happy!
They give some peace even on separation's grilling tray.
Hafez, do not be giving up all the sighing at midnight,
so They may make the mirror shine like morning's ray.

136. A CONVERSATION

I said: "Me blessed, Your mouth and lip when will
they make?"
You said: "Even as you talk, it immediately to fulfill
they make."
I said, "Your lip demands the tribute of Egypt for only one kiss:"
You said: "In this no unfavourable transaction will
they make."
I said: "Who will find the way to the fine point of Your mouth?"
You said: "Such knowledge revealed to subtle of skill

They make."
I said: "Do not be a lover of idols, stay only in God's company?"
You said: "In the street of Love, this and also that still
they make."
I said: "The Winehouse's atmosphere takes grief away from heart;"
You said: "They're happy, who in a heart, joyful thrill
they make."
I said: "Do the patchcoat and wine have any relation to religion?"
You said: "In the Perfect Master's circle, this way skill
they make."
I said: "What profit are the aged obtaining from Your sweet lips?"
You said: "With a sweet kiss the old young again still
they make."
I said: "And when does the kind Master come into the chamber?"
You said: "Not until Jupiter and moon conjoined will
They make."
I said: "It is Hafez's practise at morning to pray for Your health."
You said: "This prayer, angels of seventh Heaven's hill,
they make."

137. SLAVES

Those who wear crowns, slaves of Your intoxicated eye
are:
even sober ones, drunk with wine of Your ruby lip's sigh
are.
Drift like the breeze over to the bed of violets and see how
from Your hair's tyranny, they sad and beginning to cry
are.
Morning breeze is Your informer, mine is the water of my eye:
if not, then keeping their secret, lover and Beloved shy
are.
I am not the only one singing love songs to that rose-cheek:
Your thousands of praising nightingales, far, wide and high
are.
When You pass by, have a look beneath Your hair's long curls:
see how from right to left that they in restless oversupply

are.
Go, you who say you know God; we are Paradise inheritors:
sinners, deserving God's mercy which to them does apply
are.
Go to the Winehouse and make your face red from the wine:
do not go to cloister for there they of the dark evil eye
are.
O Khizer with happy feet, hold tight on to my hand because
I'm on foot and on horseback my companions, I testify
are.
May Hafez never be set free from that chain of twisting hair:
for the only ones who are truly free, tied to Your curls' tie
are.
From what is written on Hafez's face it can be known by one,
that the dwellers at the door of the Friend in dust to lie,
are.

138. LOVE'S PAIN AND REMEDY

When jasmine-scented ones lay, they lay down dust of grieving;
when Pari-faced ones try, they make peace from heart be leaving.
When they tie their hair they tie hearts to tyranny's saddle strap:
when they shake ambergris-scented hair, souls they're scattering.
When in a lifetime they sit with us for a moment, they soon rise;
when rising, into the heart the seed of longing they are planting.
They make pomegranate tears rain from my face when they laugh:
the hidden secret from my face, when they look they're perceiving.
When discovering they discover grief of those secluded in corners,
if knowing of those awake all night, love's face they're not turning.
Where is that one who thinks the remedy of a lover's pain is easy?
Those who think about remedy become distressed from thinking.
Those upon the gallows like Mansur obtain their desired remedy:
those delving into thinking of a remedy, find pain too distressing.
When those who are longing beg in that Presence, grace comes:
to this Court They call Hafez when They cause him to be dying.

139. DETERMINED IN LOVE

Unadulterated wine and Winebringer are two snares of the Way,
from whose rope, even the wise of the world... are very easy prey.
Although I am a lover, an outsider, drunk and one black of book,
a thousand thanks that our city friends are sinless in every way.
Don't put your feet down in the Winehouse except with respect:
for confidants of the King are those, who at its doorway... stay.
It's not the true way of the dervish and the wayfarer to be cruel;
bring wine, for men of the Path, by cruelty are never led astray.
Don't act in such a way that the Heartstealer's glory is splintered,
by servants fleeing and slaves leaping up and then running away.
Do not believe that the beggars of love are contemptible because,
these are belt-less kings and are monarchs without crowns today.
Be sensible and beware of the blowing of the wind of your pride:
with barleycorn, for thousand harvests of devotion, you can't pay.
I'm the slave of true intentions, of one colour, a drinker of dregs:
I'm not of that crowd of blue-gowns having a black heart's way.
Hafez, the majesty of Love is of the highest rank, be determined;
for lovers allow no admittance to those not determined to stay.

140. PERFECT MASTER'S DISCIPLE

I do not know what to us this face of intoxication
has brought:
who is Winebringer and wine from which direction
has brought?
What robbery this musician does with such knowledge of music,
that in middle of a *ghazal*, Beloved's conversation
has brought.
The breeze with its happy news is the hoopoe bird of Solomon,
which from Sheba's rosegarden, joy's information
has brought.
You also take cup into your hand and take the wide land's path,
for sweet-singing bird, sweet melodious composition
has brought.

A happy welcome to the arrival of the rose and to the wild rose;
joyful sweet violet has come and lily purification
has brought.
Heart, don't complain that your fate's folded like the rosebud:
for the morning wind, the soft breeze of liberation
has brought.
Smile of the Winebringer is the remedy of our heart's sickness:
lift your head, Physician has come and medication
has brought.
Preacher, don't be angry with me if I'm Perfect Master's disciple,
for you only made a promise and he substantiation
has brought.
I am boasting of that Turkish Warrior's eye that never strayed,
which upon me the dervish with one coat, an action
has brought.
The sky now submits to being an obedient servant of Hafez...
for Fate, him to Your door of Fortune for protection,
has brought.

141. CUP OF JOY

You never wrote explaining Yourself and it's many a day:
where's one I can trust to get to You a note without delay.
To the Highest Goal our desire can't reach its destination,
unless You meet our effort with some help along the way.
From bottle to flagon is the wine and the rose is unveiled;
hold the cup of Joy, and drink until merry while you may.
Candy mixed with rose juice will not cure our sick heart;
give kisses mixed with straight talking, it's better that way.
Fanatic, go from me in peace and secure your own safety;
if you stay with us drunkards you might end up that way.
Dangers of drinking you've preached, what of the wonders?
Skills of the blender don't ignore because fools have a say.
O beggars of the Wineshop, the Owner is the True Friend;
don't expect gifts from dumb animals; God's the only Way.
What great wisdom spoke the Master to drunkard friend:
"Don't reveal heart to an ignorant youth who can't pay."

Hafez burns away for the cheek that is lit up by the Sun;
give one dying of thirst a quenching and come what may.

142. DON'T WORRY

To grieve for a moment about all of creation
is worthless:
sell it for wine, because our cloak of religion
is worthless.
In Winemaker's street they don't give a cup for austerity;
what use is prayermat that for intoxication
is worthless!
Wash this many coloured coat of deceit and worldliness;
red wine's one colour and coat's colouration
is worthless.
The crown's majesty leads to pride that seduces the heart;
for to risk one's life for its shaky situation
is worthless.
When the ocean voyage began the treasure seemed close;
I was wrong: hundred pearls for raging ocean
is worthless.
Don't worry, be happy, content with your life's treasure;
for land and sea to cause heart consternation
is worthless.
It is best that you hide your face from too many hearts;
joy of taking world, for army of lamentation
is worthless.
The Beloved's direction is our only purpose and home…
any other than that blessed One's location, i
s worthless.
Like Hafez, don't you worry, and let go the selfish world:
a ton of gold to buy miser's consideration,
is worthless.

143. SOMEDAY

Except for love of those moon of face, my heart a way
doesn't take:
I advise it this way and that, but it all the advice I say,
doesn't take.
O giver of advice, for God's sake tell tale of Winebringer's image:
for an image more beautiful, our imagination's play
doesn't take.
I drink the goblet of wine secretly and the people think it is a book:
it's strange if fire of this hypocrisy, to this book someday
doesn't take.
Someday I will certainly burn this multi-coloured dervish patchcoat,
which the Wineseller's Master for single cup as its pay,
doesn't take.
The one who criticizes drunkards, making war against God's decree,
I see has stained heart: maybe he the winecup his way
doesn't take.
Those who have pure hearts take much delight in wine that's pure,
for other than the image of the Truth in this gem's ray,
doesn't take.
In the middle of crying I laugh out loud because my tongue's on fire
like this gathering's candle; but it, to it, one could say:
"Doesn't take."
With eyes and mind full of goodness you tell me to turn eyes away;
go away, for in my mind stupid advice doesn't stay,
doesn't take.
How happily You made heart a prey: I boast of Your drunken eye!
For a person, of all wild birds, than this a better prey,
doesn't take.
Generous One, some pity for God's sake: the dervish of Your street
does not know another door but Yours, and another way
doesn't take.
I have received many an act of kindness from the old Perfect Master:
who for a cup of the wine, the ways of hypocrisy as pay
doesn't take.

One day like Alexander the Great I'll bring that mirror to my hand,
if this fire takes hold of it and then suddenly me away
doesn't take.
For this verse that's fresh and sweet I wonder why the King of kings,
Hafez to be covered in gold from the head to feet today,
doesn't take.

144. WHAT EXCUSE?

I've a Beloved Who around the rose the hyacinths gathering
has:
a line written in arghavan's blood, Beloved's cheek's Spring
has.
O Lord, sun of that One's face is covered by the dust of that line;
give everlasting life to that fair One, Who beauty everlasting
has.
I can see that in every direction the soul cannot escape that eye;
it lies in ambush in every corner, and arrow in bow for firing
has.
O Ruler of the feast, for God's sake give me justice from that One;
with others that One drank wine and my head only an aching
has.
When I became a lover I said, "I've won the jewel that I desired:"
I didn't know this sea, great waves that blood are splattering
has.
You should make me feel safe from being frightened of separation
by saying: "God gives safety from eye of one who evil-thinking
has."
Don't exclude my eye from Your shape's cypress that steals heart:
by head of this fountain plant it, for it water that is running
has.
If You tie me to Your saddle's strap, please God quickly take me;
mistakes lie in delay; delay for the seeker, loss it no denying
has.
O nightingale, when rose laughs in your face don't fall in the trap:
there is no relying on rose, even if it world's beauty showing
has.

Scatter wine on the dust and witness the position of the mighty:
dust, thousand tales of Jamshid and Kay Khusrau for telling
has.
When Beloved made loose hair's noose from around lovers' hearts,
Beloved said to wind's informer: "Wind, Our secret for keeping
has."
What has happened in this path, that every great man with insight,
I see that his head upon the sill of this threshold still lying
has.
What excuse can I give for my case? That trouble-maker of the city
through bitterness killed Hafez, and mouth that sugar's filling
has?

145. WE SEEK THE ETERNAL

Heart that found the Hidden Secret, cup of Jamshid's might
has;
and for the seal-ring that was lost, concern that's only slight
has.
To the seal-ring of Solomon, tell about the happy time to come;
the Great Name of God cuts off hand that the demon's spite
has.
To the beard and mole of beggars don't give the heart's treasure:
no, give it only to the hand of One a King, that to it a right
has.
Not every tree is saved from the cold violent tyranny of winter;
I'm the slave of the strong straight cypress who roots so tight
has.
Season of happiness has come when each, like drunken narcissus,
places six petals at the foot of cup; if each, six coins bright
has.
Now, like the rose, do not hold back gold for the price of wine;
or a suspicion of all your faults the Great Knowable's Light
has.
The Hidden Secret is a story that nobody knows, or ever tells;
the path to the Sacred Place, heart's true Friend secret sight
has.

My heart boasted of independence; now a hundred works with
Your curls fragrance, the breeze that blows at morning light
has.
From whom can I seek my heart's desire? There's no sweet heart
who is used to such generosity, and also true perfect insight
has.
Hafez, from pocket of the coat of religion can one make a profit?
We seek the Eternal, and he, by way of a form, his delight
has.

146. PRESERVE

Every one who is faithful, the people faithfully
preserve;
God will always these ones, from calamity safely
preserve.
I'll only relate about the Friend in the Friend's presence;
and words of friend, the friend will trustfully
preserve.
If your desire is that the Beloved won't break the promise,
cord that is held, you will its end respectfully
preserve.
O heart, live in such a way that if your foot happens to slip,
an Angel, praying, lifting, will you, thankfully
preserve.
O soft breeze, if you see my heart at the tip of that hair,
kindly quietly tell it, its place to always sacredly
preserve.
When I said to You: "Preserve my heart," You then said:
"What's from slave's hand, God will undoubtedly
preserve."
Wealth, mind, heart and soul are surrendered to Beloved,
Who will the right of love's friendship, honestly
preserve.
Warriors, heroes, bravely watch and preserve the Master;
for he will you, like his own soul, preciously...
preserve.

Where is the dust of Your Path, so that then Hafez will,
remembering wind's breath blowing fragrantly,
preserve.

147. THE WISE BIRD

That one is not the Beloved who only a waist and hair
has,
be slave of that One's form Who beauty's perfect share
has.
Although the way of the Pari and the Huri is so enchanting,
that way of gracefulness and beauty, that One so fair
has.
With the craft of shooting arrows, curve of Your eyebrow
takes away from the hand, the bow that every archer
has.
My words sit in the heart since they were accepted by You:
yes, it is true that love's word, such impressive power
has.
In love's path, no one with certainty knows the mystery:
according to his insight, each his own conception there
has.
Don't boast of generosity to frequenters of the Winehouse:
each word a time when, each subtlety a place where,
has.
The wise bird does not go into the meadow singing its song,
because every spring still an autumn following its rear
has.
Who then will take the ball of beauty from You, when here
the sun isn't a horseman and not even the rein's share
has.
Say to the rival: "Don't try your wit and subtlety on Hafez:"
for a tongue and also its meaning, our reed... take care,
has.

148. HIDDEN LONGING

Heart's blood from our eye all over our face
goes:
one can't see what from eye upon our case
goes.
We have hidden a great longing within the heart,
so by that longing our heart to wind's space
goes.
We laid our face on the dust of the Friend's path,
so that it's right if the Friend over our face
goes.
Water from our eye is a torrent: whoever crosses it,
even if his heart is a stone, it from its place
goes.
I argue with that water of my eye day and night,
about flow that up Your street to Your place
goes.
The sun of the east tears his garment from jealousy
as Moon puts on coat, with love and grace
goes.
Hafez, to the Winehouse's street with clean heart
like a Sufi going to cell, to the honest place
goes.

149. VEIL OF THE PATH

When on the tip of your hair I place my hand, you angrily
go:
if I look for peace then you with your head criticizing me,
go.
You attack the helpless onlookers with your eyebrow's corner
that is like the new moon, which into the veil will quickly
go.
You ruin me with your wakefulness, during nights of wine:
if during the day I start to explain, you to sleep suddenly
go.

O heart, the path of love is full of trouble and is full of strife;
that one will fall down on this path who happens to hastily
go.
When the false wind of pride falls on the head of the bubble,
quickly its desire for wine goes and so does its supremacy
go.
Heart, don't boast of beauty and eloquence when you are old,
for with the world of youth, boasts such as this, do only
go.
When the black book of the black hair is completely closed,
the white isn't lessened if many extracted should seemingly
go.
Don't sell being a beggar at Beloved's door even for an empire:
from this door's shade does anyone into the Sun's ferocity
go?
You called me a 'one who breaks the promise', and I'm afraid
that this title with you, will on the Resurrection Day finally
go.
Hafez, veil of the Path is you, yourself: from within come out!
That one's happy who unveiled on this same Path, may freely
go.

150. THE FOOL

Brothers, there was a heart that at one time mine
was,
to which I told a problem, if it difficult to define
was.
A heart that suffered with me, that offered good advice
to those of heart: a helping shelter true and benign
was.
Whenever I was troubled by a calamity that came along,
it a friend and experienced worker, skilful and fine,
was.
After the eye had led me along to fall in the whirlpool,
through heart's aid my only hope of the shoreline
was.

In the street of the Beloved, it was suddenly lost by me:
O Lord, a place that seizes coats, that street Divine
was!
From searching for it my tears, like pearls, trickled down;
but my trying to discover it again, just a useless line
was.
There's no effort that has not danger of disappointment,
but has one been upset like me, who ready to resign
was?
Have compassion for me in my hopeless drunkenness,
for at one time a skilful worker this heart of mine
was.
When love was the teacher that inspired all of my words,
subtle highlight of every gathering my talk so fine
was.
Never again mention: "Hafez knows how to be subtle,"
for we've seen that he, of the fool's obvious sign
was.

151. FALLEN FOR A CUP

When the Beloved, the cup of wine in the hand
takes,
the market for fair ones, a great crash in demand
takes.
Into the ocean I have fallen and I've become like a fish,
so that me, by a hook the Beloved out to land
takes.
Each one who has witnessed Your eye has shouted out:
"Where's a policeman, who this drunk to remand
takes?"
I've fallen full of great grief at the feet of my Beloved,
in desperate hope that Beloved, me by the hand
takes.
That one's heart is full of happiness, who like Hafez,
a cup of the wine of the Eternal First Command
takes.

152. IF IT IS NOT

In the longing and searching of one who like lightning
is not,
if such a harvest should be burnt up, then it, amazing
is not.
That bird whose heart never became acquainted with sorrow,
on branch of the tree of its life, a leaf of joy growing
is not.
There's no remedy for unfaithfulness in the workshop of Love;
who can the fire be burning if an Abu Lahab existing
is not?
There is no need to have manners in the soul-sellers religion;
there is not room for lineage there… also a reckoning
is not.
In the assembly where the reckoning is, the sun is an atom:
wise, to see oneself there from manners and breeding,
is not.
Drink wine; for if one can discover eternal life in the world,
except for wine of Paradise, its source for discovering
is not.
Hafez, the union of Beloved with one poor of heart like you,
could be on that day which having a night following
is not.

153. CUP FROM SUN'S CORNER

If the wine into the winecup the Winebringer in this way
throws,
all the wise men into drinking wine, that One every day
throws.
If that One places the mole's grain under the hair's coil like this;
into the trap there are many wise birds that it to waylay
throws.
Drunken one's condition is happiness, when he does not know
whether he, his head or turban down in this pathway,
throws.

The pious fanatic's nature remains immature because of denial;
maturity comes when he, his glance the winecup's way
throws.
During day learn to be skilful; for a heart that's like the mirror,
into the dirt of darkness, drinking of wine during day
throws.
The time of the splendid morning wine is the time when night,
the screen of evening around the tent of horizon's ray,
throws.
Be careful that you do not drink wine with the city's censor:
he drinks your wine and stone into your cup to repay,
throws.
O Hafez, lift up your head with the cup from the sun's corner,
if while throwing dice, Fortune that full Moon your way
throws.

154. THE RETURN

O my heart, good news, for the breeze of the morning
has returned;
from the borders of Saba bringing good news lapwing
has returned.
Bird of the morning, prolong the sweet song, the melody of David:
for the rose like Solomon on the strong wind's wing
has returned.
Tulip, discovering scent of sweet wine from the morning's breath
and with the stain on the heart, for remedy hoping,
has returned.
Where now is a wise man who can understand the lily's tongue
so that he may ask why such a one who was leaving
has returned?
My eyes flowed water of many tears behind that departing caravan,
until to my heart's ear the sound of the bell's tinkling
has returned.
Fortune, given by God, has given me much kindness and happiness;
for that Idol with stony heart, from God interfering,
has returned.

Although Hafez beat on the door of offence and broke his promise;
see Beloved's grace, Who to our door, peace bringing,
has returned.

155. WITHOUT THE BELOVED

The rose that hasn't the Beloved's face
isn't worthwhile;
the Spring, that of wine hasn't a trace,
isn't worthwhile.
The border around the fields and the air of the gardens,
without Beloved's tulip cheek of grace,
isn't worthwhile.
The lip of sugar and the rose of the form of the Beloved,
without the Beloved's kiss and embrace
isn't worthwhile.
Dancing of the swaying cypress and rapture of the rose,
without nightingale's songs filling space,
isn't worthwhile.
Every picture that the hands of intellect have depicted,
unless it's Your image that they trace:
isn't worthwhile.
The garden and the rose and the wine are truly pleasant,
but if in Beloved's place is empty space:
isn't worthwhile.
Hafez, your life is nothing but a used old worthless coin,
to scatter it for the Beloved to efface,
isn't worthwhile.

156. THE WIND

Last night the wind gave news of my travelling Beloved to me:
I also give my heart to the wind and now whatever will be, be!
My condition has reached such a state that I make confidants
of flash of lightning at night, and the morning wind's vagrancy.
My heart in curl of Your hair wasn't protected; it didn't say:
"May where I am accustomed to stay, reach Your memory."

The value of the advice of those dear ones I understand today:
Lord, may hearts of our advisers because of You, beat joyfully.
My heart began bleeding from remembering You, when in field
the wind loosened the fastening of the rosebud's coat, slightly.
My heart remembered a corner of the peak of Your royal cap,
when the wind placed crown on head of narcissus, suddenly.
When my weak state of existence slipped out from my hand,
at morning the wind gave back life by Your hair's fragrancy.
O Hafez, your natural good soul will bring to you your desire;
souls, the ransom of the man of a good nature, always will be.

157. FOR YOU BE

O Monarch, in the curve of Your mallet, ball of the sky
for You be;
sphere of being and time and space, a plain to hit high
for You be!
All climes have proclaimed and all the quarters have let loose the
fame of Your disposition, which protection to go by,
for You be!
The hair of the Lady of Victory is drawn to Your standard's tassel;
eye of eternal success, lover that Your footsteps tie...
for You be!
O You, the writing of Mercury is all in praise of Your great glory!
Writer of the book with Royal seal, Reasoner of the sky
for You be!
Your shape that is like cypress, put to shame the Tree of Paradise;
Your wide Palace, the envy of Paradise that is on high,
for You be!
Not only are animals and vegetation and stones under Your order;
may what is in the world of order, under Your order lie:
for You be!
In sincerity, sick and broken Hafez became utterer of Your praises:
Your Grace, his Doctor and voice of praise, I don't deny
for You be!

158. THREE CUPS

Winebringer, of cypress and rose and tulip the storyline
goes,
and now this argument washed by three cups of wine,
goes.
Drink wine; Spring, field's new bride, reached beauty's limit!
There's no need for others to add to a tale that so fine
goes.
All the parrots of India have become great eaters of sugar,
now that on to Bengal this Persian sweetmeat of mine
goes.
See how the passage of verse travels through place and time!
See how this child of a night, after a year, true to design
goes.
Now look at that eye of sorcery that fascinates the devotee,
how behind it the caravan of sorcery in a steady line
goes.
Sweat drops and Beloved proudly sways; on white rose's face,
night's dew shamed by the Beloved's face, into decline
goes.
Don't leave the path for the world's flattery: for this old hag
when sitting is a cheat, when leaving as a greedy swine
goes.
Don't be like Samiri, who on seeing gold acted like an ass,
leaves Moses and then off to find the calf's fake shine
goes.
The wind of the Spring blows from the garden of the King;
and within the bowl of the tulip, from the dew, wine
goes.
Hafez, don't be silent about the love of Ghiyas ud-din's court,
for due to his cry of lamentation, your poetry so fine
goes.

159. PATIENCE AND VICTORY

I have the desire that if it from my hand out right
will come,
I'll have in hand such a thing, grief's end in sight
will come.
The plain of heart's vision isn't the place to meet opponents:
when the demon goes out, within the angel's light
will come.
The darkness of night is the close companion of the dictators:
ask light of the sun for perhaps light that's bright
will come.
At the door of the great of the world lacking in generosity,
how long will you sit, asking: "Sir, inside, tonight
will come?"
Let go of this time that is so much more bitter than poison:
after you let go, again the time of sweet delight
will come.
Do not stop begging, for you will eventually gain the treasure
from the glance of a Traveller Who into your sight
will come.
O nightingale full of love, ask only for life; because in the end
the garden is green and red rose blooming bright,
will come.
Patience and victory are the two who are old companions:
after patience comes, the time of victory's might
will come.
It's no wonder that in this room Hafez is without any cares:
whoever went to Winehouse, to madness one night
will come.

160. YOUR BEAUTY

Sun of everyone's eyesight Your beauty
be;
Your fair face more beautiful than beauty
be.
Under the Fortunate Bird of Your long-haired
falcon wings; the hearts of kings, worldly,
be!
The one who is not captivated by Your hair,
like Your long hair, thrown haphazardly
be.
The heart that is not in love with Your face,
in liver's blood drowned for all eternity
be.
O Idol, when Your glance shoots the arrow,
my wounded heart its target for archery
be.
And when Your ruby of sugar gives the kiss,
the taste of my soul from this, all sugary
be.
Each moment, great new love in me for You:
each hour, You another new great beauty
be!
With the soul, Hafez desires to see Your face:
Your glance on who desire You, like me,
be!

161. YOUR RUBY LIP

May Your beauty increasing eternally
be;
may Your face, tulip-coloured, yearly
be!
May the image of Your love in my mind
increasingly stay there and also daily
be!

The forms of all the world's sweethearts
serve Your form: like an 'n' humbly
be!
Each cypress that's growing in the field,
before the 'l' of Your form… bent fully
be!
That eye that is not entranced by You:
jewel of tears, and sea of blood only
be!
Stealing all the hearts, Your eye practices
sorcery so skillfully; such sorcery fully
be!
And wherever a heart's grieving for You,
without any patience and not calmly
be!
A one discontented, separated from You,
out of the circle of union with You, he
be!
Your ruby lip which is the soul of Hafez,
far from an unworthy lip completely
be!

162. A POET'S PRAYER

May Your body, in the need of physician's care,
never be!
May Your tender existence, hurt by Fate's snare,
never be!
All the horizons of our world depend upon Your welfare;
may accidents for You that Chance may prepare,
never be!
The beauty of the outer and inner is from Your prosperity;
may to You, outward anger and inward despair
never be!
Autumn comes to the field to spoil and to plunder its life;
towards straight high cypress may its cold stare
never be!

In that place where Your beauty is flowering so splendidly,
power of ill-doer and the ill-wisher's hateful glare
never be!
May all who with evil eye look upon Your moonlike face,
except as seed on grief's fire may his life's share
never be!
Look for healing in the words of Hafez that scatter sugar;
so a need for rosewater candy for Your welfare
never be!

163. INSIDE THE CUP

Anyone who the real winecup in the hand
does hold,
ever Jamshid's great Sovereign command
does hold.
That Water from which Khizer obtained Eternal Life,
look for in Winehouse: cup, understand,
does hold.
Fasten end of life's thread to the inside of the cup,
so that life's thread, ordered and planned,
does hold.
Together are we and the wine, the fanatics and piety:
let's now see which one Beloved's hand
does hold.
Winebringer, without Your sweet lip there's nothing
of worth that Time and the world's land
does hold.
All of the intoxicating ways that the narcissus has,
come from what Your fair eye firsthand
does hold.
My heart, from praising Your face and Your hair
each morning and evening, does expand,
does hold.
O Soul; Your Beauty, two hundred slaves like Hafez
in the pit of the chin at Your command,
does hold.

That one who beauty of Beloved's cheeks down in his vision
has,
he is then certain that he the height of vision's acquisition
has.
Like pen, on the writing of Your order we have laid our head;
perhaps it is that from Your sword it now a higher position
has.
Only that one is prepared for union with You, who like candle,
each moment under Your sword new head for acquisition
has.
The hand of only that one will have ability to kiss Your foot,
who forever his head on door like threshold of submission
has.
One day Your watcher sent an arrow straight in my poor chest:
from grief, many an arrow my chest's shieldless position
has.
I am sick and tired of this dry austerity: bring to me pure wine;
for scent of wine, power to make fresh brain's condition,
has.
If you do not gain this from wine, isn't it then enough that it,
power to keep you for a moment from reason's temptation
has?
That one who did not plant his foot outside the door of piety,
now desiring to travel, to visit Winehouse as his intention
has.
The broken heart of Hafez will be taken to the dust by the deep
stain of passion that like the tulip, his old liver's condition
has.

165. A GLANCE FOR A VICTIM

That One, for Whose hyacinth curl, ambergris great envy
has;
towards those who lost their hearts, grace and tyranny
has.
The Beloved passes like the wind past the head of the victim:
what can one do, for Beloved is life which a swift history
has.
Since the lip of Beloved is clearly the Water of Eternal Life,
then it's clear that Khizer a share of the mirage obviously
has.
Moon shows the bright sun through the curtain of Your hair:
so great then is the sun's light that it a cloud for privacy
has.
My eye has flowed a great torrent of tears from each corner,
so that Your cypress form from water, a fresh fertility
has.
It is a mistake that Your glance has freely spilled my blood;
but give it every opportunity, for it the right authority
has.
Because of my heart Your intoxicated eye now wants my liver:
bold One is drunk and maybe for roast meat a tendency
has.
It is not the way of my sick soul to ask questions of You:
happy that sick one who answer from Beloved happily
has.
When will Your drunken eye send to Hafez's broken heart
a glance that a ruined victim in every corner certainly
has?

166. THE FOUNDATION OF GENEROSITY

Messenger with news from the Chief's presence last night
did come:
from the presence of a Solomon the order to take delight
did come.
Make clay from the dust of our existence with the water of the eye,
to the ruined house of the heart, time to raise it upright
did come.
O you with garment stained with wine be careful to hide my defect,
for to visit me the Beloved with a garment pure and white
did come.
The explanations without end they told about the Beloved's beauty,
are only a word out of thousands that to be told outright
did come.
Today the place of every one of the lovely ones will become known,
for that Moon to seat of honour, setting gathering alight,
did come.
On the throne of Solomon Whose crown is the sun's place of ascent,
see the spirit of this ant, that all contemptibility despite,
did come.
O heart, keep yourself guarded from the bold eye of that bold One,
because that archer, that sorcerer, seeking another fight
did come.
Hafez, you are so stained: now ask for a favour from the Great King,
for that Soul, a foundation of generosity, to clean blight
did come.
The assembly of the King is a sea and it's the time to gain a pearl!
Hey, you who are sick of losing, time of trading overnight
did come.

167. SOME GOOD NEWS

Last night some good news to me the morning's windy air
brought,
saying: "Its face to an end, the day of work and despair
brought."
We gave our new garment to the minstrels of the cup of morning,
as a gift for this news that morning breeze then and there
brought.
Come; because for you the Huri of Paradise, the slave of the world
Rizvan, for the sake of that slave your heart that is rare,
brought.
Really, it's true we will go to Shiraz with blessings of the Friend;
what a Friend as companion, Fortune beyond compare
brought!
Many were my heart's cries that reached the palace of the moon,
when it into memory, that Moon's cheek and halo of hair
brought.
Strive with all our heart's strength; because this felt dervish cap
has many a hard knock upon kingly crowns, everywhere,
brought.
Hafez could make his flag of victory be raised to the sky, since he,
himself to the Court of the Great King, for refuge there,
brought.

168. YOU WHO GIVE

Who to Your cheek, did rose and wild rose's hue
give,
can poor miserable me, patience and rest imbue:
give.
And Who gave to Your hair the talent of being long,
can free sorrowful me and mercy, that is due,
give.
I gave up any hope for Farhad, on that day when he
handed reins of his mad heart to Shirin's lip; to
give.
If I don't own a treasure of gold, I'm still content:

Who gave that to kings, did this to beggars true
give.
The world's seen on the surface as a beautiful bride,
but he who is her groom, finds life the price to
give.
I'm content to hold garment: cypress, stream's edge.
February is here, breeze did good news a clue
give.
From Time's cleaving hand Hafez's heart is bleeding:
O Supporter of The Faith, Kivam-ud-Din; you:
give.

168. A DIFFICULT BELOVED

If I am following You, You stir up so much calamity:
and if I sit, not seeking: You get up full of brutality.
If through desire, for a moment on the highway I fall
like dust at Your foot; like wind You have mobility.
And if I'm longing for half a kiss, a hundred criticisms
like sugar from mouth's casket, You allow fluidity.
Hills and valleys of love's desert are a disastrous trap:
where's one with heart of lion not fearing calamity?
I see many deceits in that narcissus, that eye of Yours:
to reputations, with path's dust, comes perishability.
When I ask You: "Why do You mix with the others?"
Mixing my tears with blood you show me Your ability.
Ask for life and for patience: for Fortune's juggling
does a thousand strange tricks, full of inexplicability.
Hafez, come; place head on threshold of submission:
for if you should argue, Time will show implacability.

170. THE KING'S SLAVE

Inclination for world, my soul without Beloved's grace,
doesn't have.
O God, one who does not have this: that, in any place
doesn't have.
I have not seen a single trace of that Heartstealer with anyone else:
I have no news at all of that One, that One even a trace
doesn't have.
It's not right to give the stage of contentment away from the hand;
cameldriver get down, for an end this path, this chase,
doesn't have.
Each drop of night's dew is like a hundred seas of fire in love's path:
a pity, for explanation or revelation Love's subtle case
doesn't have.
Without the Beloved life doesn't have a delight that is such as that;
such as that, life that's without the Beloved's embrace,
doesn't have.
O heart, learn how to be properly intoxicated from the policeman;
he is intoxicated, yet suspicion about him the populace
doesn't have.
If the candle is your companion, conceal all your secrets from him:
for that bold one with head cut off on tongue a brace d
oesn't have.
One whom you call 'master', if you should honestly look at him…
he has the art of an arti-face, but his verse a true trace
doesn't have.
The harp with the back that's bent is inviting you to experience joy:
listen, for the old man's advice towards you, menace
doesn't have.
Story of Karun's treasure that Time gave to the wind of destruction
tell to rosebud, so that then it, gold hidden in its base,
doesn't have.
No one on surface of the whole world has a slave such as Hafez;
a King like You, one on or under the world's surface,
doesn't have.

171. O IDOL

The shining moon, the brightness of Your face
doesn't have:
compared with You, the rose the grass's grace
doesn't have.
The dwelling of my soul lies in the corner of Your eyebrow;
king, a happier place than this corner's space,
doesn't have.
I wonder what my heart's smoke will do with Your cheek:
for the mirror, power to resist the sigh's trace
doesn't have.
Not I alone have been affected by the length of Your hair:
who is there that the mark of this hair like lace
doesn't have?
I have seen that eye that has a black heart that is Your eye;
regard for any friend, that eye slightest trace
doesn't have!
O Winehouse's young enthusiast, give to me the large quart:
here is joy for priest that the cloistered place
doesn't have!
Drink your blood and silently sit, because that tender heart,
any strength to bear the seeker of justice's case,
doesn't have.
Look at the boldness of narcissus, blossoming in your sight;
such a one with eyes open, thought of disgrace
doesn't have.
Say this: "Go and wash your sleeve in the blood of the liver,"
to whoever a way to the threshold of this Place,
doesn't have.
Do not blame Hafez if he has worshipped You: O Idol, here,
one who is unfaithful to love, crime's disgrace
doesn't have.

172. HIDDEN DEFECTS

For many long years our book pawned for red grape's wine,
was;
yes, from our reading and praying, the Winehouse's shine
was.
Consider the grace of the Master of Winesellers to us drunkards:
whatever we did, in His eye of kindness, it good and fine
was.
With wine all of you should wash our book of understanding:
I saw the sky and all Who know knew that it out to malign
was.
My heart turned completely in every direction like a compass;
standing dizzy and bewildered, it in centre of circle's line
was.
Minstrel performed such a song about the painfulness of love,
the sight of the wise of the world, with blood to combine
was.
I blossomed with joy because like the rose on the stream's bank,
on my head the shade of that cypress of a tall and fine line
was.
O heart, if you know what is beautiful, seek that from the fair;
for One who said this, having insight that doesn't decline,
was.
My Master 'Rosecolour', regarding the wearers of blue robes,
didn't permit their faults to be told: or many a telling sign
was.
The counterfeit Hafez gathered wasn't passed on by his Master:
for the Master of Business, knowing hidden defect's design
was.

173. LONGING

In our circle last night, all the talk about Your hair
was:
until the heart of night, only talk of Your hair's snare
was.
The heart that was bleeding from the point of Your eyelash,

again longing for wound of bow of Your eyebrow's stare
was.
Blessing be on the wind for it brought a message from You;
and if not, no one to meet us from Your street there
was.
The world has no idea of the disturbing commotion of love:
exciter of world's calamity, Your glance's magical fare
was.
I with my bewildered mind was also of salvation's people;
the snare of my path, the curl of Your long black hair
was.
Loosen the fastening of Your coat so my heart may expand:
for whenever I was open, it from Your side, however,
was.
Be loyal to Your faithfulness and pass by the tomb of Hafez,
who went from the world and desiring Your face so fair
was.

174. I REMEMBER THAT TIME

I remember when my dwelling in Your street's vicinity
was,
to my eye from dust of Your door, gift of luminosity
was.
From being with the pure I stood up like the lily and rose:
whatever was in Your heart, on my tongue in sincerity
was.
When heart sought Divine Truths from Old Man Wisdom,
Love then explained what for him a great difficulty
was.
In my heart there was: "I will never be without the Friend."
What can one do for all of my heart's effort, only vanity
was.
Last night, thinking about friends I went to the Winehouse;
I saw winejar, blood in heart: foot in clay easy to see
was.
I wandered far and wide to find why separation's pain exists:

in this, without knowledge, teacher of reason certainly
was.
In the end, truth about the bright turquoise of Abu Ishak
was
that it gleamed brightly, but helping him to pass quickly
was.
It's a shame that all this tyranny is in this place of ambush:
it's a shame graceful generosity in that high assembly
was.
Hafez, you heard all the laughter of the strutting partridge:
he, of the grasping claws of the falcon of Fate, carefree
was.

175. DUST OF THE PATH

As long as of wine and Winehouse a name and trace
shall be,
the dust of the path of the Perfect Master our face
shall be.
When you pass by the head of our tombstone ask for grace,
for the pilgrimage of the drunken lovers, this place
shall be.
From before Time, slave-ring of First Master was in my ear;
and as we were we remain, and in this way our case
shall be.
Proud bigot, go; because from your eye and also from mine,
the Mystery of this veil's hidden: visible not a trace
shall be.
Today, lover slaying, my bold Turk went out intoxicated;
now where, blood flowing from whose eye's base
shall be?
Wherever on land is even a trace of the heel of Your foot,
for every person with Vision, the Adoration Place
shall be.
From that night my eye entombed desires, desire for You

until the Resurrection's dawn impossible to efface
shall be.
O Sir, do not censor the intoxicated, for from this old inn
none has known how the departure, from its space
shall be.
If in this way the fortune of Hafez shall give some benefit,
Beloved's long hair in hand of others, due to Grace,
shall be.

176. GOOD NEWS

Good news came: these times of difficulty
won't stay forever;
that didn't stay forever, so this obviously
won't stay forever.
Though in the eyes of the Beloved we are dust that is pitiful,
those informers on us now having security,
won't stay forever.
Because that silent doorkeeper, cuts down all with the blade,
the people living as a privileged society,
won't stay forever.
Candle, understand why union with the moth is worthwhile;
give and take until morning's luminosity,
won't stay forever.
Good news from the invisible world, Angel Gabriel gave me:
with sorrow in this world, one most surely
won't stay forever.
Regarding the image of good and bad, why cry or be happy,
for upon the page of life what we can see,
won't stay forever.
It's been said that the song at Jamshid's party went like this:
"Bring cup of wine for Jam: for Jam, he
won't stay forever."
O powerful one, use your hands and take this dervish heart:
warehouses of gold and a silver treasury
won't stay forever.
Look at palace's crystal dome, on it has been written in gold:

"Except works from hearts pure and free:
won't stay forever."
With dawn came the welcome news; singing of the final union:
"Trapped by grief's cage, a person truly
won't stay forever."
Hafez, don't ever stop longing for the Beloved's generosity;
stories of violence and times of tyranny,
won't stay forever.

177. ALL THAT REMAINED

In Beloved's home, he who was his heart's confidant,
remained,
and he who did not understand this matter ignorant
remained.
Don't blame me if my distracted heart broke through the screen;
thank God that it no longer behind screen, arrogant
remained.
Once I had a patched coat, it concealed over a hundred faults;
I pawned for wine and musician, but cord, irrelevant,
remained.
The Sufis took back their cloaks they had pawned for the wine;
in Wineseller's house, our coat given for intoxicant,
remained.
In the past others passed, patched-coats, drunk, now forgotten;
at head of every market's street, our story dominant
remained.
The memory of love's talk was the most pleasant sound I heard;
nothing else to echo around this high dome, resonant
, remained.
Except for my heart loving You from before to beyond Time,
I have heard of no other who in this work, constant
remained.
All ruby-coloured wine that I have taken from that crystal hand
became water of regret; my eye raining pearls, extant
remained.
The lover of pictures was so astonished by Your great beauty,

that his tale everywhere, on gate and wall to enchant,
remained.
The narcissus became sick and tired, trying to be like Your eye;
it did not acquire that Magic, so it sick and petulant
remained.
One day to the show to see Your long hair went Hafez's heart,
thinking to return; but caught in Your hair, luxuriant,
remained.

178. THE REAL PROVIDER

In the good times gone by, Your care for lover's welfare
was;
Your loving kindness to us, the talk of people everywhere
was.
So now remember these convivial nights when with sweet lips,
conversation about Love's Mystery and the Circle, there
was.
Although gathering's moon-faced beauties stole heart and faith,
our love was for the graceful ways of a nature that so rare
was.
If the shade of the Beloved fell upon the lover, is that wrong?
We are forever needing You, also Your desire for us there
was.
Before this new high dome and this azure arch are uprooted,
for my eye the true archway, the eyebrow of Beloved fair
was.
Dawn of beginningless Eternity to evening of endless Eternity,
our compact with love's promise and agreement, forever
was.
If on 'The Night of Power' I'm drunk at dawn, don't blame me;
Beloved came merry with wine, cup on edge of arch there
was.
If the rosary cord has snapped, please understand I'm excused;
for my arm on the arm of Winebringer with legs like silver
was.
As regards action, beggar at the King's door said this subtlety:

"At every table, wherever I've sat, God the real Provider
was."
In the time of Adam in the Garden, Hafez's poetry, beautifying
pages of the book of roses, white and red, all that were…
was.

179. THE MIRROR'S MANIFESTATION

When on the mirror of the cup, reflection of Your face's shine
falls;
the saint into longing for the cup, from the laughter of wine,
falls.
From that one manifestation in the mirror of Your face's beauty,
all this various imagination that is a mirror of mind's design,
falls.
What can a being do when he, compass-like, moves only to revolve?
Can he not move, he who in the circle of time's revolving line,
falls?
O kind sir, that time has now gone when you saw me in the cloister;
with face of the Winebringer and lip of cup, the work of mine
falls.
It is a proper thing to go dancing beneath sword of grief for You;
for whoever may be killed for You, his ending as a happy sign,
falls.
I did not fall from mosque to the Winehouse completely on my own:
this that is my end result, from the Order of Eternity Divine
falls.
Since Love's jealousy has silenced tongues of all the Great Ones,
why, mystery of grief for You into common mouths to define,
falls?
Each moment You do another kindness to me of a burning heart;
see how, worthy of such rewards, this Your beggar, into line
falls.
From pit of Your chin my heart reached, to cling to Your hair's curls;
O no, see how it escapes from the pit and into the trap's twine
falls.
On the Day of Eternity, Your face from behind veil manifested;

on face of knowledge, reflection from ray of that sublime Sign
falls.
All of this reflection of wine and various images that have appeared,
is a manifestation of face of Winebringer, that into cup of wine
falls.
One with a pure vision, through pure vision obtained the objective;
through eye that sees double, a sly one into desire of decline,
falls.
All of the Sufis are lovers and they also all play at giving glances;
but, from the midst of them, heartsick Hafez's name to malign,
falls.

180. THE SUFI'S COAT

The patched old coat of the Sufi is not all unmixed purity,
there are many religious habits that of the fire are worthy.
Our Sufi, proud of reading in the morning, used to get drunk;
look at him in the evening, for then he is seen to be merry.
It'd be good if the touchstone of experience came into use,
so that in whom is alloy, black of face that one would be.
One reared in softness and ease didn't travel to the Friend:
to be a lover one must be a drunkard… suffering calamity.
How long will you be grieving for this world that is mean?
Drink wine: it's a pity that hearts of the wise always worry.
If down on Winebringer's cheek makes such images on water,
many are the sallow faces that painted with blood shall be!
The Wineseller will take patchcoat and prayermat of Hafez,
if from hand of the moonlike Winebringer, wine flows freely.

181. THE LEAST CONDITION

Soul's breath leaves and my wish of You for me,
doesn't come;
from sleep and slowness my fortune, my agony,
doesn't come.
Into my eye, breeze sent a grain of the dust from Your street;

the Water of Life in my vision I'm unable to see:
doesn't come.
In Your hair heart made its home, experiencing sweet madness
with others there; news from it, full of misery,
doesn't come.
As long as I don't hold Your tall slender form tight in my arms,
to fruit, the plant of my heart, my desire's tree,
doesn't come.
Perhaps by Your heart-comforting face our wish comes; if not,
by any other way of arriving, our need, certainly
doesn't come.
With aim of truth, sincerely I let fly many an arrow of prayer;
what's the use, because to hit target effectively,
doesn't come.
Hafez, least condition of Love's faith is surrenderence of life;
go away, if from you, work of at least this degree
doesn't come.

182. DYING IN REGRET

I came out from my heart and work's dividend
doesn't come;
I went out from myself and inside the Friend
doesn't come.
In this fantasy of mine the time of life passed away; and yet,
the tyranny of Your long hair at last to an end
doesn't come.
My heart can tell many stories to the breeze of the morning;
but by my luck, night for morning away to send,
doesn't come.
The sighs of mine in the morning have never missed their mark:
now what happened, that to target each I expend
doesn't come?
O no, we never did sacrifice life and our wealth for the Friend:
from us this little work of love we could extend,
doesn't come.
Therefore, for the dust of Your door I will be dying in regret

that to my sight Water of Life its way to wend,
doesn't come.
The heart of Hafez became the most terrified of all mankind;
for it, out from curl of Beloved's hair's bend,
doesn't come.

183. HAPPY IS THAT HEART

Happy is that one's heart who after the illusory
doesn't go:
every doorway calls him, but by invitation he
doesn't go.
It is better for me that I don't desire that sweet ruby lip;
after sugar is there ever a fly that greedily
doesn't go?
You of such a glorious nature from beyond these worlds,
perhaps the promise Your heart gave, from me
doesn't go.
The eyes of grief's dark experience, tears don't wash away;
Your beauty spot's a vision that away certainly
doesn't go.
My book's the blackest there is, no one is worse than me;
why like pen's ink, heart's smoke into memory,
doesn't go?
Heart, restrain all this complaining and wandering about;
this going to go is useless: one going to flee,
doesn't go.
Don't try to decoy me with the crest of a mere sparrow;
bait with a falcon: pride, for prey unworthy
doesn't go.
Give me the perfume of Your hair like the eastwind has,
because my mind without Your scent, certainly
doesn't go.
Hem of Your merciful garment hide my drunkard's faults;
a small dishonour on God's Honorable Decree,
doesn't go.
Beggar that I am, I beg for the One straight as a cypress,

Whose hand into purse but for gold's treasury,
doesn't go.
Bring pure wine and give first to Hafez on this condition:
from our special circle, news of this generosity,
doesn't go.

184. IT WASN'T TO BE

My soul melted so my heart would be fulfilled:
it wasn't to be.
I burned away in this vain wish that I'd willed:
it, wasn't to be.
From searching for the treasure's talisman I desired to obtain,
I became one on whom the world's ruin spilled:
it, wasn't to be.
While searching for precious wealth of the Presence to be present,
I wander, to beg from those of generosity's guild:
It wasn't to be.
You said seriously: "One night I'll be the Chief of your circle:"
I became Your lowest slave, Your wish fulfilled:
it wasn't to be.
It is quite right if dove of my heart flutters, because it saw that
its path with twists, turns and traps was filled:
it wasn't to be.
Realizing to become intoxicated that ruby lip should be kissed,
so much blood into my heart like a cup spilled:
it wasn't to be.
Don't place your foot down in street of Love without a Guide;
by myself, for myself, a hundred moves I willed:
it wasn't to be.
Hafez devised a thousand methods through longing and thinking,
desiring obedience to him in Friend be instilled:
it wasn't to be.

185. A LOVER'S DESTINY

As for me, love for those dark eyes, from my mind's state
won't go;
this was destined by the heavens, and by any other gate,
won't go.
The spy stirred strife and torment, leaving no place to make peace;
perhaps all the sighs of dawn-risers into the sphere's estate
won't go.
Day of Eternity beyond Time, They ordered me only drunkenness;
for every portion that was on That Day given, another fate
won't go.
A safe secret place and ruby wine and Winebringer, the kind friend:
O heart, when could a work be better if it with this state
won't go?
O man of morals, for God's sake forgive us noise of drum and reed;
the Law with this idle tale is out of date, it will not rate,
won't go.
Power that I have is this, that secretly I practise my love for You;
of breast, kiss and embrace, I can't relate, not in my fate…
won't go.
One night Majnun spoke to Layla, said, "Beloved beyond compare,
to you will appear many lovers, but the one in a mad state
won't go."
Eye, don't try to wash grief's engraving from slate of Hafez's heart,
it's cut by Heartowner's sword and bloodstains from slate
won't go.

186. THE BOOK OF LOVE

In Eternity beyond Time, Your radiant beauty, glorification
struck;
then love revealed itself and with its fire all of the creation
struck.
Your face showed splendour, the angels saw but were without love;
from this flame raged into fire and Adam's clay preparation
struck.
Reason desired to light its lamp from that ever increasing flame,

lightning of jealousy flashed and the world into confusion
struck.
Then the pretender tried to enter the scene where the Mystery is;
an invisible hand at chest of that one without invitation,
struck.
Others staked their fortune upon the side of pleasure and of ease;
we who weren't strangers to love's grief for grief's vocation
struck.
The exalted soul desired to enter into that dimple of Your chin;
hands reached for chain of curls and locks locked location
struck.
So Hafez wrote joy's book of love in praise of You on that day,
when desires bringing joy to heart, his pen of cancellation
struck.

187. REMEMBER

Remember how in that sacred time, given Your glance so full
was:
obviously, our face showed a sign that Your love so merciful
was.
Remember how You blamed me and then with a look killed me;
Your sweet-tasting lip, Jesus Christ's life-giving miracle
was.
Remember when in secret Friendship we drank the morning cup;
there was only You my Friend, and I, and God also helpful
was.
Remember when my moon tied on tight a crescent-shaped cap;
servant of stirrup's arch, new-moon the messenger, global,
was.
Remember that time when I used to sit drunk in the Winehouse;
what I had then, now I need here; there, it always available
was.
Remember when the red wine inside the cup was really laughing;
between Your ruby and me, much communication, faithful,
was.
Remember how, when Your cheek lit up the bright candle of joy,

this flaming heart like the moth without any reason, pitiful
was.
Remember how, when at that Meeting Place of correct conduct,
laughing like a drunkard, the morning's red wine, mirthful
was.
Remember how You placed in order and also properly corrected,
every unpierced pearl of the poetry of Hafez, that doubtful
was.

188. FOR GOD'S SAKE

O heart, the door of the Winehouse maybe
they'll open;
perhaps the difficult knot of our difficulty
they'll open.
If because of selfish preachers they have closed the door,
for God's sake keep heart brave and happy:
they'll open.
By the pure hearts of lovers drunk from the morning cup,
soon the door with Love's prayer as key,
they'll open.
Write a note of consolation to the daughter of the vine,
that lovers cry blood from grief, and see:
they'll open.
On the death of pure wine cut the strands of the harp;
its tangled hair, young magicians, quickly
they'll open.
O God, they've closed Winehouse door; do not approve,
or the door of lies and deceit and hypocrisy
they'll open.
Hafez, this costume that you wear, when tomorrow comes
they'll tear away, and its cord you will see,
they'll open.

189. HEARTSIGHS

Pleasant is being alone, if the Beloved will with me
be;
not if I burn and You, candle of another assembly
be.
Solomon's seal-ring of power is really worthless stone;
at any time upon the hand of a demon it can easily
be.
O Lord, don't ever allow in the sacred place of Union
informers a confidence, or myself like a deportee
be.
Say to Phoenix: "Don't throw Your graceful shadow
on a land where the parrot less than kite's degree
be."
Why try to explain the desire of the lover's heartsighs,
burning words expression of burning heart obviously
be.
Our head has never lost the longing for Your country;
but my heart is far away, while I an exile over sea
be.
Even if like the lily Hafez should have ten long tongues,
in Your presence, like the rosebud he shall silently
be.

190. THE TALE OF ABSTINENCE

What a tale this my refusal, this my renouncing of wine,
is;
it is quite certain that at least the reasoning for it, mine
is.
I, nightly with the drum and harp threw down piety's path;
now suddenly I turn to this path: this a fine old storyline
is!
Until the end I did not know the path to the Winehouse:
if I didn't know, to what end then our abstinence a sign
is?
If the pious one doesn't take drunkards path he is excused;

Love is a matter that depending on the guidance Divine
is.
I'm slave of Perfect Master Who freed me from ignorance,
whatever our Master does, essence of assistance benign
is.
Prayer and pride for pious; I am for drinking and begging:
let's see which of us, the way of Your favour to incline
is.
Last night I didn't sleep from this thought a sage expressed:
"There is reason to complain if Hafez, drunk with wine
is."

191. FROM BEGINNING TO END

I fear that regarding our grief our tears the veil tearing
will be,
that throughout the world this sealed secret for telling
will be.
They say that by being patient the stone will become the ruby:
yes, it does become this, but the liver greatly bleeding
will be.
From the great arrogance of enemies, I'm completely astonished:
O Lord, forbid it if some praise this beggar ever receiving
will be.
Seeing that Your high cypress has a head that is so full of pride,
how then is it our short hand Your waist's belt, holding
will be?
I have launched the arrows of begging prayers from every side:
so that it may be that out of those arrows, one working
will be.
This palace of empire where Your form is like that of the moon,
at its threshold it's right that heads its doorstep dusting
will be.
My face has become golden from the alchemy of my loving You;
yes, dust turned into gold, by Your grace's happy raining
will be.
It's necessary for one to have many subtle graces besides beauty;

so that one, acceptable to the One Who is All-Knowing,
will be.
I will go to the Winehouse weeping and demanding to be helped;
for there, perhaps my deliverance from all this grieving
will be.
Soul, please tell our tale to the Heartowner in such a fashion,
that it not told to breeze, as news for it to be spreading,
will be.
If a great grief one day comes to you, do not have a sad heart;
go, be thankful to God, so that no greater grief coming
will be.
O my heart, be patient and don't grieve, because in the end this
evening becomes bright morning and night soon dawning
will be.
When the musk of the tip of Beloved's hair is in your hand Hafez,
hold your breath or this news sent to breeze of morning
will be.
Love for You is in my heart and love for You is also in my head:
with milk it had entered me, and it with the soul leaving
will be.
Hafez raises his head out from the tomb to be kissing Your foot,
if his dust to be spreading, Your graceful foot it treading
will be.

192. UNION WITH BELOVED

Separation day and severance night from Beloved at last
is ended;
this grief, as lucky star has passed and my fortune cast,
is ended.
All of the heart's grief and those long cold dark worrying nights
in the shadow of lovely form's long hair that's overcast,
is ended.
Although it was my way to be at first tangled by that long hair,
the problem-knot of entanglement, by Your face at last
is ended.
To the dawn of Hope worshipping from behind the hidden screen,

say: "Break out and see, dark nights work is in the past,
is ended."
False pride of face of Autumn that weary waiting Winter showed,
with arrival of footsteps of the breeze of Spring, at last
is ended.
Thanks to God that by fortune of crown that caps rosebud's peak,
the mighty thorn and pompous December wind's blast
is ended.
From now on, light will shine from our heart across the horizon,
for we have reached the Sun and the dust is in the past,
is ended.
And now with the harp and drum to the Winehouse I'll be going;
with grace of Union with Beloved, grief's story at last
is ended.
Wineseller, You showed kindness, Your goblet be full of the best!
by Your management, vine causing sickness is outcast,
is ended.
Although true consideration and praise due to Hafez no one gives,
thank God his occupation of grief beyond estimate, vast,
is ended.

193. IT'S NOT EASY

To preacher of the city this easy to understand
doesn't become:
as long as he practices deceit, he a real Muslim
doesn't become.
Learn drunkenness and be kind; for it's not really a great thing
if an animal doesn't drink wine and if it a man
doesn't become.
Divine Name of God does its work: heart, be full of happiness!
demon, by lying and cunning, a real Solomon
doesn't become.
To be worthy of God's grace it's necessary to be pure in essence:
if not so, pearl and coral every clod and stone
doesn't become.
I practise love; and I am hopeful that this great, this noble art,

like some, reason for disappointment in this man
doesn't become.
Last night You said: "Tomorrow I will give you heart's desire."
God, devise a foolproof way so defunct this plan
doesn't become.
I pray to God to give to Your nature a disposition that is gentle,
so that our poor heart hurt by You once again
doesn't become.
One with many sorrows who keeps pain secret from Physician,
without a doubt, capable of a remedy, his pain
doesn't become.
That one who trembles before the false idols with all of his soul,
without a doubt, that one worthy of the *Koran*
doesn't become.
Hafez, so long as the atom does not seek to reach to the highest;
it, a true seeker of the gleaming Sun's fountain
doesn't become.

194. YOU ANSWERED

I said: "I grieve for You," You said: "Your grief's limit
comes:"
I said: "Be my moon," You answered: "If it happens, it
comes."
I said: "Your face is a moon," and You: "Only two weeks old:"
I said: "Will it shine on me?" And You: "If that way it
comes."
"The use of faithfulness" I said, "learn from all Your lovers;"
"Such from moon-faced ones" You said, "not even a bit
comes."
I said: "Your image, I will chain my sight upon its pathway:"
"But" You said, "the nightstalker by a path inexplicit,
comes."
I said: "Vagabond of the world, scent of Your curls made me:"
You answered: "And you know, as your guide also it
comes."
I said: "I am killed from longing for honey of Your ruby lip;"

You answered: "Be a good servant for finally the profit
comes."
"When will Your merciful heart" I said, "give me some peace?"
You said: "Don't tell it to anyone until time that's fit
comes."
Then I said: "How quickly have ended the moments of ease:"
You answered: "Hafez, be silent, to an end grief's limit
comes."

195. WHAT WILL BE

He whose desire for Your cheek's down so sweet,
will be,
never to step out from Your lovers' circle his feet
will be.
When like the tulip I rise out from the dust of the grave,
scar of love for You, secret mark of heart's seat
will be.
Perfect jewel: for You, how long my eye's pupil joined
with that ocean of sorrow where all rivers meet,
will be?
May the shelter of Your long hair lengthen over my head,
for in that shadow, peace to the mad heart's heat
will be.
Water is flowing from the root of every eyelash of mine:
come, if Your inclination stream's bank to greet
will be.
Come out from screen for a moment like my heart does,
for it's not known if another time for us to meet
will be.
You turn Your eyes away from Hafez because of pride:
yes, the quality of deep blue narcissus, conceit
will be.

196. FROM THE EAST

When from the east the cup of sun, the wine in the bowl,
                    comes out;
many a tulip from the garden that is Winebringer's mole,
                    comes out.
A soft scented breeze spreads curls of the hyacinth over rose's head,
        when into the garden that hair's perfume, out of control,
                    comes out.
O heart, don't expect anything from turning of sky's inverted bowl:
        no crumb without making many problems, from this bowl
                    comes out.
The anguish of the night of separation no history has written down;
        not even a note about it, even if a hundred scrolls unroll,
                    comes out.
If like the Prophet Noah you are patient in the deluge of suffering,
        flood subsides and wish of thousands of years, your goal,
                    comes out.
One cannot by only one's own effort reach to the jewel of desires…
        it is only a fantasy that this, without the Guide's control,
                    comes out.
If by tomb of Hafez the breeze of Your grace should happen to pass,
        from that dust of his body many a shout from his soul
                    comes out.

197. WORTHY OF THE SWORD

Why is it that meadow's cypress, inclination for meadow
                    doesn't have,
doesn't become companion of rose, memory of lily also
                    doesn't have?
Since my foolish heart has departed, going into the curl of Your hair,
        from that journey, towards its homeland it a wish to go,
                    doesn't have.
Heart from hoping for union with You is no longer soul's companion:
        soul is Your slave and a desire to serve my body also,
                    doesn't have.

Before the bow of Your eyebrow I keep offering myself to be taken;
although drawn to ear, to hear, ear no sigh does show:
doesn't have.
Last night I complained about Your hair and with regrets You said:
"Inclination to me these long black curls' ear, I know,
doesn't have.
When the dark violet hair becomes twisted because of the wind...
O no, for then my heart a memory of curl it does show,
doesn't have.
If Winebringer of silver legs should give me nothing but the dregs,
who is it that a body that's all mouth like winecup, also,
doesn't have?
Breeze became a bringer of perfume: why is it that Your pure coat,
a need to make from violet's dust, Khutan's musk flow,
doesn't have?
I marvel at how perfume of Your coat coming from wind as You pass,
inclination to make from dust Khutan's musk flow,
doesn't have.
Do not spill the water of my cheek, my honour... for gift of the cloud
without the help of my tears, Aden's pearls to bestow:
doesn't have.
Hafez, who didn't listen to any advice was murdered by Your glance:
he is worthy of a sword, who an ear to hear advice, also
doesn't have.

198. BOLD THIEF

Our heart has no need of garden when it of Your face a trace
has:
its feet .are bound like cypress and like tulip a stain on face
has.
Our head does not bend down low to bow of anyone's eyebrow:
for the heart in seclusion, no need at all for any other place
has.
I'm tormented because of the violet, for it boasts it has Your curls;
witness the conceited mind this slave that is full of disgrace
has.

How can destination be reached in the wilderness in a dark night,
unless my pathway is illuminated by the light that Your face
has?
It's right if candle of the morning and myself went out together,
for we have both burned away and Beloved for us no grace
has.
Walk into the garden and then consider the throne of the rose;
see how the tulip like King's slave, cup in hand held at base
has.
It is right that in the garden I weep like the clouds of January:
see how the joyful nest of the nightingale, a crow to debase
has.
By the light of Your face, all night long Your hair takes my heart:
what a bold thief this is, that in hand the light of Your face
has!
The sick and sad heart of Hafez is longing for the lesson of love:
for the heart, neither desire to view nor be in garden's space,
has.

199. COME WHAT MAY

Secret wine and pleasure, without any substance are they:
we'll join up with drunken lovers, and, come what may!
Loosen knot of heart's strings and forget sky's destiny;
for to untie this knot no intellectual has found a way.
At the changes of fortune brought about by the planets
don't question; millions of stories the sphere could say.
With appreciation take the wine goblet, remembering it's
from dust of Jamshid's skull, Kobad and Bahman's clay.
Where Kay and Kaus went who knows and who can tell?
How did Jamshid's throne meet such a wind of decay?
In deep regret for the lip of sweet Shirin, I can still see
the blood in Farhad's eye; the tulip still blossoms today.
Come, come and let's drink wine until drunk and ruined;
perhaps then in this place of ruin a treasure might lay.
Could be tulip knew about the unfaithfulness of Time;
for since being born, she never gave the winecup away.

The breeze of Musalla's dust and the water of Ruknabad
have never let me wander or ever travel too far away.
My soul's as it is because of my grief from love for You;
may Time's wounded eye never touch Your soul, I pray.
If I don't put the cup from my hand don't criticize me:
for one purer than this companion hasn't come my way.
Like Hafez, don't take the cup unless you hear the harp;
listen, the happy heart to silk string of Joy, tied They.

200. THE BEST KIND OF SECRET

He who receiver of Fortune's gift in Eternity without beginning
is,
his cup's desire as his soul's companion to Eternity without ending
is.
At that moment when I was wishing I could renounce drinking wine,
I said this: "If this branch will bear some fruit, it then repenting
is."
Though it's granted that I threw prayer-mat on my back like the lily,
it on patchcoat, wine-rose of colour, fit for Muslim to be wearing
is?
I cannot sit in seclusion without having the lamp of the cup of wine;
for it's necessary that in the corners of lovers hearts, light shining
is.
The glow of the light of the candle and the wine, lights our seclusion:
abstinence of drunkards in the rose season, lack of understanding
is.
We are sitting among friends in the Springtime and talk is of love;
not to take the cup of wine from the Beloved, truly unbecoming
is.
Try to gain highest: to the goblet with the false jewels say: "No!"
to drunkard, juice of the grape, pomegranate of ruby for drinking
is.
O heart, if you desire a good reputation then don't make bad friends.
O soul, the proof of stupidity is when one of the bad approving
is.
Although our work may seem to be disordered, don't think it is easy:

for in this religion the great envy of kings, one who goes begging
is.
Last night the pious one said: "Hafez, is secretly drinking wine."
O pious one, the best kind of secret is the secret that for keeping
is.

201. THE LOVER'S CONDITION

If a cup of wine, never heart's grief from our memory
will take,
foundation of our occupation, Time that gives anxiety,
will take.
If reason does not lower its anchor into the sea of intoxication,
how is it that a boat out of this whirlpool of calamity
will take?
What a pity, the sky played a treacherous game with everyone:
there is not a one who over this treachery, superiority
will take.
My sick heart drags me out into the meadow for the reason that
my soul from its death the morning breeze's passivity
will take.
Way is through Land of Darkness but where's Khizer the guide?
Don't let it be that the fire of disappointment, dignity
will take.
I am love's physician: drink the wine; for this helpful concoction
brings immediate relief and away thoughts of calamity
will take.
Hafez burned away and no one told his condition to the Beloved;
perhaps, for God's sake, the breeze his note for delivery
will take.

202. KEY TO THE TREASURE

For love and drunkenness that stupid one tries to censor me,
making criticisms of the men who guard the hidden mystery.
Look at the perfection of love's mystery, not sin's mistake:

he who has no talent at all looks only at what is unworthy.
In such a way Winebringer's glance struck the path of Islam,
that perhaps only Suhaib, the red morning wine doesn't see.
From the scent of the Huri of Paradise perfume ascends when
she, taking Winehouse's dust, makes collar smell fragrantly.
Acceptance by Friend is the key to the treasure of happiness:
no one should have in this matter, a fear or any uncertainty.
Moses, the shepherd of Wadi Ayman gained his desire when
after many a year, with his soul he served Jethro faithfully.
The tale of Hafez makes the blood trickle down from the eye,
when the time of youth and old age he brings into memory.

203. ONE DAY

If again the bird of Fortune a passage along this way
shall make,
the Beloved will come once again and a happy day
shall make.
Although there is no strength in the eye to make pearls or gems,
it will drink much blood and then it a visible spray
shall make.
No one can ever find the words to tell our tale to the Beloved;
perhaps a report of it, morning breeze shall convey:
shall make.
I have given flight to the hawk of my eye towards the Pheasant:
perhaps it may bring back Fortune and a great Prey
shall make.
Last night I said this: "Will You make Your ruby lip my remedy?"
Voice of invisible messenger answered: "Yes, one day
shall make!"
The city has no lovers; yet it could be that out from somewhere
a man by himself, an offering of himself, someday
shall make.
Where is a generous One, from Whose banquet of Joy, one who
is sorrowful is drinking and winesickness to go away
shall make?
Either faith, or news of union with You, or death of the rival:

one of these one, two, or three, is what sky in play
shall make.
Hafez, if you don't leave the Beloved's doorway even for a day;
Beloved, a way here from a private district, one day
shall make.

204. THE HAPPIEST SPRING

The rose came happily, no happier Spring
is:
when in your hand cup is, no other thing
is.
Take time, and in the rosegarden drink wine,
for no more than a week, a rose blooming
is.
Enjoy fully; fully enjoy a time of happiness,
because in shell not always the pearl lying
is.
So unique is the path of Love; on this path
whoever lifts a head, a head not existing
is.
If you go to our school, wash all pages white,
because in the book, never love's learning
is.
Listen to me, join your heart to a Sweetheart,
whose beauty without need of ornamenting
is.
O priest, come to our Winehouse; drink wine
that not even in Kauther, Paradise's spring,
is.
You, Who filled Your go id en cup with ruby,
give gold to those, where no gold flowing
is.
Lord, give me a wine without any impurities,
from which later no hangover, head-aching,
is.

In Name of God, I've an Idol of silver body,
that in old Azar's temple, no such a thing
is.
With all my heart I'm slave of Sultan Uvays,
although of his servant, no remembering
is.
I swear by his crown that adorns the world:
the sun does not cap what this, crowning
is.
Only those criticize the poetry of Hafez's soul,
in whom no grace or pleasure for pearling
is.

205. BRING TO YOUR MIND

Companions, the Friend through the night,
bring to your mind:
duty of being a servant doing what is right,
bring to your mind.
The weeping and sighing of lovers in the season of intoxication,
to height of tune, harp and cymbal's flight,
bring to your mind.
When you bring the hand of hope to the waist of your objective;
the promise our circle made with all might,
bring to your mind.
When wine's reflection shines out in the face of the Winebringer,
lovers, through singing of a melody all night,
bring to your mind.
Do not be feeling grief for a moment for those who are faithful:
the unfaithfulness of Time's spinning flight,
bring to your mind.
No matter how impetuous is the steed of Fortune, when whip
You crave to use, those who are out of sight,
bring to your mind.

You Who are dwelling in the seat of honour, show some kindness:

Hafez's face with Your threshold in the light,
bring to Your mind.

206. THE FLY AND THE FALCON

O heart, joyful news, One with breath of a Messiah
comes:
by sweet perfumed breath, one's fragrance supplier
comes.
Don't complain again of separation's grief, for last night
I cast an omen and it was that a grievance rectifier
comes.
I am not the only one who is full of the fire of Wadi Ayman:
there like me is also Moses, full of hope that the Fire
comes.
There is no one who does not have a place in Your street:
because there, everyone to this way as a great desirer
comes.
No one has knowledge of where the Beloved is dwelling:
for only the ringing of the bells, to the identifier
comes.
Give a drink: for to the Winehouse of the generous Masters
with intention of requesting each drunkard as trier
comes.
If Friend inquires about health of one sick with grief, say:
"Quick! Go to him, while breath still as his supplier
comes."
Make some inquiries about the nightingale of this garden:
for I hear the crying that from the cage's occupier
comes.
Friends, the Beloved desires to make Hafez's heart the prey:
for a fly, a small prey, a royal falcon, a great flyer
comes.

207. SPRING

Good news came that Spring is here with a green coat so fine:
if allowance comes it will be spent on the rose and some wine.
Song of the birds grows louder; where's the leather wine flagon?
The nightingales are upset; who tore back the rose's veil so fine?
This old patched coat that's red as the rose I'll take and burn;
the old Winemaker won't buy it, not for a drop from the vine.
Pluck a rose today from cheek of the Wineseller like the moon;
for around the rose garden's face there grows a fine violet line.
Without a Guide of the road don't put a foot on Love's street;
for the one without a Guide is lost, and lost is that road's line.
What delight will one obtain from tasting the fruits of Paradise,
if one hasn't delighted in a peach of the Beloved's chin Divine?
Wineseller's tender looks have stolen my heart from my hand,
so that when I try to talk to others or listen, no power is mine.
Yes O friend, the ways of love are full of so many marvels that
the fierce lion in this wild domain, flees from deer's first sign.
Don't complain of suffering, because in this path of searching,
the only ones gaining ease are those who suffer without a sign.
Help for God's sake, You Guide Who knows this Sacred Path;
for end to Love's desert can't be seen, there's no horizon line.
Come and drink wine and give to Hafez the cup of pure gold;
for the sin of the Sufis is forgiven, by a King, merciful, Divine.
Hafez has not plucked a single rose from Your beautiful garden;
on this land it seems no breeze of human kindness blows a sign.
Spring is racing by quickly, please help me, Justice Giving One!
The season's already finished, and Hafez still hasn't tasted wine.

208. BREATH OF JESUS

If that Wineseller an allowance for the drunkard's need
makes,
God forgives: and turning away of every disastrous deed
makes.
Winebringer, give the wine in the cup of the measure of justice,

so beggar isn't jealous and in the miserable world, greed
makes.
Minstrel, with the lute play: "Without true death, no one died!"
Whoever does not know this melody, a false creed indeed
makes.
Wise man, if your way comes sorrow or if it is ease that comes,
attribute it to no other but God, Who what is decreed
makes.
In the workshop where there's no path for reason or for craft,
why weak imagination, a presumption of taking the lead
makes?
O God, the happy news of safety from these sorrows will come,
if the holy traveller, faith in Promise originally agreed,
makes.
Since love's pain and the disaster of the sickness of wine is ours,
the Beloved's ruby or pure wine our remedy guaranteed
makes.
Life passed by in the desire for wine and Hafez burned from love:
where's One of breath of Jesus, Who our reviving, decreed
makes?

209. THE BEST ADVICE

I wonder when of the heart's coin a complete assay They
take,
if all those recommending cloisters, their own way they
take?
The best advice I see is that all friends let go of all other work,
and a hold of the curl of the Beloved's hair today they
take.
With happiness the companions hold tip of Winebringer's hair:
and when the sky will allow it, a little rest one day they
take.
Don't boast to lovely ones of strength of your arm of chastity:
with a single rider from this tribe, a fortress away they
take.
O Lord, how eager for blood are all of those bold young ones,

for with arrow of the eyelash each moment a prey they
take.
Sweet is the dance, dancing to sweet singing and reed's voice:
especially that dance where a fair one's hand in play they
take.
So people of vision may turn Your path's dust into eye's *kohl,*
many ages have passed by: but still to Your highway they
take.
Hafez, the sons of Time do not have even a care for the poor:
it's best if the poor, a path that is out of their way, they
take.

210. A HAPPY DREAM

In a happy dream I noticed that the cup my hand was holding:
interpretation was made and the work to Fortune was passing.
For forty years I suffered difficulty and anguish, and finally I
was to find the outcome in wine that for two years was aging.
In the curling long hair of that Beloved with the hair of musk,
was that muskpod which from Fortune I was always desiring.
In the morning I was overcome by the great hangover of grief.
Fortune became generous and the cup the wine was containing.
I drink the heart's blood but there is no reason to complain;
this much, the tray of generosity as our portion was serving.
I drink blood forever on the steps of the Winehouse's doorway;
when this to me on the First Day was given, it I was drinking.
Weeping and asking for justice I make my way to the Winehouse,
for to get help there for all my sighing and crying, I was trying.
Whoever hasn't planted love or plucked a rose for its loveliness,
took care of the tulip in the path where the wind was blowing.
In the morning time I happened to pass by the bed of the rose,
bird of the garden was working: he was sighing, he was wailing!
We saw Hafez's verse that fascinates heart, praising the King;
better than a hundred letters is each line that book's containing.
Sun that seizes the lion bends before that fierce attacking King
Who, on the day of battle, turns lion into a gazelle, trembling.
One of Hafez's sayings, on leaf the rose kept writing: a verse

that in subtlety more than a hundred books was explaining.
The breeze of the garden threw fire into the nightingale's heart,
because of the secret stain that in its soul the tulip was hiding.

211. UNDER THE SURFACE

Not every beauty whose face is bright, ways of a heartstealer
knows;
not everyone who makes a mirror, insight of an Alexander
knows.
Not everyone who wears his cap slanted and sits up proudly
straight,
can do the work of the crown, or the worth of a true Ruler
knows.
There are a thousand points here that are finer than the finest hair:
not every person with a shaven head, subtlety of a Kalandar
knows.
It would be good if you learned faithfulness and kept the promise:
you'll see that the one not doing this, the role of a dictator
knows.
Clearly, the objective of my vision is centred upon Your dark mole;
for the value of the incomparable black pearl, the jeweler
knows.
Don't give service as beggars do, to gain some kind of material
reward, because the way to pay for the servants' service, the Master
knows.
I'm drowned in the water flowing from my eyes but what can I do?
Not everyone who is in the ocean, the way of a swimmer
knows.
I am the slave of whatever that daring Adventurer may want to do,
Who, the means of turning into an alchemist a poor beggar,
knows.
I staked my heart that was insane, but I did not really understand
that this being, birthed by Adam, truly an angel's character
knows.
Each One Who reigned by form and face over all of the lovely ones,
would conquer the world, if each the law of a justice-giver

knows.
Verse of Hafez that fascinates the heart will be known by one who
has natural grace, and the passwords of the 'Doorway' keeper
knows.

212. BEYOND COMPARE

To our Friend, no one in faith and nature fair
ever reaches;
to you, this concern's work is denied, it never
ever reaches.
Compared to our sincere and faithful Friend, no friend or a
confidant, by dues of ancient promise, I swear,
ever reaches.
To the people have come splendid ones, boasting of beauty:
to Beloved in grace and beauty none anywhere
ever reaches.
Into this market of Creation are brought thousands of coins:
not one, to die of Master Minter can compare:
ever reaches.
From Creator's pen are drawn thousands of fine images: but,
not one to degree and approval of our Idol fair,
ever reaches.
Heart, don't grieve about the blows of the jealous: trust God,
for to our good true heart at the end, evil never
ever reaches.
No, the Caravan of Life went past so fast and in such a way,
that never its heart's dust, to our country's air
ever reaches.
So live in such a way that if you die and you are path's dust,
from this, heart's dust to no one whatsoever,
ever reaches.
Hafez is consumed, and I'm afraid no word to explain this
to ear of the powerful King, beyond compare,
ever reaches.

213. WHAT WILL BE?

Blowing musk, breath of the breeze of morning
will be;
the old world once again to its youth returning
will be.
The arghavan shall give the jasmine the cornelian cup;
towards anemone, eye of the narcissus glancing
will be.
Nightingale suffering grief from sorrow of separation,
going to the pavilion of the rose, loudly lamenting
will be.
Don't blame me if I leave the mosque for the Winehouse:
sermon to assembly was long, away time slipping
will be.
O heart, if you throw away today's joy until tomorrow;
who then, insurer of today's wealth of living
will be?
In this festive month don't put the cup from your hand:
for this sun from one's sight, until end of fasting
will be.
The rose is priceless, evaluate its presence as a great gift:
it enters the garden this way and by that, going
will be.
Singer, it's a party of friends so sing songs and *ghazals*:
how long do you say: "This went; that, coming
will be?"
Into a cycle of life's existence Hafez came for Your sake:
prepare to say goodbye to him, he soon departing
will be.

214. REMEMBER US

When remembrance of us one day Your musky reed
makes,
reward will be this: that it, two hundred slaves freed
makes.
Majestic Salma's messenger to whom be blessing of safety,
what is it if he with a greeting, full our heart's need

makes?

O Lord, into heart of that Sovereign Shirin throw Yourself
so that then a merciful passage to Farhad she in deed
makes.

Your glances of love have now torn away my foundation,
now let's see what foundation Your intelligent creed
makes.

Your pure Essence has no need at all of any of our praises:
Who with Divine beauty, thought of adorner's deed
makes?

Take notice of: "They will give You many desired treasures,
if a ruin like me full of prosperity, Your grace indeed,
makes."

Better for king, than a hundred years of piety and austerity,
is hour of life, where he justice to those who plead
makes.

Here in Shiraz, by our desire we don't travel very far at all;
day of going to Baghdad, Hafez joyful guaranteed
makes.

215. ADVICE OF THE MASTER

Whoever from morning breeze Your fragrant scent
knew,
from a familiar friend, the Friend's familiar accent
knew.

Monarch of beauty, give the beggar's case an eye's glance,
for many tales of the King the beggar, his ear bent,
knew.

With musky wine I'll make the palate of my soul happy:
from cloaked cloistered hypocrites, it bitter scent
knew.

The mystery of God the wayfaring Seeker told to no one;
I'm astonished, because the Wineseller so confident,
knew.

O Lord, where is that confidant, so my heart can confide
what it said and what it has heard and what content

knew.

My faithful thankful heart that wasn't fit for unfit words,
from its sympathizer, words impossible to invent
knew.

If I am excluded from your street, does it really matter:
from rosebed of the world who ever faith's scent
knew?

It's not only today we drink the wine from under our coat;
over a hundred times the Wineseller this same event
knew.

It is not only today that we drink wine to the harp's tune:
often this sound the sky's dome, turning as it went,
knew.

Advice of the Master is the right essence of what is right;
fortunate is the one who heard, then action's assent
knew.

O Hafez, your role is only to praise, and to do only that;
whether it is heard or not, not even your torment
knew.

216. STRIVE

To those broken ones, who for the search their ability
is not,
if You cause a difficulty then a state of humanity
is not.

We haven't received injustice from You, and Your approval
of what judgment of the elders of the path may be,
is not.

Kaaba and house of idols are one when there is no purity:
all is not well when in house of the heart, purity
is not.

For as long as Your eye's sorcery doesn't give aid to a spell,
from the burning of the candle of love a light to see
is not.

That eye be blind whose water is not taken by fire of love:
a heart be dark where love's light shining brilliantly

is not.
Your beauty let me see the end of rope of my occupation:
may it not be, that such a fortune given generously
is not.
Whoever is not a pure mirror because of dark rust of lust;
that one's eye to look on the face of Wisdom, worthy
is not.
From shadow of Pure Bird of fortune don't look for fortune,
for fortune's long feather with black crow certainly
is not.
If I look for a blessing from the Winehouse, don't criticize:
our Master said this: "In a cloister, such generosity
is not."
Hafez, strive for knowledge and manners; without manners,
one of company in King's chosen assembly, worthy
is not.

217. THE NIGHT OF UNION

Praise be to God what wonderful wealth's given to me
tonight;
because my Divine Beloved came to me, quite suddenly,
tonight.
The moment I saw Beloved's beautiful face I bowed in praise;
thanks be to the Grace of God, I'm fortunately happy
tonight.
The seed of my infinite patience has now blossomed this Union;
I'm harvesting fruit of my patience, Fortune's with me
tonight.
My slumbering destiny has awakened and is finally approved;
it is my life's luckiest night, for I hold the guarantee
tonight.
I've resolved that even if my head's cut off it doesn't matter;
removing the world's veil, Secret shown by me will be
tonight.
My blood will write 'I am The Truth' [Anal Haq] on the earth,
if like Mansur they kill me on the gallows mercilessly

tonight.

Beloved, You possess Divine Wealth, I'm beggar at Your door,
give the gift of Your Glory, make me blissfully happy
tonight.

All the time I'm frightened that Hafez will be lost, obliterated;
because each moment I'm in possession of such ecstasy
tonight.

218. REALIZATION

Last night before dawn, freedom from all suffering
They gave me;
in the darkness of night, Water of Life-everlasting,
They gave me.

They overpowered me with the brilliance of the Divine Essence;
a drink from the goblet of Divine Light overflowing,
They gave me.

What a fortunate dawn and joyful night was that Night of Power
when the Supreme Authority of God's Commanding
They gave me.

When I swooned with awe and wonder from love for Love's Face,
the two goddesses Lat and Manat's true meaning
They gave me.

If my longing is fulfilled and my heart is in bliss, what wonder…
all of this as rightful gifts, because I was deserving
They gave me.

Now, together are my face and the mirror of the Glory of Beauty:
Beloved's Glory reflecting my true Self showing,
They gave me.

All this honey and sugar that's pouring from my pen is the reward
for patience; and a branch of sugarcane for writing
They gave me.

Angel Gabriel the invisible messenger, gave me the happiest news:
when tyranny and violence comes, patience enduring
They gave me.

It's such a wonderful miracle to be the slave of the Perfect Master:
I became His dust and the rank of the highest rating

They gave me.
The Master raised me that day to reach to life Eternal without end;
when the, writing of freedom from death, everlasting,
They gave me.
Hafez said: "The moment I fell into the snare of the tip of Your hair,
release from the chains of anguish and of suffering
They gave me."
Because of blessings I received and wishes of dawn companions,
freedom from Fate's sickness and Time's grieving
They gave me.
Hafez, rejoice, rejoice, then thankfully scatter the sugar of thanks:
Realization of the Divine Beloved, sweetly swaying,
They gave me.

219. THE TREASURY OF LOVE

Really, jewel of the treasury of Mystery
is as it was:
with that seal and mark, Love's treasury
is as it was.
Lovers are trustworthy ones who keep Love's secret;
undoubtedly, their eyes raining jewelry,
is as it was.
Ask the east breeze how all night until breath of dawn,
our soul's friend Your hair's perfumery
is, as it was.
There is not a seeker of ruby and jewel, but even so,
the Sun hard at work in mine and quarry
is, as it was.
Colour of the. blood of our heart which You conceal;
it visibly in Your lip's ruby depository
is, as it was.
Come and visit the victim destroyed by Your glance;
expecting You, the helpless one's memory
is as it was.
I said: "Your Hindu-black hair won't attack again;"
years have passed and still its robbery,

is as it was.

Hafez, tell again the tale of your eye's tears of blood;

it, in this fountain still flowing, watery,

is as it was.

220. PLANT THE TREE OF FRIENDSHIP

Plant tree of friendship that to heart's desire fruitfulness
brings:
uproot the shrub of unfriendliness that troubles countless
brings.
When you are guest in the Winehouse respect intoxicated lovers,
for, O soul, drinking what's left excessively, winesickness
brings.
Nights of close friendship count as gifts, because after our time,
sphere turns many times, many nights, days of wakefulness
brings.
The bearer of Layla's burden, whose order is to cradle the moon,
God, maybe that one's heart, direction of Majnun's distress
brings.
O heart, wish for the Season of Spring; for in every year this field
a hundred roses, thousand birds like nightingales, no less,
brings.
As my heart made a true covenant with Your hair, for God's sake
command Your sweet ruby, that an ease to its restlessness
brings.
Heart, you've fallen helpless, you bear a hundred gallons of grief;
go, drink one measure of wine so that it, away all tiredness
brings.
In this garden of the world, Hafez, his hair grey, asks this of God:
that by the stream's bank he sits and cypress into his caress
brings.

221. PLAYING AT LOVE

Because of my glancing, those without vision full of amazement go:
they know about all of it, except that I'm what I'm wanting to show.
Wise men are the central point of the turning compass of existence,
but, in this circle their heads are spinning, and this Love did know.
Boasting love, complaining of Beloved's violence... proud of lies!
Such ones who play like this at love, should know separation, woe.
God made me promise of service with lip of those sweet of mouth:
each one of us is only a slave, and service to the Great Ones we owe.
Perhaps Your dark intoxicated eye will teach to me that occupation;
if not, then the work of being both drunk and sober not all can know.
My eye is not alone in shining Your cheek's great glorious splendour:
the sun and moon are also both turning this same mirror as they go.
If our way of thinking becomes known to all of those young masters,
afterwards they'll not pledge the Sufi patchcoat: O no! Not so! No!
We are poor and we have desire for the wine and for the Minstrel:
O no, if they don't pawn woolen patchcoat: O no, if they do not go!
If the wind will carry Your fragrance to the soul's place of pleasure,
throwing reason and soul, jewel of their being away they will throw.
The bat that is blind does not ever attain unity with the shining Sun:
even those who see are astonished by what this Mirror does show.
What have you to fear pious critic, from Hafez's drinking of wine?
"The devil flees from man who knows the *Koran:*" this, now know.

222. THE CLAY OF ADAM

Last night I saw that on Winehouse's door angels knocked,
they took the clay of Adam and it into a cup they shaped.
Inhabiting eternal realms, veiled and pure Angelic ones,
upon me lying in dust, a sweet intoxicating wine poured.
Thank God between us there is peace and contentment;
to this, many a cup of gratitude dancing Huris drained.
No wonder a hundred harvests of fantasy led me astray,
when from Path, aware Adam by a grain was betrayed.
The heavens could not bear that Trust's heavy burden;
they threw dice, and on mad lover, helpless me, decided.
That is no true fire that makes the candle's flame dance,
it is where the moth's harvest by that Fire is annihilated.

Pardon the seventy two arguing sects, because unable to
see the Truth, on the door of illusion they have pounded.
No one has like Hafez torn the veil from Thought's face,
since the tips of long hair, Speech's Brides first combed.

223. BLACK IS THE WATER OF LIFE

I see friendship in no one: to all the friends
what's happened?
Did friendship and friends meet their ends:
what's happened?
Black is the water of life; where are Khizer's guiding footsteps?
Rose has lost colour, no breeze Spring sends:
what's happened?
No one tells about a friend who keeps the friendship's promise;
to those who understand true values, friends:
what's happened?
This land was the home town of friends and dust of kindness:
where are friends, why is it friendship ends:
what's happened?
It's years since a ruby came out from the mine of all humanity:
to the rain and wind and heat the sun sends,
what's happened?
Into the middle They've thrown the ball of Grace and Mercy:
no one is on field, no horseman descends:
what's happened?
Thousands of roses have bloomed: no cry of a bird has risen;
to nightingale who a thousand notes blends,
what's happened?
Venus makes no sweet music, maybe she consumed her lute:
no one wants to drink, to drinking friends
what's happened?
Hafez, no one knows all the secrets of the Divine, so be silent!
Who to ask about Fate; who comprehends
what's happened?

224. HEAD ON THE THRESHOLD

Strike a note, a melody so moving that a sigh
one may give;
sing a verse whereby the cup that's filled high,
one may give.
If on the Beloved's threshold one can lay down one's head,
the shout of highest exultation up to the sky
one may give.
This world and that, men of vision stake for one glance;
it is love, where life's coin is cast: first 'die'
one may give.
It's not the cloister that contains the secrets of love's game;
wine of the Masters, only the Masters, a try
one may give.
About great fortune that is royally assured, do you know?
Maybe this time, opportunity's ball a hit high
one may give.
The finery of the king's palace isn't fit for the poor dervish;
if struck, a fire (our ragged old coat's so dry)
one may give.
The sum totality of our desire is love, youth, drinking wine;
if sense is clear, the ball of speech to clarify
one may give.
It is small wonder if Your flowing hair robs me of security,
hundred caravans' halt: to Your thieving eye,
one may give.
I'm ashamed that I'm inexperienced: Winebringer give kindly,
so on that mouth bold with wine, kisses supply
one may give.
If the Beloved's shadow's thrown in front of my eyes stream,
water that sprinkles dust as Beloved goes by,
one may give.
With reason, wisdom and knowledge, speech can be gifted;
once obtained, the ball from centre a hit high
one may give.
Our bent and bowed back is a form that may seem wretched,
still, from bow into eyes of foe, arrows to fly

one may give.

Enticed by the idea that fortune will open door of Union;
with hope, head to threshold for ages to lie,
one may give.

Hafez, by the truth of the *Koran*, leave all fraud and deceit;
maybe ball of fortune from true men, a supply
one may give.

225. THE POWER OF WINE

Again the power over myself, that wine did waylay:
again wine showed its power over me without delay.
A thousand blessings be heaped upon that red wine,
which has now driven my face's yellowness far away.
I praise the hand that was first to gather the grape…
may the foot that first pressed down on it never decay.
Fate decreed Love for me… wrote it on my forehead:
whatever Fate has written is impossible to wipe away.
Do not boast of wisdom: Aristotle must give up life
like the miserable old beggar, when death has its day.
Go far away you pious fanatic, and don't criticize us,
for the work of God is no small thing… in any way.
Don't pass your whole life in such a way in this world
that when you are dead, "He is dead," they will say.
Be happy and don't worry and don't be showing grief,
be content: such striped satin cloth is like silk today.
From cup of Eternity, intoxicated with God's Unity
become all, who like Hafez, drink the pure wine away.

226. THE CHOICE OF DESTINY

How a verse is the reviver of a heart that is full of despair!
A subtlety we quoted from this book, this subtlety we share.
If I've gained from Your ruby lip a great ring of protection,
a hundred kingdoms of Solomon are under my seal's share.
O heart, it's not good to despair because of the enviers' lies:

when you delve into it, what is good for you may lie there.
Whoever doesn't appreciate this, my reed's raising of images:
may his form be stilled, even if he is China's famous painter.
They gave each one a cup of wine and blood of the heart:
as destiny's circle unfolds, each one takes what is there.
In the matter of the rose and rosewater the First Law was:
"That, should be market's beauty; this, a veil should wear."
It's impossible for Hafez's heart to leave love and the wine:
that which was at time's beginning, at time's ending is there.

227. A FLEETING TREASURE

That one through whom our house the angels' dwelling
was,
from head to foot being like an angel, without faulting
was.
That moon was accepted by wisdom in me because of this:
that one, a beautiful nature and true insight uniting
was.
My heart said: "I will stay in this city in hope of this one;"
being helpless, it did not know its loved one travelling
was.
That loved one was torn from my arms by a malignant star.
What can I do? Cause of this disaster, moon's revolving
was.
Not only from my heart has the secret fallen from the veil:
the sky, since it began, its practise of the veil tearing,
was.
Sweet was edge of the water and the rose and green grass;
but, it's a shame that fleeting treasure soon wayfaring
was.
Those times that we spent with this loved one were happy:
in ignorance and without worth, everything remaining
was.
The nightingale killed himself through jealousy because to
the rose at dawn, the embrace of the breeze of morning

was.

O heart, it is all excused: because you are but only a beggar,
and that one, in beauty's kingdom, head for crowning
was.

All the treasures of happiness that God has given to Hafez,
result of the evening prayers and the morning begging
was.

228. FORTUNE'S MEANNESS

Of the Beloved's mouth, fortune even a trace
doesn't give me;
Fortune, news of the hidden mystery's place,
doesn't give me.
I died from my desire and there's no way within the screen; or,
there is, but screen's holder, way to its space
doesn't give me.
I would immediately surrender my life for a kiss from Your lip:
but this, You won't take, and that, Your grace
doesn't give me.
Morning breeze drew back Your hair: see fortune's meanness,
in that it, even the wind's power to embrace,
doesn't give me.
However like the compass along the edge of the circle I may go,
Time like the point, path to the central place
doesn't give me.
Sugar in the end came because of my patience; but some safety,
Time, which of faithfulness hasn't a trace…
doesn't give me.
I said: "I will go to sleep and see the beauty of the Beloved,"
but by sighs and cries of Hafez, sleep its grace
doesn't give me.

229. IN THE EARLY MORNING

At early morning waking Fortune over to my bed
did come:
"Get up, up, for your sweet Sovereign," it said,
"did come.
Drink some wine and go with a merry head to see that One,
so that you may then see which way your Beloved
did come.
O lonely hermit, opener of muskpod, give the happy news
that the muskdeer from Tartary's desert's bed,
did come!"
To cheeks of those burning, my tears brought back a shine:
weeping, the helper of the lover, sick and wretched,
did come.
Winebringer, wine; don't grieve because of enemy or Beloved:
as our heart wished, that one has gone and Beloved
did come.
Give a winecup out of joy for the angel-face of the Beloved:
remedy for the heart sick with grief wine so red,
did come.
The bird of my heart is again longing for the eyebrow's bow:
O pigeon, be patient and wait, for falcon to be fed
did come.
Since the cloud of Spring did see the unfaithfulness of Time,
its tears on lily, hyacinth and rose, white and red,
did come.
The morning breeze heard Hafez's words from nightingale;
for it, to see the sweet basil that ambergris shed,
did come.

230. LOVE'S MYSTERY COMES

When in prayer Your eyebrow's curve into memory
comes,
the arch of Prayer cries out, for to me such ecstasy
comes.
Now do not look to me for patience and strength of heart:
into thin air the patience you saw in me obviously

comes.

The wine is clear and drunk are all the world's songbirds:
season of the lover blossoms when love's mystery
comes.
From the corners of the world, scent of well-being I sense;
happiness the rose brought; dawn's breeze joyfully
comes.
Skilful bride, do not complain about fortune's hardships;
dress bridal room of Beauty, Bridegroom skillfully
comes.
Joseph of Egypt, don't approve violence against Zulaikha,
because the injustice to her, due to love's honesty
comes.
All the blooming heart-entrancing flowers dress in jewels;
except Heartstealer Who with God's gift of Beauty
comes.
The trees that are attached to world's fruit bear burdens:
happy the cypress that from grief's burden, freely
comes.
Come Singer, sing a sweet song of the poetry of Hafez;
so I will say: "The time, joyfully into my memory
comes."

231. OPEN THE KNOT

Companions; open, knot of Beloved's long tresses,
please make!
The night is happy, so with this, long its happiness
please make!
It's an intimate gathering and friends of the circle are together;
recite holy charm, the door locked against access
please make.
Stringed instrument and also the harp proclaim this out loud:
"Ear open to message of those of Consciousness
please make."
The first advice of the Master of the gathering was these words:
"Yourselves, safe from those mean and worthless,

please make."
By the Beloved's life I swear that grief will never tear your veil,
If you, reliance on Maker's Gracious Blessedness,
please make.
There is a great difference between the lover and the Beloved:
when Beloved's disdainful, the use of humbleness
please make.
In this circle of the world, everyone who is not alive with love,
he is dead though not: prayer over his deathliness
please make.
If Hafez should be seeking from you the gift of a great reward;
gift of him, to Beloved's heart-soothing lip's caress,
please make.

232. POWERFUL RIVAL

Young love, into my head covered by hair turned white,
has fallen:
the secret that I've hidden in my heart, out into the light
has fallen.
The bird of my heart went soaring quickly along the path of vision:
eye, look and see into Whose trap, it on its quick flight
has fallen.
What sorrow that because of the dark eye. that is like the musk pod
of the muskdeer, heart's blood into liver without respite
has fallen.
Every one to whom I mentioned the heavy load of this great grief
became helpless: and back to me, burden of this plight
has fallen.
From the way of the passage of dust from the end of Your street,
comes muskpod, that into hand of breeze at end of night
has fallen.
Since Your eyelash that conquers all the world drew out the sword,
many dead ones, heart beating, on the others in the fight
has fallen.
Whoever appreciates cup, to the extent the Winehouse drinker does,
because of its perfume of paradise from senses outright

has fallen?

Even if the black stone gives its life it does not become the ruby:
what can it do? It's not right, but to it, having this blight
has fallen.

In this house where one is given punishment, I've known for a time
that whoever falls out with drunkards, truly out of sight
has fallen.

In the end, even the sigh of a heart will take its path from the fire
burning the heart, that on the wet and dry to set it alight
has fallen.

Cry out, for that bird, though weighing words, through imagination
has lost its way and into a trap, whether wrong or right...
has fallen.

Hafez, whose happy hand is holding on to the long hair of the fair,
has a powerful rival, that into his head with much might
has fallen.

233. DOES IT MATTER?

If from Your garden a flower I gather,
does it matter?

If by Your lamp, my feet's way I ponder,
does it matter?

O Lord, if in shelter of the cool shade of the cypress,
burning, I sat for a moment to recover,
does it matter?

Seal-ring of Jamshid that works hard for good fortune,
if upon ring's ruby You're the reflector,
does it matter?

My reason has gone from the house, and if this is wine
I've had, then, faith's house, I wonder
does it matter?

When the city's pious look for king and judge's favours,
if of a fair One I choose to be a lover,
does it matter?

I've spent my precious life on wine and on a fair One:
what comes from this and the other:

does it matter?
The Master knew that I was a lover and kept silent:
if Hafez also knows that I am a lover:
does it matter?

234. THE BURNING HEART

O heart, burn: benefit to come your way... such burning
will make:
a hundred disasters to be turned away, midnight praying
will make.
Reproaches of the Pari-faced Beloved you should endure like a lover:
compensation for hundreds of cruelties one eye's glancing
will make.
They tear the screen from this world to that of angels, for that one
who a great service to that cup, that is world-displaying,
will make.
The Physician of love has compassion and also the breath of Jesus,
but when He sees no pain in you, then He any comforting
will make?
Give all your actions to God and let your heart be brave and happy:
if mercy enemy isn't showing, Mercy God Who is Willing
will make.
I'm tired of fortune that is sleeping: maybe one who is wide awake,
prayer for me at the time when the morning is dawning,
will make.
Hafez burned away and did not receive the scent of Beloved's hair:
perhaps the wind from the east, his fortune to be arriving
will make.

235. THE WINESELLER CAME

To congratulate the Ancient Wineseller, the morning breeze
came;
the season of joy and sweetness and freshness and happy ease
came.
The air's breath became that of the Messiah and dust shed musk:
the birds burst into loud singing and greenness to the trees...
came.
The breeze of the Spring has heated the oven of the tulip so much,
that the bud drowned in perspiration and rose into unease
came.
Be sensible and listen and hear what I say: "Try hard, to be happy,"
invisible messenger at dawn, to my ear these words to release,
came.
I don't know what that noble lily heard from the bird of the morning;
although it has ten tongues, into silence every one of these...
came.
Throw off thoughts of separation... so you can pull yourself together,
because when Satan left... Angel Gabriel of Divine prestige
came.
At the gathering of friendship there is no room for those excluded!
cover cup's mouth: because robe-wearers it will displease...
came.
They are happy words that I spoke to you, so bring out pure wine,
for the pious have left us... and the Wineseller, us to please,
came.
Hafez, going out from the cloister and going in to the Winehouse...
perhaps to his senses, from austerity and hypocrisy's disease,
came.

236. EMPTY PURSE

Clouds of March come and blowing is the breeze of the New Year,
my longing is for wine, and the singing minstrel has arrived here.
The lovely ones are beautiful and I'm ashamed of my empty purse;
O sky... for how long will I, a shame like this shame have to bear?
There is a drought of generosity: it's wrong to be selling honour:
it's right to buy wine and rose for patchcoat's price: that's clear.

It is likely that something great will come about from my fortune,
for I prayed all of last night and the dawn of creation did appear.
With a lip and a hundred thousand laughs, rose came into garden;
you could say: "It smelt perfume of a dear one in a corner, near."
If in the drunken lovers' world the skirt was torn, does it matter?
it is also necessary that one's cloak of reputation, one must tear.
Who spoke those graceful words about Your ruby lip that I spoke?
Who bore the suffering from the tip of Your hair... that I did bear?
If Sultan's justice doesn't inquire of those who suffer from Love,
it's necessary for secluded to be excluded when peace comes near.
I don't know who shot at Hafez's heart the arrow that kills lovers!
All I know is that from his fresh verse some drops of blood appear.

237. THE RING OF SERVICE

If the Sufi drinks wine to his limit, then may it for him sweet
be!
If he doesn't, may his occupation be forgotten and incomplete
be!
The one who can give a single mouthful of wine to someone else,
with the Beloved of his desires, handed over to him as a treat
be!
Who is that horseman who is full of happiness and is full of joy?
May both worlds tied to his shoulder's flag and his coat's seat
be!
Our Master said: "The pen of the Creator did not make a mistake."
May blessings on the Master's pure sight, covering the indiscreet,
be!
The king of the Turkans listened to the suggestions of the enemies:
his, great shame for the way Siyawash he did cruelly mistreat,
be.
Eye became one of the holders of mirror of Your mole and down:
lip, a snatcher of kisses of where neck and back sweetly meet,
be!
Although from pride You didn't say a word to me the poor dervish;
my life as a ransom for Your silent pistachio nut that's sweet,
be!

Your eye, drunken narcissus, doing favours and subduing mankind,
if it drinks the lover's blood in the goblet, may it a sweet treat
be!
Hafez has become famous in the world, from being in Your service:
may the ring of service for Your hair, in his ear, this I repeat:
be!

238. THE ONLY REMEDY

Lord, in street of Winehouse in the morning a great commotion
was,
for noise of the fair, Winebringer, and candle and fire's agitation
was.
The story of love that is independent of any letter or of any sound…
with resounding shout, shrieking reed and drum's reverberation
was.
That heated discussion in that frantic circle, passing beyond debate
of the college and the proposition and the answer and question,
was.
My heart was grateful for glance of the Winebringer; but I still had
a small complaint, because lacking in good fortune my situation
was.
In that bold eye that has shown to me such sorcery, I have estimated
many a sorcerer like Egypt's Samiri sunk in a deep desperation
was.
I spoke to that One, saying: "Come and place one kiss upon my lip."
that One laughed and said: "Like this, always my occupation
was."
Star showing favourable aspect is now in my path because of this:
between the moon and between face of my Beloved, conjunction
was.
Mouth of Beloved Hafez sees as the only remedy for all this pain;
it's a pity that in time of generosity, only small the consideration
was.

239. FALLEN ON THE PATH

At morning the chance for me to drink a few cups of wine

had fallen:
wine that gives joy, from the Winebringer's lip on to mine
had fallen.
From being intoxicated, I desired that the bride of time of my youth
be restored to me as my wife: but divorce, to undermine,
had fallen.
I thought I would retire into a corner away from that intoxicated eye,
for power of patience, due to those curved eyebrows line,
had fallen.
Interpreter of dreams, give the good news, because to me last night
as my ally, in the sweet sleep of morning, the sun's shine
had fallen.
In the stages of the path of Truth wherever we may have travelled,
in the play of love, both salvation and separation's line
had fallen.
O Winebringer, give the cup again and again: in this Path's journey,
where is the poor lover who never into hypocrisy's decline
had fallen?
Moment when Hafez was composing this verse full of difficulties,
Bird of his imagination into a trap of deep longing's design had
fallen.

240. FRESH FORTUNE

If that blessed Holy Bird through my door
comes back,
to my old head, my life as it was once before,
comes back.
The lightning of my fortune has now departed from my sight,
I hope it, with my tears that like rain does pour,
comes back.
My head's crown was the dust of the sole of that One's foot:
I would behave like a king if that One once more
comes back.
If what Beloved's foot scatters are not by me made precious,
will a place exist to where soul's precious core
comes back?

I will follow the Beloved and news about me to the friends,
will come, if myself again in person never more
comes back.
Twang of harp and sweet sleep of morning is the preventer:
otherwise, on hearing my sigh, Beloved I'm sure
comes back.
I will beat drum of fresh fortune from the roof of happiness,
if to me, Moon of a journey never taken before,
comes back.
Like the moon I'm deeply longing to see the face of the King:
Hafez, pray, so the King safely through my door
comes back.

WISDOM'S FOUNTAIN

Who ever due to shame, from Your street away
goes;
finally away full of shame, never again to stay,
goes.
By the guiding light, traveller seeks way to Beloved;
it is a pity if the whole time only in idle play
goes.
O Guide of the lost heart, for God's sake some help,
for the stranger not knowing, by the Guide's say
goes.
Fate sealed the order of soberness and drunkenness:
no one can know how at the end one's own way
goes.
The caravan that has as the Guide the Grace of God,
will rest in life's joy... and off to a glorious day
goes.
Hafez, take in the hand a cup from Wisdom's fountain:
maybe from heart's page, ignorance's image away
goes.

241. THE STAR

The Star gleamed out, and the Moon of the circle's gathering
became:
consoling our frightened heart, the Companion so comforting
became.
Beloved, Who did not go to school and didn't know how to write,
with a glance, Teacher of teachers of many ways of schooling
became.
The Palace of Love and of Joy became prosperous at this same time,
when its Architect, arch of my Beloved's eyebrow's curving,
became.
Your loving glance poured out such an amount of wine to lovers, that
their sense became senseless, reason devoid of understanding
became.
For God's sake, I'll clean lip from too much wine and make it pure:
my heart from a thousand sins, one who is madly muttering
became.
Now that the Beloved placed us in the chief seat of the Winehouse:
see how the old beggar of the city, the Chief of the gathering
became!
Because of Beloved's fragrance, sick heart of lovers like the breeze,
a ransom for that eye's narcissus and cheek's wild colouring
became.
Your imagination devised Water of Khizer and cup of Kay Khusrau:
it, dream of Sultan Abul Farwis, from only a little drinking
became.
My verse is like the precious gold of existence: yes, the pure alchemy
of this copper has transmuted all the wealthy who accepting
became.
Friends, I advise you all to turn the rein away from that Winehouse:
for Hafez travelled by this path and poor from this travelling
became.

242. WHERE IS ONE?

Where is one who through friendship will be faithful to me;

who, with a reprobate such as me will act kindly, mercifully?
First, to sound of harp and reed he'll bring news of Beloved:
then with some wine, he'll do an act of friendship, faithfully.
Heartstealer, for Whom soul shrank, heart's wish vanished,
and of Whom one can't be hopeless, will be loving… maybe.
I said: "All my life I haven't loosened a knot from that hair:"
the reply: "I have ordered it like this for you, so be ready."
The sullen wearer of wool hasn't known the perfume of love:
give a hint of its intoxication and he will act out of insanity.
Friend like that was difficult to find for me, a useless beggar:
will the Sultan entertain the Bazaar's commoner, in privacy?
If from that hair that twists and turns I suffer, it is nothing:
to one coming, going, its bond and chain will do no tyranny.
The army of grief became countless: I ask help from Fortune,
until Fakhr-ud-Din Abdu-s-Samad will give some help to me.
Hafez, don't try to gain Beloved's glance that's full of magic,
or that One's hair that's black as night will do much sorcery.

243. THE TRUE MARRIAGE

My heart causes me to drink musky wine; so be it:
from fasting and hypocrisy is no fragrance sweet.
If all of the people in all creation forbid me love,
I'll do whatever the Master wishes, whatever be it.
Don't despair of grace and kindness, for the nature
of the Merciful pardons all sin and lovers in defeat.
The heart lives in hope in the ring of its prayers,
that the Friend may open a ring of hair so sweet.
To You God gave marriage of beauty and fortune;
do You need a beautifier when beauty's complete?
The world is pleasant: air stirs heart, wine's pure;
what's needed is a joyous heart, then it's complete.
The bride of the world is beautiful, but be careful,
because no one will trap this young maiden's feet.
The earth will never be without cypress and tulip,
for as another comes, another makes its retreat.
Heart of the beggar's nature don't ask, look inside;

only the honest picture, this mirror does repeat.
Coaxing You, I said: "Mooncheek, what's the harm
if You save a heartbroken one, with sugar sweet?"
You laughed: "Hafez, for God's sake, no stain is on
this moon's cheek if your kiss it happens to meet."

244. WISDOM'S FOUNTAIN

Who ever due to shame, from Your street away
goes;
finally away full of shame, never again to stay,
goes.
By the guiding light, traveller seeks way to Beloved;
it is a pity if the whole time only in idle play
goes.
O Guide of the lost heart, for God's sake some help,
for the stranger not knowing, by the Guide's say
goes.
Fate sealed the order of soberness and drunkenness:
no one can know how at the end one's own way
goes.
The caravan that has as the Guide the Grace of God,
will rest in life's joy... and off to a glorious day
goes.
Hafez, take in the hand a cup from Wisdom's fountain:
maybe from heart's page, ignorance's image away
goes.

245. BROUGHT FROM DESPAIR

East breeze at daybreak a perfume from Beloved's hair
did bring:
it immediately into agitation, the heart full of despair
did bring.
Out from the garden of my heart I uprooted that branch of pine,
for every rose blossoming from its grief, pain's share
did bring.

In fear of an attack from Your eye, I set free my bleeding heart;
but it, by dripping blood on the path, Your eye's stare
did bring.
From roof of the palace I witnessed the splendour of the moon,
which face of the sun to the wall because of despair
did bring.
To voice of Minstrel and Winebringer I went, in season and out;
for along a heavy road, difficult news... the messenger
did bring.
Whatever the Beloved may give is from kindness and graciousness;
whether Muslim beads or Christian cord, Beloved's care
did bring.
May God protect Your eyebrow; although it made me despair,
it brought a consoling greeting, and a gracious stare
did bring.
Happy that time that I freed my heart from tangle of Your hair;
a confession from the enemy, victory over Your hair
did bring.
In envy of the Beloved's fragrant hair, the breeze gave the wind
in the air, every muskpod that it from Tartary's share
did bring.
Last night, I was amazed, discovering Hafez with cup and flagon:
but I didn't object, for, he, both, in a Sufi-like manner
did bring.

246. HAPPINESS AND GOOD FORTUNE

Everyone having carefree heart and who an agreeable companion
has,
happiness as an associate and good fortune as his consolation
has.
The doorway of the courtyard of Love is much higher than Reason:
that one kisses threshold, who life in sleeve for appropriation
has.
Perhaps Your sweet small mouth is the seal of the ring of Solomon:
for it, beneath its ruby seal, the whole world as an impression
has.

The ruby lip and the musky hair, since You have this and also that,
I boast about my heart's thief Whose beauty both in possession
has.
While you are on the surface of the earth make profit from strength:
under the earth, power over the powerless, Time's compulsion
has.
O one with riches, don't look on the weak and poor with contempt:
the wise beggar sitting by the road, the chief seat of recognition
has.
Prayer of the poor removes calamities from the soul and the body:
who gains from harvest who for a gleaner lack of appreciation
has?
Breeze, tell secret of my love to that Sovereign of lovely ones, who
many Jamshids and Kay Khusraus as slaves of lowest station,
has.
If the Beloved says: "I do not desire a poor lover such as Hafez is;"
you answer: "The beggar, sitting by road, Sovereign's attention
has."

247. COMPLAINT

It's ages and my Sweetheart's greeting
hasn't been sent;
a letter hasn't been written… writing
hasn't been sent.
A hundred letters I wrote and sent, but that proud One
never sent a note for me to be reading:
hasn't been sent.
A deer-like One with the slow walk of a fine partridge,
to a terrified beast like me in hiding,
hasn't been sent.
You knew the bird of my heart would leave my hand,
yet, handwritten chain of hair curling,
hasn't been sent.
I complain: that Winebringer sweet of lip, intoxicated,
knew I was winesick: cup for drinking
hasn't been sent.

As long as I boasted of advances on the path I've made;
news from You of any stage coming,
hasn't been sent.
Hafez, be respectful because there's no room for appeal,
even if message to slave from the King,
hasn't been sent.

248. SMILE A SWEET SMILE

O You Whose pistachio mouth laughs at the tale of candy,
for God's sake, I desire that You smile a sweet smile at me!
Where my Beloved breathes with a smile that is so sweet,
pistachio compares? For God's sake don't laugh secretly!
The Tuba tree of Paradise can't boast of Your great height:
I will pass over this story, or it too long a subject will be.
If You show some sullenest or if You make some criticism,
we are not a friend of any man and do not act conceitedly.
How could one know my condition of worry and anguish,
who didn't have a heart caught in this noose just like me?
You don't want a river of blood to flow out from my eye?
Then don't bind your heart to the rosy ones' consistency!
Market of love's desire is brisk: where is that candle-face?
I'll scatter heart and soul like twigs, on that face so fiery!
Hafez, you do not give away the glances of the bold ones;
is it Khwarazm or Khujand… that your place should be?

249. COMES OUT

I'll not stop my hand from seeking my desire until my desire
comes out:
either body reaches Beloved, or soul leaving body to expire,
comes out.

Like the unfaithful, one can't be taking a new beloved every moment:
we're joined to Your street's dust until soul from form's mire
comes out.

The soul is on lip, ready to depart, and in the heart is much worry:
for soul leaves body and from Your lip, not a single desire
comes out.
Soul is under a great strain from fruitlessly hoping for Your mouth,
how will it be that from that mouth the desire of the beggar
comes out?
Pull open my tomb after I have passed away, then have a long look
at how smoke through the shroud from my heart's great fire
comes out.
Get up! On account of Your great height and standing in meadow,
the cypress goes inside itself and the pomegranate fruit's fire
comes out.
In hope that a beautiful rose like Your face comes into the garden...
breeze comes, and every moment around the field to inquire,
comes out.
Show Your face, for a whole population keeps weeping and grieving:
open Your lip, from every man and woman... a cry of desire
comes out.
Every single curl of Your hair contains a hundred sharp barbed hooks,
how will it be that this bleeding heart caught in barbed wire
comes out?
I said to myself: "My heart, you came out, away from the Beloved."
My heart said: "This is for the one who from his own desire,
comes out."
Inside that circle of the lovers they make a mention of his good name,
whenever in that crowd of lovers the name Hafez to inspire
comes out.

250. DESTINY'S ORIGINAL ORDER

If to Your face, the moon and Pleiades as a comparison
they've made;
a guess about a form not yet seen is such an estimation
they've made.
Only a part of the tale of our love that's bewildering to all senses,
are the tales of Farhad and Shirin of which explanation
they've made.

Winebringer, wine; there's no stopping Destiny's Original Order:
it is not worth contemplating changing that destination
They've made.
Never has a long eyelash and never has a glance of sorcery made
what that dark mole and also that musky hair's profusion,
they've made.
Don't look contemptuously at drunkard's cup made out of earth;
servant of cup where the world is seen, each companion,
they've made.
Don't be a stranger to wisdom, to your embrace take vine's daughter,
whose dowry, cash of reason, is the marriage portion
They've made.
Ones who are in the dust don't have a portion of the cup of kindness:
see how on the poor lovers, the practise of oppression
They've made.
Unfit to be hunted and captured are long feather of crow and kite:
this, to noble falcon and royal white falcon's discretion,
They've made.
Dust of street of the stealers of hearts has perfume that gives Life;
the lovers there, discovery of the musk of wise action,
they've made.
Our reward was only one sugar and Your lip did not pay it out to me;
You owe me justice: such sweet lips, my justification,
they've made.
Lovely Ones from the red fire of Their flowing cheeks, each moment
a breach into the hearts of the pious and their religion,
They've made.
The poetry of Hafez that from beginning to end praises Your beauty:
wherever they have heard it honestly, its acclamation
they've made.

251. THE ESSENCE OF TRUTH

Sweet One, Your beautiful form as artiface

They've made;
with sweetness of Soul, Your lip of grace
They've made.
Heart-entrancing and fair are Your cheek and fresh hair;
like shelter of ambergris at the rose's place,
They've made.
For arrival of Your form to full completion, the armies
of lovers from eyes, tears of blood's trace,
they've made.
Your curls' occupation is to spread musk; but only lately
of China's muskpod's reputation, a disgrace
they've made.
Lord, I wonder is that the face with the cap fastened on,
or the moon, with Pleiades as a necklace
They've made?
All the stories they tell of Farhad and Shirin are but tales
in praise of my love for that beautiful face
They've made.
Hafez, tell the essence of truth that is the secret of love;
except this, everything else is commonplace
they've made.

252. AGAIN TO THE GARDEN

Fragrance of musk of Khutan on the breeze of morning
comes:
what is this breeze, from which Your perfume, blowing,
comes?
Fragrance of musk of Khutan whirls from the breeze's pocket:
perhaps from country of Khata a great caravan travelling
comes.
I'll not take my heart from You as long as soul is in my body:
listen, because from my words, faith's fragrance flowing
comes.
Heart, don't use chest as shield for arrows of grief for that One:
shut the eye because through the air, arrow unrelenting
comes.

I am still comforted by the love that I have for Your eyebrow:
that One's King, to Whom remembering beggar's begging
comes.
Your foot often sunk deep into the clay because of my tears:
in Your presence, to pupil of my eye, a great overflowing
comes.
Hafez, don't abstain from wine; for again to the garden the rose
with a hundred blooming beauties, for sake of pleasing,
comes.

253. BITTER TASTE

The days of union with friends gone by,
remember:
remember all those time , O try, O try,
remember.
The bitter taste of grief is like poison on my tongue:
those who drink wine, their drinking cry
remember!
Although the friends have no more memories of me,
each of them a thousand times over… I
remember!
I am tangled up in these chains of my misfortune:
the kindness that to upright ones apply,
remember!
Although hundreds of streams flow from my eye,
stream Zinda delighting gardener's eye,
remember!
I am held tight by the grip of pain and deep sorrow:
remedy those dispellers of grief apply,
remember!
At this time there remains no faith left in anyone;
faith and that which loved ones supply,
remember!
Because this happened, Hafez's secret stays untold:
the keepers of secrets who said goodbye,
remember!

254. MINSTREL OF LOVE

My Minstrel of love a great melody and wonderful harmony
has:
each note about the hidden that is struck, a passage to see
has.
May the world never be without the sound of lovers lamenting:
for it, a note that imparts joy and also a sweet melody,
has.
Although our Master who drinks the dregs hasn't force or gold,
God Who forgives sins, covers errors, our Master happily
has.
Hold my heart with respect, for since this fly that worships sugar
began longing for You, it, pomp of the Pure Bird's Majesty
has.
It would only be justice if that King of all His neighbourbood
inquired about the condition that this old beggar obviously
has.
I showed my tears of blood to the physicians and they said this:
"It's the pain of love and burning of the heart as a remedy
has."
Do not learn the tyranny of the glance; because in love's Way,
every work has a reward, every action repayment for injury
has.
That Beloved of the young Christian who sold wine, rightly said:
"Drink to, and enjoy the joy of that soul's face that purity
has."
O King, Hafez who sits at Your court recites the *Koran's Fatiha;*
and the longing for a blessing to roll from Your tongue, he
has.

255. THE ROBBER OF THE ROAD

In this city there is not a fair one who my heart's sway

takes;
if Fortune's my true helpful friend then it my load away
takes.
Where's a happy intoxicated companion before whose kindness,
the lover with a burning heart, his longing to portray,
takes.
O gardener, I see that you are careless about Autumn's arrival;
that day comes when your beautiful rose, wind of decay
takes.
Time, the robber of the road, is not asleep, don't trust in him:
he, you, tomorrow it is certain, if he hasn't yet today,
takes.
The bellow of the ox that sounds like a shout deceives the ass:
the star Sirius, the reflection of the brilliant Sun away
takes?
In my imagination I play with all the puppets in the hope that
hearing of my performance, eye of a Director my play
takes.
All the wisdom and craft that my heart learnt in forty years,
I fear those two intoxicated narcissus eyes, as easy prey
takes.
It's certain that sorcery cannot match miracle, so do not fear:
what sorcerer like Samiri over white hand of Moses, sway
takes?
Although the Path of Love is the place of ambush of archers,
whoever travels wisely, victory from enemies on the way
takes.
Crystal goblet of wine stands in the broken-hearted one's path:
hand it away and you from your way, grief's flood away
takes.
Hafez, if the intoxicated eye of Beloved is seeking your life,
empty life's house and leave, so it, life, when it may,
takes.

256. THE NEW MOON

For the new moon, world drew celebration's eyebrow's bend;

it is right to see the new moon in the eyebrow of the Friend.
Like the back of the crescent moon my standing form is bent,
with indigo the Beloved drew the bow of the eyebrow's bend.
Do not cover up Your face and be upset by the people gazing,
the soft hair on Your cheek chants, breathes: "God defend!"
Maybe at dawn a scent from Your form swept over the field,
because from Your scent the rose tears its garment, end to end.
Neither were a harp nor the stringed lute, nor rose, nor wine;
clay of my existence the grapejuice and datewine did blend.
Come, so that to You I can tell my heart's grief and my pain;
without You, on power of speech and hearing I can't depend.
Though life be the price for You giving Union, I'm the buyer:
the good thing the wise buys, it's irrelevant what he'll spend.
Be it far from You to make my tears flow, for without You,
far from You, they as wind go into dust of Your path's end.
When I see the moon of Your face in the night of Your hair,
to my night, Your face the bright light of the day does send.
My soul reached to the lip, and not a wish has been fulfilled:
my hope has come to an end, my search never reaches an end.
With deep desire for Your face, Hafez has written some words;
read his verse and then like pearls, them in Your ear suspend.

257. THE QUEST

Last night Hafez, secluded, the Winehouse's guest
became;
he broke his promise and the winecup his quest
became.
In a dream came young sweetheart of the season of youth;
again as test for his old head, poor lover's unrest
became.
A young Master, the thief of heart and of faith, passed by;
in pursuit of that Friend, he a stranger to the rest
became.
The fire of rose's cheek burnt away nightingale's harvest;
the moth, the candle's laughing face's conquest,
became.

Yesterday, the unstable Sufi broke the cup and the flagon;
last night with a sip of wine he wise and manifest
became.
The narcissus of the Winebringer has cast such a spell that
our circle of religious readers, the sorcerers' nest
became.
The home of Hafez is now the feasting place of the King;
soul is the Friend's, heart in Sweetheart's breast
became.

258. PERMANENT PAIN

From the book of my heart and soul Your image
never goes:
that graceful swaying cypress from mind's page
never goes.
From my crazy brain that picture of Your fair face's cheek,
although time be violent and the sky in a rage:
never goes.
From Eternity my heart made a promise with Your long hair:
until Eternity, it from that in which it did engage,
never goes.
Except the load of grief You've given me, what's in my heart
has left my heart: what can it do, for that stage
never goes?
My love for You has taken such a hold in my heart and soul
that even if life goes, my love for You for an age
never goes.
If my heart should chase the beautiful ones it can be excused:
what can it do, it has pain and it for remedy's wage
never goes?
Whoever wishes not, to become mad in the head like Hafez is,
shouldn't give heart to fair... and to them to engage,
never goes.

259. ASTONISHED IN LOVE

Out of love for You, plant's shoot

of astonishment came;
in Union with You, perfect fruit
of astonishment came.
There are many who are drowned in the ocean of Union,
who at last to that highest shoot
of astonishment came.
Union did not remain, and neither did the uniter remain
there; where imagination destitute
of astonishment came.
That one was crushed by that perfection of glorification,
to whom brilliant light absolute
of astonishment came.
The very existence of Hafez from head down to the foot,
in love, deep into the plant's root
of astonishment came.

260. LAST NIGHT

Last night You came and Your cheek enflamed
had been;
see how the griefstricken heart, by You burned
had been.
The fashion of slaying the lover and of upsetting the city,
was garment on Your body that by You stitched
had been.
You regard the lover's soul as kindling for Your face's fire;
Your cheek 's fire for this work, kindly kindled
had been.
Your hair's infidelity attacked faith, and in its path made
a torch of Your bright face, it so stone-hearted
had been.
My heart gathered much blood which my eye then spilled:
O God, who had given, who by this advantaged
had been?
Don't sell Beloved for the world, for there wasn't profit
for the one gaining gold, for which Joseph traded
had been.

Although You openly said: "I will kill you without mercy,"
I saw that Your secret glance to me who burned
, had been.
You spoke to me a sweet speech: "Hafez, burn patchcoat;"
Your way of knowing worth, from whom learned
had been?

261. THE TALE OF TORTURE

Pre-ordained, by Your sword, wounded one's extermination,
was not:
if not, then due to Your glance of sorcery, a faulty ordination
was not.
Lord, I wonder how the mirror of Your beauty has such great lustre,
that in it power of my sigh to make even a small impression,
was not.
At the time when I who was a madman let go of Your flowing hair,
a thing more fit than fetters of these chains for distraction,
was not.
A thing more graceful than You did not grow in beauty's meadow;
a picture more pleasant than You in the world of depiction,
was not.
So that like breeze of morning it may be that I will reach Your hair,
anything last night except profit from night's lamentation,
was not.
From out of astonishment I lifted my head at door of the Winehouse,
when a Master in corridor to give You Your due recognition,
was not.
O fire of separation, I've suffered so much from you, that like candle,
another plan for me, but by your hand my self-destruction:
was not.
Suffering of Hafez without You, was telling of the tale of torture,
of which to all mankind, the need for a detailed explanation
was not.

262. HEART'S DESIRE

The desire for Your lip my heart forever

has:
what desire, heart from Your lip so rare,
has?
The wine of love and that cup full of desire,
my soul in cup of the heart, everywhere
has.
The madman who's captured in Beloved's hair,
his dwelling still in the calamity's snare
has.
So that Beloved may boldly capture a heart,
Beloved over rose, snare of violet's hair
has.
At last it seemed proper that I could ask this:
"What name is it our heart's stealer fair
has?"
How does that one sit easily with the Beloved,
who thinks of high and low and not a care
has?
That one's joyful of heart and is always happy,
who the friendship of the Beloved forever
has.
As the gathering is happy for a moment, Hafez
everywhere tools for joy beyond compare
has.

263. KEEP QUIET

I have honesty and integrity and this, understanding
is no one;
of all of this of the Winehouse's drunkard, suspecting
is no one.
I'm wearing this old patched coat because of this reason I'll give,
that under this coat I am drinking wine and knowing
is no one.
Don't be proud of theory and practise of the time's theologian:
because his life, from the decree of God, to be saving
is no one.

Don't be fascinated by colour and perfume, just drink from cup:
only Master's wine cleans; removing all grief's rusting
is no one.
O heart, although your eye is the watchman, be on the guard:
so that taking wealth you're holding while guarding,
is no one.
O heart, if you need to have the wage, try to be hard-working;
the one who is receiving a wage for never working,
is no one.
Hafez, in presence of One a gifted speaker, don't offer a word:
for bringing to Sea and Mine the treasure of pearling,
is no one.

264. THE OLD WINESELLER

The old Wineseller, bless his good name, said yesterday:
"Drink wine, and the memory of heart's grief, put away."
I said: "Wine will throw my name and fame to the wind,"
He said: "Do as I say, and what will be, come what may.
Since the world's profit and loss from the hand will go,
don't rejoice about gain, or moan if loss comes this way.
In the hand is nothing but wind; if you place your heart
on something, like Solomon's throne it'll finally decay.
Rose is not without thorn, honey has sting of the bee:
why think hard about it, the world is created this way.
Keep the cup full of wine, and listen with sensitivity
to the language of the cup: hear story of Jam and Kay.
Hafez, if you don't enjoy hearing advice from the Wise,
we say: may your life be long, goodbye; no more to say."

265. THE DRUNKARD'S GIFT

To whom the cup of the pure red wine of the morning

They give,
know that a place in the Most Sacred Divine Dwelling
They give.
Sufi, do not criticize drunkards, for to them, in Love's Mystery,
on Eternity's Day beyond Time, Winehouse frequenting
They give.
Winebringer, bring wine that's rosy coloured and musky perfumed:
for believers in reason, trouble to those wine drinking,
they give.
That one hasn't even a little enjoyment of the enjoyment of life,
to whom today, promise of tomorrow's joyful living
they give.
Hafez will quickly be abandoning the many gardens of Paradise,
if in Your Sacred Home of Union, to him a dwelling
They give.

266. BE PATIENT

From the sky's course, outcome of my occupation
doesn't come;
my heart bleeds from grief and the soothing lotion
doesn't come.
Although like the dog I am now in the dust of the Friend's street,
tears flow from my face but of sustenance a portion
doesn't come.
I do not gnaw upon the slightest morsel of sinew from off a bone;
so, many a wound to my tongue from mastication
doesn't come.
I swear by the heart of the Friend that I am sick of my own life;
but what help's there for helpless when annihilation
doesn't come?
The two eyes of Jacob became white because of a great longing;
yet from Egypt to Canaan the desired information
doesn't come.
As long as a hundred thousand thorns don't spring from the soil,
a rose in rosegarden from a rosebush's cultivation,
doesn't come.

To people who are worthy, from the power of the violence of Time,
greatest griefs that life, given to hand's destruction,
doesn't come.
The pompous and the ignorant raise themselves up to Saturn; but,
to highest, anything but sigh of those of perception,
doesn't come.
Sufi, wash away the rust of your heart with the water of the wine:
from ablutions and washing patchcoat, absolution
doesn't come.
Hafez, be patient; for in the path in which one is a lover, whoever
doesn't give his life, into the Beloved's attention
doesn't come.

267. THE HAPPY RETURN

O happy is the time when the Beloved Friend
will return:
for the griefstricken's broken heart, to mend,
will return.
The black and white pony of my eye I lead for Your favour,
hoping that on Royal Horseman I can depend:
will return.
Expecting Your white poplar arrow the prey's heart flees,
thinking You, hunting with arrow ready to send,
will return.
Like dust, I have made my home at the head of Your path,
hoping that by this way, Your way will wend,
will return.
If into curve of Your mallet my head doesn't go, what else?
What can I say to head, will it comprehend?
Will return?
That heart, that with tip of Your curls has made a treaty,
don't think to that heart peace will descend,
will return.
My tears will not roll like waves of the sea on the shore,
if into my embrace that waist of that Friend
will return.

What cruelties the nightingales have endured from Winter,
in the hope that a fresh new Spring in the end
will return.
Hafez's hope is, that because of the Engraver of Destiny,
that fair cypress form, to the arms I extend,
will return.

268. LOVE LET LOOSE

At head of the market the soul gamblers a proclamation make:
"Hear this, you dwellers of Beloved's district, for God's sake!
it is days now since the daughter of the vine was lost to us,
left to follow her own desire; take care, she is on the make!
she is dressed in a garment of ruby and a crown of bubbles,
she steals reason and knowledge, don't sleep, be wide awake!"
To whoever brings me that bitter one I'll pay my soul so sweet;
if in Hell that one's hiding, then my soul to Hell quickly take!
That one's a night-prowler, bitter, sharp, rosy and a drunkard;
if you find her, please quickly over to the house of Hafez take!

269. THE VIOLET'S DESPAIR

Last night the violet spoke out to the rose and a sweet sign
gave,
saying: "In the world, a twist of hair, this despair of mine
gave."
Storehouse of mysteries was my heart but Fate locked the door,
and then its key, to the hand of that Heartstealer so fine,
gave.
To Your door I came, like one shattered; for the physician only
a hint of that healing balm of Your Grace that is Divine,
gave.

You passed by poor miserable me and to those watching said:
"What a shame; such a soul this poor slain lover of mine
gave."

May his body be sound and his heart glad and happy his mind,
who to the weak, out of loving kindness, his hand benign
gave.
O you who scold and forbid wine, go and find your own cure;
tell me of any harm that to anyone, sweetheart or wine
gave.
The treasure of Hafez's heart containing the jewel of mysteries,
the whole world's wealth for the joy of Your Love Divine
gave.

270. MY EXISTENCE

My love for You isn't so flimsy that it easily from my mind
goes;
my love for You isn't on loan, that it somewhere undefined
goes.
Love for You is my existence and my heart is full of love for You:
it entered with milk and with my soul when life's resigned,
goes.
The pain of love is a terrible pain and the remedy for this pain,
no matter how much you try it, it still more unconfined
goes.
I'm the one who when night comes is the first person in the city,
whose loud cry because of love, to the sky, you will find,
goes.
If the full flow of my raining tears should enter the Zinda river,
all at once the sown field of Irak flooded and undermined
goes.
Last night I saw the face of the Beloved circled by a halo of hair,
it was as if it were a moon with cloud that around it to wind,
goes.
I said: "I will make a beginning with a kiss;" Beloved said: "No,
wait until the moon out of Scorpio, by which it's confined,
goes."
Hafez, if you drink wine to the memory of the Beloved's ruby lip,
be careful that news of it, never to enemies and their kind
goes.

271. IF GOD PUNISHED EVERY PERSON

If God were to punish every person for each and every sin,
  world would be weeping, Time screaming a terrible din.
To the Lord, blade of grass and mountain are the same:
sometimes the Maker punishes blade, forgives mountain.
All Earth's surface is because of sin… didn't you know?
Because of this, moon suffers eclipse, because of your sin.
You've a clean skirt, do you? But it will soon be known,
  tomorrow those who demand justice will see your sin.
I'm ashamed of my sins, I spend whole nights weeping,
  so that from the place I kneel green growth will begin.
At the time to say goodbye such a flood of tears I'll cry,
  so that no matter where Friend's going, rain will begin.
Hafez, when that Majesty wants to put an end to one,
  who has the strength to stop such a Monarch and win?

272. HOPING FOR HELP

Inside my head my love for You secretly
    still turns;
see how so much in this head that's crazy,
    still turns.
Placing one's heart at the mallet of Your hair's tip;
  it, like ball from head to foot, certainly
    still turns.
Though that charming heart deals cruelly and falsely,
  heart seeking faith from You, faithfully
    still turns.
From the violence of the sky and the rages of Time,
  a hundred times shirt of patience on me,
    still turns.

My helpless form, thin and weak, is like new moon,
  which a pointing-stock in the sky to see,
    still turns.

It's many days since helpless, hopeless, this kind of
nightingale, from rosegarden of beauty,
still turns.
O heart how often must I tell you, lust and desire
to give up, for this is wind that wrongly
still turns.
In love with You, tulip-cheek, cypress-shape, there
are many like us: heart spins, mind crazily
still turns.
At the end of Your street is the sick heart of Hafez:
like the east wind, it for help hopefully
still turns.

273. SLAVE'S DESOLATION

Every moment I'm complaining about the hand of separation:
O no, if the wind doesn't carry my weeping to Your location!
What can I do if I'm not weeping and I'm not crying like this?
Being far from You, I wish Your enemy shared my condition!
Day and night I suffer grief and sorrow; but why shouldn't I?
I'm far from Your sight, should my heart feel any jubilation?
Since You have gone far away from the eye of heartbroken me,
heart pours from my eye, bleeding fountains of desperation.
Hundreds of drops of blood trickle from root of every eyelash,
more came when heart complained about hand of separation.
Heart of Hafez is drowned in remembering You, day and night:
but You're free of thinking about this poor slave's desolation.

274. THE LOST HEART

If the power of union with You, promised to me
is,
what more from my own fortune left for me to be
is?
No wonder the lovers cry out around Your threshold,
because around sugar the fly always there to see
is.

What's the need for a sword to take the lover's life?
A glance for half-alive me, quite adequate certainly
is.
If in both worlds I breathed one breath with Beloved,
from both worlds that breath my gift's guarantee
is.
Since my desire is short handed because of destiny,
my power to reach Your high cypress a possibility
is?
How can one who's drowning find the way to safety?
Ahead and behind love's trying torrent obviously
is.
A thousand times I'm with You in secret; yet, again
when You see me, Your question: "Who is he?"
is.
Coloured wine is pleasant, so is Beloved's company:
Hafez has lost his heart and he like this eternally
is.

275. THE THIEF

The desire for Spring breeze, me to desert's plain
took;
breeze brought Your perfume and my peace again
took.
Wherever was a heart, Your eye took away its path;
it, not only my broken heart so sick with pain,
took.
My silver tears took the golden shine from my face;
You, giving gold for gold came, and these again
took.
My flowing tears took Your heart of stone to the path:
a stone to river's bank, my tears torrential rain
took.
Last night my love's joy tied my chain of desire for You.
Cavalry of my consciousness, grief's army of pain
took.

Glance of bold Turk's bow eyebrow shot our path away;
long hair of that slender cypress, all we contain
took.
Last night, cup of wine from Your lip gave to us Life:
wine's glory from Life-giving lip, soul's fountain
took.
Do not talk to Hafez about the nightingale's sweet voice:
Bird of a thousand songs to parrot only the insane
took.

276. THE APPEARANCE OF THE KING

At dawn when King of the East, flag on the mountains pitched,
with hand of Mercy, my Friend on door of the hopefuls knocked.
When this world's condition became clear before morning came,
He rose, and at conceit of dictators, a long good laugh expressed.
O my Fair One, last night when You stood up intending to dance,
from the hair You untied knot and on hearts of lovers, pounded.
I washed my hands of righteousness in my heart's blood that time
when Your eye, measuring wine, all sober to drunkenness invited.
What power has taught You roguery, that when first coming out,
on all those who are awake and watch all night, You descended?
My poor heart matured to memory of horsemen then out it went;
O Lord guard it... for into the centre of the horsemen, it dashed.
For Your cheek's lustre what lives we gave, what blood we drank:
when You were first seen, all those surrendering soul were effaced.
How can I in woolen cloak, bring into the trap of my noose One
clothed in hair, Whose eyelashes, at those with daggers thrusted?
My glance is to the Grace and Faithfulness of the King's Fortune;
give desire of Hafez's heart, to whom a fortunate omen appeared.
Victorious King of kings, bravest of Kingdom's people of Faith,
Whose boundless generosity at the Spring clouds openly laughed.
Since that hour when the winecup became honoured by His hand,
to memory of its wine drinkers' health, cup of Joy Time drained.
God Most High this nature has, since gaining mastery of existence;
His purity of Essence was even with the austere, equally breathed.
Hafez, from Grace of God ask for His life and reign to continue;

for heaven, amongst the people, this Coin of Fortune has minted.

277. HAIL!

Hail! Come! The flag, standard of Victory, the King,
has come!
Joyous news for sun and moon, Victory, now sing,
has come!
The veil from Victory's face the fortune of beauty has drawn;
Perfect Justice for all the complainers of suffering
has come.
The universe joyfully swings a sweet circle, for the Moon is here;
the world turns up to the heart's desire, for the King
has come.
Caravans of heart and knowledge's road are safe from robbers
that lurk by the path; now that The One, Wayfaring,
has come.
The 'Darling of Egypt', despite all his jealous brothers, to that
glorious place of the Moon, from the pit's dwelling,
has come.
To that false Sufi, that Antichrist who is so unfaithful, say this:
"Burn, for the New Coming Messiah, faith sheltering,
has come."
Morning breeze, tell Beloved that love's grief is upon my head;
smoke of fire of my heart burning, painfully sighing,
has come.
O King, from the longing desire for Your face, what will come
to separation's prisoner, now straw's fire to flaming
has come?
Do not go to sleep, for Hafez, himself, to the Palace of Grace,
from the prayer at midnight and at the dawn praising,
has come.

278. HIGHEST OF THE HIGH

Just One, drinking companion of Your cup the Sphere

be!

Tulip drowned in blood, Your foe's black heart and fear
be!

Highest of the high peaks is height of Your high position;
going on a pilgrimage, many for many a thousand year
be!

Your hair full of curls is the eye and the light of the world:
by breeze of Your fortune, Your curls may a soul near
be!

Moon of the Sphere of Justice, eye and light of the world;
forever Yours may goblet and cup full of wine so clear
be!

Now that Venus has taken to singing songs praising You,
those hearing who envy You, friends of sigh and tear
be!

Nine stages of Creation and round cakes of silver and gold
that flow on tray of Your grandeur, simple table gear
be!

Daughter of my virgin mind Your praises made a confider,
given to Your hand's favour this bride without a peer
be!

In this *ghazal* Hafez gave references of his service to You;
may witness to contract, Your servant-cherishing cheer
be!

279. THE MOON OF HOPE

The Pure Bird of the highest faith in our snare
will fall,
if Your footsteps passing by our dwelling there
will fall.
Like the rising bubble I'll throw my cap with great joy,
if into our cup a reflection of Your face so fair
will fall.
When one night, moon of hope rises from horizon's line,
hopefully on our roof, that light's brilliant flare
will fall.

When even wind isn't allowed to go into Your courtyard,
the chance for our salutation, when and where
will fall?
When I offered my life as sacrifice for Your lip I thought:
"A drop of its pure water as our palate's share
will fall."
I imagined Your hair said: "Don't make life the means;
many are the prey that like this, into Our snare
will fall."
When not even kings have a right to kiss dust of this door,
how is it to our salutation favour of an answer
will fall?"
Don't turn away from this door hopeless, go cast an omen:
perhaps to our name the stamp of fortune's care
will fall.
Whenever Hafez speaks out about the dust of Your street,
to our scent the breeze of soul's rosebed there
will fall.

280. ENDLESS AGONY

A moment's rest from grief my body doesn't know;
my heart from endless agony, into shreds does go.
Heart to head, the mist of my sorrow for You rises;
dew of the rain of grief, down from my eyes flow.
My two eyes cannot bear to see my yellow cheeks,
with heart's blood they plaster so as not to show.
This way, if one who wishes me ill sees my face,
these yellow cheeks his eyesight will never know.
For me, misfortune goes searching after calamity,
it dresses it for me like a bride and then to it I go.
Time has stolen away from me whatever was mine,
except my love for You which I will never let go.
Why shouldn't my eye weep and my soul cry out?
Shouldn't patience lessen and sorrow greater grow?
When the sky saw my joy, it measured it all out;

now it gives out grief and a limit it doesn't know.
Since the heart's Friend has taken exception to me,
how can my body look for any pity from the Foe?
If I do cry out, they say this: "He needs nothing;"
"He eats thistles" they then say if I let go; O no!
I don't grieve about this, for Great Glorious God
shuts no door unless He throws another open also.

281. THE PURPOSE OF LOVE

I said: "You made an error and thoughtless it
was:"
You said: "What to do, what fate would permit,
was."
I said: "They wrote down many faults against You:"
You said: "On page of forehead, all was as it
was."
I said: "O Moon, why have You cut off love for me?"
You said: "To Me, sky's angry; it, for love unfit
was."
I said: "Before this, You drank many cups of joy:"
You said: "Remedy, in that last cup of wine it
was."
I said: "Why then did life very quickly leave You?"
You said: "What could I do, as life so definite
was?"
I said: "God gave You the desire to unite with Him:"
You said: "Not my desire to unite with Him, it
was."
I said: "The time You took to travel was not fast:"
You said: "Maybe this was what time's requisite
was."

I said: "Why then did You go far away from Hafez?"
You said: "My purpose, like this every time it
was."

282. THE PARROT

Ha, O parrot, you that speak the mysteries still,
pray, may sugar never be lacking from your bill!
Fresh-green be your head, heart happy forever;
the line of Friend's cheek's lit up by your skill.
To friends, you told things difficult to know,
for God's sake, unravel this maze, so they will.
On our faces drowsy with sleep, splash some
rosewater and our fortune wake; let cup spill.
What chord was it that the musician strummed,
so that the drunk and sober dance to its thrill?
What opium did the Winebringer put in the cup,
that they've lost hat and head and their will?
To Alexander, They never gave Water of Life:
it's not obtained by gold, power, will or skill.
Though Reason's now the currency in the world,
compared to Love, true Alchemy, worth is nil.
Come, listen to the story of the people of pain,
there are very few words but truth's there still.
One like a Chinese idol became foe of our faith;
O Lord, keep heart and faith from such ill will.
Don't tell the drunkard's secrets to sober ones;
soul from a picture on wall, do not try to fill.
You played the part of God towards us slaves;
O God I beg, please preserve you from every ill.
By good fortune of the King's banner of Victory,
in rank of Poetry Hafez's became standard skill.

283. LOST FOR ANOTHER

If I live another time to Winehouse I'll turn my rein:

another.

Only service of drunken outsiders I'll do, never again
another.

That day is happy when I will go again with my eyes weeping:
so that again on the Winehouse door I can then rain
another.

There's no wisdom at all among this tribe: O God, some help,
so that my jewel I carry another purchaser will gain:
another!

If Beloved departed not acknowledging the code of friendship:
God forbid I should go looking for another to obtain:
another.

If circle of the azure sphere is to become my generous helper;
Beloved, in another time's circle my hand will regain:
another.

My heart's seeking ease, if Beloved's bold thieving glance and
pocket-cutting hair allows another time to cut chain:
another.

See our hoarded hidden secret; they make a ballad about it
with a drum and flute, at yet another bazaar again:
another!

Every moment I cry out with grief, for every moment the sky
for my sick heart devises and projects another pain:
another.

I repeat again: "In this afflicted condition, Hafez is not alone,
another and yet another's lost in this desert's plain:
another."

284. DO NOT GRIEVE

That lost Joseph will return again to Canaan:
do not grieve;
sorrow's cell becomes a blooming rosegarden:
do not grieve.
O sorrowful heart, your condition improves, don't despair,
this worried mind will rest peacefully again:
do not grieve.

If springtime of life is once more upon the garden's throne,
night-singer, over head rose canopy's drawn:
do not grieve.
If for a few days the revolving Sphere doesn't turn our way:
this wheel not always spins in one direction:
do not grieve.
Don't be hopeless if you don't understand what's hidden,
a secret game is played behind the curtain:
do not grieve.
When from longing for *Kaaba* you've set foot in the desert,
if you're wounded by the sharp Meccan thorn:
do not grieve.
Heart, if the flood of death sweeps away life's foundation,
when in this torrent Noah is your Captain:
do not grieve.
Although journey's stage is perilous and the goal not seen,
each road will always end at the Destination:
do not grieve.
Though we're separated from Beloved, troubled by enemy,
God causes and changes our every situation:
do not grieve.
Hafez, in your corner so poor, alone through dark nights,
while you're praying and reading the *Koran:*
do not grieve.

285. DESPAIR'S COMPLAINT

Show Your face and my existence from my memory tear
away;
tell the wind: "Harvest of those who are consumed, bear
away."
To us who have given heart and eye to deluge of calamity, say:
"From its foundation take our house by flood of despair,
away."
May fortune of the Perfect Master remain, then the rest is easy;
tell others: "From your memories, send our name forever
away."

O no, who can smell that long hair that is like pure ambergris?
Greedy heart, from the mind give all thought of that hair
away.
You said last night: "I'll kill you with these long dark eyelashes:"
Lord, from Your heart all thought of cruelty please tear
away.
Tell the heart: "Put out the flame of the fire temple of Persia,"
tell to eye: "Shine from face of Tigris of Baghdad, glare
away."
Without making an effort in this path you won't reach its end;
you must obey the Master if its Reward you want to bear
away.
Promise me I'll see You for a moment on the day of my death,
then me to the grave take, happy and free from all care,
away.
From now on my pale yellow face is in dust of Friend's door;
bring out wine and from my memory take grief's share
away.
O Hafez, take care, and think of the tenderness of the Beloved:
from Beloved's courtyard take this complaint of despair
away.

286. BRING A SCENT

O breeze, from dust of the path of the Beloved, a scent
bring;
take grief from my heart, news of where Beloved went,
bring.
Say a subtle word from Beloved's mouth that expands the soul,
from the world of mysteries a letter of happy content
bring.
From path where the Friend walks, for the watchers' blindness,
a little dust to rub on this bleeding eye as its liniment,
bring.
Foolishness and inexperience are not for those who risk life;
from that charming sorcerer, news of acknowledgment
bring.

So that my nostrils are perfumed by your favourable breeze,
from that fragrant breath of the Beloved, a little scent
bring.
I call upon your faithfulness: the dust of dear Beloved's path,
upon which not a single grain a stranger has even lent,
bring.
It's a long time since my heart has seen the face that it desires:
Winebringer, the cup that mirrors that which is radiant,
bring.
O bird of the garden, be thankful that you are so full of joy…
To those captured in cage, news of rosebed's merriment
bring.
My soul's desire is bitter from being patient without Friend;
from that sweet lip that rains sugar some nourishment
bring.
The mad bewildered heart does not break out from the chain;
a noose from the curls of that hair that is permanent,
bring.
What is Hafez's tattered patched-coat worth? Dye it with wine!
Then, to market's centre, him in drunken abandonment
bring.

287. SUCH A ONE

Fragrance from the street of such a One, O breeze
bring:
I'm weeping I'm so sick with grief the soul's ease
bring.
For our poor barren heart, pour out desired pure elixir;
that is, a trace of dust from Beloved's door, please
bring.
Where vision is ambushed, I'm at war with my own heart:
arrow and bow from eyebrow and glance: these,
bring.
I'm old through listlessness, grief of heart and separation:
for me, a cup of wine from hand of Youth, seize,
bring.

Make all those who deny taste a few cups of this wine:
and if they don't take it, running fast to me these
bring.
Winebringer, don't put off until tomorrow joys of today:
or from Fate's book, to me the line of safety please
bring.
Last night my heart went from screen when Hafez said:
"Fragrance from the street of such a One, O breeze
bring."

288. LIFE

O You, from Whose face blossoms the joyful tulip-bed
of life,
come back; without the rose of Your face, Spring's shed
of life.
They haven't even a thought about the ocean of destruction,
for whom the point of Your mouth is the pivot-head
of life.
It is no great wonder if the tears fall from my eyes like rain,
because grieving for You, time has like lightning, sped
of life.
I am alive and I am without life and this is no great wonder:
for in the days of separation, who strings the thread
of life?
There is an ambush everywhere from the army of viciousness:
thoughtfully drawing reins must be horseman's tread
of life.
The moments when there's the possible fortune of seeing You,
are for finding our role, for a secret is role of the thread
of life.
Yesterday, Beloved passed and did not even glance our way;
foolish heart, you received nothing by what was shed
of Life.
Hafez, speak out, because upon the surface of the world's page,
only this picture will remain: what you've remembered
of life.

289. HELPLESS

It's the moon's holiday time, the rose and friends anticipate:
Winebringer, see moon in King's face, bring wine don't wait!
I'd taken away my heart from the Spring season of the rose,
but the blessings of pure ones of the time carried no weight.
Don't set your heart upon the world: ask from the drunkard
  about cup's generosity and about story of Jamshid's fate.
O heart, the power of Love is very great; make a resolution:
hear the story well and open the ear to the tale it will relate.
Except for the wealth of life, I've nothing else in my hand;
where is wine so that on Winebringer's glance I can liquidate.
What does it really matter if morning meal had been missed;
with morning wine, seekers of Beloved break fast, celebrate.
I'm afraid that on the Resurrection Day, rein for rein will go
the priest's rosary and an old coat of a mad loving inebriate.
Fortune is joyful and good and the King is mercifully good;
God, guard them both from the wounded eye of Time's fate.
Drink wine to the slave's song: for upon Your jeweled cup,
  this royal pearl will with another exquisite taste, decorate.
Because it is Your universal merciful nature to offer a screen,
  cover up and forgive our heart, it is a coin that doesn't rate.
Hafez, since the fast has passed and the rose has gone away,
helpless, drink wine; opportunity left your hand, it's too late!

290. DON'T DENY

O breeze, your passing by Beloved's dwelling,
            don't deny:
   to the poor lover, news of Beloved be telling:
            don't deny.

O rose, thankful that you blossomed to your heart's desire,
      the breeze of union to the bird of the morning
            don't deny.

All of our desires depend upon just one glance of Yours:
to old friends, who are this much depending;
don't deny.
Now that the fountain of sweetness is Your sweet ruby lip,
speak out and from the parrot all its sugaring
don't deny.
When You were the new moon, I was Your companion,
now that You're the full moon, Your glancing
don't deny.
The world and all that is in it are mean and insignificant;
to those with divine knowledge this is trifling:
don't deny.
Poet carries Your glorious kind acts to ends of the earth:
provision to him for the road's long travelling,
don't deny.
Since You desire praise that is worthy of all Your virtues,
regarding this: silver and gold for my praising,
don't deny.
"Hafez, grief's dust blows away, your condition improves;
in this path, the water from your eye falling,
don't deny."

291. DON'T LEAVE

Reveal Your face and say: "Give your life and let Me
take;"
say: "Like the moth before candle give soul, let Me
take."
See our thirsting lip, don't deny the water of Your grace;
come, Your victim's head up from the dust quickly
take.
Do not leave this dervish even if he has no gold or silver;
rate his tears for You as silver, his face as gold see:
take.
Strum harp, play it; if wood lacks play, my plywood heart
use as aloe, my love as fire, as incense tray my body
take.

Throw cloak off your head and join in the circle's dance;
or go in seclusion and over head cloak of hypocrisy
take.
Draw cloak's wool off your head and draw in pure wine;
spend silver; to heart for gold, One of breast, silvery,
take.
So that Friend is friend, may both worlds be the enemy:
Fortune desert me and earth's surface the foe's army
take.
O Friend, do not desire to go, and stay a moment with us;
come follow stream's bank and cup to hand joyfully
take.
If You take leave of me: my yellow colour, water and fire
of heart and eyes, and dry lip and wet chest quickly
take.
Hafez, set up the banquet and go tell to the preacher this:
"See our feast, then from the pulpit leave from me
take."

292. FROM SEPARATION COMES UNION

Again from cypress branch comes patient nightingale's cry:
"From the face of the rose, far be ignorant one's evil eye!"
Rose, be thankful that you bloomed to your heart's desire;
do not be proud to nightingales: mad lovers easily terrify.
I don't complain against being handed the absence of You;
if absence isn't experienced, presence gives no joy to go by.
If others are joyful and happy and are pleasantly delighted,
love's grief for the Beloved is the source of our joyful sigh.
If the fanatics are hoping for Huris and palaces of Paradise:
for us, Winehouse is the palace and the Beloved's the Huri.
Drink wine to sound of harp and don't worry about grief;
if anyone says: "Don't drink," "God Forgives," is the reply.
O Hafez, why do you complain of the grief from separation?
From separation comes Union and in darkness Light does lie.

293. THE NIGHT OF POWER

It's the Night of Power, closed is the book of separating;
because of Night, there's safety from the dawn's parting.
O heart, be such a lover that the feet will never stumble,
for this Path always rewards those who are hardworking.
I'll never again turn away from being a truly honest lover,
even if stoned, driven away heart-sick by Your tormenting.
Although my heart fell from hand, You don't show face;
such cruel lack of attention towards me has me weeping!
With God's mercy, reveal a heart that is morning bright;
when I see only dark, only the night, it must be parting.
Hafez, if you want to be faithful, try to be very patient,
for the profit and loss is the result of every marketing.

294. THE ADVICE TO LOVERS

Advice I give to you; listen, and no excuse will do:
accept whatever the kind adviser may tell to you.
Enjoy those with youthful faces while you may:
to ambush life, is the deceit the old world will do.
To lovers, wealth of both worlds is as a barleycorn,
for 'that' is a small thing and 'this' is of little value.
My desire's good company, music on an instrument:
to its cry of bass and treble, I will tell my pain too.
I pledge that I'll not drink wine or commit any sin,
if in accordance with my wish, fate comes through.
A hundred times repenting, I have put aside the cup,
but Winebringer's glance made resistance give in too.
Wine two years old and Beloved of fourteen years,
are for me company of small and great that will do.
They, without my presence, made Fate, in Eternity;
so if I act a little against this, do not complain too.
Winebringer, pour in cup pure wine like the tulip,
so my Beloved's mole won't leave my mind's view.
Heart, didn't I say to you: "Beware of that long hair?"
For in this ring of chains the wind is held tight too!

Bring the cup of grace, that of the ruby and pearl;
tell the jealous: "See the Master's gift and die, you!"
"Drink wine and try hard for Union with Beloved:"
hear, this is shouted out from ninth Heaven's blue.
Who would try to hold our terrified runaway heart?
Madman Majnun escaped from chains, give news to.
Hafez, at this banquet don't tell of your repentance,
or arrows of Winebringer's glances will strike you.
Since the verse of Hafez is better than that of Zahir,
what room's left for Salman's and poems of Khwaju?

295. SHAME AT LAST

Heart, through eye you bled some, you have shame
at last;
eye, go into deep sleep so that the heart fulfils aim
at last.
Lord, wasn't it I who stole a kiss on arm of my lovely one?
You saw how the prayer of dawn, effective became
at last?
To me was given essence of this world and next by Provider;
harp's notes first, into hand Beloved's curls came
at last.
How long to snatch like wind an ear from mean harvesters?
Courage, make provisions, sow seeds in own name
at last.
Your house won't be the famous Chinese picture gallery,
but, musk-tipped pen flowing, picture you'll frame
at last.
O heart, if in the land of late nights, you stay and suffer,
breath of dawn brings news of union, Beloved came
at last.

A form like the moon knelt, and offered wine like rubies:
Hafez said: "I've quit." To Winebringer show shame
at last.

296. ONE OR TWO CUPS

O Winebringer, youth's joy to me here,
bring:
make one or two cups of wine appear:
bring.
That remedy for the pain of love that is wine,
that remedy for young, old and austere:
bring.
The sun is the wine and the moon is the cup:
sun into the middle of moon's sphere,
bring.
And because reason is obstinate in the extreme,
that rope of wine for its neck, to steer,
bring.
Throw a little water upon this my burning fire:
that fire that's like water, bring it here:
bring!
If rose has gone away, say this: "Go with joy:"
the pure wine that's like rosewater, clear,
bring.
If nightingale's singing doesn't remain, so what?
Glugging of that flagon of wine to hear,
bring.
The drinking of wine is either right or is wrong:
if it's either right or wrong, do not fear:
bring.
Don't be sad for time the wind has blown away;
the sound of the lute and the lyre to ear
bring.
Since we can only see Beloved's face in sleep,
a Medicine that makes sleep come here,
bring.
Although I am intoxicated, three or four cups
so that I may be so ruined I'll disappear:
bring.

Give to Hafez one or two large double quarts:
   if it's sin or if it is sanctity: it, over here
            bring.

297. SORCERY

Cypress, sweetly moving, so tall and straight,
   rosy-cheeked stealer of hearts, lying in wait;
   since You have stolen our heart by sorcery,
   please keep it, for the sake of God, inviolate.
Ever since I first saw Your two magical eyes,
   peace and patience have left my heart's state.
When You spread the hyacinth of Your hair,
   musk's power afterwards as nothing will rate.
Don't be unfaithful anymore, magical form;
   try hard to be faithful and to be fortunate.
Tenderly cherish me sometimes with a kiss:
   You'll enjoy fruit of life's tree, consummate.
So astonished is wretched Hafez: Your slave,
   he is without any gold or silver, it's his fate.

298. THE QUEST OF LOVE

I am that one who has opened his eye to see the Beloved's face:
   You're so kind to slaves, how can I thank You for such grace?
Say to the troubled beggar: "Don't wipe your face clean of dust;
   dust of the street of beggary is your longing's alchemical base."
Eye, along with the one or two drops that you have scattered,
O many are the glances that you have thrown at Fortune's face.
If the lover doesn't become purified with the blood of the liver,
   according to the word of love's Judge, his prayer is a disgrace.
O heart, do not turn the rein away from the Path's difficulties:
   ascent and descent, to the wayfarer should be commonplace.
What gain shall I obtain from the breeze that carries all the tales,
when in this garden, straight cypress doesn't even know the case?
In this stage of illusion, take nothing except for the cup of wine:
in this playhouse don't play any game, but love's game embrace.

Although Your beauty is independent, having no need of love,
  I'm not one who will turn from this game of love, back apace.
How can I tell to You what I see because of my burning heart?
  Ask about it from my tears, for I am not of that gossiping race.
The quest of love is the glance of beauty: if this wasn't so, then
  Mahmud of Ghezni's fortune did not need Ayaz's hair and face.
The singing of *ghazals* of Venus cannot take the lead in singing,
  where the voice of Hafez is singing songs in that highest place.

299. TRUTH'S PATH

A thousand thanks I've seen You again, I'm content;
  in truth and purity my heart's partner is now evident.
Wayfarers of Truth's Path walk the road of calamity;
  friends of the Path don't think of ascent or descent.
Grief for hidden Friend is better than seeking spies;
  secrets are not for confiding to heart of malevolent.
Be thankful that the Friend illuminates our gathering:
  even if badly treated, burn like a candle, be content.
With a half a kiss buy a blessing from one with heart;
  this, enemy's malice to soul and body will prevent.
O Chief, sadness that is on my face from grief for You,
  would possibly take me a year to tell to its full extent.
The murmur of love has to Irak and as well to Hijaz,
  sweet melody of the *ghazals* of Hafez of Shiraz, sent.

300. CAPTIVE OF LOVE

That night's happy when You come and many glances share;
  You flirt and are scornful and I humbly beg and then it I bear.
How shall the inner mystery stay hidden like that of rosebud?
  Because my heart's confidant is the breeze's sweet fragrant air.
From fortune in the highest I'd hoped I would have Your form:
  from long life I had desired that fragrant waft of Your hair.
What a great commotion it was that the Artist of Fate brought,
  when for Your narcissus, eyeliner with grace He did prepare.
How often from longing I knocked upon the door of the heart,

hopeful of the day of Union with You in this night of despair.
Why should I think of Your cruelty and the tyranny of spies?
Captive of love, from many disasters, has no grief whatsoever!
With the news the rose was coming, breeze gave soul some rest;
a thousand blessings of God be showered on such an informer!
Dust of our heart causes the eye of the enemy to be blinded:
Hafez, lay your face in dust; burn, and bear your burden there.

301. A NIGHT LIKE THIS

On way to Winehouse, lovers who hurry without delay,
suffer the same as pilgrims on the road to Mecca's way.
Separated from You, I sealed my eye from the world;
soul gave hope of fortune of Union with You, as pay.
After this, from Beloved's presence I'll go to no door;
since gaining Kaaba, from idol worship I've gone away.
From Fortune I desire a night like this until morning,
so explanation of my need for You I can begin to say.
In desire to be with that Moon in halo-canopy, Hafez,
content, burn like candle if violence comes your way!

302. BOTH THE SAME

Bride of the rose came back to the rosebed's feast of Spring;
where is the sweet nightingale to tell: "Let out a song, sing?"
Heart, don't complain about separation, because in the world
is grief and joy, thorn and rose, the degrading and inspiring.
I'm bent like a bow from sorrow, but I don't breathe a word
about giving away bowed eyebrows, that send arrows flying.
Don't tell to the enemies the story of the night of separation;
for hearts of masters of malice, the mystery aren't holding.
It was because of Your hair my heart's distress was revealed;
it isn't so range if it is the role of musk to do some informing.
A thousand eyes are looking at Your face; it's true that You
through grace, not a glance towards any one's face are giving.
O heart, if Beloved burns you, don't complain of burning pain;
breathe out about Beloved's love and the pain remain bearing.

Dust of our heart will make the eye of the enemy be blinded:
Hafez, place your face in the dust, it's the place to be begging.
Long ago, broken-hearted, I placed my face on Your threshold,
yes I did, longing and begging, in Eternity without beginning.
In this Path, what is difficult and easy are the same to Hafez.
To bird on the wing, high and low have a difference showing?

303. AGAIN

Come, so that in my poor heart will come power
again:
come, so that into my dead body, life will enter
again.
Come, for Your absence has shut my eyes in such a way,
only Your open door of Union, will be the opener
again.
Grief like Ethiopia's army, overtook my bleeding heart;
Your face, like Turkey's troop, will be its cleanser
again.
No matter what I've held before the mirror of my heart,
but for Your beautiful image, there's no reflector
again.
From the saying: "Pregnant is the night:" far from You
I count stars, and what night will bring, I wonder
again.
Don't be frightened of desert: put on pilgrims clothes!
Path's pilgrim doesn't worry, and he never travels
again.
Come; for Hafez, the nightingale with heart that pleases,
from scent of Your rosebed of Union, is the singer
again.

304. MYSTERY OF GRACE

O fresh cypress of beauty, sweetly You sway through space,
every moment Your lovers a hundred times need Your grace.

May Your beauty's garment be fortunate, because in Eternity,
to Your cypress shape They have cut a fine garment of grace.
Whoever may be desiring ambergris fragrance of Your hair,
should be content to burn like aloes for incense, and efface.
Value those who envy me, place on me, doesn't alter my value,
even if they scratch me with scissors as is done to gold's base.
The heart of the moth was burnt away because of the candle:
without candle of Your face, my heart's melting without trace.
The heart which has circumnavigated Your street's *Kaaba*,
from love for Your Home, hasn't need for Mecca's holy space.
Where is the profit in abluting the eye in blood every moment,
when I'm not allowed Your eyebrow's arch, my praying place?
Sufi who last night had renounced wine, being without You,
quickly broke resolution, seeing Winehouse's door open apace.
Like cup, drunk from being first to jar, clapping joyously went
Hafez: for last night from cup's lip, he heard Mystery of Grace.

305. THE RUBY OF YOUR LIP

Your lip hadn't come; my desire, from Your lip hasn't come:
hopeful of Your ruby's cup, a drinker of dregs I've become.
At first, from desiring Your hair I lost my heart and faith:
in the end, to me what will be the outcome of this delirium?
Winebringer, give one drink of that wine the colour of fire,
for being among those full of this love, I am in a vacuum.
One night, by mistake, I called Your hair 'musk of Tartary:'
every moment striking my body, hairs like swords become.
One day, by mistake, my name came to lip of the Beloved:
the Soul's perfume from my name to lovers will still come.
In my secluded room, sun saw a ray shining from Your face:
like the shadows on my porch, it has become troublesome.
In Eternity without beginning, Winebringer gave that ruby,
a drink from a cup of which, still causes me to be numb.
You Who said: "Give your soul so heart may have peace;"
grieving for You I gave my soul but my peace hasn't come.
Story of ruby of Your lip Hafez has made flow from his pen;
all the time from my pen Water of Life flows at maximum.

306. THE CONDITION OF BLEEDING HEARTS

Of condition of bleeding hearts, who can speak
again?
From sky, for blood of Jamshid, who will seek
again.
May the intoxicated narcissus be filled with shame
before worshippers of wine, if up it does peek
again.
Except for Plato who is sitting with the cask of wine,
to us the secret of Philosophy, who can speak
again?
Whoever became a passer of the cup like the tulip is,
from this tyranny, washes in blood his cheek
again.
Because harp spoke many words veiled by its notes,
cut its hair-like strings so that it can't shriek
again.
My heart will expand like the rosebud does expand,
if a scent of a tulip-coloured cup it may sneak
again.
Circumnavigation of Sacred House of the winecask,
if the head of Hafez will allow, Hafez will seek
again.

307. THROW!

Get up, and into golden goblet the water of delight
throw:
before the cup of the skull turns to dust outright:
throw!
Our dwelling in the end is over in the valley of the silent:
now the wild shout, up to the heaven's great height,
throw!
From face of Beloved, far is the eye stained from looking:

glance on Beloved's face, from the mirror bright,
throw!
Cypress, by your verdant head I ask you: when I'm dust,
throw shade on me, out from your head any spite
throw!
For our heart that's stung by snake of the tip of Your hair:
from Your lip, to the dispensary, antidote of delight
throw.
You know that this field that is sown is not permanent:
into its harvest, from liver of cup, the fire's light
throw!
I bathed in my own tears, for the people of the Path say:
"First be pure, then on Pure One, your eyesight
throw."
Lord, that bigot who seeing only himself saw only defects,
on his mind's mirror, smoke from sighing all night
throw!
Hafez, like rose, tear garment because of Beloved's perfume:
in the path of that form, that garment that is tight,
throw!

308. THE VEIL

One, like a singing gypsy, maker of mischief my heart has stolen:
a mixer of colours, a killer, believing promises are to be broken.
Thousand garments of piety and many patched coats of austerity,
for torn clothes of One with a moonlike face, as ransom be given.
Being thankful that in beauty's game You took ball from angel,
call for the cup and the dust of Adam with a little water moisten.
I have come to Your doorway poor and broken: show a little pity,
because except for love of You, all other feelings I have forsaken.
I am the servant of the Word that is making the fire rise higher:
not that which by throwing cold water, the fire would dampen.
Come; for to me last night invisible messenger said "Be content:
for one to try to be free from Destiny shouldn't be undertaken."
Don't be proud of your strength, for it's recorded: "By orders
of the Maker of Kings, thousands of events can only happen."

Tie cup on my coffin so that when the morning of rising comes,
terror of the Resurrection from my heart with wine will be taken.
A veil has never really existed between the lover and the Beloved.
Hafez, you are your veil: get up; your pace to the Beloved quicken.

309. THROW ME IN

Come, our cup shaped like a boat, into the river of wine
throw:
into the soul of old and the young, weeping, grief's sign,
throw.
O Winebringer, throw me into my boat and throw in the wine,
for it's said: "Do good, and it upon the water consign:
throw."
I wandered from the street of the Winehouse through mistake;
out of kindness, me back onto right path's straight line
throw.
Bring cup of the wine that's rose of colour and musk of scent:
sparks into heart of the rose of jealousy and envy's design
throw.
Although I am ruined and drunk, show a little kindness to me:
Your glance on this bewildered and ruined heart of mine
throw.
If it is necessary for you to have the sun shining at midnight,
the veil from off rosy face of the daughter of the vine
throw.
Do not allow them to give me to the dust on the day of death:
carry me to the Winehouse and me into the cask of wine
throw.
If the heart of Hafez withdraws its head one hair's tip from You,
seize it and it into the curl of Your hair's twisting twine
throw.

310. ENOUGH TO LIVE BY

O breeze, if near the bank of the river Araxes you should pass by,
kiss the dust of that valley and the musk will be from your sigh.

Salma's place, where we send a hundred greetings each moment,
rings with the clang of the great bell and the cameldriver's cry!
Kiss the Beloved's possessions and then with quiet humility say:
"I burn away from separation from You, kind One help me, try!"
I used to call the advice of advisors an instrument without sound,
but so much separation twists this ear, such advice I'd now go by.
Don't fear the making of delight by taking to the night, because
in love's city, night's prowler is friendly with the night's Chief spy.
O heart, love is not a sport to play; you must play with your life:
if not, to strike love's ball with passion's mallet isn't worth a try.
My heart happily gives up its life to the Beloved's drunken eye;
none who were sober, to anyone else gave themselves up to die.
In the sugar plantation all the parrots are taking their pleasures;
but from grief beating his head with his wings… is this poor fly!
If the name of Hafez should reach to the nib of the Friend's pen,
from this Majestic King such a great blessing is enough to live by.

311. DON'T ASK

O soul, who told to you: "The situation of our case,
                    don't ask;
wander unknown and about any friend a single trace
                    don't ask?"
Because it's Your nature to be understanding and compassionate:
        forgive a sin that hasn't happened and of past disgrace
                    don't ask.
Do you wish to be illuminated about love's bright burning fire?
        Ask about this from candle, of morning breeze a trace
                    don't ask.
That one had no knowledge of the dervish's world who to you
        spoke, saying this: "The dervish, about his own place,
                    don't ask."
Don't look for coin of the quest from the recluse clothed in rags:
        of that poverty-stricken one, for Pure Alchemy's base
                    don't ask.
We've never read the story of Alexander or even that of Darius:

except for the case of love and loyalty, of us a case
don't ask.
In the book of the wise physician there is no chapter about love:
O heart, become used to pain and for remedy to efface
don't ask.
The image drawn, that of the obligation of service that is sincere,
efface from Your heart's slate and our name and trace
don't ask.
Hafez, season of rose has come, don't talk of divine knowledge:
Discover value of time, and how and why for a space
don't ask.

312. REASON TO COMPLAIN

I've such a complaint because of Beloved's black hair,
that, don't ask;
because of it I'm so poor, helpless and full of despair,
that, don't ask.
Do not let anyone surrender heart and soul in the hope of its faith;
for I who have done this, am sorry so much I swear,
that, don't ask.
For one mouthful of wine which would not hurt even a single soul,
from the fools who know nothing, such pain I suffer,
that don't ask.
O pious fanatic, go far from us in peace, for ruby wine in such a way
away from the hand my heart and faith does bear,
that, don't ask.
My desire was to gain safety and to be secluded in a quiet corner;
but that bewitching narcissus such sorcery did dare,
that, don't ask.
It is said that all of one's life dissolves away in the pathway of Love:
they shout: "Don't look at this;" to another there:
"That, don't ask."
I said: "I'll ask of the present condition from ball of the heavens:"
it said: "In the curve of the mallet I suffer such fear,
that, don't ask."
I asked Beloved: "Your hair is everywhere because of whose malice?"

Beloved: "By the *Koran*, this is such a story I declare,
that, don't ask."

313. SUCH SORROW

I've gained from love such sorrow,
that, don't ask:
separation's poison had to swallow,
that, don't ask.
I have wandered in the world and out of all of this,
I've so perfect a Beloved to follow,
that, don't ask.
From deep longing for the dust of Your doorstep,
I have such eyes letting tears flow,
that, don't ask.
During the night, with both ears, from Your mouth
I heard words so sweet and mellow
that, don't ask.
Why do you bite lip at me and say: "Don't speak;"
I've bitten ruby lip that's so aglow,
that, don't ask.
In the poor small room of my beggary, without You
I have suffered such great sorrow,
that... don't ask.
Like the stranger Hafez, in the long pathway of love
I've come to a new stage somehow,
that... don't ask.

314. ENOUGH

Heart, on journey as companion fortune that is helping
is enough:

having garden of Shiraz's breeze as friend while travelling
, is enough.
O dervish, never again wander far from the dwelling of the Beloved;
because for you in cloistered corner, some spirited walking
is enough.
Love of familiar dwelling's atmosphere and promise of the old Friend,
as an excuse to experienced travellers who are wayfaring,
is enough.
Sit on the favourite bench in the Winehouse, drink a cup of wine:
this for you of wealth and glory of the world's dwelling,
is enough.
The heavens hand reins of passion into hands of the ignorant fool:
you who feel wise and virtuous, desire you're possessing
is enough.
Don't let yourself be accustomed to gifts of others; in both worlds,
the favour of king, and Grace that Great God is Willing,
is enough.
If from out of corner of your heart a great grief should ambush you,
for you, sanctuary of Master's gate that is protecting,
is enough.
Don't desire more than you need and don't work yourself too heavily;
for flagon of ruby wine and beauty like the moon shining,
is enough.
O Hafez, no need for you to put into practise anything but this:
for you, prayer of morning and at midnight some begging,
is enough.

315. ENOUGH FOR US

From rosegarden, One with rosy cheek blooming,
is enough for us:
from meadow, shadow of that cypress swaying,
is enough for us.
May companionship of hypocritical people be kept far away from me!
Of weighty matters, a heavy quart to be carrying
is enough for us.
They give the palace of paradise as the reward for doing good deeds:

Winehouse of Winesellers for poor lovers thirsting,
is enough for us.
Sit on the bank of the passing stream and look at life that is passing:
because this example of this world that is passing,
is enough for us.
Understand value of the world's market, and see world's miseries:
if the profit isn't enough for you, such a loss showing
is enough for us.
Beloved's with us, what need is there for us to desire anything more?
That Friend of the soul's company that's a blessing,
is enough for us.
For God's sake, do not send me away from Your door to paradise:
the end of Your street in this existence's dwelling,
is enough for us.
In our head there's not a single desire except to be united with You:
in this world and another, this objective's happening
is enough for us.
Hafez, it is unjust complaining about this watering place of fate...
to have pure nature like water and *ghazals* flowing,
is enough for us.

316. TRUE TO PROMISE

If You're compassionate Friend, true to promise really
be;
Friend of bath, closet and rosegarden, daily and nightly
be.
Do not give Your wild flowing hair to the breeze's clutches;
to hearts of lovers don't say: "Hearts wild, upset, crazy
be."
If your desire is to be sitting side by side with Khizer, then
hidden from Alexander's eye, like Water of Life, secretly
be.
Not every bird that flies has the power to sing Love's song;
come, to nightingale singing *ghazals*, a rose new to see
be.
The path of being a servant and all of the standing, waiting,

for the sake of God, give this to us; and true Royalty
be.
From captive of the Holy Net, don't take the sword away;
be careful; for what you have done to our heart, sorry
be.
You are candle of this crowd, so be one tongue and heart;
see the folly of the moth's effort and laughing lightly
be.
Love's glance is the perfection of heartstealing and grace;
rare Ones of the Age perceive, and One of them really
be.
Hafez, be silent and don't complain of the Friend's cruelty;
Who said to you: "Astonished at the face that is lovely,
be?"

317. BLISS

Your form's beautiful: each place, everywhere of Yours,
is bliss.
In heart, from grace of sugar-eating lip so fair of Yours,
is bliss.
Your form is as gracious as the rosebud that is freshly opened,
like the cypress of Paradise, here and over there of Yours,
is bliss.
Your graceful way is sweet and Your cheek and mole are lovely;
eye and eyebrow and height beyond compare of Yours,
is bliss.
My imagination is decorated by the rosegarden of Your image;
fragrance of my heart from that jasmine hair of Yours,
is bliss.
I'll die before Your eyes, although they have caused this illness;
my pain, from that face that is bright and fair of Yours,
is bliss.
In the path of Love where there is no escaping disaster's flood,
in my heart, from waiting for the scent of air of Yours,
is bliss.
Although in the desert of search each side is extremely dangerous,

heartsick Hafez goes on; for love, everywhere of Yours,
is bliss.

318. BLESSED WITH UNITY

Nightingale's only thought is that the rose his Beloved will be,
but the rose's role is only how to show grace for lovers to see.
Not everything that effaces the lover is charming to the heart:
whoever attends to grief serving it well, a Master, *Khwaja* is he.
It's no wonder ruby's value in this market's shattered by a stone,
this is a place where the ruby's heart is thrown to a bleeding sea.
Nightingale learned to speak because of the favour of the rose;
if not, then this singing and songs in his throat could never be.
One Who travelled and is Companion of many caravans of hearts,
O God, wherever that travelling One is, keep forever in safety.
When passing through the street of our Beloved, be very careful,
for if not, by wall of Beloved's street, your head broken will be.
O heart, although company of health may happily come to you,
there is no doubt you will take the road to the True Territory.
While the Sufi from being slightly drunk tipped cap to one side,
with two more cups his turban will unwind and be falling free.
Heart of Hafez that has become accustomed to Your presence,
do not think of tormenting, for it has been blessed with Unity.

319. THE RUINED ONE

Come back; to this deprived heart, the friend truly
be:
to this ruined one, the confider of mysteries kindly
be.
Of that wine which they sell in the Winehouse of Love,
give two, three cups; though it Fasting Time really
be.
O wise holy traveller, after you burn cloak of religion,
make an effort and chief of drunken lovers sincerely
be.
To that Friend Who said: "My heart looks, expects you,"

reply: "Look, surely I'm coming, so waiting for me
be."
My heart bleeds with love for that Life-giving ruby lip;
may same seal and stamp on casket of Love clearly
be!
So not a speck of grief's dust may settle on Your heart,
following my letter, may my tears flowing quickly
be!
Tell Hafez that if he is seeking the World-revealing cup,
his sights set on the Master of Jamshid should clearly
be.

320. TULIP SEASON

In tulip's season take cup and do not a hypocritical envier
become;
with the red rose's perfume and with the breeze, friendlier
become!
I'm not telling you to worship wine throughout the whole long year;
give it away for nine months and then for three a drinker
become.
If the Wiseman of Love's path should offer to you a drink of wine,
go ahead and drink, and trusting in God the Great Forgiver,
become.
If you, like Jamshid wish to be united with the Hidden Mystery,
come and be a companion of the cup and a World-revealer
become.
Although the world's doings are in a knot like the bud of the rose,
like the breeze of Spring, if you prefer, you a knot-opener
become.
Do not expect faithfulness from anyone; if you don't listen to this,
you, a fool looking for the Phoenix or Alchemist's elixir,
become.
Hafez, do not accept the ways and laws of those who are strangers,
but to those who are lovers of pure wine, a friend forever
become.

321. THE PATIENT NIGHTINGALE

If for five days, gardener to be in the company of the rose
is necessary,
nightingale patient at separation's thorns that oppose,
is necessary.
Heart, don't complain of bewilderment, bound up in Beloved's hair,
when the wise bird falls and is tied there, to take blows
is necessary.
To one who has Your hair in sight may love's glance be forbidden,
if for that one, jasmine face, hyacinth hair, both of those
is necessary.
In Path of Love to trust in piety and knowledge is unfaithfulness:
even if wayfarer has many skills, to trust God knows,
is necessary.
O mad heart, it is necessary you must endure that drunken narcissus
that's full of pride: hair and forehead's curl that flows
is necessary.
Winebringer, how long will You delay the circulation of the winecup?
When with the lovers it circulates, that around it goes
is necessary.
Who is Hafez that he doesn't drink from cup without harp's melody?
Why is it to poor lover, patience like this that overflows,
is necessary?

322. SHIRAZ

Hail Shiraz, city situated on a site beyond compare!
May the Lord preserve it from decay, is my prayer.
A hundred praises to our stream called Ruknabad;
Khizer, drinking its water, found Eternal Life there.
From between the districts of Jafarabad and Musalla,
the cool north wind the scent of ambergris does bear.
Come to Shiraz and ask for the Holy Spirit's grace,
from the man Who has gained all perfection's share.
Who here would make a mention of Egypt's candy,
when here, the Sweet Ones, of same have not a care?

O breeze of the east, what news have you to pass on
about the condition of that intoxicated One, so fair?
For God's sake do not wake me up from this dream,
for in it I see an image that is indeed sweet and rare.
Even if that Sweet One should be spilling my blood,
  heart, then it's lawful, like mother's milk to share.
Hafez, when you're frightened of separation, why not
give thanks for when you and Beloved were together?

323. TAKEN

Peace, power and sense, have from me been taken
by that stony-hearted Idol's earlobe, silver laden.
An image, a beauty, quick and playful like a Pari,
  a subtle one, moonlike one, Turk-like robe open.
With the fierce fire in me that's the frenzy of love,
  I am forever boiling like the bubbling cauldron.
Heart that's like a shirt would be free from pain,
if the wearer of that robe to my embrace is taken.
At cruelty I no longer grieve, for without a thorn
  none finds rose; honey without sting isn't eaten.
Even if rotten my mortal skeleton should become,
  the love that is in my soul will not be forgotten.
My heart and faith, heart and faith, were by that
  breast and shoulder, breast and shoulder, taken.
Hafez, your only remedy is, your only remedy is
that sweet lip, that sweet lip, that lip to sweeten.

324. THE DERVISH

I am the dervish without a care and my heart became full of fear,
because of what happened to heart, the prey, the frightened deer.
I trembled like willow's leaves for the sake of my own faith's life,

for heart's in Infidel's hand, Whose eyebrow has a bow so near.
I imagine that I'm the essence of the sea: how ridiculous this is!
In head of this mere drop are such thoughts: absurd and unclear!
I boast about that eyelash that is bold and that murders all sleep,
on tip of whose point dashes the waves of water sweet and clear.
From sleeves of thousands of physicians much blood will trickle,
if on my wounded heart they should put a hand to examine here.
In street of the Winehouse I go with my head hanging, weeping,
because I'm ashamed all of the time of what I have gathered here.
Age of Khizer doesn't last forever, neither does Alexander's realm:
dervish, don't make trouble for the world that's mean, insincere.
O friend, you are a slave, don't go complaining about loved ones:
love's state is not to complain of less or more, but to persevere!
Hafez, not the hand of every beggar reaches to belt of that waist;
bring to hand a treasury greater than that held by Karun's cashier.

325. THE WINESELLER'S SECRET

Last night a wise knower of a mystery secretly said to me:
"The secret of the Wineseller... hidden from you cannot be."
He then said: "Be easy with the way that you treat yourself,
it is the nature of the world to treat hard-workers heavily."
He then gave to me the cup which radiated the sky, so that
Venus danced and the lute player said: "Drink," repeatedly.
"O son, listen to advice, do not grieve for the world's sake:
I speak to you advice like a pearl, keep it in your memory.
"With bleeding heart still show the laughing lip of the cup:
if you are wounded, then crying like reed you shouldn't be.
"As long as you haven't been in the veil, you haven't a hint:
where Gabriel gives news, those who're immature can't see.
On the carpet of the knowers of the subtle is no pride of self:
man of wisdom, either speak what you know or sit silently."
O Winebringer, give wine: Hafez's drunken loving was known
by Lord of Unity, Forgiver of faults... Concealer of stupidity.

326. A VOICE FROM THE INVISIBLE

In the days of the king who hid errors and towards crimes was forgiving,
the professors drank from the cup and Hafez from flagon was drinking.
The Sufi came out from cloister's corner and sat at foot of the winejar;
he saw that the policeman's shoulder, the pitcher of wine was carrying.
The condition of priest and judge and their secret drinking like the Jew,
I inquired about from the Master, old Wineseller, during the morning.
He said: "Although you're initiated, this matter isn't fit to speak about:
hold your tongue and drink the wine and the veil keep on respecting."
Winebringer, Spring is coming and there is no means of obtaining wine:
give me a clue for my heart's blood is boiling from worry and suffering.
My excuses are love and poverty and youthfulness and the new Spring;
accept my excuses and then in the trail of mercy the fault be covering.
For how long will You extend Your tongue like the flame of the candle?
O Friend, be quiet, for this moth that You long for... is shortly arriving.
O King of every form and King of every truth, beyond every comparison,
no eye has ever seen the like of You and also no ear will be ever hearing.
Continue to stay, until Your youthful fortune has been finally inherited,
by the hypocrites blue patched coats from the sky that a rag is wearing.
Hafez, I tried to discover my purpose from this old inconsistent sphere:
It said this: "Go to the Winehouse and a cup of the wine be drinking."
Last night a voice reached into the ear of my heart from the Invisible:
"Hafez, sit down, drink some wine and grief no longer be suffering."

327. OPENLY DRINKING

At dawn, the invisible messenger to my ear happy news was giving:
"It is the age of Shah Shuja, so now the wine be openly, drinking."
That time has passed when the people of vision kept out of the way:
a thousand forms of speech in the mouth, and lips silent from fearing.
To the twanging sound of the harp we will be telling all those tales:
heart's like a boiling cauldron because them it has been concealing.
Wine hidden in house was being secretly drunk from fear of police:
let's now drink to Beloved's face, and shout: "Drink; keep drinking."
Last night they carried on their backs from street of the Winehouse,
the revered Imam who on his back the mat for prayer was bearing.
O heart, I give to you some guiding advice for the path of salvation:

do not glory in wickedness and of austerity don't ever be boasting.
Enlightened opinion of the king is place of the light of splendour:
when you wish to be near him, for only pure intentions be striving.
Do not exercise the mind except to give some praise to his greatness;
for ear of his heart has the Angel Gabriel as a confidant, advising.
Kings have knowledge only of the secrets of the state of the empire:
Hafez, you are a beggar who is sitting in a corner, stop this raving!

328. BITTER WINE

Bitter wine, having strength to overpower a man is my desire;
then maybe for awhile from world's viciousness I may retire.
Bring wine, one can't be safe from the treachery of the sky:
its harpist Venus plays, thirst of Mars for blood doesn't tire.
Table of this age is set for the mean, there's no place for joy:
O heart, wash from the greedy palate its bitterly salted mire.
Let go of Bahram's hunting lasso and take the cup of Jamshid:
we didn't find Bahram or his ass, and we crossed desert's fire.
To glance at poor dervishes doesn't do any harm to greatness:
Solomon with his greatness found that an ant he could admire.
Come, so that we may show in pure wine the mystery of Time:
but do not show it to those blind hearts of unnatural desire.
I drink ruby wine from the cup that is the colour of emerald:
with this I will blind pious fanatic, snake of this age, spitfire.
Shaft of the bow of Beloved's eyebrow is still aimed at Hafez:
but at the Beloved's powerful arm only a laugh it can expire.

329. GIVE

Sufi, pluck a beautiful rose; and for the pleasant tasting wine,
give
to thorn the patched religious cloak: austerity bitter as brine

give.

In path of the melody of the harp lay aside all talk and deception;
the beads and the dervish mantle for a drink of that wine,
give.
The Beloved and Winebringer don't place much value on austerity:
it, to the fragrant breeze of Spring in meadow's borderline,
give.
O Monarch of lovers, the ruby wine has attacked me in my path:
in the pit of the Beloved's chin, the heart's blood that's mine,
give.
Lord, in the season of the rose, please forgive the sin of the slave;
to cypress of the bank of the stream, pass on mercy's sign:
give.
You Who've found Your way to the drinking place of Your desire,
a drop from that great ocean to dusty parched lips of mine,
give.
You should be thankful that your eye hasn't seen a fair one's face;
we're of those who work: to us, pardon, favour of the Divine,
give.
Winebringer, when the Master drinks the wine of the morning cup,
mention: "To Hafez, awake all night, the cup of gold so fine
give."

330. HAPPINESS

River's bank, willow's shade, a poetic mind and a friend:
happiness:
heartstealing Winebringer's cheek with rose does blend:
happiness.
Hey, such a fortunate destiny, that has no idea of the value of time,
may this be pleasant... as time for you does apprehend
happiness.
To whoever's heart has friendship through love of a stealer of hearts,
say: "Throw rice on fire, you've an occupation to extend
happiness."
On the bride of nature I generously clasp jewels of virgin thoughts:
perhaps Time's gallery to me a beautiful image will send:

happiness.

Understand the night spent with Beloved is a gift, and be happy,
for when moon shines, heart's on fire, riverbank does wend
happiness.

In the Name of God, there is wine in cup of the eye of Winebringer,
that gives to reason intoxication... a hangover in the end:
happiness!

Hafez, your life carelessly passed by: come with us to Winehouse,
so drunken perfect Ones will an occupation commend...
happiness!

331. COMBINATION OF BEAUTY AND GRACE

Mixture of beauty and grace is in that one's moonlike face;
Lord, love and faith give to that one who hasn't even a trace.
That one who takes my heart is a child; and I'm sure one day
in sport will cruelly kill me and in law be guiltless of the case.
It is best that I should guard my own heart for its own good:
that one hasn't known good or bad, can't tell good from base.
I idolize one who is agile and sweet and is fourteen years old:
who has as the slave of the soul, the moon of fourteen days.
The sweet smell of milk is coming from that one's sugary lip,
but from those black eyes look, blood drips all over the place.
O Lord, where did our heart go, searching for that new rose?
For we haven't seen it in its place for over a long day's space.
If my loved one that takes the heart breaks my heart like this,
the king will quickly take that one, to all of his guards replace.
I would be thankful and sacrifice my life, if that peerless pearl
would consider the shell of the eye of Hafez its resting place.

332. IF IT WERE POSSIBLE

I have completely exhausted my fortune in this city,
I must take my load from this whirlpool's insecurity.
I'm gnawing on my hand and I am heaving many sighs,

like rose I set fire to my poor body's torn fragility.
How sweet it was last night when a nightingale sang,
from tree's branch rose listened with all its ability,
saying: "O heart, be joyful, because your Beloved
sits down often angry because of Fortune's hostility.
If you want this cruel, slow world to pass you by:
give up your own cruel words and lack of credibility.
If the waves of misfortune beat upon the sky's roof,
for the pure to get their load wet isn't a possibility."
Hafez, if it were possible to gain everlasting pleasure,
Jamshid would not have left his throne from futility.

333. DIVINE FORGIVENESS

It was last night that the invisible messenger did say
from the Winehouse: "They pardon sin, drink away!"
Divine forgiveness is busy doing its own occupation:
the happy news of mercy, Gabriel brought this way.
The Grace of God is far greater than all of our sins;
a subtlety beyond mind: silence… what can you say?
Take this crude and dull reason into the Winehouse:
so its blood, ruby wine can make bubble and spray.
Though by effort They don't give union with Beloved,
heart, try as hard as you can: don't give effort away.
My ear is united with curl of the hair of the Beloved:
my face with dust of door of the Wineseller does lay.
The drunkenness of Hafez is not really much of a sin,
in the estimate of King's mercy that hides sins away.

334. TRAVELLING COMPANION

Lord, that fresh smiling rose that You entrusted into my keeping
to guard from envious ones of the garden, to You I am returning.

My heart is that one's travelling companion; wherever the journey,
  guarding the soul and the body will be the helpful people's blessing.
Though that one wanders a hundred stages from Faith's homestead,
  may far from soul and body be the calamity of the moon's turning.
Morning breeze, if you reach to the edge of the dwelling of Salma,
  a salutation from me I am hopeful that you'll kindly be conveying.
From that long black hair, please softly scatter some musk to me,
  because it is the home of all the true hearts, it don't be disturbing.
Say this: "My heart has remained faithful to Your down and mole:
  in that ambergris long curling hair, it please sacredly be keeping."
  In that place where they drink wine to memory of Your ruby lip,
  mean is the one who any consciousness of himself is still retaining.
It's wrong to gather wealth and prestige from the Winehouse door;
  into the sea throw the wealth of whoever this water is drinking.
He who is frightened of love's suffering is not really a true lover:
  Your foot with our head, or Your mouth with our lip be joining.
The verse of Hafez, couplet of the *ghazal,* is all Divine Knowledge:
  on his soul that fascinates heart and gracious verse, be a blessing.

335. FRESH LIFE

When breeze that blows ambergris blew Your hair into a mess,
  by caressing them it brought fresh life to all those in distress.
Where is a friendly conspirator so that I may explain my grief,
  how my heart, long separated from You, suffers from stress.
A letter promising faith, morning's messenger took to Friend,
  its inscription was blood of an eye: a seal meant to impress.
Time made leaves of the rose as an impression of Your cheek,
  but hid it in rosebud upon seeing You, out of shamefulness.
You are asleep and it's apparent that there is no limit to this,
  thanks be to God for this Path, that having no end, is limitless!
Perhaps it is *Kaaba's* beauty that wants to be wayfarers' excuse:
  in its desert, hearts still alive are souls burnt without redress.
Secret love for You my heart kept secret, I told to only You;
  now see how my eye reveals all to lovers, this I must confess.
News of a trace of the heart's Joseph from the pit of the chin,
  who brings to this poor lover's griefstricken house of heaviness?

I take that tip of hair and place it in the hand of the Master;
so that He might take me out of its hand, and hand me justice.
In the morning on the edge of the meadow, from nightingale
I heard melody of Hafez: so sweet of song, voice of sweetness.

336. DRUNK WITH GRIEF

I'm drunk with grief of love for Winehouse Friend of mine:
on my wounded heart You glance arrows of grief's design.
If that cross at that tip of the end of Your hair You show,
O many is the Muslim corrupted by this infidelity so fine.
To You I join; from anything but You, I'll sever the heart:
Your lover does neither to stranger nor to relative incline.
Kindly grant a gracious glance to me whose heart is lost;
without help of Your grace my work is at end of its line.
If Your ruby lip pours out salt on my poor wounded heart,
O Ruler of Beauty's realm, where finally does hurt incline?
Before and behind me Your intoxicated eye lay in ambush;
to the wind, the harvest of all my patience it did consign.
From mouth's box of honey lay a lotion on Hafez's heart,
for it's bleeding from that knifelike glance, a stinging sign.

337. ROBE OF HONOUR

When I drink Your ruby cup, where do all my senses remain?
When I see Your drunken eye, my ear, who tries to restrain?
I am Your slave and although You are free of a need for me,
sell me to the Wineseller of the Winehouse, I won't complain.
On my shoulder I carry the jug of those who go to Winehouse:
I go in the hope that in the Winehouse a goblet I may obtain.
From desiring Your ruby lip, carrier of the water of the street
of drinkers of wine, at Wineseller's threshold makes tears rain.
Do not talk to me saying this: "Be silent, breathe in deeply:"
one cannot tell the bird in the meadow: "Be silent, refrain!"
If I search for trace of You, where's patience and where's rest?

If I tell Your tale, then who has patience left and who a brain?
Don't give wine that's matured to souls with withered hearts:
  wine is a fierce fire: those matured are wild from love's pain.
The delights of paradise never reach to the delight that comes
  when while Beloved is drinking wine, one says: "Drink again!"
When They gave me the robe of honour of the Sultan of Love,
  They shouted this: "Hafez, put it on and your mouth restrain!"

338. THE PRECIOUS PEARL

From the noose of Your hair's tip there is deliverance for no one;
You kill the poor lover, unafraid of punishment for what is done.
If the lover with burning heart doesn't go to effacement's desert,
he isn't accepted as special one in special place of the Special One.
Power of Your glance is powerful enough to overpower Rustom;
bowman of Your eyebrow's bow has archery prize from Wikas won.
In all truthfulness, I placed my life in the middle like the candle:
in all sincerity, I made my own body melt away from shining Sun.
As long as you don't burn away from love's longing like the moth,
  freedom from grief of love for you will be much less than none.
You drive such a fire into our heart that is like the burning moth,
even though from our desire for You, much dancing we have done.
Our body's dust has been transmuted into purest gold by alchemy
of love's grief for You, though it's worth less than tin to anyone.
What do the populace know about the value of the precious pearl?
Hafez, give precious pearl only to worthy, not every mothers' son.

339. CENSORSHIP, WINE AND THE BOOK

From that watcher, the heart of mine is never released:
  one who tells tales, by a teller of tales is never loved.
The censor broke the flagon and slave broke his heart:
  "Tooth for tooth and the wounded for the wounded."
The cup of wine is like Jesus, because in its pure nature
  is the speciality, that the dead by it are really revived.
Minstrel, play such a fine tune, that upon the sphere,

to be a dancer like Venus old Jupiter will be inclined.
Look for wealth from love, never seek it from reason:
so that like pure gold you will then become purified.
With heart, Hafez, from the Book of the Friend's face,
chapters 'Praise' and 'Constancy' should be memorized.

340. FAR AND WIDE

Your beauty took the whole earth from top to bottom, side to side:
of lovely face of earth's Moon, sun was ashamed and tried to hide.
If it is necessary for all creation to witness Your boundless beauty,
also, it is commanded duty that all the angels Your face have spied.
The sun of the fourth heaven borrows all its light from Your face;
and like seventh earth, its load when it is dying it must cast aside.
The soul that has not been sacrificed for You will always be dead:
body that's not Your captive deserves to be cut and sheared of hide.
If Your lip that loves the soul doesn't give me a piece of rose-jam,
when will this sorrowful body of mine escape this sickness inside?
How is it possible for your kiss to be upon dust at Beloved's foot?
Hafez, your tale of longing as proof, let the wind take far and wide.

341. FROM THAT CHEEK

Come, so that fragrance of my soul I may trace
from that cheek;
for I discovered trace of my own heart's place
from that cheek.
Huris' charms and spirituality which they've explained in books,
explanation you'll get of their beauty and grace
from that cheek.
The form of the proud cypress is left in the dust by that shape:
rose of rosegarden shamefully shrinks back apace
from that cheek.
The muskpod of China took the fragrance of musk from that hair:
perfume of Beloved, rosewater found as its base
from that cheek.
Sun became drowned in perspiration from the Sun of Your face:

thin and waning remained moon of sky's face,
from that cheek.
Water of Life is trickling from Hafez's verse that charms heart,
as souls dissolve into sweat and trickle like lace
from that cheek.

342. SINCE YOU HAVE COME

Ever since rounding the Beloved's cheek in down, Time drew the line,
the sky's moon honestly mistook Your face as another moon's shine.
From desire for Your lip, which is far better than the Water of Life,
the fountain of water flowing from my eyes and Euphrates combine.
Look at the dark mole that is upon that cheek that is silver coloured;
truthfully, all that's remaining of the moon's face is this musky sign.
Since You have come to the garden, hair loose and sweat showing,
face of red rose is like saffron and the musk and water did resign.
Sometimes longing for You, I give heart and soul like they were dust:
sometimes like duck, I quench love's fire with water, tears of mine.
If the Great Sovereign, the King, will find me acceptable as a slave,
the agreement that binds me as a slave I will welcome, and it sign.
O Hafez, the Water of Life is full of shame because of your poetry:
no one has created verse such as this out of desire for Love Divine.

343. GHAZAL TO HAFEZ

May God guard your good face from eyes of evil ways,
Hafez,
because with Us it is only all its goodness that stays,
Hafez.
Come, for it is the time of peace and of friendship and faith:
for with Us the memory of conflict isn't even a haze,
Hafez.
Although My ruby lip drank deeply from your heart's blood,
take from My lip a kiss as blood-money, see if it pays,
Hafez.
Where then are you, and the hope of Union with Me is where?

upon this garment the hand of not every beggar lays,
Hafez.
Do not give your heart to the hair or to the mole of beauties,
if you make an escape from this calamity and this maze,
Hafez.
Go, fanatic: for you have put on the patched coat of jugglers!
Come; for you have drunk dregs of griefstricken days,
Hafez.
At morning, with heart and with soul cry like the drunkards;
and, at that moment, a single prayer for My work says
Hafez.
Come and sing a beautiful *ghazal*, delightful and full of fire:
for giving joy and increasing life are your verses' ways
Hafez.

344. I SWEAR

By the power and glory and the pomp of Shah Shuja I swear,
that for sake of wealth and position I haven't fought anywhere.
Give a thankful glance to all the lovers because of this favour,
for I'm the obedient slave of you, the king obeyed everywhere.
We are thirsting for the bounty of what comes from the cup:
but we don't give you a pain in the head with too bold a prayer.
House-wine's sufficient for me; don't bring wine of Winehouse:
friend, cup's companion came: goodbye repentance forever!
For God's sake, clean and scour the patchcoat with the wine:
for from this coat I don't smell the scent of the good and fair.
Look at how they all now go dancing to the twang of the harp,
those who did not give permission to hear the song anywhere.
O God, do not make the brow and face of Hafez be separated
from the dust of Shah Shuja's court of magnificent grandeur.

345. SING THE LOVE SONG

By glory of the world-illuminating fortune of Shah Shuja's reign,
I swear that I've never fought anyone for wealth, rank, or gain.

Bring wine, for when that bright sun makes his torch brighter,
even down to the hut of the dervish, the bounty of its rays rain.
Flagon and lovely companion is enough for me from the world:
all things without these, only cause stress and to the head, pain.
Giver of advice, go and exchange all this pity for a cup of wine;
for I am the slave, and not king who is obeyed, the sovereign.
Love has sent me out from the mosque over to the Winehouse:
friend, companion of cup has come: farewell to repentance again!
Time will not make payment for merit and I've nothing but this:
where will I go to sell these goods when the market's a dull brain?
I'm sick and tired of the austerity and all the idle talk of Hafez:
play the harp and sing the love song and begin the dance again.

346. THE OBEDIENT KING

When at dawn from private room of the House of Wonder on high,
the candle of the east throws out its radiance over the whole sky;
when from the horizon's pocket the juggling sky takes the mirror,
and in a thousand ways the face of the world then does magnify,
in the hidden halls of the House of Joy of the Jamshid of Heaven,
to the music of the spheres, Venus then tunes the organ to go by.
The harp brought into twang says: "Where is he who love denies?"
The cup juggles out a laugh: "Where is he who would wine deny?"
Consider the turnings of the heavens and take up the cup of joy:
because in all conditions, this is the far better way for one to try.
The flowing curls of the mistress of the world are false and a trap:
the men of true wisdom will not look for the end of a threaded lie.
If you want the world to be happy then pray for King's long life:
for it is an existence Divinely generous, helping all, low and high.
The image of the evidence of the Eternal Grace is that of the King,
soul of world, height of practise and wisdom, light of Hope's eye.
Hafez, just like the slave does, waits at the threshold of His door:
He's obedient King of kings who are obeyed, wherever they may lie.

347. LIKE THE CANDLE

Constantly loving You, known as one of the fair,

I'm like the candle;
in the street of drunken outsiders, as night watcher
I'm like the candle.

Day and night there is no sleep for eye that's a worshipper of grief,
for sick from separation from You, weeping there,
I'm like the candle.
In this night of separation send me a written note telling of Union,
or I will burn a world, because for You, in despair
I'm like the candle.
If stallion of my rose-coloured tear had not been so hot from racing,
would it be, to the world blazing my secret there,
I'm like the candle?
In middle of water and of fire, my heart that is weak and is wasted
rains tears; its longing for You is such a bright flare,
I'm like the candle.
Mountain of patience has become soft like wax from grief for You;
in water and fire of love for You, as I melt and wear
I'm like the candle.
My day has become night without Your beauty lighting the world:
by perfecting my love for You, effacing into the air,
I'm like the candle.
Stretch my neck one night and raise my head into Union with You:
let sight of Your face illuminate my room where
I'm like the candle.
Without seeing You there is only a breath of life like in the morning;
Heartstealer, show Your face, life I'll give: I swear
I'm like the candle.
It is wonderful how the fire of love for You has caught fire to Hafez:
will I ever quench heart's fire with the eye's water?
I'm like the candle.

348. THE EXAMPLE OF THE ROSE

At morning, like heartbroken nightingale, to the garden I went;
so that I may find remedy for my brain from the rose's scent.

I gazed for a long time on the rose's face, that was coloured red,
that to the darkness of night a bright light, like a lamp, lent.
She was so proud of such youth and such beauty that all peace
out from the heart of nightingale of a thousand songs, she sent.
The eye of the exquisite narcissus was flowing water from envy:
a hundred lashes to her heart and soul the tulip's passion vent.
In disapproval the lily thrust out her tongue like a long sword:
anemone, like gossiping wife, opened mouth in astonishment.
At one time, a flagon in the hand like the lovers of the wine:
at another, like Winebringer of drunkards, hand to cup bent.
Understand joy and pleasure like the rose does, as being plunder;
because O Hafez, the messenger only delivers that which is sent.

349. THE WATCHMAN

If Fortune helps me, my hand on the Beloved's garment I'll lay:
if I hold it, what great joy; what honour, if me Beloved does slay!
This hopeful heart has not once received the advantage of mercy:
although my tale to each and every district goes out every day.
Idols with hearts made of stone, I have loved and I've cherished;
these unnatural offspring don't remember the father in any way.
From the curve of Your eyebrow I didn't find an opening at all:
it's a pity that pursuing this crooked line, dear life passed away.
When did the Friend's eyebrow begin to lead me into this misery?
From this bow no one has made desire's arrow go the target's way.
With the purpose of becoming pious I sat in corners and strangely
from each side, young master with harp and drum to me did play.
The pious fanatics are stupid, uttering charms and not conversing:
police are intoxicated: drink the cup, don't fear but don't delay.
See how the city's Sufi is eating an extremely doubtful morsel!
May this animal of such good fodder like an animal always stay!
O Hafez, if you put down your foot in the path of love's house:
the blessing of Ali, the Watchman of Najaf, shall guide your way.

350. NOTHING INTO NOTHING

A peaceful safe place and pure wine and the kind Friend;
if these are attained, these on the Grace of God depend.

World and its work is nothing but nothing into Nothing:
a thousand times, the proof of this truth I comprehend.
Find a safe place and know stealing from time is opportune:
robbers of the Path lie in ambush and on life will descend.
O I regret so much that up until now I did not understand:
the alchemy of true happiness is the Friend, the Friend!
Come; for to give away ruby lip and laughter of the cup is
an impulse, the truth of which wisdom cannot commend.
That deep beauty that is hiding in that pit of Your chin:
the deepest of thoughts can't reach to the depth of its end.
Where is one with a heart to guide us to what is good?
For in no way have we walked along the path to the Friend.
Though a low one like me doesn't reach Your waist so fine,
thinking of waist's subtlety, happiness to heart does send.
A thousand lives be the ransom for Winebringer's glance,
that moment ruby with wine like cornelian is moistened.
Is it a wonder if my tear should be the cornelian's colour?
For seal of my eye's seal-ring, with cornelian does blend.
Laughing, You spoke: "Hafez, I'm the slave of your will:"
I'm made to look a fool by You, it's easy to comprehend.

351. PATIENCE AND SEPARATION

The pen's tongue does not wish for the recollection
of separation,
or I would tell its story by making an explanation
of separation.
We are comrade of Your image ~ troop and patience's horseman,
partner of exhaustion and affliction and companion
of separation.
What regrets that all of life, hoping for union, has come to an end;
and to an end has come all of time's completion
of separation.
The head that for glory I have rubbed on the roof of the sphere,
by that One I swear I laid it on threshold's station
of separation.
How then shall I be able to open the wing in the wish for union:

my heart's bird shed its feathers on nest's station
of separation.
How can I claim union with You, because by my soul my heart
became fate's puppet, and my body has disposition
of separation.
My heart has become roast meat from the burning of deep desire;
from Beloved I drink blood from table's selection
of separation.
What help's there now that into the great whirlpool of grief's ocean
my boat of patience falls, due to the sailing direction
of separation.
The boat of my life did not need very much to be overwhelmed
by the wave of love, from ocean without limitation,
of separation.
When the sky saw that my head was held captive to love's circle,
it tied neck of my patience with the cord's action
of separation.
Who brought the disunity and separation into the world, O Lord?
May the day of disunity darken and also habitation
of separation.
Hafez, if to end of this Path you had gone with the foot of desire,
to disunity's hand no one would give rein's direction
of separation.

352. SEPARATION

May none be shattered like me by the woes
of separation;
my life has passed by wasted by the throes
of separation.
Exiled stranger, lover, heartsick beggar, mind bewildered;
I've shouldered brunt of Fortune and blows
of separation.
If ever separation should fall into my hand I will kill it;
with tears, in blood, I will pay all the dues
of separation.
Where to go, what to do, who to tell my heart's state to?

Who gives justice, who pays out, for those
of separation?
From the pain of separation not a moment's peace is mine;
for the sake of God, be just… give the dues
of separation.
By separation from Your Presence I'll make separation sick,
until the heart's blood flows from the eyes
of separation.
From where am I and from where are separation and grief?
Seems my mother bore me for grief that grows
of separation.
Therefore, at day and at night, branded by love, like Hafez,
with nightingales of dawn, I cry songs, woes
of separation.

353. DEPART

Your lip's right of salt has now given to my wounded heart
that right, so guard it: may God be with You, now I depart.
You are the pure and priceless jewel in the spiritual world:
the angels in their praising, all of Your virtues do impart.
If You are doubting my sincerity then put me to the test:
no one knows if gold is real except by the touchstone's art.
You said: "I'll become drunk and will give you two kisses:"
Your promise never ends, but for me will one or two start?
Open Your laughing pistachio lips and scatter some sugar:
make doubts of people that You haven't a mouth, depart.
If the heavens don't give my desire I'll smash them together:
I am not the type that is crushed by the sky's fateful part.
Since you will not allow the Beloved any access to Hafez,
O my enemy, a long way, one or two steps further, depart!

354. THE HARMLESS SIN

If you drink wine, pour some upon the dusty clay:
no harm in sin, that someone profits by some day.

Go and drink whatever you have, with no regrets;
ruthless Time with sword of destruction will slay.
Graceful cypress, cherish me by dust of Your foot;
on death's day don't take Your foot off my clay.
In all inhabitants of hell and paradise, men, angels,
in all the religions, selfishness is against the Way.
The sky's Architect made this house of six sides,
so that there is no way out from this pit's decay.
Daughter of the vine charms Reason's path away:
may the vine garden grow until the Judgment Day!
Hafez, by path of the Winehouse you happily went:
the true-hearted lovers, for your pure heart pray!

355. DEATH IS EVERLASTING LIFE

If thousands of enemies for my destruction try,
if You are my Friend, no fear of enemies have I.
The hope of union with You has kept me alive:
fearing separation from You, many deaths I'll die.
If from each breath of the breeze Your scent goes,
with each breath, like rose, my coat in two tear I.
Because of Your image, my eyes sleep? No, never!
My heart's patient separated from You? God deny!
Wound by Your hand's better than another's cure:
Your poison is better than antidotes they supply.
Death by Your sword's blow gives everlasting life:
my soul would be truly happy if for You I'd die.
Don't turn the rein; if You strike me with sword,
I offer my head for shield, hands for halter to tie.
How can every vision see You as You really are?
Everyone has his own limited vision to go by.
When Hafez, downcast, lay in Your door's dust,
then he was uplifted, worthy in the people's eye.

356. THE PAIN OF LOVE

If it is within my power to make it over to Your street,

my case, by fortune of Union with You, safety will meet.
Tranquility has been taken from me by that hyacinth hair;
sleep is taken from me by those eyes, like narcissi sweet.
Since the jewel of Your love polished my heart so brightly,
it's been polished clean of the rust of trouble and defeat.
I will gain life when I have been shattered by misfortune,
when the sword of grief for You makes my death complete.
What sin have I done in Your presence O Heart and Soul,
that the devotion of heartbroken me, You do not meet?
Since I'm at Your door helpless without wealth or strength,
I've neither the way of advancement on the path, nor defeat.
Where will I go, what will I do, be what, make what plan?
Because I'm extremely sick of fortune's sorrow and deceit.
Grief for You, found nowhere a worse state than my heart,
when in my poor straining heart it at first found its seat.
Hafez, with the pain of love be contented and also silent:
do not tell love's secrets to the reasonable and indiscreet.

357. ASHAMED

From giving up wine in rose season, I became so
ashamed;
from such a wrongful action, may no one else go
ashamed.
My righteousness is a trap in Love's Path, causing argument;
of the lovely one or Winebringer, I'll never grow
ashamed.
Of the blood, that last night flowed from our eye as it saw
wayfarers, that in sleep come and go, we were so
ashamed.
Your face is more beautiful than the sun: thanks be to God
I'm not, of You, in presence of sun's face's glow:
ashamed.
maybe by Compassion of God, Beloved doesn't ask my sin;
I'm worried by question, of answer I'm long ago
ashamed.
It's a lifetime but I've not turned face from Your presence:

by Grace of God, of this threshold I'm never, no,
       ashamed.
Why does cup laugh with such bitterness beneath the lip,
    if the wine did not become of Your ruby lip, so
       ashamed?
The pearl of pure water hid its face behind the shell's veil
    for the reason that it is of my verse's pearly glow,
       ashamed.
Water of Khizer drew veil of darkness, because it became
    of Hafez and his poetry that like water does flow,
       ashamed.

358. THE GLORY OF GOD

You of Paradise face, heart and soul fortifies
    in Your ruby lip like clear water of Paradise.
A round Your lip is Your fresh cover of down,
    like ants around where Paradise water lies.
Lord, do with me as You did with Abraham:
    quench within my soul these burning fires.
O friends, I haven't any strength left in me:
    for Your perfect Beauty, beauty Beautifies.
Our hand's short and the date's on the palm,
    our foot is lame and there is still Paradise.
In every corner lie hundreds of fallen ones,
    killed like me by an arrow from Your eyes.
Beauty of this poem is beyond description:
    all will agree that the sun lights up the skies.
Praise to the brush of The Painter, Who gave
    such beauty to Virgin Truth that underlies.
This verse is either miraculous or true magic:
    from invisible messenger or Gabriel it flies.
To the King of the World be absolute glory,
    and everything like this be what He desires.
No one knows how to create verse like this,
    a pearl such as this no one pierces, versifies.

From the grip of love for the fair idol, Hafez
like an ant at the Elephant's foot, now lies.

359. EITHER : OR

To the wayfarer, love is really the sufficient guide:
to find Your path many are the tears I have cried.
How will You regard the great waves of our tears,
when over the dead's blood Your boat You glide?
It is not by my own choice that I am infamous:
God, making me lost in love's road, was the Guide.
Don't splash fire of the idols' faces upon yourself
or, like Abraham did, happily over the fire stride.
Either establish yourself so you lose your desire,
or don't let feet without Guide, on a path decide.
For years I've been thinking about those couplets
an elephant driver on the banks of the Nile cried:
"Either understand the ways of an elephant driver,
or do not go to India thinking of an elephant ride.
Either, don't draw the lover's dark line on the face;
or, on the river Nile throw your coat of piety aside.
Either don't make friends with elephant drivers:
or make the house fit for the Elephant to reside."
Don't call me to Paradise without wine and Minstrel,
my joy is in the winecup, not in that water untried.
Hafez, if you have the meaning, then bring it out;
if not, then this is only a game of seek and hide.

360. SWEET IS THE CRY

Breeze of the north, bring some good news from there,
that informs us that the time of union is almost here.
O messenger from the bird's nest, may God protect you:
welcome to you, welcome, come, and come without fear!
Where is Salma and what is happening in the Zu Salam?
Where are all our neighbours, how are they over there?

The hail for the banquets is now only an empty space;
companions and the full quarts, it no longer do share.
Mansion that was secure has now completely perished:
about its past, go and ask the ruins lying cold and bare.
The night of separation has now thrown out its shadow:
see what prowlers at night, play with imagination there!
The tale of love is such that it never reaches to an end:
here, even the most eloquent of tongues split in despair.
Our tempting Turkish One does not glance at anyone:
it's a pity, all of this pride and disdain, all this cold air!
Hoping for perfection of beauty You acquired Your wish:
may God keep You far away from the evil eye forever!
O Hafez, how long will you have both love and patience?
Cry out loud, for sweet is the cry of the lovers' prayer!

361. BELOVED'S GARMENT

You stole my heart's ease with these: Your form and graces;
You give peace to none, whole world in love with You races.
O soul, sometimes my heart sighs, sometimes draws the bow:
how can I tell You what's drawn from my heart's dark places?
To those informers can I talk and describe Your ruby lip?
on the ignorant and impure... such a description useless is.
Since each day Your beauty grows more and more and more,
to compare Your glorious face to the moon's... a disgrace is.
My heart You've taken, I gave You my soul; why send grief?
We're full of grief... grief-collector not needed at this place is.
Hafez, when in love's special place you put down your foot,
hold Beloved's garment, wash hands of all but such embraces.

362. THE LOVER'S OATH

By magic of magician of Your eye, O One happy and fair,
by mystery of Your down, O fortunate omen written there,

by sweetness of Your lip of ruby that is my Water of Life,
by perfume and colour of You, fresh seal-ring of Beauty rare,
by dust of Your path, that's the shelter of all hopefulness,
by dust of Your foot, of which the pure water is an envier,
by Your cypress-like appearance, like moon, high as sun,
by Your exalted threshold, sky of glory, beyond compare,
by Your graceful walk that is like sway of the partridge,
by Your glances, like the way that a gazelle's eyes flutter,
by Your sweet nature, Your breath like morning's scent,
by Your hair's perfume like north wind's cool fragrant air,
by that red cornelian, that's for me my eye's own seal-ring,
by that jewel, that is for You, door of speech's treasurer,
by that leaf of Your cheek, that's the rose bed of knowledge,
by that enclosed garden of vision, that's my mind's dweller,
I swear that, if You will favourably regard Hafez, for You
he won't hold back life: what use possessions and power?

363. THE DOOR OF THE KING

World's possessor, defender of Religion, accomplished king,
Yahya bin Muzaffar, sovereign, who justice is administering!
Face of world, window of soul and door of heart's thrown open
by your court, shelter of Islam, protecting it under its wing.
It is necessary that wisdom and the soul are reverent to you:
for every created being in existence, your bounty's embracing.
On day of Eternity beyond Time, a black drop from Your pen
fell on the moon's face and solution to all questions did bring.
When sun glimpsed that black mole, complaining to his heart,
"I wish to heaven that lucky slave I had been," he kept saying.
King, from the hum of your banquet the sky sings and dances;
may your hand never let go of skirt's hem of this humming.
Drink wine and give the whole world, for the neck of your foe
is caught in your noose, your hair: caught in that chain's sling.
Revolution of the heavens is converted to the course of justice:
be happy that the wicked tyrant, his objective is now missing.

Hafez, when door of the king of the world is way of subsistence,
concern for your own livelihood it is quite useless to be having.

364. THE POOR STRANGER

I smell breeze of love's fragrance and see lightning of union flashing;
come, O breeze of the north, for fragrance of Your form I'm dying.
O singing guide of the camels of the Beloved, stand and then unload;
I have no more patience: for the beauty of the Beloved I'm longing.
Heart, give away all the complaints about the night of separation:
be thankful that the day of union, the night's screen is now lifting.
Since the Beloved is desiring to have an excuse to have some peace,
one can disregard the spy's violence no matter where it's happening.
Come, for with seven folds of the eye's screen, shedding like the rose,
on the workshop and on the place of Your image I have been writing.
In my straining heart there's nothing but the image of Your mouth:
may there be no one else like me, following such a vain imagining.
I do not show that I am upset with some advice the Beloved gives;
anger with one's own soul, even if one tries, one can't be showing.
My heart has been hurt from being trodden on by the foot of grief:
of its condition there is not even an acquaintance who is knowing.
Murdered by his love for You has become the poor stranger, Hafez;
but, come and pass by our dust, for lawful to You is our bleeding.

365. A MAGIC CHARM

For every subtlety I expressed in praise of such fine graces,
everyone hearing said: "Milk flows from the Highest Places."
"When will You show mercy to this poor soul?" I asked.
You said: "That moment, union not subject to life's trace is.
At the Beginning, love and drunkenness seemed so easy;
in the end the soul tired and worn out from the chase is.
This subtlety, sweet singing Hallaj sang before decapitation:
"To question theologians now, the wrong time and place is."
I've given my heart to a Friend, fair and bold and delicate,

Who having an agreeable disposition, such pure grace has.
Once, like Your eye, I used to go straight into the corner;
now, like Your eyebrow, leaning to drunkenness my place is.
I've cried hundreds of thousands of tears like Noah's flood;
yet, from this heart's screen, Your image it never effaces.
Sorrow's mine: no entrance to that door Heartstealer gave:
although I used every type of go-between, from all places.
Beloved, Hafez's hand is a magic charm against the evil eye:
I wish I could see it on Yours... where its proper place is.

366. CHIEF OF THE AGE

If to my hand it comes that I can sit down with my Heartowner,
from fate's cup I sip wine, from union's garden the rose I gather.
The bitter Sufi-burning wine will not take my life's foundation:
Winebringer, lay Your lip on my lip, take my sweet life as barter.
Perhaps I will go mad; for from love for You, from night to day
I talk to the moon and in sleep I see the Pari, an angelic dweller.
Your lip gave sugar to drunkards, Your eye gave wine to drinkers:
I'm so disappointed for I don't have that or this, I have neither.
On night of departure from couch I go to palace of dark-eyed Huri,
if as I surrender life, You're the candle making my pillow brighter.
As every grain of dust the wind brought was a gift of Your grace,
because I'm an old servant, Your poor slave's condition remember.
Not all who write verses full of imagery are pleasantly accepted:
I take the rare partridge... for my royal falcon is so much swifter.
If you don't believe this, then go and ask the painter of Cathay;
for Mani himself is envious of images my pen's nib puts together.
"Good morning," cries nightingale, "where's Winebringer? Get up!
For last night's loud twanging of harp, in my head grows louder."
It's not the work of every one to be faithful and speak the truth,
I am slave of Chief of the Age, Jalal-ud-Din, the Truth Speaker.
From me, not Hafez, hear the mysteries of love and intoxication;
nightly, friend of moon and Pleiades, with cup and goblet I gather.

367. WINEHOUSE'S HIGHWAY

Please allow us to be travelling by the Winehouse's highway;
for we're all needing a drink, obtained through that doorway.
On the First Day when we boasted of love and drunkenness,
the condition was that the only path we tread was this way.
In this world where the throne of Jamshid the wind takes, it
isn't worth suffering grief best to drink wine come what may.
Let's see if it's possible for us to hold on to Your waist's belt;
for we're sitting in the heart's blood like the ruby's red ray.
Preacher, do not go and give advice to those who are insane:
we in the dust at Friend's feet, from Paradise turn eyes away.
While the Sufis are getting caught up in the dance's rapture,
we get caught by love's magic and lift our hands and sway.
Dust is as valuable as the ruby because You sprinkled wine:
we helpless lovers are much less than dust before You, today.
Because life that is so precious will very soon be leaving us,
at least allow us to look at Your face before we go far away.
Hafez, when there, is no way to the tower of Union's palace,
upon the dust of this door's threshold, our head let us lay.

368. FAMILY FRIENDS

Hasn't the time come for friends to show pity, to relent;
and for those who have broken the promise, to repent?
Haven't they received news of him who was left behind,
he whose chest contains the fire of grief and torment?
If friends knew what had happened to the wounded one,
they would come to him and made their pity evident.
Season of Spring has come and the hills are green again:
why don't the young minstrels sing, full of merriment?
My tears reveal about me what my heart has concealed:
listen to the dumb speaking: what a great wonderment!
In these months the things the wind blows are for gain:
but for us, the pleasures of Spring, are not given assent.
O sons of our Uncle, give us a portion of your kindness:
for the gift of greatness is a trademark of the excellent.

You who have power over all of the kings of the world
give pity; God repays you: Fortune returns what's spent.
Every one of the friends is wealthy and full of hope...
but poor Hafez has only poverty and a constant lament.

369. MY WAY

At dawn I tried to repent, saying: "Guide me God, I need You,"
but Spring came and stopped repentance, so what else can I do?
If I must speak of the truth, it is not difficult to understand,
while the friends drink wine I look on, for I'm not allowed to.
Look here I am really mad, so pass to me the cup that cures,
for with this feasting table of happiness I am finally through.
A form as grand as a Monarch I place upon throne of the rose,
with hyacinth I make You a bracelet, jasmine a necklace too.
Eventually, the Friend's face blossoms for me, a glowing rose;
as for the heads of my enemies, hard stones, and rightly too.
Though I'm Wineshop beggar, when I'm drunk it's fair to say
that I control the stars above and I'm beyond the sky so blue.
My way isn't one of abstaining from what those others forbid,
so why accuse happy drunkards and mad lovers who are true?
Like laughing lip of the rosebud, in memory of King's order,
I take wine and drink from the cup, longing to tear coat in two.
If I'm lucky and obtain a kiss from Beloved Friend's ruby lip,
joyfully young again I become and I'm born again totally new.
Hafez has now become so upset about drinking wine secretly,
to everyone, with harp and wine he will tell this mystery, too.

370. NEW WAY'S DESIGN

Come, so we may scatter the rose and into the cup wine
we'll take,

we'll tear apart roof of the sky, a whole new way's design
we'll take.
If an army should raise grief that will cause blood of lovers to flow,
Winebringer and I are content... its foundation into decline
we'll take.
We will pour out the rosewater into the cup of the red-coloured wine:
into revolving censor of the breeze... sugar sweet and fine
we'll take.
Minstrel, as a sweet instrument is in Your hand, sing a sweet song:
singing of love, waving hands, dancing, head down the line
we'll take.
O breeze, carry our dust to that sacred district where that Beloved is,
it may be that our glance, to see that King Who is Divine,
we'll take.
One person boasts of having reason, another weaves ignorant words:
come, and these disputes before Ruler, to justly define...
we'll take.
If your desire is for paradise of Eden, come with us to the Winehouse,
so that you into Kauther's pool from winejar's bottom line,
we'll take.
Beloved, illuminate our gathering with the brightness of Your face:
singing a song for You, head where Your foot does incline,
we'll take.
In Shiraz they don't appreciate the art of poetry and of conversation:
Hafez, come; ourselves to another land that won't confine,
we'll take.

371. NOT MY DOING

Often, many times I have said it, and once again I will say,
that it's not my doing, that with broken heart I go this Way.
In front of the mirror They have placed me like the parrot;
what the Eternal Master behind it tells me to say, that I say.
Whether I am the thorn or rose, it's due to Gardener's hand
that reared and gave to me nourishment, to grow day by day.
O friends, don't go blaming me, heart-broken, astonished;
I have a jewel and seek the sight of Master Jeweler to assay.

Although it is a sin for rosy wine to stain the patched coat,
do not criticize me; with it I wash hypocrisy's colour away.
The laughing and weeping of lovers is from some other place:
in the night I am singing and I am moaning at dawn of day.
To Hafez was quoted: "Don't smell dust of Winehouse door:"
reply this: "Don't stop me, for there I smell musk of Cathay."

372. THE TALE OF LONGING

With Your black eyelashes, a thousand holes in my faith You've made;
come, so out from Your languishing eye a thousand pains I'll persuade.
Hey, Companion of my heart, from Whose memory friends have gone,
may no day come when I sit for a moment and thoughts of You fade.
The world is old, without foundation: justice for this killer of Farhad!
Its deceitful craft and trickery have made me with sweet life dismayed.
The world that goes and stays I ransom for Beloved and Winebringer:
for world's sovereignty as humble companion of love, I have displayed.
If instead of me the Friend chooses the stranger, such is the judgment:
if instead of the Friend I prefer my own life, may it unlawful be made.
Nightingale shouted: "Good morning!" Winebringer where are You?
Get up, for inside my head last night's wine, intoxication has sprayed.
From tormenting fire of separation I drown in perspiration like a rose:
O night wind, from that sweat-taker of mine, a cool breeze persuade.
From me and not the preacher, hear mysteries of love and intoxication:
nightly with cup and goblet, with the moon and Pleiades... I stayed.
The tale of longing that is told in this volume is true beyond a doubt;
certainly it has no error, because Hafez, it completely to me, relayed.

373. INTOXICATED

From my hand I've lost religion and reason, O Loved One;
I ask You, from my love for You what have I so far won?
Grieving for You, I have given to the wind life's harvest;
as dust at Your precious feet, I still keep promises done.
Though I'm meagre as an atom, see how enriching is love:
desire for Your face has joined me to Love's mighty Sun.
Bring wine; for it's a lifetime since for sake of salvation,

I've sat in a quiet corner and from ease and pleasure run.
Advice-giving preacher, if you're sober why talk to dust?
I am greatly intoxicated and I hear advice from no one.
Before the Friend, how can I raise up my shameful head?
What service could this hand give to such a Perfect One?
Hafez burns away; Beloved soothes not with these words:
"I wounded his heart, but ointment lid's already undone."

374. DRUNKEN LOVER

Wineseller come back, because to serve You I want to try;
for Your sake, praying for Your welfare and longing am I.
From Your cup of perfect happiness and home of Grace,
show escape from this long, dreadful night, so I can fly.
Although surrounded and drowning in ocean of darkness,
Love's friend I've become and of the lovers of Mercy am I.
Religious academics, don't blame infamous drunken lovers:
for it was ruled like this by the Court of Destiny on High.
Drink wine, for being a drunken lover wasn't my choice:
I've inherited this gift; wine I have never needed to buy.
I am one who has never left this place where I was born;
now, because I want to see You, addicted to travel am I.
This form that seems far from Your door of hospitality,
still has a heart and soul living in Your presence so high.
High mountain, a wide sea ahead, exhausted and injured:
sure-footed Khizer pray for me, strength to knees supply.
Breeze from the East, if coil of musky curls you breathe,
beware of my jealous revenge which on you I won't deny.
At the target of Your eybrow's glance I placed wit's end;
arrow is drawn, I am waiting, when You want to, let fly!
Hafez is ready to give up life for the eye of Your glance;
this selfish whim still hopes that life won't pass him by.

375. PEACEFUL PLACE

Happy news: to Zu-Salam, the thornless tree, has come salvation;
praise be to God, the Great Giver of blessing beyond expectation!

Where is bringer of happy news, bringer of good news of victory,
so I may scatter my soul, like gold at his foot, from gratification?
Truly, hearts of all those who broke the promise became broken:
in Masters of Wisdom's opinion, promises are full of sanctification.
When the King turned back, what a rare picture was to be seen
by this enemy who had gone, departed for house of termination!
The enemy tried to obtain a blessing from a small cloud of hope,
but to eye that was searching, it gave nothing but moisturisation.
Into the Nile of sorrow he fell and the sky reproaching him said:
"Now you are sorry, when you gain nothing from mortification."
Winebringer, come: for it is the rose's season and the time of joy:
bring the cup; don't suffer any more or less of grief's deliberation.
Listen to the cup, about how this world, this newlywed old shrew,
slew her husbands Kay Kobad and Jamshid… an abomination!
"Heart, don't look for kingdom of Jamshid, seek the cup of wine:"
in the garden of Jamshid this was nightingale's song of inspiration.
When You spill blood of enemy like You spill the flagon's wine,
take the cup of Jamshid and with the lovers have a celebration.
In a corner of the Winehouse Hafez has his place that is peaceful,
like bird has his home in garden and lion in forest his habitation.

376. WHAT CAN I DO?

O cypress, with the rose and rosebud, without You,
what can I do?
How can I hold hyacinth's hair, with lily's cheek too,
what can I do?
It's a pity that I did not see Your face because of enemies' criticisms!
When I have no mirror, with what dull iron does imbue
what can I do?
Go, you critic; and do not criticize those who are drinking the dregs:
if this is what One Who arranges Fate chooses to do,
what can I do?

When the lightning of jealousy leaps out from the hidden ambush to
do Your command: I, whose harvest is burnt through,
what can I do?

Since the King of the Turks has approved of casting me into the pit,
if Rustom's grace does not seize my hand to rescue,
what can I do?
If fire of Sinai doesn't give me assistance by a little light that makes
way through Wadi-i-Aiman's night show through:
what can I do?
You're spilling my blood with separation's arrow that cuts the heart:
do You say to Yourself "Bright eye, strong and true,
what can I do?"
Hafez, Paradise in the Highest is the dwelling that I once inherited:
having my home in this place of only wasted residue,
what can I do?

377. BURN AWAY

I'll not stop Your hand even if with sword You slay
me;
I will thank You even if with many arrows, You flay
me.
I say this: "Shoot Your arrow in our eyebrows' direction,
then, because of Your hand and arm, dead will lay,
me."
If the grief of the world should knock me from off my feet,
except for cup, who takes my hand to steady and stay
me?
Shine out... you Sun of the morning of all hopefulness;
for the hand of the night of separation does waylay
me.
Master of the Winehouse, answer my cry for some help:
for I'm old... and with a drop, to youthfulness relay
me.

Last night, by Your long flowing hair, I swore a pledge
that with my head, forever at Your feet, I would lay...
me.
O Hafez, this your old patched coat of piety, burn away:
I wouldn't help it burn, even if as fire I did portray...

me.

378. DAWN'S CANDLE

You are the dawning and I am the candle in the room at morning:
smile towards me and see how for You my life I am surrendering.
In this heart are such stains of love for Your hair that entrances,
that when I go, the bed of violets on my grave will stay, growing.
I've opened the door of my eye upon the hope for Your threshold,
hoping You'll look; but me away from Your glance You're sending.
O armies of sorrow, how can I thank you? May God forgive you,
for on the day I am friendless, my breast you will not be leaving.
I'm slave of the man of vision, who though he is black of heart,
weeps a thousand tears when of my heart's suffering I am telling.
Our Idol is displaying such glorious splendour in every direction,
but not a single eye is seeing all these glances that I keep seeing.
If over dust of the grave of Hafez the Beloved goes like the breeze,
I'll rip shroud from longing, while in that narrow place I'm lying.

379. FORTUNE

Since Your auspicious shadow upon my head fell,
fortune has become my slave, prosperity as well.
It's years since fortune has passed away from me;
with union blessed by You it has entered my cell.
No one should see me awake in this, Your time;
for in my dreams I imagine Your image so well.
Grieving for You I pass my life; but without You,
do not think I live a moment, if the truth I tell.
The cure for my pain no physician could know;
without Friend I'm heartbroken, with, I'm well.
You say: "Don't bring your load into this street,"
by Your soul, I will never leave where You dwell.
All are the slaves of a king and obey his minister;
Hafez is a slave of the Monarch Who rules so well.

380. THE SLAVE OF THE KING

At morning Gemini placed before me the *Koran's* preserving:
which means: "The slave of the King I am," I was swearing.
Winebringer, come; from the help of fortune that's effective,
because of God I'll be gaining all that which I was desiring.
Don't try to lead me astray by praising Khizer's pure water:
from King's cup the dregs of Khizer's fountain I'm drinking.
O King, if I bring the throne of learning to the ninth heaven,
I'm still slave to Your Majesty and at Your door I'm begging.
For a thousand years I was draining dregs at Your banquet:
how could my passionate nature all this drinking be leaving?
If You do not believe all of what I'm saying about the slave,
I'll quote some perfect speech to now prove what I'm saying:
"If I tear away my heart from You and lift away my love,
to whom will I give this love, to where this heart be taking?"
Complete love for the King, in the Beginning was my promise:
along the highway of life, to this promise I'm still travelling.
Since the heavens strung Pleiades in the Name of the King,
then I am less than whom, if in pearl of a verse I am praising?
Since I've been fed from the King's hand like the falcon is fed,
why then should I ever care upon the pigeon to be preying?
O King that captures the lion, will Your shadow ever shrink
if in the territory of Your peaceful shade I'll be sheltering?
It is very strange, that I have no wing made out of feathers,
yet the only wish in my mind is for the Simurgh's dwelling.
My verse won a hundred heartlands by faithfully praising You:
it could be truly said that Your sword is my tongue flashing.
If like the breeze of the morning I then passed by a rosebed,
the cypress I wasn't loving and the pinetree wasn't desiring:
I scented Your fragrance and to the memory of Your face,
the Winebringers of joyfulness, one or two cups were giving.
It's not Your servant's custom to get drunk on a few grapes,
I struggled for years, I became old while Winehouse haunting.
May my name be effaced from the work-roll of all the lovers,
if other than loving You at any employment I am working.
O You, Whose face has more lovers than the sun has atoms,
how can I, less than an atom, reach to You and be uniting?

Show to me who it is who will deny the beauty of Your face,
so that with the knife of jealousy, his eye I can be removing.
The shadow of the sun of Sovereignty has now fallen on me;
now, about sun that comes up in the east, I'm not worrying.
The aim of my actions is not to make the market's trade brisk,
I do not sell any praises and for any favours I am not paying.
The soul of Hafez is the friend of the Prophet and His family!
God, the Lord, my King, is the witness to what I am saying.

381. BELOVED'S STREET

In pursuit of the path to my home, without a care
I'll be?
Dust of beginning of my Beloved's street, is where
I'll be?
As I can't bear the grief and suffering of being a stranger,
to my own city I will go, my own monarch there
I'll be.
I will be one of the confidants of the holy veil of Union:
of the servants of my own Master, beyond compare,
I'll be.
Since the outcome of life is unknown, at least it is better
that on that eventful day, with that Beloved fair
I'll be.
My way has forever been that of a lover and a drunkard;
I'll try once again, and involved in my own affair
I'll be.
Hafez, perhaps Grace of Beginningless Eternity guides:
if not, to endless Eternity, ashamed of me forever
I'll be.

382. COMPLETELY RUINED

You want peace from us, when to drunkards an invitation
we said?
"Goodbye to safety, because of that eye full of intoxication,"

we said.
Open Winehouse door, for nothing is revealed by the monastery:
if you believe this or if you do not, this was the revelation
we said.
Winebringer, because of Your eye I have become completely ruined;
for calamity from Friend, a thousand words in appreciation
we said.
We said this: "Your shape's the boxtree, bringing same to the fruit:"
why did we make a comparison, why is it this falsification
we said?
If You do not forgive me, You will in the end suffer many regrets;
keep it in Your mind that in Your service this proclamation
we said.
My liver is all blood like the muskpod and this was rightly deserved,
for with Your hair the word 'China', as mistaken comparison
we said.
Hafez, you've become fire, but it didn't take effect on the Beloved:
you could say, through rose's faithlessness, to wind a fiction
we said.

383. THE DRUNKEN NIGHTINGALE

It was forty years ago I made this boast of mine:
"I am the lowest servant of the Master Divine."
Never, thanks to kindness of the old Wineseller,
    has my cup been empty of the luminous wine.
In glory of Love is true drunken lovers' fortune:
    a Chief seat in the Winehouse was always mine.
Don't think ill of me for being such a drunkard,
    my coat is stained but shirt purely does shine.
I'm falcon of the King's hand; O Lord, how have
    they taken from my memory that home of mine?
It's a pity that a nightingale like me, with tongue
    so sweet, in the field with silent lily does repine.
The climate of Persia fosters the mean... where
    is Friend to fold tent with, and from land resign?
The good Turan King showered many gifts on me,

and these became a collar on that neck of mine.
How long will Hafez drink from cup under coat?
At Khwaja's party, this veiled secret I'll consign.

384. THE ROSE SEASON

God forbid that in the rose season I should ever give up wine:
how could I do this, when I boast of this intelligence of mine?
Come here Minstrel, so that all austerity and knowledge gained,
to the service of harp and lute and voice of reed I can consign.
My heart has become tired of the loud arguments of the college;
now for awhile I'll do the service of the Beloved and the wine.
There was no faithfulness in Time: so bring the winecup to me,
so that I'll tell of how Jam and Kaus and Kay ended their line.
I don't fear the 'black book'; for on the Day of the Gathering,
I shall close a hundred books like this, by God's Grace Divine.
Where's morning's runner of messages, so I can make complaint
to Fortunate One's happy feet, about separation night of mine.
Since in Eternity beyond Time, with wine They mixed my dust,
to enemy mention this: "Then why should I the wine decline?"
This borrowed life, that the Friend has loaned in trust to Hafez,
when one day I see Your face then its surrenderance I will sign.

385. EXISTENCE

The dust of my body is the veil that is over the Beloved's face;
happy is that moment when from this face the veil I will efface.
Such a cage as this is not fitting for such a sweet singer like me;
I will go to the rosebed of Rizvan, for I'm the bird of that Place.
It is not revealed why I have come here, or where I was before:
it's a shame, a shame, that I'm so careless of my place in space.
How may I make my circuit of the expanse of the Holy World,
when in this place of mixture I'm tied to a plank of body-base.
Although my true home and dwelling is the gallery of the Huris,
why is my native place the street of the winehouse addicts' race?
If out from my heart's blood there rises the fragrance of musk,
don't be surprised: I suffer with Cathay's muskpods they chase.

Don't take notice of my tunic with thread of gold like the candle,
because inside tunic, hidden fires are consuming the whole place.
Come, and take this selfish existence of Hafez away from himself
due to Your Existence no one hears from me of mine one trace.

386. LOVER'S OCCUPATION

If the dust of the sole of my fair One's foot gives light,
on the tablet of vision a dusty line I'll certainly write.
If to me should come Your request for me to give life,
at that moment, like candle I'll give my life outright.
If You do not get verified that basic coin of my heart,
in Your path current coin floods from my place of sight.
Don't shake Your garment from dusty me: after death
from Your door I won't be blown by the wind's flight.
I am drowned in longing for Your embrace; but I hope
that waves of my tears will take me to the shore alright.
The two long plaits of Your hair gave a great promise
to console lovers; then they stole my peace outright.
Today, be faithful to me, do not turn Your head away;
think of my grief hand lifted in prayer, in the night.
O breeze, send me fragrance of perfume from that cup:
my winesick grief needs help from that perfume's delight.
Praising tip of Your long hair is my verse's occupation,
therefore I'm conspirer of musk of Tartary when I write.
Since Your ruby lip is like the dear soul to me, Hafez;
that moment I bring my soul to the lip, my life's right.

387. ALL THIS AND MUCH LESS

It is so; in times like these, see the good advice I present:
my belongings I take to Winehouse and there sit content.
Except long-necked flagon and the Book, I've no friend;

so that I'll seldom see this world's traitors, so malevolent.
I take cup of wine in hand, keep far away from hypocrites;
in all of Creation only with pure of heart I will frequent.
In this old stained coat I was often proud of being right;
ashamed, before Wineseller's face and rosy wine, I repent.
Above mankind I shall raise my head, free like the cypress,
so I can raise up my garment from the world's sad lament.
On heart is tyranny's dust; O God Most High, don't allow
my sun bright mirror to be dulled by such a malcontent.
My straining chest carries its heavy load of grief ah well!
My grieving heart's not able to take the load's punishment.
I'm servant of Master of the Age; don't worry, my heart;
if I asked I would get what I deserved from the firmament.
If I'm Wineshop drunkard, or Guardian (Hafez) of the city,
all this you see, I am, and much less than what I present.

388. GET UP!

Get up, then to the Winehouse the patched Sufi garment
we'll take;
patchcoat and idle talk to the market where they're spent,
we'll take.
We shut our ears and then escaped all the nonsense of the preacher:
like uninformed, how long is it that talk that's irrelevant
we'll take?
So that all of those in strict seclusion will take up the morning cup,
harp of the morning to the Wineseller's doorway's vent,
we'll take.
Our journey brought us to the path of the wandering drunken lovers;
ragged woolen coat and prayermat of idle talk, to present,
we'll take.

If the pious fanatic should plant in our path the thornbush of blame,
then him from the rosegarden into prison for punishment
we'll take.
May we be fully ashamed of our woolen patchcoat that is stained,
if with skill and excellence, for miracles, encouragement

we'll take.
If heart doesn't understand value of time and does no work of worth,
then from harvest of time, shame is the only monument
we'll take.
Great troubles rain down from this vaulted roof so quickly get up!
So shelter in Winehouse from disasters that are imminent,
we'll take.
For how long shall we be lost like this in the long desert of desire?
We'll ask the way and perhaps our steps to what's relevant
we'll take.
That same covenant that we made with You in the Wadi-i-Aiman,
like Moses who said: "Let me see," to that appointment
we'll take.
We beat the drum of Your glory from the turret of the ninth Heaven:
pennants of love for You, to roof of Heavenly battlement
we'll take.
Tomorrow in the plain where all stand up, the dust of Your street
on the top of our head, to bring glory and enrichment,
we'll take.
To drink the wine secretly is not the sign of one who is generous;
wine, this mediator, to the Lords of generous assessment
we'll take.
Hafez, don't spill lustre of your face's water on each miser's door:
to Judge of all needs, it's best that need, for attainment
we'll take.

389. WE MAY FIND

Get up, so that from door of Winehouse, an opening
we may find;
so that sitting in the path of Friend, our meaning
we may find.
We do not have provisions for the road to the Friend's sanctuary,
perhaps at door of Winehouse, provisions from begging
we may find.
Although our tears stained with blood are running, to dispatch
them to You, one who's pure and uncompromising

we may find.
May taste of sweetness of grief for You be forbidden to our heart,
if due to pain of grief from loving You, justice coming
we may find.
One can't describe upon vision's tablet the point of Your mole,
unless from the eye's dark pupil, ink for writing
we may find.
My heart and soul tried to find the means from Your sweet lip:
Your lip said with sweet smile: "Maybe a meaning
we may find."
Since the fragrant remedy is just what the mad sick heart needs,
from Your hair this perfume for which we're longing
we may find.
Since one cannot find grief for You except in the joyous heart,
in hope of grief for You, maybe a heart rejoicing
we may find.
Hafez, for how long will you sit down at the door of the college?
Get up, so that from Winehouse's door, an opening
we may find.

390. IMAGE OF YOUR FACE

When the image of Your face comes into the eye's rosebed,
for the sake of seeing You, heart to window of eye is led.
Come: for when You arrive, rubies and pearls are scattered
from chamber of heart, and treasure of our eye is spread.
I don't see a single place… that is worthy for You to rest:
I am of this world and in this corner of the eye is my bed.
My heart said on that first day when I saw Your fair face:
"If any harm comes, my blood will be on the eye's head."
At morning my flowing tears were thinking of ruining me,
if liver's blood hadn't seized the skirt of the eye's thread.
Hoping for happy news of meeting You, night until dawn
on wind's path I placed luminous lamps of the eyes, ahead.
I call on You from good manners, not to strike Hafez's heart
with arrow, heart's stitcher, making mankind's eyes misled.

391. THAT DAY WILL BE HAPPY

That day is happy when from this desolate dwelling
I go:
searching for soul's peace and for Beloved, travelling
I go.
Although I know the stranger doesn't find the place's path,
by the sweet fragrance of that wild long hair flowing,
I go.
Despite a sick heart and a powerless body; like the breeze,
out of deep longing for that cypress that is swaying,
I go.
My heart is worn out from fearing the prison of Alexander:
I tie my heavy load and to Solomon's Land travelling
I go.
Since those Arabs in the light don't worry about our load,
Persians, give some help, so that happy and rejoicing
I go.
If on Your path it's necessary to go on head like pen's nib,
then with the heart wounded and with eye weeping
I go.
If one day this grief comes to an end, then I have vowed
that to Winehouse's door, joyful and a song singing,
I go.
From deep longing for You, dancing like the mote dances,
to the lip of the fountain of the sun's bright shining,
I go.
And if I don't take a path out from the desert like Hafez,
along with star of the Chief of the Age, journeying
I go.

392. IN THE WINEHOUSE

In the dwelling of the Master, God's Light bright and clear
I see;
remember and write down this wonder, what it is and where

I see.

O Lord, who is this drinker of the dregs in the Winehouse I wonder?
His door, the touchstone of all need, prayer-arch of all prayer
I see.

Pleased with dignity of role as lover and drunkard and one in love,
due to the instructions You graciously gave, all of this here,
I see.

O leader of the pilgrims, don't boast to me of such a fine honour;
you see only the house, but God Who owns house and leader,
I see.

From musk pods of China and musk of Tartary, nobody has seen
what each morning at dawn from soft scented Eastern zephyr
I see.

In the circle of all the creation, except for the point of Unification,
there is nothing; how and why are questions that are unclear,
I see.

From the long flowing hair of the beauties I will take musk away;
a long way off is such a thought, or it's a 'musk take' here
I see.

Heart on fire, tears streaming, weeping nightly and sighing at dawn:
all of this because Your sweetness can't be seen, is my career
I see.

Suddenly my thoughts are ambushed by an apparition, Your Face;
to whom can I describe the insights, that in this veil forever
I see?

Friends, do not criticize Hafez for glancing with love at beauties;
for he loves you too, and when looking, only of God a lover
I see.

393. STRANGE CONDITION

"Friends, it is best to try and be happy in the season of the rose:"
this is a saying of the Perfect Master, let's listen so the soul knows.
In no one there is generosity and the time of joy is soon passing by;

the solution to it is that we sell the prayermat for wine, I suppose.
It is an air that is pleasant, that gives happiness: O God send to us
one of graceful form, so we can drink wine to a face, coloured rose.
The organist of the sky is very skilful and is also a highway robber:
how to complain of this grief, if we moan, who hears, who knows?
The rose has blossomed and we have not spilt wine upon its glory:
so with fire of desire and disappointment our complaining shows.
We draw some imaginary wine out from the cup that the tulip has;
stay away evil eye: for without wine and Minstrel, we've our woes.
Hafez, this is a very strange condition, to whom can one reveal it?
For we are nightingales from whom in the rose season, silence flows.

394. LOVE STRUCK

Last night, with a torrent of tears, sleep's pathway
I struck;
in memory, Your face's down on water to portray
I struck.
In my vision was Beloved's eyebrow, so my coat burnt up;
a cup to memory of that sacred prayer archway
I struck.
In my sight the face of the Friend's form shone with glory;
on light on that Moon's cheek, kiss from far away
I struck.
My eye on the Winebringer's face, ear on wail of the harp;
in this way, with eye and ear, an omen to convey
I struck.
I pictured the ideal of Your face until the morning dawned;
upon the workshop of my eye, all sleep until day
I struck.

My Winebringer took up the cup to the tune of this *ghazal*;
I sang song first, then to pure wine without delay
I struck.
Every bird of thought, that from tip of joy's branch flew,
back again into the cage of Your curls to obey,

I struck.

For Hafez, the time was happy; fortunate omen I brought

to friends: long life, wishes granted in every way,

I struck.

395. DON'T FORGET TO REMEMBER

Last night I said: "I'll drive from mind this longing for Your face;"
You said: "Where is a chain to secure this madman in his place?"
I called Your form the cypress, and in anger You turned from me:
O friends, what will I do, for my Idol's upset, and truth won't face?
Heartstealer, excuse me, for I didn't weigh the words that I said;
be gracious so that in my verse many weighty words one can trace.
I suffer from a pale yellow face because of a tender pure nature;
Winebringer, give winecup, so the rose's colour I'll give to my face.
Breeze from the dwelling of Layla, for God's sake for how long
will I overthrow a fourth of the world and flood that ruined place?
I, having taken that path to treasure of Friend's boundless beauty,
afterwards will make a hundred beggars rich, and Karun a disgrace.
Moon of faithfulness, don't forget to remember Your slave Hafez,
so that I may pray that Your beauty will every day gain more grace.

396. THE SOURCE OF A HAPPY HEART

My eyes cry an ocean; patience to wilderness
I'll cast;
my heart into the ocean from work's duress
I'll cast.
From my narrow sinful heart I will heave such a sigh,
into Eve and Adam's sin, fire of forgetfulness
I'll cast.
Sky's arrows too long I've suffered, give wine; a knot
into the quiver of Orion, from drunkenness
I'll cast.
Yes, upon this moving throne, wine dregs I will spill;
into azure dome the harp's resonance, no less,

I'll cast.
Where Heartowner lives is source of the happy heart;
there, myself if my struggles fortune bless,
I'll cast.
O moon, sun-crowned, loosen Your coat's fastening;
at feet, like Your long hair, my lovesickness
I'll cast.
O Hafez, since reliance on Time is a foolish mistake,
no more, until tomorrow, today's happiness
I'll cast.

397. A NEW KIND OF LIFE

Last night, the drunkenness of Your eye overpowered me,
but I created a new kind of life from Your lip's generosity.
My love for Your long hair didn't happen today, it's ages
since I was drunk with this cup like a new moon's beauty.
From constant patience this subtle knowledge came my way:
I never stepped from Your street's end to sit with tyranny.
Do not expect peace from me who stays in the Winehouse:
for I have boasted of being the drunkards' servant eternally.
There are so many dangers from death's side in love's path:
be careful not to say that when my life's ended I am free.
What concern from now on do I have for arrows of envious,
when tied to bow of Beloved's eyebrow I experience unity?
I'm allowed to place a kiss on the casket of Your cornelian;
for despite Your violence, I've not broken love or fidelity.
That Idol, that Warrior, stole heart and from me departed;
have pity on me if the grace of the King isn't handed to me.
Greatness of knowledge of Hafez that rose to the heavens,
was brought down low by my grief for Your high boxtree.

398. RELIEF AND CONSTERNATION

From Beloved is my relief and my consternation
also;

my heart is given to You, my life in submission
also.
To those who say: "That's far better than beauty;"
say: "This, our Beloved has; that in profusion
also."
The splendour of Your face is One in both worlds;
what is hidden I have told you, what is open a
lso.
Friends behind the hidden veil, we will talk to you,
and it will be a tale that's forthrightly spoken
also.
That intoxicated narcissus eye has shed our blood;
tip of that tangled black hair hadn't compassion
also.
Place no reliance on the course of the mean world;
this goes for me spinning sphere's illumination
also.
That Beloved be remembered Who took our blood,
meaning to break word and love's obligation
also.
When the nights of union have finally passed away;
then gone away are all the days of separation,
also.
Often, imagining Your mole these eyes cried blood;
in private, in secret, and then out in the open,
also.
Bring wine, for the Judge, the lover does not fear,
nor powerful light of Monarch's constellation
also.
The Man of Reason knows that Hafez is a lover; and
Asaf, right hand man of the Court of Solomon,
also.

399. MUCH BETTER

In the secret home of my heart's ease, sweet Idol fair
I have:
'The horseshoe in the fire,' from Whose cheek and hair,

I have.
Lover, outsider, drinker of wine: from that Huri, like the Pari
all of these titles I'm told and I now loudly declare:
"I have."
If You keep me completely helpless in such a manner as this,
I'll keep Your hair disheveled, with a morning prayer
I have.
If You should take one step towards the drunkards' dwelling,
the sweetest of sweet verse and purest wine to share
I have.
If the orange down on the face of the Friend displays itself
painted this yellow face with bloody water, I swear,
I have.
Bring the arrow of Your glance from the flow of Your hair;
for a contest with my wounded beaten heart, forever
I have.
A tip of the hair is in my hand and the other the Friend has:
with this tip of hair, a great struggle, here and there,
I have.
O Hafez, since the grief and joy of the world will both vanish,
it is much better that a heart that hasn't even a care,
I have.

400. SUCH A CHIEF

Promised to me was vision of the Beloved, kiss and embrace
too;
to fortune I owe many thanks and to Time for such grace,
too.
Go away in peace pious critic; if I am destined to be very lucky,
in my hand will be the winecup and Beloved's curls like lace
too.
To love madly and to be a drunkard is not worthless we declare:
wine tastes so good and so does the lip of such a lovely face
too.
O heart, I give to you the good news that Reason has vanished:
the world is full of love's wine... lover of wine is in his place

too.

The time has gone when the eyes of ignorance waited in ambush;
enemies from our midst have gone, of tears we haven't a trace
too.

It isn't wise to give the heart and mind to the forces of separation:
seek a good book with quiet heart, bring flagon to the place
too.

Since Your beauty overflowed to become the tulip and the rose,
Cloud of Grace, on us dusty lovers gracefully rain grace
too.

As all of the creation lives in hope of Your sweet fragrant mercy,
full Sun, don't keep from us the shade of Your kind embrace
too.

You capture people of knowledge and teach them to respect God;
You gained Your wishes from Asaf from Solomon every trace
too.

Such a Chief of country and religion, whose generous right arm
gave minefields of jewels; from left, oceanic pearls of grace
too.

So illuminating and so understanding a man, that at dawn the sky
paid homage by surrendering existence and all stars did efface
too.

This ball in the universe is prize that is won by Your judgement,
the same goes for this high ceiling dome and blue sky's face
too.

It's Your light-fingered purpose to spin into a steady motion this
earth that's stuck in space, which has a stable central place
too.

Until the time when the sky's movement and turning of the globe
causes change of years and months and movement of space
too,

Without such Chiefs may the Halls of Your Great Glory never be,
may Winebringers, cypress-straight, rosy-cheeked, be in place
too.

A humble Hafez, who in praise of You scatters pearls like these,
in Your presence was struck dumb, ashamed, full of disgrace
too.

401. SERVICE IN THE WINEHOUSE

Long, hard service in the Winehouse for many a long year
I've done;
the work of all the fortunate Ones, in my poor beggar's gear
I've done.
Our critic has not even perceived a scent of the truth; listen to what
I say in his presence: because no backbiting you will hear
I've done.
Until I bring that sweet strutting partridge into the snare of union,
much expecting that the time of ambush soon comes near,
I've done.
Falling and rising like the breeze I now go to the street of the Friend,
to basil and the rose, many a prayer for help to come here,
I've done.
Path's snare is the Heartstealer's hair and glance is disaster's arrow:
O heart, think of all the advice on actions, for your career
I've done.
As Your street's dust won't endure our troubles any more than this:
O generous Idol, the making of troubles almost disappear
I've done.
O Merciful One Who hides defects; cover eyes that see mistakes,
from the open deeds that in the corner of seclusion here,
I've done.
God forbid that I do not fear the reckoning of the Resurrection Day!
The omen of tomorrow I'll consult, and today's good cheer
I've done.
From the right of God's throne, Faithful Spirit is shouting: "Amen!"
When prayer that the Lord of country and faith does hear,
I've done.
O Monarch, I've the hope of the summit of all glory because of this:
Prayer begging to kiss threshold of Your Majestic atmosphere
I've done.
I'm Hafez at religious gathering, drinker of dregs where it's friendly:
see how boldly the changing of my career, it would appear
I've done.

402. DEAD DRUNK AND HALF CRAZY

My arm's too short and my heart a sorry case is;
I'm ashamed, when brought before glorious faces.
It could be my hand will reach those long curls;
if not I will go crazy, without their embraces.
Ask my eyes about the turning of the spheres:
I don't sleep, I count stars until dawn's trace is.
Through magic, I kiss the lip of that great cup:
revealed to me the secret of Time and Space is.
Thank heavens I've not the strength in my arm:
my good luck, to never hurt the human race is.
I've made a prayer for the Winesellers: why not?
I return the favours of such kind generous graces.
From the dust of sorrow you will not raise me,
though my eyes rain pearls in teardrops' places.
Don't pity me drinking blood of my own grief,
for my teacher, that musk-deer of the chase is.
From the Winehouse of love such a wine I drink,
that of sense and wakefulness there no trace is.
Dead drunk and half crazy though Hafez may be,
from his generous Master his hope for grace is.

403. IF

If fate once more took me to the Master's Winehouse door,
coat and prayermat I'd gamble, no matter what the score.
If today I ring bell of repentance… like the fanatic does,
tomorrow, Winehouse doorman for me won't cross floor.
If like the moth, the freedom from all care is given to me;
except for that cheek like the candle, I will fly no more.
If You won't embrace my heart, for like a harp I'm slack,
cherish me like a reed with Your lips, Your breath outpour.
Relationship with the female angel I don't want; for it is
truly error if with another I play, when I need You more.
I talk of the situation of my bleeding heart to not one soul:

except a knife of grief for You, no close friend is in store.
Still hiding in my chest, would be passionate love for You,
if my secret wasn't told by my eye's wet skirt's downpour.
From the cage of dusty clay I became the bird on the air,
desiring that perhaps Falcon will prey upon me and score.
If every hair upon the body of Hafez were really a head,
like Your hair, at Your feet I'd lay every head and more.

404. BEGGING

Don't give Your hair to breeze, or You'll give wind to destruction
of me;
don't give foundation to contempt, or You'll take life's foundation
of me.
Do make me independent of roseleaf, through illumination of Your face:
do give exultation to Your form, so I'm free of cypress' domination
of me.
Don't be well known in the city, or my mind will drive me to mountain;
don't show scorn like Shirin, or You'll make a Farhad-like creation
of me.
Don't drink wine with others, or You'll make me drink my heart's blood;
don't remember other people, so You'll always have a recollection
of me.
Don't twist Your hair into curls, or You will then chain me up in prison;
don't make Your face more lustrous, or You'll wind up destruction
of me.
Don't be friendly with strangers, or You'll make me be beside myself;
don't let Yourself worry about others, or You'll cause lamentation
of me.
Don't be candle of every gathering, so that me You will not consume;
don't turn Your head away, or to heaven will call the depravation
of me.
Do show pity to miserable me and arrive soon to hear my complaint;
do this, so to dust of Asaf's door is no complaining representation
of me.
Do no more violence like the sky is doing so that You won't kill Hafez:

do be kind, so that favourable fortune makes justifiable restoration
of me.

405. MY CRY

O Beloved, what complaint from grief of love for You
I'll make;
from grief for You, my cries the whole night through
I'll make?
My frenzied heart passed long ago hoping it might gain remedy:
perhaps with tip of Your hair a tight chain for it too
I'll make.
It is because of the tip of Your hair that I suffer such anxiety;
where is time and strength so an explanation that's true
I'll make?
What I suffered during the time that I was separated from You,
it's impossible that an explanation in one letter to You
I'll make.
Whenever I have the longing to look at the face of the Beloved,
picture in the mind of Your lovely face for me to view
I'll make.
If I knew that this way would help me to gain union with You,
I'd give heart and faith, and much more of an effort too
I'll make.
O preacher, go far away from me and don't speak such stupidity,
and never my ear, open to hypocrisy from one like you,
I'll make.
I'm a drunken lover of one colour, associate of Beloved and wine,
with all hypocrisy I'm through: this promise that's true
I'll make.
Hafez, there is no hope of gaining freedom from such ignorance;
since fate is set out like this, a plan to get me through
I'll make?

406. IT'S NOT RIGHT

If around the curls of Your long hair again my hand should lay,

there are many heads that like balls with Your mallet I'll play.
Your long flowing hair is long life to me, but there is not even
a tip of a hair of this long life in my hand today, I'm sad to say.
O candle, give to me the order to have a rest: because tonight,
before You, like burning candle, from heart's fire I burn away.
That moment when like the flagon I give up life with a laugh,
I wish that Your drunken ones many a prayer for me will say.
Since the prayer of one stained like me is not really a prayer,
my melting and burning in Winehouse isn't less in any way.
If Your image comes into the mosque and into the Winehouse,
of Your two eyebrows I'll make the lute and shrine, to pray.
If one night You illuminate my lonely room with Your face,
I'll raise my head and shine over the world like break of day.
Worthy of much praise is the result of my effort in this Path,
if in longing to please Ayaz's desire, my mind is thrown away.
Hafez, to whom shall I be mentioning the grief of the heart?
Except cup, it's not right my secrets with another should stay.

407. WITH THE KORAN'S BLESSING

For years, to drunken lovers to be of service, my objective I made;
until due to understanding, I sent greed to prison and it obeyed.
I did not find by myself the path to the home of the Pure Bird;
this journey, with the guidance of the bird of Solomon, I made.
Whether one is abstaining or drunk is not in my hand or yours;
whatever the Lord of Eternity has told me to do, that I obeyed.
Through the Grace of Eternal God I still greedily desire Paradise:
although keeper of door of the Winehouse was often my trade.
My old head has this, that it is comforted by Joseph's company:
this is reward for patience, that in the room of grief I displayed.
O Treasure of desire, throw Your shade on my wounded heart;
for from much desire for You, this house into ruins I have laid.
I repented and said: "I'll not kiss the Winebringer's lip," and now
I bite my lip because my ear listened to what the foolish relayed.
Contrary to what is usually said, go seek the desire of the heart;
for I acquired peace of heart from that hair that's all disarrayed.
If in Divan, assembly of *ghazals*, I sat on chief seat, why wonder?

For years as servant of the Master of the Divine Divan, I obeyed.
Rising at morning and looking for salvation, this was like Hafez:
whatever I made, because of blessed fortune of the *Koran,* I made.

408. HAFEZ'S PRESCRIPTION

My head is happy with the wine, and with a loud shout I cry:
"To look for the breeze of Life from the cup, I try and I try."
No sullen pious austerity sits on the face of the winesickness;
disciple of patch-coated, joyful-natured drinker of dregs, am I.
If the Perfect Master doesn't open the Winehouse's door to us,
on what door shall I knock and on what remedy shall I rely?
Do not criticize me for the way that I grow in the meadow:
as They allow me to grow, I grow, and with no how or why.
From the centre you don't see the monastery and the tavern:
God is the Witness and wherever He may be, with Him am I.
The dust of the path of seeking is the alchemy of happiness:
of that dust's perfume of ambergris, I'm the slave until I die.
From longing for One tall of stature, an intoxicated narcissus;
by the stream's bank, with the cup, like the fallen tulip I lie.
I'm infamous for confusing minds: and the Beloved's eyebrow
has caught me like ball in its mallet's curve, ready to let fly.
O giver of advice, what advice do you give, because you know
that not one who believes but one who promises peace am I.
As Hafez prescribes, bring wine; so that by the goblet's grace,
washing down the dust of hypocrisy, the heart I may purify.

409. BOASTS LIKE THESE

Come Sufi, off forever coat hypocrisy has tied,
we take;
with the line that cancels, away writings of pride
we take.
Alms and offerings of tall monastery we spend on wine;

fake sackcloth to wash in Winehouse, purified
we take.
We will happily leap the walls and from the rival's table
take wine: through the door, the lovely Bride
we take.
Fate's secret that's mysteriously hidden behind the veil,
from its face in a drunken way this veil aside
we take.
Let's begin to work, or embarrassment will be our dues
on death's day, when life's load to other side
we take.
If tomorrow they won't give us the garden of Paradise,
heavenly youths and the Garden's Huris, aside
we take.
A glance from Your eyebrow, and with the polo mallet,
golden crescent moon, ball of sphere so wide,
we take.
Hafez, beyond all proper limits are boasts such as these;
from underneath blanket why my feet outside
we take?

410. SOMETIMES

It's a lifetime since every day searching I go here and over there,
every moment my good reputation I throw away with a prayer.
So that my day will not pass without my moon, the light of love:
a net upon the path I've set, and thrown a fowl into the snare.
So that I may gain some news of the shade of the straight cypress,
I send love's commotion from all sides to One walking Who is fair.
I know that it will bring grief to an end and also colour to wine:
this sigh shedding blood, each dawn and night I heave into the air.
Where is Aurang and where Gulchihra and where Mihr and Wefa?
I can only now rightly claim that as a lover, to them I compare.
Although I know that peace of heart doesn't give heart's desire,
I think of the perfect situation and gain omen that it lasts forever.
Even though I'm not myself and like Hafez have given up wine,
in the banquet where souls gather, sometimes I drink a cup there.

411. THE HOLIDAY

Today is the holiday of the new moon, and I've decided today
to take winecup, and in return give the thirty days fast away.
It has been days since I've been separated from wine and cup:
I'm feeling ashamed that such a mistake as this came my way.
From now on I'll not sit in seclusion, even if to set an example,
pious fanatic of the cloister chains my leg to make me stay.
The preacher of the city gives me saintly advice; but I know
that I will never again accept the advice that anyone may say.
Where is one who gave up life in the Winehouse door's dust,
so I may lay my head on his foot and before him die today?
I drink wine… and on my shoulder is the prayermat of piety:
O no, if information of my imposture comes the people's way!
The people say: "O Hafez, listen to the wise old man's words:"
but old wine means more to me than a hundred old men today.

412. A BANQUET

Youthfulness and playing the game of love, and wine of ruby hue,
a friendly gathering, the close companion and wine plentiful too:
the Winebringer's sweet mouth and that sweet-speaking Minstrel,
sitting with the right kind of friends, and companions who are true:
the lovely One, graceful and pure and envied by the Water of Life,
heartstealer's beauty and sweetness that turns the new moon blue:
a place for a banquet, captivating the heart, like highest Paradise,
a rosebed with borders having the peaceful mansion's garden view:
the rows of sitting well-wishers and the servants all full of respect,
friends who know Mysteries, companions desiring friendship too:
the cup that's rose-coloured and bitter, light and delicious to taste;
its sweet point: ruby of beautiful form; its story: wine that's new;
the glance of the Winebringer that sword-drawn, plunders wisdom:
the hair of Beloved that to capture heart… spreads a trap through;
knowing subtlety, a teller of jokes, like Hafez… sweetly speaking:
freedom teacher like Haji Kivam, enlightening all as to what to do:

whoever doesn't want such company, may his heart's joy be ruined;
whoever doesn't seek this happiness... his life become unlawful too.

413. SURRENDERANCE

Many times in the dust of Your foot, our face there
we have laid;
yes, aside all hypocrisy, argument and being unfair,
we have laid.
We have now entrusted our soul to those two bewitching narcissi;
our heart in that long Hindu-black hyacinth hair,
we have laid.
We have not taken the country of safety and ease with the army:
nor the throne of sovereignty with the arm of power
we have laid.
In the corner of hope, like those that watch for the new moon,
the hopeful eye on the curve of that eyebrow fair,
we have laid.
Like that violet without the caress and grace of Your narcissus,
on the knee, our head from wine and lack of care,
we have laid.
We have laid down the heavy burden upon our poor weak heart;
to be tied tight by a single hair, all of this affair
we have laid.
Let's see what magic is dispensed by sorcery of the Friend's eye,
for again life's foundation on the eye's magical stare
we have laid.
The arch and porch of the college and the arguments of learning,
in pathway of joy and rosy face of Beloved so fair
we have laid.

Reputations of many generations of ancestors with good names,
in path of the cup and of love and the Winebringer
we have laid.
We are sensible and intelligent for on the hand and on the foot,
using heart, the chain of the curl of that hair, there,
we have laid.

Hafez, try to obtain love: for the payment of wisdom and sense,
both aside, for sake of Beloved with chain-like hair,
we have laid.

414. THIS BUSINESS

I am in love with the youthful, joyous, freshly-blossomed fair face:
praying to God I have asked that from this grief joy I can embrace.
I am a lover, drunkard and looking for love; and I will say it openly
so You will know that I'm endowed with merits not commonplace.
The shame of my patched coat stained with wine has come over me,
a hundred hypocritical deceits I have sewn on each patched space.
O candle, happily you are burning away out of longing for that One;
see, I am also in this business, belted and ready, standing in place!
The profit of any work fell from my hand from such bewilderment:
I've gained in grief that which of heart and soul I've now but a trace.
All night each night I'm a guardian of the sacred place in my heart,
so perhaps it will happen that the full moon will to me stroll a pace.
I go to the Winehouse like Hafez, wearing the appropriate garment:
so it could be that me, newly-blossomed Heartstealer may embrace.

415. BOAT FOR THE BLIND

Time's grief is such, that of its limit even a sign
I don't see;
medicine to remedy this, except for this wine,
I don't see.
The conversation of the old Wineseller I will not give away
since by doing this, an advantage that is mine,
I don't see.
No one gives to me a drink although I'm sick for the wine;
O no, look: in the world a single heart benign,
I don't see.
Take the highlight of all life from the sun of the winecup:
fortunate ascendant of Time, staying in my line
I don't see.

The only sign of a true-hearted one is still in being a lover:
keep advice, for with city's preachers this sign
I don't see.
A thousand regrets that these eyes are blinded by weeping:
Your face, with these double mirrors of mine,
I don't see.
Since Your form has departed from the stream of my eye,
except running water in place of cypress-pine,
I don't see.
I grasp this boat of Hafez's Divan; in this ocean, except for
words that comfort heart with speech Divine,
I don't see.

416. THE SLAVE OF LOVE

These words I speak openly and my heart's happy about it:
I'm the slave of Love and of both worlds I'm free, I've quit.
I'm the bird of the heavenly rosebed: what story can I tell
of how I fell into separation's snare, a fate that is unfit?
I was an angel and my home was up in the highest Paradise;
by Adam I was brought down into this ruined cloistered pit.
Shade of Tuba tree, attractions of Huris and brink of Pool:
end of Your street has caused me to forget about all of it.
On heart's blackboard is the straight 'A' of Beloved's form;
what can I do? For my Master taught no other letter but it.
No astrologer has ever worked out the star of my fortune;
O God, when Mother Earth did bear me where did I fit?
Since I became ear-ringed slave at Love's Winehouse door,
a new sorrow comes every moment and I'm greeted by it.
My eyes pour out the blood of my heart, as it should be;
why lose my heart to a Beloved of others, why did I do it?
With the tips of Your curls wipe the tears from Hafez's face,
or flooding may sweep away my foundations any minute.

419. SERVANT AND SLAVE

You, Who like dust of the path, me to be trampled by tyranny gave;

I kiss the dust and beg for pardon because for You to come I crave.
I am not that one who moans about violence from You: God forbid!
I am Your old faithful servant and I am Your well-wishing slave.
I have securely tied my long-time hope to the curl of Your long hair;
to make short my hand of searching: may it never like this behave.
I'm an atom of dust, a mote, and I have a fine time in Your street:
O Friend, I'm frightened that I'll be taken by a wind's sudden wave.
I am the Sufi of the cloister of the Holy Place: but now it happens
to be, that my responsibility is Wineseller's cellar, a cloistered cave.
At morning, Winehouse's Master gave the cup revealing the world,
and to me in that mirror, the information about Your beauty gave.
Get up, and with me the sitter by the roadside, come to Winehouse;
so that you may see haw I rank at Master in that circle's conclave.
You passed by intoxicated and You had no thought at all of Hafez:
Your beauty's coat may catch alight from how my sigh does behave!
At the head of the candle of Your form I'm flickering like the flame,
although I know my desire for You will soon put me in the grave.
At morning I was happy when the shining monarch of the east said:
"Although I've much sovereignty, of the Great King I'm the slave."

420. MY HOPE IS THIS

Although like the winejar, from the heart's fire fermenting am I,
I drink blood and press seal on the lip and myself to silence apply.
To openly desire the lip of the Beloved is to try to take one's life:
look at me who in a matter such as this, with soul I try and try.
How can I be free from the heart's grief when with every breath,
the Hindu-black of the Beloved's hair, a ring in my ear does tie.
I do not put on this patched coat because of a religious fervour:
over this head, hiding a hundred secret faults, I let this veil lie.
I who have the desire not to drink unless it is the purest of wine,
what will I do if to Perfect Master's words my ears I don't apply?
God forbid that I don't have any trust at all in my own devotion!
Extent of my trust is that from time to time a cup of wine I try.
My hope is this, that despite the enemy, on the day of reckoning,
gift of His forgiveness won't place sin's burden on my back to lie.
My Father Adam sold garden of Paradise for two grains of wheat;

if I don't sell it for grain of barley, then an unworthy son am I.
If the Minstrel of the gathering conducts love's way with the hand,
at the time to sing Hafez's verse, all my sanity from me will fly.

421. KING OF THE INTOXICATED

When the slanderers criticize me and on it I deeply meditate,
I remember I did not invent love and wine, I came too late.
Because the giving up of the wine by new drunkards is hopeless,
can notorious ones like me hope to change such an initiate?
Call me: 'The King of the Intoxicated,' for I've lost all reason;
because of this I'm beyond creation, both the small and great.
On Your forehead with my heart's blood make a mole's mark,
so all can see I'm for You, beyond religion, given up to Fate.
So take me on trust and for God's sake, you go your own way;
if you look closely in this dervish's coat, a low score I'd rate.
Breeze, send these verses raining heart's blood to that Friend,
Who punctured vein to my soul with eyelash black and straight.
Withdraw your cloak from my heart that is bleeding because
if you come near my wound, its condition may be your fate.
If I am a drunken lover or if I'm a Master, what is it to you?
Guardian of my secret I'm Hafez, my time I won't complicate.

422. A WAYFARER'S VOW

If from this place of wandering to my Home, should ever
I go,
when I go there once again, with wisdom and with much care
I go.

If I should return in safety to my native land from this journey,
by the pathway to the Winehouse, I'll make a vow that there
I go.
To relate what has been revealed from travelling and journeying,
to Winehouse's door with the harp and the winecup I bear,
I go.

From now on my hand is bound to the chains of Beloved's hair;
chasing the desire of my mad heart for how long: forever
I go?
If again I see Your eyebrow's curve that's like the arch of prayer,
I'll bend so low, so thankfully, and to give a thankful prayer
I go.
That moment's joyful when, like Hafez, from the Chief's kindness,
from Winehouse to Home happily drunk, with Friend so fair
I go.

423. THE LONG DESERT

Though my work in Your long hair is tangled through,
I've the hope it will be unknotted by the mercy of You.
My face is not red from joy, no, it's because my cheek
is reflecting like cup with wine, heart's blood through.
The Musician's tune will take me out from my own self
help; if due to this, melody's veil I've no entrance to.
All night, I am the guardian over my heart's plateaus
so none but You can enter when the screen turns blue.
Fortune's eye is asleep to Your stories so enchanting;
where is a favourable breeze to wake and make me new?
I'm that poet-magician who with the sorcery of speech,
from reed of pen makes sugar flow and honey rain too.
With a hundred hopes I began across this long desert;
Guide of my long heart, don't leave me without a clue.
As I cannot see You in the path of this wind's storm,
to whom can I give message to take my words to You?
Last night was said: "A many-faced hypocrite is Hafez;"
except for Your door's dust, with whom have I to do?

424. FRUITLESS THINKING

I'm the friend of the fair face and the heart-captivating hair,
I'm mad from the drunken eye and wine that's pure and rare.
You ask: "Say one word of Promise of Eternity's Mystery."
When I drink two cups of wine I'll tell you then and there.

When for lover there's no escape from burning and patience:
I, who stand like the candle, with the fire one cannot scare.
I am Adam of Paradise, but during this particular journey,
I have been captured by the love of the young and the fair.
If Fate helps me so that I can carry my load to the Friend,
the Huris will wipe dust from off my bed with their hair.
Shiraz is the mine of the ruby lip and the quarry of beauty;
I, the poor jeweler, because of this am in such deep despair.
From the many intoxicated eyes that in this city I have seen,
O God, although now I don't drink wine, I am merry I swear.
From all six sides it is a city full of glances of lovely ones:
I have nothing; if I did not, of all six I'd be the purchaser.
Hafez, bride of your true nature wishes to become known:
but I haven't a mirror and because of that I sigh in despair.
Hafez burns away from the heat of such fruitless thinking:
where is the Winebringer to throw water on my fire's flare?

425. WE WILL LIFT OUR HANDS

We will lift our hands up high one night and then a prayer
we will make;
for despair from separation, help to come from somewhere
we will make.
My sick heart fell from my hand: o my friends, bring to me a little
help, bring the Physician to the bedhead and remedy for despair we
will make.
Through no fault of mine, You, upset, struck with sword and went;
for God's sake come back to me, so that peace in this affair
we will make.

O heart, look for aid from hearts of drunken lovers, for if you don't,
it's a difficult occupation, and God forbid that a fault there
we will make.
In the path of lust through which our heart became a temple for idols,
we will let fly sighs like arrows: war against lust, beware,
we will make.

Root of my joy became withered: where is path to the Winehouse?
So that growth and blossoming in that water and that air
we will make.
The shadow of the mean paltry bird does not do even an ounce of
good; search for shadow of blessed Huma, Bird beyond compare,
we will make.
Heart went, leaving note's melody: where is Hafez sweet of tone,
so that with his sweet words and *ghazals,* harmony so fair
we will make?

426. A MISTAKE IN CALCULATION

From the friends, the eye of friendship's expectation
was ours;
but in this matter, honestly a mistake in calculation
was ours.
When the tree of friendship will give the fruit, now let us see;
for we have gone and seed planted for germination
was ours.
Many a subtle thing has happened and yet we didn't complain:
never the way of throwing aside dignity's observation
was ours.
It is not the dervish's way to be holding lengthy discussions:
or else, the right to tell You of our passed situation,
was ours.
The intention of Your eye was to deceitfully go into battle;
we didn't know this, and only a peaceful intention
was ours.
When from love for others You gave Your heart's existence,
the uprooting of all hope of having Your unification
was ours.
You said: "O Hafez, you gave to Us your heart all by yourself
from no one, the intention of gaining tax collection
was Ours."

427. MESSENGER OF GRACE

Welcome, bird with the blessed feet; welcome, messenger of grace!
Your coming is happy; what of the Beloved, which way, what place?
O Lord, Grace of Eternity beyond Time be Guide for this traveller,
so the enemy is trapped, and all desires the Beloved gives with grace.
There's no limit at all to the long story of myself and of my Beloved:
if there is no beginning, then also there is no ending to such a case.
Because hair of the Heartstealer tells me to tie thread around waist;
go, kind sir, for upon our body the patched coat is unlawful to place.
The bird of my soul that sings out from the top of the Sidrah tree,
has at last cast the grain of Your mole as bait into this trap's space.
Proud rose brings grace that's limitless: Your face please kindly show!
Cypress shows unpleasant elegance: for God's sake move, with grace!
How can it be fitting for sleep to come to my eye that rains blood?
Can he who has such a sickness sleep, that one whom it will efface?
I said: "You don't show any pity to me with a heart that is broken:
I complain that this is what You do and it's time changes took place."
It is fitting if Hafez has the inclination to go towards Your eyebrow;
in the corner of the archway of prayer lies the eloquent man's face.

428. CLEAN OF IMAGINATION

Lovers, hearts handed away, without care, full of intoxication
are we;
close companions of cup, with love having close association,
are we.
There are many that draw back bow of censorship in our direction:
because from eyebrow of Beloved, letting loose our occupation
are we.

O rose, it was only last night you drained the morning cup away:
anemone, that before being born gained stain's classification,
are we.
If the Perfect Master became upset by us being repentant, say this:
"Make wine pure, because standing still, ready for correction,
are we."

O Guide of the Path, we wait for the orders from You: give a glance,
so that You give me what is due, for far from Path's direction
are we.
Take no notice of wine that is streaked like the red tulip and goblet;
see how, streaking this stain on our heart's bleeding condition
are we.
You spoke, saying: "What is this extremely colourful imagination?"
Hafez: "Don't say it is false for slate clean of imagination
are we."

429. A CONTRACT

Don't shoot my heart with arrows, for I die
before the glances of Your melancholic eye.
Passing all limits is Your portion of beauty;
give me alms, for the miserable beggar am I.
I'm the bird whose song, morning and night,
rises from rooftop to the Heavens most high.
Fill up the cup, because although I'm old, with
Love's fortune I'll make young luck leap high.
My heart became so full of the Friend that
from my mind all thoughts of myself did fly.
Nothing but the score of musicians and wine,
be added by The Pen to my account on High.
That Last Hour when no one talks of others,
the ancient Winemaker's favours I'll magnify.
With apples of Paradise and honey and milk,
a fanatic, a child, tries to trick one such as I.
With the Winesellers I am holding a contract:
at the hour of sorrow, nothing but cup take I.
Happy's that hour I'm free from intoxication,
and the king and his vizier I'll be able to defy.
Within this heart there is a great treasure,
though I'm poverty-stricken in the foe's eye.
Away from Hafez I took my heart that time,
when I took the Winebringer as my only ally.

430. THE LOVER'S PROMISE

Give up love for the Beloved and for the cup of wine,
I will not;
I've renounced a hundred times and once more resign
I will not.
Paradise's garden, Tuba tree's shade and the palace of the Huris,
see as an equal to street's dust of the Friend of mine,
I will not.
The teaching of the lesson of men of insight is but a single hint:
I have uttered that hint and repeat once again the line,
I will not.
Out of anger the pious fanatic said to me: "Go and give up love."
O brother, the need to have an argument is not mine:
I will not.
I am at least pious enough that with all the beauties of the city:
from top of pulpit, glance their way and make a sign,
I will not.
I will never get any information or knowledge about my own self;
because, lift my head in the Winehouse where I recline,
I will not.
Criticizing, the preacher said: "Wine is forbidden, do not drink:"
I said: "My eye sees, but allow ear to every ass incline,
I will not.
The Perfect Master tells a tale that is reasonable and acceptable:
'Excuse me if your absurdity, make a belief of mine...
I will not.' "
Hafez, the threshold of the Perfect Master is the place of Fortune:
from the kissing of the dust of this sacred door, resign
I will not.

431. AN IMAGE OF YOU

At the front of the Winehouse we have placed aside the morning prayer:
we've placed all gained from prayer in path of Beloved beyond compare.
The harvest of hundreds of wise ones of learning is made to burn away,
by the mark that upon our mad frenzied heart we have branded there.

Lord of Eternity without beginning gave us the treasure of love's grief
ever since then we have turned our face towards this desert of despair.
One cannot be more of a hypocrite than this, while in a patched coat:
   by being drunken lover we have found the foundation of this affair.
   From now on we will never again open our heart to the love of idols:
we have placed the seal of Beloved's lip on this house's door, forever.
That kiss, for which the pale pious fanatic gave us his hand to receive,
   from this time on, only the pure lip of the cup of wine shall ever bear.
Thanks be to The Almighty, that like us, without a religion and heart
was that One, Who we acknowledged as wise and as being our Master.
How will this battered vessel go when the end finally comes its way?
For we have set forth our life in the desire for the pearl that is so rare.
We're also contented like Hafez was, in having only an image of You;
O Lord, we relied on You when we were either friendless or a beggar.

432. BEFORE AND AFTER

Upon the eye's drawing board Your face's form I drew with a line:
good fortune to see and hear image of Your form, was never mine.
Mine: mine was the hope of lordship, now I seek to be Your slave:
mine was the desire to have kingdoms, now to serve You I incline.
Although searching for You I am equal in force to the north wind,
I have never reached the dust of Your form's moving cypress-pine.
   I did not find in the night of Your hair hope for life's bright day:
   the desire of heart for form of Your round mouth, I made resign.
   It was the fault of Your dark eye and neck that fascinates heart,
   that, like a wild deer fleeing from mankind, was the fate of mine.
What teardrops I've scattered from desire for Your sweet fountain;
   what graces I have purchased from Your ruby, that seller of wine.
What arrows of glances You let loose on my poor wounded heart;
what burdens of grief I suffered where Your street's end has its line.
O breeze of the morning, bring a little dust from Beloved's street:
I breathe a scent of wounded heart's blood, from fresh land Divine.
A breeze like the rosebud passed over my head from Your district,
I tore apart my poor heart's veil to make such a fine perfume mine.
I make an oath, by the dust of Your foot and light of Hafez's eye,

that without Your face, no splendour from eye's lamp I saw shine.

433. WE HAVE COME

To this door, not looking for riches and glory,
we have come;
for shelter here from fortune's pain and misery
we have come.
We wayfarers of love's stage, journeying from non-existence,
all this way, to this existence's wide country,
we have come.
We saw fresh down on Your cheek and from Paradise's garden,
searching always for this grass of love to see,
we have come.
Having treasure whose treasurer is Gabriel the faithful spirit,
arriving at door of the King's house, in beggary
we have come.
O Vessel of Grace, where is Your anchor of lasting patience?
In this ocean of generosity, drowning in iniquity,
we have come.
Honour is leaving; O cloud, O cleaner of sins, rain, rain, rain,
because black of book, owing to our activity,
we have come.
Hafez, throw off this woolen cloak and set fire with sighing,
for to follow, sighing, behind Caravan's journey,
we have come.

434. WE PLEDGE

We will speak no evil at all, and to injustice incline
we will not:
blacken one's face or make blue the cloak of mine,
we will not.

It is wrong to expose the wealth or poverty of the rich or poor:
it is wise advice that be working for evil's design
we will not.
In wayfarers' sight we will happily travel in the world peaceably:
be thinking of black horse or golden saddle's shine
we will not.
We will not write down falsely on the book of true knowledge:
mix the page of magic with Truth's Mystery Divine,
we will not.
If the sober one forbids us to have the winecup, it's better that
we don't attend to him: give him the refined wine,
we will not.
If the king will not drink with respect from the drunkard's lot;
work for him, making truth and clarity combine,
we will not.
The heavens shipwrecked the vessel of men of much wisdom:
it's wise if our trust to this inverted sea, consign
we will not.
If one who is envious speaks an evil and a friend is very upset,
say this: "Be happy, for to the fool, our ear incline
we will not."
Hafez, we will not pay any attention if the enemy speaks lies;
if he speaks truthfully, Truth be trying to define
we will not.

435. AFTER LONG ABSTINENCE

With Beloved I made a promise, that as long as I've heart that's beating,
for well-wishers of Beloved's street, as for my own life, I've deep feeling.
Due to that candle of Chigil, I see light in the purity of my heart's closet:
from that moon of Khutan comes my heart's lustre and my eye's shining.
Since I have won a place of shelter to the desire and wish of my heart,
about the venom of all the evil speakers in the crowd, am I ever caring?
If a hundred armies of beauties should be in ambush to attack my heart,
praise and thanks be to God, that I've an Idol that an army is shattering.
O watcher, for God's sake for a little while tonight keep your eyes shut,
for with Beloved's silent ruby lip, a hundred words I will be murmuring.

When I walk proudly into the rosebed of Your favour, praise be to God,
that for neither tulip nor white rose nor for the narcissus I've any longing.
Hey, O old wise man, do not go and forbid me to go into the Winehouse;
for by giving up the winecup, I have a heart that the promise is breaking.
My wine is that which is pleasant tasting, and Beloved's a fair picture:
"No one has beloved like this Beloved Who I have," I'm proudly saying.
It's right that I should boast like Solomon about Your ruby lip's seal ring;
what fear's there of Satan when the Great Name of God I'm possessing.
After long abstinence like this, Hafez was renowned for drunken loving;
should I worry, while in world Amin-ud-Din Hasan, me is protecting?

436. THE PEARL

Who am I that Your fragrant mind should now remember me?
You're so gracious, may the dust of Your door my crown be!
Who taught You such generosity to slaves, Heartkeeper: reveal!
Coming from informers about You, such a favour I can't see.
O Holy Bird, may Your blessing be my guide along the way,
for the road's long to my destination and new to this are we.
Please, O morning breeze, take this my service all of the way,
say: "At dawn I will pray to You, please do not forget me."
Happy is that day when I leave the house and lift up my load;
at Your road's end, friends will ask what has become of me.
Guide me to the secret place for drinking the wine with You,
because from the world's grief and worry I will then be free.
Poetry of the highest order can captivate this entire world;
so poets sing and the King feeds pearls from Kingdom's sea.
If you seek the pearl of Unity Hafez, cry a whole sea of tears,
then in that ocean from your eyes, a persistent deep diver be.

437. MY CONDITION

On me You looked... immediately my suffering became great again;
on You I look and suddenly I'm drawn to You by a greater strain.
My condition You never ask: why keep to Yourself, I do not know;
but to heal me You never try: it could be You don't know my pain.

It is not the right way to just throw me in the dust and move on;
come by and ask after me and the dust of Your Path I'll be again.
I won't stop holding on to Your garment until I am dust; and then
when over my clay You go, Your garment my dust will clutch again.
Grief of love for You has taken my breath: how long do You give?
On me You heap destruction and never allow me to breathe again.
One night in the darkness, I looked for my heart among Your curls:
Your cheek I saw and from Your ruby lip the cup again I did drain.
Suddenly, the heart I gave You was lost in the tangle of Your curls;
to Your lip I gave my lip, sacrificed my heart and mind and brain.
When You went away without us, seeking greener fields and plains,
my tears were blood that flowed down these yellow cheeks like rain.
To Hafez You be kind, and tell the enemy to surrender up to death;
when You do such kind favours, of his cold breath I don't complain.

438. TO ABSTAIN IS MADNESS

I'm not that kind of lover who the Beloved and cup gives away,
   such an action I don't do: the police will repeat what I say.
For years I criticized those who repented, and I would be mad
   if of the wine I were to be repentant, when it is the rose's day.
Love's the pearl and I'm the diver and the Winehouse is the sea:
   I've plunged head in there: where it's lifted, come what may.
I've many treasures, for I have many rubies and pearls of tears;
   can I ask from that high star the sun, when these I can display?
Although I'm a beggar I've in my hand the treasure of Royalty;
   can I be greedy for Sphere's help when it helps meanness stay?
Tulip holds cup and narcissus is drunk, and I'm called impious:
   I've complaints; o Lord, who can I ask to bring Justice my way?
In rose season you preach: "Be an abstainer," I nod and wink;
   I'll leave so I may hear what the Beloved and cup have to say.
If the grace of Beloved's pleased that the lovers are in the fire,
   if I glance at Paradise's fountain, my eye shuts straight away.
If I should become stripped like the old willow that is barren,
   out of shame before rose's face, can I lift my head some day?
When breeze washes the bud of the rose with the dew of grace,
   call me sick in the heart if eye to page of book should stray.

Although stained with poverty's dust, shame be on my spirit
if I wet garment with the water from sun's fountain's spray.
The reliability of the promise and pledge of the sky is minimal;
I make a pledge with the flagon and with cup a promise I say.
O my bold disturber of the city, draw the rein for a moment,
so with tears of pearls and face of gold I may pave Your way.
Last night they said: "Your ruby lip gives sugar;" but for me,
as long as my mouth cannot taste it, the truth of it can I say?
From fortune I wish for arch of prayer, Your eyebrows curve:
so to it at morning and evening, love's lesson by heart I pray.
When I'm gaining Paradise paid in cash today right in my hand,
should I trust in the preacher's promises of a forthcoming day?
Besides complete poverty, my face like moon would be dirty,
if I took the gift that the high star the sun, offered my way.
Last night Your ruby lip kept making false promises to Hafez;
but I'm not one to believe in fables, however strong their sway.
Hafez, be sensible, abstaining in rose season is simply madness:
say: "I take refuge with God" and turn mind to that other way.

439. RESURRECTION

Where is news of Your arrival so that life I won't have to bear?
I'm the Bird of Paradise, I'll leave world's cage then and there.
By Your love I swear that if You should call to me, Your slave,
I would never again desire mastery of this world or any other.
Lord, promise to pour a shower from Your cloud of guidance,
before I'm blown away like a handful of dust by the wind's air.
Idol, sweet melodious mover, arise and show Your tall shape;
I will rise and my desire for life and the world will disappear.
Although I'm old, one night take me into Your close embrace,
so with dawn I may rise from Your embrace: young, forever.
Don't sit at my tomb unless there is wine and also the musician;
so that by Your call I'll rise, dance, and Your fragrance share.
Don't believe that from the dust of the entrance of Your street,
sky's tyranny or time's violence can take me away from there.
On the day that I'm due to die let me see You for one breath,
and then like Hafez I'll give away life and the world forever.

440. THE BELOVED'S COUNTRY

At the time strangers say evening prayers, I begin weeping;
  moaning like the strangers, my story I begin to be telling.
  Remembering Friend and my country I weep so bitterly,
  that from the world the use of travelling I'm abolishing.
I'm from the country of my Beloved, not strangers' cities;
  O Divine Protector, to my friends cause me to be reaching.
Guide of the Path, for heaven's sake a little help so that
  again in street of Winehouse my banner I may be raising.
How will reason hope to cope with me being an old Master,
  when once again with a beautiful young one I am playing.
Except for east breeze and north wind, no one knows me;
  for my friend, except wind, I've no companion, nothing.
The air where the Friend is dwelling is our Water of life;
  O breeze, from dust of Shiraz, me a fragrance be bringing.
My tear rushed out and told my crime from face to face;
  of whom can I complain, for traitor in my house is staying.
From the harp of Venus I have heard that at dawn it said:
  "I'm pupil of Hafez, sweet of note, voice sweetly singing."

441. TO THE THRONE

Though old and brokenhearted and without any power
          I am,
whenever I remember Your fair face, youthful forever
          I am.
Thanks be to God, that whatever I asked for He gave to me;
  beyond the limits of my hope and happiness altogether
          I am.
As friends would wish it, the cup of wine is now in my hand;
  I'm on Eternal Fortune's road, at Throne beyond fear
          I am.
Young rosebush, the best of fortune to you, enjoy its fruit;
  in the garden under your shade, still the world's singer
          I am.

In the Beginning I had no knowledge of world's cry of grief;
You see how from grief for You, now the expert learner
I am.
Ever since Your eye looked towards me and caused calamity,
at the end of this Time safe from that terrible disaster
I am.
The door of Reality became visible to this heart on that day;
therefore, now one who is at Your doorstep a dweller,
I am.
To the Winehouse Fate has ordered me, for now and forever;
not desiring to go and not desiring to stay, however,
I am.
When not old in years and in months, that faithless friend
passed by me, like life; through that, now much older
I am.
Last night, good news was given to me by the Grace of God:
"Hafez don't worry, coming back to be your Forgiver
I am."

442. THIS LUNATIC SPHERE

What's all this conflict in this lunatic sphere
I see?
On every horizon there is hatred and fear…
I see.
Everyone tries to turn all their time into a profit;
it's out of control, and each day more severe
I see.
All the daughters are at odds with their mothers;
every son wishes misfortune for his father,
I see.
Brothers do not have any compassion for brothers;
there is no understanding… of son by father,
I see.
Fools are interested in sweet rose-water sherbet;
some wise men live but with a bleeding liver
I see.

The Arab stallion is broken by a heavy saddle load;
upon the neck of the ass is the golden collar,
I see.
Listen to advice of Hafez kind sir, go and do good;
better than a trunk of jewels, this advice here
I see.

443. A CONSULTATION

Visible from edge of the garden is the Monarch's jewel, the rose:
O Lord, may its coming bless cypress and jasmine, both of those.
This Royal One now happily is sitting down in the rightful place,
for now every one sits in his proper place, none comes and goes.
To the seal-ring of Solomon give good news of the happy result,
now that hand of Satan's shortened by Great Name that overflows.
May this house prosper to endless eternity, from the door of which
every moment breeze of Yemen with sweet mercy's perfume blows.
Majesty of Pashang's son Afrasiyab and his sword taking the world,
in all places where stories appear is a story that everyone knows.
Polo-pony of the universe became obedient to You under saddle,
royal horseman, since You've come on field, give ball many blows.
In the kingdom, stream for irrigation is the water of Your sword:
now You plant tree of justice, so root of ill-wishes never grows.
If it doesn't blossom after this, despite fragrance of Your sweetness,
from Iran's plain the musk of China flows out and blows and goes.
The recluses in corners are in expectation of the sweet splendour;
so place cap on a slant and take off veil so that Your face shows.
O breeze, I tell request to Winebringer of the banquet of Atabak,
so that from that cup that scatters gold, some to me then goes.
I had a consultation with Reason and it said: "Hafez, drink wine!"
Winebringer, in accordance with advice: give; see that wine flows.

444. THE OLD MAN'S ADVICE

O light of my eye, there is something I want you to hear from me:
since your cup is full, make others drink and yourself drink fully.
Old men speak words from experience and this to you I have said;

hey, my son, listen to my advice so that then old you will also be.
The hand of Love doesn't place the chain on the one who is sober:
if you wish your hand to draw the Beloved's hair, give up sobriety.
The rosary and the patchcoat don't give to you joy of intoxication;
demanding to be helped in this matter, the Wineseller go and see.
There's no need as regards life and property when there are friends:
ransom a hundred lives for the Friend, listen to this advice clearly.
Satan's temptations are really plentiful on the long path of love:
be careful, and to Angel's words listen with the heart attentively.
Subsistence became ruined and the means of joy does not remain;
O harp, make long the wailing: O drum, beat loudly, triumphantly.
Winebringer, may it be that Your cup's never empty of pure wine!
Look with a favourable eye upon the drinker of dregs... that is me!
When You pass by intoxicated in Your garment that scatters gold,
give the present of a kiss to Hafez, who wears the wool of poverty.

445. ON TOP OF THE FIRE

That tall, cypress of form, bold and flirtatious glancer
of mine,
has shortened the tale that was long and was austere,
of mine.
O heart, you saw that despite old age, knowledge and austerity,
what with me it has done: that Beloved's eye's stare,
of mine.
Because of all the water of the eye I sit here on top of the fire,
because in all directions, of secrets it was the revealer
of mine.
I said: "I'll conceal the trace of love under hypocrisy's cloak,"
but a revealer of the secret was the tear, the informer
of mine.
That Friend is intoxicated and does not remember the friends,
but Winebringer be remembered, for You're the helper
of mine.
I fear that my faith will be destroyed, for the arch of prayer,
Your eyebrow, bears away the presence of the prayer
of mine.

Like the laughing candle I'm weeping and laughing over myself
what effect has my burning, stony-hearted destroyer
of mine?
I depict a picture on water with my weeping: so now how long
will it be until the truth replaces this illusory picture
of mine?
That moment when life of King Mahmud came to an end he
bitterly kept giving soul, saying: "Where's Ayaz fair,
of mine?"
Lord, when will that breeze be blowing, from whose perfume,
the fragrance of mercy will become the great helper
of mine?
O pious fanatic, since there is no gain by the prayers you make,
what harm is from nightly drinking, burning, prayer
of mine?
Hafez burned away from sorrow: o breeze, tell of his condition
to the King, helper of friend, and of enemy destroyer,
of mine.

446. INCURABLE

However much of my grief I told to many a physician,
no potion they discovered for this outsider's condition.
The casket of love doesn't place its own seal on itself;
O Lord, don't ever let the enemies gain their ambition!
To that rose that is in the thorn's power for a moment
say: "You should be ashamed of nightingale's position."
O Lord, allow a stable condition; so that eyes of lovers
may once again in loved ones' faces, find illumination.
To Friend we've related all about our secret sufferings;
one cannot conceal such pain as this from The Physician.
O Benevolent One, at the table of Unification with You,
how long shall we be one of those without a portion?
Hafez wouldn't be a disgrace, crazy in the world's eyes,
if he had listened to the sane ones' constant admonition.

447. BEAUTY

O You, bright as moon and fresh as Spring is Your face
of beauty;
Your mole and down are the circle and centre of grace
of beauty.
Your eye full of intoxication hides fascination of enchantment;
in Your restless long floating hair lies the resting space
of beauty.
No moon like You shone from the Gallery of Perfect Excellence,
no cypress like Your form arose in a streaming place
of beauty.
By Your beauty the age of the captivating of hearts is full of joy;
by Your grace, the days are fully feeling the embrace
of beauty.
From the cage of Your curls and bait of the grain of Your mole,
no bird of heart in the world is not prey to the chase
of beauty.
Nurse Nature, throughout the whole of life is always gracefully
cherishing You tenderly; in the breast's close embrace
of beauty.
Fresh down around Your lip is that violet that is growing there,
because it's drinking Water of Life from fountain's base
of beauty.
Hafez has given up all possibility that he will ever see Your equal;
there is only Your fair face, in the place, of the race...
of beauty.

448. THE RAISING OF THE ROSE

Spring, and the rose raised rapture and told repentance to depart,
from joy of seeing the rose's face, tear grief's root from the heart!
The soft morning breeze came and rosebud, possessed by passion
has gone out of itself by tearing its tight fitting shirt wide apart.

Heart, learn the way of truth from the clear purity of the water,
seek straightness from the field's cypress and know freedom's art.
The bride, that rosebud with the jewel and with the sweet smile,
has exactly in the same way, stolen both my faith and my heart.
Frenzied cry of nightingale and moan of bird of a thousand songs,
to unite with the rose, out from the house of mourning, did start.
See how the violence of the breeze caused curling around the rose:
see how the curls of hyacinth's hair on face of the jasmine dart!
Hafez, seeking the tale of the story of Time from the cup of wine,
is decision of Minstrel's word and order Perfect Master did impart.

449. LIKE STEEL INTO SILVER

Like the rose, all of a sudden because of Your scent,
I tear apart from the collar down, my body's garment.
You could say the rose in the garden saw Your body,
for like drunkard, with body's garment it was violent.
I bear life with difficulty, because of my grief for You;
but how easily You took the heart from me is evident.
You turned away from friends at the word of enemies,
no friend would ever with the enemy become content.
Don't, so that the heart-burning sigh from my chest,
may rise like smoke by the way of the window's vent.
Your body is in the garment like the wine's in the cup,
Your head into the breast, like steel into silver went.
Candle, rain tears from your eye like the cloud does;
fire of your heart, to all people is an obvious event.
Don't break my heart and then throw it under the foot,
because in the tip of Your hair it has pitched its tent.
Because Hafez has chained up his heart to Your hair,
do not trample on his exertion with discouragement.

450. THE LESSON OF LOVE

When I am dust for Your path, Your coat You throw
from me:
if I ask: "This heart return," You turn face... and go
from me.

To everyone in Creation You show the red rose of Your cheek;
if I ask: "Hide it from them," You hide face's glow...
from me.
If I die like candle before You, You laugh like morning light;
grief now overcomes me, You take heart full of woe
from me.
To my eye I stated this: "At last see the Beloved, completely;"
reply was this: "Perhaps you want blood to flow
from... Me?"
You thirst for my blood, these lips thirst for Yours; so when
I win desire from You, will You take reward and go
from me?
Friends witness, that for Your mouth I offered life and soul;
see, for such a small thing, You hold Yourself in tow
from me.
If like Farhad... my life should bitterly be lost, do not worry,
as many stories sweet and sorry will stay, that flow
from me.
Hafez finish this, the lesson of Love; for if you keep reading,
a love story from every corner... will come and go
from me.

451. NEVER

For God's sake, with the patchcoat wearers, sit
never;
Your face from the helpless drunkards, hide it
never.
There are many stains on those with patched-coats:
the drunkards' house is happy: stains on it...
never!
You are of a delicate nature, and of power to endure
handful of heavy patchcoat wearers, are unfit.
Never.
I never see any pain in those who are like these Sufis;
to gain pure bliss, drinkers of dregs never quit:
never!

Come and see the dishonesty of all these hypocrites:
flagons and bleeding hearts loud harps admit?
Never!
Since You have made me very drunk, never sit sober;
You have given me elixir and poison isn't fit:
never.
The ruby wine is all foaming with the desire for You;
opening of wine-red lip and tipsy eye to omit:
never!
Hafez has a full heart that is like a seething cauldron;
his heart is boiling, never be incautious of it:
never!

452. AT THE END

Than of the thought of wine and cup, much sweeter
will be what?
Now let us look and see, at the end of this affair,
will be what?
Why suffer sorrows of the heart when there is no time remaining,
one could say: "When heart and time are not, there
will be what?"
Drink wine, do not grieve and don't listen to advice of imitators:
for the talk of the masses, to credit of the listener
will be what?
Say to bird of little endurance: "Eat your own grief," for on it,
the mercy of that One Who has planted the snare,
will be what?
Truly it is better if your hand is working for your heart's desire;
finally, to one with desire not attained, you're aware,
will be what.
Last night the Master of the Winehouse kept saying this enigma
that is on the line of the cup: "At the end, there
will be what?"
I took Hafez's heart from the Path with drum and harp and *ghazal*:
let's see then, reward of me, infamous everywhere,
will be what?

453. THE GREATEST FORTUNE

Do you know what great fortune is? It's the Friend, to see:
  choosing to beg in the Friend's street, instead of royalty.
It is quite an easy thing to give up the desire to stay alive;
  but, to give up the sweet friends of the soul, isn't so easy.
With heart folded tight like bud, into rosegarden I'll go;
  where my garment of good reputation I will tear off me.
Now, like the breeze, tell the hidden mysteries to the rose;
  now, from nightingales hear the playing of Love's mystery.
Firstly, do not hand away the kissing of the Friend's lip;
  or, lastly you may regret, gnawing hand and lip you'll be.
Gain much from friendship: from this house of two doors,
  once we leave it, such an opportunity we'll never again see.
You could say it seems that the King has passed by Hafez;
  Lord, bring the thought of this dervish into Your memory.

454. HEART AND SOUL

Come through the door and fill our small room with light,
  perfume the souls of all of us with a fragrance to delight.
To eye and eyebrow of Beloved I've given heart and soul:
  come, come to the arch of window, see through our sight.
Breeze of garden of Paradise, from dust of our gathering
  take to Paradise this perfume and its incense burner light.
Beauty's splendid rays became veil of eye's knowledge:
  rise and come and make the Sun's pavilion full of light.
The star of separation's night doesn't shine; so come now
  to this house's roof, turn lamp of moon to bright white.
Since under Your hand are the lovely one's of the earth,
  glance at the jasmine and raise up the pinetree a height.
Winebringer, too many tall tales are much wasted breath;
  don't hand away Your special work, fill the cup up right.
It's not our business to hope to receive union with You;
  give I.O.U. for ruby of sugar to be given to me on sight.
Kiss the lip of the cup and then give it to the drunkard;

and with this subtlety, perfume a wise palate's delight.
If theologian should give this advice: "Don't be a lover,"
give him cup and to freshen his brain, him then invite.
Because graceful qualities and sweet ways meet in You,
lift Your head like the candle in all companions' sight.
I am tired of this cover-up, this patched coat of religion:
give me a Sufi-killing look, make me Kalandar outright.
After serving pleasure and loving those fair moon-faced,
work with your heart on the verse of Hafez, then recite.

455. THE POLISH OF LOVE

Drink ruby wine and the faces of those moon of forehead fair,
see:
despite what some say about religious laws, their beauty there,
see.
Under garments covered with gold patches they have nooses hidden:
the length of their hands, even though short sleeves they wear,
see.
They don't bow down their head for the harvest of the two worlds:
the knowledge and pride of these beggars gleaning their share,
see.
The Friend does not loosen the frown from the frowning eyebrow;
Grace of One without a care and without heart full of despair,
see!
I do not hear about the promise of love from anyone at all anymore;
conspirators and the faith that some of the friends did swear,
see.
The way to be released is that one should become a captive of love;
the mind, that sees the future of those who about it still care,
see.
The dust of the heart of Hafez is taken away by the polish of love;
purity of the pure mirror of those of faith that's pure and rare,
see.

456. SEE!

A subtlety fascinating to the heart I say: "That moonface's mole,
see:
tightly bound by the chain of that hair is my reason and my soul:
see!"
I criticized heart, saying: "Don't let your nature be a wild beast's:"
then it replied: "That deer's bold half drunken eye is in control,
see!"
Curl of the Beloved's hair is the morning breeze's place for seeing;
by every hair a hundred lovers are bound by both heart and soul,
see!
Those who are worshippers of the sun don't know of Heartstealer:
O critic, please don't see the sun's face: Beloved's face as the goal
see.
See how sun's limbs tremble from envy of that One's moonlike face;
from that ambergris perfumed hair, blood in liver of musky bowl,
see.
Beloved's heartstealing hair laid the halter on the neck of the wind;
how that Indian-black hair traps the Path's lovers' part and whole,
see.
In searching for that special One I have gone far away from myself
no one will see a one like that One, even if they from pole to pole
see.
It is right if Hafez rubs face down in the corner of the prayer-arch;
O critic, for God's sake, the curve of that eyebrow's inverted bowl,
see.

457. A TEMPTING OFFER

Monarch of box-tree shaped ones, Sovereign over all sweet-lipped,
whose eyelashes pierce centre of all ranks that have been pierced,
Passed by intoxicated and on me, a dervish, glanced and then said:
"O you; O you eye and light of all those who are sweet-speeched,
Empty of silver and empty of gold how long will your purse be?
Be my slave and from those of silver form, fruit will be enjoyed.
You are not less than a mote, an atom, you are so much greater;
be a lover and ride whirling into where swirling sun is enclosed.

Don't rely on the world; if you have a goblet with wine within,
　drink; enjoy those of Venus forehead, tenderly, delicately formed."
Our Master the wine measurer, his soul always be happy, said:
　"Don't keep company with those whose word cannot be trusted.
Hold on to the hem of the Friend's garment, break from the foe;
　be a man of God and from Satan safely pass, don't be deceived."
In the morning in meadow of tulips I said this to the soft breeze:
　"Who are the martyrs that these bloody shrouds have wrapped?"
It answered: "Hafez, both you and I do not know this mystery,
　let only the ruby wine and those of silver chin be mentioned."

458. PRAYER OF A BROKEN HEART

Make a veil of musky hyacinth for Your roseleaf, that's to say,
　hide Your face with Your hair and make a world in ruins lay.
Scatter the sweat from Your face on the borders of the garden,
　so that full of rosewater You make flagons of our eyes today.
Gracefully open Your drunken narcissus eyes, so full of sleep;
　make the eye of the lovely narcissus from envy in sleep to stay.
Season of the rose is now hurrying to depart like life departs;
　Winebringer, in circulating the rose-coloured cup don't delay.
Smell the violet's perfume and take a hold of the Idol's hair,
　look at lily's colour and then resolve to take the wine away.
Like the bubbles, open your eyes upon the face of the goblet;
　from the bubbles, the worth of this house's endurance weigh.
Since the way and means of slaying the lover belongs to You,
　with the enemies drain the goblet and then criticize us today.
Hafez is seeking to obtain union through this path of prayer;
　Lord, accept those who have a broken heart, when they pray.

459. THE WORSHIP OF WINE

O Winebringer, it's morning, the goblet full of wine
　　　　　make:
　hurry, for the sky's revolution will never a decline
　　　　　make!

Before this perishing world becomes finally totally ruined,
us, ruined with a cup of the red wine from the vine
make!
Sun of wine caused appearance of the bowl from the east;
if you are looking for glory, sleep forced to resign
make.
When the sky one day makes pitchers out of our poor clay;
be careful, and our skulls, bowls full of wine Divine
make.
We are not the one for austerity or penance or foolish talk,
talk to us about the cup of pure wine, no other line
make.
Hafez, worship of wine is the only work that's worthwhile:
get up, by facing resolutely to the good work, a sign
make!

460. LOVE'S FEVER

When You come, say *Koran's* opening verse over the sick one's bed;
open Your lip, for the ruby of Your lip gives new life to the dead.
That One came inquiring and said the opening verse, then went;
where's one's breath so that after that One my soul may be sped?
O You Who are Physician to the sick, look at my face and tongue:
on my tongue this sigh's breath is from load on my heart like lead.
Although fever made my bones hot with love and then departed,
from my bones the fire of this love has never like the fever fled.
The condition of my heart stays like Your mole on its fiery land;
because of Your two eyes my body became a sick powerless shred.
Quench the burning of my fever's heat with the water of the eyes,
and feel my pulse to see whether of life it shows even one thread.
That one, who had given me the bottle of wine to get some peace,
why does that one, with my bottle, to the Physician quickly tread?
Hafez, your verse has given to me a mouthful of the Water of Life:
leave Physician alone and let my prescription's mouthful be read.

461. OUR LAW

They say about me all over the city: "A lover is he,"
still… I do not hate and I do not feel any jealousy.
We're faithful and happy and contented in criticism;
faithlessness is worry and our law is not to worry.
I asked Winehouse Master: "What path's the Truth?"
He asked for winecup, said: "Conceal the Mystery."
From beauty of Creation's garden what do we want?
"With eye's pupil of your face pluck rose's beauty."
With wine, I destroyed my reflection on the water,
so that I could destroy the picture I'd made of me.
I tie my trust to the tip of Your long flowing hair;
why should I try, for nothing else exists for me?
Downy cheek of friend teaches love for the Friend;
to praise such a beautiful face is also praiseworthy.
We will turn the rein from church to the Winehouse,
because with the jobless preachers, no time have we.
Kiss only Beloved's lip Hafez, and the cup of wine;
kisser of preacher's hand, don't you ever try to be.

462. MORE THAN THIS

To us intoxicated lovers glance our way,
more than this;
to Winehouse door show the pathway,
more than this.
Thank You for the grace that flows to us from Your lip,
it's wonderful, but give a little more I say:
more than this.

To that One Who simplifies this crazy mixed-up world,
say: "Make explanation in a subtle way,
more than this."
How can I not lay my heart at such beautiful young feet?
Time never birthed beauty on any day,
more than this.
The critic said to me: "Besides grief, what is from love?"

"Wise sir," I said, "it has meaning today,
more than this."
"Take up the cup" I say, "drink away and kiss the lip;"
for my soul, answer none could say,
more than this.
The reed of Hafez's pen is a sweet branch of sugarcane;
take it, in garden no fruit is a higher pay,
more than this.

463. EXPECTATION

Because we are separated from You, on the fire we
turn;
O Lord, our separation is a calamity, this calamity
turn.
Moon parades splendidly on the blue stallion of the sky:
so pride will end, Your foot to Rakhsh the mighty,
turn.
Intoxicated, gracefully move to plunder reason and faith:
slant cap on Your head and house of body gracefully
turn.
Shake Your long lovely curls towards and against hyacinth;
all around the field, like morning breeze, fragrantly
turn.
O Light of drunkard's eyesight, I'm deep in expectation:
wailing of the harp make, and to the cup quickly
turn.
When on Your cheek Time writes down the happy lines,
Lord, from our friend, any writing at all of calamity
turn.
Hafez, except for this, your lot from beauty is nothing;
if you are not content with this, then Fate's decree
turn.

464. THE DESTROYER

Give just one glance and the whole market of sorcery

shatter;
with one glorious glance, the face of magician Samiri
shatter.
Give to the wind all the heads and turbans of the whole world:
that is, by slant of cap on Your ear, by hearts' robbery,
shatter.

Tell to the hair this: "Give up the way of pride and arrogance;"
tell to the glance this: "The army of all that cruelty…
shatter."
Move out gracefully and take the ball of beauty from everyone;
chastise the lovely Huri and the splendour of the Pari
shatter.
With Your gazelle eyes use Your glance to capture sun's lion,
with Your eyebrows, bow used by Jupiter for archery
shatter.
When from breath of the breeze, hyacinth gives out perfume;
with tip of Your perfumed hair, its whole perfumery
shatter.
O Hafez, when the nightingale boasts about being so eloquent,
then you by using the old Dari language, its vocabulary
shatter.

465. A SACRED BIRD

Bird of my heart is a sacred bird and God's Throne is its nest;
it is tired of cage of the body and of world's way is distressed.
When the bird of the soul flies from the top of this heap of dust,
at the threshold of Palace's door, falcon finds its place of rest.
Yes, when the bird of the heart soars, its nest is Paradise's Tree;
know that the perch of our falcon is the top of Throne's crest.
On the head of the whole world will fall fair fortune's shadow,
if our bird expands wings and feathers over the East and West.
Its dwelling is only the highest Sphere, not in both the worlds;
its body is from the mine, but its soul from Beyond is Blessed.
The bower of the Splendour of our bird is in the Highest Place;
its nourishment is Paradise's rosebed that Beloved did manifest.

O Hafez, distraught through ecstasy, since you proclaim Unity,
on the page of man and angel, let your pen of Unity be pressed.

466. BRING BACK

O Lord, home to Khutan that musk-deer over there,
bring back;
and that straight swaying cypress into field's air
bring back.
Please send a favourable breeze and revive our fading fortune,
my soul has left my body so please, it to its snare
bring back.
Since from Your command the moon and sun reach their rank,
leave and return my Beloved, that moon face fair
bring back.
By searching for that ruby of Yemen our eyes have both bled;
O Lord, to Yemen that constellation's bright flare
bring back.
These are our words: "We don't want our life without You;"
just one word, O runner, O news-taker, messenger,
bring back!
O blessed bird with the happy helpful walk, please go quickly;
the words of crow and kite to Pure Bird, the Anka,
bring back.
O Lord, that One Whose homeland was once the eye of Hafez,
from desire for wandering, to this home-dweller,
bring back.

467. A CITY SUCH AS THIS

If the ruby from Badakhshan's rocky slate
comes out,
water of Rukni like sugar from the Strait
comes out.
Here in the city of Shiraz, a one who steals the heart,

lovely, flirtatious, graceful: from each gate
comes out.
In the dwelling of judge, teacher, priest and policeman,
wine that is rose of colour and is first-rate
comes out.
In the pulpit during such hypocritical acts of ecstasy,
from preacher's turban hashish to evaporate
comes out.
In the gardens, cry of nightingale with twang of harp,
and voice of minstrel, morning and late,
comes out.
In this city, grieving from being distant from Beloved,
Hafez, from house, with heart in a sad state,
comes out.

468. THE CLOAK OF SOVEREIGNTY

O You, cloak of Sovereignty truly fits shape and height
of Yours,
crown and seal-ring are decorated by that jewel so bright
of Yours.
With each moment, out from the imperial cap there keeps rising
the sun of victory, attracted by that cheek's moonlight
of Yours.
Although the sun of the sky is the eye and the lamp of the world,
its eye that gives light is dust from what foot does excite,
of Yours.
The Bird of Fortune's summit of glorious splendour is wherever
Huma's shade of the canopy, scrapes the earthly might
of Yours.
In spite of the thousand differences in the law and in philosophy,
a point never escaped unexplained by wise heart's light
of Yours.
The true Water of Life is dropping from the beak of eloquence of
that sweet-talking parrot, sugar-eating reed of delight,
of Yours.
What Alexander searched for and what Fortune did not give him,

was a drink from cup's pure water, life fresh and bright,
of Yours.
There is no need to tell of need in the presence of Your majesty;
for no secret is hidden from judgement of what's right,
of Yours.
O Monarch, in the old head of Hafez, youth has put the hope that
he will gain pardon (giving life, forgiving his sins' blight)
of Yours.

469. IN ENVY AND REGRET

O You, China's musk is blood-price for dust of that pathway
of Yours,
the sun's reared in shade of the border of that cap's fray
of Yours.
The narcissus sent her proud glance out beyond her limit: You move!
O soul, be sacrificed for glance of that dark eye's display
of Yours.
Drink my blood; for with a beauty that is like this, not even an angel
in his heart could come to write down the sin of that way
of Yours.
You are the cause of the people's ease and the sleep of all the world;
from that, my eye and heart's border became place to lay,
of Yours.
All night, every night, I wake and then I cry like every star cries out,
in envy and regret for that face like the moon's bright ray
of Yours.
All of the friends who sit with friends are separated from each other;
I am together with the shelter of where threshold does lay,
of Yours.
Don't be friendly to those unworthy ones: because like good fortune,
may he be Your friend who wishes happiness for each day
of Yours.
When people are presented tomorrow on the day of the Gathering,
possibly in the middle may fall upon me, the glance's sway
of Yours.
Hafez, don't keep longing to gain favour, for when the end comes

the harvest of grief is set on fire, by smoke of sigh's way
of Yours.

470. THIS FINE NOOSE

O You; You Whose beauty is so bright, the sun is but a mirror;
  Your mole is a beauty spot, muskpod's but an incense holder.
With tears I washed the courtyard of my eyes, but it's hopeless;
  there is nothing to tempt Your form to such an empty corner.
This point of darkness that has become the centre of all Light,
  is simply the reflection of Your mole, in the Vision's theatre.
Where is the good news of Your coming feast of the new moon,
  that congratulating her I can return to Fortune without a fear?
From Your eyebrow like the new moon where's the special rise,
  so that the sky in the heaven is our slave, with ring in its ear?
You are the Sun of Beauty, You are all grace and gracefulness;
O God, may You never set, until the last Resurrection and after.
Poor heart, how are you, lost in the luxurious curls of that One?
  The soft morning breeze gave troubled warnings of your affair.
Your form is so pleasing that no illustration comes close to it
by the Decorator, Who drew Your eyebrow with a musk so rare.
Perfume of the rose has risen: come by the door of friendship;
  Your fair face is fortunate omen that our Spring is nearly here.
To the Kind Sir's notice, which of these difficulties will I bring:
  will I tell of my own need or of Your disgust at such despair?
The head of many a gallant one Hafez, is held in this fine noose;
  stop all this desire to possess, for it is not within your power.

471. GOD'S BOUNDLESS MERCY

By the soul of the Wineseller, by my thanks for generosity
of His,
I swear that in my mind is no desire but the servant to be
of His.
Although Paradise may not be the dwelling of sinners, bring wine,

because I am the one who is always begging for the mercy
of His.
The lamp of lightning that flashed from that cloud is so bright,
that to our dry harvest it set the fire of love so fiercely,
of His!
Bring wine, for to me last night Gabriel from the invisible world
brought news: "For all of creation is the boundless mercy
of His."
If you see a head that is upon that threshold of the Winehouse,
do not kick it, because unknown is the Plan, purposely,
of His.
Don't go and look with the eye of contempt at intoxicated me;
never are austerity or inequity without the Will, eternally,
of His.
My heart has no inclination towards repentance or to abstinence;
but, for the Kind Sir's Name I do my best, for that glory
of His.
Heart, don't be worrying about the limitless Grace of the Friend,
for everything in creation receives that boundless bounty
of His.
That old patched coat of Hafez is forever in pawn for the wine;
perhaps the dust of that Winehouse is the natural quality
of his.

472. ROYAL BEGGAR

The violet is much tormented by that musk scented hair:
Yours;
rosebud's cover is torn by that heart seducing laughter:
Yours.
O my rose of sweet perfume, do not consume Your nightingale,
for night after night, full of sincerity, he has one prayer:
Yours.
Witness the great strength of love! See how his pride and glory
dared to knock sideways the sovereign crown: this beggar,
Yours.
Tell the enemy and the friend, that everything that is intended,

all the violence that's in the world, for Your sake I bear:
Yours.
At one timer I became upset if the angels happened to breathe;
now, cloak of the world's criticism for Your sake I wear:
Yours.
Love for You is my destiny and dust of Your door my Paradise:
love for Your face is my nature, Your Will my pleasure:
Yours.
Although patched coat and austerity don't mix with cup of wine,
by painting this picture, I endeavour in Your Will to share:
Yours.
The ragged coat of the beggar of Love has treasure in the sleeve:
to Royalty quickly arrives that one who was Your beggar:
Yours.
The palace balcony of my eye is the place of rest of Your image;
it's a place of prayer. O my Sovereign, Your place is there:
Yours.
Wine's hangover and love's passion, leave my head that moment
when this mind full of longing, is dust at doorway there:
Yours.
Your cheek's a pleasant garden, especially in the Spring's beauty
when sweetly speaking Hafez is the bird, singing songster:
Yours.

473. A JOYFUL RING

The down of the Beloved's cheek by which the moon is eclipsed,
is a very joyful ring, but a way out of it has never yet existed.
Eyebrow of the Friend is the peak of Fortune's arch of prayer:
rub your face there and ask from the Friend for what is needed.
O you, drinking dregs of Jamshid's circle, keep your heart pure,
because the cup's a mirror that shows the world, yes it is indeed!
Conduct of monastery's men turned me into a worshipper of wine;
look and see all the smoke by which my blood became blackened.
Say to the devil of grief "Say and do whatever may be possible,
for away from you with the Winesellers I have been sheltered."

Winebringer, on the pathway of the sun keep the lamp of wine;
tell it that the torch of the morning, by it will be illuminated.
Sprinkle a little water on the day book's record of all our deeds;
perhaps it is possible that the letters of sin by it will be effaced.
The beggar of the city constantly has a thought in his mind that
the day will soon come when by the King he'll be remembered.
Hafez, who made straight the arrangement of the circle of lovers:
from the space of the banquet's place, may he not be displaced.

474. HEART'S BLOOD

Rosebush of joy blossomed: Winebringer with cheek of rose
is where?
Breeze of Spring blows: pleasant tasting wine that flows
is where?
Each new rose brings to the memory the One with the cheek of rose;
but where is ear that listens, the eye that attention shows
is where?
In the banquet of pleasure's circle there is no fragrant ball of desire;
dawn's breath, soul-sweet, musk that Friend's hair throws
is where?
O breeze, I cannot keep enduring the rose boasting about its beauty;
I splash hands in heart's blood: God, the One beauty shows
is where?
The candle of the morning has boasted cruelly of Your cheek of rose;
enemy's tongue became long: shining sword for such foes
is where?
You said: "Perhaps you're not really longing for kiss of My ruby?"
I died from such longing, but the will and power that grows
is where?
Although in speech, Hafez is the treasurer of the treasure of wisdom,
yet about grief given by selfish Time, he who speech knows
is where?

475. THAT EYEBROW

I have an eye that is bleeding because of the eye of that bow,
that eyebrow;
world will be full of commotion because of that eye and also
that eyebrow.
I'm slave of that bold One's eye, Whose face when drunkenly asleep
is a beautiful rosebed, and a musky canopy does over it grow:
that eyebrow.
Body is a crescent moon from grief, because on seeing such a musky
line, where is the moon in the sky's curve, daring enough to show
that eyebrow?
You with an unfaithful heart, You don't tie down veil of Your hair:
I fear my arch where I pray, heartstealing curve will overthrow:
that eyebrow.
To mind of secluded, rosebed's beauty is of Your forehead's beauty:
on garden's border is one who strolls and does come and go:
that eyebrow.
May the bow of the great beauty of Your intoxicated eye be strung
forever, which by Your aim fires arrows at the moon from that bow:
that eyebrow.
The spies are careless, for every' moment from that eye and that
forehead come a thousand signs to us, for between them is, incognito,
that eyebrow.
Because of such beauty no one will speak again of the Huri and of
the Pari, saying: "The eye of this is like this and that can also show
that eyebrow."
Although Hafez is the wise bird when it comes to being one who is
faithful, yet that eye made a prey of him with arrows from that bow:
that eyebrow.

476. WHAT NEWS OF THE BELOVED?

What news of Beloved do you, messenger to the true lover,
say?
What's happened to rose and nightingale the sweet singer?
Say!
Don't worry, we are initiated into the sacred abode of Love;

to the familiar friend about the Friend please now utter:
say!
To me a poor wretch, read a letter from that honourable One:
from that great Monarch, a message to this poor beggar
say.
From the snare of Your long curls, You threw hearts in dust;
where's ours, since for Love we told it goodbye forever?
Say.
If once again you are fortunate to go past that blessed door,
with a greeting like the good servant and after a prayer,
say:
"In the Path of Love there is no dividing of the rich and poor;
so, Monarch of beauty, what do You to this poor beggar
say?"
To whoever said: "Dust of the door of the Friend is like kohl;"
"What you are saying is seen by this eye, is quite clear,"
say.
To the exacting Sufi who forbids us entrance to the Wineshop,
"Repeat what you've said in the presence of our Master,"
say.
The wine that sparkled so much in jar it took the Sufi's heart;
"When will it then sparkle away the goblet, Winebringer?"
Say.
When with that maze of dark curls You made two long plaits,
O soft breeze of the East, what mystery do they gather?
Say.
Last night, because of my crying, the bird of the fields wept;
soft breeze, so at last you know what does nightly occur:
say.
Comfort to the soul is the speech of the Knowledgeable Ones;
breeze, with respect, ask the Mystery; to us a clue transfer:
say.
Although we are worthless, please don't think of us like this:
tell all our sins to the King's wise forgiveness, 'A beggar'
say.
Hafez, if you are admitted to that Feasting Table, drink wine;
yes, and for God's sake, "Hypocrisy I give away forever,"

477. TIME OF REAPING

When at wide green sky and sickle of crescent moon I was looking,
I remembered my own field's sowing, and the time of the reaping.
I said: "O fortune, the sun has now risen and you are lost in sleep:"
The answer was: "Despite what happened, don't worry, be hoping."
If you happen to go pure and free like the Messiah to the heavens,
to the sun there will reach many rays of your bright light shining.
Don't you ever trust in the false star, because that thief of the night,
that old trickster, the crown of Kaus and Kay Khusrau was stealing.
Go and tell to the sky that it should not be boasting of grandeur:
in love the moon is worth a barleycorn, Pleiades for two is selling.
Although the ear may be heavy with an ear-ring of gold and ruby,
the season of beauty is a passing thing, this wise advice be hearing.
May the evil eye be far from Your mole, for on beauty's chessboard,
by advancing a pawn, over the moon and sun the game it is winning.
Anyone who does not plant green faith's seed in field of the heart,
reaps a yellow face from what one produces at the time of reaping.
In this circle be like the tambourine that's surrounded by the ring;
don't go out of your circle even if you happen to suffer a beating.
The fire of hypocrisy and deceit will burn the harvest of religion;
Hafez, throw this woolen patchcoat away and then be wayfaring.

478. FAITH'S FORTRESS

The Beloved said: "You went out, upon the new moon to gaze:
go, shame on you, for it's My eyebrow-moon that should amaze.
"It is a whole life since your heart has been a slave of My hair;
don't be careless of being on the side where your friendship lays."
Don't value the scent of intelligence above Beloved's black hair;
there, a thousand muskpods at half a barleycorn they appraise.

In this old sown field the seed of love and faith will be sprouting,
at that time when at long last arrive the final harvesting days.
Winebringer, bring wine; and then I will tell to you the mystery
about the old star's secret and the new moon's wandering ways.
At the end of each month the lack of sight of the moon is a sign
of the fate of Siyamak's and Zhu's crown: a mere waning haze.
Hafez, threshold of the Perfect Master is the fortress of faith:
read the lesson of love to him and then listen to what he says.

479. YOU HAVE COME

O You with those long chains of curling hair,
        You have come;
    good luck to You: to help the mad in despair,
        You have come.
For a moment don't be contemptuous, and change Your ways;
    for those who are most needy, as their helper
        You have come.
I'm the ransom for Your straight form; because for peace or war,
    no matter what, of unworthiness to be reliever:
        You have come.
From that ruby lip You create and blend both water and fire;
    far be evil eyes from You, sweet magic-maker,
        You have come.
Blessings be on Your tender heart, for You do nothing but good
    for one who is killed by Your glance; in prayer,
        You have come.

Thinking nothing of my abstaining You come to steal my heart;
    to my hiding place intoxicated, without a care,
        You have come.
Although with every glance Your eye steals my heart from me,
    I regret that You love strangers, not that here
        You have come.
Hafez, you said: "Again garment of religion is winestained;
    perhaps, back from religious practices there,

you have come."

480. TORTURE

A letter to the Friend with the blood of the heart I wrote:
"Really, I feel terrors of Judgment Day when You're remote.
A hundred signs of separation from You I have in my eyes:
these tears of our eyes are not alone in what they denote."
Although I tried, no gift from that One was obtained by me:
whoever tried The Tried, repents; 'trying,' he'll never quote.
I asked physician about 'a friend's' state and was answered:
"Being close to 'beloved' is torture; distance is the antidote."
Suddenly the East breeze shifted the veil from off my Moon:
it was like the sun before noon when away the clouds float.
I said: "If I stay around Your street it brings me criticism:"
but, by God, a love without criticism is unworthy of note.
Since Hafez is now a seeker, exchange a cup for his sweet life,
so that from it he may taste Your gift, soothing his throat.

481. DO NOT LEAVE ME

O Beloved, don't leave me, for the light of my eye
　　　　You have:
the soul's peace and help for the mad heart's sigh
　　　　You have.
May no harm come to You from sick envious eyes of people,
　　for in taking of hearts by beauty, greatest supply
　　　　You have.
Lovers cannot keep their hands from touching Your garment;
　　You've torn their shirt of patience, You can't deny
　　　　You have.
Don't have a worried heart: you also reach the day of union,
　　for poison of the Beloved's absence in oversupply
　　　　you have.
O judge of the age, do not forbid me to be loving that One:
　　I'll excuse you, for never seeing that One, as alibi

you have.
Hafez, about this criticism that the Friend has given to you:
Your foot out from blanket under which you lie
you have?

482. YOUR FACE'S GLORY

O You, from glory of Whose face lamp of vision is illuminated,
such an intoxicated eye as Yours the world's eye never sighted.
A sweet beauty like You, full of grace from head down to feet:
the world never saw a trace like You, and God has never created.
Every pious fanatic who saw Your ruby that is a seller of wine,
threw away the mat for prayer and the cup for wine clutched.
Your eyebrow and drunken eye intend to spill the lover's blood:
sometimes this one ambushed; sometimes that one bow stretched.
For how long like the fowl, half-killed, lying in blood and dust
from wound of Your bow's arrow, has heart's pigeon fluttered?
Every moment smoke rises from the fire that burns in my heart;
for how long shall I upon the fire like aloe-wood be scattered?
If fortune that is frightened of me became for me quite tame,
from Your mouth I'd gain wish of my heart that's frightened.
If Your eyebrow is not inclined towards Your cheek, why is it
that it, like my bent shape, is always bent when it is sighted?
If You should place Your lip on my lip I will gain immortal life,
at that moment when from the lip, my sweet life has alighted.
For how long like Your own hair will You throw back my heart
into bewilderment and confusion, my eyes having enlightened?
The thorn of separation has fallen at Your foot from confusion;
it has no rose from Your rosebed, where one with You is united.
This verse is our stock in trade and if You happen to enjoy it,
write down into a book these pearls that Hafez has created.
If You will not take my hand I'll give information to the Chief,
that by that eye You've taken hearts of poor lovers, uninvited.

483. LET GO

To heart's wish is the ambergris-scented breeze, soft and low,

that out of longing for You, early in the morning does blow.
O bird of good fortune, please be the guide along the roadway:
From longing for Courtyard's dust, my eye's water does flow.
Remembering my thin body that is drowned in heart's blood,
from the twilight district the new moon they will then know.
When from the world I depart one day from love of Your face,
a red rose instead of the green grass from my grave shall grow.
I am that one that breathes without You: how shameful it is!
Perhaps You'll pardon, if not, an excuse for sin please show.
Dawn learned from Your lovers that are in the Path of Love,
that intense longing ripped the night's shirt from top to toe.
Do not allow Your tender heart to suffer grief because of me:
at this moment Hafez cried: "In Name of God," then let go.

484. INSPIRED WISDOM

Doorstep of Masters' dwelling was sprinkled, swept like new;
wise Friend sat at the entrance, welcomed young and old too.
Wine drinkers standing at service were all prepared for action;
canopy was fixed above crown, a cloud above heavenly blue.
The brightness of cup and flagon obscured light of the moon;
cheeks waylaid young Masters and shielded the Sun from view.
From ardent moving of graceful Winebringers sweetly working,
sugar spilt, white rose wept petals and harp broke strings too.
The Bride Fortune in her chamber, despite her graceful ways,
pencilled indigo, and on her musky hair spread musk through.
The Angel of Mercy taking the cup of delight into the hand,
into the faces of Paris' and Huris', dregs, for rosewater, threw.
I gave to him my greeting and laughing my way, he said this:
"Sufferer of vine's disease, you're wine sick whatever you do:
did one ever do what you, with lack of judgment have done?
Your tent to pitch in waste, from treasure house you withdrew!
Union with awakened Fortune I'm afraid they won't give you,
for in sleepstruck Fortune's embrace, you're lying asleep too."
The heavens hold the lead of the horse of King Nasrat ud-Din;
come and see, angels have clasped hands on his stirrup's shoe.
So that perhaps shoe of his stallion the crescent moon may be;

from vault of heaven, a hundred kisses on his ground threw.
Wisdom inspired of the Hidden, for sake of honour and glory,
a hundred kisses on his majesty gives from the heavenly blue.
Come to the Winehouse Hafez so that to you I may present
a thousand ranks whose prayers are answered, for your view.

485. THE WINESELLER'S APPRENTICE

I went last night to the Winehouse, eyes with sleep's sign stained;
my patched coat was wet and prayermat was with wine stained.
The young apprentice of the Wineseller came over and called out
in a loud voice: "Wake up wayfarer, don't to sleep resign, stained.
Wash, wash yourself properly and then come to the Winehouse,
so that by you this ruined place won't fall into decline, stained.
Pass through the time of old age in purity, and don't be making
the honourable robe of old age by youthful coat's design, stained.
By longing for those mouths so sweet, how much longer will you
make the jewel of your soul by the melted ruby's shine, stained?
Be pure and clean and come out from the pit of your own nature;
unclean water doesn't enjoy purity, to filth it will incline, stained.
Those who were familiar with the path of Love were drowned
in its ocean; but by water they were never, not one sign, stained."
I answered: "O worldly soul, what is the harm if in Springtime,
the book of the rose becomes with a little pure wine, stained?"
He said: "Hafez, don't score off your friends with your subtle wit:
no, in your graciousness, all kinds of anger do combine, stained."

486. YOU WALKED

You walked, trailing Your garment that was with gold embroidered,
in envy of You a hundred with moon faces, collars of hemp ripped.
From the heat of the fire of wine, around about Your cheek sweat
like drops of dew trickling from off the leaf of the rose, dropped.
A pronunciation that's sweet and fluent and a shape tall and lovely:
a gracious face that fascinates the heart and an eye sweetly placed.

Your ruby lip that refreshes soul was born of the Water of Grace;
Your sweetly moving box tree-form, in all daintiness was cherished.
Look at that ruby that fascinates heart with that rippling laughter,
look at that way of sweetly moving and that walk that's so reposed.
That Beloved dark of eye, has departed and has now left our snare;
friends, what solace can I give to this poor heart that is frightened?
Be careful as much as you can that you don't hurt people of insight;
because the world will not keep faith, o eyes that are enlightened!
For how long will I endure reproaches because of a charming eye?
O Beloved that is so well chosen, one day let one glance be directed!
Because of the help of the Master I will utter many words of thanks,
if into my hand there should fall that fair fruit when it's matured.
You have listened to every evil that the enemy has uttered about us;
O Lord, may the evil tongue of the adversary be completely severed!
If because of Hafez Your heart that is noble is grieved and is upset,
relent and come back: of what we said and heard we have repented.

487. ALL ELSE IS ILLUSION

Early at dawn, still feeling the previous night's intoxication,
I took the cup and harp and flute without procrastination.
I gave Reason some provisions for the road by way of wine,
packed him off with City of Intoxication as destination.
The Wineseller then delivered to me a glance in such a way,
that I gained security from Time's deceitful inclination.
From Winebringer with eyebrow arched like a bow I heard:
"O you who are such a target for the arrow of reprobation,
Like the belt, you will never gain profit from that waist,
because within, you are seeing nothing but your creation.
Go, go and set up your trap to try to catch another bird,
for Pure Bird's nesting Place is beyond your calculation."
All are One, the Friend and the Minstrel and Winebringer:
all else is illusion, only water and dust, an hallucination.
Give to me the ark of wine, so that happily I may sail out
over the waves of this sea, with unseen shore for navigation.
Who will gain a reward from union with a beautiful woman
who is always busy playing at love with her self-adoration?

The stranger has vacated the house, so now drink some wine,
because O pure man, then you are alone, in this habitation.
Hafez, our existence in life is an enigma, a puzzling riddle;
and only an enchanting fable comes from its investigation.

488. DESIRE FOR THE WINEHOUSE

The candle became the moth to the bright lamp of Your face;
because of Your mole I have not even a care for my own case.
Reason, who bound all those who were mad because of love,
from perfume of Your hair's curl, joined the madman's race.
From the good news the candle gave up its life to the breeze,
when it brought a message to it from the candle of Your face.
It matters if my soul went to the wind due to Your hair's scent?
A thousand precious souls are ransom for the Beloved's grace.
Who ever saw the grain that was better than Your dark mole,
placed on the fire of Your face's lovely cheek's radiant place?
I fell off my feet last night I was so frightened from jealousy,
when I saw the hand of my Idol in a stranger's hands' embrace.
What plans we have devised and all of them without a profit!
On the Beloved all our devices became merely a laughing case.
I have sworn an oath by the round form of the Beloved's lip,
that except for tale of the cup my tongue won't take a trace.
Do not tell the tale of the college and cloister, for once again
desire for the Winehouse fell into Hafez's head's empty space.

489. THE LONGING FOR YOUR FACE

From that ruby my heart desires, comes constant delight;
praise be to God that my desire will come to me alright.
O arrogant fortune, hold the Beloved close to Your breast:
now drink the cup of gold; now ruby, heart's delight, bite.
They repeat tales about us, that we are always intoxicated,
those ignorant old men and those priests lost in the night.

We have done repentance due to the preaching of the pious,
and for what the devotee does, pardon from God we invite.
O soul, how can I explain to you all about this separation?
Eye with a hundred tears, a soul and a hundred sighs unite.
May the infidel not see the grief that the cypress has seen,
because of Your form and the moon from Your face's light.
There's nothing that pleases more than a lover's patience:
from God ask only for patience; patience ask for outright!
Patched garment is the same as Christian cord of the path;
Sufi, the use of this method, throw far away out of sight.
My time was happy for awhile because of the Beloved's face;
due to union with Beloved, a hundred times: "God is right."
I will not turn my face away from the path of Your service,
from the dust of Your door I'll never raise my head upright.
The longing for Your face took from the memory of Hafez,
the lesson of the morning and also the prayer of the night.

490. PATIENCE IS BITTER

If in the pathway of that Moon the sword should rain,
our neck there we would lay, if this God would ordain.
The regulation of piety we've also fully comprehended;
but with our luck gone astray where's remedy for pain?
We seldom recognize the priest and seldom the preacher:
either give us the cup of wine or of talk, silent remain.
I was drunken conspirator and lover and then repenter;
I ask for pardon from God, O God pardon once again!
Reflection from the sun of Your face didn't fall on us:
O Mirror Face, from Your hard heart, what great pain.
Bitter is this patience and so fleeting is this life of mine,
how long will I experience this, how long will I remain?
Hafez wouldn't have been with a broken heart like this,
if to advice of a friend he had listened with his brain.
Hafez, why do you complain if it is Union you desire?
in season and out, grief's cup of blood you must drain.

491. FEASTING TIME

It's feasting time and season of the rose: Winebringer, wine bring!
Who has seen the cup without wine in the rose-season, in Spring!
My heart is sore and sick because of this austerity and this piety:
Winebringer, give some wine so that my heart may be expanding.
The Sufi gave some advice about the longing of lovers yesterday;
today I saw him drunk; piety to the wind he did quickly fling.
The one or two days of the rose remaining, know how to enjoy;
if you are lover, with smooth-faced Winebringers, joy be seeking.
O companions, the rose is going, why are you sitting carelessly,
without Beloved and cup of wine and harp and sound of string?
You know how happy is appearance of morning cup in the circle,
when the reflection of Winebringer's cheek in the cup is falling.
At the banquet of the prince when the minstrel makes the music,
if it's possible, of the sweet elegance of Hafez's verse he will sing.

492. MY FATE

Since the Winehouse is the fate that God to me gave;
fanatic, why in me see the sin that seems so grave?
Upon one, given winecup in Eternity beyond Time,
this old sin at the Resurrection, will they engrave?
Say to the double-faced Sufi, the cloaked hypocrite,
"Your hands are too long for short sleeves to save:
you wear that pious garment because of hypocrisy,
to deceive slaves of God from the Path you crave."
I'm slave of drunkards' spirit, headless and footless,
who see both worlds as not worth one straw's wave.
Since I have gained my desire from the Winehouse,
I'm black-hearted in the college and church's nave.
Hafez, go! Don't beg before every beggar's doorway;
your own desire, only "God's Will," will surely save.

493. WHAT IS THIS?

All of a sudden, Your veil up You have thrown:

what is this?
Out from the house intoxicated You have flown:
what is this?
In breeze's power is Your hair, under spy's orders is Your ear:
in this way, to all contentment You have shown:
what is this?
You're Monarch of beauties and have become the beggars' gift:
are You sure this state's worth You have known?
What is this?
Did You not recently give into my hand the tip of Your hair?
And then me, from off my feet You have thrown:
what is this?
Each one is intensely involved in throwing love's dice: with us
in the end the dice crookedly You have thrown:
what is this?
Hafez, when Beloved came to stay in your heart full of worries,
door to strangers to leave, you haven't shown?
What is this?

494. THAT IS BETTER

Union with Beloved, than life that could last forever,
is better;
O Lord, give to me only that, because that, I do swear
is better.
You struck me with the sword and I haven't told it to anybody:
for the mystery of Beloved with enemy not to share,
is better.
O heart, stay forever as the beggar in the street of the Beloved,
for as the wise saying goes: "Fortune's eternal care,
is better."
O pious one, please don't keep inviting me to. travel to Paradise:
the apple of Beloved's chin, than all the gardens there,
is better.
If one were to die, with the brand of slavery, at that threshold,
that, I swear, above the crowns of the world to wear,

is better.

That rose that has been crushed under the foot of our cypress,
if its dust to crimson arghavan's blood one did compare:
is better.

In the Name of God, go and make inquiries of my Physician,
and ask: "This one, helpless, when and also where,
is better?"

Young man, don't turn your face away from an old man's advice:
old man's wisdom than fortune of one young and fair,
is better.

One night the Beloved said: "Than the precious pearl of my ear,
no eye has seen a jewel that in the world, anywhere,
is better."

The speech that comes from the mouth of the Beloved is a jewel;
but, all that which is spoken by Hafez, that is so rare:
is better.

495. WHY?

Heart, why to Beloved's street, your way
you don't make?
Tools of union you have, yet work's assay
you don't make.

The mallet of desire is in hand yet the ball you don't strike;
the falcon such as this is in hand, but prey
you don't make.

This blood that still makes great waves inside your heart,
why is it to colour fair face, please say,
you don't make?

Creation's breath doesn't become musky, for unlike wind,
the dust of the Beloved's street your way
you don't make.

I'm afraid that from this world the rose you shall not win,
for a move to bear thorns of rosebed gay,
you don't make.

Into the dust you throw cup that is full of wine and joy;
of tomorrow's drought, thoughts of today

you don't make.

In sleeve of your soul are a hundred muskpods; sacrifice of
them for Beloved's curls, it's true to say,
you don't make.

Go Hafez! How is it that your service at Friend's court,
while the whole world does homage pay;
you don't make?

496. DON'T COMPLAIN

Heart, the moment when intoxicated with rose-coloured wine
you are, hundred times richer than Karun, though without goldmine,
you are.

In the stage where they appoint the seat of honour to the poor
beggar, there above all in rank and also in importance, I would define
you are.

In path to the dwelling of Layla, on which there are many dangers,
first step's first condition is that of mad Majnun's design…
you are.

I have shown to you the centre of love: hey, do not make a mistake!
If you do, then when you look, outside circle of Love's line
you are.

The caravan has gone and you are asleep and in front the desert lies;
how do you go and what do, and who asking its way's sign
you are?

Drink a cup of the wine and be throwing some of it at the heavens;
how long having a liver of blood because time does malign,
you are?

If you look for crown of kingship, then show essence of your nature:
if it is true that of the descent of Jamshid and Firidun's line
you are.

Hafez, don't complain of being poor, for if this is your gift of poetry,
then no one could be happy if like this, showing sorrow's sign
you are.

497. THE GREAT SULTAN

Praise be given to God for the justice of the great Sultan:
the Ilkhanide, Ahmad the son of Shaikh Uvays bin Hasan.
It's good if you call that one the soul of the whole world:
Shahinshah descended from Shah, Khan and son of Khan.
Those who have and haven't seen you know your fortune;
O you, worthy of God's Grace, are such an excellent man!
If the moon rises without you they will break it into two:
the fortune of Ahmad and also the miracle of a Godman.
Your fortune's splendour takes heart from king and beggar;
far be the evil eye, for you are soul and the loved human.
Curl locks on the forehead like the Turks: in your fortune
in the bounty of a Khakan and energy of a Ghengiz Khan.
Although we are far away we drink goblet to your health,
for distance doesn't exist in the spiritual journey's span.
From the clay of my Persia no rosebud of ease blossomed;
excellent is Baghad's Tigris: wine is sweeter than in Iran.
To the lover's head that isn't the dust of Beloved's door,
when does peace come: his head's like that of a madman?
O morning breeze, please bring the dust of Beloved's path,
so that to make his heart's eye be clear with it, Hafez can.

498. A PLEA AND AN OMEN

King of all the beloveds of the world, help my grief my loneliness;
without You my heart reaches my soul, come and ease this distress.
Desires and distances have caused me to be kept far away from You;
so much that from my hand strength to be patient is more than less.
Pain for You is my remedy upon the couch of disappointed desires;
Your memory is my closest friend in the corner of all this loneliness.
We are the central point of the compass in the circle of our destiny:
whatever You wish is grace and law is whatever You may express.
In the world of the drunken lover is no thought or opinion of self
in this religion, pride and being self-opinionated is unfaithfulness.
O my Lord, to whom can it be presentable to mention this subtlety:
though present in everything, Beloved's face is veiled nevertheless.
Last night I spoke, complaining to morning breeze about Your hair:

the breeze said: "It's a mistake, give up this thought, this madness:
  hundred morning breezes keep dancing where this chain is found:
heart, it is your companion if wind's length you don't try to guess."
Winebringer, without Your face the rose of the garden has no colour;
  move Your box tree shape so that You fill garden with gracefulness.
The rose of the garden of the world won't remain this fresh forever:
  come and help the poor weak ones at the time of such powerfulness.
Because of this circle of blue I have a bleeding heart; give the wine,
  so that in the goblet of glass I may be solving all this difficult mess.
Hafez, separation's night has gone, morning's fragrance has come:
  mad lover of madness, happy fortunate omen be in your happiness!

499. THE RANSOM

Breeze came bringing the fragrance of Hima and increased my desire;
  to Su-aad, the Beloved, who will convey my greeting, this I inquire.
To hear the message of the Friend is happiness and health and peace;
  for dust of Friend's door, my life to be the ransom you may require.
Come to the exile any evening and witness the tears from our eyes,
like the pure red wine that in the glass of Damascus one does admire.
If I inclined towards Paradise and did not fulfil the promise I made,
  may sleep never be pleasant and where I sleep, peace never acquire.
If the bird of happiness should sing in praise of the Dweller of Arak,
  the moaning of my pigeon from those gardens would then conspire.
The day of separation from the Beloved will soon come to an end;
  removing of the tents from the hills of Hima I can almost admire.
O that time will be happy when You enter safely and to You I say:
"What a blessed arrival, where You have arrived is all You require."
  I am hopeful that because of good fortune I will quickly see You:
You joyfully giving out orders, and I being the slave that You desire.
Although I have nothing worth anything in the company of kings,
please accept me as a slave for any reason that clarity may inspire.
I have become as slender as the new moon from being far from You,
although Your face like the moon, I have never been able to admire.
Hafez, your shining verse is like a string of pearls from good water,
for it surpasses verse of Nizami in the place where grace does attire.

500. COME OUT

O heart, if from pit of chin's hollow
    you come out,
everywhere you go, quickly in sorrow
    you come out.
Possibly the sky won't help you with a little water,
    if thirsting, from life's fountain's flow,
    you come out.
Be aware, because if you listen to lust's temptations,
    like Adam, from Paradise's meadow,
    you come out.
Like the breeze I send You such sweet blessings that
    from bud, like a rose joyfully aglow,
    You come out.
In the night of distance from You, soul is on brink;
    it's the time, that like moon on show,
    You come out.
On Your door's dust I shed a hundred rivers of tears,
    maybe like cypress, moving so slow,
    You come out.
Heart, in house of blame and grief why do you stay?
    By Monarch's fortune, it's time you go:
    you come out.
Hafez, don't grieve; that moon Joseph will come back;
    and again from that room of sorrow,
    you come out.

501. SUCH WAS FATE

If letter to us had been written by that musky fragrant long hair,
the world, existence's page, wouldn't have folded then and there.
Although separation will not bring about all of the fruit of union,
I wish to God the world's Gardener hadn't sown this seed to bear.
Do not allow it to happen, that Your pen's reed should be split!
It had no love far from You, or it would have told me, with care.

If the creation's Architect hadn't drawn Your image upon love,
He wouldn't have mixed love's atoms with Adam's clay, I swear!
Fanatic, quickly tell me your tale, for I have the cash in my hand:
Friend that is like an Angel and a house like Paradise to compare!
Do not sell for the garden of Iram and for the power of Shudad,
a bottle of wine and a field's borderline and a lip sweet and rare.
To the sky, have my ignorance and your wisdom any difference?
To the blind, between beauty and ugliness, a difference is there?
I'm not the only one to make Idol's house the Kaaba of my heart:
at every step taken, there are churches and cloisters everywhere.
One can never make oneself happy in the hotel where love waits:
if a golden pillow is there, sleep with a brick I'm happy to share.
O wise heart, for how long will you be caring for a selfish world?
It is such a pity that such beauty loves such ugliness as is there.
The stain that is upon the patched coat is the ruin of the world;
where's wayfarer with whole heart? One pure of nature is where?
Why did Hafez let that tip of Your hair fall away from his hand?
Such was fate: what would he do if his hand had still stayed there?

502. YOUR OWN FAULT

You, lovers separated from You, You think it's right
to keep:
the lovers away from Your embrace and out of sight
to keep.
Give a little help with a little water to the desert's thirsty one,
due to this hopeful reason: God's Way is Your delight
to keep.
O Soul, You have taken my heart and I've now forgiven You:
keep it more safely than me, who You wouldn't fight
to keep.
We will endure the fact that all the others are sharing our cup,
if You think that this is right, then for You it's a right
to keep.
Fly, in presence of the Simurgh is not the place for you to be;
you will not keep your position and cause us a plight

to keep.

It's because of your own fault that you are outside this door;
who are you complaining to and what is this blight,
to keep?
Hafez, others look for shelter and advancement by serving kings;
you, having done no work, expect a gift that is bright,
to keep?

503. PRIDE

O you, you who are always so full of pride,
you will be excused if love for you is denied.
Don't spend time near to those mad with love,
for you are known to take wisdom as a guide.
Intoxication of love is not in your head: go;
grape's wine, your drunkenness has supplied.
The yellow face and sighs strained with grief
are the signs of sickness that lovers can't hide.
The garden of Paradise is without any beauty,
without lip of the Huri and the wine purified.
It is necessary that you try to love that Moon,
though you, like sun, are known far and wide.
Hafez, give up caring for your name and fame;
search for winecup, for you are winesick inside.

504. THE GUARDIAN

O you, in the street of the Winehouse your dwelling
you have;
you are your time's Jamshid, if hand the cup holding,
you have.
You who spend night and day with the Beloved's face and hair,
may opportunity for happiness, morning and evening,

you have.
You who choose seclusion, united with happiness of the heart,
understand this moment as worthwhile, when longing
you have.
O breeze, those on fire with love are waiting in your pathway,
expecting that news from Beloved Who was travelling,
you have.
Although You are not constant when it is time to be faithful,
I'm thankful that violence's consistency continuing,
You have.

Your fresh mole is the pleasing seed of the joy of all pleasure,
but on border of its field, what a means of trapping
You have!
I sense the soul's fragrance from the laughing lip of the goblet;
kind sir, inhale it, if for it a good sense of smelling
you have.
Will it be a wonder today if a stranger seeks from You a name?
For the One Who in the city a Great Name is having,
You have.
The sky has become generous since it stopped being so violent;
O soul, yours is such a way: a movement overpowering
you have.
Many the prayer of the dawn will be the guardian of your soul,
because like Hafez, a slave that during night is rising,
you have.

505. CROWN OF THE SUN

O you: over the moon the veil of the musky flowing hair
you throw;
you are kind because some shade on the sun's bright glare
you throw.
What will happen to us from your cheek's colour shining like water,
now that your own magical image upon the water there,

you throw?

You have taken the ball of beauty from the world's beauties: be
happy! Look for Kay Khusrau's cup, for Afrasiyab down forever
you throw.

You buried the treasure of your love in our heart that was desolate;
shadow of your mercy on this treasure, ruined, in despair,
you throw.

Every one played love's game differently with the candle of your face:
from the centre of this, moth into fear beyond compare
, you throw.

Though I'm ruined because of drunkenness don't reject my devotion:
because with hope of a reward, me into this same affair
you throw.

When in the glorious place of splendour you lift our veil for a glance,
from shame the Huri and Pari, back behind veil from despair
you throw.

You stop those awake from sleeping, and then by concocting an
image, suspicion on the hordes of sleepers about a night prowler,
you throw.

From longing for the drunken narcissus and ruby that worships wine,
Hafez who is sitting in a quiet seclusion, into wine's snare
you throw.

To capture the hearts you throw that chain of your hair on his neck
like the noose of Khusrau: of necks, you being the master:
you throw!

O you, Nasrat ud-Din Shah Yahya, you: the land of all the enemies
into water, from foam of your sword flashing fire's flare,
you throw!

O you, glorious ruler, proud like Darius, you: the crown of the sun
from the height of the mighty in the dust of the verandah
you throw.

Drink wine from cup that reveals the world, for on Jamshid's throne,
from face of Beloved Who is desired, down the veil you tear,
you throw.

Safe shelter from your sword glistening like water, which you made
lions thirsty for, and with which, those heroes into water
you throw!

O You, in Whose radiant face the manifestations of Royalty shine,
and in Whose thought are concealed philosophies that are Divine,
in the country of the people of Faith, God bless Your pen's reed:
from drop of its ink, hundred streams from Water of Life combine.
Splendours of the seal of the Great Name do not shine on Satan,
realm and seal-ring are Yours, order what You wish with a sign.
Whoever may show any doubts at all about authority of Solomon,
at the intelligence of such a one, laughter of bird and of fish align.
Although sometimes the hawk puts cap of sovereignty on his head,
the usage of Sovereignty is only known to the Highest Bird's line.
Your sword to which the sky from its generosity gives great lustre,
without the help of an army, alone, would make the world resign.
Your pen's reed writes an amulet for friend: "More and more life,"
and for the enemy it writes a spell: "Life to decline and decline."
O You, Whose Being's elements are created from honour's alchemy;
and You, Whose fortune's completely safe from any ruinous design.
The ruby with the red face becomes the colour of withered grass,
if the bright flash of Your sword should fall on quarry and mine.
O King, hear the slave's complaint that is witnessed by the Judge:
it has been much more than a lifetime since my cup had any wine!
I know that Your heart will pity those poor lovers awake all night,
if from breeze of the morning You ask about that condition of mine.
Winebringer, bring a little water from fountain of the Winehouse,
so we may wash our monastery's patchcoats, full of pride's design.
Ever since the way of true Sovereignty was in the family of Adam,
none like You has known this subtle Art's essence in a way so fine.
You've such an angelic nature that the sky has given up violence:
since You are world's shelter, oppression's left this world of mine.
Since lightning flashed upon the sin of Adam, the Height of Purity,
how can we now claim to be sinless, does it really fit into our line?
O Refuge of created beings, Giver of all gifts that are worthwhile!
Show me Your generosity, because towards me calamities incline.
Hafez, since the King has mentioned your name from time to time,
don't show grief because of fate, ask for pardon and to King resign.

507. TALE OF GRIEF

O You, Beloved, the tale of Paradise is a story about Your street,
the description of Huris' beauty is a sign of Your face to repeat.
The breath of Jesus is only one small laugh from Your ruby lip,
the Water of Life is only one splash from Your mouth so sweet.
Every fragment of my heart has been joined to a story of grief,
each line of Your qualities is joined to a verse of Mercy replete.
If You had not freely given Your perfume in trust to the rose,
how would it be a holder of incense where angelic souls meet?
If the bright image of Your face should be appearing in the fire,
come O Winebringer, for then I won't complain of hell's heat.
The smell from my roasted heart filled the whole of creation,
this great burning of my heart deep into heart of all does eat.
O heart that's full of stupid knowledge, your life has passed by:
you had a hundred means of winning, but gained only defeat.
Is it known what was Hafez's purpose in telling this tale of grief?
It was to gain your attention and from King a favour to entreat.

508. PLEDGED FOR WINE

That I've pledged for wine this patchcoat of mine,
is best;
that this meaningless book drowns in pure wine,
is best.
How I have wasted my life: the more that I think about it,
in the Winehouse's corner to fall drunk and recline,
is best.
Since the considering of advice the poor do not consider,
heart full of fire and full of water that eye of mine,
is best.
I will not tell the people the pious fanatic's condition:
this condition, for the harp and the lute to define,
is best.
Since the course of the sky is a way without head or tail,
in head desire for Winebringer, in hand the wine,

is best.

I won't take my heart from an owner of hearts like You:

if I do suffer torment, to do so in Your hair is fine,

is best.

Hafez, since you have become old, leave the Winehouse;

drunkenness and longing, to Youth to consign,

is best.

509. NOT THE RIGHT THING TO DO

When with us You make a killing, there's no mercy that You know;

You burn up all capital and all interest, and no humanity You show.

The ones full of grief from calamity have a deadly poison to drink;

be careful that You, the danger of upsetting this tribe do not sow.

As it's possible to take away our grief with the corner of Your eye,

it is not the right thing to do, if our remedy You do not let flow.

Since out of hope for You our eye is the ocean, why then is it that

on the ocean's shore, for some recreation, passing by You don't go?

All stories of violence they've concocted about Your gentle nature

are words of self-interest, for such actions from You do not grow.

O you pious fanatic, if our Beloved should show to you such glory,

from God except for wine and Beloved, desire you wouldn't know.

Hafez, pray in adoration to Beloved's eyebrow, archway of prayer;

except from the depth of sincerity, the prayer from you can't flow.

510. THE SCHOOL OF TRUTH

O ignorant one, try, so that a Master, open-eyed,

you'll be.

As long as you're not traveller, how is it Guide

you'll be?

In the School of Truth, at the feet of the Master of Love,

listen, O son, try; one day Father true and tried

you'll be.
Eating and sleeping have kept you from Love's threshold;
arriving at Love, when food and sleep is denied,
you'll be.
If on your heart and soul the Light of God's Love shows,
by God I swear, brighter than the sun magnified
you'll be.
With hands wash copper of existence like men on the Path,
and gain Love's Transmutation: gold, alchemized
you'll be.
If a moment plunged in God's sea you be, don't think that
having a hair wet with water seven seas wide,
you'll be.
If the face of God is the only thing that is in your sight,
then no doubts remain, for with Vision clarified
you'll be.
Even if foundation of your existence is blown to the wind,
do not think that in your heart, shaken inside,
you'll be.
Hafez, if it is Union that you desire, then it is necessary
that the dust at the door of Wise Perfect Guide,
you'll be.

511. DON'T TELL THE ENEMY

Don't tell to the enemy the secrets of love and of intoxication,
so without knowledge he'll die through suffering self adoration.
Although being weak and powerless, be pleasant like the breeze,
for in this Path better than body's health is this incapacitation.
How is it possible for one to be veiled, sober in the safe corner,
when of wine's mysteries Your narcissus gives me information?
Be the lover; if this you don't do, one day world's work will end,
and your purpose you'll not know from workshop of Creation.
At the threshold of the Beloved beware of allurements of heaven,
so that you won't fall from highest to the dust of degradation.
Though life is lessened by the thorn, the rose asks for its pardon;
the bitterness of wine is small beside the delight of intoxication.

Sufi, drink the cup; in preparation make the great flagon Hafez!
O you, short of sleeve, how long your long-handed occupation?

512. NOT FOR A MOMENT

O heart, do not for a moment be without love and drunkenness;
go, at the time when escaping into Existence from nothingness.
If you see a wearer of the patchcoat, go and do your own work;
every place turned to in prayer is better than self righteousness.
In the law of the religion of Love it's unfaithful to be immature;
the way of being drunken lover is that of maturity and alertness.
As long as you see your own wisdom, Divine Wisdom isn't yours;
I'll say this: "So you may be free, give up all self centredness."
All of these problems that have arisen I'd foreseen on that day,
when you would not sit with us for awhile out of perverseness.
O my Monarch, for the sake of God, Your hair has destroyed us;
how long will such a blackness practise such long-handedness?
In the Masters' circle last night, how well that beauty told me:
"If you don't worship idols, with pagans what's your business?"
O soul, love will be consigning you to the power of that flood:
you think like lightning you will escape flood's powerfulness?
Hafez looked away from the Path until he saw Your lovely hair;
he was full of his greatness, then became the dust of lowliness.

513. TAKING AND GIVING

Listen to my advice so yourself free from grief's care
you make:
"You'll drink blood, if search for more than daily fare
you make."
In the end you'll become merely the clay for the maker of pots;
think now of your jug, so that it full of wine's snare

you make.

If you happen to be one of those who is always desiring Paradise,
O born of Paradise, how long, joy from earthly pleasure
you make?

It's not possible to boast of reclining on the cushion of the great,
unless fully prepared, the load that greatness does wear,
you make.

How can your heart be receiving the inscription of Divine Grace,
unless of selfish impressions, the page pure and clear
you make?

Many rewards are Yours, O Monarch of those so sweet of mouth,
if a glance to Your poor Farhad, heart full of despair,
You make.

Hafez, if you give everything you do back to the Merciful One,
the Grace God has given, to be full of great pleasure
you make.

O breeze of the East, work in the service of Master Jallal ud-Din;
until with scent of lily and rose, full the world's air
you make.

514. GENEROSITY

If to voice of nightingale and dove, wine you won't be drinking,
how can I be curing you, because the last remedy is in burning.
When the rose lifts off the veil and the bird shouts: "You, You,"
don't put cup away from your hand, why: "No, no," be crying?
While the Water of Life is in your hand don't be dying of thirst;
do not die because: "From water comes all things that are living."
Stock up on riches from colours and perfumes of the Spring;
for robbers of the road, Autumn and Winter, are soon pursuing.
Time doesn't give a single thing that it does not take back again:
don't look for kindness from meanness, what it gives is nothing.
How can the pomp of royalty and its power have real stability?
Of throne of Jamshid and crown of Kay only a tale is remaining.
"To hoard an inherited treasure is the same as being an infidel;"
this, with drum and pipe, Minstrel and Winebringer are advising.
They engraved on the hail of the Garden of the Place of Refuge:

"He who bought the world's favours, will gain a terrible grieving."
Generosity didn't remain. I'll stop this talking: where is the wine?
To memory of the soul and generosity of Hatim Tai, be giving!
Fragrance of God won't be perceived by the miser: come, Hafez,
take cup and practise generosity, to be your surety I'm willing.

515. TRUE VALUE

For awhile, with a tranquil heart on Your face like a moon to gaze,
is better than wearing a king's crown and a life of honourable days.
By God I swear, that I am envious of my eye being on Your cheek:
on such a One's tender face, like this it's really disastrous to gaze.
My heart has gone and I don't know what has become of the exile,
for life has departed and from no place no news comes and stays.
My breath has come to an end and my gaze hasn't fully seen You;
except for this I do not have a desire remaining, no wish in me lays.
O breeze, do not disturb the tip of the hair of that One like a Pari,
thread of a hair of Whom, Hafez a thousand lives as ransom pays.

516. YOUR BEAUTY AND MY LOVE

Your great beauty took my love with it… to reach perfection:
be happy, for this united love and beauty has no interception.
I imagine that an image that is more beautiful than this form
could never appear; not in all power of heart's imagination.
When I'm with You for a moment, a year is only a short day;
the blink of an eye without You is a year by my calculation.
We would have accomplished delight for the whole of our life,
if only one day of life with You was given up to Unification.
Beloved, how may I see the image of Your face while asleep?
For when I am not asleep… my eye sees only my imagination.
Give some pity to my heart, because from loving Your face,
my body became thin like crescent moon, from exhaustion.
O Hafez, don't complain, if it's Union with Beloved you want,
you'll have to bear load greater than this through separation.

517. DRUNK WITH HAPPINESS

In the old Pahlavi language from a branch of the cypress,
nightingale last night, a lesson of spirituality did express:
"Come, because the rose has displayed the fire of Moses,
from the bush you can learn the subtlety of the Oneness."
Birds of the garden are making melodies and telling jokes:
so Master may drink wine, *ghazals* in Pahlavi they address.
Sleeping peacefully on mat of beggary makes a happy time;
the kingly crown is not fit to sit on such a mat's happiness.
  Jamshid took nothing from the world except for the cup:
  do not tie your hearts to the world, don't try to possess.
I am equally dervish and beggar, yet I don't value as equal,
the old ragged cap and hundred kingly crowns that impress.
  How well the enduring peasant spoke to his son, saying:
  "Eye's light, except what you sow, reaping hasn't success."
  Your eye darkened the house of man because of a glance;
  Yours isn't winesick, because You're drunk with happiness.
  Hear this wonderful tale of fortune turned upside down:
  the Beloved killed us with Jesus' life giving breath's caress.
  Drink to the verse of the slave and don't strain your heart:
  behind you will be dust on what this world does possess.
Perhaps Winebringer gave to Hafez more than was his share,
because tassel of the Master's turban is a disorderly mess.

518. THE RIGHT OF FRIENDSHIP

Come, given to us for far too long, this spite
you have;
too long been ignoring old friendship's right,
you have.
Listen to my pen's advice, for this pearl is worth more
than stored gems and jewels that shining bright

you have.

To the cry of the poor drinkers sick for the wine, come:
if, before God, any of the wine of last night
you have.

But how can you show your face to the lovers of wine,
if the mirror of sun and the moon's high light
you have?

O learned one, be sensible, don't speak out against love,
unless with the love of God some spiteful fight
you have.

Haven't you, inside, any fear at all of my burning sigh?
You know a woolen coat that's easy to light,
you have.

Hafez, I've never seen verse more beautiful than yours,
which, by the *Koran,* in your heart held tight,
you have.

519. THE METHOD

I have imagined the eyebrow on One moon of form in my eye;
image of One with fresh down, pictured in this place have I.
My hope is that the method which my love has now patented,
will reach from the bow of that eyebrow, to You to certify.
My head left my hands and my eye burned with expectation:
the Adorner of the banquet is the desire of my head and eye.
My heart is worried and weary; I'll set fire to the patchcoat:
come and see, it will be a wonderful sight, this I won't deny.
In the place where lovely ones strike with sword of the glance,
is it a wonder if the head which has fallen, at a foot does lie?
Since because of Your face I now have moon in my bedroom,
do I have any need for the twinkling of the stars in the sky?
I, the dervish, have given the rein of my heart to that One Who
doesn't need crown or throne, for that One is Highest of High.
What does separation or union matter? Seek the Friend's Will:
from that Friend, except for Friend, any wish is a selfish lie.
On the eventful day, you make our coffin out of the cypress,

for we will be departing with the mark of One Who is High.
Because of rapture, fishes would bring up pearls to scatter
if Hafez's boat should reach to the sea, on that you can rely.

520. WOULD HAVE BEEN

By Your soul I swear: if giving my life in my power
would have been,
for certain, it then as Your slave's humblest offer
would have been.
And if my heart had not been bound at all to Your hair by its base,
where then in this dark heap of dust my comforter
would have been?
I wish to God that You had entered by my door like a flash of light,
so that then upon my two eyes Your latest order
would have been.
Like the sun of the sky, the perfect climate is Your beautiful face:
if only in Your heart, You just a little kinder
would have been!
Even in sleep I don't see You, so what hope then is there for Union?
Since this was not so, we wished to God the other
would have been.
The cypress would have confessed to being the slave of Your form,
if the ten tongues of the proud lily its confessor
would have been.
When would a cry of Hafez have fallen out from behind the screen,
if as companion of birds, he not morning's singer
would have been?

521. I WISH TO GOD

If the Beloved's heart had been kind, everything fine
would have been;
if Beloved had been kind, our mind not ready to resign
would have been.
If both Time and Fortune had cherished me and then honoured me,
the dust of Your threshold, honour's throne of mine

would have been.

I would have asked: "What price is breeze from the Friend's hair?"
If a thousand lives given for every tip of hair's twine
would have been.

O Lord, how would that order for our heart to be happy be lessened,
if from malice of Time, it covered by safety's sign
would have been?

If the image of You had not been the barrier of the water of the eyes,
a thousand fountains flowing in every corner of mine
would have been.

I wish to God someone had given to me directions to Your street,
then I, free of garden and rosegarden's illusory design
would have been.

I wish to God that You had come out from the veil like the teardrop,
so that on my two eyes Your latest command's sign
would have been.

If the circle of love had not closed off the way of the Path like this,
heartbroken Hafez, not like point inside circle's line
would have been.

522. DROWNING

Perhaps you have never sat by a pool's edge, full of deep longing;
   or you would know that your problems come from self-loving.
I now call upon you by God, Who has chosen you for His slave,
   that none other than this ancient slave, you should be choosing.
From now on we'll be united to beggary; because in love's stage,
there's no helpful remedy for wayfarer, except helplessly begging.
Respect and humility made You Monarch of those moon of face;
You are worthy of a hundred such as this: on You be all blessing!
If in safety I take the pledge of love, then there is nothing to fear;
   it's easy to be without a heart, no faith is difficult to be bearing.
If I become impatient with tyranny of the enemy, what can I do?
For a lover who is helpless the remedy is to be patiently waiting.
From Your slave who is sincere listen to some impartial words,
O You, Who are the goal and vision of ones who Truth are seeing.
One such as You, Who is tender and has a pure heart and nature,

it is best that with those that are evil You should not be sitting.
It's a pity for me that You should walk into view in the meadow:
You're fresher than wild white rose, lovelier than red rose blooming.
Rose, it's wonderful that with Your grace You still sit with thorn;
it appears that You understand that by this, someone is gaining.
A morning breeze arose from rosegarden out of longing for You:
You're like lovely scented red rose, scent of white rose wafting.
From the left and the right you may see the trickle of my tears,
if you're sitting for a moment in the place from which I'm looking.
Candle of Chigil, You have this delicacy that fascinates the heart;
You are worthy of gracing where great Jalal ud-Din is feasting.
The torrent of streaming tears takes patience from heart of Hafez;
O pupil of my eye, come quickly and help me, for I am drowning.

523. THE DUST OF CONTENTMENT

Happily, the heavens have helped you on the day of judgment:
how may you give thanks, what to bring in acknowledgment?
In that street of Love they do not value the rank of kingship;
confess to service, claim the servant's right to be an attendant.
Say to that one, who when falling, God grasped by the hand:
"For you, despair of one who was falling was the instrument."
Winebringer, come by my door with the reward for news of joy,
so that You will make grief leave my heart for even a moment.
In the path of rank and lordship there is many a great danger,
it's best that light of burden, passing by this height you went.
The sultan thinks of the army and desires treasure and crown,
the dervish has a peaceful heart and a corner of contentment.
The success of desire is to the limits of thought and of spirit;
the king may be generous but Grace of God is more pertinent.
If I am allowed I will utter only one word that is a Sufi word,
light of the eye: "Peace," is better than war and being violent.
Hafez, from cheek don't wash dust of contentment and poverty,
for this dust is better than alchemy's most important ingredient.

524. I WOULD NOT EXCHANGE THIS

Two understanding friends, two gallons of vintage wine,
    some leisure and a book, in a field's corner to recline:
I would not exchange this, for this and the next world,
    though multitudes pursue me and condemn and malign.
Whoever sold contentment's riches for world's treasures,
    did Joseph of Egypt, for a paltry priced bill of sale sign.
Come, for this workshop of the world becomes no less
    by your devout austerity, or by my drinking of the wine.
On the Fateful Day, with wine we need to tell our grief
    for at such a time as this there is no one who is benign.
Sit in a corner with a happy heart, and bear witness that
    no mind to think of so strange a disaster does incline.
I keep seeing my fair One in the hand of the unworthy:
    this is how the heavens pay for the service that is mine.
O my heart, try to be patient; for God will never allow
    a seal-ring so priceless, on an evil one's hand to shine.
From the fierce winds of change it is impossible to see
    that in this field the red and wild white rose did recline.
From the hot storm that has blasted across garden's edge,
    it is odd rose's colour and jasmine's scent don't decline.
In this calamity Hafez, the time became sick with anger;
    where's physician's advice, Brahmin's wisdom to define?

525. PERISH THE THOUGHT

In all the corridors of Winesellers there is none like me, distraught;
in one place patchcoat's pawned for wine, to another book is brought.
    There is a great deal of dust upon the heart that is a royal mirror;
from God I ask for friendship of One, pure and bright of thought.
    I've made streams run from my eye to my garment, so that perhaps
in my breast, they may plant the One straight of form I have sought.

Bring to me the cup, the boat; for without the face of the Beloved,
from heart's grief each corner of my eyes a great ocean has caught.
I have become repentant due to the hand of a beauty selling wine;
I will not drink wine unless by One Who is beautiful, it is brought.
Perhaps the candle's tongue will tell the mystery of this subtlety;
if not, then the need for the moth to hear speech is really naught.
To me the lover, do not talk about anything except the Beloved;
except for the Beloved and the cup of wine, what I need is naught.
If the narcissus boasted about the way of its eye, then don't grieve:
one who is blind, by the one who has sight, has never been sought.
How pleasant it was to me when in the morning this saying from
a Christian, the drum and reed at Winehouse, to my ears brought:
"If Hafez represents the type that being a good faithful Muslim is,
it's a pity if after today there is a tomorrow: perish the thought!"

526. IF YOU WOULD COME

While sleeping last night I saw the full moon's ascension
would come;
from its face's reflection, to an end the night of separation
would come.
So what is the explanation of the arrival of the much-travelled Friend?
I hoped that the Friend's glorious gift and beautification,
would come.
Winebringer, such a blessed Omen and One so worthy of mention,
often to my door with the flagon and cup for circulation,
would come.
It would have been good if in sleep that One had seen the homeland,
and then as our Guide, to pass on to us the recollection,
would come.
Whoever has made You to be the Guide on the road to the stony heart;
I wish that his foot to a large stone, making a connection,
would come.
If through power and gold to our hand had come that gift of Eternity,
then it's true that Khizer's Water as Alexander's portion
would come.

I would have scattered all my soul for that soother of the heart, if only
that One like pure Soul, into my heart to give benediction
would come.
May the time be remembered when to me from the roof and from door,
Beloved's message and Heartstealer's note of explanation
would come.
Where would Your watcher have obtained such a power to do tyranny,
if one night to the Ruler's doorway a victim in expectation
would come?
How do the immature ones of the Path understand the longing of love?
Seek, then One with heart of ocean and Chief's occupation
would come.
If someone else happened to write in the same way that Hafez writes,
then it, to arouse the King's natural artistic appreciation,
would come.

527. DUBIOUS FATE

This is a time Beloved, when for many days You made us wait:
not treating Your servants like the others do is not appropriate.
The corner of Your eye's approval never did become open to me;
in this manner You keep those with insight in this anxious state.
Neither rose nor nightingale escaped from stain of grief for You;
You make sure they complain, ripping coats, for they're desperate.
It would be best if You covered Your arm when You keep hand
in the heart's blood of Your lovers, which You use to decorate.
O heart, you that are the father of experience of where it ends,
why is it that love and faithfulness of young ones you anticipate?
Heart and faith have both departed but I am powerless to speak,
for You keep my heart burning, and both of them I can't relate.
Although being drunken lover and worthless outcast are our sins,
a lover said: "You keep making the slave like this: a reprobate."
O you, searching for delight of unity in the coloured patchcoat,
hoping for help from the ignorant: amazing, but unfortunate!
O eye and lamp, since you are narcissus of the garden of vision,
why keep me with broken heart and a head with a heavy weight?

Since the breeze read Your beauty's page to rose and nightingale,
You keep making them all distraught and You make them wait.
From the other world's mine is the jewel of the cup of Jamshid,
yet you desire it from clay of the potters: is that appropriate?
Hafez, don't give away day of safety by being full of reproaches;
What are you expecting from this world that has a dubious fate?

528. THE ROSE AND THE NIGHTINGALE

One morning I walked into the garden to pick a rose,
when suddenly, into my ear a nightingale's song arose.
In love with the rose and so terribly afflicted like me,
into that meadow's breeze his call of complaint goes.
Yes, upon the grass of that garden I have often walked:
concerned with rose and nightingale my thought flows.
Rose is with thorn, nightingale is companion of grief:
it's still the same with these, will always be with those.
Since the nightingale's cry made its mark on my heart,
all patience to endure this separation, from me goes.
In the garden of our world many a rose has bloomed;
from it, no one without thorn's wound, picked a rose.
Hafez, in this circle of life there is never a hope of joy;
it has a thousand pointed defects: no perfection grows.

529. THE FAVOUR OF FORTUNE

With that beautiful writing, on Your cheek rose-red
You drew;
that line across the page of rosebush and rosebed
You drew.
My tear that had been cloistered in the hidden house of the eye,
from behind its seven doors, it into the open instead

You drew.
Each breath remembering that winestained lip and drunken eye,
my feet, that from seclusion to the Winehouse sped,
You drew.
You said: "It is fitting you tie your head to our saddlestrap;"
it would be easy, if this heavy burden off this head
You drew.
Come back, so that with Your cheek I can repel that evil eye!
fresh rose, from this thorn, Your garment's thread
You drew.
Hafez, what else would you expect from the favour of Fortune?
Wine you tasted and curls of the Heartowner's head
you drew.

530. NOT A DROP

From Heartstealer, who'll bring mercy written with a quill?
Where is east wind's postman? Some kindness, if he will!
I make no complaint; but the Friend's raincloud of mercy
gave not a drop of dew: a field of thirsty hearts waits still.
In the path of Love, I came to know that Reason's advice
is like night's dewdrop that wrinkles a sea no one can fill.
Come; for although my patchcoat's bestowed to Winehouse,
to see me obtain from this even one cent, you never will.
For a reed of his sugarcane, why don't they value the man,
who makes a hundred sweet scatterings from a single quill?
My heart's sick of hypocrisy and drumming under blanket;
come, so I'll plant my banner on Winehouse's windowsill.
The roadside doctor knows nothing about love's sufferings;
dead heart, get one of Jesus-breath then no more you're ill.
Heart, the babble of 'how and why' gives only a headache;
take the winecup and from your life, rest a moment: still.
Come drink; a valuer of time sells this and the next world
for one cup of pure wine: yes, that a lovely One will fill.
Love has no use for the ways of pleasure and also of ease;
if companion of us lovers you are, then grief's poison swill.

O king, in this hand of Hafez is nothing of value for you;
  humble prayers during night and morning are his only skill.

531. NEW SPRING BREEZE

From Friend's street, New Spring's breeze comes, fragrant and slight;
  if you look for help, from this breeze the heart's lamp you may light.
If like rose you have a little gold, for God's sake spend it on pleasure,
  for the fault of Karun was that to gather gold was always in his sight.
I have the wine that's as pure as the soul and yet the Sufi criticizes it:
  O God, may an unhappy fate not fall for a day, on one wise and right.
The path to fulfillment of desires is the renouncing of all our desires;
  the crown of perfection we stitch when the renouncement is outright.
I do not know why the turtle-dove laments by the bank of the stream:
  perhaps she has also like me, grief that continues both day and night.
Your sweet companion has left you O candle, so now you sit all alone;
  in Heaven's will, equal are contentment and your burning out of sight.
I will say a little to you behind the veil: "Come out like the rosebud:
  it's Master's order that in five days Spring makes everything bright."
The wonder of knowledge should not exclude one from being merry;
  come Winebringer, for to clown comes the greatest portion of delight.
O heart, go and drink wine, practise love and give away all hypocrisy:
  I wonder whether a better lesson than this, your learning could incite.
Go to the garden, so from nightingale the heart may take love's secret;
  to gathering's circle come, so from Hafez, *ghazal* singing you'll recite.

532. WITH DIFFICULTY

Of that wine of love, that gives to immature ones maturity,
  although it's the Ramazan month, a large cup bring to me.
Days have passed and still the hand of poor me hasn't held
  arm of One silver of limb, leg of One's form like box tree.
O heart, although the dear guest is the fasting of Ramazan,
  know it's coming as a gift and its departure as favour see.

At this time the wise bird doesn't fly to the cloister's door:
where preaching's practiced, a trap is set for every assembly.
I don't complain about the malice of pious fanatics, because
when a morning dawns it's followed by a night very quickly.
When my Friend walks out into the meadow to have a look,
postman of the breeze, take to that One a message from me:
"Where is Companion Who drinks pure wine day and night;
don't You know one drinking dregs; have You no memory?"
Hafez, if Master of the age does not give your heart justice,
with difficulty you will get desire: selfishly, deliberately.

533. SECLUDED

Upon the outskirts of a land at the break of day,
a wayfarer to a companion this enigma did say:
"O Sufi, wine can only become pure when it has
in the wine flagon, completed a forty day stay."
Unless seal-ring is on finger of a Solomon's hand,
what special power does that engraving convey?
God frowns on that patchcoat a hundred times,
where a sleeve has a hundred idols hiding away.
Although darkness is within, maybe from Beyond
a lamp will light one who in seclusion does stay.
Although generosity is only a name without trace,
still present your need to One Who is noble, today.
O Lord of the harvest, You'll be amply rewarded,
if to the gleaner a little more attention You pay.
In no one do I see cheerfulness and enjoyment:
no medicine for the heart or faith exists today.
There is no hope of aspiration for lofty spirits,
no image of love on page of a forehead does lay.
The wise man has no knowledge of what's certain,
neither does Hafez, secluded, reading all the day.
Show to me the door of the Winehouse, so that I
may ask the Knower where in the end I will stay.
Though the nature of the beautiful is to be cruel,
may be you'll find mercy coming your sad way.

Since Irak became my Sulaima's place of habitation,
through longing I endure the whole of this duration.
Hey, camel driver of the possessions of the Beloved,
my longing for your charge goes on without cessation.
My heart's now bleeding from not seeing the Beloved;
now all evil falls upon all of the days of separation!
Throw your wisdom into the Zinda stream, drink wine
to shouts of the youths of Irak in loud acclamation.
Minstrel, sweet singer, sweet speaker, please compose
in Persian verse, a sweet melody in Iraki modulation.
Sound of the harp and Winebringer's hands clapping,
bring the time of Youth back into my recollection.
So that I may scatter on friends my remaining life,
give the wine, make heart happy with intoxication.
Winebringer, come; give me the heavy quart of wine;
God wanting one to drink from a full cup is salvation.
Be in agreement with the well-wishers for a moment;
understand as profit the times of friendly jubilation.
Spring of life is passed in the pasture of Your care:
time of union, may you be under God's protection!
Opportunities of union passed and we weren't aware:
see how now I am in the midst of all this separation.
O daughter of the vine, you are a pleasant bride; but
a possibility of divorce comes with your reputation.
It's right that the Messiah Who was always Himself,
should with the Sun alone have had an association.
Old age forbids me to be uniting with pure beauties,
except kissing cheeks and an embrace for variation.
Do not regard as mean my tears from missing You,
as many a sea comes from small streams' collection.
It's not our fortune to have communion with friends;
Hafez, the *ghazals* of Irak sing, sing, in lamentation!

535. THE MARKET'S PROFIT

In the morning I told the breeze the story of my deep longing;
it replied: "On Compassion of the Lord you should be relying."
Pen's reed has no tongue to make known the mystery of love:
beyond the power of expression is the explanation of longing.
Tie your heart to Layla's hair and in actions become a Majnun;
for to the lover, words of reason are hurtful and worth nothing.
Hey, Joseph of Egypt, being kept so busy by Your Sovereignty,
ask Your Father where finally His love for His Son was going.
The enchantment of Your magical glance gives remedy and pain,
curl of Your musky hair caresses the heart, and is also binding.
The world's old and beautiful but has never been compassionate:
what do you want from it, why ask it for what you're desiring?
If there is profit from this market, it's with the happy dervish:
God, make me happy; a dervish's contented happiness be giving.
Morning prayer, evening sigh are key to the treasured objective;
go by this path, so that then the Heartowner you'll be finding.
How long shall a Pure Bird like you, a high flyer, crave bones?
O no, that shadow of fortune on the unworthy you are casting.
Hafez, don't give your heart to lovely ones: see treachery that
to men of Kashmir and Samarkand, tempting ones were doing.
Dance to tune of Hafez of Shiraz, dance and whirl: you dark
eyes of Kashmir and you beauties of Samarkand, start dancing!

536. ON YOUR BREATH

O Winebringer, here is cloud's shade and stream's bank in Spring;
do what Your heart feels is right: what to do… I am not saying.
Fragrance of one colour doesn't come from this picture; so get up,
and with pure wine, stained and tattered cloak of Sufi be washing.
The world has a mean nature so don't be relying on its generosity;
O you who know the world, from it consistency don't be seeking.

Open your ears and listen to this lament the nightingale sings:
"Kind sir, be not worthless and stupid, rose of Grace be inhaling."
Two pieces of advice I give; listen, carry off a hundred treasures:
"Enter by ease's door and on the path of guilt don't be striding."
You search for the true Beloved's face? Then make mirror clear;
if not, from iron and brass, rose and wild rose is not blossoming.
Before you have become the dust in the Winehouse, in the pavilion
of the Winehouse for space of one or two days be always striving.
Out of gratitude that one more time you've experienced Spring,
plant deep the root of goodness and the rose of Grace be inhaling.
You said this: "The perfume of hypocrisy comes from Our Hafez."
You brought a great fragrance and on Your breath be a blessing!

537. PRAYER OF THE EXILE

The blessing of God (so long as the nights continue;
as long as two or three stringed lutes respond too),
be on the valley of Arak and on that One over there,
by my home on the hill's bend above the sandy view!
I am one who says the prayers for the world's exiles:
perpetually praying, my prayer I continue to renew.
O God, wherever the exile may turn his face to next,
keep him safe, eternally protected, I ask this of You.
O heart, don't grieve: in the chain of Beloved's hair,
condition of being mad with grief becomes easy too.
I die from intense loving: O if only I'd knowledge of
when bringer of happy news of Union comes through!
Your love's at all times the only means I have of peace;
my comfort in every situation is remembrance of You.
Until Day of Judgment, that deep core of my heart
for You still burns madly, where it is black of hue!
How can Union with Royalty like You be accomplished
by me who is infamous and a careless drunkard too?
From Your face's down, hundred beau ties are drawn:
may Your life see a hundred glorious years through!
May blessings be on that Omnipotent Master Painter,
Who around the moon draws the crescent line so true.

We need Your existence, for without You as a goal,
it would be hard to give up position, possessions too.
God has full knowledge of what is the desire of Hafez;
this knowledge of God is enough, for me this will do.

538. THE CHEMISTRY OF HAPPINESS

A greeting as pleasant as friendship's perfume I send
to that One Whose eye is lit by radiance: the Friend.
A blessing like the bright light of the heart of the Pure,
to that Candle of the cell of all who devoutly attend.
I do not see even one of my companions in his place;
heart bleeds from grief where's Winebringer, to mend?
Where do they sell the wine that overcomes the Sufi?
Because of hands of hypocrites, patience is at its end.
My companions ripped apart friendship's pact so much
that how friendship existed you wouldn't comprehend.
Do not turn your face away from street of the Master:
they sell that Key there, that difficulties will unbend.
Although bride of the world has a beauty that's limited,
beyond limit her unfaithfulness she often does extend.
If my broken heart is allowed to gain desire, it wouldn't
desire from stony hearts, embalming fluid to mend.
I'll teach to you the chemistry of preparing happiness:
from evil companions separate yourself, I recommend.
O you lustful soul, if you would take your leave of me,
in beggar's poverty I'd gain sovereignty... without end.
Hafez, don't be complaining about the violence of Time:
slave, work of the Divine Master, do you comprehend?

539. AT THE DOORWAY OF THE WINEHOUSE

At dawn, Winehouse's invisible speaker wishing me well did say:
"Come back, for you are an old friend of this place's doorway."
Drink a portion of wine like Jamshid, so you have knowledge of
the Angels' Mystery, from cup that shows the world in its ray.
At the doorway of the Winehouse there are drunken Kalandars,

who give the crown of true Royalty and who also take it away.
A brick beneath the head and feet resting upon the seven stars:
see the true nature of power, and position of real dignity's way!
Our head is joined to door of the Winehouse, the roof of which
is joined to the sky, although its wall is only the humble clay.
O you traveller of the Path, if you're aware of God's Mysteries,
to beggars of the Winehouse's doorway, show courtesy today.
Heart, if They should give to you the kingdom of true poverty,
your least territory will be from the moon to where fishes stay.
Unless you have Khizer as a companion, don't travel this road,
for it is a road in the dark: fear the danger of losing your way.
If you do not know how to beat upon the door of true poverty,
the Chief's seat and Turan's royal crowd do not let slip away.
O Hafez, be ashamed of relating your desires so full of greed:
what work have you done that you demand two worlds as pay?

540. DELUGE

O no, my heart is full, full of pain: O if only I had a remedy!
Heart dies from loneliness, if only a friend would come to me!
Who has any hope of help from the sky that is swiftly passing?
Winebringer, bring a cup, so that peaceful for awhile I may be.
Get up, and let's give our heart to the bold One of Samarkand;
    its breeze sends us scent of Oxus river, blowing fragrantly.
I said to a witty man: "See our position;" he laughed, saying:
"It's difficult, a strange state, a world of madness and worry."
I burned away in a pit of patience for that candle of Chigil;
king of Turkistan hasn't a care for us, where can a Rustom be?
In the path of being a lover the danger is safety and pleasure;
may that heart be wounded that from pain wishes for remedy!
For all with desires, no path leads to street of drunken lovers;
wayfarers burning all are there, the immature you won't see.
In this dusty world of ours, to hand comes not one true man;
it's necessary to make a new world and a new man is necessary.
Hafez, what weight does weeping have, weighed against Love?
In this deluge, seven seas a little night dew would seem to be.

541. TWO-GALLON CUP

Winebringer come, for the cup of the tulip is already full of wine:
how long will we keep ranting and raving in this drawn-out whine?
Give up all pride and contempt: for Time has been witness to the
wrinkling of Caesar's robe and fall of the crown of Kay's royal line.
Be sensible, for the bird of the garden is ceaselessly intoxicated:
wake up, for sleep of nothingness follows, persuading us to resign.
You branch of fresh young Spring, softly and gracefully you wave;
may the cruel blast of the Winter's wind never hurt you or malign.
Without any reliability is the sphere's love and also its movement:
pity a human being who may feel secure from its deceitful design.
Tomorrow it's the wine from the stream of Paradise and Huri for us;
but today there's Winebringer, face like moon, and the cup of wine.
Morning breeze brings back memory of the promise in youth's time:
generous Youth, give that elixir of life, cause my grief to decline.
Don't give attention to pride and royalty of the rose: by scattering
each petal, the executioner the wind, with its foot will undermine.
Fill a two-gallon cup to toast the memory of generous Hatim Tai;
so that to be closed forever the misers' black book we can consign.
Wine that gave colour and grace to the crimson arghavan's blossom,
gives out in sweat from the face, Grace of the True Nature Divine.
Carry the cushion to the garden, because the cypress like a servant
is standing in attendance and reed has girded loins ready for a sign.
Listen to how those Minstrels of the meadow have made harmony
of the melody of harp and lyre and voice of lute and reed combine.
Hafez, fame of the magic of your sweet enchantment has reached
to the limits of Egypt and China and to Rum and Rai's borderline.

542. A DIFFICULT AFFAIR

It's a city full of graceful ones, beautiful forms everywhere!
O friends, it's the greeting of love if you want to trade there.
The eye of the sky has never seen youth more fresh than this:
never has a fairer quarry ever been handed over to a snare.
Who has ever seen a body that is created so much like a soul?
On this garment, may no particle of a mortal's dust be there.

Why send away from Your presence one as broken as me?
A kiss or an embrace was the great expectation of my prayer.
The wine's good and pure, so hurry because the time is right;
that again Spring will arrive next year can one now be aware?
In the garden are the companions like the tulip and the rose,
each filling cup to the memory of the face of a friend so rare.
How shall I unravel this knot, how to unfold this mystery?
It's painful, severely painful: it's difficult, a difficult affair.
Every thread of Hafez's hair is in the hand of a flirt's hair;
living in a land like this, there are difficulties everywhere.

543. STAY WITH US

O breeze of the east, the fragrance of that musk-scented hair
you have;
stay with us as a token, for its perfume that is so very rare
you have.
My heart which contains the jewels of the mysteries of beauty and
love, one can place in Your hand if intention to guard it with care
You have.
Fitting for You is a garment that is proud of its beauty, and that
alone, because all kinds of colours and perfumes like roses so fair,
You have.
It's right to boast about You as having kingdoms of beauty like the
sun, for many servants with faces that are like moons, I declare
You have.
One can't speak at all about those pleasant qualities that can't be
seen, except to say this: many a watcher with a suspicious stare
You have.
Rose, how can melody of the nightingale be a pleasing sound to You,
when ear inclined to birds who utter mistrust and despair
You have?
My head became confused by Your drink: may it be pleasing to You!
What wine indeed is it, that in the flagon that's over there
You have?
O cypress beside river, don't keep boasting about your great height;
if you reach my Beloved, head hung low in shame and despair

you have.
I prayed for You and laughing under Your lip You said this to me...
"Who then could you be, and with Us what is this affair
you have?"
Hafez, do not look for the jewel of love in the corner of the cloister,
place your foot outside if inclination to find a treasure rare
you have.

544. FOR SAKE OF LOVE'S EXISTENCE

For sake of love's existence are men and angels of Paradise;
so that you can obtain great happiness, show a few desires.
If you are not prepared for Vision… do not look for Union,
for Jamshid's cup is useless when there are Visionless eyes.
How long the drink of the morning and the sleep of dawn?
Midnight prayer, weeping all morning, are far better tries.
Come and buy our kingdom with Your beauty's prosperity,
do not neglect this business, or to Your lot, grief… applies.
Kind sir, show a great effort, do not be without some love;
for nobody buys a slave who has no skill and never tries.
A door to astonishment was where all information led me;
I am for intoxication now, and where no information lies.
O dainty player of sorcery, what kind of puppet are You
that You're never hidden from vision nor before our eyes?
A thousand true loving souls burnt up from being jealous,
for You are candle, morning and evening, of another's skies.
The prayer of those sitting in corners turns away calamity;
why don't You look at us… from the corners of Your eyes?
Who will take this message from me to the Chief, the Asaf:
"Remember these two lines my old Dari language versifies?
'Come, so the way of the world's desires opens to my eyes;
if one looks hard one drinks wine… gives up grief's sighs.'"
May the crown never lie crookedly on Your beautiful head,
You're worthy of throne, crown and fortune that beautifies.
The Path of Love is such a dangerous road full of wonders
if you don't take the Path of Safety: in God our Safety lies!
With the perfume of Your hair and cheek, in all directions,

the morning breeze blows perfume and the rose glorifies.
To that One Who guided me out of this land of darkness,
my prayer at midnight and my weeping in the morning flies.
Because of prayer of Hafez, it is the hope that once again
I will trace my Layla in night's path, moon lighting skies.

545. LIFE SPENT LOVING YOU

You, for Whom we are united to sorrow forever,
I've spent my whole life loving You, but I don't care.
Do all know how happy are the dogs of Your street?
If only it were my fortune to wander nearby there!
Beloved, my secret has been divulged by my tear;
You, knowing my condition take pity on my despair.
O crowd of sincere lovers, don't expect faith from
the beautiful, for strangers to faith are all the fair.
We've passed by the Water of Life with lip still dry;
O Winebringer, for my thirst a drop You can spare!
I've given away religion and the world, loving You;
loving You, my love for all wealth went to the air.
If on threshold's dust of Your doorway Hafez dies,
it's certain that Life without end will be his share.

546. DON'T REGRET

From envy of Your cheek the rose is drowned in sweat;
cup of wine sweats from Your comelian and can't forget!
It is hail upon the tulip or it is rosewater upon the rose,
or water upon the fire, or Your face is wet with sweat.
From eye shot that bow, that eyebrow; heart then went
stumbling, out of control, and was lost from the outset.
No, I'll not keep my hand away tonight from Your hair:
caller to prayer, go, shout: "Come, pray," don't forget!
Place the harp in the hand of the minstrel for a moment,
say this: "Strum its cord awhile then sing a beautiful set."
Get the stove alight and put the aloe-wood on the fire;
about the harshness of winter, cold and wet, do not fret.

If after this, fortune should be holding you in contempt,
in presence of the Monarch of Rai, say that you're upset.
The King, Whose unbounded generosity exceeds horizons,
caused historians, fame of generous Hatim Tai to forget.
Take that one who would surrender his life for one drop,
take such a one's life and give him a cup to pay the debt.
As in Banu Amir, the tribe of Majnun, many will go mad
if coming out from tribe of Hagy another Layla they met.
Put the reed and the winecup's lip on the minstrel's lip;
it's right that under the fingernail the harp's string is set.
Bring out the cup of wine, and like Hafez do not grieve:
don't ask when were Jamshid and Kaus, and don't regret.

547. THE COUNTRY OF THE HEART

Bring wine, and hangover that I have please take away;
for with wine, the suffering from wine, one can way lay.
Except for the Idol's face and for the wine of the grape,
lamp of the friendly gathering doesn't shine a single ray.
Don't have pride in the magic of Your seducing glance,
for I have proven many times that pride does not pay.
Professor, you give much advice saying: "Don't try love:"
"No one can profess to be a professional in this," I say.
The soul of the man with heart, is alive because of love;
you're excused if you don't have love, but now go away!
By being deceitful only once, I handed away integrity:
it is a pity austerity, integrity and chastity didn't stay.
Fortune of union came and pain of separation passed;
country of the heart turned again to prosperity's way.
Hafez, one cannot tell everyone the secret of the heart,
tell only one who has suffered Beloved being far away.

548. ONE BEYOND COMPARE

Breeze, the scent of Beloved fair
you have;

the full musk perfume of that air
        you have.
Beware, don't you show long-handedness;
    any business with that long hair
        you have?
O rose, what are you beside that fair face?
    It has pure musk, the thorn's tear
        you have.
Sweet basil, you and that One's fresh down?
    It is fresh and you, a dusty smear
        you have.
Narcissus, you and that One's drunken eye?
    It is so merry and you, a sick fever
        you have.
Cypress, compared to that One's high form,
    some value in garden to compare,
        you have?
O Reason, compared with that One's Love,
    power at all to escape that Snare
        you have?
O Hafez, one day you will reach to Union,
    if in the waiting, a lasting power
        you have.

549. DETACHMENT

Unfaithfulness is throughout the human race;
of faithfulness, no one shows even one trace.
Good skilful men hold out hands of beggary
for survival, to those who are mean and base.
In this age, today, anyone who is worthwhile
hasn't from grief a moment's breathing space.
While in great luxury lives the ignorant fool,

now, all his possessions are prized like grace.
If the poet gives out poetry as clear as water
from which the heart gains the light of Grace,
they don't give him a grain, because of greed;
even if his face is the same... as Sanai's face.
Yesterday, Wisdom was whispering in my ear:
"Go patiently here, resourcelessness embrace.
Make contentment your work and burn up,
for in all this grief resourceless is your case.
Come Hafez, listen with soul to this advice:
if you fall off feet, head will find its place."

550. CARELESSNESS

O fanatic; go, with whatever hope you may profess,
for like you I am one who is filled with hopefulness.
What does tulip hold in its hand except for the cup?
O Winebringer, bring what You have; show kindness!
Bring me into the circle of all of those who are mad,
because intoxication is much better than soberness.
Abstain from me O Sufi, O abstain from me, abstain!
I have repented of being abstinent, this I do confess.
For God's sake, give up repentance in the rose season,
for how long the rose season stays one cannot guess.
O friends, the fresh Springtime of life has passed by;
no longer does Spring's breeze, meadow's edge caress.
Hafez, come and drink the wine that is ruby-coloured;
why do you let your life pass by in such carelessness?

551. YOUR PURPOSE

Since Your purpose here, whatever it be, in full share
You have,
what care is it that for condition of the poor in despair
You have?
From the slave demand his life and heart and also take the soul;
even over the free man, command applying everywhere,
You have.

You've no waist and for a moment I'm in astonishment as to how
in middle of the crowd of lovely ones, title of 'The Fair'
You have.
No painting could portray the whiteness of Your face because
of musky black line of down on the arghavan's red flare
You have.
Graceful One, drink wine forever, for You're soul's light forever;
especially now, when the head heavy with wine's fever
You have.
Don't criticize or be violent against my heart any more than this;
do what you can do when occasion arises: give whatever
You have.
If a hundred thousand arrows of violence are within Your range,
to take life of me who is shattered, within Your power
You have.
Always endure the tyranny of those who watch us, and be happy:
this is a small and easy thing, if Beloved beyond compare
you have.
And if in a moment to hand should come union with the Friend,
go; for whatever desire may be in the world, it to share
you have.
Whenever you remember ruby of the Beloved's lip or hear of it,
in Your mouth is sugar when you say whatever there
you have.
Hafez, when you carry off the rose from the edge of the garden,
care for weeping and wailing and the gardener's despair
you have?

552. CAPTURED

If swaying like the cypress into the rosegarden You should go,
from envy of Your face, each rose, thorn's sharpness does know.
From Your hair's unfaithfulness every circle is in commotion,
because of Your eye's magic, each corner a sick man can show.
O intoxicated eye of the Beloved, don't sleep like my fortune;
because from all sides in pursuit, an alert one's sigh does flow.
The coin of my soul is that which the dust of Your path scatters,

although as far as You are concerned, soul's cash value is low.
O heart, don't ever express an opinion about Heartowner's hair;
when an opinion becomes unclear, what action can then follow?
I had lost my head, and for some time this matter did not end;
my heart was captured, and pity for a captive You don't show.
I said to You: "Become the pivot in the middle of our circle:"
laughing, You said this: "Hafez, within which circle do you go?"

553. YOUR STREET'S END

My soul is sacrificed for You, for You are the Soul and Beloved!
My head is sacrificed for You, if not I will have a spinning head!
I don't find it easy to get up when I am at the end of your street:
those who know something's difficult, don't say it's easy instead.
Immature ones don't have endurance of a moth with burnt wings;
fragile ones don't reach the path where souls are scattered ahead.
To be satisfied during Your absence could be from inexperience,
to sit at ease in Your presence could from astonishment be bred.
It is those who watch You that have revealed Your heart's secret;
how can the matter of a great secret stay concealed, never said?
So that the plant of Your form may remain fresh and moistened,
it's necessary that You should plant it deep in my eye's riverbed.
One day I saw my heart in the curve of Your hair and said to it:
"How have you been O prisoner, are you living or are you dead?"
My heart replied: "Yes, what can you do if you don't envy me;
because the palace of the Great Sultan is not every beggar's bed.
"Hafez, it is true that to be in our company is beyond your limit,
it's quite enough if you watch out like a dog at this street's end."

554. HOPING IN VAIN

Because today in the realm of beauty You are the Sovereign,
perhaps Your lip may allow your lovers their desire to gain?
To heartsick lovers how long will You be proud and scornful?
Until when, will all the sick ones be given cruelty and pain?
How long down in depth of deep melancholy like Your eye,
how long like Your hair will this twisting restlessness remain?
The pain and also the violence that I suffer because of You,

I know if You knew a little about it, Your mercy I'd obtain.
In the occupation of being a lover one must have equipment
such as a heart like a fire and eyes that great oceans rain.
I remained in separation: O morning breeze, send the perfume
of hopefulness from Your garden of union to me once again.
Although I'll rise at the Resurrection hoping to be with You;
because of shame I'll not raise head from the dusty domain.
If I should drink an amount of the wine of union with You,
for as long as I'm still living I'll never again sober remain.
We are the powerless slave and You are the powerful Ruler:
You can scornfully kill me and me You can forcibly retain.
In the end, show some pity for poor Hafez's bitter condition!
How long will he be contemptible and how long hope in vain?

555. THE DRUNKARD'S CRY

O Winebringer, if Your love is for the wine,
hey, before us then bring nothing but wine.
In Winehouse sell prayermat and patchcoat;
bring to me a fill of the juice from the vine.
If your heart's alive hear the drunkard's cry
in rosebed of soul: 'O living One, Divine!"
O possessors of sorrow, come to the remedy;
when compared to Love, both worlds resign.
In Love's path, a poor honest beggar's worth
is more than riches of Hatim Tai's goldmine.
That Idol, Paradise-face, like Sultan comes;
the city's crowd is following in a long line.
The people all gaze upon that beautiful face;
cheek perspiring through modesty does shine.
How long will Hafez grieve because of You?
When will it stop breaking, this heart of mine?

556. IT'S CERTAIN

There is not a more pleasant place than the Winehouse's street;
even if a sumptuous haven this old head should happen to meet.

Why should I go on keeping all that I desire hidden from you?
It's the flagon of wine and a pleasant place, One fair and sweet.
My place is the Masters' corridor and fields of my native land;
my pleasure is beautiful faces; that, truly one can never defeat.
Why do you listen, for in this age is there no one as mad as me?
This is only the word of one inwardly useless, outwardly sweet.
Be respectful and don't talk of the condition of the corridor;
for a subject like this, not even a Brahmin or a Rajah can treat.
Beloved, how can anything else but You be here in our heart?
Because except for You, we care for no one: no one, I repeat!
Show pity on the heart of Hafez that is wounded and is ruined,
for it is certain that after today a terrible tomorrow we meet.

557. THE SONG OF GOD

It's morning, from the clouds of January is falling dew:
prepare the morning cup and make it a gallon cup too.
Drink the cup's blood for it's blood that's lawful blood:
be occupied with cup for it is an occupation fit to do.
And if at dawn the winesickness gives to you a headache,
with wine you should break head of the sickness in two.
Winebringer, be on hand, for grief is in ambush for us:
minstrel, this way of singing you should always pursue.
Give wine, for harp has told the secret in my ear, saying:
"Be happy and listen to what this old Master tells you:
Hafez, by independence of drunkards, drink wine I say;
so you'll hear the Song of God, Who's independent too."

558. SPREAD YOUR WINGS

Fruitless and full of desires, all of my life passed in vain:
son, give to me a cup of wine, so old age you can attain.
From Sinai's Tur lightning flashed and I turned towards it:
perhaps to you, I can bring this flaming torch once again.
Such sweets are in this city that those falcons of the Path
with the position of poor pitiful flies, contented remain!
Last night with many servants, I went to door of Beloved

Who said: "Friendless, helpless; whose help do you retain?"
So for a moment, like incense we hold Beloved's garment;
on a fire we lay our heart for sake of sweet breath's gain.
He whose heart is bleeding needs to be like the musk pod;
one known for sweet breath, a sweet breath must retain.
The caravan's gone, you're asleep in the place of ambush,
yet unconscious of many clangs of the bell, you remain.
Spread your wings and from the Tree of Paradise sing out:
it's wrong that this cage, a bird like you should contain.
How long desiring You, will Hafez run in every direction?
The path to your desired objective, may God make plain.

559. THE STORY OF MY LONGING

I wrote the story of this longing and full of tears was my eye:
come, for from grief caused by Your absence, I'm going to die.
Through deep longing many times I have said to my two eyes:
"O you dwellings of Salma, where does your lovely Salma lie?"
This is a very strange happening and is a wonderful occurrence:
it was I who was almost dead, yet the Killer, against me did cry.
Has any person the right to complain about Your pure garment?
For You are as pure as dew that drops on roseleaf from the sky.
When the Pen of Creation wrote the Law on the water and earth,
glory to the tulip and the rose, the dust of Your foot did supply.
Winebringer, get up: the breeze has begun to scatter ambergris;
bring along juice of the grape, pure and fragrant, for us to try.
Not a trace of me remains without Your praiseworthy presence;
it's true, that only from Your face a trace of true life I can spy.
If you want success then do not be lazy, for as the saying goes:
"For wayfarers, road's provisions are expertness, alertness of eye."
How can Hafez give a truly faithful description of Your beauty?
Like all of God's Divine attributes, all comprehension You defy.

559a. VISION

Thank God that a vision of Your face has been given to me;
the sun of Your beauty illuminates the eye of my destiny.

In my heart's gallery I painted all the loneliness of my day,
in those colours that tell me of the day when You I will see.
When mercy's shade is upon my head because of Your love,
the Pure Bird of luck and Destiny throws His shadow on me.
I was told that You would arrive and my heart gave thanks:
for my grieving heart, this was a time to bring joy to me.
Beloved, be bold and place Your foot towards Hafez's eye,
for a home is made for You in his eye that shines brightly.

560. SPILL THE BLOOD

Who will to the kings, from me who is the beggar, a message convey?
"In Wineseller's street, two thousand Jamshids for cup is price to pay."
I have become ruined and I am infamous, and yet I still have the hope
that with the help of powerful Names, I'll gain a good name someday.
You Who sell the Alchemy, give a glance at our gold that is impure,
for we do not possess much capital at all, and with it a trap we lay.
Priest, don't try to drive me from the Path with the old rosary beads:
when a crafty bird falls into a trap, that is never the successful prey.
O you pious ones, go away; piety has left us, we've drunk pure wine:
we have lost sense of honour and our reputation we've thrown away.
I wonder about the faithfulness of the Beloved: there is no enquiry,
not one greeting has been written, not even a note: nothing to say.
I'm longing to be at Your service; kindly buy me and never sell me:
the poor slave doesn't fall into such good fortune as this every day.
To which place can I take my complaint and to whom can I relate:
"Your lip was our life, yet You not even for a moment would stay."
If this wine's immature and if this companion happens to be mature,
wine immature is better by a thousand than a mature thousand I say.
Let loose the arrow of Your eyelash and spill all the blood of Hafez,
for no one will take revenge when it's One such as You Who does slay.

561. HEART, FAITH AND YOUTH

People spoke, and they were saying: "A second Joseph You are:"
when I looked more closely, truly You were better, better by far.

You are much sweeter than they say You are, by a sweet smile:
O Monarch of all the lovely ones, You are the Shirin of this era.
One cannot make comparison between Your mouth and rosebud:
of such a fine narrow mouth the rosebud will never be possessor.
If the cypress should stay at home because of Your straight form,
please move: for You outsway the cypress, so moving You are!
You said a hundred times: "I give your desire from this mouth:"
why are You all tongue? To the free lily, You are quite similar.
You said: "I will give your desire and I will also take your life:"
I'm afraid You'll not give my desire yet take my life as a memoir.
Through shield of my life Your eye causes many arrows to pass;
who has seen the drunken eye with bow both strong and regular?
When You banish one, it's like a tear leaving the eye of mankind;
to be sent from Your sight for even a moment causes great despair.
Don't send away from Your presence Your Hafez, griefstricken;
from love for Your face he gave his heart, faith, and youth so fair.

562. THE SECRET

Your lip I kiss and then I drink its wine away:
to Water of Life my feet have found the way.
I cannot tell Your mystery to all those others;
I can't see another to compare with You today.
Cup keeps kissing Your lip and drinking blood;
rose keeps seeing Your face and melting away.
Rose brought throne from seclusion to garden;
fold like rosebud austerity's carpet, it aside lay.
Give the cup of wine and forget about Jamshid:
who knows when Jamshid lived, or when Kay?
O moon like Minstrel, stretch hands on the harp,
so I may shout praises as those veins they play.
Don't leave the drunkard winesick like that eye:
Winebringer, remember lip and give wine today!
The soul's not willing to be leaving that body,
in whose veins blood of cup flows on its way.
When bird of the morning cries: "You! You!"

don't give cup away, cry: "Hooray! Hooray!"
Hafez, hold back your tongue for a little time;
from reed, hear what the tongueless does say.

563. THE MIRAGE OF IMAGINATION

I'm drunk with love's cup, Winebringer more wine be bringing!
Fill the cup, for without wine, gathering has no light shining.
My love for that moonlike face behind veil, doesn't penetrate;
so, Minstrel strike a melody, Winebringer some wine be giving.
My shape is bent like the doorknocker, so that the doorman
will not away to another door from this door, me be sending.
United are our hopes and our expectations to see Your face;
united are our desire for Union and late at night our dreaming.
I'm drunk from Your two eyes and gain less than a question;
I'm sick for Your rubies, but at the end there is no replying.
Since no eye has the power to contain the Sun of Your face,
O heart, what gain can your eye retain from such worrying?
Don't stain your hand with intention of gaining cup from which
you know, in the end not a drop of water you'll be attaining.
O Hafez, why did your heart set out for an imagined Beloved:
when was traveller's thirst quenched by a mirage's shimmering?

564. THE KING'S ROSEGARDEN

"Demand wine, scatter roses; from Time what are you looking for?"
This, the rose said at dawn to the nightingale: can you say more?
Take the cushion into the garden so that you may smell the rose;
drink wine, and Beloved's, the Winebringer's lip and cheek, explore.
Let's discover who is lucky enough to gain Your laughing rosebud;
O bough of the beautiful rose, who is it that you are growing for?
Proudly sway the box tree and resolve to come out into the garden,

so from Your shape cypress may learn Your heart's captivating lore.
Today, when your market is full of the shouts of the purchasers,
get a few provisions for the road, out of wealth from merit's store.
As the candle is in the wind's corridor, it's good for you to go out
and take what will be profitable from what goodness has in store.
That hair, where each curl is worth hundreds of China's muskpods,
would bring great happiness if its scent from kindness had its core.
Each bird comes into the King's rosegarden with a different song:
nightingale makes melodies; out of Hafez's mouth, prayers pour.

565. FRESH SPRING

It's a fresh Spring: try, so in Spring, happy of heart
you are:
many roses will blossom when of clay a small part
you are.
The harp keeps giving to you advice from within the veil;
it's only of value when valuing what it will impart,
you are.
I'll not say now with whom to sit and also what to drink:
you will know this, if one who is wise and smart
you are.
Every leaf in the field is a volume of a very different kind;
it would be shameful if careless of each one's part
you are.
Although road leading from us to the Friend is terrifying;
going is easy, if knowing stages before you depart
you are.
Worries of the world will take much of your life's wealth,
if always involved in problems that stop and start
you are.
O Hafez, if the highest fortune should give you some help,
the prey of that Beloved excelling in beauty's art
you are.

566. LOVE'S ENTREATY

Breeze of morning of happiness, bring a sign
that you know
to a certain One's street; pass at that time
that you know.
Messenger of Mystery's place you are, so my eye's on Path;
don't order, gently urge in the way so fine
that you know.
Say this: "My poor soul slips from my hand; for God's sake
give from Your ruby soul-refreshing wine
that You know.
"Why shouldn't my hope be tied to Your gold woven belt?
Form, in that waist is a subtlety Divine:
that, You know.
To us, image of Your sword is of one thirsting, and water;
You take Your captive and slay with a Sign
that You know.
These words I've composed in a way no one else will know;
a favour: take them the way You incline,
that You know."
So for Hafez in this matter, Turkish and Arabic are as one:
tell Love's story in every tongue sublime
that you know.

567. WINE OF SELFLESSNESS

From the gallon-sized flagon drink the wine of Unity;
so that from heart you pluck root of grief's futility.
Like the cup of wine, still keep the heart expansive:
like corked wine bottle, why keep soul in captivity?
When from flagon you have a mouthful of selflessness,
you will never boast again of your own self's ability.
Be like the stone at your foot, don't be like the water:
your coat will be wet if you mix deceit with instability.
Secure the heart to the wine, so that then like a man,
you cut off neck that holds hypocrisy and false piety.
Get up and be like Hafez, make an effort; so that then,

yourself at Beloved's feet you may throw in humility.

568. THE MOMENT RECOGNISE

Make the most of the present time, for you know that time flies;
O soul, if you want to know life's essence, the moment recognize.
In exchange for giving one's desire, the heavens ask for one's life;
try, so that you can take your share of happiness from the skies.
Hear the advice of lovers and enter through the doorway of joy:
to be occupied with a passing world, isn't worth a lover's sighs.
Don't boast of being a drunkard to the sober: for one can't tell
the physician with no experience, about pain one must disguise.
Gardener, whenever I may pass by, may it be unlawful for you
to plant in my place a cypress other than the Beloved I idolize.
One who breaks bottles has no idea of the worth that the Sufi
places on this household utensil: there a pomegranate ruby lies!
Quickly You go and spill the people's blood with Your eyelash:
O my soul, you follow; fear of being left behind in you does rise.
O honey lips, don't try to stop prayers of those awake all night;
guarded by the One Name is seal that on hand of Solomon lies.
I kept my heart out of the way of the glance of Your eye: but,
Your brow that has a bow by its forehead, takes me by surprise.
My brothers, have compassion for me, longing for my Joseph:
grief of old man of Canaan, longing for his son, I now realize.
Wine's desirable delight will murder the repentant sober one;
O wise man, do not be repentant for it is a step that is unwise.
Enter by my door one day so that I may clap hands with joy,
saying: "Truly, essence of light as my Guest, fills my eyes."
Show some kindness by giving some peace to the heart of Hafez;
O You, curl of Your hair gathers up all troubles to tranquilize.
O Idol with a heart of stone, if You have no more care for me,
I'll go and tell another Master and my condition I'll emphasize.

569. LOOK CLOSELY

I am one who wishes You well, and I know that You know of it:
You see the unseen and read the unwritten; that, You must admit.

When angels bowed in praise of Adam they kissed Your ground,
for they admitted that Your beauty contains Humanity infinite.
In God's Name, curl of Your hair is now the Collector of hearts:
may You always be safe from that breeze that tries to uncurl it.
I've the hope that with Fortune Your waist's belt I'll make loose;
O sky, for the sake of God, the knot from the forehead unknit.
Shake Your hair loose and make the Sufi dance and start playing,
so You throw off many idols that on each patch of his coat do sit.
Fragrance of the hair affair ones sets alight the lamp of our eye;
Lord, a gathering such as this: don't allow breeze to disperse it.
How does the critic know the mystery of the lover and Beloved?
The eye that cannot see the secret mystery, can not it transmit.
To be angry with another wayfarer is not an intelligent action:
while remembering the easy times, to difficult conditions submit.
It is a pity, joy of being awake all night left like morning breeze;
O heart, you know value of union when by separation you're hit.
Hafez, your imagining of the curl of Beloved's hair fascinates you;
look closely, so that inside ring of impossible luck, you don't sit.

570. YOU SHOULD BE

I made a thousand efforts, so that my Beloved
You should be;
so that my grieving heart's fulfiller, as desired,
You should be;
So that for a moment to room of sorrowful lovers You'd come;
so for a night, consoler of my heart that's grieved
You should be.
Because You made my eye's lamp keep alive through the night,
my hopeful heart's helper Who is near my bed
You should be.
At midnight in sleep's dream I see this desire appearing to me:
that instead of streaming tears, by me embraced
You should be.
When I have a heart that is bleeding because of that cornelian,
then keeping my secret, if I have complained,
You should be.

When Monarchs of great beauty act with generosity to slaves,
into the midst, Lord of what for me is decreed,
You should be.
The rays of the sun would become too slender a prey for me,
if suddenly like a deer, as prey to be followed,
You should be.
Three kisses You promised as my portion from Your two lips,
if You do not give to me, to me then indebted
You should be.
In that meadow where the loved ones take the hand of lovers,
if Your hand should take a hand, my 'Beloved
You should be.
I'm the Hafez, guardian of city, but I'm not worth a barleycorn:
unless due to Your own generosity my Beloved
You should be.

571. JUICE OF THE VINE

O mouth, you look like a casket of precious pearls, beautiful, fine!
How perfectly around Your face curves the new moon's thin line!
This fantasy of Union with You is now pleasantly deceiving me;
let's see what game is played by the form of this fantasy of mine.
The heart left and the eye bled and the body broke and soul shed:
in love there are many such marvels, every one with another sign.
Heart bled from Your hand and memory of Your drunken eye;
I have been injured by injury: does love toward me ever incline?
If Your nature doesn't change then it will never change again, and
then the lover will remain here and the Master over there recline.
O rider of camels who has departed from the area of my dwelling;
if you meet the inhabitants of Najd, my condition to them define.
Heartstealer thought to spill my blood was lawful in love's game;
O gathering of Judges, to me what does love's decision consign?
Because of longing for the Inhabitant of Najd my eye never slept;
the heart because of rapture dissolved in anguish that was mine.
For sake of God, there in the Zat-i-Raml my Beloved was staying,
the wise ones ran away when their eyes to this fawn did incline.
If you have knowledge and are wise then don't let four things go:

security and the Beloved, the quiet safe place and the pure wine.
Give wine; for although I became one black of book in the world,
can one ever be hopeless of the Grace of the Eternal and Divine?
Winebringer, bring to me a cup and bring me out from seclusion;
so that from door to door I may wander, then to beggary resign.
O Hafez, since the picture that Time paints never stays the same,
don't be complaining and don't worry and let us drink the wine.
In the time of the Master of the Age the cup of the heart is pure;
come, make me drink cup purer than pure water: juice of the vine!

572. THE ONLY GUIDE

With those plaits Salma tied my heart tightly;
every day my soul cries: "Come, die for me."
For God's sake, give heartbroken me, kindness:
though enemies hate me, give Union, free me.
You who criticize because my love's for Salma,
at that face you should take a look, and see.
To the Beloved completely surrender the heart,
drown like me in a sea of friendly conspiracy.
Now we shall have to advance to You our soul:
You stubbornly held my heart stolen from me.
Grief for You has swallowed my helpless heart,
and good fortune of my poetry deceived me.
Fair form, in the grief of love, longing for You,
to the Lord of fortunate slaves, bound are we.
Into dark twisting curl of Your hair went Hafez:
into the dark night… with God the Guide only.

573. DETACHMENT'S MIRROR

God's light, in detachment's mirror you'll be able to see;
enter by our door, if a seeker of Eternal Love you be.
Give wine; if our sin's name all Hell has written down,
on its fire falls Mohammed's miraculous water of Mercy.
You try to juggle the moments: it is against the Law;
the Messenger of God said: "Never tricksters are We."
If with the splendour of Grace you go into the world,

lily and cypress and rose going with you will also be.
Use time to make the heart's slate clean of your self?
If with heart and soul to wisdom's street your path be.
Hafez, the bird of your heart is imprisoned by desire;
you slave of corruption, don't talk detachment to me.

574. SULTAN OF THE FAITH

Heart, be slave of the King of the world and you a King
will be;
and you, forever protected by God's Grace, God-Willing,
will be.
I'd not buy a thousand of those false devotees for a barley-corn:
say to hypocrites: "From hilltop to hilltop your dwelling
will be."
Since Mohammed will speak for me on day of The Resurrection.
You can say today that my sinful body full of suffering
will be.
Anyone who is not the friend of Ali is unfaithful to the Faith,
whether he, devotee of the age, or on the path travelling
will be.
O Ali, today I'm full of life and it's because of my love for You:
tomorrow, by Imam's pure Soul, You for me witnessing
will be.
That tomb of the eighth Imam, Riza, the Sultan of the Faith,
kiss reverently with soul, and you at that gate, staying
will be.
If you don't gain the strength to pluck a rose from the rosebush,
you at least at foot of the rosebush, grass that's growing
will be.
The man of God is the devotee who tries hard to be truly pure,
whether clothing is white or whether black the clothing
will be.
Hafez, follow the path of giving service to the King, Imam 'Ali.
Then you, on the Path like those on the Path, travelling
will be.

575. SELECT FRIENDS ONLY

On all of those who claim Our love, the demands are mystifying;
Our lovers always look for suffering as being for them a blessing.
Adam was exiled from Paradise, and it happened for a purpose:
Our All-Powerful Nature, We made him on this earth be seeing.
Noah received distraction, tossed about by tempest and waves;
Moses, through mysterious rod, with power We were endowing.
Solomon's seal-ring was arranged to be stolen, taken by a demon;
Jacob, finality of Our decree and will was made to be realizing.
Abraham We even had tested by throwing him into the flames;
although in submission of Our Will, his son he was sacrificing.
Zakaria suffered the ordeal of being sawed from head to foot,
John, because of Our verdict, to be murdered We were allowing.
Mohammed the chosen, broke his teeth in battles for Our cause;
Job patiently withstood the withdrawal of all material blessing.
Hasan, he had to taste death through a dose of deadly poison;
Husain in crusade at Kerbala was allowed to know beheading.
Strangers don't have access to Our blessings through such pain,
select friends only to feast of disgrace and torture We're inviting.
Pharaoh, he was denied all this headache and this giddy pain,
ready for Our trials and tribulations, him We were not finding.
Shudad, upon him We conferred untold wealth and great riches,
that then goaded him a heaven upon earth to try to be creating.
We pamper all Our enemies and We slaughter all Our friends,
and to challenge Our decree and its ends, no one can be daring.
Hafez is eternally lamenting these agonies and these sorrows…
maybe his diseases will prove to be the remedy, and the curing.

576. THE WILD DEER

Hello, O wild deer of the desert, where are you?
Receiving most of my love and my care are you.
Two lone travellers, perplexed, a friendless pair;

wild beasts, whispered curses lurk here and there.
Come, so of each other's condition we can inquire;
if we can, we will seek what the both of us desire.
For I can see that in this desert is only confusion,
having no oasis of joy, no happy green profusion.
Companions, who'll be the companion to loners?
Explain, who will be the friend of the strangers?
Perhaps Khizer's blessed footsteps will now arrive,
for from fortunate help great deeds come alive.
Perhaps time of generous Grace Divine has come,
for: "Leave me not alone," as my sign, has come.
Awhile ago a drunken lover who was on the way,
to wayfarer crossing a land did courteously say:
"O Wayfarer, what do you have in your bag there?
Come, if it is the grain, use it as bait for a snare."
He answered him by saying this: "I have the grain;
but the Simurgh is that Prey I desire to obtain."
The other said: "How will your hand find a trace,
for we haven't found trace of It's nesting place?"
Don't hand away cup of wine and base of the rose,
be careful of Time, power-drunk; be on your toes!
When that straight cypress joins with that Caravan,
with cypress-branch, watching the path is the plan.
You departed, turning my happy disposition sad;
when did companion make companion feel so bad?
You struck the sword of separation so mercilessly,
how could my poor offerings be possibly accepted,
when wealthy sun from purse, its riches scattered?
The edge of the pool of water and bank of estuary;
a dewdrop, then talk to oneself about a memory.
Remembering the departed, remembering friends,
be in sympathy with what the April cloud sends.
When the running water is weeping before you,
give it some help; the water of your eye pour too.
No courtesy at all did the old friend to me display;
O Muslims, Muslims, for God's sake help today!
Over my head the water of separation has passed;

in this condition, courtesy is unfit to be grasped.
Perhaps auspicious feet of Khizer can help convey
these lonely forms to those forms long gone away.
Why do I try so hard to change my own destiny?
from the star of my Fate, why do I try to flee?
From now on I take path of the Friend's street;
if I die in that Path, then my death I will greet.
The exiled strangers who hear of my condition,
will above my dust sit for awhile in meditation.
Strangers remember strangers stranded far away,
because the memorials of one another are they.
O God, You are remedy of those without remedy.
You know the remedy for me and those like me:
like how from night You make daylight shine;
You bring out from this grief the joy that's mine.
I've much to complain about, separated from You;
that this place could never contain this tale is true.
Pay regard to the pearl and leave the shell alone;
by that way, a bad reputation is left to its own.
Explaining essence, my pen's reed brings in its fish;
from the fish and pen ask the explanation of this.
Companions value each other then comprehend,
when they know hearts' explanation, end to end.
Truthfully, word of giver of advice has promised
that the Orderer of separation is also ambushed.
With wisdom, the soul we mixed and then kneaded,
and the seed produced from this we then planted.
Apparent in this mixture is the gift of joy; in this,
the essence of poetry and the soul and the body is.
Come; from this perfume full of hope so fragrant,
seek the soul's perfumed place, its fragrant scent.
For this pod of musk is from pocket of the Huri,
it is not from that deer that from man does flee.
In this valley, listen to the sound of the torrent:
here, hundred guiltless ones blood's a grain spent.
Here, They scorch the wings of Gabriel with fire,
so that children who play with fire can admire.

Who has the power to speak, to say a word here?
O Lord, in this valley, is freedom's sword here?
Go Hafez, and stop filling space talking of this;
Make your speech short, for God, knowing all is.

577. BOOK OF THE WINEBRINGER

Winebringer, come. That wine that ecstasy brings,
  that to the soul all perfection and mercy brings,
  give; give me, so broken-hearted I have become,
  from both of those, long-parted I have become.
Winebringer, come. The alchemy, elixir that gives
  treasure of Karun and the long life Noah lives,
  give; so that They may throw wide open the door
  to your face, of long life and prosperity's store.
Winebringer, come. That shining fire Zoroaster
  kept searching for behind the dusty clay cover,
  give, give me; in the law of the drunken outsider,
  does fire worshipper or world worshipper matter?
Winebringer, come. Wine that boasts to have seen
  the way of the cup of Jamshid into the Unseen,
  give; give me so with the aid of the cup I may be
  like Jamshid, always aware of world's mystery.
Winebringer, come. Give cup of Jamshid to me,
  don't try to delay, give it to me now, instantly!
Of having crown and treasure Jamshid said rightly:
"Not worth a barleycorn, this house is transitory."
Winebringer, come. That cup, like Salsabil, wide is,
  that to Paradise still the heart's honest guide is,
  give, give me; for truly spoke the lute and reed:
"Swallow of wine, will the crown of Kay exceed."
Winebringer, come. Love, the Virgin, intoxicated,
  that's there within Winehouse to be discovered,
  give; give me, ruined of reputation I wish to be;
Wine and the winecup my ruination I wish to be.
Winebringer, come. That liquid that all cares bums;
  that if a lion drinks, into a burner of forests turns,

give, so to the sky that captures the lion I can go;
so the cage, this tired old world, I can overthrow.
Winebringer, come. The wine the Paradise Huris
make rich by mixing with the angels' ambergris,
give; so that it on the fire as perfume I may place,
to sweeten Reason's brain for an Eternity's space.
Winebringer, come. Wine from cup, a reflection
that to Kay and to Jamshid sent communication,
give; so that with the voice of the reed I can say:
"When was Jamshid and where is Kaus, today?"
Winebringer, come. That wine that gives Royalty,
of which the heart gives the evidence of purity,
give me; because I was once the King of my heart,
now I'm stained and from King I have had to part.
Give me wine, that from stain I can become pure,
grow strong, from thoughts of fear become secure.
Give wine and upon face of Fortune look and see;
make me ruined, then in me see Wisdom's treasury.
As the Garden of Souls is my true native ground,
why am I jailed here, to a plank of flesh bound?
I'm the one who when taking the cup in the hand,
sees in mirror what's there, whatever the demand.
While intoxicated, the door of austerity I'll beat;
of being Royal in beggary I'll boast, I will repeat.
For when drunken Hafez should feel like singing,
the lyre of Venus from the sky gives him blessing.
Winebringer, come. Fear the faithlessness of life;
with wine petition, beg for Endlessness of Life.
Because the wine will lengthen your life so much,
always a door to the Unseen opens to your touch.
Winebringer, come. Spread a banquet with wine,
for faithfulness with none is the world's design.
The bubble of wine reminds us of this condition:
how Kay Kobad's diadem wind took to extinction.
Winebringer, come. From wine seek heart's desire,
because I saw no peace of heart without wine's fire.
If body shows patience in uniting with the soul,

then possibly heart is separated from winebowl.
Winebringer, come. Make full this cup, that I may
explain to you the condition of Kisra and of Kay.
Winebringer, come. Can you be safe from Time,
when it intends to kill you for not even a crime?
Winebringer, come. Don't show arrogance to us,
for in the end you are dust and not of the Furnace.
Make the goblet full of wine, for wine is so good,
especially when it's pure, without any falsehood.
Winebringer, come. Wine of a sweet-basil breeze,
gold and silver I've lost, but give it to me please.
Winebringer, come. Pure bright ruby wine give;
how long will boasting and cunning design live?
Sick and tired of the beads and patched coat am I;
pledge them both for wine, and then it's goodbye!
Winebringer, come. From the Masters' corridor,
don't go far, for in this corner is 'Soul's treasure.'
If one says: "Don't go to Winehouse's corridor;"
"Goodnight," is how such a one you can answer.
Winebringer, come. The goblet coloured with red,
from which heart gains joy, soul with bliss is fed,
give to me that it may release me from suffering;
show me path to the Banquet's special offering.
Winebringer, come. That wine that is soul's food,
that like life is needed to heal sick heart's mood,
give; so out from the world I can pitch my tent,
and my canopy I can pitch above the firmament.
Winebringer, come. That cup like sun and moon
give, so that above the sky I may place my throne.
Winebringer, come. With old wine, cup after cup,
make me completely intoxicated, fill up the cup.
When You make me drunk with Your pure wine,
in drunkenness I'll sing You sweet songs of mine.
Winebringer, come. Now that, thanks to Your face,
ambergris-fragrant Paradise is this feasting place,
take the cup, do not be afraid, in it is happiness…
in Paradise the taking of wine is not lawlessness.

Winebringer, come. Since wine I can never give up,
come then and help with that last remaining cup.
Because of sphere's revolutions I'm ready to die,
running fast towards the Master's corridor come I.
Winebringer, come. That wine that gives delight,
give; so that on Rakhsh's back I may then alight,
and to the field like Rustom we will turn our face,
galloping to heart's desire into the fight we'll race.
Winebringer, that cup that is red like bright ruby,
that opens to heart, door of the time of ecstasy,
give; so that all reason I can annihilate and then
raise for the world my standard of intoxication.
In a moment we boast of the cup of the Moment;
we throw the wine's water on grief's fiery lament.
For today we are drinking wine with each other,
it's an easy time to drink; will there be another?
For those who have prepared the banquet of joy,
who were also taking part in the banquet of joy,
from this low place of cages, devil-dwelling caves,
departed and took dust of regret to their graves.
Who has been victorious over this turquoise dome?
Who found happiness in this ten-day-long home?
That time of youth went to the wind, departed;
and he who understood Justice happily departed.
Winebringer, give wine. For as long as I breathe,
the both worlds my feet will trample underneath.
Be quick and give to me the heavy quart of wine;
if not in the open… then secretly make it mine.
He for whom on elephant's back drum was struck,
at him they beat death's drum… ending his luck.
When rays of light announcing the dawn appear,
each moment in my ear, words of the Huri I hear,
saying: "Bird, sweet of song and sweet of speech,
stretch your wings, break out of the cage, reach.
Nest on top of six levels of azure palace's dome;
rest in your place, in that stage of Soul's home.
You are victorious over fortune like Manuchihr;

you have known that in the time of Buzurjmihr,
how they wrote upon the cup of Naushiravan:
'All earlier traces of us, you will not find, O man;
Listen to this advice from us, learn how works
the subtle turnings of Fate, and Fortune's quirks:
that this is the stage of grief and of suffering…
in this place of snares, joy is usually missing.'"
We are joyful, we don't grieve over pain and grief
if we have nothing, then all is equal in our belief.
What is Jamshid's cup, Jamshid the King is where?
Where did Solomon go and the seal-ring is where?
Of all of the philosophers alive, who understands
when Jamshid, when Kay Kaus walked the lands?
After they took the step into the non-existence,
only their name in this land was their subsistence.
Why do you tie your heart to this fleeting place?
Once you pass away, this house you'll never face.
It is only a madness to attach to this your heart:
it is not even acquainted with friendship's art!
You'll not find in this house of six doors a place
you desire, or even the delight of a joyful space.
Winebringer, give that water of the nature of fire,
so that I can become free from the fire of desire.
For inside the fire there's my heart that's aglow;
give wine, so on the fire some liquid I can throw.
O Winebringer, give that wine that is ruby of hue,
that steals colour from the ruby and sapphire too.
Quick, give the water that from fountain does run;
no, that is not running water… it is liquefied Sun.
On this sky of five folds, degrees numbering nine;
one can pitch one's square tent with a cup of wine.
Above the pillarless roof of the nine-vaulted sky
one can go, if… out from one's self one will fly.
If you are wise, get up, and of the madhouse be;
don't spill self-respect, the dust of Winehouse be.
Don't be bound to this place's dusty heap, O no;
for then suddenly like dust, to wind you will go.

Winebringer, come. Give that Royal goblet to me,
that gives joy to the heart and soul, increasingly.
That goblet's meaning is: 'infinite perpetuality,'
this wine means to us: 'selflessness and charity.'
Youth has departed like Yemen's fast lightning,
life has departed like a swift breeze of morning.
Give up this house of six doors and make a stand;
come, of this nine-headed snake, wash the hand.
In this path your head and your gold quickly lay;
if you are Wayfarer, the soul also you must pay.
To Mansion of Permanence running quickly go;
everything's impermanent but God; this, know.
Winebringer, that jewel that awakens soul, give;
remedy to sick heart give… and make heart live.
Since Time snatched the cup from Jamshid's hand,
what good is it if all the world was his command?
Winebringer, give me that water that has frozen up,
make this dead heart live with juice from the cup,
Because every brick that on the terrace we tread,
was once an Alexander's or a Kay Kobad's head.
In bowl above is nothing but blood of kings there;
in this desert is nothing but the dust of the fair.
I've lately heard that someone, mad, wine loving;
cup in the hand in the Winehouse, kept on saying:
"Because of that mean course the sky does turn;
the most unwise, the most from joy does learn."
Winebringer, give that bitter, sweet-tasting wine;
for from Beloved's hand, wine… is sweetly divine.
578. THE BOOK OF THE MINSTREL

Minstrel come; where are You? Strike lute's strings
so that the Royal song into my memory it brings!
Come, to drunken ones, greetings in the song send,
blessings to the loved-ones gone for so long, send.
Minstrel, come and tune up the joyful instruments,
with a song and a *ghazal* let now the tale commence.
For grief's burden has nailed my foot to the ground,

get me stirring, by union's sweet rhythmical sound.
Minstrel, bring out a vision from behind the screen;
let's see what doorkeeper of the Sanctuary has seen.
The voices of the minstrels prolong in such a way,
that Venus the harpist you will make dance today.
Minstrel, bring close together the harp and the drum,
with a sweet melody invite all of the lovers to come.
Strike such a path that the Sufi into ecstasy goes,
Union through drunkenness will soon end his woes.
Minstrel, on the organ strike hard with Your hand;
rid my heart of all worldly worries, this I demand.
Perhaps my poor heart will then discover some peace,
when it is freed from that stain of grief's disease.
Minstrel, come: don't be upset by any of my wishes,
if You've no harp, on tambourine place Your fingers.
I've heard that when the wine causes such an aching,
there's soothing balm in the drum's low throbbing.
Minstrel, where are You? The rose is now blooming,
the fields are full of the nightingale's loud singing.
Truly, it is good if to the boil my blood You bring,
that harp's throbbing breath with a thud You bring.
Minstrel, come; tune up the lute, make it like new;
a song, a melody of a whole new order, begin anew.
With this one tune the remedy for my suffering send;
tear my heart, like the patchcoat from end to end.
Minstrel, what harm's there if You did a kind deed,
and my heart is inflamed by the song of Your reed;
if me, out from my sorrowful thoughts You did bring,
if You then shattered the household of my suffering?
Minstrel, where are You? A sweet melody now strum;
to us who've nothing, allow a kind greeting to come.
Because without us soon the old world desires to be,
much better than the role of royalty is that of beggary.
Minstrel, sing, chant that chant, take melody higher;
for the destitute helpless, You're the remedy supplier.
Show to me the way of Irak upon that stringed lute,
I'll show how from my eyes is Zinda stream's route.

Minstrel, come now and listen to all that I am saying,
about this matter understand wisdom I'm imparting:
"Since grief brings an army, tighten Your company,
with harp and reed and drum and lute of harmony."
Minstrel, of the mysteries a true confidant You are,
with reed breathe sympathetic breath of conspirator.
If heart has grief with wine drown the grief to death,
blow breath into a reed, for the world's but a breath.
Minstrel, come; where are You? Upon that lyre play;
O Winebringer, with wine fill that flagon all the way.
So let us sit together and together joyfulness make,
let's pleasantly rest a moment, happy madness make.
Minstrel, from my own verses, bring a *ghazal* along:
to the twanging of the harp, bring it out into song,
so that I'm enraptured by the dance I'm embracing,
because of the dancing, patchcoat I'll be forsaking.
One can by intoxication pierce the pearl of mysteries,
because when selfless, one cannot have any secrecies.
Minstrel, I'm grieving, two-stringed instrument play;
with God's One string, three-stringed instrument play.
Minstrel, practise this new kind of song to its peak,
to the companions with the voice of this music speak.
Do Your work, make the soul of great ones rejoice;
singers Parviz and Barbud, remember with Your voice.
Because to cause us calamity Time still does intend,
I'm for intoxication and calamity of eye of the Friend.
In this blood-splattering plain of The Resurrection,
the blood of a cup You could spill, and also a flagon.
I am amazed when I look at this sphere's direction:
I don't know who dust will next take to destruction.
The deceitfulness of this world is an obvious affair;
"Pregnant is the night:" let us see what it will bear.
Come, beware not to pledge to this world your heart;
on the top of the bridge one has no permanent part.
Truthfully, this ruined world is the stopping station
that Afrasiyab's palace has seen as its destination.
Truthfully, a stopping station is this desert of waste,

where Salm and Tur's army went astray and were lost.
Where's Piran's judgement, his army's leader is where?
Where's Shaida the Turk, sword he did bear is where?
Not only did his palace and halls the wind blow away,
    even his tomb no one at all remembers to this day.
This one (Hafez), to be wielder of a pen, Fate decreed;
    those to be given to the sword, Fate saw as the need.

579. SOVEREIGN

Young again like the garden of Iram became earth's terrain,
    from the light of happiness of the king, taking its domain.
He is lord of sunrise and sunset being in the east and west;
    he is lord of conjunction and is sovereign and does reign.
Sun that nourishes the land, and monarch dispensing justice,
    he rules by giving out justice and like Kay is the sovereign.
Chief of those sitting on that throne of: "Be, and it was;"
    he is the maker of kings of the whole of the world's domain.
He is the faith and the joy of the world, having the glory
    that tightly holds forever the steed of Time, by its rein.
The time and the age's Dara and sun of the realm's Shuja;
    Khan who is prosperous, youthful king of kings mundane.
A moon, by whose radiant appearance the earth has shone,
    the king, by whose great spirit, Time great glory did rain.
The power of the Simurgh cannot reach up to the height
    where hawk of his spirit nests; an attempt would be in vain.
His order is current like the wind over the land and the sea;
    his love like the soul, the bodies of man and genie contain.
Your form is the realm of beauty and beauty of the realm;
    your aspect is the world's soul and soul's world, I maintain!
Your throne is envy of sieges of Jamshid and of Kay Kobad;
    your crown's that for which Dara and Advan sought in vain.
If the flashing of your sword should pierce sphere's thought,
    Gemini's limbs would be separated and never joined again.
You're the sun of the land and wherever you happen to go,
    like the shadow great fortune is following in your train.
The elements never brought forth a jewel like you in any age,

in a hundred ages no star like you did the heavens ordain.
The soul doesn't stay with body without your appearance:
marrow doesn't stay in bone unless your favour it does gain.
Every piece of knowledge that's not written down in books,
your pen on the tip of its tongue, the answer does retain.
Who can make a comparison of your hand to the cloud?
One drops only a drop and the other a heavy purse does rain.
Compared to your height of glory the sky is only a doormat;
compared to generosity's sea, your kindness does remain.
You are sun of sphere of knowledge, crown on reason's head;
you are light of eye of learning and soul of country's brain.
By you, knowledge is blessed and reason gains splendour;
by you, law is protected and faith's safety you do maintain.
O Monarch who is sublime of majesty and highly exalted;
ruler without an equal and dignified of rank and of reign!
O sun of all the country, in the presence of your fine spirit
Shaigan's fabled treasure is like a feeble atom that is vain.
A hundred such treasures are less than only the small drop
that from sea of generosity you give, expecting no gain.
Innocence with a face that is veiled lives in your dwelling:
under your tent, fortune all its belongings does maintain.
The sphere, the tent of the sun of the great wide blue sky,
makes a canopy and a support out of cloud and mountain.
This painted satin that has nine folds and is painted gold,
a high awning over your royal pavilion does now sustain.
Since the Kayan kings in the kingdom of Solomon, no one
found such store, treasury, army, too weighty to maintain.
While you're in rosebed's centre and from your men's courage,
there is commotion in India and in Ethiopia they complain.
You pitch your tent in Rum's plain and throb of the drum
went to the desert of Sistan and on to India's distant plain.
Since you have built the yellow palace, great fear has come
to Kaiser's mansion, order in Khan's house one can't maintain.
From Egypt to Rum and all the way from China to Cyrene,
who is there that is equal to you in power and in domain?
Next year they shall bring the Kaiser's crown to your head;
from China to your court they'll bring Khan's tribute again.

You thank the Creator and all of the creation thanks you;
fortune gives you joy, through you the people fortune gain.
See how you keep going towards rosebed and rosegarden,
you go with slave, steed of happiness, which you constrain.
O you who are one who is inspired by ranks of holy angels,
a blessing comes to your pure heart each time it does rain!
Clearly manifested to your heart is what the Omnipotent
keeps hidden behind screen of the hidden, there to retain,
the rein of your desire the sky has placed into your hand,
saying this: "Who then am I? I am at your desire's rein:
if it will help your endeavour, then I give you my body:
if you wish for a gift, my goldmines are all yours to gain.
Where are your enemies? Throw them under your foot!
Where is your friend? Give him to me so I can entertain!
My desires are all expecting to be of some service to you:
by all my praising of you, my name eternal shall remain."

580. CHIEF OVER ALL THE WORLD

Of such charming of hearts one cannot very easily be boasting,
there are a thousand subtleties here, but this you are knowing.
In the matter of beauty there is more besides a sweet mouth;
one can't boast of being a Solomon by having only a seal-ring.
Charming of hearts of a thousand realms doesn't reach to that,
which by your skillfulness, in a single heart you're containing.
What dust you stirred up and out from my worldly existence!
May your steed never tire, although him you are always urging.
You're sitting with drunken lovers and are lowering your head:
for there are treasures in this helpless hopeless unreasoning.
Bring the cup of many colours, so that a hundred rare stories
I may tell and yet the being a Muslim I will not be breaching.
Because I've stood in the dust of the drinker in the morning,
intoxicated in Winehouse's street, watch at door I'm keeping.
I never let a fanatic who is a worshipper of the outward go past,
who beneath the religion's robe, the secret cord was not hiding.
In the name of your hair that binds hearts, give to us a favour,
so that you, from being wild like it, God will then be saving.

Don't turn your eye that gives favours away from Hafez's state,
or else to the second Chief, his condition I'll then be telling.
Advisor of the rank of King, Chief over all the earth and time,
from whom mankind's state and genie are joyfully prospering,
Kivam, Pillar and Fortune of the world, Mohammed son of Ali,
from whose face, glorious rays of Almighty God are gleaming.
You're the most praiseworthy quality in Nature: with honesty
and true judgment, mastery over the world you are claiming.
It is in your honourable enduring fortune and it is rightly so,
that your high spirit the world of effacement isn't mentioning.
If the great treasure of your generosity was not given as help,
the whole surface of the earth would be desolate and rotting.
You're one, the frame of whose body has no corporate matter;
you are of the Angel's essence wearing human being's clothing.
What measure of magnificence is it then possible to establish,
where you are not the highest in all the degrees of thinking?
Inside sacred chamber of Angels of the realm of Holy World,
the highest music of the soul is your pen's reed scratching.
The clinging sweetness of Lordship reaches you, because from
generosity upon all kind ones, both sleeves you're scattering.
How could I ever be explaining your generosity of the past?
For that merciful work that is done, may God give a blessing.
How shall I explain your bolts of thunder that are powerful?
From these calamities like a deluge let us to God be fleeing.
Since the bride of rose has gone to the field's bridal chamber,
there is not a soul's conspirator except the breeze of morning,
for the sake of the rose's Monarch, by the hand of the breeze,
the canopies of the red anemones by the tulips are opening.
From the efforts of the fragrance of the breeze of Springtime,
it comes to such a state that this brute, of grace is boasting.
How sweetly it came to me in the morning when a nightingale
raised the rose, and shouting at rosebud was eloquently saying:
"Why do you sit with such a sad heart, come out from the veil,
for in the great flagon is a real wine like ruby for drinking."
For a month don't allow yourself to drink to the rose's beauty,
or then for another month you'll drink the wine of repenting.
Be thankful for criticism of unfaithfulness that has come out,

and try, so that from rose and wine, happy dues you're taking.
God forbid, it's not the way of cherishers of Faith to be cruel;
the Law of God is full of grace and of mercy and of blessing!
Does that careless one know of the secret of "I am The Truth,"
who by God's attractions, doesn't find The Divine attracting?
See how within the veil of the rose, the rosebud still continues
to make arrow of ruby and at your enemy keeps on shooting?
Winebringer, it is the Chief's house of joy: so do not let it be
that without the cup of wine, a heavy heart one is showing.
Breath of morning, you were the hope that was there, because
you dawned because of love and night's darkness was ending.
It's been brought to my notice that at times you remember me;
but into your special gathering, me you are still not calling.
You do not want me to speak and this is the greatest cruelty!
If this is not so, then why all this argument about speaking?
Of all Hafezes of the world, no one like your poor slave here,
has philosophic graces with *Koranic* mysteries been blending.
My praising will give to you a thousand years of permanency,
for one like you, cheap is such precious wealth of praising.
I have made my speech long, but I am also still hopeful that
over this, the skirt of pardon you will cause to be covering.
On the surface of the garden until the coming of Springtime,
morning breeze with basil's line, a thousand images is painting.
For you, in garden of the King, from the bough of hopefulness,
from long life, rose of fortune and joyfulness, be blossoming.

581. THE FALCON WITH THE GOLDEN WING

When dawn's white breath, scent of soul's life sweetly
takes,
to heart a sweet message on earth through air softly
takes.
Veiled cloud upon earth brings a thousand scents of rose;
horizon is rosegarden's colour, such a glow it lightly
takes.

Melody of the harp invites the morning cup in such a way,
that path to Master's door, saint from cell quickly
takes.
When upon his face the sky's king draws the golden shield,
with dawn's sword and horizon's rays, the world he
takes.
The falcon with the golden wing, despite the black crow,
makes for the high azure dome and sky's nest royally
takes.
To earth's feasting table go: because it is a pleasant sight
where tulip, cup of wine, arghavan and rose's beauty
takes.
What does it mean that the rose shows her face on earth?
What fire's in soul that bird at dawn to song joyfully
takes?
If in head of Hafez the thought of being a king is absent;
why then with tongue for sword, the entire world he
takes?
See how impulsively the breeze, like a mad lover playing,
now lip of the rose, now the curls of basil freely
takes!
I'm like that one whose blessed breath is the breath that
in the white of dawn, dark dust from the world he
takes.
Why am I the one who griefstricken, regretful, frightened,
to point of the compass, the circle of sphere quickly
takes?

The depth of my heart I open to no one, that is the best:
for Time is so jealous and it suddenly toward envy
takes.
Whoever should give out the secrets like the candle does,
at night like a wick, his tongue the scissors quickly
takes.
Where is my moonfaced Winebringer, Who with kindness,
to his own half-intoxicated one, cup of wine fully
takes?

That one brings me news from the Friend and later a cup;
joy, from that kind moon's cheek, my ease so easily
takes.
If the song of our gathering the musician should bring out,
melodic paths of Irak and of Isfahan, it occasionally
takes.
You are an Alexander, who like Khizer dwells in Courtyard,
and from gracious dust of the doorway, Life Eternally
takes.
You are the beautiful face of kindness, Shaikh Abu Ishak:
under your feet, the country, rosegarden's beauty
takes.
When he is ascending, it's to the high sky of being a Lord;
as the first step of such a rank, the two Polestars he
takes.
He is light of eye of Mahmud's family, whose enemy flees
from the flash of fire that from his sword brightly
takes.
High as moon is the wave of blood when his sword's drawn;
the arrow of constellations he hits, when his bow he
takes.
His luminous wisdom puts to shame the bride of the East;
rightly, leaving the East, nightly off to Morocco she
takes.
So great is your glory and grace that whoever is your slave,
holding and praising your Gemini garment to safety
takes.

From Mercury many thousands of 'congratulations' come;
your thought "Be, and it was," into formation fully
takes.
Arcturus the Lancebearer, who is always on the lookout,
day and night, spear in hand, your envious enemy
takes.
Your stallion, which the sky sees gracefully performing,
the reaches of the milky way is the lowest place he
takes.

Fortune shall be yours from bearing of small misfortunes,
for this order is his own design, that Jupiter freely
takes.

The purpose of Fate and Time was to prove you in this way,
so that on your heart, impression of aspirant's purity
takes:

If this is not the case, then highest is the Book of Books,
which, when examined closely, test of Time clearly
takes.

The wise and the witty hero is that one, who, every time,
thinks deeply first, then that way he believes in, he
takes.

Safe from sorrow's bitterness is palate of each man's soul,
whose mouth is sugar and food of praise to you he
takes.

He eats of the fruit of Life, who in all involvements looks
firstly at himself and the way he believes in only
takes.

When he sees no reason to fight, hand reaches for winecup;
when it's time to act, the sword that takes life, he
takes.

Do not turn face hopelessly from kindness hidden deeply,
for in the hard bone, soft sweet marrow still securely
takes.

After a really long period sugar becomes perfectly sweet:
so, its place in the narrow straight cane, it initially
takes.

That place where left and right, flood of viciousness comes,
eventually out from the middle, to the side of safety
takes.

Why grieve about it? Whatever the situation, mountain is
strong and firm: not even the waves of a stormy sea
takes.

Though now your enemy struts, head high with arrogance,
you be happy; for his rein, his arrogance certainly
takes.

Although he slanders this fortunate household with words,

for wife, children and house, Justice payment fully
takes.
Long, long be the term of your life; because your fortune
is a happy gift from God, that upon man and genie
takes.
The Chief of the Kings of words is Hafez, for whole fields
of riders, with Ali's spinelike sword of speech… he
takes.

582. SO MUCH IN LOVE WITH YOU

Adored One, so much in love with You, so much I am,
that with my existence completely out of touch I am;
although weak and without power at all, as such I am,
if a thousand lives allowed once again to clutch I am,
throwing them all at Your blessed feet to touch I am.
When will I be fortunate enough to be the supplicater,
brought in the presence of You, the heart comforter,
and of the heart's hidden secrets to be the explainer?
O if only a mighty falcon like You, such a high flyer,
would give this honour to this poor nest where I am.
Although in Your nature it natural to be so hurtful is,
don't You do any harm, for that not very helpful is.
If it is, that of iron and of brass Your heart not full is,
pass at last, my Friend, over this my head so foolish,
then remember that the dust of Your threshold I am.
"Because with such severity You have struck me dead,
from now on the path of Mercy Your feet must tread,
on Your heart, faith's writing You must write," I said.
But not one thought of union with us is in Your head:
and knowing my star and my fortune far too well I am.
O You Who tied Your waist's cord from near and far,
to soon be taking the blood of Turkey and of Persia,
although where I make my home is mean and darker
than the dwelling of other slaves, no one is any truer;
but I'm afraid that marked by Your radiant eye, I am.

Nothing, except for faithfulness from You, I'm seeking;
beyond rose of faithfulness my eyes are never seeing;
except on the path of service to You, I'm not walking;
never of Your mysteries to a single soul I'm speaking,
and never singing Your praises to anyone at all I am.
Never the door of faithfulness I opened, this I admit;
neither did I to love add love, nothing I added to it:
nothing at all of the amount of whatever I did was fit;
in the end, You and I, never friendship we could knit:
Your promise is broken, but still keeping same I am.
If with the sharpened sword You cut the head off me,
taking leave from the street of faithfulness I'll not be,
and even if from limb to limb they then tear apart me,
the seal of my love for You will not by me broken be;
except when as bones, scattered high and low, I am.
All those who are looking for the trace of love's way,
except for the way that leads to my tomb, never stray:
and when they are looking at my poor miserable clay,
if over my head at my tomb Your name they then say,
making a shout that is rising out from the soul, I am.
If before me should troop a brigade of great beauties,
every one much purer than Canopus' bright purities,
from You to another, I'll not give my love's abilities:
I would be insane if in selling Layla's fair securities,
gaining those territories of Arabia and of Persia I am.
I've become, through longing for You, O Form so fair,
distracted and dark of heart like Your long dark hair;
though I don't reach Your street, not a night is there
when from separation from You out of black despair,
that not storming the sky with my loud wailing I am.
O You, You with Whom Union is such great happiness,
may You be staying in such an everlasting joyfulness!
On Your own Hafez, why do You scatter this distress?
Every order that against me You so urgently impress
is easy to take: as long as from You, not far away I am.

583. MAN'S BEST FRIEND

The dog has more honour on which to depend,
than that man who hurts the heart of a friend.
It is necessary for this true saying to. be proved
so that in the heart it sinks, not to be removed.
Man eats with you, with his hand on the table;
shut outside on the threshold the dog is unable.
It is a pity, for dog is faithful until his death;
while that man thinks it is right to break faith.

584. LISTEN WELL

O breeze of morning, my heart is one of sorrowfulness,
with your fragrance my soul is scented with happiness.
By the rosebed's border in the morning a passage make;
to the cypress and to the rose from us a message take.
Say: "O rose, before that face, don't boast of beauty;
for the weaver of rush doesn't know gold-embroidery.
O cypress, before that height don't say you are tall,
for compared with that height, to the smallest you fall."
Winebringer come; because it is the season of Spring,
don't take any notice of the one who is not drinking.
With a song and with that red wine keep on drinking,
for as long as you are able; and do not be delaying.
Don't allow your ear to hear the morals of the teachers,
whether it's their own advice or gabble of the preachers.
In the garden, to you the nightingale keeps on singing:
"In season of rose, cup from the hand don't be giving."
Understand as great gain, having the rose's enjoyment;
drinking wine, resolve to make your only employment.
Don't ever be careless: because this occasion will pass,
each breath that passes, time of joy's season will pass.
For a moment listen well to this advice Hafez is giving:
"God knows everything, and winecup keep draining."

585. ONLY A BRIDGE

Whoever enters this world that's full of commotion,
in the end, it's necessary he goes to tomb's location.
This world is like a bridge to the next world's road,
a place without permanency and a desolate abode.
Don't set your heart on this bridge that is full of fear:
prepare provisions for the road and do not stay here.
Opinion of men of understanding is: this old mansion
is transitory; there is no treasure in this place of ruin.
Truthfully, the wise have pierced the pearl of truth,
who have named this place: "An inn without a roof."
This inn is not fit to be staying in: move on from it!
This world leaves no one remaining: move on from it!
From friendship with wealth and rank, far away sit:
your wealth is the snake and your rank is the pit.
Suppose I grant that you are Bahram Gur the great;
into the grave's snare you'll fall, whether soon or late.
I said to you: "If you are not blind, the grave see,"
and: "Don't for a moment without work, sitting be."
There's no help, no escape for anyone from this stage;
not for beggar or king or youth or those of old age.
You, who draw your skirt so proudly over our clay,
Hafez wishes that the *Koran's 'Fatiha'* you'd say.

586. ONLY GRIEF

I have had nothing from the life I have had
, but grief
I have had nothing from love, good and bad,
but grief:
I've never for a moment had a sympathetic companion;
I have no one, no consoler when I am sad,
but grief

587. FROM ALI

For courage from 'Ali, plucker of the door of Kheiber,
ask:
the secrets of generosity from the Master of Kember
ask.
Hafez, if you are sincerely thirsting for the Grace of God,
from its fountainhead, the Winebringer of Kauther,
ask.

588. A VICTIM

If like me the victim fallen into the snare
you become,
intoxicated with wine of the cup forever
you become;
we are drunken lovers who burnt away the whole world;
do not sit here, or an infamous one there
you become.

589. ONLY SORROW

From this world's salty desert man receives only sorrow,
and finally he cries his life out as his sorrow does grow.
That one's happy who into this world has never entered,
and he is happy whose exit from it does quickly follow.

590. MY DISCOVERY

Your soul has completely covered me in deepest ecstasy,
I desired You but grief was holding my heart tightly;
if I'm unable to find You in the place where one prays,
in the Winehouse of Love Your lips are my discovery.

591. THE PRICE

Beloved may only be embraced by one who'll give away
silver and gold and heart and sanity: give all away today;
once a beauty full of scorn refused to hear my words:
I did not have gold, although words like pearls I did say.

592. IF YOU DECIDE

If You should happen to be leaving Your Sacred Home,
my prayer is that You hear cry of one who does roam;
and if You decide to rest in my house for a short time,
never, even in Your mind, take to wind, fly for home.

593. GIVE AND TAKE

O my Beloved, while this life of mine I can be offering
to soft down of Your cheek: I can never be leaving.
For my soul's sweet nourishment, for Your lip's ruby,
two hundred thousand jewels I would never be taking.

594. VIOLET'S VIOLENCE

The violet down will grow around Your lip of sweetness,
then the violet will blow and pillow tulip with a caress;
a thousand hearts will be driven to the depth of despair
from smoke from that flame that from Your cheek rises.

595. PATHWAY'S DUST

Upon my sorrow smile with Your heart full of kindness,
like the sun that shines on the earth's dark filthy mess.
Do not criticize me even though I am pathway's dust,
to waste Your words on mere dust is surely worthless.

596. DEPRESSION

Time ruined and crushed me under foot of oppression;
happiness with another I've not had in my possession.
From cup of world I haven't drunk pure wine or dregs,
and none could spend a life in such dark depression.

597. DISCONTENTED

It's true that to You allegiance is sworn by all countries,
that before the seal-ring You wear, all are on their knees;
You're contented, but when You and I part, for me it's
ten yards of shroud and three of earth under the trees.

598. DRAWN BY PARADISE

When Paradise drew Your features, O my fair Beloved,
and each line of beauty that fascinates hearts, pencilled:
for a pen Paradise chose for the work the purple violet,
and on unknowing rose petals, there Paradise traced.

599. A LENGTHY AFFAIR

Like a beggar tightly I clung to Your long hyacinth hair,
and I cried: "Devise a remedy for me, full of despair:"
You answered this: "Take My sweet lip, let My hair go;
hold on to sweetness, let go of life, it's a lengthy affair."

600. LIKE THE BUBBLE

Since the bud of the rose the flagon's drainer
becomes,
the narcissus desiring wine, the cup's holder
becomes.
That one will have a happy heart who like the bubble,
from desiring wine, the house's demolisher
becomes.

601. THAT OLD WINE

That old wine that is prepared in the village give to me,
and I will make life's covering new with embroidery:
make me drunk and unconscious of the world's affairs,
so, o faultless man, I may reveal the world's mystery.

602. BECAUSE OF YOU

O You, because of You both the sun and the moon lay
their forehead upon Your garden's dust, night and day:
with a hand and a tongue and a heart, don't plant me
on expectation's fire and then without a care go away.

603. SEEK

Sit down with the Friend and the cup of the wine
seek,
a kiss from lip of that cypress, limb of rose so fine,
seek.
If the wounded one is seeking to have his wound eased,
say: "Ease from Barber's Son's razor's fine line,
seek."

604. SOURCE OF LIFE

For as long as the Heavens our destiny ordering
shall be,
then ever your occupation with joy ascending
shall be:
that cup that you drink from the hands of Taktamun,
the source of life which is always long-lasting
shall be.

605. WORTHLESS

To gain a world's fortune through tyranny
, is worthless;
gaining existence's joy by grief and worry,
is worthless;
the joys of the whole world for seven thousand years,
for five days of despair, worry and cruelty,
is worthless.

606. I'LL SLEEP

In pool of blood through grief for You tonight
I'll sleep,
far away from the couch of peace and delight
I'll sleep.
If You don't believe then send to me Your own image,
to see how impossibly, without You in sight,
I'll sleep.

607. I DIE

Because of longing for Your kiss and embrace,
I die;
because of grief for Your glistening lip's grace,
I die.
Why do I make this story so long? I will make it brief
come back, for out of expectation for Your face
I die.

608. WATER OF LIFE

O Soul, since with You I have brought a night into day,
I'm not a man if I breathe when You have gone away;
I don't fear death after this, because the Water of Life
I drink from Your sweet fountain, a glistening spray.

609. HOW LONG?

For how long is this violence and oppression
of Yours?
all people are upset by this foolish aggression
of Yours.
The sword stained with blood is in the hand of the lover;
if it reaches You, blood is on head's decision,
of Yours.

610. THE CUP'S LIP

Never, never separated your lip make
from the cup's lip;
so your desire from world, you take
from the cup's lip.
Since in the world's cup sweet and bitter are combined,
take this from Beloved's lip, that take
from the cup's lip.

611. A DROP OF BLOOD

You said this: "I'm yours and so have no more concern,
make the heart joyful, to patience give all your concern."
What heart? Where's patience? That which You call heart
is only a drop of blood and there is so much for concern.

612. SUCH CRUELTY

For loving the Beloved's face, against me
don't complain:
against those with hearts full of misery,
don't complain.
Sufi, since you have knowledge of the wayfarers' ways,
against the drinking man, with cruelty
don't complain.

613. NEITHER: NOR

Neither the tale about that candle of Chigil
one can tell,
nor condition of the heart, burning still,
one can tell:
in my tired heart there is grief because there's no friend
who about grief which the heart does fill,
one can tell.

614. WITH GOLD

Those lovely ones of the world one can bait
with gold;
because of them, happily one can't enjoy fate
with gold.
See the narcissus that possesses the crown of the world
how its head also bends, from being straight,
with gold.

615. SOME CONSOLATION

A moon whose shape was straight like the tall cypress,
straightened her face while holding mirror in her caress.
When I offered her the handkerchief she then said this:
"You seek union? At least your imagination isn't a mess!"

616. LION OF GOD

Loosener of knots and Awarder of heaven and of hell
don't leave us, or from feet we'll fall, You know well.
For how much longer will the wolves keep snatching?
Lion of God, show Your claws and the enemy dispel.

617. EXCEPT

Except Your image, nothing comes into that sight
of ours,
except Your street, no other path holds delight
of ours.
Although to all in Your time a sweet sleep does come,
God, I swear it never comes to eye, day or night,
of ours.

618. FAR TOO QUICKLY

You, Your eye: deceit and sorcery
keep raining from it;
hey, many swords, war's weaponry,
keep raining from it.
Too quickly You became wearied and upset with friends;
Your heart: stones that do injury,
keep raining from it.

619. STRANGE!

Every friend who boasted about faith an enemy
became:
every one with a spoiled garment, one of purity
became.
They say: "Night's pregnant with the unknown." Strange!
Since she knew no man, how is it pregnant she
became?

620. SAY SOME WORDS

Soft breeze, in great secrecy my tale relay
to that One,
my heart's fire with many a tongue portray
to that One.
Don't speak in such a way that makes that One annoyed,
say some words: my heart's sad tune play
to that One.

621. AND YOU SAID

I said: "What's Your lip?" "Water of Life," You told me.
I said: "Your mouth?" You: "An excellent ball of candy."
Then I said: "Your speech?" And You said: "Hafez said
it is joy of the prayers of all who speak with subtlety."

622. MY MOON

My moon Whose face the sun's shining renown
took,
around that One's cheeks down, Kauther's gown
took;
then throwing all the hearts into the pit of that chin,
the pit of the mouth with that fine musky down
, took.

623. EASY TO SEE

When that musky moon takes the garment off the body,
there is not an equal to that moon in pure fair beauty;
one can see the heart in that breast for it is transparent,
like the hard stone in crystal water, it is so easy to see.

624. BE ON YOUR GUARD

The torrent came and took the ruined habitation
of life,
and then it began to fill up the cup's limitation
of life.
Kind sir, be on your guard; because the porter of death
soon takes all the belongings from the habitation
of life.

625. KEEP HOPING

Keep hoping for the sky's fortune in every possible way;
yet, from Time's turns, like a willow tremble and sway.
You said this: "After black, there's not a colour coming:"
then why did my black hair become white, can you say?

626. EYE'S SORCERY

The sorcery of Your eye that Babylon's sorcerers taught,
O God, I swear, that sorcery has never left its thought.
That hair that has put the ring of slavery upon beauty,
may it, by the pearl of Hafez's verse, be forever caught.

627. THE RIGHT WAY

With the wine, on a stream's bank, to sit,
is the right way;
to be far away from grief of the hermit
is the right way.
Because our precious life is lasting only ten short days,
for lip to smile and face to be freshly lit,
is the right way.

628. FROM YOU

You, the veiled rosebud is filled with sham
e from You;
the drunken narcissus is sick and also lame
from You.
How then can the rose with You ever become an equal?
for it takes moon's light and that also came
from You.

629. YOU GAVE

At first, faithfully that cup of union to me
You gave:
when I became drunk, me the cup of tyranny
You gave;
when with both eyes weeping and the heart full of fire
I became Your path's dust, me to wind quickly
You gave.

630. NOT RIGHT TO BE

Towards those good men to be bad,
it's not right to be:
in desert of the demon that is mad,
it's not right to be.
Of one's own way of living to be glad,
it's not right to be,
and proud of the learning one's had,
it's not right to be.

631. SPIRITUAL WINE

By shade of Your hyacinth hair, jasmine
is nourished!
Pearl of Aden by Your lip's ruby so fine,
is nourished!
Soul is nourished by Your lip that by wine
is nourished;
with wine that's Spiritual Your form Divine
is nourished!

632. ANOTHER!

Daily my heart under another burden does lie,
another!
A thorn because of separation is now in my eye,
another!
I keep trying and trying and Fate is calling and calling:
"It's another work, beyond all you may try:
another!"

633. LET THE WINE FLOW

Why is it necessary to foam like wine because of sorrow?
With the army of grief, why is it necessary to fight so?
Your lip is fresh so do not keep the goblet far from it;
over the fresh lip it's very pleasing to let the wine flow.

634. SEASON OF YOUTH

This is now the season of youth, and that wine
is best;
for all grief to go to drunkenness and to resign,
is best.
All of the world from end to end is ruined and spent;
to be totally ruined in this place of ruin is fine,
is best.

635. SWEET BELOVED

Come back, because of Your beauty my soul is waiting;
come back, from being without You my heart is hurting.
Come back, for without Your face, O my sweet Beloved,
from eye of my head that's spinning, a torrent's flowing.

636. COME

Take wine that gives joy, about it be discreet
and come,
with mean watcher don't try, leave Your seat:
and come.
Don't hear rival's speech who says: "Sit down, don't go."
O fair Idol, listen to me, get up now I repeat,
and come.

637. EVIL DAY

The separation that to the soul of poor me to stay
came,
"On heart's wound, piece of salt," you could say
"came;"
I was so afraid that one day I'd go far away from You,
and You surely saw that to me such an evil day
came.

638. THEY DON'T RECOMMEND

Those sweet talkers often a promise to the end
don't take:
visionaries, away from love soul don't send:
don't take.
When the Beloved is to your wish and also to your desire,
lovers, your name they don't recommend:
don't take.

639. WHAT HAS CAUSED IT?

The twist and the turn of Your hair,
what has caused it?
Your intoxicated eye's sleepy stare,
what has caused it?
Since no one scattered on You the petal of a single rose,
head to toe Your rose-scented air,
what has caused it?

640. THE RECOGNISER OF LOVE

That long pathway to You, many a thorn of grief
has:
where is the wayfarer that feet not wanting relief
has?
Do you know one who recognizes love? That one who
on face of the soul, the light of breath and belief
has.

641. TEAR AWAY YOUR HEART

O son, from the mother of time tear away your heart;
hold what is left of that husband who was torn apart;
O heart, you will become one who has no knowledge,
if like Hafez, your happiness from her face does start.

642. IT'S OBVIOUS

I grasped Your belt hoping Your help I would obtain,
or that I would gain whatever that belt did contain;
it's so obvious what Your waist gains from Your belt;
now let me see what it is that from Your belt I'll gain.

643. HAJJI AHMED

Acceptable to heart of the high and acclaimed by the low,
sweet of note, harmoniously moving, full moon on show.
All throughout the city of Shiraz, famous is the player
of the instrument, who by name of Hajji Ahmed does go.

644. I PERCEIVE

The wing of the bird of joyfulness beating I perceive;
or is it the scent of the rosebed of longing I perceive?
Or is it the tale that from Your lips the breeze is telling?
Anyway, it's truly a wonderful tale for telling I perceive.

645. ALL YOU NEED

The Sweetheart lovingly playful, and minstrel and reed,
quiet corner, time to play, bottle of wine, is all you need.
When veins and muscles become warm with wine, indeed
for barleycorn to Hatim Tai I'd not for generosity plead.

646. I WEEP

More than the candle, when You are not near,
I weep:
like flagon of wine, many a rose-coloured tear
I weep.
I am like the cup of wine; because from broken heart,
my blood, whenever the wail of the harp I hear,
I weep.

647. A GREAT MISTAKE

It is truly a great mistake for one to glorify
oneself,
and out of all of the creation to go and magnify
oneself:
it is right for one to learn from the pupil of one's eye,
to see everyone else and not to only ever spy
oneself

648. SOCIETY OF THE WORTHLESS

My soul is sacrificed for that One, Who worthwhile
is;
if you place my head at those feet, it a peaceful pile
is.
Do you desire to understand all the truth about hell?
Truthfully, hell the society of the worthless and vile
is.

649. WISE ADVICE

To pound all the horizon from end to end in a mortar,
and the sky's nine arches with heart's blood to smear,
to be captive in a prison for a hundred years and a year,
is better than being with a fool for a moment, I swear.

650. GATES OF HAPPINESS

Until the desire of my wounded heart gratified
shall be,
until my body without its king, the soul, inside
shall be:
I am forever hopeful that from the Great Court of God,
gates of happiness thrown open high and wide
shall be.

651. DRAW IN

Friend, your heart from doing violence to foe,
draw in;
with a happy face, that wine that does glow,
draw in.
Loosen button of your collar to the worthwhile man,
hem of your garment from the worthless also,
draw in.

652. IF ONLY

O if only Fortune had been much more helpful to me,
or the turn of Fate's wheel had turned out to be lucky!
If only old Age could place a foot firmly in the stirrup,
because from hands of Youth, Time took reins playfully.

653. STAR OF ANGUISH

The loss of a long life because of chasing a wish,
                    have I;
what gain from the turnings of the inverted dish
                    have I?
Every single person to whom I said: "I was your friend,"
became my enemy: O no, what a star of anguish
                    have I.

654. IN MEMORY

Friends, when your hands meet and when you embrace,
you forget this sphere that is turning around in space,
when the turn comes to me and I am not in my place,
have a drink during that time from memory of my face.

655. TODAY

Today, when the breaking of a promise is so easy to see,
where's a friend who in the end doesn't become enemy?
Because of this state I've taken hold of solitude's shirt,
so through eyes of enemy, that friend will not see me.

656. YOU MADE ME

My Friend, to the wishes of the enemy
You made me;
I was Spring, then like Autumn's severity
You made me.
In Your quiver, I was straight like an arrow; why is it that
bent like a bow, slave to Your victory,
You made me?

657. OPPOSITES

I'm so weak and exhausted, helpless and deep in poverty;
and You are so self-sufficient, so proud and beyond me:
but if You place me on the fire I will patiently sit there,
but if I place You on the horse You don't sit, You flee!

658. THE SIGH

Friend, do not sit careless of the fierceness
of the sigh,
for fire may reach you from fire's closeness
of the sigh.
Beware that in your own street you don't underestimate
weeping at night and morning's restlessness
of the sigh.

659. IN HAND

For how long, the heart's grief from Fate do
you have?
Leave world and its possessions that to accrue
you have.
Seek Friend and a little stream and foot of the rosebush,
now in hand, wine that is a mouthful or two,
you have.

660. MY RESOLVE

Much room for grief for You in this heart
I've made;
pain for You, remedy for my heart torn apart,
I've made;
the more violent that You become towards my heart,
the firmer my resolve that I'll play my part,
I've made.

661. NOTHING ELSE

I said: "What is Your sweet dark mole that I can see?"
You said: "You are so silly and stupid, beyond all pity;
for there is no mole in the mirror of Our fair beauty:
it is nothing else but your eye's pupil that you see."

662. HOW IS IT?

Like face of my Beloved, my tears rose-coloured
became;
from my heart, my eye full of blood that bled
became.
Gracefully my Beloved spoke to me, saying this to me:
"O dear friend, how is it that your eye so red
became?"

663. HOMESICK

If a person for a long month should remain wandering,
even if strong as a mountain, only a straw is remaining.
Although the poor stranger may dwell in another land,
when he remembers his own land, then he begins sighing.

664. THE KNOWER

O Lord, since of all needs the Accomplisher

You are,
both the Judge and the sufficient Apportioner
You are;
why should I relate to You all the secrets of my heart,
since of all the hidden mysteries, the Knower
You are?

665. DIVINE

In all of the form, the expression of the Divine
You are,
the mirror of everything that's lovely and fine
You are!
Nothing in this world can exist by itself without You;
wherever we look we find that all we define:
You are!

666. YOU!

The only aim of my love and my heart's desire
is You,
the only source of this love's passionate fire
is You!
Whenever I look on the world and on Time, I see that
all is You today and all tomorrow may acquire
is You!

667. YOUR WILL

Give to me all the joy of Unification,
if it's Your Will;
or the pain of sorrow from separation,
if it's Your Will.
I don't say this to You: "What will You give to me?"
Give whatever is the due proportion:
if it's Your Will.

668. ANOTHER QUESTION

If You turned to me, from all the world I'd turn away;
if You dealt to me harsh justice, to death I'd go today!
Each day I cry out a hundred times: "O pure Creator,
from me, a handful of filth, what comes Your way?"

669. WHICH WILL BE THE GREATER?

It was Your Almighty Infinite Power that created me;
I've been nourished by Your Love and help, given free:
if I am put on trial for a hundred years and still I sin,
which will be the greater, my sin or Your great Mercy?

670. SHOW NO MERCY

O King of the world, show Your mercy to me so poor!
O soother of wounded hearts, Your balm on mine pour.
Don't let Your enemies live, don't listen to their advice:
give pity to Your own, and pity Your enemy no more.

671. EVERY MORNING

Every morning I tell You all of the secrets of my heart.
At Your Court each day this same request I impart:
"O You Who love slaves, I'm Your slave, loyal and true;
please help the work of one hurt by oppression's dart."

672. HOW?

O You, the place where You stay all men turn to pray;

all hearts that Fortune helps: You've looked their way.
That one who turns his face away today from Your face,
how will he manage to face You on the Judgement Day?

673. NOT A THOUGHT FOR ME

O King, who can compare with Your kindness, learning?
How could I be so daring as to sit where You are sitting?
What lies, what stories have been concocted by my foes,
that today, now, not a thought for me You are having?

674. THE ROPE OF LOVE

I am resigned to be the slave of the One Who loves me,
so that around my neck is tied the rope of Love to see.
What do you know of delights of Love and lover's joys?
He only drinks this cup, who a lover of the taste will be!

675. ONLY THE PICTURE

Your mind didn't think about the One Who is Almighty,
and you don't care at all for searching for the Divinity;
O no, you were caught up so much in only the picture,
you forgot Who created it: the Painter you didn't see!

676. UNTIL

Until you're humble, without pride and less than nothing,
you can't walk path to Paradise, or anyone be guiding.
Truly, until you have been drinking the world's poison,
sweet water of Paradise's Kauther you can't be tasting.

677. INCOGNITO

Although not drunk, as an inebriate
you must appear;
although not mad, yet as a hypocrite
you must appear;
until the secret of your faith is understood by the world,
idolater who with outcasts does sit,
you must appear.

678. SWEET

To my heart You softly said: "Your utterance:
sweet!
From where comes your gentle heart and essence
sweet?
If your heart bums like incense does in the fire of love,
shall My brain not be scented by its fragrance
sweet?"

679. STATE OF HUNGER

Like on lute, my fingers stray over Your curls and play,
my heart and Your lips are tuned in harmony all day;
Your mouth, that sweet pistachio nut, is my daily food;
Lord, my wounded heart in a state of hunger does stay.

680. THANKS TO YOU

The night has passed by, but I only told half of my tale;
I thanked You, although with troubles You I did assail:
I know I was bold and presumptuous, and yet I give to
You thanks that Your compassionate nature won't fail.

681. UNHAPPY DIFFICULTY

O lips that are like pure sugar, which I can no longer see,
kept distant, there is no rest each day and night for me.
O Beloved, my heart has lost all blood from separation,
O come just one time and see this unhappy difficulty!

682. RETURNING TO DUST

Absence tears my heart with pain, for You I'm longing;
I'd die for just one look at You yet I can't be hoping
to see Union arrive: from longing I die, I'm departing;
and from desire for You, to dust I am now returning.

683. PUNISHMENT FOR UNFAITHFULNESS

The day of separation has sent me far away from You,
now far from Your face I worry and I'm impatient too;
if I were to look at another's face, then, faithfulness
to Your beauty would cause blindness to quickly ensue.

684. YOU KNOW THIS TOO

Since that sorrowful day when Fate took me from You,
none have seen my lips smile, for this I cannot do;
this long separation causes my heart such deep sorrow:
I know this; You Who created me, You know this too.

685. THAT AND THIS

You, enflaming soul to bliss, once it was Unification,
and today I only experience the hellfire of separation!
It is a pity that in the volume of the book of my life:
"That, for one day; this, for another," was the notation.

686. DEADLY ENEMY

I said: "You're a lovely One Who is like a cypress, to me;

and perhaps a Friend to my poor sick heart You'll be?"
I thought that I'd found in You a Friend good and true,
I didn't know that You were really my deadly Enemy.

687. BECAUSE OF THIS

I said: "If You never become at all unfaithful to me
I'll never leave You, the back of me You will never see;
because of this I do not know why You are so distant;
O, if only You hadn't made me love You so dearly!"

688. THE FORGETFUL ROSE

O rose, the nightingale's sweet song You are not hearing;
You're fortunate but all with nothing You're forgetting.
You don't have a thought for those who are separated,
for separation's bitterness You've not had to be tasting.

689. ALMOST SELF-SUFFICIENT

That One with an angel's face Who my life was seeking,
as angels do, kept out of sight; it was so very upsetting
I said: "There's no kind word from Your closed lips?"
The answer: "Except your worthless life, I want nothing."

690. DEPENDING UPON

My heart, proof of love for Your lovely face
can show,
for like one burnt by fire, my heart love's trace
can show.
I don't offer my life to Your heart, but to Your fair face,
depending on whether Your heart to me grace
can show.

691. NOBODY

It's a pity, for there is no one to plead my need
for me;
no one to be a friend in either word or deed
for me!
If I were somebody, then somebody would be a friend,
but because I'm a nobody, nobody will plead
for me.

692. I'D LIKE TO SEE TOO!

The Friend remain faithful? That, I'd like to see
too!
Peace from that One's tyranny? I'd rest peaceably
too!
Can I be faithless when You are the whole of my life?
A life of faithfulness? That, I'd really like to see
too!

693. PLEASE EXPLAIN

My inconsistent One, You have left me for no reason;
You've been unfaithful and Your promise have broken.
Since You've become so distant, at least please explain
why at first You're my Friend, then leave me forsaken.

694. I WILL DEMAND

See what You did when You sent me off into
separation:
we're cut off separated, since You sent me to
separation!
If I should happen to return again to the One that I love,
I will demand, I'll ask: "Why put me through
separation?"

695. BURNT TO DUST

Due to floods of hot tears, blindness came to my eyes;
from much cruelty my heart burnt up, from many fires;
and when You found me burnt to dust on Your path,
You gathered up all my dust and threw it to the skies.

696. THORNS

I said: "Maybe You will not laugh at being my Friend:
those rubies beautifying Your lips I'll gain in the end."
I did not know then that the fair garden of Your face
would give roses to others and on thorns I could depend.

697. LAMP OF CHIGIL

O Lamp of Chigil, is it possible for me to forget You?
For that load that I carry gets heavier, it's true, it's true.
Pain through love for You that my heart experiences,
my heart knows, my heart knows, and I do, I do, I do.

698. PAIN OF DEEP SORROW

Deep in my heart's ocean many priceless pearls are there,
it's a pity if they remain unpierced, unstrung to compare!
Who speaks about the pain of grief that one can express?
It's a pity, for the pain of deep sorrow one cannot share!

699. THE BITTER CUP

My heart's bird fell into snare's strife of grieving
for You,
then on its neck fell the sharp knife of grieving
for You.
I despise the sickly-sweet sherbet of the cup of Destiny
since I drank the bitter cup of a life of grieving
for You.

700. COMPLETELY CRAZY

Raging flames burn my heart but You can shelter me:
my soul is troubled and suffers many a great difficulty.
Don't blame me if all I say seems wild, out of control:
You know through love for You I'm completely crazy.

701. WISHING

If only my pen had a tongue, and then it could impart
my sorrow without end, bitter grief and pain of my heart.
If only arms of my Friend were there around my neck,
or I were beheaded... to death I could quickly depart.

702. TAKE MY MESSAGE

O breeze, kindly take my message to Beloved and say:
"From this anguish do not be feeling grief in any way:
joy and peace for Your bed, sleeping all night through,
of him always awake, did a thought reach You to stay?"

703. UNTIL BREAK OF DAY

From grief, last night I didn't sleep until sun's first ray;
my eyelashes pierced rubies until sun came up to stay.
I can't tell my pain and grief to anyone, they're so great;
I only told it to my sorrowful heart until break of day.

704. EXCEPT ME!

In Your street, no one is poor and homeless,
except me!
Near Your dwelling, no one stays friendless,
except me!
I'm the only one imprisoned by the chain of Your hair,
for no one, from loving You, has this madness,
except me!

705. MY PLIGHT

You are with me in every thought, each day and night;
You are always with me in spirit, and truthfully I might
mention that in this deep grief that comes from the love
I have for Your face, I am existing; and that's my plight!

706. FAITH'S FULL EXPRESSION

If You should strike me with that knife of oppression,
I will not leave You or take notice of its deep incision;
freely I will sacrifice myself to You because I believe:
"One owning my heart deserves faith's full expression."

707. WHAT WORTH OR NEED?

What worth are friends who haven't felt Fortune's blows?
What joy exists for hearts where happiness never glows?
My Beloved Who was the pupil of my eye has departed:
what need have I now for an eye that no light knows?

708. MY HEART'S STORY

If I should speak of my wounded heart's deep despair,
hundred hearts with grief like mine, apart I would tear;
it would take a whole lifetime's patience and sympathy,
for you to hear the story of what my heart has to bear.

709. THE DIVINE LIGHT

You are a lovely Moon and the sun is a slave of Yours:
as he is Your slave, glorious light he constantly pours!
Because all things are illuminated by Your bright face,
out from the sun and the moon the divine light soars.

710. LIFE'S GREAT JOY

I have spent all my days thinking of Your fair beauty,

I've passed each night painfully longing for sweet unity;
my heart spills over from love for Your soft fine down,
and life's great joy has been when You, I'm able to see.

711. YOUR FORM

Your small mouth with the pistachio nut does contend;
Your cheek, tulip's crimson colour with itself does blend.
With pleasant grace and humour You speak so sweetly!
Your form's silver limb and thigh, silver light does extend.

712. LONGING TO STAY

What subtle and complex ways are used by my Beloved:
once coy, then scornful, then fascinating then bored!
Longing to stay with the Beloved, my poor heart desires
the chance for the Beloved's company to be enjoyed.

713. PUT IT ON MY HAND

Go and get the wine, Joy's falcon:
put it on my hand;
like a beautiful one is that flagon:
put it on my hand.
With that curl that coils around itself chain me tightly,
for I am insane: go and chain it on,
put it on my hand.

714. MORE THAN DAY AND NIGHT

Black as shadows cast by the sun is shade of Your hair,
the full moon's light is eclipsed by Your face so fair;
evening bears a banner behind Your cheek's dark mole,
attendant of Your moon-like face is dawn in full flare.

715. ONLY WITH BRIBES

My soul had been caught by my Friend's twisting hair,
without success it tried escaping that entwining snare;
I gave my life as a tribute to the eyebrow of my Friend,
such a One must be bought with bribes like an officer.

716. WORRIED

If for a hundred days You do not happen to see me,
You don't even question anyone as to where I may be;
I ask many hundreds of people to tell me where You are
if only one day passes and You I don't happen to see.

717. SHINING EYES

When I talk about the soft and glossy surface of satin,
I know about its texture from Your cheek's silky skin,
and if I wanted to know all of the story of Narcissus,
to read it all, Your sweet shining eyes I would look in.

718. IT'S TRUE

I'll become dust by the road because of my love for You,
the enchanting mole on Your cheek will be my ruin too;
to the wind I'll be thrown by Your hair's twisting curls,
Your eye will throw me into black despair, yes it's true!

719. THE HAPPIEST HEART

Your beautiful bright cheek is love's camping-ground,
and Your curls, small chains, one another go around.
One moment with You is worth living countless lives;
heart complaining of grief for You: no happier is found.

720. SWEET PRISON

By Your chin's dimple every heart's peace is disturbed,

and that dimple is a prison that is barred and is locked
on every heart that You have taken and thrown into it;
and prison door by sweet scented ambergris is guarded.

721. YOUR SHINING GRACE

Your shining grace has made the glorious sun Your slave,
wanting to be of service, written contract to You he gave;
it's possible that he didn't have paper on which to write:
writing it on moon's bright face was how he did behave.

722. HOME OF THE ROSE

When across the garden breezed, comforter
of the rose,
it glorified nature when it became beautifier
of the rose;
when you find the garden's corner sheltered from the sun,
call out for cheek of the tulip and the shader
of the rose.

723. FAITHFUL TO LOVE AND WINE

It's said that those who in this life wine are not drinking,
when they are finally dead, up their souls will be rising;
but I'm remaining faithful to love and wine in the hope
that my dust when rising up, their scent will be retaining.

724. HERE AND AFTERWARDS

It is said by some that in Paradise is found the blessed,
many Huris with dark eyes, delicious wine unmeasured.
If I've the preference to have wine and the Beloved here,
what is wrong? For afterwards, by all such joys are shared.

725. EXCEPT FOR ME

O Friend, who except for me, will see You as friendly?

Who except for me would bear Your cruelty patiently?
I will tell everyone of Your tyranny wherever I may be,
then no one will ever desire to steal You away from me.

726. SCENT OF WINE

Wind of death, when head falls from shame and agony
and my life's tree is torn up, is there even a possibility
that my clay will be turned into the winejar? For scent
of the wine which will wet it, will give life back to me.

727. LONELY

Today, when lovers far from the Friend are sorrowful,
it's not a time when friends are humourous and joyful,
it's not because I don't have wine that I'm not drinking:
the wine's here, but friends to share it are not plentiful.

728. QUICKLY BRING

In cups without any decoration, that wine of ruby
        bring;
the Friend Who's close to everyone, Who is free:
        bring!
Because You know that this dusty world blows away,
    disappears like the passing wind: winecup quickly
        bring.

729. WHILE IT'S POSSIBLE

While Time continues I'm not free of grief for a moment;
it's possible that even the wine no joy to me will present.
While it's possible, get up and drink when morning comes;
when we're no longer here, many dawns will be recurrent.

730. WINE

In the same way that the lip is nourished by that wine,

that wine refreshes and nourishes the soul that's mine;
from that wine my body is fed and is made like new,
by that mysterious wine, that is Mystical and Divine.

731. THE WINE OF LOVE

Drink wine, the wine of Love, for it is everlasting
Life;
yes, it is the essence, true essence of this passing
life.
Now is the time for roses and tulips and happy friends:
enjoy an hour of bliss that passes, as this is lasting
Life!

732. WHATEVER OUR SHARE!

You Who are always holding the cup, what harm's there
if You should think of us: why leave friends in despair?
Except for the tears from my eyes I haven't ruby wine,
but wine is in Your cup, so drink, whatever our share!

733. THE BEST THING TO DO

To make heart happy with wine is the best thing to do,
to forget past desires and to smile and to be jovial too;
to place all problems of life aside for a brief moment,
which is given for awhile on loan to me and also to you.

734. COMPENSATION

Now the time has again arrived when drinkers happily
take pleasure in the wine and the lute's sweet melody;
to compensate for this short life that passes so quickly,
they drain winejar's blood and from cup drink freely.

735. WHEN ROSES BLOOM

I said: "If in my determination all my friends participate,

when roses bloom, perhaps for the wine… I will wait!"
From rosegarden, nightingale sang an answer: "Fool, when
roses bloom how can you give up wine… please state."

736. TO REMEMBER YOU

The rose that blossoms on the tree of friendship is lovely,
it fills my heart forever with happiness and with ecstasy;
I search for the company of the rose because the perfume
brings into memory the fragrance of the One loved by me.

737. LOVE

Fresh wine of the time of our Youth's rose tree
is love,
that Life that is lasting forever is true currency
is Love.
Do you look for the Water of Life like ageless Khizer?
Understand that the fountain that gives Eternity
is Love.

738. THE ROSE'S SLAVE

See the rose in the beautiful garden that only joy knows,
one moment clouds rain tears yet laughing is the rose.
The cypress is the rose's slave, even though it's boasting
it's free because it is tall and because it proudly grows.

739. THE SONG OF LOVE

Now to the rose, the song of love sings the nightingale,
when rose pretends to dislike it, nightingale starts to wail.
Nightingale then begins to be subtle, mellow and sweet,
until on rose's lips that are full of sugar, smiles prevail.

740. THE WORLD WILL BE THANKFUL

If winning the hearts of the poor is what you wish to do,
gaining respect of those who today are discreet too,
don't criticize the Christian, the Muslim and the Jew,
and all the world will be thankful and recommend you.

741. GOOD ADVICE

Although it is the right thing to be careful of mankind,
it's best that to no one in word or action one is unkind.
Although you will not find any faithfulness in this life,
it's best to leave all the seeds of all tyranny far behind.

742. WHAT THEN?

If the world to your will you could bend,
what then?
Or make it read your life's book, start to end,
what then?
Even if you lived as you wanted to for a hundred years,
and another hundred: when it's all at an end,
what then?

743. NO LOSS OR GAIN

O heart, we're with One Who is all kindness,
so don't ask;
like Him, this Mercy we talk of is endless,
so... don't ask.
Whatever we do or don't do, and in actions good or bad,
we don't lose or gain, so to fear is useless:
so... don't ask.

744. WITHIN MY WORDS

Within my words there lies many a treasure and jewel,
you'll find in there many an unpierced priceless pearl.
Each subtle pleasing thought taking hold in your heart,
out from my insane bewildered heart at first did swirl.

745. THE DESERT OF AMBITION

O you, who in that endless desert of ambition wander,
for how long will you, the sun with dirt try to smear?
If your head's pushed into lion's mouth through greed,
wouldn't the earth for ages have sought you as lodger?

746. JUST AS WELL

When death uses sword, shield as protector
                is worthless;
possessions, fame and gold one can gather
                is worthless.
Although I can see in the world both the good and bad,
        it is good that some good stays: the other
                is worthless.

747. TIME TO BE SILENT

O Hafez, the pages of this discussion fold up, put away;
give away the pen of false complicated reasoning today.
The time to be silent has now come and so keep silent;
fill your goblet full of that wine, and then silent stay.

748. MUZAFFAR, THE DICTATOR

Don't set your heart on the world and its possessions,
because from it no one has experienced faithfulness.
No one ate the honey from this hive without a sting,
or took date from a garden without thorn's sharpness.
Whoever has set alight a lamp for a number of days,
once alight the wind blows it out with great quickness.
Whoever without a care set his heart on this world,
I could see that to help his enemy was his willingness.
That warrior-king, that monarch who seized the world,
from whose sword blood spilled without forgiveness,
sometimes he broke an army with only one attack,
sometimes with a shout he split army's immenseness.
Without a cause he sent to prison chiefs and lords,
cut heads off guiltless heroes, with unreasonableness.
On hearing his name when it reached to the desert,
fearing his grasp, cubs were sent off by the lioness.
When in the end he subdued Shiraz, Tabriz and Irak,
and at last the moment arrived for his contentedness,
the son who was in the world by the light of his eye,
drove a nail into his eye and gave to him blindness.

749. BRING THE WINE

Winebringer, bring the wine that is the elixir of life, so the
fountain of immortality on my dusty body You may make.
I've my eye on circulating cup and soul on my hand's palm;
by Master's head: you don't give that, until this You take.
Don't shake wine from Your garment like rose in the field,
because at Your feet I have my head, and my soul I stake.
O Minstrel, on the second and third chord of the lute sing
the praises of that Moon, Who in beauty has no namesake.

750. NEWS

Into the ear of the slave, the announcer of news cried
from the Lord of Unity: "There is no God but He!"
And then: "Dear friend, he whose portion's the lowest,

the truth is: by force he won't gain the highest degree.
"With water of Zam-zam and Kauther one can't make
one's Fortune white, when woven black by Destiny."

751. RELY ON GOD

O wise man, don't set heart on this or that man's generosity,
no one has knowledge when success for a work is brought.
Go and rely on God, for don't you know that my pen's nib
wrote something quite different to everything I'd thought.
King of Hurmuz didn't see me yet gave a hundred favours;
king of Yazd saw me, I praised him, yet I received naught.
O Hafez, this is the way that kings are, so don't be grieving:
may Ruler, Giver of sustenance, give them grace not bought.

752. UPON THE THRONE

On the emerald roof of the Heavens,
Gabriel the Holy Spirit, the happy one,
shouted in the morning: "O Lord, in
fortune and power that's never undone,
upon the throne of the king remain
Mansur Muzaffar, Muhammad's son!"

753. FIVE WONDERFUL PEOPLE

In the time of the rulership of the Shah, Shaikh Abu Ishak,
country of Ears due to five wonderful people became fair;
the first, a monarch such as him, one who gave kingdoms,
who nurtured his own soul, and gave joy its rightful share.
The second was the Guardian of Islam, Shaikh Majd ud-Din,
the heavens record that a better judge wasn't here or there.
The third, one of Truth's 'Substitutes' Shaikh Amin ud-Din,
who opened doors that were closed, by his blessed prayer.

The fourth, Azd, the Monarch of Learning, who composed
in the name of the king 'The Stations,' an exposition so rare.
The fifth, Haji Kivam the Merciful, whose heart was a sea,
who from justice and kindness, name of 'The Good' did bear.
They all departed and left no one like them after they went,
may the Great and Glorious God forgive all of them forever.

754. AND IF

If in reality, the beggar had been in his essence truly pure,
in the water, the pivot of his shame's pole would have been.
If the sun had not mocked the stars, then is it possible that
not full of pleasant wine, his golden bowl would have been?
And if the mansion of the world were not destined for ruin,
its foundation stronger and more whole would have been.
If Time had not inclined towards mixing of metals, its work
in the Master's hand, Who knows the goal, would have been.
Since this Liberated One is all that this Age could produce,
for this One, respite from Time's control would have been.

755. A REQUEST

O friend, choose the time for me speak to the Master,
in a private place where the breeze a stranger shall be.
Open with a witty greeting and happily cause a laugh
with a subtlety within which heart's pleasure shall be.
His generosity then courteously ask of in this manner:
"It to me permitted, that weekly measure… shall be?"

756. GOOD AND BAD

You question yourself about your good and your bad?
It's necessary for you to have another judge? You forgot?
Stay far away from the bad and work towards the good;
do not play games and toy with life or it will soon rot.
Since you know that God is the One Who will provide,
don't keep the heart, through greed, tied in a tight knot.
God will give help to whoever will be obedient to Him;
to him He will give ample aid when he expects it not.

757. FAITH AND MORALS

From the Book of Morals I will read to you
the verse about faith and about generosity:
"If one violently slashes your liver from hate,
give to him gold like the mine of liberality.
Do not be less than the tree that gives shade:
rain fruit upon stone-throwers, like the tree.
Give pearl to whoever takes your head off
from oyster remember subtlety of humility."

758. IT'S NOT UNTRUE

Hall and college and debate of learning, arch and corridor;
what is it worth when the wise heart and seeing eye is not?
Although house of judge of Yazd is a fountain of learning,
it is not untrue that there vision's knowledge to spy is not.

759. LET US FLY TO GOD

Speak to those jealous of our Master, saying: "Don't approve
of any evil; for Time, a reward, except for evil,
doesn't give.
Don't cause strife; because due to reason or too much thinking,
sky into our hands the rein of commanding's skill,
doesn't give.
Even though they spread the whole world in Jamshid's sight;
he, his jewel, the cup 'that shows the world', still

doesn't give."
Let us fly to God and if the arrow should rain from the sky,
it to us, the power to enter Sanctuary on the hill,
doesn't give.
I swear by the right due to the favour of our Haji Kivam, that
for his own welfare, he a consent to such peril, doesn't give.

760. A MESSENGER HAS COME

O king! From Paradise, bringer of happy news has come;
Rizvan of throne and like the Huri and Salsabil of hair,
Sweetly speaking with pure meaning, soothing the heart,
beautiful and graceful and telling jokes and being fair.
I said: "Why have you now come to this poor dwelling?"
Answer: "For feast of the king, who is beyond compare."
Now the messenger is tired of his poor one's company,
call him to you and ask of his heart's desire, whatever.

761. THIS DARK HOUSE

In this dark house how long shall I sit hoping for the Friend,
sometimes hand in teeth, sometimes head on knee, grieving?
Patience ended when the wolf cornered it in the lion's den;
Reason fled when in the dove's nest the crow began singing.
O blessed bird, come and bring that news of a happy fortune;
maybe the time that once was, to the people will be returning.

762. CALL FOR CUP

O Winebringer, fill the cup; for the Master of the feast
gives what one desires, and the secrets doesn't declare.
Here, Paradise is available so renew pleasure and ease,
because God does not record sin against servants there.
Harp's melody is pleasant and hail is the place to dance,
Beloved's mole is heart's bait, Winebringer's hair is snare.
Friends wish to be friendly, companions are respectful;
attendants are of good repute, all sitting kind and fair.

O Winebringer, time will never turn better: be happy;
O Hafez, call for cup: never a better condition was there.

763. YOUR COMPANION

O king, the army of God's Grace is your companion;
    get up, if a plan to seize the world then
        you make.
From the height of glory you've knowledge of your
    origin, and service for the hearts of men
        you make.
Apart from the magic of this rusty blue vault's colour,
    according to Law of God, an occupation
        you make.
One turning ten into seven and a half made no profit;
    it's opportune, so seven and a half into ten
        you make.

764. A QUESTION

O one of such high descent with essence pure of hate and greed;
O one of such auspicious star, one free of deceit and hypocrisy;
with such greatness as yours, when does it then become lawful
to take honours from the angel and give them to the unworthy?

765. THE BEAUTY OF THIS VERSE

The beauty of this verse is beyond an explanation;
to splendour of the sun does a person need a guide?
Blessings be on brush of the painter who gave such
wonderful beauty as this to meaning's virgin bride.
Regarding its beauty, reason can't find comparison;
regarding its grace, comparison nature can't provide.
This verse is either a miracle or it is of true magic;
these words, Gabriel or Invisible Voice did guide.

No one can utter a great mystery in such a fashion;
like this, no one knows how to pierce a pearl inside.

766. A DREAM

O monarch, O just one, O one with ocean hands, lion of heart!
O you whose great glory has many arts to proclaim your estate!
All of the horizons were captured and all quarters were subdued
by commotion of the happiness and fame of such a king's state.
It could be that an invisible voice has told you of my condition,
how my day that was radiant, has become a dark night of late.
That which in three years I had received from king and adviser,
all in one moment was snatched away by the sky's mallet: fate.
Late last night while I was sleeping, in my imagination I saw that
at morning I happened to go secretly to the king's stable's gate.
There, tied up in the stall was my mule that kept eating barley;
he pushed nosebag aside, saying: "Do I know you?" as he ate.
I do not have any idea at all as to the explanation of this dream;
you interpret it, for in comprehension near you no one does rate!

767. KEPT GOING

At morning, from great grief my power of making poetry
    took exception to the slave, and on fleeing,
        kept going.

It kept imagining about Khiva and the Jihun river's bank;
    from the land of Solomon, it complaining,
        kept going.
That one kept going who alone understood language's soul;
    from my body the soul, as I kept looking...
        kept going.
When I spoke to my soul I said: "Old helpful close friend!"
    Reply was harsh and it, heartsick and weeping,
        kept going.
I said: "Who will not utter speech that is sweet to me?"

For that sweet tongue, sweet verses knowing,
kept going.
I pleaded and pleaded: "Do not go;" nothing came of it:
it, due to the king's merciful glance not coming,
kept going.
O king, kindly call him back; what does one on fire do,
who, from such disappointment overflowing...
kept going?

768. THE NATURE OF TIME

They do not see or hear of the malice of the sky,
for their eyes are blind and their ears don't hear.
There are many with pillows of the sun and moon,
who in the end will have clay and dust as their bier.
What's armour worth against the arrows of destiny?
Is Fate's penetration stopped by shield and spear?
If you make the fortress walls out of iron and steel,
death knocks down door when the moment's here.
Don't be proud of pleasant light, drink and pleasure:
darkness follows light, in sugar is poison to fear.
That door They open to you, don't desire to open it;
path They show, don't leave for lust: is that clear?
In your path is a pit, so don't go with bowed head;
in your cup is poison, if untasted don't bring near.
Look at dust of sphere and see the nature of time:
fold carpet of desire and tear in two greed's gear.

769. HIDING OUT

Yesterday a friend sent a message to me that said this:
"O you, ink of whose pen gives insight to pupil of eye,
Now after two years, fortune has brought you home,
you don't leave the Khwaja's house, why is this, why?"
I replied to him by saying: "Please, please excuse me:
not taking this path due to selfishness or conceit am I;
the judge's officer has placed an ambush in my path,
the summons like a deadly viper in his hand does lie.

If I set foot outside of the threshold of the Khwaja,
he will take me off to prison, disgraced in every eye.
The district of the Khwaja is my fortress; for there,
if anyone should mention that debt-collecting spy,
with the aid of the Khwaja's servants' powerful arms
I will break his mad skull with all the blows I let fly!
Is there room for joking? Since B and E were united
except for serving the Khwaja no final cause have I.
May his door forever be wide open to heart's desire;
with pure love, in his service, be the belted blue sky!"

770. A SWEET BUY

The rosejam of my verse took away the sugar from the violet:
it therefore, the envy of sugarcandy and of fawnheel became.
Bitter be the mouth of that one who complains of this candy!
Dust on head of one who seeking sweetwater's denial became!
Every one who was born blind out from his mother, in his life
the buyer of a lovely one full of beauty, do you feel became?

771. WASTE NOT

Brother, in passing away, swift
like the clouds is opportunity.
Know that life is very precious;
if it is wasted, ah what a pity!

772. FRIDAY THE SIXTH

It was the morning of Friday and it was the sixth day of Rabiu,
when from my heart quickly went that moon-faced one's face.
In year of the Flight, seven hundred and sixty four (A.D. 1362)
like a hailstorm the heavy news fell on me, such was the case!
What worth is it for one to sigh and to grieve and also regret,
when without a profit my life passed away and left this place?

773. FRUIT OF PARADISE

O soul, that fruit of Paradise that came into your hand,
why didn't you sow in heart, why from the hand let go?
If they should ask of you for the date of this event, say:
"It from 'Fruit of Paradise' (A.D.13 76) you can know."

774. FRIEND ADIL

Brother Khwaja Adil's rest be without worry
because after he had lived for fifty nine years
he departed, going to the garden of Paradise;
God be glad with his nature, actions and tears!
Always say: "Friend Adil" (meaning A.D.1383)
knowledge of year of death from this appears.

775. MERCIFUL DIES NOT

When the Merciful One, God Who does not die,
saw this king who doesn't stop doing good deeds,
God made him associate of His mercy, so that
the date as... 'Merciful dies not' (1384) reads.

776. INCLINATION FOR PARADISE

Turanshah, the Khan of the world and Chief of the age,
who sowed nothing but grain of good deeds in this field,
in middle of the week on twenty-first of month of Rajab,
after leaving this smoky stove went to rosebed far afield;
to one who inclines towards truth and speaking the truth,
for his death... 'Inclination for Paradise' (1385) will yield.

777. BY DEVOTION

Baha, u-l-Hakk va Din: happy be his place of resting!
Imam of the Sunnat and Shaikh of the congregation.
When departing from this world, to men of excellence,
to eminent lords, of this couplet he made recitation:
"If one has the strength to put one's foot on this path,
one can gain association with God through devotion."
The date of his death can be obtained in this manner:
calculate (A.D.1380) from 'By devotion: association.'

778. DEATH OF ISMAIL MAJD UD-DIN

The Chief of the Sultan-Judges, glory of religion, Ismail,
whose eloquent pen in treating the law did never cease:
it was in the middle of the week, on the eighth of Rajab,
when he left this house that is without order or peace.
Know that his dwelling is in the corner of God's mercy;
from 'God's Mercy,' (A.D.1355) find date he did decease.

779. DEATH OF GIVAM UD-DIN

Givam ud-Din, the great pillar of faith and state, at whose door
in homage, the heavens to kiss that dust there bent the knee;
in middle of the month of Zu-l-Ka'dat, from existence's place,
despite all of his might and his glory, under the dust went he.
Since hope of generosity no one any longer has from anyone,
letters of his year's death are (A.D.1362) 'Hope of generosity.'

780. ON YOUR DUST I WEEP

It's Springtime, and the rose and tulip and the wild white rose
have come up from the clay: in the dust, where are you today?
I go like the clouds of the Spring, and bitterly I weep as I go,
so much on your dust I weep, that you will rise from the clay.

781. A HYPOCRITE

Who is the one who'll go and tell to the sultan:
from time's violence cat-camels have come to light.
Upon the prayermat of the judge sits a hypocrite,
and to the rank of lordship has come a catamite.
Hypocrite said: "I'm eye and lamp of the world."
"I'm Dara and Firidun's seed," said the parasite.
You who are the Chief of the Age, for God's sake
tell to king, whose Fortune is the greatest height:
"King, don't let the will of such as these be done;
be one who does His Will, and show your might!"

782. THE GREEN GRAIN

Eat that green grain that is so easy to digest,
whoever eats a grain puts Simurgh on the spit.
That grain that throws the Sufi into 'ecstasy:'
a hundred elations, Simurghs, in a grain of it.

783. BEST WISHES

Years and blessings and wealth, offspring, throne and power,
be yours in kingship that is perpetual, free of every care.
Joyful year, omen auspicious, state peaceful, property ample,
firm foundation and race abiding, throne lofty, fortune fair!

784. SIXTH OF THE MONTH

Chief of wearers of turbans, candle of the circle's unity,
master of lord of conjunction, Haji Hasan, Kivam ud-Din,
754 years (A.D.1353) from Flight of 'The Best of Men,'
when the sun was in Gemini, and Virgo the moon was in,
on sixth of the month of Rabi'a in the middle of the day,
on Friday, by the decree of the Creator without any sin,
the bird of his soul that was the Huma of the holy sky,
left for Garden of Paradise, from world's troubled coffin.

785. UNDER THE PATCHCOAT

When will a little peace come so I may serve the Perfect Master,
and from the Master's advice, make young the fortune of mine?
I have been for many a long year a caretaker of the Winehouse,
and the rest of my life to service of that threshold I will resign.
Yesterday the censor saw me with the flagon and he broke it;
from now on under the patchcoat I'll put the flagon of wine.

786. SALMAN

The wisdom of my mind questioned Reason last night:
"O peerless one of the favours of the Creator's mercy,
which is the peerless jewel of verse in the world, from
which the market of the pearl of Uman loses currency?"
It answered by saying: "Listen to me and not to those
saying, it this one's elegy and that one's *ghazal* must be.
Do you know the most accomplished one of the time,
by means of sincerity, not by deception or insincerity?
Prince of accomplished ones, king of country of speech
is Salman, Master of the world, religion, faith's beauty."

787. IT'S NECESSARY

What regrets for that bright robe of youth's days!
If only it had been embroidered with permanency!
O no, what grief what pain, that from the stream,
the water of existence will be passing so quickly!
It is necessary to be cut from family and friends,
this has been passed down by the sky's decree.
Every brother must at some time leave his brother
because of birth by father, unless they Farkads be!

788. LAST MESSAGE

O breeze of Spring, if you possibly can,
By way of faithfulness and of kindness
take news from me to the Friend, say:
"Secretly, that one burning, in distress,
is dying; and from desire is saying...
'You, without You, life is lawlessness.'"

789. COMPLETELY IMPOSSIBLE

Man, the race of Adam, with knowledge is a complete man;
he becomes completely a brute when knowledge isn't his.
For one to act without knowledge is complete ignorance;
O soul, finding God in ignorance, completely impossible is.

790. DUST OF MUSALLA

The lamp of the men of spirituality is Khwaja Hafez,
his brilliant candle shone from the Light of Glory.
When in the dust of Musalla he did finally dwell,
the date: 'Dust of Musalla' (1389) told the story.

791. THE LUTE AND THE CUP

This lute to many a feast has brought exhilaration,
this cup has served many a guest with anticipation.
O believers, come; for the Winehouse entices: come,
listen to the lute, drink from cup, gain beatification.
Of the Koran, Puranas, Vedas and the Zend Avesta,
their wine and music will give a clear explanation.
Believer, come and feel breathing through your soul
and through your heart, the breath of inspiration.

And if the world should try to catch you in its trap,
    with all your might show your complete rejection.
Innumerable wise men have rejoiced when this lute's
sweet subtle caress soothes their hearts' lamentation.
Innumerable kings have smiled to drink of this cup,
    when their souls have been filled with consternation.
Innumerable poets, because of these two charmers,
    drowned pain when grief made them its occupation.
This lute and this cup have gained all the wisdom of
life's experiences of all East and West's population.
They know and they can tell the ancient secrets of
Solomon's and Jamshid's private room for relaxation.
They know of the famous thrones filled with pride,
    of many shattered crowns and robes of destruction.
They know the miraculous fruit of highest Paradise,
    which on the trees of the world will not gain fruition.
They give all of this to the gathering that they cherish,
    during feasts; to all blessed with Spirit's clarification.
Against the armies of worries they have declared war,
    and this they've made clear by an open declaration.
They give garment of flame for today's bitter cold,
    and for the fire of grief the pure light's emanation.
Whoever's mind is melted by this magical lute's music
will fully understand each mystery's inner solution.
Whoever's veins are filled with this cup's Divine elixir,
    answers riddles to which none can find explanation.
Whoever takes the riches of them both will instantly
    understand black Satan as a joke, an hallucination.
These strains and streams of tone and of taste of lute
and of cup, turn an old inn into a heavenly location.
If a pious saint drinks of both their breath and blood,
    he will sit, drunk with bliss, on the top of creation.
He will soar through many dazzling skies of pleasure,
    filled with Divinity and clothed in mad-intoxication.
And he will sink through tossing seas of great wonder,
    still holding tightly to every quest's final destination.
Contented with joyful peace and crowned with safety,

he will ignore each threat, each poisonous accusation.
And when life ends he'll speed to the highest Heaven:
his bliss will last beyond test of death's extermination.
So twang the lute and clink and kiss the cup, is request
of dying drunken Hafez... his final farewell declaration.

792. COMES MY WAY

Beloved, to wind You've thrown being friendly:
is this the promise of companionship, with me?
For how long will You keep this wounded, this
heart so full of anguish, in the prison of worry?
I see no freedom from Your locks of hair, so...
for how long will You treat the sick... cruelly?
Though You burn me up in Your heartless fire
this broken-hearted one dealt with You fairly,
in the hope that You would take pity and then
wash Your hands of all oppression and cruelty!
Now... I've no hope that upon Your lover You
would take pity... me, this desperate one, *me!*
Now, the best thing is face up to You again...
and to never give up, to go on the way bravely!
Better that from patience I do not turn away...
then maybe heart's deep desire comes my way.
Winebringer... from that night's leftover wine
give me a few cups of the lover's wine, divine!
For as long as I have all of my five senses left,
make sure in Your hands wine stays, sublime!
The orchard's birds are all singing beautifully
like David from all their nests of love, a sign!
Minstrel, do not let instrument leave hands...
go on singing the melodies with a longing line
with a heart burning as though of aloes-wood,
in memory of being with Beloved... that, time.
For long fire of grief and anguish in this heart
has kept flames in chest, thriving like a vine!

When the end of separation cannot be seen...
best to not turn the face from One... Divine!
Better that from patience I do not turn away,
then maybe heart's deep desire comes my way.
Beloved, even if in love's torture, dying am I...
heart from Your love's pain never taking am I.
If my cries were to pierce the turning spheres,
sun and moon would cry, "Suffering... am I!"
The bow of Your eyebrow continues to shoot
arrows of love's glances, then swooning am I.
And even if my pen happened to be Mercury,
not able to describe for You my longing am I.
Through the anguish of love I've become old
though a child in love's ways... learning am I.
I imagine I should sit down quietly like Sa'di
and gaze upon patience be fastening... am I.
Master... when this cruel time has separated
us and placed in a prison of worrying am I...
better that from patience I do not turn away,
then maybe heart's deep desire comes my way.
Beloved, Who makes made-up beauties shrink,
unveil Your moon-like face so I no longer think
about this world and break my pledge and once
again of pure wine I shall joyfully take a drink!
Beloved, through eyes my secret has been told;
separation begins love, end in a heavenly wink.
Anyone who took up suffering of loving You,
to wind life's capital threw without one blink!
Heart, in fire of deep love, in cauldron of pain,
burn like aloes-wood; from both, don't shrink!
And... because now this longing I have to kiss
the feet of You, Perfect Master... I truly think
that if it's not allowed for me to do so then I'll
go on trying and asking, from it I'll not shrink.
Better that from patience I do not turn away...
then maybe heart's deep desire comes my way.
Beloved, stature like cypress, jasmine scented,

body with the beauty of a rose, fully flowered;
Your cheeks make night's full moon feel small:
come, distance burns soul... I'm down-hearted.
Enticed by beauty-spot, caught by long hair...
the bird of my heart by Your locks, is trapped!
As desire is not obtained by trying, striving...
helpless, I've to be with separation, contented.
Now, so here I am, distressed by separation...
only the heavens know how this will be ended.
Being far from You, except for trying, longing,
from Time my destiny nothing has received...
O Hafez, but for Beloved here, wine and cup,
what other desire has existence ever pursued?
Better that from patience I do not turn away...
then maybe heart's deep desire comes my way.
O You, the comfort of my soul, O so restless...
O You, the hope of my heart that is hopeless...
I'm happy with the pain of loving You for in all
ways the fire of grief for You is my accomplice.
O beautiful Beloved, that moment You left my
embrace I've lost any desire for other pleasures.
Longing for union with You, Sweetheart... I am
passing this life in separation... full of distress.
Tonight, my flood of tears will shoulders cover:
even in death hands, I'll not let go Your dress!
From longing of my broken and burnt up heart,
that has not in the least bit been one to possess
even though as I have often stated I keep trying
and trying but all that I gain is a lack of access:
better that from patience I do not turn away...
then maybe heart's deep desire comes my way.
Wound of Your love's pain is heart's soothing:
my love for You is a friend of heart's confiding.
Locks of Your hair are like a noose for my soul:
Your ruby-like lip is the gem of my heart's ring.
Your eyebrow's like my soul's police-inspector,
and... Your eye is now this heart commanding!

You are in my heart staying and I'm in the fire:
I don't care what happens to heart, I am caring
only for You as heart burns up from separation!
Under the weight of separation that's crushing
I'm at the end of my rope and must choose now
between the two: give up life, or heart be losing!
Hafez, what occurs if a light from One you see?
When realm of Union my heart is not calling...
better, that from patience I do not turn away...
then, maybe heart's deep desire comes my way.

793. THAT ONE AGAIN

The King, sanctuary of people and the Way,
is worthy of being hailed each night and day!
King, gives fresh fruits in a world that rots...
for faith throws roses from garden in a spray.
That One, is Master of Master of any time:
for the time that One's the Ruler of the day.
Those signs of good fortune from that One's
forehead keep on shining out with every ray!
In the passing world that splendour, dignity
and perception is like the North Star... I say.
In the ring of that One's rank the azure dome
is studded tight like a gem that is on display.
That One's sword is like an iron wall that is
standing tall... between faith and infidelity!
Pearls are strewn when that One takes pen;
with sword in arms both fit that One again.
O that exalted Lord with shade so merciful!
O bud of King's rosegarden, O so plentiful!
In fragrant royal garden never has sprouted
a cypress so tall with a face O so beautiful.
You are not only bright sun of the sphere of
perfection of beauty but radiant moon, full!
Your good fortune is the gift of God for the

morning praises of Your lovers, one and all.
Time's wheel has put Your name's seal on
its patent: You can order all to rise, or fall!
Your radiant beauty, power, highest rank,
majesty... prove You're of those Spiritual.
It's true Your name from moon to Piscus,
or sky to the fish, will recall and will call!
Time's wheel, humorous colours wearing,
rare pearl like You in oyster is not having.
Master, robe on Your body feels honoured...
quick perception's etched on Your forehead.
New bride of spirituality is fascinated now
by Your form and nature and all You liked.
Your royal grandeur's rays of light… Your
fame in this city, by Your face is achieved.
Sky's brocade is less than Your majesty…
renown of Your justice, to highest reached.
Your gathering's atmosphere, so friendly,
all the time bright sun its wine consumed.
With purpose of Your blessed face seeing
all the tulips into an eye have now turned.
Master, to be accepted by You in the ear
the 'lu-lu' has become 'la-la', enraptured!
Master, the sphere is merely the doorbell
of Yours… Saturn listening for its knell!
Master, while You have God's blessing,
may You only rapture keep experiencing.
May the Wheel of Time lay in Your lap
everything Your heart could be desiring.
Blessed be Your right hand's companion
and may the Divine Your left be holding.
Your hand is never empty of the aid that
in a battle is a weapon You are weilding.
From the flourish of Your shining sword
this realm is a paradise it is decorating!
May Your knowledge spill over, as long
as Time's wheel on feet is still standing.

May all of Yours stay true and steady...
Your high state and Your honour aiding.
May all creatures such as Hafez preserve
peace, in shade of Your fortune... abiding!
May protection of this world and next be
Yours for as long as all life goes on, only.
Beloved, moon bright as You isn't in sky;
cypress tall as You in any field isn't high.
Radiant sun I compared with Your face...
it's good as it goes but Yours is not a lie!
How can we really describe Your beauty,
as in all ways none can do it, so why try?
No bird who has flown towards You ever
to begin to return to the old nest will fly!
A heart not head over heels in love with
You has no soul on which heart can rely.
Beloved, what arrow is still to be shot at
my heart... by bow of brow of Your eye?
Your eye hasn't even glanced at me once:
it is drunk... and world for it is only a lie!
Your closest one is looking out for You...
cares not for those heart-broken such as I.
Ruler of the day You are faithful's helper:
You are the highest, my refuge, protector!
Winebringer, if You hear of desire of mine
don't mention anything to me except wine.

In winehouse sell the prayer-mat and coat,
and in return get the wine pure and so fine.
If you've a heart that is alive with longing,
hear from the drunkards the Truth Divine!
Smelling the cure, with pain of love arrive:
compared to love all worlds are a mere sign.
In path of love, see heart's secrets as than a
thousand Hatim Tais* more generous, fine!
Idol, beautiful as an angel, like a monarch...
came into the city and all followed in a line!

People saw that beautiful face as modestly
perspiration that trickled down, did shine.
Master, tell me, how long will Hafez wail?
"How long will heart be broken?" I whine.
While friends with the pain of love for You
with pleasures of world I've nothing to do?

APPENDIX:

HAFEZ~of~SHIRAZ

The Life, Poetry & Times of the Immortal Persian Poet

(In Three Volumes)

BOOK ONE: THE EARLY YEARS

(The Opening 180 Pages)

Hail Shiraz: city situated on a site beyond compare,

may the Lord preserve it from decay... is my prayer.

A hundred praises to our stream... called Ruknabad;

Khizer... drinking its water, found eternal life there!

From between the districts of Jafarabad and Musalla,

the cool north wind the scent of ambergris does bear.

Come to Shiraz and ask for the Holy Spirit's Grace,

from the man... who has gained all perfection's share.

Who here, would make a mention of Egypt's candy...

when here, the sweet ones... of same haven't a care?

O breeze of the East, what news have you to pass on

about the condition of that intoxicated one... so fair?

For God's sake do not wake me up from this dream...

for in it I see an image, that is indeed sweet and rare.

Hafez, when you're frightened of separation, why not

give thanks for when you and Beloved were together.

In the Name of God. My name is Muhammad Gulandam and it was my fortunate destiny, my *kismet,* to be the pupil then the friend of Shams-ud-din Mohammed, who is now famous throughout the known world as 'Hafez of Shiraz'.

It was I who collected his poems together into one book, his *Divan*... at the insistence of him and his and my teacher and friend Khwaja Haji Kivam. This story that I am about to tell you began in the twenty-seventh year of the last century, the fourteenth century after the birth of Jesus the Christ in the Christian calendar or as we call it, the eighth century in the Islamic calendar (calculated after the *heija* or flight of Mohammed the Prophet).

In many ways it could be this century or possibly the next or in four centuries or in seven centuries time. The rich are still becoming richer and the poor, poorer. Dictators still seek power and kill and maim and imprison innocent people to obtain it. Most monarchs, or whoever is ruling, over-tax the common people and grow fat, as do their relatives and courtiers. Many of the priests and clergy splutter forth from their pulpits to the masses and in their private lives hypocritically take no notice of their own words and seek power in the Name of the Lord through their fearful influence at Court and with the Law. As it is said... 'A false lamp gives no light'.

Meanwhile, lovers love and drunkards drink and minstrels sing and poets create songs and poems and life goes on unchanged. But is that really so? No, I don't think it is. Something is different now... because of Hafez and others such as him. But really, there is only *one* Hafez.

Ah, he was and is... *unique*. His songs are still singing in my ears and heart, as though it were yesterday. Let me tell you his story as it was told to me by himself, his friends the minstrels Hajji Ahmed and Abu Khan, by Khwaja Kivam, Obeyd, Khaju, Nabat, the poet-princess Jahan Malek and the others so dear to him, and of course... what I remember myself.

By my soul, let me take you back over seventy years to 627/1327 when he was seven. I am old now, but... the *himma,* the power of my heart, my creative imagination as Ibn 'Arabi calls it, is still fresh and clear. I met Hafez when I was eighteen and he was twenty-four. It all comes back. Ah, how I still love that man so much, his small and ugly body, his sparkling wit, his infectious laugh, his eyes... his *burning,* glorious eyes. His songs, *ghazals...* his poems!

Ah, Shiraz... Shiraz, turquoise and golden domes of its hundreds of mosques gleaming in the early morning light as I look out through this window. Shiraz... famous for its gardens, wine, poets and beautiful women. Almost miraculously, we Shirazis were spared the atrocities and genocide that the Mongols had committed in most of our country. The depth of depravity and cruelty of the Mongols towards us Persians has probably not been equaled in all of known history.

Some historians claim that Shiraz was built from the ruins of Persepolis, and others state that it was founded by the Arabs at the time of the Muslim conquest. Other traditions claim that Shiraz was built on the site of a city named Fars or *Pars* (which became the name for our province, *Parsa* becoming 'Persia') and was named after Fars who was the son of Masus, the son of Shem who was Noah's son. Incidentally, Noah the great Spiritual Master, is known to have been a vintner and after his great boat landed on that mountain called Ararat in the nearby land of the Turks he brought his family here and planted the grapevines he brought with him... some say he founded our fair city almost ten-thousand years ago and Shiraz has become famous for the grape that bears its name. In our history Noah was called Yima (Jamshid). The three wise men or Zoroastrian Perfect

Masters (*Qutubs or Magi*) are said to have set off from Shiraz to go to Bethlehem to recognize the Christ (*Rasool*). Persepolis was built some two thousand or more years ago near Shiraz, dedicated to the great Spiritual Master Zoroaster who settled here some eight thousand years ago... although some say less than two-thousand years ago, but they stupidly confuse him with the last of the head priests of that faith who bore his ancient name.

By my old eyes... Shiraz is still such a beautiful city, known for its variety of markets, being on the trade route from Europe to the Far East. All of the agricultural produce of our province of Fars comes to our capital, which is a bustling, lively city. Our grains, vegetables, fish, fruit, honey and of course wine are known all over Persia and elsewhere. Each market and bazaar has its own specialty... and craft and art flourished in Shiraz before Hafez's time as it does now. The gold and silverware and the beautiful books with their fine miniatures are bought by rich patrons for their libraries and palaces from Shiraz's workshops and this has been so for as long as I can remember.

During this time that Hafez lived, there was a change in the art of miniature painting in Shiraz due to a new way of looking at the world that he brought about and because of a master-painter friend of his who I will later tell you about, that led to the great masterpieces are now appearing here and in Tabriz and Herat and elsewhere. Shiraz is also an important centre for the buying and selling of Persian carpets and cotton-goods... cotton being grown in the valley. Because our city is a cosmopolitan centre on the long silk-road to China many merchants pass through here from all the known world bringing not only merchandise but also news of many distant, fascinating lands.

Shiraz and its outer villages are more than twenty miles in circumference with a population of about 200,000 souls with the number in the central city behind the walls being nearly 60,000 and the area there just over five miles in circumference. It is a cosmopolitan city with peoples arriving constantly from all over the country and from foreign places. We Shirazis speak many languages apart from Persian and old Pahlevi... Turkish, Lori, Arabic and Hebrew.

Ibn Battuta the traveller from Tangiers, whose book *Rihla* or 'Travels' is now in my library... and who Hafez and I met and befriended, passed through Shiraz twice during our lifetimes and described our blessed city as follows: "Shiraz is a densely populated town, well built and admirably planned, well-known and has a high place among cities. It possesses pleasant gardens and far-reaching streams, fine streets and excellent markets. Each trade has its own bazaar. Its inhabitants are handsome and clean in their dress. In the whole East there is no city that approaches Damascus in beauty of bazaars, orchards and rivers and in the handsome figures of its inhabitants, but Shiraz. It is on a plain surrounded by gardens and orchards and intersected by five rivers, one of which is the stream known as Ruknabad, whose water is very sweet and excellent to drink, very cold in summer and warm in winter and gushes out of a fountain on the lower slope of a hill called al-Qulai'a. The principal mosque of Shiraz, which is called the 'old mosque' is one of the largest of mosques in area and most beautiful in construction. Its courtyard occupies a wide expanse paved with marble and is washed down every night during the summer heats. The leading inhabitants of the city assemble in this mosque every night and pray the sunset and night prayers in it. On its northern side is a gate leading to the fruit market which is one of the most admirable of bazaars and to which I for my part would give the preference over the bazaar of the Courier Gate at Damascus.

"The people of Shiraz are distinguished by piety, sound religion and purity of manners, most especially the women. These wear boots and when out of doors are swathed in mantles and head-veils, so that no part of them is to be seen and they are noted for their charitable alms and their liberality. One of their strange customs is that they meet in the principal mosque every Monday, Thursday and Fridays to listen to the preacher, sometimes one or two thousand of them, carrying fans in their hands with which they fan themselves on account of the great heat. I have never seen in any land an assembly of women in such numbers."

Hamd Allah Mustaufi wrote in his book *Nuzhat al-Qulab* in 739/1340 about Shiraz as it was when Hafez was twenty and I was fourteen, "The city of Shiraz has seventeen quarters and nine gates... the city is extremely pleasant to live in but its streets are very filthy, hence it is impossible for any one to go about in these streets and not be defiled. The climate is temperate and here all trades may be followed. At most times sweet-smelling herbs are available and are sold in the market. The water is from underground channels called *qanats* and the best is from the conduit of Ruknabad... but the biggest *qanat* is called Qalat Bandar that runs under the tomb of the poet Sadi, which never needs repair. During the spring floods the rivers rush down from Mount Darak and passing outside the town flows off into Mahaluyah Lake. The crops are of medium produce and very often go up to famine prices. Of fruits, the grapes known as *mithqali* are excellent. The population are lean and brown-skinned; they are Sunnis of the Shafi'ite sect; some few being Hanafites and there are also Shi'ahs. Further there are many great *sayyids* of noble lineage here... who hold the Traditions of the Prophet and as traditionalists they are for the most part excellently esteemed. The people of Shiraz are much addicted to holy poverty and they are of strict orthodoxy... so that they are content to do but little trade. Hence there are many poor folk, though they refrain from begging, and do not fail to practice some means of livelihood... while the wealthy folk are mostly foreigners. Hence few Shirazis are very wealthy, and most of the people strive after good works and in piety and obedience to the Almighty have attained a high degree of godliness. Never is this city devoid of saintly persons, for which reason it was also called the Tower of Saints... but indeed, at the present day, it should rather be called the Robbers' Haunt by reason of the lack of justice and bold greediness that is too common here... The revenues of the city go to the Treasury, and at the present time they amount to 450,000 *dinars*."

The nine gates mentioned by him are the Istakhr on the north side, the Darak Musa on the west opposite the Darak Mountain; the Bayda Gate on the west that adjoins the Murdestan quarter; the Kazerun Gate at the south west corner in the direction of the city of Kazerun and in the Kazerun quarter; the Salam Gate on the southern side opposite the cemetery of al-Salam; the Fasa Gate in the south-east; the *Now* or New Gate on the east side in the quarter of the same name which also contained the New Garden; the Dowlat Gate on the north-eastern side in the Bagh-e-Now quarter, named after

Sheikh Doulat who was a warrior killed in battle during the Arab conquest... and lastly the nearby Sa'dat Gate.

As for the past seven hundred years Shiraz had been ruled over by non-Shirazis and in the past two hundred by those of Turkish or Mongol origin, we had strangely accepted the idea that they were born to rule over us and the ruler of Shiraz, Mahmud Shah as we shall soon see, though not Turkish himself had a Turkish wife... Tashi Khatun, who was greatly loved and influential in her own right endowing many public buildings including a college and often paid her respects at the tomb of the Spiritual Master Ibn Khafif known as Shaikh-e-Kabir who was credited with having brought Sufism to Shiraz some four hundred years ago.

Junaid Shirazi, the poet and historian of our city, who passed on to the Lord some few months before Hafez, wrote in his book on Shiraz about the shrines of the many Saints and Spiritual Masters who have graced this place with their blessed presence and where Shirazis weekly or even daily go on pilgrimage, usually a surprisingly joyous and relaxed occasion with a picnic-like atmosphere and a chance to socialise with family and friends. There are many important pilgrimage shrines apart from that of Shaikh-e-Kabir that is in the northern Darb-e-Istakhr quarter. Junaid Shirazi tells us in the words of a pious undertaker who was taken by a young dervish to the garden of Haft-tanan or the bodies of seven saints, which became a sacred site during our lifetime...

"I went with him to a place in Musalla area which was walled and that in those days was called Samdal. The young man then said to me, 'Wait here!' For about an hour I waited and then suddenly I heard, 'God is the greatest!' I quickly entered and discovered the young man was dead and lay in such a way that he was facing the Qiblah. I was amazed and I wondered how I'd wash and then bury him as I was alone... but suddenly six people were there carrying burial sheets and they then helped me to get him ready to be buried. They then lifted him and carried him outside that building. I couldn't follow then so I washed and dressed and went outside. I was amazed to see that there was no wall and only open fields and not a sign of anyone. I sat down and prayed and I fell asleep. In the morning when I woke I saw a new grave that had been watered recently. I realized it was the young man's grave.' " Junaid Shirazi adds, "Some time later next to this grave others appeared until there were seven. The identity of the seven was unknown and today seven blank stones mark them."

An understanding of the multi-layered and interlocking and often conflicting structure of Shirazi society over the past century is essential to the understanding of the story I am about to unveil. On top, as we have already mentioned, was the ruler... and although he was in power, he usually did not directly control the everyday goings-on of our city. All of that was designated to officials such as the ministers for police, tax-collectors, bazaar regulators, who were appointed by the prime minister. The prime minister's life was often shortened if he antagonized in some way his master, or if the king was deposed, as will often be tragically seen in the following pages.

As the king and his prime minister's power and responsibility usually covered much of Fars and not just Shiraz, it was necessary that the chief-judge become an important head of this ruling class who acted in the king's name, but was also understood to be the representative of the ordinary citizen and thus was the bridge that could be crossed in either direction as we shall often see in the life of Shiraz's much beloved Chief Judge Majd al-Din who saved us all on two occasions and like succeeding chief-judges were sent on important peace missions to other rulers by their kings. Even the nobles of the city would pay them daily visits to judge family matters. The ruler and the chief-judge could criticize each other but rarely did, as each was greatly dependent upon the other.

The group that was most powerful and influential amongst the nobles was the fourteen hundred *sayyids* or descendants of the Prophet who received from the government yearly stipends. These were the Alavis, whose large family could trace themselves back to Mohammed's son-in-law Ali, but even so were of the Sunni faith even though there were a small number of Shi'ah in Shiraz and the tomb of Ahmad Musa, the brother of the eighth Imam of the Shi'ites was respected and visited by most Shirazis no matter their religion. The Shirazi *sayyids* controlled much wealth in the city and did so by endowments of colleges and individuals and events. Such wealth and power also meant they were somewhat independent from the ruler and their ruler, their *naqib*, like the chief-judge wielded much power upwards and downwards.

Apart from the ruler, prime-minister, chief-judge and *naqib*, the various trade guilds leaders and neighbourhood groups were of much importance in how the city functioned. The king had to have the support of such organizations leaders or bosses who had the responsibility to keep order in the bazaars and seventeen quarters and if the city was under siege they oversaw the battlements and security of all the gates. These bosses tried to control the street ruffians, young so-called 'heroes' and gangs that were potential mobs that could be for or against the rulers.

Under these chiefs were the common workers who could easily join the mobs in the street if the occasion arose and the ruler was hated. Some were ridiculed by the nobles and called drunken rogues and reprobate-outsiders (rindan), ruffians and no-hopers... but such young men saw themselves as heroes (pahlawan), and believed in the lore of chivalry... and their groups welcomed and fed and housed strangers and gave protection to the weak and vulnerable when violent times befell the city. Hafez always identified himself with the rindan but Hafez's rindan belief was more about an inner philosophy of rejection of the outer forms of hypocritical society and religious dogma and rituals and a freedom to reject reason in favour of love and divine-intoxication.

Apart from the chief-judges, leaders of the sayyids and the bosses of the guilds and neighbourhoods there was another group who wielded great power although they were not appointed by the ruler. These were the sheikhs and their families. The shaikhs were the head-preachers and Sufi leaders, such as the evil and powerful black-magician Shaikh Ali Kolah who claimed he could control the jinn... and was a deep and dangerous thorn in Hafez's and all our sides for over thirty years.

Shiraz during the 8th/14th century contained more than five hundred mosques and colleges (madrasses) and Sufi retreats and other religious foundations endowed by the aristocratic, wealthy, old, established families who were as a social group the most powerful and of whom the Baghnovi, Fali-Sirafi, Alavi-Mohhamadis, Arabsh-Hoseini, Bozghash, Mosalahi Beiza'i, Salmani, Ruzbehan and

Zarkub families were the most influential... occasionally marrying into each-other (but often only with in-laws, as with the Alavi-Mohammadis who were *sayyids*), and holding many of the positions of chief-judges, judges, preachers, scholars, historians, Sufi masters and teachers. Our famous chief-judge, Majd al-Din, who was revered by all us Shirazis and saved our city a number of times was from the Fali-Sirafi family. Most of Shiraz's religious establishment came from these fifteen or more noble families.

At the time that I will begin our story, when Hafez is seven years old, Shiraz for some time has been under the benign administration of Sharaf al-Din Mahmud Shah Inju, who is said to be a descendant of the Court poet and mystic Ansari of Herat. Mahmud Shah was appointed by Amir Chupan Salduz the chief-commander of the ruler of all Persia, the son of the Mongol khan (king) Uljaitu who had ruled from the majestic capital he built called Sultaniyeh near Zanjan south-east of Tabriz... Sultan Abu Said Bahador. He succeeded his father Uljaitu in 717/1317 at the age of twelve. Mahmud Shah was sent to Shiraz as the tax agent to administrator all the personal holdings of the sultan, and because of his mastership in this control of the finances of the whole province of Fars he received a fortune for himself of an income each year of at least a million *dinars*. He had become independent and powerful in Fars with the exception of some of the mountains and plains where robber bands still raped, murdered, looted and plundered.

As the years passed and the young sultan, Abu Said, became embroiled in a power struggle and intrigues at Court, the taxes that were supposed to come from Shiraz (the second richest city in his kingdom) dwindled. Mahmud Shah seized the opportunity and used the taxes to protect the city by building many large brickworks with tall towers that are still used today as lookouts. The bricks of rammed-earth were baked then carried to rebuild the tall, thick wall that had been constructed over 300 years earlier that surrounds our city and is of 12,500 paces He also cleared the moat that had been added at the turn of the century. He dropped some of the many taxes and helped the city's poor and the poets and artists... and because of his generosity he and his family are greatly loved by our people. Mahmud Shah had finally returned to Sultaniyeh, the newly built Mongol capital near Tabriz, and left the governorship of the province of Fars to his three oldest sons Jalal al-Din Masud Shah, Ghiyath al-Din Kaikhosrau and Shams al-Din Mohammad. Kaikhosrau, the second eldest son was put in charge of Shiraz in 726/1326.

Let us now return to a year later, 727/1327. Within this year the Turks will capture Nicea... in Europe the English king Edward the second will be killed by his wife and her lover. In Italy the painter Giotto passes away as does in France the German mystic Meister Eckhart who stated this profound truth 'God exists because I exist and I exist because God exists'. In India the cruel king Mohammad ibn Tughluq shoots a poor blind man from a cannon and has a cripple's limbs torn off because they are unable to follow his command to vacate Delhi and move to his new capital at Daulatabad hundreds of miles away.

And on this particular day Hafez is seven years old and his life is about to be changed forever.

The sun is slowly rising behind the hills, less than two hours walk from this city of Shiraz. The golden light moves down the hillside then across the plain and slowly reaches the city. The light from the sun creeps over the fields and villages outside the walls of the city and reaches the clear, sparkling stream... Ruknabad!

As the small, ugly-looking boy, frantically runs... on either side of the narrow street the sun hits the walls and the fronts of the dilapidated mud-brick houses and the many run-down shops of the Yazdi quarter.

The cry of the *muezzin* from the minaret above one of the turquoise and golden-domed mosques in the distance calls the faithful to prayer. He looks down over this fabled city with the sun creeping over its great wall, along its seventeen quarters, its streets and alleyways, across its numerous rooftops, gardens and orchards and sees the small boy, coal-dust smudged over his tear-stained face and covering most of his clothes, running through the narrow backstreets where some Shirazis already bend in prayer, or open windows and yawn and stretch and look down at him... fascinated by his mad dash, so early in the morning.

A large, swarthy-faced man finishes washing his neck on a rickety balcony and throws water from the bowl and the running boy looks up and is hit full in the face which causes him to tumble head-over-heels and come to an undignified halt. Two older boys wrestling outside the door of a tumbling-down house stop and look across and laugh with some malice. They pick themselves up and run in the direction of the sorry-looking seven year-old, who on seeing their blurred shapes coming in his direction, pulls himself to his feet and scampers off again.

The older boys look up ahead at their prey's racing backside and find the sight quite comical... they point and laugh. Now and then with an anxious glance back in their direction the desperate boy is certainly not amused! He scampers past donkeys, countless tethered horses, camels, goats, cats racing for cover, barking dogs and flying chickens. People look down and across in amusement, or amazement or disgust, or sleepily try to wake up.

From the roof of a building a crow looks down on the running trio... caws twice, then soars into the sky and hovers, then follows them scrambling through the streets until finally the crow descends.

On some of the rooftops and small gardens women now hang out washing and on one a girl tugs at the hem of her mother's dress and points frantically down at them... dashing past.

The crow perches on the top of a cypress and looks down into the street at the front of the *attar's* shop selling fruit and small containers of perfume, as a man with a greying beard and his son of about fifteen years begin to place fruit in boxes arranged out the front. The bird swoops down and plucks a grape from a box as the boy runs out and shouts, but with a smile on his face, an interesting face.

"Hey *you!* You didn't have to steal that! You could've *asked!*" He grins up as the bird.

From inside his father calls out to him.

"What is it Mahmud?"

"Nothing father, just another hungry creature of God!"

He shakes his head and then looks into the street and is flabbergasted as the two shrieking boys rush past chasing the... by now, terrified-looking, shabbily-dressed, ugly little boy.

"*Oiy!* You two! Leave that kid alone! *Oiy!*"

As the chase continues the streets get wider and the houses larger as they race across the small bridge over an open water channel or *qanat* and from a balcony of a mansion a young, very pretty girl about six years old looks down. She is fascinated by what she is seeing as she chews on a thin stick of sugarcane.

From inside the house her mother calls out.

"Upon my head... Nabat, remember, no sugar before breakfast!"

Nabat frowns, then giggles.

The cawing crow looks down at the scene and blinks a yellow, glassy eye, amazed at what the morning has already brought forth... and still so early! The bird flies off following the running threesome towards a small garden-park. The crow soars down towards the trees as the sun's light now speeds over the tops of most of them. It lands on a branch and looks at the two older boys now lying exhausted and gasping for breath. The now-distraught, small, puffed-out boy is shortly afterwards banging on the door of a medium-sized house when finally a fat, bearded, self-important looking man in his forties opens the door and stares down disdainfully at this dirty, sobbing child.

"You? My God, look at you... Shams-ud-din! What are you *doing* waking me up so early in the morning, you *stupid, filthy boy?* My sister Ulya should teach you some manners!"

"Uncle, my name is now *Hafez,* as I've told you so often before! Uncle... it's... it's father, Baha-ud-din... he's *so* sick! Mother told me to run to you to get a doctor for him, we... don't have the money anymore, you must help! I... *ahhh...*"

He collapses from exhaustion.

"By my soul, how embarrassing... still, no one much about at this hour. I'll have to do as she asks, but first I'll have to get her ugly little wretch inside."

He bends over, holds his nose with one hand and with the other grabs hold of Hafez's shirt and looks up and down the street then drags him inside calling out... *"Haroun! Where are you, you good-for-nothing... get up and go and fetch the doctor and tell him to ride immediately to my poor sister's house! Haroun! Get up!"*

*

Baha-ud-din is near death now. The doctor shakes his head at Hafez's mother who turns to her three sons and her brother Sadi and drops down beside her husband and sobs on his chest as he coughs, then whispers, "My two big boys, almost grown men. You will have to go to my relatives in Isfahan... I have written to them, they will give you apprenticeships... you will have a life, I'm not worried about you. It is you my dear wife, my Ulya... and my Shams-ud-din, my little memorizer... my 'Hafez' that I worry about. Come here son, come here my *special boy*."

Hafez now throws himself into his dying father's arms, sobbing uncontrollably.

"Ah, do not be frightened of separation my boy, without separation there is no union, always remember that. You have a great gift my little 'Hafez'... in a few more years you will have memorized the whole of the *Koran* which took me many years, but don't stop there... study hard and keep writing those poems of yours, I like them... and where I am going I'll be listening for them. Now, you must be the man of the house from now on and look after your sweet mother here. Sadi! I've something to ask of you. I know we haven't always seen eye-to-eye but I know your sister here and our son will be welcomed into your home when I'm gone, that will be very soon now. It is all His will. Do not refuse the request of a dying man! "

Sadi wipes a tear from his eye and nods his agreement as Baha-ud-din coughs, then continues.

"Ah... now I can go to meet God in peace. My family, destiny has dealt us a heavy blow but perhaps from all this suffering we will all come closer to the Almighty, perhaps... *ahhhh*, my time has come..."

He breathes his last as he clutches the hands of his sobbing wife and small son... and now his other sons are on the floor weeping as outside the howling of a dog can be heard and nearby... the cawing of a crow.

*

Hafez helps up the dirty brown puppy that has just crashed headlong into the old cart full of his clothes and other possessions that he has wheeled into the alleyway. He looks at him and smiles.

"By my soul, are you alright... a bit dizzy, eh? Can you see me now? I'm your friend... Shams-ud-din, but I'm now called Hafez, because I'm good at remembering."

He hugs the puppy and the puppy looks like he is in paradise, he has finally found a home.

"Don't worry, you're safe now. I'll look after you and you, well... you'll look after me too. Won't you boy? God willing!"

The puppy licks his face and he laughs. Hafez's mother calls out from inside the house.

"Son, have you finished loading the rest of your things into that cart yet? You know we have to be out of here soon."

Hafez looks up, stops laughing, both he and the puppy look a bit uneasy.

"Almost Mother, just one more thing to go in!"

He smiles at the puppy, wraps it in a thin blanket, pats its head.

"Now boy, you have to keep very still and quiet, or it's back on the street for you and big trouble for me. You see, mother might not understand and my uncle Sadi definitely wouldn't. My father, well… he's passed on now and my brothers have been sent to work in Isfahan… but we've got each other, as long as we use our wits." The puppy licks his hand as he gently places it under a bundle in the cart.

A short time later Hafez and his mother who is about thirty-six but looks older, red around her eyes from weeping but strong-looking, poorly dressed… trudge through the streets of the Yazdi quarter of Shiraz. She is carrying two large bags and he is pushing his cart. As they slowly walk by people stop what they are doing and stare at them. Two old ladies stop and watch them and chat.

"The poor things. She has lost her husband that good-hearted coal-merchant you know, a terrible fever. And he left them with many debts. She's had to send her older boys away."

"By the spirits, I hear they are moving up town to her brother's place, cheaper than hiring help I suppose."

Two boys about Hafez's age, perhaps a bit older, stare at them as they pass by. The taller boy shouts at Hafez, "Good riddance! Hey, ugly-head, don't scare too many people where you're going like you did at our school!"

His father smacks him on the backside as the other boy laughs. Hafez grimaces and his mother looks sadly down at him.

"Don't worry son, it's not how you look on the outside that's important, but... who you are on the inside, and I know you're someone special, remember that."

Through clenched teeth Hafez replies.

"Yes Mum!"

The puppy growls. His mother looks worried.

"What's that?"

"Just... my tummy!"

"We'll have breakfast soon as we get there if it pleases God! Not too far, son."

*

It is a medium sized house in a forgettable street of one of the middle-class quarters... Kazerun, near the Kazerun Gate. Hafez's mother knocks on the door, that after a long wait finally opens. Sadi looks down at them annoyed and embarrassed, yet resigned to his fate. Worriedly, he looks up and down the street to see if anyone has seen them.

"Upon my eyes, Ulya... quick, around the back, down that alley, and make sure you leave that broken-down cart in the outside shed, Shams-ud-din."

He slams the door in their faces. Hafez is shocked.

"I've never liked him!"

They turn towards the alley. His mother looks sternly in her son's direction.

"Shams-ud-din! Enough of that! If it wasn't for my brother we'd be on the street, begging! He's been good enough to let us live with him and pay for your new clothes. Be grateful, you'll need them at your new school."

Hafez turns as the come to the garden gate, shocked.

"*New* school?"

"Of course! It's nearby and I hear it's very good. *Nice* children go there."

"But Mum, just when the kids had got sick of teasing me!"

They enter the unkempt back garden and head towards an old shed.

"Upon my soul! These *nice* children won't do that!"

"Oh... *no?*" Hafez grimaces.

She drops her bundle beside the shed and sits on a small bench, smiling at him.

"Have you been making up any more of those poems son? I like them. Any new ones?"

Hafez grins as he pushes the cart outside the shed.

"I thought up one on the way over here. Thought I'd give it to Uncle. Like to hear it?"

"Wonderful! Tell me it!"

"Alright Mum, here it is...

You question yourself... about your good and your bad?

It's necessary for you to have another judge? You forgot?

Stay far away from the bad and work towards the good;

do not play games and toy with life... or it will soon rot.

Since you know that God is the One Who will provide,

don't keep the heart, through greed, tied in a tight knot.

God will give help to whoever will be obedient to Him;

to him, He will give ample aid... when he expects it not.

Hafez finishes upon his knees, after 'performing' in greatly exaggerated speech and acting, much to his mother's amusement.

He stands as she hides a laugh, coughs and now says, "Hmmm, very interesting... but, I'm not sure if my brother would appreciate it. Come on, put your cart in that shed and I'll take these things inside so that we can get something into that poetic, growling stomach of yours. I think your father was right, my little 'Hafez'... you do have some talent as a poet, though whether that will help or hinder you in the future I'm not too sure. Don't take too long my boy!"

Hafez is soon hiding the puppy in the unused garden shed.

"Now Rustom! That's what I'll call you, a real brave fighter. Rustom... keep quiet in there and I'll bring you some food, soon... God willing!"

The puppy licks his face, then yelps.

"Shhhh... quiet! I'll be back!"

He shuts the door, runs across the unloved garden, opens the door and enters the back of his uncle's house. Perhaps he's taken too much time? He runs down the long hallway and slides on his stockinged feet on the polished stone floor and crashes into a large, expensive-looking pot on a tall wooden stand. It flies up into the air, stops, then begins its deadly descent. He looks up, shocked and then reaches out and just catches it in time, a mere fingers-width from the hard, mirror-like floor.

"Phew! *That*... was really close!"

He looks over to see a pair of fat, bare, hairy feet and now he looks up to see an enormous stomach looming overhead, then the frowning face of his uncle looking down at him. He is… *not amused!*

"I'll take that, you clumsy little idiot!"

Sadi bends down and grabs the expensive vase out of Hafez's tight grip and lifts it only to see it suddenly slip from his own greasy fingers… breakfast is always so messy! Once again the hard polished floor beckons the falling vase. Again Hafez makes a brilliant catch. This time the shocked face of his uncle changes to a grateful and pleased grin!

"Well done, my boy! You've quick reflexes and strong hands, even if your face looks like… well, let's just say it's a bit *unusual."*

Hafez's smile turns to a scowl as he pulls himself up then throws the vase high in the air towards his flabbergasted uncle who, finally, holds onto it… *just!* Hafez brushes himself off. Sadi is furious again!

"Upon my head! Don't brush all that coal dust onto this nice clean floor! I think you'd better have a bath and put on some new clothes before you have breakfast. After all, you are staying with a poet of some importance, a literary figure with a reputation to keep up! This isn't the house of… a… a coal merchant!"

Hafez's mother Ulya walks up, eyes ablaze.

"That'll be enough of *that,* brother! He'll eat *now…* if it pleases God! He's starving. He'll bathe afterwards, thank you. And there's another thing… there's nothing wrong with the honest dust of a coal merchant!" She pushes her son ahead of her towards the kitchen.

After eating, Hafez is in the shed feeding some scraps to a hungry Rustom who is wolfing them down!

"It's not much, but wait 'til lunch, I'll bring more. I've got to have a bath now, later I'll find a way to give you yours."

Rustom looks worried.

"I'll be back when I can and we'll go off and explore the place. Alright?" He bends down, Rustom licks him on the face making him laugh.

Shortly afterwards the small naked body of Hafez climbs into a steaming bathtub helped by his mother, sleeves rolled up.

"It's not too hot. I tried it."

She pushes his head under the water, laughing. He pops up, spluttering. She rubs his hair with soap then ducks him under again, he comes up gasping for breath.

"Mum, enough! Enough! I'm old enough to do it myself you know?"

"Alright then... you can!"

She backs away and sits on a small bench, smiling at him.

"Have you any more of those songs, those poems you make up? Your father liked them and I like them. Any more new ones?"

Hafez grins through the bubbles.

"I thought up another one at breakfast. Dedicated to dear Uncle like the one I told you out the back. Like to hear it?"

"Wonderful! *Sing* it to me this time!"

Hafez begins to sing in his boyish, out of tune, comical voice...

The dog has more honour on which to depend,

than that man who hurts the heart of a friend.

It's necessary for this true saying to be proved

so that in the heart it sinks, not to be removed.

Hafez stands up, soapsuds covering his hair... dramatically throwing his arms about. His mother is almost falling off the bench in hysterics as he sings and mimes the rest of the short song...

Man eats with you with his hand on the table

Shut outside on the threshold, dog is unable...

His mother is trying not to laugh, spluttering, covering her mouth with her hand as he continues...

It's a pity (his hand is thrust over forehead) *for the dog is faithful until death* (he stands up straight, salutes, a brave look on his face, seeing distant horizons)...

While that man, (he does good impression of his uncle... stomach out, sly look on face) *thinks it's right to break faith...* (arms flung out as if to dismiss someone).

He loses his balance and falls back into the tub, feet flying into the air, suds and water fly skywards and out and over the floor. His mother falls off the bench in hysterical laughter, gasping for breath, tears streaming down her face. His soapsuds-covered face appears out of the water, wanting approval... all enthusiastic, realizing a great opportunity has been created.

"Mum, you liked it? Mum, can I, can I get... a... dog... a *little* puppy? It'd be a great friend you know. Since Dad died I've no one to play with... *I'm lonely.* Except for you of course, but, you're always so busy and, well, *different...* you know."

His mother pulls herself together and places the bench upright, wipes her eyes, brushes off her clothes, sits down and looks at him with sad eyes.

"I understand. Would it help, my dear? Would it *really* make such a difference?"

"Oh *yes* Mother, it *really* would!"

"Well then, I don't see how it could do any harm..."

Hafez's face lights up with happiness and disbelief.

"Oh, thank you Mum. I'll go out and bring him in, *now...* you'll love him... he's in the shed, I've named him Rustom... he's very, very intelligent and brave too!"

She can't believe what she's hearing.

"You little rogue! You could sing your way into anyone's heart couldn't you? What a little poet you are, and a talker!"

Hafez suddenly looks concerned.

"Mum, I've just thought about, what about... Uncle? He probably thinks dogs are 'unclean' like many do!"

"Every creature of God is blessed. You were read the story of the Seven Sleepers from Maulana Rumi's *Masnavi* by your father and also from that wonderful book comes these lines my son...

Majnun was seen patting a dog and kissing
it and as he did he could not stop swooning;
he was pacing around it and as he circled it,
he stooped, gave it sugar-julep: it slurped it.
An idler passing said, "O half-mad Majnun
what hypocrisy's this that you've now done?
Mouth of a dog is always some filth eating...
and a dog its private parts is always licking."
Then he went on at length about dogs' faults:
not a scent of truth has one seeing only faults.

"Now Shams-ud-din, listen to our dear, loving Majnun's wonderful reply...

Majnun said, "You are seeing only the body;
go in and see with my eyes... see what I see!
This dog's a talisman sealed by God's hand;
this dog is the guardian of dear Layla's land!
See its hopes, heart, soul, wisdom in its face,

where it's chosen to make its dwelling-place.

It is the dog with a blessed face, of my Cave;

no, more, it shares my grief, perhaps my grave.

The dog that is staying in the abode of Layla,

how could I to the lions even a hair of it offer?

O and since to her dogs, a slave is every lion,

no more talking! Silence! Goodbye, walk on!"

"By my soul Mother, that is so true! I feel that my puppy Rustom is like that, a talisman sent by God for Father! I will never forget that poem. How could I, I'm... *Hafez!"*

"You leave my brother to me, I know how to handle that one. Now, only one rule... he stays out 'on the threshold' like in your poem, alright?"

"Alright. Now, can I show him to you?"

"Upon my soul, I don't see why not! Let's get you dressed and we'll go out and meet this wonderful mastiff."

"Mum, he's just a little puppy."

"Just like you!"

They both laugh.

*

It is six days later when another crow flies over the city, soars down to a fenced-in courtyard with a tall cypress in the middle of it and rosebushes along the walls and flies over to a long verandah leading to the inside classrooms and caws twice. On the verandah there are about fifteen children, at or near Hafez's age, sitting on mats at low desks, with writing slates and chalk. The teacher stands up front, a handsome young man in his late-twenties. Beside him stands another taller man of about the same age with long ringlets of hair hanging on his cheeks, wearing a loose black caftan and a strangely bell-shaped, black leather hat and a boy of Hafez's age, tall and thin, also with long ringlets, black caftan... but with a small leather cap on his head. From beyond the back row of the children the bird watches him as their teacher speaks.

"In the Name of God! Children... now, quiet *please!* Today for your poetry and history classes I have a special treat for you. Standing next to me is a friend of mine, a fellow teacher and I believe he will one day be recognized as one of Shiraz's great poets. His name is Shahin and he is of the Jewish faith and of course lives in the Jewish quarter, and beside him is his son... Musa. As today is a Jewish holiday and he does not have to work, he kindly agreed to come and talk to you and read from a long, epic *masnavi* poem he has recently completed called the *Musa-Nameh* or 'Book of Moses'. The book is written in our Persian language but with the Hebrew letters.

"First he will read a poem that opens the book about our young ruler whom we all love, the Sultan of all Persia... Abu Said. First, can anyone tell us how old Abu Said was when he became Sultan?"

"Sir, he was only twelve years old and it was ten years ago so now he is twenty-two." A boy at the back answers immediately.

"Correct Zak... he was only four years older than most of you here and carried the burden of all of us on his young shoulders. Our own beloved ruler Mahmud Shah was appointed governor over all of Fars and Abu Said has no reason not to approve of *him* so I can assure you all that we will have a stable government for many years to come. Now I call on my friend the poet and teacher to read his opening poem in *masnavi* form in praise of our young sultan... please Shahin..."

"Thank you Mirza for such a kind introduction. I will read the opening poem and then perhaps we can have a chat about the rest of my book and I'll read some of it...

On the great Sultan Abu Said... son of kings, reigning king,

kind ruler of all... let only great fortune and victory be falling.

He is Faridun of this age and he is a present day Alexander,

and... may the eye of the evil one look upon his face... never!

Towards the kingdoms of the world he shows only generosity,

and he carries the crown of Faridun on his head for all to see!

Soldiers in numbers beyond counting, many complete armies

he assembles, as he does what's right... justice everyone sees!

From one end of the world to the other... each and every king

from every possible direction... a tribute to him they all bring.

Since the time of Jamshid such a sun that is shining so bright

in this old world of ours has never, never seen the day's light!

Everywhere he has established true justice and also fairness,

because of such good fortune all his subjects know happiness.

If way back in the past, in the storybook time of Naushirvan,

lamb and wolf drank from where the same spring of water ran...

and now, in time of this king, no wolf who for blood is thirsting

would ever be brave enough at house's gateway to be appearing.

King takes from our world each seed that may sprout tyranny,

hearts of who are his enemies... he rips to shreds immediately!

Because of his great fortune all the world's people are fortunate:

everyone hearing his name can himself as a happy person rate.

Each province he rides through has joy from his stirrup scattered:

Abu Said is essence of happiness, 'Be he happy,' is always said.
And also... may it never be taken... that crown of his royalty,
from off his head that is so venerable and may God Almighty
be his Companion, his Friend wherever he may happen to go,
and may his crown and his throne never receive bad luck's blow.
And may those who are jealous of him be chained up each hour,
and may Destiny grant that each victory be in his hand's power.
Each moment's sweetness come again from his sweet embrace,
and may his life be more fruitful than any of our human race.
And may his name so fine for each age of Time continue to live:
may his nights be lucky, days like New Year... prosperity give.
May he always be happy and joyful through all his life's days:
may he never encounter an enemy from Time's tyrannical ways!
And may his hand forever hold the brimming wine and the cup,
may he always be feasting with joy for him forever coming up!
May he never be needing anyone but the Great Judge of us all,
and may he his Companion the Lord of Creation always call.
O Lord, please from his fair beauty keep the evil eye so far away,
and may such perfection increase, hour by hour... day by day!
And may disaster never upon his throne and on his crown fall:
may good fortune be his, bright as the sun... shining on us all.
May great God watch over him and see that he is safe always,
and may the Lord of Creation be his Friend for all of his days.
May winds of disaster blow far away from his royal parasol...
may all in the world be prosperous, as is always his final goal!
May slaves, kings, caesars, stand forever in service at his door...
joy his friend 'til Final Day seals his work in peace, forever more.
Hafez is in a state of shock, mouth open... paralyzed. All the

other children are clapping or cheering. He realizes that standing before him is a *real, live* poet… and perhaps a great one. His heart is thumping so hard he thinks everyone must be able to hear it. He places his hand over it to try to muffle the sound.

Their teacher raises his hands for quiet and Shahin continues.

"Thank you all. I don't think I've ever had such a reception to my poetry even amongst our own people, have I Musa?"

His son smiles lovingly at him and shakes his head.

"No! Never! Not that I read my poems to anyone that often. Now, how many of you know the story of Moses in the *Koran?*"

Only Hafez slowly raises his hand. Mirza their teacher says, "We are all studying the holy *Koran* but have yet to read the Moses story… it will come up next reading, God willing. You, the new boy with your hand up, your name is Shams-ud-din isn't it?"

"Hafez."

Shahin is more interested now.

"Why do you say your name is Hafez?"

"Because I am memorizing all of the *Koran* and I'm good at remembering!"

There are a few sniggers of disbelief from some of the other students.

"Really? That is very admirable… *Hafez.* So, you know the story of our Moses, eh? *Who* do you think he was?"

"Someone who loved God and tried to obey Him and finally saw Him."

"Hmmm… *very* good. Now, what part of his life would you like me to read to all of you Hafez?"

"Sir, where he sees God… for that is also my great ambition."

"Ah, somehow I knew you would say that! I can see it in your eyes young man, you are a seeker. Musa, please get comfortable... go and sit with our young *Hafez* over there."

Musa happily sits next to Hafez and they grin at each other... new friends!

"Now listen children, for the story of Moses is not only a story for us Jews but as you will soon read in the *Koran* it is a story for all Muslims too... ah, here it is...

And then, Moses in great sorrow began to cry:
"O You Who are Immortal, one desire have I:
be merciful, remove the veil, show Your face...
allow me see Your face for only a short space
of time, for my desire to see you in my heart
is so great... my heart is ripping itself apart!"
To gain sight of God the prophet kept crying,
his head and beard in the dirt he was rubbing.
Suddenly, the Divine Voice said: " O Moses,
that one... he will die the moment he sees Us:
he will not stay in the world, within an hour
over soul he holds dear he will have no power.
For no human eye can take this Divine Light:
you need much distance for My Face to sight.
Now go down and tell Joshua the son of Nun,
to the army immediately to go, happily to run
and when there all the people he should seek
out and about when sun rises tomorrow speak:
say that none at that time, (this is a warning)
except for Aaron, should not home be leaving.

Tell them to keep their sheep and goats inside

and all should not go out… none to go outside.

O Moses, this is what I am now commanding

and is My order… now this to you I am telling:

listen, tomorrow night you must go out happily

to that great mountain made of emeralds… see

where there is some flat ground… and you will

see a mound: don't worry, happily on it sit still.

Moses, be awake and of yourself be in command

for tomorrow I will come quickly past there and

you'll see nothing except My back in that glade,

even if out of iron, steel or stone you were made.

So that you in this world can continue on living

the complete story about this to you I'm telling."

Moses kissed the ground when he heard all this

and happy, with cheeks glowing like roses, this

man of pure nature then left that place quickly

to where Nun's son Joshua waited, him to see.

Moses told Joshua all that God to him revealed

and told him to join the army away in the field.

When Josua reached his friends that brave man

told them immediately with feeling, God's plan.

To each he went and told each of them to beware

because it was the command of God that "There

shouldn't be a living being straying from its abode

or happen to be wandering plain or the open road:

and not a single human or an animal should stray

around or near Mount Sanai at all… in any way.

Be aware... listen well to that Judge's command:

if you wish to be safe and to have a steady hand,

and want your souls inside your bodies to stay,

then this His command do not defy in any way."

Then wise, old prophet Moses, in depth of night

towards that emerald mountain made his flight

to that place where that Judge, the Ancient One

of days and nights, had told him earlier to come.

Walking, longing to Unite with Friend burned

in him. Suddenly, all was full of Light, he turned

and fire upon mountain and stones was falling,

and heavy mountains down were sent crashing.

The mountain and desert, the earth and heaven

due to that Divine Judge's order... were shaken.

And all the world was full of light neverending...

which, with every moment, kept on expanding.

All of a sudden, Moses from the path looked up,

saw His Divine Majesty... his senses gave up.

That man so pure, became nothing but spirit...

being beside himself, his soul's garment he split.

A cry came out of the lover at that very moment

he saw his Divine Beloved enter what was rent.

As He passed in front, Moses looked and he saw

the One and from fear he passed away as before.

Prophet Moses fell, tears from his face flowing...

in the dust his beautiful face he was then rubbing

as he cried out, "Creator, Hidden, Manifested,

Ancient, Almighty, Omnipotent, One Blessed:

forgive all the mistakes the sinful world makes,

to all asking forgiveness, give them all it takes.

All of my people please, please now You forgive:

absolution for their crimes and mistakes, give."

And he cried like this to God beyond compare…

Creator's glorious reply in His voice did declare:

"O Moses, now raise high your head and rejoice.

Rise, do not strike face, no tears, hear My voice!

I now forgive them completely… all those worthy

are forgiven, so let mind and heart be worry free!"

"Children, I must stop now. Hafez, hey are you alright? Musa, what's wrong with him?"

"He seems to be awake father but is… somewhere else."

"Slap his face, son!"

Musa gently does as told.

"Harder Musa!"

Musa slaps him as hard as he can and Hafez turns to him and shouts, "Eh… *watchit!* Oh, I'm here. I was there, with him, Moses. Sir, why have you stopped? Never before have I been so close to seeing His face!"

Shahin smiles gently at him and gestures to Mirza that all is fine.

"Sit down children!" Their teacher Mirza shouts.

"Hafez, please come to my house with my son Musa and I will read you more, but I'm afraid the other children have had enough. Mirza?"

"Yes Shahin, perhaps so. We have a short time left. Now children, who would like to read out their homework, a *ruba'i* styled poem on how you feel about life."

No one except Hafez puts their hands up. The young teacher is annoyed.

"No one? Right. Ah? You, new boy... Shams-ud-din. I notice you have your hand up. What about you?"

"My poetic name is... Hafez."

"Oh, I forgot, *Hafez*... I must *remember* that."

He laughs, then whole class laughs at the pun, except for Hafez and Musa sitting down the front. The teacher's arms go up for silence.

"Well now, if you have a name as a poet... then you must have written a poem, a *ruba'i*. And, I expect it to equal one by our mathematician, our fine astronomer-poet Omar Khayyam. Please come here, face the children and read it."

Hafez gets up and walks up... no slate in hand.

"No slate? Of course, one who *remembers*, eh... *Hafez?*"

Hafez, embarrassed, smiles. Children snigger or giggle. Most are boys, but there are four girls.

"Go on! We haven't got 'til the end of time, young man!"

Hafez gulps, looks at Shahin who smiles at him then at the leering, curious, laughing or expectant faces of the other students, now he clears his throat and begins...

I've nothing from the life I've had but grief: (he stretches out one arm and puts one hand on heart)

I've nothing from love, good and bad, but grief: (his hand goes to his brow)...

Mirza is fascinated... the children have mouths agape!

I've never for a moment had a sympathetic friend;

I've no one, no shoulder when I'm sad... but grief.

He dramatically lifts his arms and lets them fall and his head falls also. The girls sigh or sniff. Some boys snigger, then wait. The young teacher Mirza is not sure how to react.

"That's, eh... interesting, er... Hafez! Do you have any more?"

Hafez doesn't look up.

"Many, Teacher!"

"Oh... so, you *are* a poet... at eight years old?"

"That is my *earnest wish,* God willing!

"One more then. And... children, pay attention, one of you lot will be the next to read. Go ahead!"

Hafez looks up, slight smile showing the awareness he has a captured audience. He stretches his arms out...

It's a pity there's no one to plead my need... for me;

no one to be a friend in either word or deed for me!

He kneels on one leg, both hands on heart... eyes to the heavens, dramatic...

If I were somebody, then Somebody would be my friend... (he raises one hand up, with one finger up)...

But because I'm nobody, (his hand changes and his forefinger and thumb make a zero) *nobody will plead for me.* (He drops his hand and head).

Two girls and Musa and Shahin applaud but the boys look disgusted. The teacher sighs, then helps Hafez to stand.

"Very dramatic and well written too! But, a little too... *sad.* Let's have a *happy poem* now. Back to your seat."

Hafez quietly walks back to his place and Musa hugs him.

"Someone else? Yes?"

A large tough-looking boy stands up and swaggers to the front and the teacher smiles and says...

"Well Abul, now cheer us up!"

Abul has a sly look on his face as he begins...

It seems to me... one would be... a fool

to befriend one that looks like a ghoul,

it's easy to see... with a face like that...

such a one shouldn't be let into school!

He claps his hands and bursts out laughing. All the others except Musa, Shahin and Mirza also burst out laughing. Hafez turns red with anger, fists clenched. The teacher finally splutters, smiles and covers his mouth with his hand. Hafez leaps from his place and head-butts the boy and they begin to fight, rolling over. The other children go wild, shouting and screaming and jumping up and down. The teacher grabs the two fighters by their collars and pulls them apart.

"Abul, back to your place at once. Err... *Hafez*... go to the head teacher now and get your punishment and you'll be staying in after school. You have to learn to control your temper young man!"

Hafez slouches out of the room. Musa sadly watches him go!

Some hours later outside the school the sun is setting and Musa is waiting, when suddenly the large gate opens and Hafez, walking uneasily, comes out and not noticing Musa or anything, walks off, head bowed, shuffling. Musa catches up with him.

"Hafez, Hafez, wait, let me walk home with you. You sure gave it to that big oaf!"

Hafez wearily looks up.

"Oh, it's you."

"My father said I could wait for you and bring you to our house soon. You know many don't like us because we are Jews!"

"So what? Same God isn't it? There *is* only one!"

Musa kicks a stone through the air.

"Yes, I suppose so. Most of your classmates wouldn't have anything to do with me, it's their parents I think. I really liked your poetry. One day I want to write poems too, like my father."

"By my soul, I think he's a *great* poet Musa. You want to come to my place and play with my dog Rustom?"

"You've a dog? I thought you didn't have anyone to play with?"

Hafez picks up a flat stone and skips it across the road where it narrowly misses a man staggering out of a winehouse.

"Oops! Oh? That! I wrote those poems before my mother and I went to live with my uncle and got Rustom, after my father died. C'mon let's run, it's getting a little late! Just enough time to get up to a little mischief!"

*

It is six months later and Hafez and Musa have become firm friends. They are laughing as they pick up sticks and throw them for Rustom to fetch again as they turn into the main thoroughfare only to be stopped by a darkish young man in his twenties dressed in strange clothes. He speaks in slow, stumbling Persian.

"I... am looking... for the grave... of your good... er... great poet and traveller... known as... Sadi!"

Hafez replies in Arabic, "It is quite a way but we will take you there, kind sir. He is my favourite poet... the same name as my uncle who only *thinks* he is a poet."

"Ah, upon my head, you speak the tongue. He is one of my

favourites too, not only because he was a great poet and storyteller and moralist but he was also one of the most amazing travellers that ever lived and I hope to follow in his footsteps in that regard, I'm afraid I'm no poet..."

Hafez reverts to Persian, "Well *I am*... aren't I Musa, a poet and small and... odd-looking like Master Sadi?"

"Yes, you should have heard the fine but sad *ruba'i* he recited at school the first day we met, it made me cry. His father is dead you know?"

"You mentioned that your friend's father has died. What is your name boy? You speak Arabic and so young... how come?"

"My father taught me and I am memorizing the *Koran*... that is one of the reasons I am called 'Hafez'... also my good memory."

"Hafez eh... I'll *remember* you my friend. But I will speak in my very bad Persian from now on so that your friend here will not miss out on our enlightening conversation."

They both laugh as they begin to walk in the direction of the stream called Ruknabad.

"And you sir, what is your name please?"

"Abu Abdullah Muhammad, call me Ibn Battuta... travelling with a few companions throughout God's world like our beloved Sadi. I'm from North Africa, Tangier to be exact, kind sir!"

Hafez smiles as he whispers, "I'll *remember* that."

After some time they come to the banks of the Ruknabad canal and sit down under a shady tree for a rest and Ibn Battuta takes three oranges from his shoulder bag and says as he hands one to each of the hungry boys and a piece of bread to Rustom... "Hafez, your father is dead so I have been informed by your friend Musa here. Perhaps you can recite to me the poem you read at school about what a loss you feel, perhaps I can console you in some small way."

Hafez bites into his orange, eating the rind as the others wince and begin to peel theirs and they all silently eat their fruit and finally he replies, "You know it is strange... the way I feel about the man whose tomb we are about to visit. In some ways I feel that perhaps I *am* him come back to life again in a new body. You know, in many religions they believe that this is possible? He only died about thirty years before I was born and he lived to well over a hundred years old... (somehow, I know that won't be *my* fate). Sometimes when I read his poetry I believe it was I who wrote it. I'll give you an example... how like his life was, to what mine has started out to be. He too was small and... *odd-looking* and his father died when he was about the *same age* as me when my father died and later he wrote this poem from his *Bustan* which expresses what I feel about my father's loss better than I ever could. It goes...

> *You should protect the orphan... whose father is dead,*
> *brush mud from his clothes, stop pain hitting his head.*
> *You don't know how hard for him living happens to be:*
> *when the root is cut away... does life exist in the tree?*
> *Do not hug and do not kiss that child that is your own*
> *where an orphan can see it... so neglected and so alone!*
> *If the orphan cries tears, who will comfort his suffering?*
> *If he loses his temper... who his rage will be believing?*
> *You make sure he doesn't cry, for surely God's throne*
> *begins to shake violently from the orphan's sad moan.*
> *With pity that is infinite and with tenderest of care*
> *wipe tears from his eyes and brush dust from his hair.*

There's not a shield of parental protection over his head

sheltering him: you be that protector he needs instead.

When the arms of a father around my neck could fold…

way back then I was crowned like a monarch, with gold.

Back then, if even a fly should come and alight upon me:

not one heart… many, were scared by what they'd see!

But now, if I'm taken captive and they do what they will,

I call out loud, but no friend comes, no matter how shrill!

Sorrows of orphans I can always understand… and share,

way back in my childhood… I tasted the orphan's despair.

Tears are running down Musa's cheeks and even Ibn Battuta wipes one from his eye as he studies the strange boy sitting before him.

"Listen young man, and you obviously are a young *man* because of all you have suffered… you are not just a boy, are you? No! Let me tell you this… you still have a mother don't you, who really loves you and an uncle who is kind enough to help you, eh?"

Hafez nods.

"Well, you have much more than many others I have encountered on my journeys so far… boys your age begging in streets for a crust to keep them alive… no parents, no friends… nobody! Understand?"

"And you've got this wonderful dog… Rustom! I don't have a dog. But, I've got a father but he's always writing, my mother died when I was born." Musa looks away, tears in his eyes.

Hafez puts an arm on his shoulder as Ibn Battuta says, "See… your young friend here seems worse off than you and on top of all his troubles he has to take the brunt of insults for being a Jew. Now listen Hafez, if you promise me you'll stop being sorry for yourself and live in the present and get on with your life and become as fine a poet as Sadi I'll recite to you my favourite *ghazal* by him. Is it a bargain? Yes? Good! Now, let me see if it comes back to me... ah... yes...

> *Listen to this: so precious are the sighs that burn the heart,*
> *for whether they come or go, they help the days to depart.*
> *I wait through the night for one with a face like the dawn*
> *that to the grace of morning makes a new radiance start.*
> *If once again I happen to see that sweet face of my Friend,*
> *all Eternity my lucky star I'd be thanking from my heart.*
> *Why should I fear mankind accusing me, for a brave man's*
> *heart serves as his shield, to ward off the slanderer's dart!*
> *The successful one is that one who many a failure endured:*
> *New Year's Day comes because a cold winter did depart.*
> *Many a careful lover may for long be longing for his Layla,*
> *but only a Majnun who burns his harvest wins that heart!*
> *Your slave am I, so go and find a game that is in the wild*
> *for no chain is required for a bird that is tame at the start.*
> *That one is truly strong who throws both the worlds away,*
> *of which monks attached to the world cannot have a part.*
> *Tomorrow doesn't exist and yesterday's completely spent:*
> *Sadi, today is the time to bring contentment to your heart.*

Now Hafez wipes away a tear from his eye as he stands and walks over and hugs the sitting Ibn Battuta and says, "Kind sir, I did not know that poem of Master Sadi's but I can assure you that it is now placed firmly in my memory and has also become one of my favourites of his. May God bless you and all you hold dear forever for revealing this great lesson to me... I'll never forget it or you, how could I... I'm Hafez!"

They all laugh and hug each other and continue towards the tomb of Sadi. It is quite a while later that they approach the buildings surrounding his grave that he had built in his long lifetime to give shelter, nourishment and doctoring to tired travellers. Musa turns to this weary traveller from so far away and excitedly shouts.

"Sir, why don't you stay here! Travellers like you are very welcome here! That is why Sadi had this large building built!"

"I would love to Musa, except it would perhaps be an insult to my host who has made a small room available for me back in the city."

"And who may your host be, if I may ask?" Hafez is curious, as he can not imagine turning down the blessed opportunity of sleeping so close to the grave of such a great soul. Once he had tried to sleep there himself but they did not believe his story that he had travelled alone from Yazd. All he got for his trouble was a kick in the backside there and a bawling out from his distraught mother when he finally got home, long after it was dark. Perhaps it will happen again if he can't convince this strange traveller to visit their homes on the way back and collaborate their unbelievable excuse.

"It is quite a story my friend. First let us pay our respects to the great man and after I wash a few of my dirty clothes at what I have heard are some small cisterns that Sadi had constructed for such a practical purpose, I'll tell you the full story. Don't worry if we are late getting back for I'll visit your houses and explain what helpful citizens you both have been!"

Musa and Hafez grin at him then at each other as the three of them walk towards the tomb surrounded by a grove of cypress trees.

Later as Ibn Battuta is ringing out the last of his washing and hanging it on the tree to dry in the wind that has blown up he sits down next to them and quotes another *ghazal* of Shiraz's favourite poet…

About the long dark night what would that one know

who is wrapped in luxury's garment… and is all show?

The man who is wise knows the outcome of love so he

does not make a beginning of it from the very first go!

I tried hard to avoid surrendering my heart to anyone,

but with both eyes open how's it possible not to do so?

Look out for calamity from arrow of that One's glance

for it will never return again… once it has left the bow!

It must surely be because of coquetry of the pheasant,

that the destiny of the falcon's eyes is to never let go.

Police inspector's on the track of the drunken outsider,

but never bothers the Sufis' flirting that all now know.

Tell everyone who is loving the rose to leave and to be

enduring the cruelty of the thorn… tell them all to go!

O you, you who have yielded your heart to the Archer,

you've to take off your shield… down it quickly throw!

Whatever you expect at Beloved's hands is a kindness,

be it disdain or honour, whatever Beloved does bestow.

The hand of Majnun was grasping at the skirt of Layla:

head of Mahmud lay in dust at Ayaz's foot… long ago!

There is not another nightingale able to sing like me…

there's no minstrel who with a voice like mine does go!

Everything of value is derived from a particular source;

sugar is coming from Egypt and Sadi Shiraz did grow!

"Ah, what a poet my friends, you are so blessed that he was born in this wonderful place and you are today blessed because of another great soul. When I rode into Shiraz a few weeks ago I and my companions had but one desire... to find the illustrious chief-judge, Shaikh Majd al-Din Ismail, the marvel of the age..."

Hafez's mouth falls open in amazement, "You... you have met, him..."

"Please, no interruptions my young friend... a good story needs no explanations. Where was I? Yes... as I reached his blessed dwelling in his seminary when he was going out to the afternoon prayer... I saluted him and he embraced me and took my hand until he reached his prayermat and he indicated to me that I should pray beside him. After this all the notables of the city came forward to salute him as you would have heard is their custom every morning and evening. He then asked about my journey and the lands I had visited and gave orders that I should be lodged in a small room at his famous seminary, the Majdiyeh... so that is why I cannot stay here."

"Of course, it would be an insult to such a revered soul. Please tell us how you knew beforehand about him... before you came here." Hafez's eyes are aglow with anticipation as Ibn Battuta smiles then clears his throat.

"Aghhh... Shaikh Majd al-Din is held in the highest esteem by the king of Irak, and I will now tell you two boys why. The then king of Irak, Sultan Uljaitu had as a companion (while he was still an infidel) a Shi'ite theologian and when the king embraced Islam together with the Tartars, he showed the greatest respect for this man who persuaded him to establish the Shi'ite faith throughout his dominions.

"At Baghdad, Shiraz and Isfahan all of the population prevented the execution of the order and so the king ordered the judges of these three cities to be brought to him. The first of them to be brought was your esteemed chief-judge Majd al-Din. The sultan was then at a place called Qarabagh, which was his summer residence and when the good judge arrived he ordered him to be thrown to the dogs that he had there..."

Hafez and Musa swap anxious glances as Ibn Battuta raises his bushy eyebrows, then continues... "These are enormous dogs my young friends, *enormous*... with chains on their necks, *trained to eat men!* When anyone is brought to be delivered to the dogs, he is placed without restraint in a wide plain... the dogs are then set loose on him and he runs but finds no refuge, they overtake him and *tear him to pieces* and *eat all his flesh*..."

Hafez and Musa gulp simultaneously as Ibn Battuta wets his dry lips and then continues, "But when those dogs were let loose on Majd al-Din they would *not* attack him... they wagged their tails before him in the *friendliest* manner..."

The boys leap into the air and cheer and laugh and Rustom barks and eventually the smiling traveller holds up his hand for silence so he can continue.

"Now the sultan, on hearing about this showed the *greatest reverence* and respect towards him and renounced the doctrines of the Shi'ites. He gave the judge many presents including a hundred of the villages of Jamkan about sixty miles south of here, one of the best districts of this province of Fars. End... of story!"

"One day I'm going to meet him and perhaps he'll tell me *how* he tamed those vicious dogs!" Hafez looks determined.

"Well, if we don't make a start for your homes soon I might not be able to tame your vicious parents, eh boys... let's get a move on."

As they leave the tomb's surroundings of the great poet Hafez whispers to his friend Musa, "I tell you, one day they'll all sing my *ghazals* just like they sing Sadi's today and I'll meet the chief judge and he'll become my good friend!"

"You know Hafez, you're a strange one. It's so difficult to tell when you're joking and when you're not."

As the sun begins to set the odd-looking foursome head back towards the walls of the city, domes of the many mosques glowing golden and turquoise in the fading sunlight.

*

"I am amazed at how quickly you have been able to memorize our script and how well you now read my *Musa-Nama*, my 'Book of Moses'." Shahin looks across from his desk at the eight-year-old Hafez and smiles at his young student.

"Sir, it is not the gift of my memory that makes me want to read your poetry that has become so dear to me... but my desire to know the story of God working through man, not only in the culture of *our* country but in *all* countries since our father Adam was amongst us. You remember the promise that you made to me when you accepted me as your student when Musa brought me here for the first time?"

"I made a number of promises to you then... and you made one to me, to be a good friend to my beloved son Musa who is often a lonely child and as I am either teaching or writing most of the time. He has loved and admired you since that day we all met at your school. I'm so happy that you have kept your promise to me and I of course will always be in your debt."

"O no, teacher, it is I who will be in your debt. Musa is my closest friend, besides my mother of course... and I too was a lonely boy until our wonderful friendship began. You see, it is not only the Jews and those of other faiths beside Islam who are often ridiculed here... we who are... different-looking also find it hard to get close to others. Sir, may I ask you... a question, that perhaps you may not rush to answer?"

"Of course my friend, there are no secrets between fellow-lovers of the Almighty One. As they say, 'Seek the truth from a child!'"

"Why do you not wed again and find a new mother for Musa? I notice many beautiful, young Jewish women in the streets around here whenever I come to study with you or to see Musa?"

"Ah, Hafez... how can I explain? Miriam... was the great love of my life and after she left us I made a promise to God that I would dedicate the rest of my life to teaching and writing about His work amongst our people and the people of our country... your country too. I must admit that sometimes I regret that promise when like you I admire our beautiful women... but, understand this... once you make a promise to God it is sealed, and one cannot go back on it. Now tell me... repeat to me the promise that I made to you, besides teaching you to understand our script and allowing you to read my work."

"Ah, teacher, you remember... you are just joking with me!"

"Yes Hafez, I am. All of my library is now open to you for you to borrow one book at a time, all the Jewish and Christian Biblical texts, all the Persian works... including my favourites... the *Shah-*

Nama or 'Book of Kings' of our great epic poet Firdausi... and all the Sufi works I cherish so much... those of the Master Rumi and our beloved Sadi and Farid-al-Din Attar and of course those of my other favourite, Nizami. Altogether I have over two hundred books Hafez and if as you say you wish to borrow and copy one at a time I do not know how long it will take you to read and write your way through all of them."

"A much shorter time than might think sir, for just as some are hungry for food or wine all the time... I have a great hunger for the words of God and those of His lovers. Sir, I was just reading this section here in your great *masnavi* poem on Moses and I have some questions. It is the section that comes immediately after that which you read at our school when we first met."

"Please, go ahead and read it to me, I'll try to answer anything you may ask my young friend."

"Let me see... yes... here it is... you remember Moses asks the Lord to forgive his people and finally the Lord says...

"I now forgive them all completely... all those worthy
are forgiven, so let your mind and heart be worry free."

And then you go on to say that the Lord continues to say...

"Because with the forebears of your people a promise
I made upon My Soul, I gave my Word, nothing less:
that Canaan by me to them will eventually be given
in trust and their opponents in fear, out shall be driven.
Amorites I'll drive out and I'll drive out the Jebasites,
no Perizites will stay there, the same for the Hivites.
Not a Girgishite will be still there and all your enemies
will be down and away from there and then to please

and to fulfill that promise of My generous Soul, then
that place I will give them, beautiful, pristine as Eden.
Now listen O Moses, because this is about you... see
and truly know the innermost meaning of this mystery,
because I've ordered it to be such as this since Eternity:
in Canaan, your foot to set down there, never will be...
son of Imran, from going over there, you are stopped!"
When he heard this the colour in Moses' face dropped
away, tears flowed out like Oxus river upon his chest,
and while they flooded, in his heart... inside his breast
he thought: "Although Canaan, my eyes will not see,
there's no reason to grieve, these two eyes shouldn't be
crying and sorrowful... because when all of my people
see that place and with happiness over there do settle,
for You Who know all our secrets, this do understand
that it'll be like two hundred times I'll see that land."
Then Prophet Moses inside himself this secret saw...
joy came back like an open rosebud that inside he wore.

As he finishes Hafez puts the book down and begins to weep.
Shahin, tears in his dark eyes, stands and walks over and places his
hand on Hafez's small shoulder.

"Do not weep Hafez... he was one of the most fortunate of the
Beloved's lovers."

"Ahh, teacher... it is so beautiful... how you have written this...
it hurts me inside my heart to read it. My heart goes out to you my
teacher, for are you not like Moses, your hero? You will never see the
land of your forefathers either. It must be so difficult to be... in exile."

"You are right my dear and admirable friend... but also... you are missing something. Although I am a Jew and all Jews have a special love for their original homeland, my home and most of my ancestors that I can trace back to are here... in Shiraz. So in my way I *am* home... for we are all the children of Adam and one day I will write a book about the beginnings of all of us. Also my friend, you may not know but the history of our people is linked to this land. You know of Queen Esther, of King Ardashir and Cyrus... of Mordacai? No? Ah, one day I must tell their story too. Now, Musa is patiently waiting for you. Select your book and go with him."

"Yes, teacher."

Hafez walks to the bookshelves and is selecting an old copy of the story of Genesis.

"Ah huh? Begin at the beginning... the first poet, prophet and Spiritual Master or *Qutub*... our father Adam."

Hafez grins and turns and walks out through the low doorway to his other Jewish friend playing with Rustom in the small garden.

*

Hafez would later tell me that at the time when he was barely in his teens and had been working as an assistant in a drapery shop for a few years due to their poverty (his uncle Sadi having only enough income from his poetry readings to support himself)... he would spend every lunchtime in a nearby eating house (even though he always ate the lunch his loving mother Ulya made for him and he would only ever order a single glass of sweet black tea) where the regular clientele were all well-spoken, inquisitive and intelligent workers from the nearby woodworkers, other drapery establishments, a doctor and a few writers and poets.

He was always fascinated by their high level of conversations and good manners towards each other and the respect they gave to the Persian language even although they were all from different backgrounds, professions and religious and ethnic groups and ages. Though his mind was relatively unformed in comparison to their intelligence they always asked his opinion and respected it. They never became tired of explaining some difficult word or philosophical concept or piece of poetry or significance of some historical event. He decided that he wanted to be just like them... erudite, intelligent, well read and cosmopolitan. They already had great respect for him because he had memorized the *Koran* and many of the great Sadi and Nizami's poems that he would often be called on to recite.

However, because he had to leave school at such an early age he sometimes got mixed up when he spoke and at the most this would produce some gentle laughter and chiding from the group. This did not stop him from continually asking questions of them or trying out his latest poetic creation upon them... usually a *ruba'i*.

On this particular day which would become famous in the history of Shiraz as will become apparent some pages into the future... young Hafez has cleared his throat a couple of times until the woodworker (later on to achieve a new name and lasting fame by his actions) Mahmud, turned to Hafez and says...

"Yes young man you wish to contribute something again to our little gathering of like minds?"

"Yes sir, two *ruba'i* that I composed at breakfast this morning!"

"So... what is it about Hafez, bread and curds and jam?"

Good-natured laughter and grins all around as Hafez grins back and answers... "Noooo... Mahmud, perhaps tomorrow they will be, God willing... they are about what we were talking about yesterday. You, Moshen... you were saying it is not right to be over-proud of one's learning and intelligence so I was thinking of that and these lines came to me...

Towards those good men to be bad it's not right to be:
in desert of the demon that is mad, it's not right to be.
Of one's way of living to be glad, it's not right to be...
and proud of the learning one's had it's not right to be.

"Excellent young Hafez, excellent!" The cries come from all quarters.

"Please the other one now." Moshen the doctor smiles at him.

"This one came out of something Mahmud said about how it is impossible to truly express the grief that sometimes is inside when we lose someone near and dear to us or when someone doesn't return the love we feel for them...

Deep in my heart's ocean many priceless pearls are there,
it's a pity if they remain unpierced, unstrung to compare!
Who speaks about the pain of grief that one can express?
It is a pity, for the pain of deep sorrow one cannot share!

Silence from all, now many deep sighs, the ultimate appreciation.

"Ah Hafez... I take back what I said yesterday, grief can be truly expressed and you have done it my young friend, wonderfully! Now it is time for all of us to leave and go back to work. Ah... life is full of surprises isn't it? We really do not know what is around the next corner. As it is often said, 'Let us think of tomorrow when tomorrow comes!' "

Musa turns around and looks back at Hafez who looks around at the people in the street, most of whom are dressed differently from the people in the quarter of the city where he lives with his mother and uncle... an almost totally Muslim district.

"Wait Musa, not so fast... my legs are a lot shorter than yours you know. Hey, there certainly are a lot of Jewish people in Mahalleh and some Christians like our friend Peter... but, tell me those people over there in those long white clothes, aren't they the followers of the Prophet Zoroaster?"

"Why yes, they are *gabrs* of course... they have their own district too but my father tells me there are only a few hundred or so left in our city, most having moved to the Deccan in India over the centuries since the Arab conquest. Lately some have moved in here, not all of our people are happy about that. You've seen them before. You know... they call God Ahura-Mazda and they pray at their fire temples and they take their dead to a place outside the city walls called a 'Tower of Silence' and the vultures come and eat their dead flesh, nothing goes to waste. Understand? They were here before you Muslims came along and us Jews and the Christians. Some people say Zoroaster came here and settled with his followers over 7000 years ago. They are nice, gentle people!"

"Of course I've read about them and know there are some in our city. I've seen so few of them over on our side... must stick with their own."

"You know Hafez I was just thinking, those *gabrs* as you Muslims derisively call them... they, and some Christians too own and operate all the winehouses, yet most of the customers are you Muslims, funny isn't it? Once you're not allowed to have something you all want it! Ah, here we are. I told my father I'd be bringing you home and he was very happy and said he'd have something special for us to keep us going until dinner time. Also he has just finished his long *masnavi* epic poem about King Ardashir and Queen Esther called *Ardashir-Nama* or the 'Book of Ardashir'. He said he wants to read some to you and he has some new books you might like to look at and borrow. He told me that you are a 'born poet'."

"He's right! You know Musa I composed my first *ruba'i* even before I went to school. And about four years ago as I was skipping along on the way to school I composed my first *kit'a*... or fragment of a *ghazal*. Each time I spun around the rhyme word came... just like a spiral it was, came out of nowhere... it was about my father and brothers. I was missing them I suppose. Think I'll write mainly *ghazals* from now on, they just seem more natural for me... and Sadi's my favourite poet. If only I could write like him!"

"Your uncle?"

"No you fool... ah ha... I see... kidding me again!"

"Left yourself open for it my friend. I loved that *ghazal* of yours we sang at the bazaar. That minstrel Hajji Ahmed seems to like your songs!"

"Yes he does. Whenever he sees me he asks for something new."

"Why don't you tell me the *kit'a* you were talking about, you know... the first *ghazal* you attempted? Let's sit down next to that rosebush over there on that old seat... it's my special seat you know, where I go to talk to God. It kind of feels right saying prayers and thinking about important things there!"

"Thanks for letting me sit on it then my friend. Ah... that's better, my feet were getting quite tired. Now let me think... ah, yes... here is the poem...

What regrets for the bright robe of my young days!

If only it had been embroidered with permanency!

O no, what grief, what pain, that from the stream,

the water of existence will be passing so quickly!

It is necessary to be cut from family and friends...

this has been passed down... by the sky's decree.

Every brother must at some time leave his brother

because of birth by father, unless they Farkads be!"

"That is very sad Hafez... and *very mature* too, lots of big words. Don't you ever wonder how your brothers are and what they are doing?"

"Occasionally my mother gets a letter from Isfahan. But it is like I don't know them now. I have memories of them but they are all I have. One day perhaps I will go to Isfahan and see them again. The oldest one is married now."

"And tell me, what are 'Farkads?'"

"They are the stars... the two brother stars in Ursa Minor. I find astronomy a fascinating study, don't you?"

"Not really, what use is it? Are you reading anything new at the moment?"

"Yes... I *borrowed* a copy of Auhadi of Maragha's *Jam-i-Jam*, 'Cup of Jamshid', from my uncle. It is a truly great *masnavi* of over four thousand five hundred couplets and is so popular it sold over four hundred copies a month after it came out, and at a good price too! I love his other poems and have made my own versions of some of his *ghazals*. He must be at least sixty by now and my uncle says he is living in Isfahan and is not well. If I had the money and was allowed to I'd go there to see him. I really would like to meet him and thank him for all he has given me through his poetry. Listen, here is a short *ghazal* of his I like very much...

Autumn will follow many a spring after you've passed away,
and many an evening, many a morning, many a night and day.
Even though the World seems fair, don't give your heart to it:
don't believe it's a real friend caring for others come what may.
If today like a scorpion you're stinging whoever you can find,
your companion in tomb will be snakes, in shame you will lay.
Try to be a comfort to those sick to soul... that's worth doing:
for to cause trouble to others is worthless... the evil, easy way.
Look not down on Earth's humble creatures with selfish pride:
for you don't know what hidden hero in the clouds of dust lay.

"Hmm, a bit depressing but makes you think doesn't he? Perhaps he'll come to Shiraz some time. Oh, there's my father calling to us to come inside. I hope he's made those sticky sweet buns I like so much. They say they were the favourites of my great namesake and that they originated in Egypt. You'll love them, eat as many as you like... and Rustom too, c'mon boy!"

A half an hour later Hafez licks his honey-sticky fingers and looks up at Musa's father and smiles and says, "Your sticky buns are worthy of a *ruba'i*... I might write one about them one day." Rustom barks in agreement from outside.

"Hafez, you know how to get your way and you certainly know how to make one feel good. Now you boys go and wash your hands and then come into my study and I'll read you some of my new book as I promised."

A short time later the two boys are sitting on the rug in the book-lined study facing Shahin as he looks down at his low desk then across at them.

"Hafez, do you remember when you first came here and I had just finished my *Musa-Nama?*"

"Yes, Khwaja!"

"Hafez, you are thirteen now, almost a man, and I have long ago stopped teaching you. Please stop calling me Khwaja or sir or teacher. Call me Shahin!"

"Yes... Shahin! I remember like it was yesterday for it was one of the important days of my life. Because from that day on your own wonderful poetry and the works of so many great Master poets and lovers of God became available to me and continue to do so... thanks to your generosity, my teach... er, Shahin. I also remember that you said to me that soon you would begin to write epic poems about Adam and the story of Queen Esther, from the biblical texts you have lent me. I know that over these past five years you have been writing the story of this Queen Esther... and Musa has just told me that you have finally finished the book and today we will hear you read from it for the first time. We both feel very excited and privileged... Shahin, to be the first to experience what I know will be another masterpiece!"

"Ah, my friend... you are too kind, and once again know the right thing to say. I hope that it is worthy of your compliment. But first, I must educate you a little to how I have set my story... for the one that I tell is quite different to that in the biblical texts and in the epic poem of our great Master poet Firdausi. I have drawn from both of these sources but from others also, including the book of al-Tabari who died over four hundred years ago and wrote 'The History of Prophets and Kings' and from the stories of Ibn Khalaf that were written over two hundred years ago. Of course I have also called on my own intuition, my creative imagination, dreams and occasional visions through which the Lord has revealed to me aspects of the story that up until now have never been told.

"In this story and through the heroic personage of Esther, the most beautiful woman of the time... we see how two peoples... the Jews and the Persians, became unified for the first time and how her son Cyrus, or Kay Khusraw as we often call him, the product of the Jewish Esther's marriage to the Persian king Ardashir... freed the Jewish people and caused the rebuilding of our Temple.

"I think you are both old enough now to understand how a man can desire to have a woman by his side... as the companion of his heart, like Miriam was to me and like your mother was to your father Hafez... a special woman who is the 'love of your life'. Well, eighteen hundred years ago our king, Ardashir, had yet to find that one... he had to let his first wife Queen Vasthi go after she had betrayed and tried to poison him. Now he was lonely. He told his servant, the priest Hegai, to bring him each night for a week from the harem one of the virgins for surely one would be the one to touch his heart. But after a week his heart was still unsatisfied even if his body was. Musa, why are you blushing? You understand what I'm saying, so now listen...

There is nothing better than a friend who is loving:

is it possible without heart's friend, to keep living?

If one is in the presence of that one who is loved...

one feels more alive than all life that can be lived.

Life's wonderful with friend like that as companion:

without... time not worth a barley-grain drags on.

Hegai saw the king was burning away from this...

such deep longing in his heart instead of true bliss;

and he then the king's growing desperation knew,

that he was in search of a friend and beloved true.

He waited for the right time to go to him and then

approached him suddenly one night in the harem:

he rushed over to the king like a lion in his service

and to him the secret of Esther he did then confess:

"There's one, an idol rare, beautiful beyond compare,

in knowledge too: one unique... never has ever there

in this world been one seen her like, not among huris

of Paradise as well... and if her cheeks your eye sees

on a special night and even if it happen in a dream...

your eyes would not want to see another moonbeam.

Our moon beside her full moon is but a mere crescent,

alongside her straight form the cypress seems... bent.

Be calm... and then go and take her into your embrace

and see the fountain that will be your drinking place!

When it's that one that you hold, a thousand Vashtis

are merely boats blown away on the water's breeze!

In learning and grace and also in incomparable beauty,

in understanding and in worthiness and in speech she

is beyond compare throughout the whole world... so

a pitcher upon the hard stone you must never throw!

In your possession is one O so fine... a priceless huri,

this one who is so beautiful is yours... and so you see

that there is nothing to be worried about... and so why

do you bring grief on yourself... let all your worry go by,

because in the past ten months I have been teaching her:

she's good, nothing bad is in her, desire to learn is in her.

She never even asked me a single time for a cup of water:

not one person, has ever received any trouble from her...

so, that now I to you, the secret of her have finally told

that I have been keeping... do not just sit there, be bold

and... do something! But, about her... do not be upset:

raise your head and your eyes on the fourth heaven set:

that beautiful idol that's beyond compare go and marry

and drink deep without worrying of that one's sincerity

until your peace of mind and your heart returns to you

and in your desired position you sit, a man made anew!"

When he had heard all of this from his devoted servant

who was completely sincere and honest, to him he went

and answered: "All this that you've said to me is right...

for it's only my peace of mind that you have in your sight.

What you've said is true... so when day comes tomorrow

also comes the seed of my future happiness that I'll sow.

To my arms I'll cause to be brought that beautiful Esther,

all of my mere fantasies I will end and I will send to her

many asses piled high with gifts, musk and much jewelry,

and I... will be the one who will go give her... the dowry!

With her I will drink deeply from the sweet cup of union!"

His words were the cause of light rising towards heaven

and the population of the world heard the great clamour.

That mirror of much grace and that one of most glamour

came... like a flame flashing from a cup of fine crystal...

at sunset the king sat on the throne, a glorious mortal...

and because of shame Venus and Mercury raced away:

world turned gold, rubbish heap's dust rose, flew away.

Shahin stops reading and looks up into the rapt faces of his captivated audience.

"Well son, what do you think so far?"

"Papa, it is... wonderful, beautiful beyond description!"

"And you... our young poet, be honest with another poet now!"

"You are the real poet Khw... Shahin. Compared to your verse my poor efforts are pale shadows. This Esther, she reminds me of someone. Do you think that someday one so beautiful and intelligent as her could look at one... like me?"

"Ahem, yes, Hafez. I suppose, through the Will of the Almighty, anything is possible. I can assure you that in the eyes of one in love the beloved becomes that one's king or queen. It is often said, 'Heart finds a way to heart.' As it is getting late and we have only a short time remaining before you must head for home Hafez I will quickly tell you both what happens over the next six or seven pages and then read you one more passage before we call an end, eh?"

"Yes father, but please don't leave anything out."

"Leave nothing *important* out!" Hafez gets himself comfortable as Shahin reads awhile to himself and as he turns pages he says...

"So, in the morning the king commanded his vizier Firuz to open the

treasury and take to her gifts that are beyond your imagination boys.
I'll just tell you a few to give you a small example... two hundred
beautiful male and female Turkish and Chinese slaves, a hundred
wonderful fast horses, a hundred royal jewels... the list is almost
endless. And so Firuz carried out his master's command and went
with great fanfare with many soldiers as guards to Shush where they
were with great pomp presented to Esther's uncle Mordacai for her.
Then Firuz returned to Ardashir. When Mordacai saw all the vast
array of gifts he realized that material wealth is a passing thing and
God's mercy is worth much more and endures forever. So, he called
for his orphaned niece Esther to be brought to him and to her he
said...

> O you most beautiful one, O one who is... O so sweet...
> your manners are beyond reproach, bearing is complete:
> the One Who keeps us all has given to you abundantly
> what He has given to the nine spheres, turning silently.
> Listen to me now, give to me your complete attention,
> hear well what I give you, these few words I mention,
> and if you take them to heart then surely you'll become
> immortal in both worlds: the one here and that to come.
> The light of God can be seen manifested in your face...
> from a distance can be seen your natural shining grace.
> O child, listen well, for this now is the advice I give you:
> advice that's sweet and good and pleasant and is true...
> listen, when the time comes and with Ardashir the king
> you are intimate, be careful that it you're not forgetting!
> Be careful to keep a watch always over wisdom's spirit,
> and... that fear of God inside your heart... preserve it!

Be careful to never be involved in an action that is evil,
and veil yourself from all sin and crime and all ill will:
Do not go and be foolish and cause troubles to anyone.
the world everyday raises up from the crowd someone
and entrusts to that one some new powerful position...
but allowing one's heart to believe in it is prostitution.
Look at the treasure unseen within the oyster's shell...
that, comes from the raindrop that from the cloud fell:
for when that special drop is plucked out of the sky,
drop melts and in the end... that, as a pearl does lie:
and then when finally the diver plunges into the sea,
an oyster shell out from its darkest depth brings he!
It is similar to the way that a lion discovers his prey...
he throws it on the ground like one throws sand away.
And then that pearl is pierced through its pearly navel
and not a bit of shell stays on it... although the shell
has fed pearl... each shell must finally give it freedom
and let pearl know fully the joy of it being taken from
the shell... for pearl was only a day or two in the shell,
enjoyed shell and then it into another's possession fell.
And... because in the end the pearl could not be staying
always in shell's mouth... in the depth of the sea living,
beyond help... it put on itself the covering of patience...
and endured all thrashing blows of Time's persistence.
Listen, the throne and high position stay with no one...
so what is known by inexperience? What's to be done?
It's clear... don't think about throne's importance today:
think about tomorrow and take care of all who fall away.

And do what's necessary to do: don't you try to oppress

those who are unfortunate... and try hard not to stress

yourself... about anyone. If you do nothing that's wrong

you will not have to be frightened of evil for very long...

so try to be inactive... try not to be harmful to yourself.

One more piece of advice you should hear from myself,

which I have for a very long time kept within my heart:

beware that your faith and ancestry to none you impart."

"Then he kissed Esther and early the next morning Hegai came and had Esther dressed as the king wanted. The ancient capital city of Shush was in a great state of excitement as Esther, veiled in jewelry, in the middle of much pomp and ceremony walked from her palace to that of the king. There she was showered with gold, musk and precious jewels and was taken by female attendants to the king's bedroom where the Zoroastrian priest had her contracted in marriage to Ardashir. The king then sat on his throne and drank wine with the nobles and being able to wait no longer to be with her and remove her veil and see her for the first time he drunkenly began to walk towards his bedroom...

Just like the partridge goes strutting towards the hen,

the king went towards his wife waiting in the harem.

This fortunate monarch was now so impatient to unite

with that one who now sat on the throne in his sight.

All of the female servants then quickly left that place

but for her nurse who that moon's side still did grace.

Full of joy and happiness with a smile and no defense,

the king pulled the veil from that moon's countenance.

When his eyes caught sight of her cheek, like the night

his mind was taken away and he then fell out of sight
as into a dark well... a road-weary traveller overcome
by the journey... she, seeing he had senseless become
lifted his head up and onto her thigh and as he awoke
he saw it lay on the lovely thigh lying under her cloak!
Now she stood and then sat herself down by his side,
as he held curls of his beloved's hair she did not hide.
It was then that the bright sun the dark night did see:
witness the beauty of Venus in evening's court did he.
Her radiance brought him into complete astonishment,
many cries of blessings for her beauty he truly meant.
All through the night until break of the following day...
with his heart ablaze and in exultation, with her he lay.
Through marriage and love and friendship he now had
received the longing of his heart from that rare beloved.
Then, when the face of the bright sun begun to smile...
as it saw the world it flashed its radiant teeth, while
all of the earth was transformed into a garden of glory,
smiling with such radiance and bright from such purity.
The king now stood up happily due to Esther's embrace,
still wanting to keep looking at his loved one's face...
his love for her had so taken a hold of all of his senses,
that on plucking the rose for thorns he had no defenses.
In his mind it was only as the moon he thought of her...
her fair cheeks he loved more than his soul or any other.
Ardashir the king, placed a bejeweled crown so heavy
on that moon's head... making her queen, like Vasthi
was and gave her all titles that previously Vasthi held.

Each moment he tried to please her, nothing he withheld:

the empress of the whole world he conferred... upon her!

Seven years had gone since the start of his rule did occur.

He had married the moon and it was now that the king

was happy with this union as he was in the beginning.

If Vasthi, his previous queen, ever came into his mind...

on his head like a crown, Esther he would always find.

If one is in sunlight then does that one the moon need?

If one is wearing the crown, no need for hat... agreed?

And so each day and every night... Ardashir, the king

burnt up from impatience... her loveliness to be seeing!

There, inside that palace... he was staying for six days

with her with cheeks like roses, glowing beauty's rays.

When dawn upon the seventh day rose up, he too arose

gathering himself up, on throne... he did finally repose.

"Now Hafez, it is almost dark... it is time for you to leave. Next month we all have two days of holidays. Would you like to go riding on a trip outside of Shiraz and I will finish off this story for the both of you in a very special way?"

"Yes please Shahin, I've never been further than the 'God is Great' gate at the pass."

"Like all Persians you ride a horse of course and have access to one like Musa and myself?"

"Umm... just a small, old donkey that belongs to my uncle but he rarely rides it as last time he did he went to the winehouse and got drunk and fell off the poor beast and hurt his head. That was his excuse the following morning for his thumping headache."

"The donkey may slow us down a little but we will have enough time and if we go slowly I can tell you more of the story of Esther, Ardashir and Mordacai along the way."

"Good, Shahin... I always knew that donkey would be of some use one day. Now I must go, my mother will be getting worried. I will come here early in the morning next week with a sleeping rug and some food in a bag. I'm very excited by this mysterious journey and I can't wait to hear more of your marvelous epic. Goodbye!"

They embrace each other and now Hafez opens the door and runs off towards the street still visible in the twilight.

*

It is the following week as Hafez on Sadi's old donkey, Musa and Shahin, on horses... ride towards the 'God is Great' Pass on their mysterious journey promised by Shahin. Hafez calls across to Musa... "Musa, I only wish Ibn Battuta would return from his travels so he could be with us on *our* great journey!"

"Yes, he'd be surprised that the Lord has blessed you with such a beautiful stallion for your travels!"

"Musa, I am beginning to believe that your wit has taken a turn for the worse. Shahin, tell him to stop. Blame my uncle for this poor, slow beast... not me!"

Musa scratches his cap.

Hafez slaps Musa's horse on the rump. They ride faster for awhile then Shahin tells them not to tire the animals as the sun rises higher on the horizon as they pass the tomb of Sadi on the right and approach the 'God is Great' Gates and the Pass through the mountains heading north.

Over twelve hours later the ancient, magnificent ruins of Persepolis has a haunting grandeur in the background in front of the setting sun as Hafez, Musa and Shahin sit around a small campfire, their horses and donkey grazing nearby as Shahin quietly speaks, "I wanted the two of you to get some idea of the atmosphere and grandeur of those bygone days while I continue my story of the beautiful Esther and King Ardashir. Listen, imagine that time, the creation of the founder of our country, saviour of the Jews, Cyrus...

After Esther became the beloved of the king of kings...

she discovered dignity, respected position it did bring.

The heart of the king found great delight in that huri

and from her two cheeks... only a fair light he did see.

The time he was with her brought happiness, pleasure:

he loved being and making passionate love with her.

Because of the Will of the Greatest Father of us all...

she became pregnant and when time for birth did fall

the gates of purity were opened wide by the Almighty

for her to give birth to a beautiful boy, cheeks so sunny

and worthy of Jamshid's throne and the bright crown.

From the child's birth joy in the king's heart was sown,

and all fear and oppression from the world he banished.

The tax that was on caravans due to him now vanished:

to the poor he generously gave much gold and money...

in Shush no poor remained because of such generosity;

and even the poor ascetic had his suffering removed...

by the king, with gold... that away he then gambled.

Esther was full of happiness, with her newborn boy...

she offered prayers thanking God for her unending joy.

Two loving nurses made for the child she then chose...

to teach and help him, nurture him like cypress grows.

And when the boy named Cyrus reached the age of four

like spring tulip his face, that princely jewel was more...

for he grew tall like a cypress and when he was away

from dawn to sunset the king was worried all the day.

The wise Bishutan said one day to courageous Ardashir,

"The time has arrived for the eyes of the prince to clear

and open to understanding good and bad, more and less,

and not a day of his should be seen as being worthless."

Hearing his vizier's advice the king knew it was sound,

he called the wisest men to him to prepare the ground.

To each of the wise men he gave gold, gifts and his son

so every one of them should then teach him as the one

to know what the great should know... make him bright

with knowledge and with courage and with what is right.

And when he'd turned fourteen years old fortune spread

its wings over his head and in all Iran's cities it was said

that in all courts of brave heroes there was not one who

fought war like him... in his hand, steel like copper flew.

*

The sun is blazing overhead as Shahin shields his eyes and points to the large, rectangular tomb. He turns to Hafez and Musa and says... "On the ride here I told you what became of Esther and King

Ardashir and Mordacai. I also told you how over thirty years King Cyrus united many countries into the Empire of Iran and in doing so he founded our country... and united all warring factions and brought about peace everywhere. I also told you how he allowed us Jews to return to our homeland and to rebuild our Temple... thus fulfilling the wishes of his mother. A Zoroastrian, he loved and respected all beliefs... he was truly a great unifying force in the world and he came into existence because of a beautiful and wise woman. Down that valley was his capital on the Plain of Pasargadae. But, here stands his tomb reminding us all that even the good and mighty must pass on, listen boys...

Every rose not welcomed because of many a sharp thorn
finally lies scattered in dust with petals torn and worn.
For just one day it lives or two or three, not many more:
in the end death finishes off whatever had come before.
And the way that all form goes away is the same as this:
it is Time that wrecks revenge, not a thing it does miss!
During that year Cyrus was satisfied and he was happy:
on the high throne of good fortune he sat for all to see.
Although upon that most exulted of thrones he did sit,
his sense of fair justice... never did he lose one bit of it!
Well he looked after all he had inherited from his father
and while he did the Almighty's protection he did incur.
The king's glory was great and his prayers where then
fulfilled because of the Almighty One's Merciful Pen.
When finally his tired body like a cypress became bent,
of his own companionship all his interest became spent.
In the depth of his heart he knew worry and deep despair

and became worn and thin through the grief lying there.

A day came when a number of times out loud he cried...

then disaster rocked him this way and that... he sighed

when it reached deep his soul: he then gave it all away

and like a tall cypress he crashed down and there he lay.

From out of his fallen body his soul immediately rose up

and left behind good and bad... this and that it gave up.

His attachments fell away as he fell from throne to grave:

he died and all royal affairs to others left behind he gave.

They cleaned him and clothed him in silk and other finery,

put musk on head as a crown, camphor on chest like ivory.

From hand to hand they passed all of his personal armory

and then opened the crypt... there lay him down gently.

He died, just like all who are born eventually have to die:

because not a one in this world can stay... not you, not I.

We are made from the earth and to it we must return...

even if that greatest mystery of all we happen to learn!

*

In 734/1334 Mahmud Shah and his oldest son Masud Shah are relieved of their positions by Sultan Abu Said for supposedly enriching themselves and not passing on all the taxes to the sultan. Sultan Abu Said replaced Mahmud Shah with Amir Muzzafer Inak, a Mongol officer. In fear of losing his wealth and power Mahmud Shah decided to kill his rival and with his followers chased him to the palace walls at Sultaniyeh wherein Amir Muzaffer sought refuge with the sultan. The palace was then attacked. Abu Said was enraged by this but Mahmud Shah's great friend the prime minister Ghiyath al-Din Rashadi intervened on his behalf and while many of the conspirators were executed Mahmud Shah was imprisoned in Tabarak castle in Isfahan and Masud Shah in Anatolia. The sultan soon sends Amir Muzaffer with many soldiers to take power here and take hold of the treasury and all revenues, which amount to 10,000 silver *dinars* a day! Amir Muzaffer is preparing to send to Sultan Abu Said what is left in the treasury but before he can do this Kaikhosrau has him arrested and packed off with his men back to Tabriz.

On this particular day Hafez's mother hums a sad tune as she cleans up her son's room, putting clothes in his small closet. She shakes her head, then bends down and picks up a slate Hafez uses to write his poems on in chalk... as Rustom, now a grown dog, wanders in and curls at her feet. She pats his head fondly and begins to read with her sweet, sad voice...

The rose that blossoms on tree of friendship is lovely...

She remembers Hafez, about ten, Musa... taller, but sickly-looking, with his leather cap on, and their friend the fat boy, Peter (with different clothes... a Christian) with Rustom, running through a rose garden in Musalla, pine trees in the background. She imagines the full face of a blooming rose and the four petals become the four faces of the four friends lying on their backs, facing up to the sky, smiling...

it fills my heart forever with happiness and ecstasy...

Ulya imagines Hafez all by himself in the moonlight smelling the beautiful rose…

I search for company of the rose because the perfume…

Eyes closed she can see Hafez, about six, looking into his father's bearded, kind face (he is about forty), as he pulls down a rose for Hafez to see and smell…

brings into memory the fragrance of one loved by me!

Ulya opens her eyes to Hafez's bedroom and wipes a tear from her eye and pats Rustom, who looks up at her with a sad but understanding look on his face. On the windowsill a bright coloured, small bird alights and chirps… looking on happily. She smiles up at it then looks down at the next *ruba'i* poem and she begins to read…

If winning hearts of the poor is what you wish to do…

She looks out the window and imagines Hafez and his two friends walking arm in arm through the marketplace of a poor area of Shiraz, laughing and shouting this poem. Rustom, runs alongside, an equal, barking happily… the 'four great friends'.

gaining respect of those who today are discreet too…

People smile out at them and laugh good-naturedly, some point and smile, some frown, some shout abuse as a dumb-looking young boy throws a tomato at them. Hafez catches it and takes a bite (to the astonishment of the thrower) and passes it on to the others who do likewise and Rustom gets the biggest piece…

don't criticize the Christian… (Peter breaks off from the others and enters a church in the Armenian Christian quarter waving goodbye)… *the Muslim…* (Hafez heads off with Rustom towards the mosque in the distance)… *or the Jew…* (Musa walks off alone towards the small synagogue in the Mahalleh quarter)… *and the world will be thankful and recommend you!*

She puts down the slate, smiling and looks up at the bird on the window ledge. She talks to it.

"My, aren't you a beautiful little one!"

The bird chirps then sings and Rustom stands up wagging his tail, demanding attention.

"And so are you beautiful Rustom, of course!"

She lets him lick her hand as she looks down at another new *ruba'i* poem…

In your street, no one is poor and harmless… except me!

She imagines Hajji Ahmed, the orphaned, gypsy, minstrel boy, who is now about seventeen and has already made the pilgrimage to Mecca single-handedly and is a close friend of her son wandering the lonely streets at night with a small bag, clothes old and tattered, his battered *tar* over his shoulder…

Near your dwelling no one stays friendless, except me…

It is night and Hajji, a shadow, looks up at a balcony where a beautiful woman looks out at the moon and sings…

I'm the only one imprisoned by the chain of your hair…

Hajji stares at the long locks of a gypsy girl as she dances, while he plays and sings…

for none from loving you has this madness… except me.

Hajji sits under his favourite tree, hands on head. She imagines Hafez sitting in the corner of his room, hands on head. Hafez's mother sits on his bed with her hands on her head as she places the slate closer to her.

"Who is this about, Rustom? Is it him or Hajji or someone else? It's so sad that we're so poor that he's had to leave school and work in that drapery shop. And he studies so hard at night. What a memory... he can already remember the whole of the *Koran*, our holy book. Sometimes I think he studies too much. So little sleep and he is only fourteen."

*

It is the beginning of spring of 735/1335 and our ancient *Nowruz* Festival... celebrating the coming of the vernal equinox and the New Year. *Nowruz* which is celebrated by Muslims, Jews, Christians and Zoroastrians and all other sects in Shiraz and throughout our land lasts for thirteen days and can be traced back over 10,000 years to King Jamshid (who is also called Yima and Yama and some say is the same personage as Noah, the original founder of Fars). Some few thousand years later Prophet Zoroaster improved the calendar to 365 days, five and a bit hours.

A month before the festival begins we all get busy giving our abodes a good clean out. Then ten days before we place seeds of lentils, barley, wheat and other grains and vegetables in round earthenware plates so that when *Nowruz* arrives the sprouts are grown as high as one's finger. We buy or make new clothes for the celebration to come. Then a minstrel like Haji Ahmed is named Hajji Firuz and he roams with his minstrel friends throughout the city with his face painted black, red clothes and conical hat with tassels creating much mirth and singing...

Here's Hajji Firuz
and it's Nowruz.
All know, I know,

now is *Nowruz*.

And crowds form around him and the other minstrels and they listen to them playing the tambourine, the *tar* and the *kamancheh* and the people laugh at his jokes and dance and many give them coins as he sings...

Greetings to you my lord,
lift your head... my lord!
Look here at me, my lord,
do me a favour, my lord!
My own lord, billy goat,
why not smile, my lord?

Then when finally the celebrations begin bonfires are lit and we jump over them shouting for our sallow cheeks caused by winter pass and the fire's red glow replace the gloom. Then we have a party through the night and the fire's ashes are taken into the fields and are buried like the ashes of winter now passed.

During the many ritual feasts of *Nowruz* everyone visits relatives and friends... and on the last day any unattached female is allowed to go almost anywhere without her veil. Love is let loose in Shiraz! Perhaps this O so popular *ghazal* of Master Sadi's gives a better feeling of *Nowruz* than I could with all that explanation...

Hey, get up! Because the winter is passing away
and the door of the garden pavilion is open today.
Place upon the dish the oranges and the violets...
place chafing bowl in bed-chamber without delay
and tell to this curtain to be quickly moving aside
immediately from where upon balcony it does lay.
Hey, get up! Because breeze of New Year's dawn

is strewing all the roses along that garden's way.
In this season of the rose it is totally impossible to
expect the lovestruck nightingale in silence to stay.
The sound of the drum cannot be silenced under a
blanket, nor can love be shut away anywhere today.
Fragrance of the rose and dawn of the New Year...
and sweet sound of the nightingale... singing away
have brought about sale of many garments, turbans
and many are the houses and shops now in disarray!
Our head is lying upon that breast of our Beloved...
so now let the rival's head upon anvil forcefully lay!
The eye that the lover is raising towards his Beloved
does not flutter if a shower of arrows comes his way.
O Sadi, if your hands are able to be reaching the fruit
then let the cruelty of the Gardener: come what may!

*

Hafez is now fifteen. He walks with Hajji Ahmed the minstrel
through the enormous garden of Musalla where young women walk
in twos and young men watch and sometimes approach them with
poems and songs or small gifts of their attention and intentions.
Hafez turns to Hajji and excitedly shouts...

"Haji Kivam is my hero! He is one of the greatest men in the
world! Now the *Koran* is being truly revealed to me after these two
years of studying with him... it is a book about God's love for
Himself manifested and how Himself manifested should love Him
back!"

"Shut up Hafez you are giving me a sense of... not knowing, as usual! How can you talk about loving God when we are in the only week in the year when all Shirazi women... may they remain the most beautiful in the world... are allowed to go around unveiled in search of a suitor. Have you no sense of priorities? My God, look at that young beauty over there, and her mother obviously also still a great beauty."

Hafez stares in a state of shock across the rosegarden at the breathtakingly beautiful thirteen year-old Shakh-e-Nabat (Branch of Sugarcane) with her thirty year-old mother. He turns to Hajji Ahmed clutching at his heart as if it may burst from his chest.

"Hajji! My God, it's *her!* I'd know her anywhere... my destiny! Look how beautiful she is! Unveiled of course... but then she always will be, as is their Turkish custom."

"By all the spirits, obviously you're smitten my young friend. Here is your chance... fifteen is not too young to be a suitor and in a year she will be of age. Let your heart do your talking for you and go over and introduce yourself with a spontaneous *ghazal* declaring your love. Look! Wait a minute... there, over there... that handsome young prince Abu Ishak and his entourage approaching them. I hear he is something of a poet... he certainly is a handsome, confident peacock, and closer to her age by a year. Look... he's bowing to her."

"He *is* handsome and a lot taller than me as you can see. But, looks aren't everything... are they? Hajji! I don't know how I'd feel about him if he won her hand. I suppose he's a much better possible catch than I am."

Hajji grins.

"That's the understatement of the year my friend. Catch and match! Look... it seems her mother is impressed by his manner."

Nabat's mother is laughing at something he has said... but Nabat is not so impressed and is now turning and walking away towards a large cypress... leaving Prince Abu Ishak looking as shocked as her mother who now bows to him and rushes after her tempestuous daughter.

Hafez laughs then turns to Hajji.

"Lord, did you see that Hajji? It seems she is not so easily impressed... not by wealth, position and good looks! Perhaps there is a chance for someone with the opposite of all those... plus, love and the ability to write... umm... passable verse, eh?"

"Unbelievably, I think you may be right there Hafez. Hmm... if *you* weren't so mad about her I'd be kneeling at her feet right now declaring *my* admiration... she really is a little beauty. See, they are alone again now, he and his friends have reluctantly wandered off in a state of shock. Now is your chance, it may never come again. Remember our proverb, 'You must climb a ladder step by step'. Do you want me to accompany you?"

"No! You're too handsome Hajji... and talented. She might ask you to sing and then I'll be forgotten. You wait here. My God, my heart is beating so hard I think she may see it through my vest. At least the first couplet for a *ghazal* has come into my mind! In the Name of God..."

"Go with God my brave friend!"

Hajji grins as he watches Hafez walk towards Nabat then scratches his dirty turban as he sees that Nabat is now watching

Hafez approach... and he can just hear what she is saying to her mother.

"My God, Mother... "

"What my dear?"

"An ugly, little boy is approaching with eyes full of... oh, forget it. I refuse to recognize his horrid, little existence... *you* talk to him. *But...* don't send him away *immediately*. Perhaps he has a poem or speech in praise of me. If he does, make *sure* he recites it loud enough for me to hear. *Here he is...* I'll stand over there and turn away!"

"Nabat... I don't understand, if he's such a loathsome creature why..."

Hafez bows deeply to her mother, then to Nabat who quickly turns her head away as Hafez sighs then opens his trembling lips.

"B... b.b.by the B.b.beauty of the Almighty... who has graced you and your daughter with a reflection of that Supreme Beauty, madam... let me introduce myself... your e.e.e.eternal servant and your daughter's also. I am Hafez... student and poet come on this b.b.eautiful *Nowruz* day to express a *ghazal* in honour of that unique one over there... your incomparable d.d.d.daughter, the most perfect rose of Shiraz... perhaps the *whole world!*"

"By my ears you are a very eloquent young man. But I am a little poor of hearing, you will have to speak much louder when you recite this poem of yours. Why are you waiting... get on with it!"

Hajji sees Hafez glance across at Nabat and sees that she is looking back over her shoulder with interest... Hafez almost faints from the sight of her beauty. He tears his eyes off her and back to her mother.

"Yes, dear, gracious, beautiful lady... IS THIS LOUD ENOUGH? YES? I'll begin then...

Mixture of beauty and grace is in that one's moonlike face...
Lord, love and faith give to that one who hasn't even a trace.
That one who takes my heart is a child; and I'm sure one day
in sport will cruelly kill me and in law be guiltless of the case.

Hafez glances at Nabat and sees that her cheeks are flushed... blushing or angry? He continues...

It is best that I should guard my own heart for its own good:
that one hasn't known good or bad, can't tell good from base.
I idolize one who is agile, sweet and almost fourteen years old:
who has as the slave of the soul, the moon of fourteen days.
The sweet smell of milk is coming from that one's sugary cup,
but from those black eyes look, blood drips all over the place.

Nabat's mother looks shocked, but not as much as Nabat as Hafez gulps then bravely continues...

O Lord, where did our heart go, searching for that new rose?
For we haven't seen it in its place for over a long day's space.
If my loved one that takes the heart breaks my heart like this
the king will quickly take that one, to all of his guards replace.
I would be thankful and sacrifice my life, if that peerless pearl
would consider the shell of the eye of Hafez its resting place.

Hafez is now on his knees before her mother but he is looking across at Nabat who Hajji sees turn around and flushed with anger, fists clenched is fuming as Hajji whispers, "By my eyes, she is even more beautiful when she's furious. I'm afraid Hafez you don't know what you've got yourself into with that one!"

Nabat finally shouts at her mother, "Mother, tell that... that... that horrible *little... ugly* boy that he should take his attention and himself *elsewhere!* My love will only be given to one who not only has a fine appearance but also has *fine manners.* How *dare* he call me a *child!* Tell him to go away! *Now!*"

She storms off as her mother nods to Hafez then rushes after her calling out, "Nabat! Wait for me young lady! I didn't think the poem was *that bad...* in fact it had a certain honest charm, and... the *young man's* manners were really impeccable! *Nabat!*"

Hajji slowly walks up to the distraught Hafez, head in his hands, "Couldn't help but overhear the poem Hafez. Brilliant as usual, but I'm sure that young lady isn't interested in the honest feelings of your heart this time. One good point, she stayed and listened to all of it... she didn't do that to the prince. I'd say you were reasonably successful! C'mon, let us see if there are any other available females in the gardens that I can test my musical skills upon!"

"She called her Nabat!"

Hajji places his arm on Hafez's shoulder and they walk off through the blooming rosegarden.

.

"Who is that banging on the front door? You know my brother doesn't like to be woken too early in the morning, it puts him in a bad mood for the rest of the day. Go and see who it is!" Ulya calls out to her son.

"At least *he's* been able to get some sleep which is more than I can say for *some* of us... who work all night and not drink the night away!" Hafez shouts back as he walks to the front door and opens it to a red-faced Peter who has obviously been running all the way from his home.

"By my soul Peter don't collapse out there... come in, what in the world has happened to make you run all the way over here. Come and have some water and settle yourself a little and tell us what's happened, but quietly... his majesty is sleeping, not that he'd wake up after what he probably drank last night!" He helps the overweight Peter down the hallway to the kitchen where his mother is preparing breakfast... sweet black tea, eggs and hot bread.

"Peter, you look terrible. Sit down, lie down if you want to. What has happened? Wait, have you had breakfast? No? Then whatever you have to tell us can wait young man. Tea and eggs? Hafez, get the extra plate."

"Ow... mother, can't it wait... someone might be dying!"

"Is anyone dying Peter? See son, he's shaking his head. Now leave it until we all have eaten... and no gobbling your food down."

Some time later a full Peter (after two glasses of tea and four pieces of bread and the same number of eggs) rubs his sizable belly, sighs then begins to tell the waiting Hafez and his anxious-looking mother what brought him calling on them so early.

"Hmm, perhaps I need another tea and an egg before I begin."

"No you don't Peter you've had too much already... please get on with it, the suspense is killing us!" Hafez looks across at his mother who grins her approval.

"Worth the try! Anyway, you know how about eight weeks ago

many of Amir Muzaffer's soldiers were ordered back to Sultaniyeh because Sultan Abu Said feared an invasion by the Khan Uzbeck of the Golden Horde... and that left Kaikhusrau back in power here until Masud Shah returned after being released from prison due to the influence of the sultan's prime minister and he was welcomed back by all of us and a sullen Kaikhusrau had to allow his older brother to take the reins of power? How a month ago he decided after talking to his mother Tashi Khatun and his two brothers here that it was probably a good time for him to go to Sultaniyeh and beg Abu Said to release his father still in prison in Isfahan? Anyway, we all know he left, leaving the second oldest brother Muhammad in charge here while he was away on his mission that we all have been praying for to be a complete success."

"Get to the point Peter... that is old ground." Hafez shrugs towards his friend as his mother stops him.

"Shusssh... let him tell his story in his own way son."

"Hmm, where was I? Yes, well as you both know one of our neighbours was one of the advisors accompanying him... and last night they returned home and a short while later he came banging on our door screaming to us to let him in and hide him!"

"Hide him? That doesn't sound right, does it?" She looks across at her son who gives her back a grave shake of the head.

"Anyway, finally my father calmed him down and got the full story out of him. It seems they finally found Sultan Abu Said on the battlefield with Sheikh Hussein... who, incidentally, greeted Masud Shah quite warmly. Masud Shah asked Abu Said for a note to allow him to go to Tabriz and procure his father's release. Abu Said talked with his advisors and returned and said, 'That is impossible. But I offer *you* governorship of Shiraz and Fars like your father once possessed, but unlike him you must *pay* due homage to me... and I mean *pay,* not become a thief like your father became.' And our Masud Shah answered him saying, 'Whatever my father did he did for the city of Shiraz, Fars and *all* of its people who he loves so dearly and not for himself... he always lived a simple life and believed in love and not hurting others. It seems to me from your problems at the moment and from rumours I hear about your prospects in the near future that there is no reason why I should pay any allegiance to you when I have the full support of my family and my people. Unless you release my beloved father I will return to my people and declare myself sole ruler and you can send another army to take Shiraz as before but this time we will be ready for you, but I can't see you doing that in the foreseeable future. So, I must take my leave and bid you farewell. I do not think we will be meeting again.' And with a slight bow he and our neighbour and the others left and began the ride back here, but... on the way back Masud Shah was talked into calling in on a cousin of our neighbour's at the Court at Sultaniyeh. And this cousin told them that a little over a year ago Sultan Abu Said had a very interesting visitor, one who he had called to his Court. You both surely know about Mubariz al-Din Muhammad Muzaffar... the ruler of Yazd?"

"A little, that he like his father ruled Maibad near Yazd. His father died of poisoning some twenty-two or so years ago and the thirteen-year old Mubariz took over and even at that age was said to be a fierce and brave warrior. He made Maibad his capital some four years later, ruling from a large fortress there."

Hafez stops talking and takes a sip of what is left of his tea as his mother continues, "Around the same time the administrator of Yazd, Atabeg Yusuf Shah, was giving the king, Uljaytu, many headaches and Uljaytu confessed to his soon-to-be successor, his son Abu Said that he would like to find a way to get rid of him. So he invited Mubariz to his court and gave him Yazd. Mubariz was so fierce a fighter that the war didn't last very long… Yusuf Shah escaped as is usual with most so-called leaders." Hafez's mother stops talking and goes and puts the big black kettle on the fire for more tea.

"Correct, both of you!" Peter takes up the tale again. "Well, of course he was very popular with Uljaytu and the young and impressionable Abu Said… a hero, famous… praiseworthy! So, since then… what is it… seventeen years, he has been fighting various bands of marauders and has just about wiped them all out and has become highly skilled at fighting and… ambushing and is said to have turned his ambitious eyes in *other* directions.

"Anyway, Mubariz secretly visits Sultan Abu Said last year and the adoring ruler confers upon him the title of Amir Zada… 'birth by king'… can you believe it? Then, they retire with a few advisors and later the word leaks out that Kirman and Shiraz were mentioned by 'Amir Zada'. I don't think we have heard the last of this 'hero' my friends.

"So anyway, now here is the *really* bad news! When Masud Shah arrived home last night his treacherous brother Kaikhusrau, whom it seems has become addicted to power, having had it here for the past nine years, had convinced the soldiers that had remained here to support him as many of them were still loyal… so, when Masud Shah entered the castle he was arrested along with his other brother Muhammad and Kaikhusrau has declared himself our new ruler and our neighbour escaped and fled to us and now is hiding elsewhere in Shiraz!"

"May God save us all!" Now Hafez's mother is shaking as Sadi enters the kitchen and shouts, "What is this infernal racket sister, anyone would think there has been a disaster!"

"Out of the mouths of babes and drunkards," Hafez mumbles as he crosses the floor and hugs his mother as Sadi bellows.

"Well sister... where is my breakfast and what is this... this... fat friend of yours doing here *Shams-ud-din?*"

"In the Name of God... look who is talking," Peter laughs as he walks towards the door.

·

It is the last days of 736/1335 when Hafez's uncle rushes into the kitchen sweating profusely and gasping for breath.

"Sit down brother, what's the matter with you... your poor heart has enough to do pumping blood to your, er... *large* body without you forcing it to undergo such a strain! You haven't been *running* have you? Hafez, get your uncle some water... he looks like he's about to expire!"

As Hafez brings the water-jug and a cup Sadi collapses and now slowly is getting his breath back as he gasps...

"I... I... was... down... in that winehouse around the corner... ah, thank you *Shams-ud-din...* that's much better. Yes! Where was I?"

"In the winehouse, as usual… and call me *Hafez* please!" Hafez grins at his mother who frowns back as Sadi scowls at him.

"Still calls himself *Hafez*… and *he* thinks *I'm* the arrogant poet! Anyway, the postman who does the ride to Tabriz and back came in for a drink and announced to everyone there the astonishing *news!*"

"What news?" Hafez is interested now.

"Ah huh? News… oh yes… extraordinary! Good and bad news I suppose, who knows? It's a matter of time…"

"Brother, just calm down and *think* and tell us *the news!*" Hafez's mother winks at him.

"Yes, yes of course… the news, what was it? Ah… huh! Now I remember. Nearly four weeks ago on the thirteenth of *Rabi'u* (30th of November) Sultan Abu Said's wife, the famously beautiful Baghdad Khatun, went to him on the battlefield, slept with him and… poisoned him by… Shams-ud-din, don't listen to this… after they had performed the sexual act she wiped his body with a towel impregnated with a deadly poison. He's dead, the sultan is with us no more! It is rumoured she was jealous of all the attention he was paying to her young, beautiful rival Dilshad Khatun. Afterwards Baghdad Khatun was put to death in an unbelievably cruel and unspeakable fashion. I almost fainted when I heard! No, I can't describe it to you! You want me to sister? Hmmm. She was murdered in her bath… the Greek slave named Lu'lu who'd become a powerful amir beat her to death with a club. Her almost naked body lay there for many days, only a small part of her anatomy being covered… one can only guess what part! They say she was a most beautiful and extraordinary woman! I'd liked to have met her! I wonder what she thought of elderly, distinguished poets?"

"Uncle Sadi, she'd probably have murdered you too... after hearing your poetry! Back to the *extraordinary news!*" Hafez jumps up and begins to pace excitedly around the room.

"Hmmm, he thinks he's funny. You know I have just finished reading a book where young Sultan Abu Said was described as 'a brave and brilliant ruler of majestic appearance, generous and witty... a good calligraphist, composer and musician and of fine moral character'. Your fat friend Peter wouldn't have approved of him as he destroyed many Christian churches, and I don't think I would have liked him as he did the same to many of the winehouses... and with what he did to our beloved Mahmud Shah, perhaps he got what he deserved, which reminds me... yes... more news! What happened next? Ah... huh! Arpa Khan, the nephew of Hulagu Khan the king before Uljaytu was appointed Sultan... immediately... how can I tell you this terrible event? He sent an order from Sultaniyeh to Isfahan to the prison to... ah... remove the head of our beloved ex-ruler Mahmud Shah!"

"God, take him into Your bosom!" Hafez's mother's face is in her hands and she is gasping.

"My God, what will happen next?" Hafez looks at his uncle, eyes wide with astonishment.

"Yes, it's terrible... good and bad news as I said. Anyway, a number of the amirs didn't approve of what Arpa did or of his ascension to the throne and they set up a rival sultan in Musa, a true descendant of Hulagu... and not just of his brother. Musa has promised that if he defeats Arpa in the coming battle he will allow the sons of Mahmud Shah to peacefully go to Tabriz and collect what is left of the body of their father and return it to Shiraz for a proper burial." Sadi raises his bushy white eyebrows.

"Now let us hope Kaikhusrau will allow his brothers to accompany him if that should come to pass... he's a fool to think the people of Shiraz will accept him... Masud Shah, the oldest brother is our true monarch!" As Hafez raises his arms high to emphasize the point he accidentally falls back onto his backside to the laughter of Sadi and his mother.

"*Pahlawan* Hafez, you hero, show us what you'll do to Kaikhusrau if he won't hear the voice of the people!"

Hafez kicks him in the backside.

"Ouch! Not *that* hard! That hurt!"

His mother laughs as Sadi sits back on the cushion and sighs.

"Perhaps... I should go back to that winehouse and try to... er... discover any other news, eh?"

·

Hajji grins at Abu and says, "Hah... Abu, stop laughing it wasn't *that* funny, although Hafez's uncle was quite absurd at the time! Listen, it is now five months since *all that* happened. Arpa Khan has been killed by Musa in that battle and the new sultan, Musa, has as he said he would, kindly invite that traitor Kaikhusrau and his brothers to go to Tabriz to bring back to Shiraz the body of their father. I'm still surprised that Kaikhusrau agreed to let them all go, including their mother the tragic and much loved Tashi Khatun but, I suppose he is trying to win approval of us all who all hate him and he probably thinks that if they are all with him on the journey they can't be plotting to overthrow the rotten shit! Anyway, they should arrive here from what I've heard in the next week.

"But, listen... there's some more interesting news. See that fellow, yes... the strange-looking, tall, thin one with the odd clothes and the comical face with the wispy beard, in the corner, drinking alone? *Don't point!* Yes, *him!* I met him here about a month ago. He's a poet and writer and a teacher. I'd say, what... about thirty-five? He's originally from a village near Qazwin. His family the Zakanis were descended from the Arabian tribe of Khafaja who had settled there long ago.

"What I've heard is that he was attached to the court of the recently gone-but-not-yet-forgotten Sultan Abu Said in Sultaniyeh and wrote a book in Arabic of 'Chosen Proverbs' called *Nawader al-Amthal*. He writes some beautiful, subtle *ghazals*... I must sing you some soon. Anyway, he returned to Qazwin a few years ago and taught there and wrote his book 'The Joyous Treatise', *Risala-i-Dilgusha*. I tell you Abu, you've never heard such rib-tickling, ribald, scandalous Arab and Persian stories. He is *very* funny, but also a serious man. Shall I call him over and introduce you to him?"

"Of course, he sounds... different, my friend."

Hajji waves and catches his eye and gestures to him to join them. He lopes over.

"Abu Khan, my favourite minstrel (other than myself of course), meet Obeyd Zakani... a rare poet, a unique wit and a learned gentleman!"

They embrace and Obeyd sits as Hajji orders more wine and food.

"By my sorry arse I don't know about the 'gentleman' Hajji... I'll admit to all the other compliments, though many of my many critics wouldn't."

"And have you found employment?"

"Yes, at one of the poorer colleges... teaching classes in Arabic and Arabic Literature, *Koranic* Studies, Social History, Persian Poetry, Astronomy (with a little Astrology thrown in, but don't tell anyone) and Lexicography."

"Hmm, listen Obeyd, there is a young, very talented friend of mine, his poetic name is Hafez... and he is unhappy with his teachers at some of his night classes right now. He works at a drapery during the day takes night classes and studies in the early morning. I'll tell him to give you a trial. He is, I think you will discover... unique, in every way!"

"Upon my unbelievably handsome head, when does the poor boy sleep? Good! I need more students, you wouldn't believe the amount of money I owe. I wrote a *ghazal* about being in debt, that was when I first went to Sultan Abu Said's court. I finally got a position with one of his minister's at the time, Khwaja 'Ala al-Din Mohammad. Perhaps I could change the name at the end and try to get to the ears of Kaikhusrau through one of his ministers? I'd like your opinion on that!"

"Let us hear it then," Hajji grins at Abu who scratches his ear and nods.

"Ah... let me remember it, fifteen years is a long time. I was twenty-one then and very wet behind the ears. I thought humour mixed with honesty might have some effect."

"And did it?" Abu asks.

"Yes, surprisingly it did for awhile. I wrote my 'Arab Proverbs' then and dedicated it to 'Ala al-Din out of gratitude for introducing me to the court. What stories I could tell you. Do you know the poet Khaju Kirmani... he was there? I wouldn't be surprised to see him turn up here one day and find some way to gain the attention of whoever is in power?"

"No Obeyd, I don't know of him... Hafez probably does, he reads everyone... the poem, please!"

"Yes Hajji. One day I must tell you about my many years at that court that Fate has now blown to the wind. The debt-ridden *ghazal* my friends...

Others enjoy all their happiness... while sickly with debt am I:
others, have affairs and business: but unluckily, with debt am I.
My duty to God, debts to His subjects weigh my neck down:
discharging duty to God or all who plague me with debt, am I?
More than before are my expenses and debts beyond measure:
thinking of expenses, mentally dealing vaguely with debt am I.
I complain: the only papers I possess are summonses for debts:
fearing only those witnesses, who'll accuse me with debt, am I.
In the city I have debts... and in the suburbs I also have debts:
deep in debt in the street and in the store... only with debt am I.
From early in the morning until late at night I'm always anxious:
how to now beg for a loan... when so absolutely with debt am I?
While all of those others who are in the grip of debt run away,
praying for a loan from the Almighty to help me with debt am I!
To the winds like the pride of beggars my pride I've also thrown:
at other beggars doors seen begging frequently, with debt am I.
If the Khwaja doesn't talk to king about my desperate state...

how, poor Obeyd... me, finally... not to be without debt, am I?

"Then there is a final couplet where I call on 'Ala al-Din by name to save me. What do you think? I hear the renowned, rich and generous Khwaja Haji Kivam might be worth telling it to. Doesn't he have the ear of Kaikhusrau?"

"Yes, he does... I think he'll find your *ghazal* quite amusing. If you like I could sing him it and a few of your other *ghazals* next week when I will be seeing him, and if he likes it... who knows. But I wouldn't hold your breath in regards to the present treacherous piece of shit who has stolen the throne... I hear he dislikes all poetry and music and his one interest in life is hunting, torturing and killing his subjects?"

"Ah, perhaps I should wait until his time has come and he goes the way of all arseholes into the steaming, stinking pit. My friend, but how kind of you to mention me to the rich and generous Haji Kivam. How can I repay you?"

"I was just telling Abu here about your outrageous book of Persian and Arabic stories. Please, entertain us now with a handful of them... we've already had one good laugh tonight, but as you know, one can't have enough of a good thing... and with laughter one forgets oneself and one's troubles."

"As good as done! Hmm... talking of 'Ala ad-Din reminds me about a beautiful slave boy that he had named Arbuz which as you know means 'goats-around'. At a drinking party one day 'Ala ad-Din asked Maulana Sharaf ad-Din Ka'bani, 'Maulana, do you fuck donkeys?' Maulana replied, 'If cows are around I'll fuck 'em, if donkeys are around I'll fuck 'em and if 'goats-around, I'll fuck him too!"

"Stop laughing Abu, it's not that funny! Here is the wine. Ah! That's better! 'Lubricate the throat', as the conscientious whore said! Now let me delve into my memory. You know I'm from Qazwin... well, from Zakan near there... and you know about the people of Qazwin? You don't? I'll fill you in my friends. Listen, a man who was a Qazwini had a son who fell into a well. His father shouted down to him, 'Son, listen, don't you go anywhere until I go and fetch a rope to pull you up!' Eh? Get the idea? Here's another, a man from Qazwin who was armed with a huge shield went out to fight the heretical Assassins whose main fort was situated at Alamut near Qazwin. They fired a stone from their fort that hit him on the head and he shouted at them, 'Hey, you... are you so blind that you can't see this shield that's so big? How come you go and hit me on the head?' Eh... hah... hey Abu you'll spill your wine, friend!

"Another? I can tell these jokes because I come from the place... although I must tell you that when I told them there, they didn't go down all that well not like they are with you. In fact, it's one of the reasons I came here. The folks at home don't seem to appreciate my sense of humour. I heard you Shirazis not only love wine, poetry, women and song... but also a good laugh... even at the expense of yourselves! Eh? Don't worry, I'm working on a collection of Shirazi jokes my friends, contributions gratefully accepted.

"Listen, there was a Qazwini who was returning from Baghdad in the summer. He was asked what he was doing there and he replied, 'Sweating!' Been to Baghdad in summer Hajji? You'd be sweating too! Another? A group of Qazwinis return from fighting the heretics and each had a head on the end of a spear, except for one who had a foot! Someone asked him, 'Who killed him?' He replied,

'Me!' 'Why did you not bring his head?' 'Because before I got there and killed him, they'd already taken his head!'

"Careful Hajji, don't choke! Listen, a man from Qazwin mounted his horse backwards. Someone informed him of this fact. He replied, 'It's not me... it's the horse that's backwards!' Eh? Typical, I can assure you. Had enough? No? Alright... another, a man from Qazwin lost his donkey and went around the town declaring he was happy about it. Someone asked him why. He replied, 'If I'd been on the donkey I'd have been lost for the last four days!'

"Here's one, you ready? Went down the wrong way Abu? Never let that happen my friend, can be very unpleasant and... painful! Listen, one night a policeman saw a Qazwini who was drunk (might have been me). The policeman shouted at him, 'Get up so I can take you off to jail!' The man from Qazwin replied, 'If I could get up I'd much rather go home!' Sounds like me right now.

"This is a good one... there was a man from Qazwin who had an axe and each night he'd hide it and lock the door. His wife asked, 'Why'd you put the axe in that spot?' He answered, 'So the cat can't find it!' 'What would a cat do with an axe?' She asked. He replied, 'What a foolish woman, the cat stole six pieces of meat worth such a small amount, so do you think I'm going to leave out an axe lying around that I paid so much for?'"

"Enough, enough... I can't stand it anymore Obeyd, my stomach is hurting me. I'm aching all over!" Hajji is shouting.

"No Obeyd... don't stop, I'm addicted! Please, just one more, short and sweet!" Abu grins at him.

"Alright Abu, just one... for you only, don't listen Hajji... don't think of a camel. Thinking of one? Good! Now you won't hear it.

Abu... there was a man from Qazwin, in fact I knew him well... looked a lot like you, anyway he lost his ring, somewhere inside his house. I found him out in the street searching for it. When I asked him why he looked for it outside he said, 'Because it's too dark inside the house!' "

*

High up on the brickworks lookout-tower the small figure of Hafez is now seen pointing frantically as he shouts, "They are coming! They are coming! There they are! I can see the dust from their horses... it must be them!"

Hajji nods at Abu and shouts back to Hafez...

"Come down now Hafez... we'll meet them at the gate!"

A half-hour later they join most of Shiraz's citizens lining the streets of the fruit market leading to the main northern gate, the Isfahan Gate. All our businesses, schools, colleges and winehouses are closed for the forty-day period of mourning that is about to begin.

The people wait silently, some praying, heads bowed or in hands, all standing at a respectful distance from the centre of the streets leading the short distance to the Old Mosque where the casket containing the headless body of Mahmud Shah will be placed in the vast courtyard paved with marble... for prayers and speeches by his sons and various clerics and dignitaries before it is carried to its final resting place beside the tomb of one of our greatest saints Ibn Khafif who brought Sufism to Shiraz.

By noon the sad procession is nearing the street corner where Hafez stands with his mother and uncle, Sadi. Hajji Ahmed, Abu and the other minstrels stand a little way further off and now Hafez notices them being joined by a tall, thin, strange-looking fellow with a wispy beard that he hasn't seen before.

Finally he turns to see passing the gold casket lying on the bier drawn by two death-black horses being led by the hand. Two of the mourning brothers walk on each side looking tired and greatly saddened by their father's fate that their long journey gave them time to contemplate. Unpredictable times!

At the front on the right Kaikhusrau, twenty-eight, stout and ruddy-faced... in looks taking after his esteemed father, sweating profusely and wiping his dust-laden face. Behind him is Masud Shah, now thirty, of medium height, heavily bearded, weeping. On the left side of the bier rides the third-oldest son Shams-ud-din Muhammad, sitting tall, dark, hawk-nosed, straight and proud upon his Arabian steed, in full regalia, staring stiffly ahead. Behind him, sitting on a smaller, white horse is the youngest... recently turned fifteen, Abu Ishak, extremely handsome, wiping a tear from his dusty eye as the bier followed by on foot, the grief-stricken wife, Tashi Khatun, still heart-wrenchingly beautiful for her forty-six years, being helped by on one arm Majd al-Din and on the other Haji Kivam. Her unveiled face (as is their custom) touches everyone's heart and a loud sighs fill the air that seems to Hafez to be suddenly all taken away. He faints!

When he regains consciousness the first face he sees bending over him is Hajji's and Hajji tells me years later that Hafez blinks once then comes out with the following short poem...

Brother, in passing away, swift
like the clouds is opportunity...
know that life is very precious:

if it is wasted, ah what a pity!

Then he assures his mother, uncle and all around him that he feels better and the crowd disperses, many to follow the procession to the Old Mosque. His mother and uncle Sadi decide to go home to rest before the afternoon's ceremonies but they cannot talk Hafez into doing the same. He accepts Hajji's invitation to go to his room for refreshments and is introduced to the concerned-looking Obeyd Zakani.

"Hafez, meet a new friend, Obeyd Zakani from Qazwin. A poet, a teacher and a very humourous fellow!"

"Really? Poet *and* a teacher, in that order?" He looks up and smiles at Obeyd now grinning down at him.

"Not a poet who can compose while unconscious like you my young friend. Perhaps I should try it some time. Hajji… grab that rock over there and drop it on my head!"

They all burst out laughing.

"I've heard about you Hafez. I'm teaching at one of the colleges. Perhaps you'd like to sit in on my classes and see if you want to join any of them, I can assure you will not be bored."

Hafez bows to him and says, "An invitation impossible to refuse! Hajji, let us get those refreshments before I faint again."

"Is it true you memorized the *Koran* before the age of nine?" Obeyd takes his arm as they follow Hajji and Abu.

"Yes, I'm blessed with a remarkable memory… but sometimes I can't even remember to have breakfast!"

*

It is nearly two years later and Hafez at Khwaja Haji Kivam's invitation is riding his own newly bought young, unpredictable donkey with Haji Kivam on his magnificent white Arabian steed past Musalla to the north of the outskirts of the city near the 'God is Great' Pass at the entrance to Shiraz.

"You know my friend that stupid execution by this power-mad lunatic Kaikhusrau of the good friend and ex-minister of our true king Masud Shah, the Amir Fakhr-ud-din Phirak, is the last straw as far as Masud Shah, I and many others are concerned. Do not be surprised if the rightful heir to the throne disappears down one of our blessed qanats in a short while and escapes this beleagued city to Isfahan where that city's most powerful people are still loyal to him… and where he could assemble quite a sizable army to take back our beloved city. Also, do not be surprised if some generals and a sizable number of soldiers leave their posts and join him. Yes my friend I think it will not be long now when you poets will be in favour once again… and not a moment too soon eh? I think that delightfully irreverent and uproariously funny friend of yours Obeyd Zakani would agree to that eh?"

Hafez grins his approval as he tries to control his donkey. He has been easily convinced to go on the trip when he is told *who* they are going to visit… a beneficiary of Haji Kivam's wealth and kindness, the great Master of miniature painting Ahmad Musa who he knew had been resident in Shiraz for some months but he had never seen him… as he was something of a hermit and shunned his own fame.

As they are taking their time because of Sadi's cantankerous new donkey, Haji Kivam explains to Hafez the purpose of their visit.

"You see Hafez what this profound man is doing with our great art of miniature painting for the book is similar to what you could to do with poetry through the *ghazal*. He is now almost fifty years old. Nearly seven years ago he became the master of all the painters in the royal studios at Tabriz under Sultan Abu Said's respected prime minister Ghiyath al-Din Muhammad, one of the sons of the great Rashid al-Din and the great friend of course of Mahmud Shah. Ghiyath al-Din, an inspired and generous soul had received the ministership some ten years ago and apart from reviving the destroyed atelier or art-studios named Rashidiya of his famous father... he organized with the poet and scholar and historian Hamd Allah Mustaufi of Qazwin (another minister and a friend of his father's and of also of our recent arrival that peculiar fellow Obeyd Zakani by the way: he writes to me that he has a 'brilliant and original mind')... a major revision of our national epic, Firdausi's *Shah-Nama*... the 'Book of Kings' four years ago... using many of the copies that I had in my private collection. Incidentally, in that recent letter from Mustaufi he states he could soon be coming to Shiraz to write a book about our fair city. Did you know that he recently completed a long *masnavi* poem of about 75,000 couplets, the *Zafar-Nama*, that is a continuation of the *Shah-Nama*. Of course Firdausi's epic of over 60,000 couplets has been illustrated before, but never like this... on such a grand scale, about two feet high by a foot and a half wide, with one thousand one hundred and twenty pages and a hundred and twenty magnificent masterpieces of illustration.

"When Sultan Abu Said was poisoned by his wife Baghdad Khatun and the succeeding rulers started killing each other, as I told you yesterday I invited Ahmad Musa and the master calligrapher Maulana 'Abd Allah and Ahmad Musa's brightest assistant Amir Dawlat Yar, (who is expert at drawing and was once a slave of the Sultan)... to Shiraz... to continue under my patronage the work they had begun shortly before the young sultan's murder and finish their important work in peaceful surroundings. They hope to finish the *Shah-Nama* in about two years and next they will begin work on a book on the Ascension of the Prophet, a *Miraj-Nama*. Ahmad Musa says he will not flinch from honestly portraying the wonderful face of Muhammad... he is a brave man as well as a genius. Not far to go now, just through those trees over there."

"Why is their studio and residence way out here in this small forest?" Hafez asks as he can now just see a grand two-storied mudbrick building in the clearing amongst the chenar trees up ahead.

"You know, the alchemy of mixing the minerals and plants, dyes and precious stones... grinding and fixing... for painting can be very dangerous. Explosions occur... painters have been known to lose fingers, hands, have become blind and have even been killed. They cannot have people living nearby, too dangerous. Many also lose their eyesight at an early age because they strain their eyes for a long time painting such small paintings with brushes that sometimes consist of a few cat hairs... and after they become blind they then sometimes become blind-toolers of the leather covers for the books. That, my friend is real dedication to an art and a craft... and what do they often receive as pay... a mere pittance, but of course I pay them well. It is not a profession for the faint-hearted my friend. Come, they are expecting us. I was here last week and told them I'd bring you today at this time and of your interest in advancing your learning of calligraphy from Maulana."

As they pass through a somewhat untidy small rosegarden and approach the impressive front door they can hear an argument going on inside... "But *Master*, I tell you if we use any more blue in that cloak it will disturb the whole picture, it's *too* bright!"

"Please let me decide that Dawlat, just do as I told you and afterwards we will see the result... remember the saying, 'The village with two headmen falls into ruin!' "

"But Ahmad... Master..."

"DO IT!"

Silence. Hafez grins his lopsided grin at Haji Kivam as Haji Kivam knocks.

"Ah! That will be Khwaja Kivam and his young friend Hafez... open the door Dawlat. Get a *move* on man!"

The door is opened by a dark-skinned, scowling, thickly-bearded, stoutish fellow of around forty years who says quietly to Haji Kivam, "Upon my head, sometimes I feel like killing him... but he's probably right, usually is!"

Kivam turns and winks at Hafez and quips, "We both know someone just like that don't we my friend? Ah, Dawlat meet Hafez. I told you about him last time."

"Yes, congratulations on your poems young man and may you compose many more!"

"Thank you!"

They now walk past him into the enormous studio-room and are immediately greeted with joyful enthusiasm by the thin, greying

Master-Painter Ahmad Musa who has the most amazing piercing, sparkling eyes Hafez has ever seen. They capture Hafez and he feels as though he is searching deep inside to his soul but at the same time he is minutely observing his outward appearance so that after about thirty seconds of this Hafez know that he knows him as well as he knows himself. It is like being examined by God. Suddenly Ahmad Musa embraces him and a wave of bliss rushes through his body and wraps around his heart. He feels like weeping he is suddenly so happy. He holds Hafez in front of him and smiles at him as he says to a grinning Kivam, "You are right my friend, a fine and loving soul. Hafez, welcome to our... eh... miniature world... where like God we view all things as being equidistant and of equal value but of course some beings are more conscious of their real nature... that is the only difference, my young friend. Now, before you go into the other room to have your first calligraphy lesson from Maulana I'll show you what we do here and what we have done. You still standing there gaping Dawlat? Get back to work! *All of you... get back to work!*"

Suddenly Hafez is aware of the twenty or more boys and young and older men sitting at the low benches hunched over sheets of paper, pencils and thin paintbrushes in their delicate hands. At Ahmad Musa's fierce command they are all now back at work and seem oblivious of us as they stroll and the Master-Painter begins to enlighten Hafez... "These eight students on the left are drawing backgrounds and figures under the supervision of myself and of course Dawlat who is best of all drawing craftsmen. Those on the right are painting in what the others have drawn... usually the one painter working on the one page... of course the calligraphy has already been done in the other room which you will see later. I have designed the contents of the pages in consultation with Dawlat and Maulana. The illustrations we are all working on though are examples from the lives of the various rulers of the past are also about the life of our now departed patron Sultan Abu Said."

Hafez bends down and looks closely at first a page of fine drawing and is amazed to see a thin line spiraling from the top of the page passing through the eyes of the various animals and figures of the humans until the spiral ends in what obviously will be the centre of the picture... a raised hand of a powerful looking figure in an old-fashioned costume. He asks his host about this.

"Master Musa, why is this line drawn through the eyes of all the figures in a spiral?"

"Ah, young poet, the question is the one I hoped you would ask. Look at the form of the *ghazal* that our friend the Khwaja here tells me you have the potential to perfect... is it not a spiral? Even the Arabic root of the Persian word *gazl* means... spinning, thread, twist! As you well know in the first couplet or *beyt* which is called *matla*, meaning orient or rising... the rhyme appears at the end of *both* lines... and this couplet has the function of setting the stage or stating the subject matter and feeling of the whole poem. In a way it is the same as the following couplets where the first line does not have to rhyme and so the poet can let the heart have full rein... be spontaneous, while the second line *must rhyme* with the same rhyme as the previous couplets, quite difficult, and so the mind must take over and become a vessel for the longing and logic of the heart. As the first line of the first couplet is created from the heart, whatever comes out in the end... becomes the rhyme. The expansion and contraction of the heart... *kabz* and *babz* as the Sufis say. If the *ghazal* is looked at as a line it would be thus..."

He bends down and picks up a piece of paper and a fine pencil and draws an elongated circle and from the side a spiral of seven loops, the last loop's line continuing on up to the centre of the first circle.

"This is the shape of the *ghazal* in a visual sense... in the last couplet as you know where the poet uses his poetic name or *takhallus*, such as yours...'Hafez'... the poet can detach himself and thus answer the feeling or question posed in the first couplet and enlarged upon in the subsequent couplets. If this was looked as side-on one would see a ball or pearl. Some have likened the couplets of the *ghazal* to pearls on an invisible string to be hung around the loved one's neck... the final or *maqta* couplet being the clasp couplet. I prefer the image also of the *ghazal* that reminds me of my childhood... remember skipping stones across the water of a pond? The first couplet is the throw, the other couplets the skips on the water and the last couplet the descent to the bottom of the pond of the stone. Viewed visually this also is a spiral as are all things in nature... breath is a spiral and words come from breath... the great clusters of stars I am told by our astronomers are in a spiral... most of our great architecture is based on the spiral. In fact the *ghazal* is the oldest form of poetry... the first being composed by Adam, the first *Qutub* or Perfect Master, the *Rasool*, on the death of his son Abel... the *ghazal* is nearly always about, love, longing, loss... do you wish to hear it?"

"Yes please!" Hafez answers this extraordinary man and he notices that all the students place down their pencils and brushes and turn to face the Master as he steps back and clears his throat...

"Adam says…

The lands are changed and all those who live on them…

the face of the earth is torn and surrounded with gloom;

everything that was lovely and fragrant has now faded,

from that beautiful face has vanished the joyful bloom.

What deep regrets for my dear son, O regrets for Abel,

a victim of murder… who has been placed in the tomb!

Is it possible to rest, while that Devil that was cursed

who never fails or dies… up from behind us does loom?

"Then Satan replies…

'Give up all these lands and all of those who live on them;

I was the one who forced you out of Paradise, your room,

where you and your wife were so secure and established,

where your heart did not know of the world's dark doom!

But you… you did escape all of my traps and my trickery,

until that great gift of life… on which you did presume

you went and lost… and from Eden the blasts of wind,

but for God's Grace, would've swept you like a broom!'

They all shout and clap and Hafez feels a strange prophetic sense of foreboding of loss of a son or offspring as Ahmad Musa takes his arm and leads him along to look down at another painting in progress.

"My young friend, I hear that Obeyd Zakani is one of your teachers. We have been close friends since the time he was at the court of Sultan Abu Said. What a wit he is… but also a fine writer of *ghazals* as is Khaju Kirmani who was also there at that time but who was not so friendly with Obeyd. A strange man is *that* most noteworthy court poet. It would not surprise me if Khaju turns up in

Shiraz in the near future as this city seems now to be the centre of art, learning and spirituality in our country that is now so wracked by upheavals and treachery amongst the ruling classes and fear and uncertainty amongst the people. Kivam tells me of your great potential as a composer of the *ghazal*. I have told you one secret that may be of help... now I tell you another that you should never forget. As the Great Shaikh, the Master Ibn 'Arabi has so clearly expressed... it is necessary to use the creative imagination of the power of the heart, the *himma,* to try to see the creation through God's eyes and not ours that are limited due to our ignorance and selfishness and false desires. To God, everything and everyone is of equal importance to the Creator but some of course are more conscious of Him... and all are a reflection of the drama of His creative actions... the past, present and the future.

"Now, look at these four illustrations of ours from the epic of Firdausi and I will tell you their secret... the various levels that they can be understood... what we are trying to do with our history, our art and our understanding of fate and the hand of the Almighty. You know the story of the extremely beautiful Baghdad Khatun and the young Sultan Abu Said? Of course you do... she is still the topic of feverish conversation everywhere. I tell you I have never seen a more beautiful creation of the Almighty. But, such beauty inspired many emotions in her and others... love, desire, greed, jealousy and also hate.

"The daughter of Amir Chupan she was married to Amir Hasan. Young Abu Said fell madly in love with her and wanted to meet her and take her from her husband through her father. Chupan kept putting the sultan off by taking him on hunting trips and military expeditions. After Chupan was executed the sultan married this beautiful woman. In 732/1332 she was caught plotting by letters with Amir Hasan her former husband to assassinate the sultan. They were caught out and later pardoned by Abu Said. As you know this was the young sultan's greatest mistake for she finally poisoned him and was later... er... executed. In this miniature depicting Zal's love for Rudaba... and here in this half-finished one he is working on showing the discovery of their letters... and this one still in drawing form of the king Ardashir's love for Gulnar... a member of the harem of Ardavan, and finally this illustration that I have only recently completed of the plot by the former king's daughter to poison Ardashir. I have not only told the story of our distant past but also of our recent past and perhaps our present and future intrigues at court. The secret I am trying to express to you Hafez is that many of these paintings can be interpreted on many levels and times and stories. You could, for instance, as a poet write of a 'king' and be also writing of God, or a *Qutub* or Master or of a beloved that one adores. Through such multi-leveled meaning one is protected but one is also seeing the situation closer to that which in reality is the true situation through the 'eye of God'... all as a reflection of the hand of the Creator. Of course, the more limited the knowledge of the observer of as in your case the listener... the fewer levels the painting or poem will be appreciated. You understand?"

"Yes master, you have perfectly articulated something I have been trying to appreciate for a long time and now I think you have turned the key for me to grab hold of my destiny and be able to create the songs that I know are laying in my heart and mind and are waiting to be set free!"

"Ah, we pray for that don't we Khwaja Kivam? Now I will show you into my studio where you can look at the finished illustrations while the Khwaja and I discuss some matters of utmost urgency and importance for the future of Shiraz."

He leads him to a small side room, his own studio. He sits him down at a low flat table then goes to a cupboard and gently lifts a large parcel wrapped in silk from it and places it on the table before him.

"Please be careful... it is the result of years of hard work and inspiration by myself, Maulana, Dawlat and others. It is the culmination of all of our illustrative art that came before it and I believe will change all painting and book-illustration from now on. What I have tried to do is create a truly 'Persian' type of painting... not just the purely realistic Chinese-influenced painting that we all created before it. The books that we are illustrating now are even more our own style and we are developing a new kind of looking at the world. Now enjoy our national epic Hafez, our Book of Kings, our *Shah-Nama* by our great epic poet, Firdausi... and I will answer any questions you may wish to ask me after you have finished."

He smiles and Hafez carefully unwraps the massive parcel and gazes with wonder at the beautiful calligraphy for some minutes then turns into the inside of the magical unbound pages and stops reading the book that he knows so well and is transported back in time by the fantastic images into our glorious past.

He turn the leaves from right to left and looks at the wonderful miniatures depicting the early days, some three thousand years ago... Kayumer, the first king.

Hafez reads...

He reigned over all the earth for years almost thirty,

like a sun on the throne... his goodness all could see,

as the full moon was shining over the high cypress...

from seat of king of kings he shone out in kingliness.

He looks at breathtaking paintings depicting his son Siyamak and his death through Ahriman. Siyamak's son Hushang and his fight with that black demon.

He remembers Firdausi's couplets he learnt at school now so vividly represented...

That blessed one Siyamak... he had left behind a son,

his grandfather's minister, Hushang, a princely one...

the black demon, though through fear raised the dust

into the heavens... his claws were hanging slack just

as Hushang saw his plight and stretching his hands

like lion's paws made the earth narrow where stands

that lustful demon... flaying and striking off his head

and scornfully trampled him, though he was now dead.

He is amazed as he gazes on the pictures depicting the reign of Jamshid and Mardus and his son Zuhak and the misrule of Zuhak and then the birth of Faridun who goes to war with Zuhak who is killed and so the reign of Faridun begins.

He stares at an amazing painting of his sons bravely fighting a dragon and he stops turning the pages when he comes to a poignant and disturbing painting of the good king Faridun mourning over the head of one of his three sons... his favourite Iraj, who was the most humble but the bravest of them and because of this was given the kingdom of Persia, Iran, the greatest gift received by the three of them.

The two other brothers were jealous of this and wanted more. Iraj, on his father's advice who wanted peace between the three brothers, agreed to give Iran to them and went to tell them but was murdered by his brother Tur and his head was sent back to Faridun who is depicted in the painting by Ahmad Musa as overcome by his terrible grief. Hafez remembered the couplets...

He bore a golden casket and in it was strapped
the head of Prince Iraj, in painted silk wrapped.
The good man came forward, face full of sorrow
when approached Faridun he wailed the truth. O
they raised the golden casket's lid... all gathered
there had believed the words of he who had cried
the story, and taking off the painted silk shroud
the head of Prince Iraj made them cry out loud...
Faridun fell from his steed... and then all his men
tore shirts, dark eyes horrified, looked away then.

Faridun holds the head of his beloved son wrapped in folds of silk and cries into his son's lifeless eyes as three women, full of sorrow, bend over the tragic father and son. He is full once again now with sadness and foreboding about a prophetic feeling for his own son... in some distant future? This adds to the feeling he had when Ahmad Musa recited the first *ghazal* by Adam on the death of his son Abel. A sudden rush of terrible fear shakes his heart and he brushes away a tear and turns the thick pages again slightly dreading what he may be about to experience.

His apprehension is quickly forgotten as he gazes in awe and wonder at the bird that symbolizes God, the *Simurgh* taking the infant, white-haired Zal back to its nest.

Hafez remembered the couplets that he had loved so much at school…

She swooped down from the clouds and with her claws

she snatched the infant Zal from those hot, rocky jaws,

then carried him off quickly to that mountain… Alburz,

where were the nest and those young offspring of hers…

when her brood saw the infant weeping bloody tears,

they all lavished such love on him he lost all his fears,

his face of such purity caused them to be astonished…

the Simurgh… the tenderest, love upon him lavished.

And Hafez suddenly wonders how any infant to be born to him in the future will look… more like his mother or him? That would be too cruel of the Almighty… he usually avoided mirrors but it would be impossible. He turns the pages again and sees the now grown boy Zal shooting a waterfowl watched by two attendants and some women… a dramatic and perfectly executed painting by the Master and as he looks at it he wonders if he will ever have a boy-child and he begins to imagine all the father-son activities they'll be able to enjoy together.

He reads further and sees the birth of the son of Zal, the hero of fabulous strength, Rustom…

No one had ever seen a thing so strange… like a lion

was this baby… a hero so fair and tall to look upon.

Men and women wondered when on him they gazed,

no one knew of such an elephant child being birthed.

And now Hafez sees how he and Zal go off to war against the invader Afrasaib. He marvels at a miniature of Rustom fighting a rhinoceros. He slowly turns pages and sees Rustom slaying

Isfandiyar, another invader. He now is staring in disbelief at the complicated crowded scene of the bier of the body of Isfandiyar being hauled by a horse through the streets surrounded by grieving longhaired mourners... a stunning depiction Hafez thinks.

He senses that perhaps a long time has passed so he quickly glances at other miniatures until he comes to the story of Alexander, or as we call him... Iskander. He lingers over paintings of him fighting a dragon, building a wall against Gog and Magog, fighting two wolves, conversing with a talking tree, visiting the city of the Brahmins in India, fighting the Indian army in strange horse-like monstrous chariots and now he stops and dwells on him emerging from the dark path to the water of Life, which he never found as he could not relinquish power over others. He thinks deeply about that and turns the pages until he is gasping at one of Ahmad Musa's masterpieces... the bier of Iskander. How can he truly describe this great painting and the profound effect it has on him to anyone? Never before has grief, the dignity of death and the majesty of the one who has died been so faultlessly shown.

Hafez remembers...

They bore the golden bier out onto the plain
and on the earth the cries of grief did rain...
men, women and children... if one counted,
it would over hundred thousand have passed.

Again he is thrown into a feeling of dark apprehension and he says a prayer to God hoping that he hasn't been given dubious gift of foresight or even... heaven forbid, prophecy. Hafez shudders away his fears then wraps the pages once again in the silk and goes in search of Ahmad Musa and Haji Kivam his mind full of questions and feeling a little apprehensive before his first of many lessons with the master calligrapher Maulana 'Abd Allah.

*

Three months later Khwaja Haji Kivam gestures to Hafez as the others leave his class in *Koranic Studies*. Hafez, recently turned eighteen is growing a beard to try to lengthen his almost non-existent chin... rushes over to his teacher and bows deeply.

"Hafez, stop that bowing... how many times must... oh, forget it. Listen, it is a month now since Masud Shah returned from Isfahan and with the help of the people (quite a few of whom lost their lives *as usual*)... defeated that treacherous brother Kaikhusrau and executed him and assumed power in the palace again. But... that has made possible what I really wanted to talk to you about. You know we have often discussed the poetry of the great Auhadi of Maragha and how much you love his work. You drive me mad with your quotations from him. Well, I've some truly wonderful news. It seems he travelled from Isfahan and has arrived here at the invitation of Majd al-Din. I met him last night and he is everything you think he is and much more, I assure you. He will be in Shiraz for only a short time and then he will make the long journey to his birthplace in Maragha up north towards Tabriz. He says he will lay down his sick, old body for good. He's not a well man Hafez... but his mind and his heart, they are very fine indeed. Anyway, I had a chance to tell him about you and your love for his poetry and he asked me to invite you to the palace tonight when he will give a reading to the royal family. You'd like to come with me?"

"My God! Would I! Khwaja... God seems to be making all my wishes and dreams come true. I don't know how to thank you. Perhaps I can quote another of his *ghazals* as payment? Listen Khwaja...

You who my heart loves, tonight far from me don't go:
O You, light of my eye, I love You so dearly... don't go!
I am not really afraid if someone else leaves my sight...
but You, Beloved, Sweetheart, I have to see... don't go!
Angel, my house becomes a paradise when You're here:
angel, from this Paradise if it's a possibility... don't go.
Your eyes that are sleepy are intoxicating me tonight...
don't leave me intoxicated, even more sleepy... don't go.
I love Your face... why use separation to be hurting me?
Momentarily, from lover waiting desperately, don't go.
My heart that keeps wasting away needs a cure... You:
heart's cure, away from me, waiting patiently, don't go!
Because Auhadi became dust at Your feet, out of faith,
stop all of this resisting and be faithful finally... don't go!

"Don't go... on Hafez, please enough! Your face at the moment is thanks enough for me young man. Please, think of some poems of yours... for the king, Masud Shah, may ask you to recite some. Our odd fellow Obeyd Zakani should also be there... it appears his brand of strange wit is in favour at the court at the moment, although sometimes I wonder whether I was still sane when I introduced him to the king! Now, go and dress yourself in your finest and I'll see you at the palace gates at dusk. Go with God my friend!"

"Teacher, I... don't know how..."

"Go! We have a great bond Hafez. I have never had such a pupil as you. We'll always try to help each other on the true path! Yes?"

"Yes, Khwaja... but, what can I offer you?"

"Yourself, Hafez... your unique self!"

·

The great, fierce ball of a sun is setting over the palace as Hafez in his best coat and turban, although both frayed a little... walks up to the waiting Haji Kivam surrounded by many of our city's well-wishers coming from all walks of life.

"Ah... by my eyes, there you are Hafez! Good! We can go inside now, our friends here are beginning to wear me out with all their questions... most of which are unanswerable if one wants to keep one's head! You haven't been in the palace before have you? It's nothing! Really! An illusion like everything else, except the Almighty. Don't be intimidated by it or anyone in it, ever. Promise? Remember *this* then! Now, yes... guards... it is I Haji Kivam, yes the same as I always am. Yes. Enter, Hafez! I am truly looking-forward to tonight and the poems of our beloved Auhadi, aren't you?"

"Yes teacher, it is a dream come true for me. I only wish Musa could be here. Tell me, do you really think the king will ask me to recite?"

"It's possible, he has heard of you from me and Majd al-Din... and remember that time Hajji Ahmed sang that *ghazal* of yours to him. And of course you met him when we all rose up and freed the whole family. O... more good news! How could I have forgotten. You remember our journey some three months ago to see the beautiful *Shah-Nama* of Ahmad Musa and his helpers? I mentioned that

Hamd Allah Mustaufi could be coming to Shiraz to write a section in his new book about our city… well, my young friend he has arrived and now lives with me and you will meet him tonight. perhaps he will share with us all a little from that long masterpiece of his, his *Zafar-Nama*… eh? Much to look forward to. So much!

"Ah, now we are finally at the door. Yes, yes… I'm Haji Kivam as you well know, yes… here is my invitation. Yes, he is my guest. Hafez… you have it? Good! Open the door! My God Hafez, if the people love their monarch so much and they *do*… in fact *they* are the reason he sits on the throne right now, why all this security? Fear of assassination plagues all rulers I suppose. Let us go in. Listen, pay no attention to all the grotesque sumptuousness and the ridiculous finery my friend… it's all a trap that you and I have nothing to do with. I am a rich man, a very rich man… but, my riches come from doing the work of the Lord and what I give away or build are only the result of His great generosity to me and all I can do is pass on that beneficence."

They pass along the wide corridor flanked by luxurious curtains, wall-hangings and golden shields and implements of war and finally come to a high door when once again Haji Kivam must show his credentials even though he is obviously known and loved by all the guards.

"Ah, it's such a bore! Anyway, we are about to enter the great hall… the court of the king. Bow to him exactly as he does to you, for there is really no difference in the eyes of God between you and him. Do whatever he does but do it with your heart my friend."

As they walk towards the throne Hafez looks across from the king and his entourage of brothers, mother, clergy and nobles to a small, elderly figure that he assumes is Auhadi talking animatedly to Majd al-Din and the mysterious old dervish is standing behind him alongside a tall richly dressed man with a white beard and strange turban who must be nearing sixty that he assumes must be Hamd Allah Mustaufi. Hafez finds that he can't keep his eyes off the small man's presence and as they reach the king he stumbles and falls forward onto his knees much to the amusement of the king. He looks over to the left to see a grinning Obeyd Zakani who tips his untidy-looking turban as the king laughs and mutters, "That's not necessary young man, but perhaps one day it will become so."

He looks across at his two brothers.

"Your majesty, I'd like to introduce you to my young pupil and friend, already a fine poet and a rememberer of the *Koran*... Shams-ud-din Mohammed, known as Hafez."

Masud Shah bows slightly and Hafez copies him exactly, much to Obeyd's amusement and many others at court.

"Yes! I know of you and have come across you on occasions when I needed your service. My daughter Jahan Malek is always telling me what a fine poet you are. You are welcome and may come back here again. I appreciate your love for our city. Please make yourself comfortable. You know everyone? My brothers? Abu Ishak like Jahan is also a talented poet. I think he has mentioned you to me... it seems you are both enamoured of the same fair young lady? Eh? Obeyd... please, set the stage with a few of your, hmm... terrible, but very funny stories!"

As Haji Kivam and Hafez move to the side Obeyd walks before the king and bows.

"Your majesty, how kind of you to ask. No poems? No funny stories yet, for how can one not pay homage to our special guests Auhadi of Maragha and Hamd Allah Mustaufi of my hometown of Qazwin, whom I must say is a special mentor of mine? I had the great fortune to hear Auhadi's *Jam-i Jam...* 'Cup of Jamshid' read by him in its entirety some six years ago in Isfahan and will treasure that occasion for the rest of my life, even if I did fall asleep towards the end of the four and a half-thousand couplets. Eh... just joking sire... no... I as most others... was entranced until the end, *the following day!* Another joke! The depth and breadth of this popular work is breathtaking, and it will probably leave me breathless to quote just some of the one hundred and sixteen headings that I discovered... *On the beginning of Creation, On the origin of Man, On Man's superiority to the animals, Advice on kings to be just, On the etiquette of attending upon kings, On marriage and procreation, On bad women...* I still remember some lines from his... *Some advice to bad women,* which I'll quote to you...

Although a woman looks beautiful in your eyes,
on ruining your house her ugliness you despise.
A bright candle in the home is a modest woman:
a bold woman is always a disaster upon a man!
A woman who is pious makes her man feel pride:
a Godless woman causes a man to run and hide;
and having taken all from his table and waterjug
she takes up her veil and sees her slippers fit snug
and finds and drags him to the judge and cries...
"Give my dowry back soon... now, if you're wise!"
A sober woman, that one who agrees to obey you

is like a kernel living inside your nut... it is true!

A wicked woman will be a torment to your heart:

get rid of her quickly or your misery she will start.

If your wife's inexperienced rebuke her immediately:

if she won't cover her face... shroud her completely.

Never place a pen in the hand of a wicked woman:

far better you cut off your hand than that, O man!

It is right for a husband to become one of mourning,

than for his wife a black book on him to be writing.

God has made the wheel and it's lawful for women:

tell them to leave pen and paper for husbands, men!

"Some words of advice I have never forgotten, and if I should ever tie the knot of wedlock I'll be the one who wears the pants and wields the pen. Sire, your young, petite and beautiful daughter the poetess Jahan sitting over there, I can't see her giving up writing her lovely poems if she met the right man, but then our poet Auhadi here says a *wicked* woman and she certainly isn't that, even though some people criticize her for writing poetry and 'acting like a man'.

"But now, let me get back to Auhadi's 'Cup of Jam'. Other themes in this remarkable, long *masnavi* poem include... *On the education of children, On miserliness* (I've had knowledge of this subject, sire), *On repressing lust and birth control* (no comment), *On the state of judges and justice* (I'd like to comment but I'd be locked up immediately), *Reproof to wicked lawyers* (let me at them!), *On the benefits of travel, On seeking a guide and a leader, On the virtue of sleeplessness* (I can't really vouch for that), *On silence* (don't worry, one day I'll shut up!), *On abstinence* (don't do it!), *On trust in God*... and so on until we reach the second part of the book full of

Sufi discipline and practice. I will now quote to you a poem from it about real love that has always stayed in my memory…

> Jesus the Messiah was with his friends one day:
> with his disciples… with whom his secrets lay:
> on the subject of love he made an explanation…
> talking, and then concealing this dispensation.
> In the middle of his talk his companions did see…
> that he was tired and upset… weeping openly!
> Then they asked him for a sign, for love's proof:
> he said: "Tomorrow is Abraham's fire, the truth!"
> When upon the following day he went on his way
> and finally on the gallows cross his foot did stay,
> he said: "If any man should still be standing here
> then surely this is the proof of love… one can bear.
> One who towards God should be turning his face
> that one a cross his back must in the end embrace.
> Until his body has been fastened to gallows cross,
> to Heaven his soul can't make the journey across.
> For the body, four sharp nails are the prescribed toll:
> heaven… is the candlestick of the candle of the soul.
> The claim of the true friend for proof is not lacking:
> even so, soul from your body you must be severing.
> How then can any man be said not to have a father?
> Is not your Heavenly Father sufficient, eh kind sir?
> He who knows how to bring the dead back to life…
> how can that one ever take even an enemy's life?"

"Now sire let me talk for a little while about our other honoured guest Hamd Allah Mustaufi whose great historical work should need no introduction, but I'm afraid it does as when I mentioned his masterpiece of seventy-five thousand couplets, his continuation to the *Shah-Nama*... his great *Zafar-Nama* to other students than my own and many notables in this city very few except for Khwaja Haji Kivam, God bless his soul, had read any of it. A great shame sire, a great shame indeed! If we are ignorant of the truth about the past how can we distinguish the reality of what daily presents itself to us? I am being serious now! And he has given us the honour to come here to immortalize this fair city in his next book! I think I will have to wake up the citizens of this city with a complete reading of this master work. The whole 75,000 couplets! I estimate four days sire! Agreed? I see your mouth fall open. A joke of course... but, I will explain to you all the contents of this remarkable history and quote a mere page from it. Ten thousand couplets have been given over by our esteemed author to the seven and a half centuries that his poetic history covers... that is, twenty-five thousand couplets to the Arabs, twenty thousand to the Persians and thirty thousand to the Mongols. Hamd was forty years old when he began it and he finished it some five years ago after fifteen years working on it. A remarkable achievement. This short passage about the fall of our town of Qazwin to the blood-thirsty Mongols always impressed me and it is as authentic as one could get for it was told to the author by his grandfather who was a witness to it some one hundred and twenty years ago. Listen closely...

Then to the town of Qazwin, Subutáy
like some raging tiger came so quickly.
When year six one seven [1220] stood
that fair town became a lake of blood;

Shaban (October) passed seven days
when it was filled with woe to amaze.
The governor of the ill-fortuned town
Muzaffar of name, a ruler of renown,
by the Caliph had gained command...
to control all the fortunes of that land.
When came the hosts of war's dire fate
rock-firm he had closed the city's gate.
On wall the warriors took their place...
all towards the Mongols set their face.
Three days they kept the enemy at bay,
on the fourth they forced a bloody way.
Fiercely they did enter Qazwin town,
heads held high before were now down.
No quarter there those Mongols gave:
days were ended of each chieftain brave.
Nothing could save all there from doom,
all were gathered into one common tomb.
Alike became great and small, old, young,
those lifeless bodies in the dust they flung.
Men and women shared a common fate,
that fortune-forsaken land, lay desolate.
And many a fair one in that fearful hour
sought death to save her from that power.
Chaste maidens of the Prophet's progeny
who shone like asteroids in Virtue's sky,
fearing lust of that army, ferocious host...
cast themselves down, gave up the ghost.

Most people in that land are of Shafi'ite;

and one in a thousand there is a Hanafite

and yet they counted upon that gory plain

twelve thousand Hanafites with the slain!

In heaps on every side all the corpses lay,

and upon lonely path and broad highway.

Uncounted bodies filled up every street...

one could not find a place to set one's feet.

From fear of the Mongol soldiers searching

here and there the people kept on running...

some seeking refuge to the Mosque did go,

hearts filled with anguish, souls full of woe.

That fierce foe made so terrible their plight,

climbing into the arches some hid from sight.

Those ruthless Mongols burning torches lit

until tongues of flame leapt upwards into it.

Roof, vault, arch in burning ruin finally fell,

a heathen's holocaust... of Death and Hell!

"Ah, I can see that you are all now depressed by this brutal but honest account of just a tiny instance of the disaster that fell upon this land at the hands of the godless Mongols. The power of Hamd's verse my friends. You all should read his masterpiece. Sire, you ask for humourous stories from my 'Joyous Treatise'? I'm happy to oblige. Let me first properly introduce the work that I finished some time ago in Qazwin... so now, The Introduction...

"Praise God for his blessings, gifts, grace and His kindness and praise on Mohammed and his family. Now, let me continue. Myself, the creator of this work (may God fulfill his wishes)... *I say,* that the virtue of speech that is the difference between man and animal has two forms: serious and... well, humourous... and the worth of the latter to the former is quite obvious. Listen, we all know that seriousness that goes on for too long a time becomes boring and something funny too often produces light-headedness and all dignity is forgotten. Way back in the past the old men said...

If you are serious all the year around, body wastes away,

and your dignity is eaten... if you consume jokes all day.

"But, my friends... humour is fine if with it you vanish grief and lighten the heart and the wise men have said, 'humour, when you talk... is like salt in cooking'. And the poet says...

Give consolation to your heart that's griefstricken

with wine... and with humour cure its affliction:

but when doing this you should be careful not to

exceed what salt is added to a culinary creation.

"You should all spend some time studying all the different kinds of humour and do what the poet says who wrote...

Although unity and study of Koran are most important,

some madness and light-headedness are also relevant!

"Now sire, give me a subject and I shall tell you some stories!"

"Hah, hah! You are a witty man Obeyd! Yes, let me think. Ah... hmm, ah hah... because I am of royalty and so are my family... *some* of who have a sense of humour, let your stories be about us... royalty, if you dare!"

"Ah, your majesty... I gather I'm forgiven before I tell these fanciful tales? Eh? I see you nodding. I have many witnesses! Now let me see... ah yes. A king had three wives... a Persian, an Arab and a Coptic wife. One night he slept with the Persian and said 'What time is it?' She answered, 'It's almost morning!' 'How could you possibly know?' he asked. 'Because the smells of the flowers and grasses fill the air and birds sing, sire,' she answered. The next night he asked his Arab wife the same question and she replied, 'Morning's almost here because my necklace's beads are cold and they're making me cold.' On the third night he asked his Coptic wife and she answered, 'It's morning as I've got to go to have a pee!'

"Sire, friends, it's not that funny, please... a little decorum. Ah, that's better! You have heard of Talhak, the jester of Sultan Mahmud? Yes, everyone knows Talhak, a funny fellow. Anyway, Talhak's wife gave birth. Sultan Mahmud asked him, 'What is it?' Talhak answered, 'What else do poor people have born to them... a boy or a girl!' The Sultan asked, 'Is anything else born to the great?' Talhak replied, 'A thing that abuses people and destroys them.'

"Yes, sire... I can see that I have reached the limit of your tolerance, although you are still smiling... which is more than I can say of your advisors in the clergy. One must remember what Kamal Isfahani wrote over a hundred years ago that is even more relevant today...

The poet who is not one who satirizes...
is like a toothless, clawless lion, no less.
A patron who's tight-fisted's a real pain
for which there is no remedy but abuses.

"Now let me introduce to you and to all gathered here tonight... the *incomparable*... Auhadi of Maragha... may he stay in our hearts and minds forever!"

As Obeyed backs off towards his previous position the small, old, sickly-looking poet shuffles forward helped by a concerned-looking

Majd al-Din. Finally they make it over to the entertaining position before the king and his entourage in front of the assembled crowd of over two hundred nobles, clerics and courtiers. Hafez notices that Auhadi does not bow to the king but talks to him as an equal.

"Masud Shah, I have come to Shiraz to finish my work and go home to Maragha and drop this rotten form! Part of my work here is to tell you and all assembled here the truth about this place and great God Almighty. So be it! I met Obeyd in Isfahan some years ago and he is a good soul, a fine writer of *ghazals* and a person who through humour touches our weaknesses... our blind-spots. I hope my humble poems can do the same. Listen, all of you to a poem inspired by one of Shiraz's greatest... your beloved Sadi...

Give little attention to those courtiers so agreeable,
see their promises as a dream that is so perishable.
If through selfishness your name becomes honoured,
understand your shameful honour as dishonourable.
When the cup of good fortune comes into your hand,
when raising glass... think of hangover if you're able.
Your restless soul reminds one of an untamed camel:
place a rein on it to be led or it will be uncontrollable.

He sways a little as he finishes the poem to a deathly silence and Hafez goes to come to his aid but is held by the strong arm of Haji Kivam who whispers to him, "He is alright. Let him be."

"Friends, such silence is the greatest applause. It is good that you are all taking what I said into your hearts. There is not much time left for many of us, our time has almost come! Now I'd like to recite to you a *ghazal* I wrote on my long journey to your fair city...

You listen, think about those who inherit, who work never:

who was he whose wealth you got... who're you, the heir?

He amassed it, but he did not spend it... so it stayed here:

use it well so when you've gone... others good from it bear.

Gold's a ghoulish thing and woman a chain upon your neck:

he who's crazy for both is haunted and a chain must wear.

Don't worry a lot about your children... God knows more

than His servant how to look after his brood so don't fear.

Don't play with lust and passion, only curses they'll bring:

even Jafar's wing won't help you escape such curses, hear?

This lust and this craving of yours are an ocean of trouble:

you can't swim, can you? Why you waves of life go near?

To wash your coat and turban is worth as nothing to you:

wash hands of worldly lust is real washing... is that clear?

Do not think of the wrongs that others may or may not do,

it is deeds you do you should think about... this, now hear.

Truth is not absent in these sayings that Auhadi tells you:

if you truly hear my advice... real Fortune away you'll bear.

Again silence greets his finishing the poem. Everyone is stunned by the power and straight-forwardness and bravery of his verse. He now coughs twice then goes straight into another poem as Hafez notices the frowns on the faces of all the royal brothers...

For how long will you be proud of your beard and turban?

Take that Friend as your friend: all else give up, O man!

Suddenly he falters... coughs and splutters.

"My... argh... friends, I was trying to remember this *kasida* that seemed relevant for this time but... arghk... my old mind, can anyone help me... remember it?"

Hafez breaks from the audience and strides out to his side and bows deeply.

"Master Auhadi," says Majd al-Din, "let me introduce you to… Hafez, a local poet and great admirer of your work… if anyone can remember that poem of yours it is this young fellow."

"Ahhgh… Hafez… yes, Khwaja Kivam has told me of you. Go ahead! Please… *be my memory.* I give you my blessing."

Hafez bows again to him and Majd al-Din then he turns to the king and continues the poem at the top of his extraordinary voice…

Such rushing about will only fill your heart with grief:
soul gathering quiet strength when resting is the plan.
Try to remove all the smell and colour of your own self
so He holds you tightly in His embrace: try, if you can.
Until you see your mistake you'll be hopelessly looking
for truth and beauty in the lovely cheek behind the fan.
If you are able to do what He wants you to do for Him,
He will do whatever you ask… to rely on that you can!
He is all family you need… give up all others instantly!
When will you free yourself of your family and the clan?
Ask yourself this now: when will you be free of yourself?
You who worry God: where, who's your God? Eh, man?
Who is it in you who speaks about 'me' and about 'us'?
Who's it that decided evil and good for you, a charlatan?
If there's any 'others' please go… point them out to me:
you're alone, yes? Can others shout as loud as you can?
To be as One, is not something that can be easily seen:
there is no hypocrisy in what I am saying: I've no plan.
Really, if seeing and Union were one in fact and action,

when the eye saw the thorn, blood from it would've ran!

He gave to you a cup... don't spill it, you drink it all up.

When I give you another cup hold it as tight as you can!

The face of the Master is the only One and all of others

from out of the Mirror and holder of Mirror ran, O man!

The die that makes the coin and the king's image are one:

a lie are all the numbers, that gold and silver coins span!

There is only one sap that supplies the flower that is on

the rosebush and the cruel, sharp thorns... understand?

The fire, pomegranate and orange get their colour from

the sun that gives them all life and that is in the Plan!

A thousand circles can come from out of the point of the

compass each time the join is enlarged by a slight span.

All of the world is revealing the total vision of the One:

look for it if you can see, then see It if you possibly can:

every thing, in silent voices, are praising that only One:

even the sand in the plain and rock on the hill... O man!

The end of the poem's recital is greeted by much applause from all directions as Auhadi turns and bends down and whispers in Hafez's ear, "Thank you my friend, it seems it's not what you say but how you say it, eh?"

"No, it is both kind sir. Without your words of wisdom they would be mere words as was originally said by Firdausi... 'He who has knowledge has power.'"

"May God bless you always Hafez. *Now, Masud Shah...* it is time for my young friend here, Hafez... to recite to you and all here one of his own poems!"

"Excellent idea! Hafez, what have you to offer your king?"

"First a *ghazal* I love deeply of Master Auhadi here that we could *all* learn from…

They said to rose, "A nightingale is such a small thing,

how could you any love affair with that one be having?"

The rose replied, "One nightingale praising me is better

than ten Simurghs… that upon mount Kaf are staying!"

One pure heart for You, is better than an army of men:

than a kingdom, soul with no hypocrisy's a better thing.

Anything coming to one through honesty is wonderful,

but when done dishonestly it's worth less than nothing.

With all your skill seek the Presence of the Almighty…

but, use it also, to avoid those who are you blindfolding.

"Ah, silence… you are all obviously stunned by its beautiful simplicity and honesty as I first was when I heard it. Now, as requested, a freshly composed *ghazal* sire, but I hope… one that will be long remembered by all gathered here tonight on such a special occasion. I dedicate this poem to Master Auhadi who has blessed us with his presence at last and whose poems have meant so much to me… and to whom I will always be grateful…

When at dawn from private room of House of Wonder on high,

candle of the east throws out its radiance over the whole sky…

when from the horizon's pocket the juggling sky takes the mirror,

and in a thousand ways the face of the world then does magnify,

in the hidden halls of the House of Joy of the Jamshid of Heaven,

to the music of the spheres, Venus then tunes the organ to go by.

Harp brought into twang says: "Where is he, who love denies?"

Cup juggles out a laugh: "Where is he who would wine deny?"

Consider the turnings of the heavens and take the cup of joy…

because in all conditions this is the far better way for one to try.

The flowing curls of the mistress of the world are false... a trap:

the men of true wisdom will not look for the end of a threaded lie.

If you want the world to be happy... pray for the king's long life:

it is an existence Divinely generous, helping all... low and high.

Image of the evidence of the Eternal Grace is that of the King...

Soul of world, height of practice... wisdom, light of Hope's eye.

Hafez, just like the slave does, waits at threshold of His door...

He is obedient King of kings who are obeyed, wherever they lie.

"By my soul, most interesting Hafez! That 'king' was not just me was it? Yes? What dear? Ah, my daughter Jahan tells me that she was deeply impressed by your *ghazal* young man and asks if you could come to the palace to correct her poems and wha... yes dear I understand, I *will* pay the young man, if you could also she asks be her teacher and friend? Well? Hafez? Are you dumbstruck?"

"Yes sire... for the first time in my life!"

"I gather it is a 'yes' then... one may on occasions say no to one's king but *never* his beautiful and at times willful fifteen year-old daughter! Please, something else from you!" Masud Shah smiles down at him.

"Sire, I wrote this poem about my teacher Obeyd Zakani and what I know is his desperate financial circumstances and I heard the rumour that you were about to dismiss him from your court. I will recite it to you...

O king! From paradise, bringer of happy news has come,

Rizvan of throne and like the huri and Salsabil of hair,

sweetly speaking with pure meaning, soothing heart,

beautiful and graceful and telling jokes and being fair.

I said: "Why have you now come to this poor dwelling?"

Answer: "For feast of the king, who's beyond compare."

now the messenger is tired of his poor one's company,

call him to you and ask of his heart's desire, whatever.

"Thank you Hafez. I don't know if I agree with your description of Obeyd as a beautiful and graceful angel, a great exaggeration of a pupil for a teacher I fear. Anyway I will look into his financial position. It is not I who find the presence of Obeyd at court uncomfortable." He looks across at the clergy.

"But, you ask of nothing for yourself? I hear you work in a drapery shop, what is there to laugh about at that? Remove those people from my court who are laughing and never let them return! I don't care what distinguished family they may be from! You study at night? Yes? Now I am tired as you must always be, young poet… and I can see my dear mother is even more tired than I. This court is dismissed!"

*

"Hafez, have you heard the latest news of the intrigues going on at the palace?"

"No Obeyd, my teacher, I have heard nothing as of yesterday."

As they walk across the small courtyard of the *madrassa* where Obeyd teaches and Hafez and his fifteen other pupils continue to listen in amazement at his knowledge, skill and often strange but informative behaviour.

"A friend of mine, one of the guards at the palace, visited me this morning when he finished work and revealed that last night the king Masud Shah, without the knowledge of his long-suffering mother, accused his brother the faithful Muhammad of conspiring to remove him from the throne!"

"My God! What about Abu Ishak!"

"No! It appears he wasn't at all involved. Anyway, Masud Shah *says* he got word of a plot through one of his spies in the court and had him arrested... but my friend says no such a plot existed!"

As they walk down the long corridor Hafez almost has to run to keep up with the long-legged teacher in his untidy old clothes and his fast-unwinding turban flying out behind his nodding head.

"Yes! Yes! He arrested him... and before his mother could talk him out of it he'd been taken from the city this morning to the fortress of Safid where I suppose he'll be imprisoned for as long as Masud Shah thinks he should stay there... out of sight, out of mind, eh? I don't think the people of Shiraz are going to approve of such an action. They like Muhammad and he could become a martyr in their eyes, dangerous for Masud Shah's future. When you go to see Princess Jahan next ask her about it if you can... and also put in a good word for me to her, I'm crazy about her."

"And twenty-five years older and as poor as a servant or a beggar!"

"Ah huh, and I'd beg her to let me *serve* her... if she'd give me half a chance. I hear she is not attached to material wealth, age or position so I'm ideal for her, in fact I could teach her a few things, especially about umm... poetry."

"My dear learned teacher of *ethics* and social *morality*, sometimes I wonder about you!"

"Ah huh, here we are my *innocent* friend. Both late again. I'm starting to be influenced by *your* bad habits. Take your place at the front as usual.

"God be with you all and me especially, for I need all the help I can get! On the way here I was telling our Hafez the news about how the king Masud Shah last night imprisoned his brother Muhammad in the fortress of Safid, all because of an unfounded rumour. The fears brought on by fear and ambition, eh? Of course, the concept of Justice is not even given a thought here. There is no trial, no judge, no pleading… and so perhaps there is no Justice for those of our highest aristocracy. In the book that I am presently writing 'The Ethics of the Nobles' I deal in chapter four with Justice, way back in the past and in this present age. Now I will combine my two classes in Law and Social History… to try to enlighten you all at this timely moment in the history of this fair city with a reading from my book that I hope all of you and your family and friends will purchase when it finally goes to the copiers, whenever that may be. Hmmm, yes… here it is, now listen!

"In the past the great men believed Justice to be one of the four virtues and on it they based the foundation of this and the next world. They believed… 'Heaven and Earth stand straight due to Justice,' and to put into practice the *Koran's* message… 'God orders you to practice justice and to be generous.' So, the kings, amirs and nobles always tried to practice justice and do the *best* for their subjects and soldiers and by doing this they had good reputations. They believed in this so much that they helped to encourage the ordinary people to be true in all their dealings and partnerships and they said…

Be just, because in the country of the heart

the Prophet reigns where justice does start.

"The view of our teachers *now* is that this quality of Justice is the *worst* of all the attributes and that you lose too much by being just... and they have a thesis on this which they have proven by clear arguments. They say, 'The foundation of sovereignty, lordship and mastery is *punishment,* since men will not obey any one until they fear him; all will feel themselves equal... the foundations of administration will be undermined and the order of public business disorganized. He who practices Justice (which God forbid!) refrains from beating, killing and fining anyone... and doesn't intoxicate himself and quarrel or be angry with his subordinates, *him none will fear.* Then the people will not *obey* their kings, nor sons their fathers, nor servants their masters, while the affairs of the lands and the people will lapse into chaos. And so it is that they say...

Kings to obtain one of their objects,

will often kill... a hundred subjects.

"And they further say, 'Justice bequeaths disaster.' What proof indeed can be more convincing than this... that so long as the kings of Persia played the tyrant, like Zahhak the Arab and Yazdigird 'the Sinner' (who now confer distinction on the chief seats of Hell, together with other later potentates who followed them), their Empire increased and their realm flourished. But when the reign of Khosrau Anushiravan came, who, by reason of his weak judgement and the policy of his feeble-minded ministers chose the attribute of Justice... in a little while the pinnacles of his palace fell to the ground, the Fire Temples which were their places of worship were extinguished... and all trace of them disappeared from the face of the earth. The caliph of the faithful and confirmer of the laws of religion 'Umar ibn Khattab (may God be well pleased with him), who was noted for his justice, made bricks and ate barley-bread, while his patchwork cloak, as they relate, weighed seventeen *maunds*. On the other hand... Mu'awiyya, by the blessing of Injustice, wrested the kingdom from the hands of the Imam Ali (may God ennoble his countenance). Nebuchadnezzar did not establish himself as king, nor become eminent in both worlds, nor did his empire increase... until he killed twelve thousand innocent prophets in the Holy City and cast into bondage many thousand more. Ghengis Khan, who today, despite his enemies, stands supreme in the lower depths of Hell as the exemplar and guide of all the Mongols, ancient and modern, did not attain to the sovereignty of the whole world until with ruthless sword he had destroyed millions of innocent people.

"You all look at me with eyes wide and many with mouths open. Why? Open your eyes even further and see what is happening and open your mouths for longer and say something to someone about it! Listen to this and open your ears wider! It's recorded in the histories of the Mongols that last century when Baghdad was conquered by Hulagu Khan he ordered the remnant of the inhabitants who had escaped the sword to be brought before him. He then enquired into the circumstances of each class... and when he was acquainted with them, he said... 'craftsmen are indispensable,' and gave them permission to go about their business. To the merchants he commanded that some capital should be given, so that they might trade for him. From the Jews he was content to take a tax, declaring them to be an oppressed people... while the eunuchs he consigned to return to the harems and look after them for him. He then set apart the judges, sheikhs, Sufis, hajjis, preachers and persons of note, beggars, religious mendicants, wrestlers, poets and story-tellers, saying... 'These are superfluous creatures who waste God's blessings,' and ordered all of them to be drowned in the Tigris, thus purifying the face of earth from their vile existence. As a natural consequence sovereignty continued in his family for nearly ninety years, during which time their Empire daily increased... until, when poor young Sultan Abu Said conceived in his mind a sentimental passion for Justice and branded himself with the stigma of this quality. His Empire quickly came to an end and the House of Hulagu Khan and all his endeavours were brought to naught through the aspirations of Sultan Abu Said... I know as *I was there* and bore witness to what I am telling you today. And so it can be truly stated...

When a man's time is almost run out

he only does that which has no clout.

"Blessings rest on those great and well-directed persons who guided mankind out of the dark delusion of Justice into the light of right guidance in the proper direction!"

*

Hafez enters Abdullah's small eating-house and grins at Hajji and Abu who are already eating from plates full of *maqilba*, a porridge of meat and animal fat, sheeps intestines, meatballs, beans and wheat, leeks, onions, turnips, beets and carrots... a specialty of Shiraz. Now he is ordering the same from the aging, limping, good-natured Abdullah and takes a glass of tea from his tray and finally sighs, then sits and joins his friends.

"May God be with you both! Couldn't wait, huh? Smells... almost good! I have some important news. I just saw Haji Kivam and he told me the latest news about our new young prince, Abu Ishak. We all wondered where the king Masud Shah sent him... what was it, eight weeks ago?"

"At... mbbnm, least." Abu is talking with his mouth almost full.

"Whenever. Anyway, first he went to Yazd to try to talk Amir Mubariz Muzaffer into attaching that province onto Fars... talking to him about peace, but it seems he left the city with Mubariz's laughter ringing in his seventeen-year-old ears."

"Aghm, went down the wrong way. Ah, that's better. Send a boy to do a man's job and what would one expect."

"Right Hajji! You are not only a handsome face eh? Now listen to this. Ah, here's my food. I'll tell you after I've finished this."

A short time later Hafez is pushing his plate to the side and is draining the last of the sweet black tea and then calls to Abdullah for another.

"Now, where was I?"

"Outside Yazd with laughter following our handsome, but brave young prince." Abu finishes his third glass of tea.

"Yes, outside Yazd. Well, then he went to Kirman and was also without success there. So he quietly returned home, we didn't know that did we? Anyway, he convinced his brother Masud Shah that such an insult on the both of them should not be left alone and they decided to make a surprise attack on Mubariz. So the king provided his youngest brother with troops and the set off in the dead of night some six weeks ago. But Mubariz was too clever and was awake to his tricks and when the war started he was ready for him. He returned yesterday, this friend of Haji Kivam. A general, he was there. The prince and the others should be back in a few days. It seems they laid siege to Yazd and had captured it in a few days. Much greater number of soldiers he said. But... Mubariz had escaped with some men to the castle-fortress of Maibud, about three hours march away. It seems it's quite a spectacular castle on a hill surrounded by nothing but desert sands.

"Abu Ishak discovered that was where he'd fled and so he took some of his soldiers there and laid siege to it. Now it gets interesting. It seems this ruler Mubariz Muzaffar is a man of great courage and is not as stupid as our king originally thought. When night came he and some of his small band of men would leave the castle by some secret passageway and silently attack the camp of Abu Ishak, kill whoever they wanted to... burn the tents and equipment and escape back to the castle without any loss of life. This happened time and again and each time they got away with such daring acts almost without a loss of life to him or his men.

"Now listen to this... the fearlessness of the man! On one night he and his men attacked the camp where the prince was, killed some of his guards and highest-ranking soldiers, stole ten of his best horses and returned to the fortress unharmed. Abu Ishak was astonished by this daring act... but he was also furious that such a thing could happen. So, he gave orders that each night *five thousand* of his horsemen should ride out and wait in ambush for his brave foe. This they did and that night when Mubariz and about a hundred of his men attacked as usual Abu Ishak's encampment these horsemen surrounded them and other troops raced forward and also attacked them... but, listen to this... Mubariz and his hundred soldiers fought off these many thousands of Abu Ishak's foot and horse soldiers and finally made it back to the castle... with *only one* of Mubariz's soldiers being captured.

"Eventually, this *one man* was taken to the tent of Abu Ishak. Abu Ishak placed a robe of honour upon his shoulders then sent him with safe-conduct to Mubariz to tell Mubariz to come and talk to him. Mubariz refused to do this but letters began to be exchanged. Now, listen to this... according to the general who was there and told Haji Kivam in words full of amazement... Abu Ishak had begun to develop a great respect and admiration for this man and said out loud, 'I'd really like to see him again... and when I've seen him I'll leave him alone.' And so, Abu Ishak waited outside the castle and Mubariz stood at the gate and saluted him. Abu Ishak shouted to him, 'Come down here, I guarantee your safety!' Mubariz shouted back, 'I have promised God that I'll not come down there to you until you have come up to me and entered my castle and after that I'll come down to you!' "

"Hmmm, clever fellow this Mubariz." Hajji grins at Abu.

"Clever, but is he trustworthy?" Abu gestures to the old waiter for another tea as Hafez clears his throat and continues.

"Anyway, the prince finally accepted these conditions and soon he entered the castle-fortress flanked by ten of his highest ranking soldiers. The one who talked to Kivam was one of them. As they passed through the gate Mubariz dismounted from his horse and walked up and bent down and kissed Abu Ishak's stirrup and then walking in front of him led him and his companions into his private rooms in the castle where they all had something to eat. After this Mubariz rode with Abu Ishak into his encampment and later Abu

Ishak told Mubariz to sit next to him, placed one of his own robes on his shoulders and presented him with a large amount of money. They finally came to an agreement through the intermediary Shaikh Al-Islam Shaha-ud-din Ali, one of the well-known Islamic scholars and leaders in Yazd, that Masud Shah would be recognized as his ruler and Mubariz should govern the province and now Abu Ishak is returning home."

"I have a strong feeling that we haven't heard the last of this, this extraordinary ruler, Mubariz Muzaffar!" Abu gulps his tea.

"Kirman is still under his control... God forbid but I wouldn't be surprised if Masud Shah's eyes turn again in that direction." Hajji strokes his beard.

"Hafez, get back down now behind the wall again! One of those arrows could easily hit you!" Hajji calls out as Hafez climbs down the stairs to join him and Abu and Obeyd Zakani, each armed with a staff ready for action.

"Well, tell us what you saw!" Obeyd is not smiling for a change.

"I fear there are too many of them and they are well-armed, not like most of us. Perhaps we can hold out for another day or two... but, I think I saw what looked like a large battering-ram being uncovered amongst Pir Hussein's troops at the rear. Who would have thought that the brother of our ruler Masud Shah, Muhammad... would have had the courage after over a year of imprisonment in the fortress of Safid to escape and make his way to the camp of Pir Hussein the Chupanid, known by all not only to be ambitious but quite ruthless!"

"He must have had some help. Perhaps Pir Hussein sent someone in there to free him, then he could march on us with a 'legitimate' heir to the throne... there are still many here in Shiraz who feel Muhammad was terribly wronged by his brother. Masud Shah and the people of our city have stood up to Pir Hussein admirably even though his troops outnumber ours. I'm beginning to fear that we'll lose many of our brave people before this battle is over. It's been a week now and Masud Shah must have lost at least half of his army. God only knows how many ordinary people have been hit by those showers of arrows. When they finally break through the gates they'll be baying for blood... ours! I really don't like the look of it my friends." Hajji wipes the sweat from his face then turns to see Musa running along the side of the wall towards them.

"Here comes your friend Musa, Hafez. He looks excited about something."

Musa can't speak, he is so out of breath from running. They all wait while he recovers.

"Haah... that's better. I was outside the palace with Peter and my father. A small crowd is there, most are at the walls. Anyway, an official came out to the gate and made a proclamation. He said that the king is truly grateful to the people for their support in this time of great crises, but... it is hopeless. He has sent a message to Pir Hussein and his brother Muhammad that at noon, in two hours, the gates will open and they can march into the city to the palace that they will discover to be devoid of his presence. I heard from the official that he has escaped with a few guards and advisors down a tunnel that leads from the palace to one of the larger underground qanat that will take them well beyond the outskirts of the city and to safety. The official also said that Tashi Khatun and her son Abu Ishak and Princess Jahan Malek have decided to stay, they feel Muhammad will not let Pir Hussein harm them."

"Hmm... perhaps Masud Shah will go to Isfahan?" Hajji looks at the others.

"Unlikely," Obeyd cuts in, "from what my friends at court have told me, my guess is Masud Shah will probably go to Lauristan to find someone powerful to help him to try to take back Shiraz."

"So, we have two hours before they march into our city. We may not be able to use arms against them my friends... but, I for one am not going to welcome them with open arms! I'm going home for a bite to eat, and to arm myself with our strongest weapon now... words! I'll see you all back here at noon." Hafez walks off.

"He has courage you must admit... even if he can be a little foolhardy sometimes, but his idea of something to eat sounds fine to me. You are all invited back to my room for some... eh, meagre refreshments."

They're all grinning now and shaking their heads, knowing how 'meagre' Obeyd's refreshments will be and they go their own ways shaking their heads, leaving him standing there all alone, scratching his head and shouting.

"Nothing wrong with cress, dry bread and water... is there?"

Two hours later they have all returned to the same spot on the wall and now Hafez's mother the veiled Ulya is also there.

"I wrote a short *masnavi* that applies to him and I'd like to hurl that at him with my mouth! What do you think Mother?"

"Well... er... yes, but not so loud... he's not so far away and he doesn't seem to be moving on!" His mother is not so sure.

"Yes, Hafez, throw a poem at him... the incisive word is greater than the sharp sword and the truth lasts longer than any army!" Obeyd grabs Hafez by the arm and squeezes it.

"Give it to them Hafez, from all of us in Shiraz... all of us everywhere who have been forced to be under the fist of someone who we don't want and have no say about it! Tell him the truth... a greater truth!"

Musa is shouting now as Hajji Ahmed who has been listening begins to play his old *tar*, nods at Hafez who grins then nods back then Hajji strums harder as Hafez sets his face towards the unwanted conquerors and calls down to them as they pass in their shining armour through the gate then stop to listen to him...

Whoever enters this world that's full of commotion,
in the end, it's necessary he goes to tomb's location.
This world is like a bridge to the next world's road,
a place without permanency and a desolate abode.
Don't set your heart on this bridge that is full of fear:
prepare provisions for the road and do not stay here.
Opinion of men of understanding is: this old mansion
is transitory; there is no treasure in this place of ruin.
Truthfully, the Wise have pierced the pearl of truth,
who have named this place: "An inn without a roof."
This inn is not fit to be staying in: move on from it!
This world leaves no one remaining: move on from it!
From friendship with wealth and rank, far away sit:
your wealth is the snake and your rank... is the pit.
Suppose I grant that you are Bahram Gur the great;
into the grave's snare you'll fall, whether soon or late.

I said to you: "If you are not blind... the grave see;"

and: "Don't for a moment without work, sitting be."

There's no help, no escape for anyone from this stage;

not for beggar or... king, or youth or those of old age.

You... who draw your skirt so proudly over our clay,

Hafez wishes the Koran's 'Fatiha'... you would say.

Hajji takes up the poem and begins to sing it through again as the people nearby dance and sing along.

Pir Hussein turns to Prince Muhammad who has also been watching Hafez's performance.

"That strange-looking small fellow, that poem... I couldn't hear all of it, but did he not mention Bahram Gur?"

"That was a great compliment... to *you*... for he was one of our greatest ancient kings, renowned for his strength and courage!"

"But did he not fall into a pool and was never seen again after he was chasing a wild ass or *gur* and so that is how he received his name. Was that fellow calling *me* an *ass?*"

"Look at these... my people, now... look at the minstrel singing and the people grinning and dancing to that song, they are *praising* us... they are jubilant to see us! Did they not throw down their few weapons and open the gates and welcome us?"

"Hmmm, I wish I could have heard the rest of that poem. Let us move on to the palace... these 'people of yours' make me nervous! There is something about them that I don't trust, I just can't put my finger on it. Any trouble from them and they'll feel my anger across their stupid necks! Onward march!"

"Hafez, did you see him looking up at us and talking to Muhammad? My heart almost stopped. If he heard all of that poem of yours..."

Up on the steps Ulya turns to her son and shakes her head and looks worried. Hafez grins, "Mother, you worry too much... he is a fool, an ass but a dangerous one... and Muhammad should watch his back!"

"Perhaps he is, but you know the story from Maulana Rumi about Jesus and the fool?"

"No mother, I don't!"

"Jesus saw a fool coming towards him from the opposite direction over a hill and Jesus turned around and ran away from him. You cannot change a fool, it is dangerous to try! A fool can only be changed by his own experiences, remember that!"

"Hmmm, then I'll have to give up on uncle Sadi!"

"Your uncle is not a fool Hafez, he is just full of himself. Behind all that bluff and bluster he has a kind soul. Now let us all go home before our new ruler realizes you called him an ass to his face and comes back."

Hafez waves to Hajji who continues singing as they walk down the stairs.

*

The drapery shop's interior is colourful with rolls of beautiful fabrics stacked to the ceiling. Persian carpets cover the floor. Hafez is rolling up some brightly coloured cloth. His boss, Selim, a tall, thin Turk aged about forty, with a wispy beard and fez cap, shows a middle-aged, large, dourly dressed woman a dark silk fabric as her poorly dressed maid looks on, bored stiff.

"But, *madam*, this silk is the finest made in China."

Madam is a well-known snob of the Turkish nobility.

"I don't care if it's made of *angel's wings* my good man, it's too rough for perfect skin *like mine*."

Hafez looks up, a mischievous grin on his face.

"*Madam*, such *thin* skin as yours deserves to be covered *completely*, er… in nothing but the finest."

She turns and looks down towards him, not sure if she is flattered or insulted, then she grimaces as she looks down into his ugly face, smiling sweetly up at her. Selim frowns.

She clutches her throat.

"By my eyes, good sir, *whom* may I ask, is *that* disgusting-looking creature?

"That, is one of my assistants.., acquired six years back as a kindness to his uncle, but I'm beginning to wonder if I should have been *so easily* persuaded."

He glares at Hafez, then turns back to the two women.

"But, *madam*, he is right about one thing, you *deserve* only the very finest. Hafez, go fetch that special silk that has *just arrived!*"

He winks in Hafez's direction. Hafez nods and walks through the archway to the storeroom where great rolls of various fabrics are piled on racks to the ceiling. In one corner a parrot sits on his perch, chained by one leg. He stops eating from a bowl as Hafez enters. Bobbing up and down the parrot 'talks' to Hafez.

"*Poet, thinks he's a poet!*

Poet or parrot!"

Hafez stops and turns and laughs then imitates the parrot in voice and movement.

"You, you are a parrot

and... I, I am a poet.

All will soon know it,

so don't talk such rot!"

He goes over to the bottom row of some dark coloured rolls and slowly pulls out a long dark one. He turns to the parrot and winks...

"You would not believe it...

if she knew she'd have a fit!

He sells the sack as silk...

like baby takes mother's milk!"

The parrot is excited, moving right and left, bobbing up and down.

"Mother's milk, mother's milk,

sack as silk, sack as silk!

Free me, free me!

No one will see me!"

Hafez throws the heavy roll onto his shoulder.

"One day or night, my friend, I promise. When the time is right!"

The parrot dips his head.

"Promise, a promise!

Free me! Free me!"

Hafez nods back, then walks out and into the shop where the woman is waiting impatiently. In the distance there is a noise of a crowd disturbance and she is angry.

"By my soul, what took you so long you ugly brute? Who were you talking to?"

Hafez drops the roll that almost hits her foot. She shrieks as she jumps back. Selim is angry. Hafez mumbles, "A prisoner of this shallow world dear lady, like all of us."

Madam is flustered now.

"What? Sir, what is this little, ugly, raving idiot talking about?"

"Who knows madam? He thinks he's a poet, they're all mad! Now, this is the finest you'll find in the whole world!"

He rolls it out on the floor before her. She feels it with her fingers and looks impressed.

Suddenly through the front door the crowd noise becomes deafening and they all turn towards it. Hajji Ahmed the minstrel friend of Hafez rushes in, excited, shouting, "Hafez! Hafez, come quickly!"

"What is it? Not mother?"

He runs up to him, knocking the woman forward into Selim's lap, head first! Hajji grabs Hafez's shirt and begins to drag him doorwards.

"The soldiers of Pir Hussein are taking Tashi Khatun and her son Abu Ishak to be interrogated, probably imprisoned! The people are out on the street awaiting them. We *must* help!"

Selim, recovering, points at Hafez and shouts.

"If you leave, Hafez, then don't bother to *ever* come back!"

Hafez shrugs, hands outstretched… what else can he do?

"I'm off. I've had an offer to work in a bakery with my friend Peter anyhow! Haji Kivam arranged it. But first I'll get my jacket."

He runs out the back. The agitated parrot spies him as he picks up his patched jacket and calls out…

"Free me, free me! Parrot… or poet!

Poet... or parrot! What will you be?"

Hafez grins at him, rushes over and unclips the chain from its leg and opens the window. The shocked parrot looks at him, then flies to the window and looks back and calls out...

"Free! Free me!"

He flies through the window and up into the blue and looks down on the buildings and the crowded streets and sees a column of soldiers marching in the direction of the drapery shop, the crowd outside is thick and loud. He swoops down and lands on the roof of the building opposite the shop and watches. Hafez and Hajji run from the drapery shop and push to the front of the crowd. Hafez looks up to see the parrot and waves.

Suddenly the troop of soldiers enters the end of the street and the crowd silently waits. The soldiers march on either side of the street pushing them back. In between the soldiers the eighteen-year old Abu Ishak and his mother, (usually unveiled as is the Turkish custom but now veiled to hide her shame), following, upset and weeping. As they reach the woodworkers shop opposite Selim's drapery she suddenly stops.

For some reason the soldiers and her son also stop. A hush comes over the crowd in anticipation. Hafez and Hajji gaze at her, mouths agape as she lifts her veil to reveal her beautiful, tragic, tear-stained face. There is an intake of breath by the large crowd. She looks across towards Mahmud (later to be called Pahlawan meaning 'hero') the woodworker friend of Hafez, smiles... and Hafez and Hajji, frozen, as are everyone else, wait for whatever will happen next. She calls out in an anguished, heart-wrenching voice.

"Is it right, O you men of Shiraz that I and my son are to be taken away from you in this humiliating way? Am I not Tashi Khutan, the wife of your once beloved, generous ruler, Mahmud Shah?"

Mahmud the carpenter suddenly shouts... "WE WILL NEVER LET THEM TAKE YOU OUT OF SHIRAZ... WE WON"T LET THIS HAPPEN! FREE THEM!"

"Free them! Free them!"

The parrot screeches.

Hafez takes up the cry with passion!

"FREE THEM... NOW!"

The great crowd roars together... "FREE THEM... NOW!"

The soldiers look startled, frightened by the size and passion of the crowd that now pushes forward led by Mahmud, almost breaking their chain of arms around their captives.

She drops to her knees and raising her arms implores the people of Shiraz, "Please, kind friends, dear people of Shiraz... *Free me... free him!*"

She turns and points to her handsome son.

Hafez and Hajji crawl through the soldiers' legs and rush to catch her as she falls sideways in a faint. The crowd goes wild, weapons appearing as if by magic... swords, knives and clubs and the chain of arms of the soldiers are broken as they are engulfed and the crowd... men, women and children rush to her son and untie his hands. Many soldiers soon lie dead or dying in the street and those that remain flee in the opposite direction, terror on their faces. Abu Ishak rushes up to where Hafez is cradling his mother's head with his hands. He is almost crying with emotion.

"Thank you, my friend. I'll look after her now. I'm Abu Ishak."

"Kind sir, I'm called Hafez... at your command... like all of us people of Shiraz. What do we do now?"

Mahmud the woodworker shouts an answer, "Let's get rid of Pir Hussein!"

As one voice the whole crowd begins to shout…

"HUSSEIN MUST GO… HUSSEIN MUST GO!"

From the rooftop the parrot parrots them, then takes off and flies low over the heads of the crowd and he flies all over Shiraz as he screeches out the cry that becomes a catch-cry throughout the whole of the city…

"Hussein must go! Hussein must go!"

From high above the city it can see the seventeen quarters of the city and its vast wall with its nine gates. It can see its gardens, empty: all the people of Shiraz are in the streets and alleyways and all are heading towards the great palace where the dictator, Pir Hussein resides.

"Hussein must go! Hussein must go!"

The parrot keeps screeching the clarion call.

From the city the same cry of the crowd rises to meet that of the parrot and spread further.

The parrot swoops down towards the section of town where Hafez worked in the drapery shop… in the Khargh-tarrashan quarter. As he flies along the street he can hear music and tramping feet and coming down the street towards him. Marching arm in arm in a line with hundreds of lines of marchers behind them are Hafez and Hajji, now joined by Obeyd with an assorted collection of Shiraz's citizens, ruffians and so-called rogues… including the new hero 'Pahlawan' Mahmud.

Hajji turns to Hafez and shouts above the din… "Prince

Muhammad may have finally been disloyal to our king but he was still *of* the royal family and had been wrongfully imprisoned by Masud Shah... and for Pir Hussein to murder him and think he could rule our beloved city without the loyalty of the people was the height of stupidity! Now he has created a martyr in Muhammad in the eyes of the long-suffering population! We have risen up against others before him and we'll do it again! Hafez, we need a new song now to help kick this bloody cruel and hateful dictator Pir Hussein out."

From an alleyway the minstrel Abu Khan and three minstrel friends rush out and join the marching throng and they all begin to repeat after Hafez as he suddenly sings out...

Except for Your threshold, in the world my shelter is nowhere

my place of safety, except for this one door, there is nowhere!

People rush from alleyways and join them. Hafez's mother and a barking Rustom and Peter and Musa and Shahin rush out of other alleyways and run to the centre of the line and they join arms with Hafez, Hajji and the minstrels and Pahlawan Mahmud. Hafez hugs her and they grin at each other... then old Rustom barks and takes up his marching position out the front, the proud leader of the throng! Suddenly a group of six soldiers rush out from behind a building, but on seeing the size and fervour of the crowd, weapons raised, they instantly rush back and hide, watching in fear as the mob marches by singing as one with Hajji...

When the enemy draws out the sword we throw away the shield:

except weeping, lamenting and sighing, our rapier is nowhere!

Hafez, now clear of the marching crowd, walking backwards into the now limping Rustom, stumbles then recovers and facing them sings out loud, conducting them with his arms...

If Time should send some fire into harvest of my life... I say:

burn; for not worth a blade of grass... it, I declare, is nowhere!

The crowd repeats the last line with gusto...

Burn; for not worth a blade of grass... it I declare, is nowhere!

The crowd turns into the wider streets of the Bagh-e-Now quarter with more prosperous houses and shops on either side: veiled beautiful women come out on the balconies and front doorways and lift their veils to peek down and at the handsome, young, marching minstrels. Hajji Ahmed and his friends leap out to the front line of the crowd and all the minstrels bow and wave to the women and now Hajji Ahmed sings up to them...

I'm the slave of the fascinating narcissus eye of that fair form,

whose wine of pride's glance at anyone, anywhere, is nowhere!

The marching crowd crosses the canal bridge and turns into the street where many of the richest citizens live in Shirviyeh and there up on her father's mansion's balcony, looking down, fascinated, is the seventeen-year-old beauty, Nabat! Hafez, on seeing her, can't stop himself... he runs from the line, tripping, then recovers and pushes to the front of the minstrels and sings up to her with his deep, unusual, memorable voice as they march by...

Because I see the many traps of the Path... in every direction,

my shelter... except for safety of your long hair... is nowhere!

Embarrassed by this and by the crowd turning and looking up at her looking down at Hafez's exaggerated display of affection, she sticks her nose up in the air and stiffly strides inside, only to trip over something and stumble forward, to the laughter of the minstrels and some of the crowd. Hafez grimaces, in agony for causing her such embarrassment.

The parrot flies up and sees that they are now about to converge with another street and on the other side yet another street and another marching crowd coming from the quarter of Murderstan. The parrot screeches, but his voice is beginning to weaken.

"Go! Go! Must go!"

He flies down to street level and spies, heading the crowd from the Vakil Bazaar side, Mahmud Attar (now twenty-six) and his father the greengrocer and perfume seller and an old strange-looking dervish or holy man on the other side of Attar, arms linked. They join up with Hafez and the minstrel's crowd. They all smile and laugh now and hug each other and resume the line, now much wider. The old dervish begins to shout to the crowd and the onlookers another verse of the stirring marching song that he creates...

You do what's desired... but don't go looking to do any injury:

in our law, except for this... existence of a sinner is nowhere!

The crowd of many thousands sing out the verse as it is met by three other marching crowds from Sar-Bagh and Kalimiha as they reach the front gates of the great palace. Attar steps to the front and shouts out to the vast sea of faces his own couplet of the *ghazal*...

The eagle of violence has drawn out his wing over every city:

body bent bow of recluse, arrow sigh of repenter, is nowhere!

The crowd roars and then sing out, deafeningly... as one...

Except for Your threshold, in the world my shelter is nowhere;

my place of safety, except for this one door, there is nowhere!

They rush forward and push open the tall gate and rush into the courtyard where stand a long line of soldiers, swords raised. The crowd stops, facing the soldiers, now sing together...

When the enemy draws out the sword we throw away the shield:

except weeping, lamenting and sighing, our rapier is nowhere!

Suddenly, the leader of the guards throws down his large scimitar and then all his men do the same. The leader of the guards calls out to the crowd...

"We have won, people of Shiraz! Pir Hussein has fled the city! But, God help us all if he returns from Tabriz with a larger army!"

The people of Shiraz roar out in surprise and happiness and laugh and kiss and hug each other and throw turbans and hats into the air and one just misses the parrot, who looks down squawking at the remarkable scene...

"Oh! Oh! Go! Go! Must go! Must go!"

He flies off toward the setting sun as Hafez, his mother, Rustom and Peter, Musa and Shahin turn and head for home. Then 'Pahlawan' Mahmud, Hajji Ahmed and the minstrels, followed by Attar, his father and the old dervish, go off down the street in the other direction. Hajji strums on his *tar* as they saunter off, he sings.

Why should I turn my face away from the Winehouse's street,

for in the world a better way for my feet, I swear is nowhere!

They wander off towards Zal's winehouse. As Hafez, his mother and friends pass by the house of Nabat again his mother Ulya turns to him and quietly says...

Don't give treasure of the heart of Hafez to each hair and mole;

such a trust, to be under each black mole's power, is nowhere.

She smiles and wags her finger at him, he looks away, his two friends dig him in the ribs as Rustom licks his hand and Hafez reaches down and lifts up his old friend and from the balcony the half-hidden face of Nabat wistfully watches the odd-looking group wander off down the street towards the setting sun.

A few months later an old vulture soars up from the empty Tower of Silence and flies in hope towards the walls of the city surrounded by the tens of thousands of soldiers of the army supplied by Sheikh Hasan-e-Kuchek in Tabriz to Pir Hussein, and he has been joined by Mubariz Muzaffer and his soldiers from Yazd, a fearsome combination indeed!

Hafez stands quietly with his mother and Musa and Peter along with thousands of Shiraz's depressed-looking population staring down from the top of the wall at the vast army of foot-soldiers, soldiers on horses and camels, their bright metal armour gleaming in the late-afternoon sunlight.

Hafez looks along the parapet sees Hajji Ahmed and waves at him then down to the thousands waiting at the city's gates, swords and knives and clubs, sticks and stones at the ready. He sighs.

"It's useless! We might be able to hold them off for a few days but with those long ladders and battering poles they'd soon be inside. It will be the end for a lot of us and many of them! If only Masud Shah and his family had stayed with his small army and had joined us... perhaps..."

"No," Hafez's mother cuts in, "he was right! In his proclamation he told the truth son... and it's about time everyone here put down their weapons and accepted it before there is a bloodbath... *our* blood! He had only a thousand or so men behind him and that army down there looks as large as our whole population. As he said... he will not forget us and return when the time is right and he refuses to shed innocent blood in a futile attempt to stop Pir Hussein. It is time for us to use commonsense and be prepared to wait."

"Look! *LOOK!* It's Majd al-Din! Abu said he'd been asked to talk to Hussein for us!" Hajji Ahmed shouts to them.

"*Majd al-Din! Majd al-Din! Our saviour!*" The cry goes out and soon all attention is focused on the hunched figure of Majd al-Din assisted by the old dervish from the march on the palace as they walk slowly to the tall gate and Majd al-Din calls out in his powerful, loving voice... "Open the gate O people of Shiraz so that I can talk of peace with Pir Hussein, for no one's blood will be shed today or any day over this. Open the gates!"

"*OPEN THE GATES!*" The cry of the people fills the air.

Slowly the tall, heavy gates creak open and in ensuing pregnant silence like the sound of something divine then a command goes out from amongst the camp of the waiting soldiers then the order to 'withhold arms'. The foot soldiers with their bright, heavy-metal plumed helmets, shields and chest-plates engraved with flowers and prayers, bows and large quivers packed with arrows and swords at the ready... stand to attention as the two old men walk towards them.

"They really didn't need all that uncomfortable armoury even on their poor horses... did they son? Must be hot and exhausting marching all the way from Tabriz in all that steel. Look at those on horseback with their long lances and ornate shields and scimitars! I must say they do look a splendid sight... all that colour and shining metal... even if they all look so serious."

"Look, here comes Pir Hussein on horseback surrounded by his generals to welcome the two of them. His armour is made of silver and gold. That wouldn't stop one of our arrows from a strong arm!

Musa, don't you even think of it! Our man is a Man among men and he is *one of us*... it will be alright. God is with us today! He has stopped! He is dismounting! He salutes *our* man! They are talking, now they are going into his tent! We are saved, mother! Compared to those wild man-eating dogs Majd al-Din so easily tamed, old Pir Hussein should be tamed in no time at all. O... he is our greatest living hero! And did you see who was with him? He was with us when we marched on the palace... I wonder who *he* is?"

Less than an hour later, just as Hafez entertaining everyone, came to the end of an exciting *masnavi* about exactly what had happened up to that moment... they emerged from the tent, smiling broadly. Success!

Majd al-Din with the dervish behind him with Pir Hussein behind him strode to the wall and shouted... "Upon my soul, we have his word! I believe he is an honest man. He says he will try to be a better ruler than Mahmud Shah and he offers you all his friendship and asks forgiveness for his past actions! Mubariz Muzaffer and his men will return to Yazd, that is agreed. Listen, I have asked for a day, to give us all time to prepare ourselves to welcome a guest and perhaps a friend. We Shirazis are more welcoming then anyone else on Earth!"

A great roar goes up as he and the dervish pass through the gate into the loving arms of the people of their beloved city.

*

It is twenty-five hours later and as clear and real to me now as it was back then in 740/1340 when I was twelve and stood with my mother and father and older brother in the street outside our house that was lit up in that dusky light between day and night when finally a sacred, timeless moment came in the wondrous light among the large joyous throng as they slowly walked through and *with us*... the three of them, each as one of us!

Hafez told me years later that they'd gone back to exactly the same place with the same friends when Majd al-Din and the old dervish dressed in old clothes and smiling brightly went through the gate and walked over to hug the waiting Pir Hussein. They turn and walk back towards the gate waving to the waving people on the wall lined with burning candles and each Shirazi holds one aloft and shout as one...

"GOD... IS GREAT!"

As they walk through the gate the minstrels begin to play and soon they look up and stop as Hajji Ahmed begins to sing down to them with Hafez, his mother and two friends looking on...

Companions, the Friend through the night, bring to your mind:
duty of being a servant doing what is right, bring to your mind.
Weeping and sighing of lovers in this new season of intoxication,
to height of tune, harp and cymbal's flight, bring to your mind.
When you bring the hand of hope to the waist of your objective;
promise this circle made with all our might, bring to your mind.
When wine's reflection shines out in the face of the Winebringer,
us lovers, by singing this melody all night, bring to your mind.
Do not be feeling grief for a moment for those who are faithful:
the unfaithfulness of Time's spinning flight, bring to your mind.
No matter how impetuous is the steed of Fortune, when whip
you crave to use, those who are out of sight, bring to your mind.
You who are dwelling in the seat of honour, show some kindness:

Hafez's face with your threshold in the light, bring to your mind.

Hajji has sung to the three of them and Hafez can see they have understood the *ghazal* perhaps even more than he did when he composed it at Hajji's that afternoon and they'd gone through it three times with Abu and the others. The three men bow to Hajii and then two turn to Hafez who has bowed with Hajji and the others when they finished, Pir Hussein has just thrown Hajji a bag of gold coins and is still smiling at Hajji who is now looking at Hafez as Majd al-Din calls to him, "So young... *Hafez!* I will not forget you, my companion appreciates your songs too!"

The old dervish nods to Hafez then takes his companion by the arm and they all continue into the city.

Some time later as they turn into our street and I feel an oncoming, passing, enlightened presence amongst those many candles of our hope and faith.

*

A few weeks later Hajji Ahmed, strolls down a street in Shiraz, two minstrel friends follow him and they all play their instruments as Hajji sings. He points to the distant hills and the nearby river as he sings the first couplet...

If the ruby from Badakhshan's rocky slate... comes out,

water of Ruknabad... like sugar from Strait comes out.

Young beautiful women poke their heads out windows or stop what they are doing and gaze through their flimsy veils at the handsome minstrel as he sings...

Here in the city of Shiraz, a one who steals the heart,

lovely, flirtatious, graceful: from each gate comes out.

Hajji gestures to the other minstrels and points up to the balcony of an expensive-looking dwelling at a number of important-looking people and sings...

In the dwelling of judge, teacher, priest and policemen,

wine that is rose of colour and is first-rate comes out.

As they pass a mosque in the distance Hajji gestures towards it and sings...

In the pulpit, during such hypocritical acts of ecstasy...

from preacher's turban hashish to evaporate comes out.

When they near a small garden another minstrel on hearing them rushes out and joins then as Hajji continues to sing loudly...

In the gardens, cry of nightingale with twang of harp,

and voice of minstrel, morning and late... comes out.

Suddenly Hafez leaves his uncle's house and on seeing Hajji nods and then joins him as Hajji continues...

In this city, grieving from being distant from Beloved,

Hafez, from house, heart... in a sad state... comes out.

Hajji gestures for Hafez to join in and Hafez moves to the front of the group and a crowd of our citizens watch and some dance as he sings another *ghazal* in his inimitable voice...

I'm the friend of fair of face and heart-captivating hair,

I'm mad from the drunken eye and wine pure and rare.

"Say some Promise of Eternity's Mystery," you say:

when I drink two cups I will tell you then and there.

When for lover there's no escaping burning, patience:

I who stand like candle, with the fire one cannot scare.

I'm Adam of Paradise, but on this particular journey,

I've been captured by love of the young and the fair.

If Fate helps me so I can carry my load to the Friend,

huris will wipe dust from off my bed with their hair.

Hafez gestures towards the beautiful veiled women watching and some shrink back disgusted by his ugliness as he sings...

Shiraz is the mine of the ruby lip and quarry of beauty;

I, the poor jeweler, because of this am in such despair.

From the intoxicated eyes that in this city I've seen,

O God, though I don't drink wine, I'm merry I swear.

From six sides it is a city full of glances of lovely ones:

I've nothing; if I did not, of all six I'd be the purchaser.

Hajji steps forward, taps Hafez on shoulder and sings to him...

Hafez, bride of your true nature wishes to be known...

Hafez shrugs with regret and answers him...

but I've no mirror... because of that I sigh, in despair.

Hajji replies, touching his hot forehead...

Hafez burns away from heat of such fruitless thinking...

Hafez, looks around, asking, searching, twinkle in his eye, he gets down on one knee in a begging posture and sings...

where's Winebringer throwing water on my fire's flare?

Then he stands and he and Hajji sing the first couplet again, as a duet...

I'm friend of the fair face... and heart captivating hair,

I'm mad from the drunken eye and wine pure and rare.

When they finish the crowd cheers. They all bow, then Hafez, Hajji and the minstrels wander off.

*

Sadi has a half-grey beard now and is carrying even more weight. He is trying to compose a *ghazal*. Hafez tiptoes into the room and watches his uncle as he talks to himself, "Now, let me see. This first line is good, but I can't seem to find the next line to finish the first couplet. Yes, it flows...

More pleasant than enjoying the garden and spring, is what?

Now, what rhymes with 'what'... how long will I have to wait this time for the rhyme to come?"

Hafez quietly walks up behind his uncle, looks over his shoulder and with a mischievous glint in his eye says... " 'What'... Uncle... 'what'... turn it into a refrain, a *radif*... what about...

Where is Winebringer to ask; "The cause of waiting, is what?"

His uncle turns to him and stands up, spluttering, red in the face.

"What! Er... why don't you have any respect for your uncle or his poetry? Who gave you the right to finish that couplet? Who, I ask you?"

"No one Uncle; I just heard your line and the other line simply... popped out!"

"Popped out? *Popped out!* And I've been trying to find that line for the past two hours and from you it just... *popped out!* I wish you would *pop out* of my life for awhile and leave me in peace. What have I got for my kindness... letting you and your mother live with me since your father died? Nothing but *problems.* I know you work mixing the flour at the bakery all night and give one quarter of your salary to my sister Ulya, another quarter to your teachers, another to the poor and keep only a quarter for yourself... admirable... also that you continue to study and you'd learnt the *Koran* off by heart by the age of nine and because of that and your fine memory, *Shams-ud-din,* you always use *'Hafez'* as your pen name when you write those... er youthful attempts at poems... but to actually keep calling yourself *'Hafez'*... what a big head you have young man! Just because you have had some influence with your attempts at poetry in the streets and went once to the court of Masud Shah is no reason to get such a big head! Listen my boy, there's only one poet in this house and his name is Sadi."

"Sadi *is* my favourite poet."

"I am? You study my poetry and one day you might be some kind of poet, but let me tell you, you're not the genius you think you are. How old are you now?"

"Twenty-one."

"Twenty-one and still working in that bakery and not even married yet... but who'd want to marry you, with *that* face. What are you studying at classes now with Hajji Kivam and that lunatic Obeyd Zakani and those other so-called teachers?"

"*Koranic* Studies, Astronomy, Society, Jurisprudence, Turkish, Persian History and Literature, Arabic and of course the lives of the prophets and saints and our great poets like Firdausi, Nizami, Attar, Rumi and Sadi..."

"Ah Sadi, my namesake. One day you know, *Shams-ud-din,* all of Shiraz will sing my poems like they sing his today. What do you think?"

"What is impossible can become possible through the Will of God!"

"Yes, yes... eh? I suppose it can? Poetry, I've had enough of it for now. I think I'll go down the road for a cup of wine in a place that's fine. Wine, fine... you get it *'Hafez'*... a rhyme?"

Sadi walks out of the room and as soon as he has gone Hafez says to himself...

"O Uncle Sadi, your rhyme is tardy, to compare yourself to Master Sadi, is surely, foolhardy! Ah, this couplet of his, let me look at it. Now that looks to me like the beginning of an interesting poem. Maybe I'll just finish it... us fellow-poets should help each other out, shouldn't we?"

Hafez sits down and begins to write.

An hour later Sadi, drunk, enters the room that Hafez has recently vacated.

"Ahgh... now back to that damned *ghazal*, that poem. Ah, that Shams-ud-din... that 'Hafez'... he'll drive me crazy some day. Thinks himself a poet. The day he becomes a poet I'll stop drinking wine... *no*, no... ah... I'll, I'll... drop dead... *no*, no... the day he becomes a poet I'll never write another line! What's this? Why, why the young scoundrel has finished my poem, *my poem!* How dare he! How dare he!"

He reads it out aloud... confused and angered by it...

More pleasant than enjoying the garden and the spring, is what?
Where's Winebringer to ask: "The cause of waiting... is what?"
Every moment of happiness that comes your way, take as a gift:
no one is ever delayed, the end of all things be knowing, is what.
Bond of life is tied by only a hair, so you try to be intelligent...
take care of your own grief, for the care of time's grieving is what?
The meaning of the 'Water of Life' and of the 'Garden of Iram'...
except for the bank of stream and wine, pleasant tasting, is what?
The sober one and intoxicated one are both from the one family....
to whose glance will we be giving our heart, our choosing is what?

What does silent sky know about the secret within the screen?

O philosopher, to argue about who the screen is holding, is what?

If God didn't make allowance for slave's ignorance and error...

meaning of the Almighty's Grace and of this pardoning, is what?

Sober one desires wine of Paradise's Kauther and Hafez the cup:

between these, that which the Almighty is preferring... is what?

As Sadi finishes the poem he realizes some of the message and how it is directed at him. Spluttering, he throws it to the floor and leaves the room shouting at the top of his voice, "How dare he! Come here *Hafez!* Er... *Shams-ud-din! Shams-ud-din!* Your poetry will drive all who read it insane! Mad, I say... mad, mad! You'll drive *me* mad!"

*

Made in United States
North Haven, CT
29 April 2024

51913952R00450